TALES OF
NORTH AMERICAN INDIANS

TALES OF THE NORTH AMERICAN INDIANS

SELECTED AND ANNOTATED

BY

STITH THOMPSON

INDIANA UNIVERSITY PRESS

BLOOMINGTON

FIRST PUBLISHED 1929
FIRST MIDLAND BOOK EDITION 1966
LIBRARY OF CONGRESS CATALOG CARD NUMBER: 66-22898
MANUFACTURED IN THE UNITED STATES OF AMERICA
pa. ISBN 0-253-20091-1
12 13 14 15 16 92 91 90 89 88

TO MY PARENTS

JOHN WARDEN THOMPSON
ELIZA McCLASKEY THOMPSON

PREFACE

D URING the past century the untiring labors of a score or two of field workers have gathered from the North American Indians by far the most extensive body of tales representative of any primitive people. These tales are available in government reports, folk-lore journals, and publications of learned societies. Unfortunately, the libraries in which more than a small portion of them can be examined are few, and even in the largest libraries the very wealth of material serves but to confuse the general reader who seeks without undue expenditure of time to acquaint himself with American Indian tales.

To meet the obvious need presented by this situation, this collection has been prepared. The editor has sought to make available in the compass of a single volume typical examples of such of these tales as have gained any general currency. Some tales are common to the tribes of a single culture area, some to the whole East or the whole West, and some are known over practically the whole continent. Indeed, few tales worth telling are confined to a single tribe. The assiduous reader soon learns to recognize many recurrent patterns or types, which transcend geographical and linguistic boundaries, and which form the basis of most of the tales in the various collections. In recognition of the persistence of these types, the editor has endeavored to secure representative versions of each of the better-known tales; then, by means of comparative notes, to show the extent of the distribution of each tale and each motif; and, finally, to present the material in such wise as to be obvious to the general reader.

The unit of arrangement of the volume is thus the tale — not the tribe or the culture area. That each area has characteristics peculiar to itself the editor shows in the Introduction, but for the purpose of this volume the tale-type has been chosen as the most logical basis for classification. Only the first chapter, that on mythological tales, follows a geographical order. It is hoped that the geographical arrangement of the notes will give adequate recognition to the significance of tribe and culture area.

In his choice of the texts of the tales the editor has striven to use a full, well-told example of each tale. With the following exceptions, he has given the texts as they appear in the original collections. (1) In stories about a single hero, the spelling of his name has been standardized. (2) Certain Indian names have been changed in spelling in order to be more easily pronounced by the general reader. Occasionally an Indian word has been omitted entirely when it did not add to the meaning of the story. (3) In several places irrelevant episodes have been omitted. These changes are always indicated.

For valuable assistance in the preparation of the volume, the editor owes much to his graduate students of the past few years, especially for making his notes on various motifs fuller than they would otherwise be. To his wife he is grateful for much assistance in many indispensable parts of the undertaking. Particularly to his friend, Professor Archer Taylor of the University of Chicago, he desires at this time to give thanks for his encouragement and detailed advice at nearly every stage of the work.

For courteous permission to reprint tales, acknowledgment is hereby made to the American Museum of Natural History, to the American Folk-Lore Society, to the Canadian Geological Survey, to Professor Franz Boas for the Jesup North Pacific Expedition Papers, to the Field Columbian Museum, to the University of California, to the Carnegie Institution, to G. P. Putnam's Sons, and to Wellesley College.

                                              STITH THOMPSON

BLOOMINGTON, INDIANA

CONTENTS

INTRODUCTION xv

CHAPTER I

MYTHOLOGICAL STORIES

    I. SEDNA, MISTRESS OF THE UNDERWORLD (Eskimo)   3

   II. SUN SISTER AND MOON BROTHER (Eskimo) . .   4

  III. GLOOSCAP (Micmac)   5

  IV. MANABOZHO   8

          A. MANABOZHO'S BIRTH (Menomini)   8

          B. MANABOZHO'S WOLF BROTHER (Menomini) . 10

          C. MANABOZHO PLAYS LACROSSE (Menomini) . 11

    V. THE WOMAN WHO FELL FROM THE SKY (Seneca) . 14

   VI. THE BEGINNING OF NEWNESS (Zuñi) 17

  VII. RAVEN'S ADVENTURES 19

          A. RAVEN BECOMES VORACIOUS (Tsimshian) . 19

          B. THE THEFT OF LIGHT (Tsimshian) 22

 VIII. THE CREATION (Maidu) 24

  IX. THE CREATION (Kato) 30

CHAPTER II

MYTHICAL INCIDENTS

    X. THE LIZARD-HAND (Yokuts) 38

   XI. DETERMINATION OF THE SEASONS (Tahltan) . . 38

  XII. MARRIAGE OF THE NORTH AND THE SOUTH (Cherokee) 39

 XIII. DETERMINATION OF NIGHT AND DAY (Iroquois) . 39

 XIV. THE THEFT OF FIRE (Maidu) 40

  XV. THE SUN SNARER (Menomini) 42

 XVI. THE MAN WHO ACTED AS THE SUN (Bella Coola) 44

XVII. THE MAN IN THE MOON (Lillooet) 45

XVIII. ORIGIN OF THE PLEIADES (Onondaga) 46

XIX. THE BAG OF WINDS (Thompson) 47

XX. THE BIRD WHOSE WINGS MADE THE WIND (Micmac) 48

XXI. THE RELEASE OF THE WILD ANIMALS (Comanche) 49

XXII. THE EMPOUNDED WATER (Malecite) 51

XXIII. THE ORIGIN OF CORN (Abanaki) 51

CHAPTER III

TRICKSTER TALES

XXIV. MANABOZHO'S ADVENTURES (Ojibwa and Menomini) 53

XXV. THE TRICKSTER'S GREAT FALL AND HIS REVENGE (Menomini) 57

XXVI. THE DECEIVED BLIND MEN (Menomini) 59

XXVII. THE TRICKSTER'S RACE (Blackfoot) 61

XXVIII. THE EYE-JUGGLER (Cheyenne) 63

XXIX. THE SHARPENED LEG (Cheyenne) 64

XXX. THE OFFENDED ROLLING STONE (Pawnee) . . . 64

XXXI. THE TRICKSTER KILLS THE CHILDREN (Arapaho) 66

XXXII. WILDCAT GETS A NEW FACE (Uintah Ute) . . . 68

XXXIII. THE TRICKSTER BECOMES A DISH (Lillooet) . . . 68

XXXIV. COYOTE PROVES HIMSELF A CANNIBAL (Jicarilla Apache) 70

XXXV. THE BUNGLING HOST (Thompson) 71

XXXVI. COYOTE AND PORCUPINE (Nez Percé) 73

XXXVII. BEAVER AND PORCUPINE (Tlingit) 75

XXXVIII. THE BIG TURTLE'S WAR PARTY (Skidi Pawnee) 75

CHAPTER IV

HERO TALES

XXXIX. THE SUN TESTS HIS SON-IN-LAW (Bella Coola) . . 78

XL. THE JEALOUS UNCLE (Kodiak) 87

XLI. BLUEJAY AND HIS COMPANIONS (Quinault) . . . 93

XLII. DUG-FROM-GROUND (Hupa) 97

XLIII. THE ATTACK ON THE GIANT ELK (Jicarilla Apache) 101

XLIV. LODGE-BOY AND THROWN-AWAY (Crow) 104
XLV. BLOOD-CLOT-BOY (Blackfoot) 108
XLVI. THE SON-IN-LAW TESTS (Timagami Ojibwa) . . 113
XLVII. THE JEALOUS FATHER (Cree) 116
XLVIII. DIRTY-BOY (Okanagon) 120
XLIX. THE FALSE BRIDEGROOM (Gros Ventre) 124

CHAPTER V

JOURNEYS TO THE OTHER WORLD

L. THE STAR HUSBAND — TYPE I: THE WISH TO
        MARRY A STAR (Timagami Ojibwa) 126
LI. THE STAR HUSBAND — TYPE II: THE GIRL EN-
        TICED TO THE SKY (Arapaho) 128
LII. THE STRETCHING TREE (Chilcotin) 130
LIII. THE ARROW CHAIN (Tlingit) 131
LIV. MUDJIKIWIS (Plains Cree) 135
LV. ORPHEUS (Cherokee) 145
LVI. THE VISIT TO CHIEF ECHO (Tsimshian) 148

CHAPTER VI

ANIMAL WIVES AND HUSBANDS

LVII. THE PIQUED BUFFALO-WIFE (Blackfoot) 150
LVIII. BEAR-WOMAN AND DEER-WOMAN (Lassik) . . . 153
LIX. SPLINTER-FOOT-GIRL (Arapaho) 154
LX. THE EAGLE AND WHALE HUSBANDS (Greenland
        Eskimo) 160
LXI. THE FOX-WOMAN (Labrador Eskimo) 161
LXII. THE WOMAN STOLEN BY KILLER-WHALES (Tahltan) 162
LXIII. THE ROLLING HEAD (Cheyenne) 163
LXIV. THE BEAR-WOMAN (Blackfoot) 164
LXV. THE DOG-HUSBAND (Quinault) 167
LXVI. THE YOUTH WHO JOINED THE DEER (Thompson) 169

CHAPTER VII

MISCELLANEOUS TALES

LXVII. THE DESERTED CHILDREN (Gros Ventre) . . . 174
LXVIII. THE PRINCESS WHO REJECTED HER COUSIN (Tsimshian) 178
LXIX. THE FATAL SWING (Osage) 184
LXX. THE SKIN-SHIFTING OLD WOMAN (Wichita) . . 186
LXXI. THE CHILD AND THE CANNIBAL (Bella Coola) . . 190
LXXII. THE CANNIBAL WHO WAS BURNED (Haida) . . 193
LXXIII. THE CONQUERING GAMBLER (Chilcotin) 194
LXXIV. THE DECEIVED BLIND MAN (Smith Sound Eskimo) 195
LXXV. THE GIRL WHO MARRIED HER BROTHER (Shasta) 196
LXXVI. THE SWAN-MAIDENS (Smith Sound Eskimo) . . 198
LXXVII. THE DEATH OF PITCH (Tsimshian) 199

CHAPTER VIII

TALES BORROWED FROM EUROPEANS

LXXVIII. THE SEVEN-HEADED DRAGON (Ojibwa) 201
LXXIX. JOHN THE BEAR (Assiniboin) 205
LXXX. THE ENCHANTED HORSE (Malecite) 208
LXXXI. LITTLE POUCET (Thompson) 218
LXXXII. THE WHITE CAT (Chilcotin) 222
LXXXIII. CINDERELLA (Zuñi) 225
LXXXIV. THE TRUE BRIDE (Thompson) 231
LXXXV. THE MAGIC APPLES (Penobscot) 238
LXXXVI. MAKING THE PRINCESS LAUGH (Micmac) . . . 241
LXXXVII. THE CLEVER NUMSKULL (Micmac) 248
LXXXVIII. THE FOX AND THE WOLF (Menomini) 254
LXXXIX. THE TAR-BABY (Cherokee) 258
XC. THE TURTLE'S RELAY RACE (Arikara) 258
XCI. THE PEACE FABLE (Wyandot) 259
XCII. THE ANT AND THE GRASSHOPPER (Shuswap) . . 260

CHAPTER IX

BIBLE STORIES

XCIII. ADAM AND EVE (Thompson) 261
XCIV. NOAH'S FLOOD (Thompson) 262
XCV. THE TOWER OF BABEL (Choctaw) 263
XCVI. CROSSING THE RED SEA (Cheyenne) 264

NOTES

ABBREVIATIONS USED IN NOTES AND BIBLIOGRAPHY . . . 269
COMPARATIVE NOTES 271
LIST OF MOTIFS DISCUSSED IN THE NOTES 361
SOURCES ARRANGED BY CULTURE AREAS AND TRIBES . . 368

BIBLIOGRAPHY 371

MAP OF TRIBES AND CULTURE AREAS

INTRODUCTION

NEARLY three centuries have passed since the first American Indian tales were recorded by Europeans. The Jesuit Fathers in their Relations beginning with 1633 report tales current among the tribes with whom they had come into contact. From them we have at this early date rather good versions of the Iroquois creation myth (No. v of this collection), of "The Sun Snarer" (No. xv) and of "The Empounded Water" (No. xxii). These tales have the same form when collected in the twentieth century as they had in the early seventeenth.

Though tales were reported sporadically during the next two centuries by travellers and explorers, it was not till the second quarter of the nineteenth century that any considerable body of this folk-lore became available. Through the labors of Henry Rowe Schoolcraft, the legends of the Ojibwa and their neighbors were reported at some length. Unfortunately, the scientific value of his work is marred by the manner in which he has reshaped the stories to suit his own literary taste. Several of his tales, indeed, are distorted almost beyond recognition. Nevertheless, he introduced to the civilized world a considerable body of Indian legend. Among these tales was the myth of Manabozho (No. iv), though he caused great confusion by adapting to his myth the name of the Iroquois hero, Hiawatha. Through the poem of Longfellow, the details of this myth have become a part of American literature. Another mythical tale known anew through the work of Schoolcraft was "The Sun Snarer" (No. xv), already mentioned as reported by the Jesuits. He also tells a number of trickster incidents (for example, Nos. xxiv, xxv, and xxvi). His work serves as a landmark in the history of the recording of American Indian tales.

A result of Schoolcraft's sentimentality has been the attitude of a large part of the general public toward Indian tradition. All sections of the country have acquired legends of "lovers' leaps." The courtship of Hiawatha and Minnehaha, the least "Indian" of any of the events in "Hiawatha," has come for many readers to stand as the typical American Indian tale. If a collection of authentic tales, like the present, can help correct so erroneous an impression, it will have been well worth preparing.

Since Schoolcraft's day collecting has continued. Most of it in the sixties, seventies, and eighties of the past century was done faithfully and well. Too little regard, indeed, was paid to the preservation of variants, or to reproducing carefully the style of the native narrator. But such embroidery as appears in the otherwise excellent volumes of Rink's Eskimo or Rand's Micmac tales seems to be in diction rather than in incident.

Beginning about 1890, largely through the influence of Professor Franz Boas and others inspired by the desire to make their work of scientific value, collectors have been covering the entire continent in an increasingly efficient manner. A number of agencies have contributed to the very gratifying results thus attained. The Bureau of American Ethnology in its reports and bulletins, the University of Pennsylvania Museum, the American Museum of Natural History, the American Folk-Lore Society in its memoirs and in the *Journal of American Folk-Lore* have issued tales from every quarter of the continent. Several universities and societies have devoted themselves to the cultivation of particular areas. Thus the Field Museum has specialized in tales of the Pueblo and Plains tribes; the University of California has confined itself largely to the tribes of California; the Jesup North Pacific Expedition, to the tribes of the North Pacific Coast; Columbia University, to the North Pacific Coast and to Oregon; and the Canadian Geological Survey, to the Central and Eastern Woodland tribes. The American Ethnological Society has issued in text and close translation a series of studies covering the continent. These are of especial value to students of linguistics and of literary style. Aside from all these organized efforts, independent collectors such as Cushing for the Zuñi, Curtin for the Modoc, the Wintun, the Yana, and the Seneca, and Grinnell for the Blackfoot, the Cheyenne, and the Pawnee, have added to the store of available material. Some idea of the extent of recent collections and of the manner in which the whole territory north of Mexico has been covered will be gained by an examination of the list of sources on page 368. No other primitive people has such an extensive and accurate record of its myths, tales, and legends as the North American Indian.

After even a limited perusal of a few representative volumes of these tales the reader will begin to recognize certain general types of story that prevail in nearly all parts of the continent. Further reading but confirms the prevalence of these fundamental types.

Prominent among these will be found mythological stories dealing with the world before it was in the present state. The primary purpose of such tales is to show the preparation for the present order of affairs. They often treat of demigods or culture heroes. They explain origins of animals, or tribes, or objects, or ceremonies, or the universe itself. The true creation myth, as Professor Boas points out, is almost wholly lacking, but origin myths of a sort are found over a large territory. The Zuñi myth (No. vi) and the California myths (Nos. viii and ix) are about as clear examples of the creation myth as are to be found. Stories of the "Glooscap" type (No. iii), in which the culture hero (in a world assumed as already existing) acts as an originator of various aspects of culture and is responsible for many changes in topography, are much more prevalent. In the Southwest and the Southeast, migration legends tell of the emergence of the tribe from lower worlds in mythological times.

Aside from such rather well-developed mythological tales, there are a number of separate incidents or episodes that evidently belong to the same world of thought. The whole purpose of such tales is to explain by some happening in an earlier world the existence of some phenomenon in present-day life. Without the explanation the tale is pointless.

Attempts at exact definition of "myth" as distinguished from "tale" seem futile. As Waterman has pointed out in his study of the explanatory element in North American mythology, it is quite certain that no satisfactory classification of tales can be made on the basis of whether some phenomenon is explained or not. By far the greater number of explanations he has studied are not organic: they are not necessary to the story, but are added as an ornament or for other reasons. The same explanations combine freely with a great number of different tales. Nor can more successful classification be made on the basis of ritualistic significance, or on that of personification. All these things appear and disappear — the tale remains as the only permanent element. In this volume, tales involving an earlier world and primarily devoted to explaining present conditions have been classed as mythical. But no sharp line can be drawn. Certainly no real difference is found in published collections, whether the author calls his book "myths," or "tales," or "legends."

A second class of tale is that relating the deeds of a trickster. Sometimes the buffoon is a human being, but more often he is an animal endowed with human characteristics. Usually it is quite impossible to tell whether animal or person is in the mind of the narrator. The distinction is never very clear. In the most human of these tales, such as the Manabozho cycle (No. xxiv), the animal nature of the trickster seems always in the background of the narrative. Sometimes the trickster appears outside his proper cycle and confusion between the two natures is especially marked. Such is true, for example, in the version of the "Son-in-Law Tests" here given (No. xlvi).

To the civilized reader, perhaps the most incongruous feature of the trickster tales is the frequent identification of the buffoon with the culture hero. Such identification is found over a large part of the continent. In one set of tales, for example, Manabozho is a beneficent being, bringing culture and light to his people (No. iv); in another (No. xxiv), he is the incarnation of greediness, lust, cruelty, and stupidity. As Professor Boas has shown, even the acts of benevolence of such trickster demigods are often mere accidental by-products of baser motives. Raven steals the sun that he may more easily satisfy his greed; incidentally, his people receive light. While it would be going too far to say that none of the trickster demigods is altruistic, one must always remember that most of the culture heroes are also tricksters and that even in their most dignified moments they are prone to show something of their dual nature.

A third large division of American Indian tales concerns the life of human beings under conditions at least remotely resembling the present. To be sure, in all of these the marvelous occupies a large place. Transformation, magic, otherworld journeys, ogres, and beast marriages abound. But the characters are thought of as distinctly human. The general background is the tribal life and environment. The resemblance to the European tale in method and material is often striking. The characters and the setting are usually as vague as in a story from Grimm, the events as definitely established by convention. Motivation is usually weak, frequently quite absent. But to the average educated reader this type of tale is often more interesting than either the mythological story or the trickster cycle. We seem to have at least a partial expression of the life of the people from whom the tales come.

A large group of these stories we may call "hero" tales, for they concern themselves with the exploits of a hero (or often of twin heroes). As will be seen from an examination of our fourth chapter, the tales usually relate attempts made to kill the hero and his successful escapes from death. He often deliberately seeks dangerous enemies and overcomes them. Frequently the hero is subjected to tests by his father-in-law — an incident bearing very interesting resemblances to the European Son-in-Law Test theme.

From one area to another the hero differs in type. On the North Pacific Coast the heroes of even this kind of tale may be of the animal-human type (for example, No. XVI); in California and on the Plains his supernatural birth is stressed (Nos. XLII, XLIV, XLV); the unpromising hero turned victor is common on the Plains (No. XLIX), the Plateau (No. XLVIII), and among the Iroquois. Twin heroes are frequent on the Plains and in the Southwest.

On the North Pacific Coast the hero cycle merges with the next to be mentioned — tales of journeys to the other world. In these stories there is, from the point of view of the civilized reader, a confusion of worlds. Usually the "other world" is pictured as above; sometimes as below; sometimes as across a vast river or sea. The cosmological concepts of the particular tribe are always in the background of these tales, and a real understanding of what the narrator has in mind can often be gained only by a serious study of the religious ideas of the tribe. In spite, however, of tribal differences, such simple concepts as a star-world, a sky window, a rope to the sky, a rainbow-bridge to the upper world are to be found everywhere. For example, "The Star Husband" (Nos. L and LI) is told over the entire width of the continent.

In the discussion of the trickster cycle, mention has been made of the confusion between man and animal. This same confusion exists in the many stories of beast marriages. Animals carry off human girls or marry human husbands. They have offspring — sometimes human, sometimes animal, sometimes capable of becoming either at will. Sometimes the animal spouse is a transformed person. The tales regularly end with the transformation of the animal spouse to human form, or with an escape from the animal.

All the classes of tales thus far discussed are sufficiently widespread to attract the attention of the casual reader. A number of stories of relatively wide distribution are much more difficult to classify. These have been grouped into a chapter to themselves (chapter VII).

In the stories of certain tribes the recent influence of the Europeans is very apparent. The French in Canada, the Spanish in the Southwest, and the negroes in the Southeast have contributed many tales to the tribes in their respective territories. Usually the Indians recognize these definitely as borrowings. European phraseology, background, and ideas abound. Not fewer than fifty well-known European tales are current among the American Indians. Several good examples of such tales, as well as of Bible narratives, form chapters VIII and IX of this collection.

As the discussion of types has several times implied, there is a difference in the tales of the American Indian as we pass from one culture area to another. The same themes may — usually do — appear, but there are differences, nevertheless. Certain kinds of tale or hero or setting may be favorites with one tribe and not with another. Explanatory stories may prevail here; hero myths there; trickster tales in a third tribe A few words will serve to characterize the various areas.

The Eskimos are poor in explanatory myths and trickster tales. Insignificant animal stories and accounts of monsters and pursuits occupy a much larger proportion of their mythology than the selections here given would indicate. As a whole, their stories have a very low level of interest. (Nos. I, II, XL, LX, LXI, LXXIV, LXXVI.)

The tribes of the Mackenzie River district have little to distinguish their tales from those of their neighbors. As they approach the Eskimos to the north, the Coast tribes to the west, the Plains and Plateau tribes to the south, their stories show corresponding change.

In contrast the Plateau area gives us collections of marked individuality. A wandering hero-trickster changes topography

and gets into mischief. Journeys to the upper world, unpromis-
ing heroes and heroines, and animal marriages are frequent.
These peoples have borrowed freely from the Europeans. Their
trickster cycle contains both Plains and Pacific Coast elements.
(Nos. XVII, XIX, XXXIII, XXXV, XXXVI, XLVIII, LXVI, LXXIII,
LXXXI, LXXXII, XCII, XCIII, XCIV.)

Tales of the North Pacific Coast are of a considerable variety.
No more than the peoples already discussed do they possess a
real creation myth. The trickster — Raven in the north, Mink,
and Blue Jay farther south — is very active. Tales based on
ritual or social rank are frequent. The sea is ever present, and
in place of the animals of the Plateau, these tribes tell stories
of whales and salmon. Tales involving the other world are
prominent. (Nos. VII, XI, XVI, XXXVII, XXXIX, XLI, LIII, LVI,
LXII, LXV, LXVIII, LXXI, LXXII, LXXVII.)

The interest of the teller of tales in California seems to be two
things only — the creation and the deeds of the trickster. A
few other animal tales are present. One feels that, with the
possible exception of the Eskimos, the range of interest is least
among the California Indians of any tribes on the continent.
(Nos. VIII, IX, X, XIV, XLII, LVIII.)

In the Plains the range of interest is extraordinarily wide.
Practically every class of tale current anywhere occurs here.
If there are any favorite types they are the trickster and the
hero tales. In certain parts of the area (for example, among
the Caddoan tribes) the origin myth is important. (Nos. XXI,
XXVII, XXVIII, XXIX, XXX, XXXI, XXXII, XXXVIII, XLIV, XLV,
XLIX, LI, LIV, LVII, LIX, LXIII, LXIV, LXVII, LXIX, LXX, LXXIX,
XC, XCVI.)

In general spirit it is hard to distinguish between the tales
of the Plains and those of the Central Woodland. The trickster cycle in almost all its parts is common to the two areas.
The mythology of the Central Woodland tribes is nearly uniform, whereas the Plains tribes show great divergence. The
Manabozho cycle prevails through most of this area. (Nos.
IV, XXIV, XXV, XXVI, XLVI, XLVII, LXXVIII, LXXXVIII.)

The Northeast Woodland has been in such constant contact
with Europeans that the native tales, except among such remote tribes as the Naskapi, have been almost crowded out.
In the culture-hero cycle, myths explaining topography are
prominent. Animal marriages and trickster tales are frequent.

The Glooscap cycle is notable as an account of a culture hero not combined (or certainly to a very small extent) with a trickster. (Nos. III, XX, XXII, XXIII, LXXX, LXXXV, LXXXVI.)

No other tribes show such thorough independence in their tales and detachment from other sections as do the Iroquois. Though their origin myth has much in common with that of the Central Woodland, the rest of their tales show little outside influence. The reader is impressed with a great monotony of motivation and treatment. Accounts of cruel uncles, wicked brothers, cannibalistic mothers, flying heads, and ravaging monsters are given but slight relief through an occasional trickster tale or a beautiful myth of otherworld journeying. (Nos. V, XIII, XVIII, XCI.)

Animal tales and migration legends mark the collections from the Southeast. The animal cycle has become so greatly influenced by the "Uncle Remus" tales as to be at least as much negro as Indian. (Nos. XII, LV, LXXIX, XCV.)

The tribes of the Southwest desert land have many interesting stories of the emergence of the tribe from lower worlds and its final establishment in its present habitat. Their hero tales are usually connected with their mythology. The trickster cycle of the Plains is also prevalent. Among some tribes (for example, the Navaho) there is a tendency to string many tales into a long and complicated myth. (Nos. VI, XXXIV, XLIII, LXXXIII.)

After due consideration is given to the differences in the various areas, however, these will not be found nearly so striking as the likenesses. Generally speaking, though proportion varies, the same classes of tales are found everywhere on the continent. The practised reader immediately recognizes a tale as characteristically American Indian, whether it comes from California or Labrador.

In spite of the intrusion of stories from the whites during the past few centuries, the body of older American Indian tales is very clearly established. These tales have been here for a very long time — long enough for the incidents to travel over the entire continent. That they have some sort of relation to myths of the Old World seems in many cases most probable, but until the exact nature of parallels has been studied and a large number of them traced, speculation is perhaps unwise. Certain very clear instances of ancient migration of tales from Asia even now appear, but only very careful and detailed investigation will make any larger generalization safe.

The American Indian tale offers ample material for much profitable study. The groping toward literary style, the attempt to narrate interestingly, the primitive conception of humor — such are only a few of the possibilities of their use for the student. To the general reader they hold out great attractions as a characteristic product of our native Americans. We may well be grateful to the faithful collectors who have gathered such a wealth of material for our profit and enjoyment.

TALES OF THE
NORTH AMERICAN INDIANS

CHAPTER I

MYTHOLOGICAL STORIES[1]

I. SEDNA, MISTRESS OF THE UNDERWORLD[2]

(ESKIMO: Boas, *Report of the Bureau of American Ethnology*, vi, 583)

ONCE upon a time there lived on a solitary shore an Inung with his daughter Sedna. His wife had been dead for some time and the two led a quiet life. Sedna grew up to be a handsome girl and the youths came from all around to sue for her hand, but none of them could touch her proud heart. Finally, at the breaking up of the ice in the spring a fulmar flew from over the ice and wooed Sedna with enticing song. "Come to me," it said; "come into the land of the birds, where there is never hunger, where my tent is made of the most beautiful skins. You shall rest on soft bearskins. My fellows, the fulmars, shall bring you all your heart may desire; their feathers shall clothe you; your lamp shall always be filled with oil, your pot with meat." Sedna could not long resist such wooing and they went together over the vast sea.[3] When at last they reached the country of the fulmar, after a long and hard journey, Sedna discovered that her spouse had shamefully deceived her. Her new home was not built of beautiful pelts, but was covered with wretched fishskins, full of holes, that gave free entrance to wind and snow. Instead of soft reindeer skins her bed was made of hard walrus hides and she had to live on miserable fish, which the birds brought her. Too soon she discovered that she had thrown away her opportunities when in her foolish pride she had rejected the Inuit youth. In her woe she sang: "Aja. O father, if you knew how wretched I am you would come to me and we would hurry away in your boat over the waters. The birds look unkindly upon me the stranger; cold winds roar about my bed; they give me but miserable food. O come and take me back home. Aja."

When a year had passed and the sea was again stirred by warmer winds, the father left his country to visit Sedna. His daughter greeted him joyfully and besought him to take her back home. The father, hearing of the outrages wrought upon his daughter, determined upon revenge. He killed the fulmar, took Sedna into his boat, and they quickly left the country which had brought so much sorrow to Sedna. When the other fulmars came home and found their companion dead and his wife gone, they all flew away in search of the fugitives. They were very sad over the death of their poor murdered comrade and continue to mourn and cry until this day.[4]

Having flown a short distance they discerned the boat and stirred up a heavy storm. The sea rose in immense waves that threatened the pair with destruction. In this mortal peril the father determined to offer Sedna to the birds and flung her overboard. She clung to the edge of the boat with a death grip. The cruel father then took a knife and cut off the first joints of her fingers. Falling into the sea they were transformed into whales, the nails turning into whalebone. Sedna holding on to the boat more tightly, the second finger joints fell under the sharp knife and swam away as seals; when the father cut off the stumps of the fingers they became ground seals.

Meantime the storm subsided, for the fulmars thought Sedna was drowned. The father then allowed her to come into the boat again. But from that time she cherished a deadly hatred against him and swore bitter revenge. After they got ashore, she called her dogs and let them gnaw off the feet and hands of her father while he was asleep. Upon this he cursed himself, his daughter, and the dogs which had maimed him; whereupon the earth opened and swallowed the hut, the father, the daughter, and the dogs. They have since lived in the land of Adlivun,[5] of which Sedna is the mistress.

II. SUN SISTER AND MOON BROTHER [6]

(ESKIMO: Boas, *Report of the Bureau of American Ethnology*, vi, 597)

In olden times a brother and his sister lived in a large village in which there was a singing house, and every night the sister with her playfellows enjoyed themselves in this house. Once upon a time, when all the lamps in the singing house were extinguished, somebody came in and outraged her. She was unable to recognize him; but she blackened her hands with soot and when the same again happened besmeared the man's back with it.[7] When the lamps were relighted she saw that the violator was her brother.[8] In great anger she sharpened a knife and cut off her breasts, which she offered to him, saying: "Since you seem to relish me, eat this." Her brother fell into a passion and she fled from him, running about the room. She seized a piece of wood (with which the lamps are kept in order) which was burning brightly and rushed out of the house. The brother took another one, but in his pursuit he fell down and extinguished his light, which continued to glow only faintly. Gradually both were lifted up and continued their course in the sky, the sister being transformed into the sun, the brother into the moon.[9] Whenever the new moon first appears she sings:

Aningaga tapika, takirn tapika qaumidjatedlirpoq; qaumatitaudle.
Aningaga tapika, tikipoq tapika.

(My brother up there, the moon up there begins to shine; he will be bright.
My brother up there, he is coming up there.)

III. GLOOSCAP [10]

(MICMAC: Rand, *Legends of the Micmacs*, p. 232, No. 35)

The tradition respecting Glooscap is that he came to this country from the east, — far across the great sea; that he was a divine being, though in the form of a man. He was not far from any of the Indians (this is the identical rendering of the Indian words used by my friend Stephen in relating the sketches of his history here given). When Glooscap went away, he went toward the west.[11] There he is still tented; and two important personages are near him, who are called Kuhkw and Coolpujot, — of whom more anon.

Glooscap was the friend and teacher of the Indians; all they knew of the arts he taught them.[12] He taught them the names of the constellations and stars; he taught them how to hunt and fish, and cure what they took; how to cultivate the ground, as far as they were trained in husbandry. When he first came, he brought a woman with him, whom he ever addressed as Grandmother,[13] — a very general epithet for an old woman. She was not his wife, nor did he ever have a wife. He was always sober, grave, and good; all that the Indians knew of what was wise and good he taught them.

His canoe was a granite rock.[14] On one occasion he put to
sea in this craft, and took a young woman with him as a pas-
senger. She proved to be a bad girl; and this was manifested
by the troubles that ensued. A storm arose, and the waves
dashed wildly over the canoe; he accused her of being the cause,
through her evil deeds, and so he determined to rid himself of
her. For this purpose he stood in for the land, leaped ashore,
but would not allow her to follow; putting his foot against the
heavy craft, he pushed it off to sea again with the girl on it,
telling her to become whatever she desired to be. She was
transformed into a large, ferocious fish, called by the Indians
keeganibe, said to have a huge dorsal fin, — like the sail of a
boat, it is so large and high out of the water.

The Indians sometimes visit Glooscap at his present residence, so says tradition; this is in a beautiful land in the west.
He taught them when he was with them that there was such a
place, and led them to look forward to a residence there, and to
call it their beautiful home in the far west, — where, if good,
they would go at death.

The journey to that fair region far away is long, difficult,
and dangerous; the way back is short and easy. Some years
ago, seven stout-hearted young men attempted the journey, and
succeeded. Before reaching the place, they had to pass over a
mountain, the ascent of which was up a perpendicular bluff, and
the descent on the other side was still more difficult, for the
top hung far over the base. The fearful and unbelieving could
not pass at all; but the good and confident could travel it with
ease and safety, as though it were a level path.

Having crossed the mountain, the road ran between the
heads of two huge serpents, which lay just opposite each
other; and they darted out their tongues, so as to destroy whom-
soever they hit. But the good and the firm of heart could dart
past between the strokes of their tongues, so as to evade them.[113b]
One more difficulty remained; it was a wall, as of a thick, heavy
cloud, that separated the present world from that beautiful
region beyond. This cloudy wall rose and fell at intervals, and
struck the ground with such force that whatever was caught
under it would be crushed to atoms; but the good could dart
under when it rose, and come out on the other side unscathed.[15]

This our seven young heroes succeeded in doing. There they
found three wigwams, — one for Glooscap, one for Coolpujot,

and one for Kuhkw. These are all mighty personages, but Glooscap is supreme; the other two are subordinates. Coolpujot has no bones. He cannot move himself, but is rolled over each spring and fall by Glooscap's order, being turned with handspikes; hence the name Coolpujot (rolled over by handspikes). In the autumn he is turned towards the west, in the spring towards the east; and this is a figure of speech, denoting the revolving seasons of the year,[16] — his mighty breath and looks, by which he can sweep down whole armies and work wonders on a grand scale, indicating the weather: frost, snow, ice, and sunshine. (Such was Stephen's very satisfactory explanation.)

Kuhkw means Earthquake; this mighty personage can pass along under the surface of the ground, making all things shake and tremble by his power.

All these seven visitors had requests to proffer, and each received what he asked for; [17] though the gift did not always correspond with the spirit of the request, it oftentimes agreed with the letter. For instance, one of these seven visitors was wonderfully enamoured of a fine country, and expressed a desire to remain there, and to live long; whereupon, at Glooscap's direction, Earthquake took him and stood him up, and he became a cedar-tree.[18] When the wind blew through its boughs, they were bent and broken with great fracas, — making a thunder-storm that rolled far and wide over the country, accompanied by strong winds, which scattered the cedar-boughs and seeds in all directions, producing all the cedar-groves that exist in New Brunswick, Nova Scotia, and elsewhere.

The other men started, and reached home in a short time.

One of them had asked for a medicine that would be effectual in curing disease. This he obtained; but, neglecting to follow implicitly the directions given, he lost it before he reached home. It was carefully wrapped up in a piece of paper, and he was charged not to undo the parcel until he reached home. His curiosity got the better of his judgment; he could not see what difference it could make if he just looked at his prize as he was going along. So he undid the parcel, and *presto!* the medicine slipped out on the ground, spread and slid in all directions, covering up the face of the earth, and vanishing from sight.[19]

On another occasion several young men went to see Glooscap in his present abode. One of them went to obtain the power of winning the heart of some fair one, which all his unaided skill had failed hitherto to do; an hundred times he had tried to get a wife, but the girls all shunned him. Many of the party who started on this perilous expedition failed to overcome the difficulties that lay in their way, and turned back, baffled and defeated; but several of them succeeded. They were all hospitably entertained; all presented their requests, and were favorably heard. The man who sought power to captivate some female heart was the last to proffer his petition. Glooscap and his two subordinates conferred together in a whisper, and then Earthquake informed him that his ugly looks and still more ugly manners were the chief hindrances to his success; but they must try to help him. So he was handed a small parcel, and directed not to open it until he reached his own village; this he took, and they all set off for home together. The night before they arrived, he could restrain his curiosity no longer; he opened the parcel, the foolish fellow! Out flew young women by the scores and hundreds, covering the face of the earth, piling themselves in towering heaps, and burying the poor fellow, crushing him to the earth under the accumulating weight of their bodies. His comrades had cautioned him against disobeying the mandate, and had begged him not to undo the parcel; but he had not heeded the caution. They now heard him calling for help, but he called in vain, they could not help him; and his cries became fainter and fainter, and finally ceased altogether. Morning came at last. The young women had all vanished, and the fragments of their comrade were scattered over the ground; he had been killed and ground to atoms as the result of his unbridled curiosity and disobedience.

IV. MANABOZHO [20]

A. MANABOZHO'S BIRTH

(MENOMINI: Skinner and Satterlee, *Anthropological Papers of the American Museum of Natural History*, xiii, 239)

In the beginning, there was a lone old woman living on this island. Nobody knows where she came from, nor how she got here, but it is true that she dwelt in a wigwam with her only daughter. Wild potatoes were the only food of the two women.

Every day the old woman took her wooden hoe and went out to gather them. She packed them home and dried them in the sun, for in those days, there was no such thing as fire in that part of the world.

One day her daughter begged to go with her. "Mother, let me go and help you; between us we can dig more potatoes than you can alone." "No, my daughter, you stay here," said the old woman; "I don't want you to go. Your place is at home caring for the lodge." "Oh dear! I don't like to stay here alone all day," teased the girl; "it's so lonely when you are gone! I'd much rather go with you. There is another old hoe here that I can use. Please let me go too."

At last, the old woman consented to her daughter's pleading; the two armed themselves with their tools and set out. After a little journey they came to a damp ravine. "Here is the place where I always come to gather the potatoes," cried the mother; "you can dig here too. But there is one thing that I must warn you about, when you are digging these potatoes; I want you to face the south. Be sure not to forget this. It was because I was afraid that you could not be trusted to remember that I never brought you here before." "Oh, that's all right, I won't forget," cried the girl. "Very well then, you stay right here and work; I am going to dig over there."

The girl set to work with a will, and enjoyed her task very much. "Oh how nice it is to dig potatoes!" she said, and kept up a running stream of conversation with her mother as she labored. As the time passed by, the daughter gradually forgot her promise and at last turned round and faced in the opposite direction as she dug. All at once there came a great rushing, roaring noise from the heavens and the wind swept down where she stood and whirled her round and round. "Oh, mother! Help! Come quick!" she screamed. Her mother dropped everything and rushed to her aid. "Grab me by the back and hold me down!" cried the girl in terror. The old lady seized her with one hand and steadied herself, meanwhile, by catching hold of some bushes. "Hold me as tightly as you can!" she gasped. "Now you see why I told you to stay at home! You are being properly punished for your disobedience."

Suddenly the wind stopped. The air was as calm as though nothing had happened. The two women hastily gathered up their potatoes and hurried home. After that the old woman worked alone. Everything went well for a while, and then, one day the daughter complained. "I feel very strange and different, mother; there seems to be something within me." The old woman scrutinized the girl narrowly, but made no answer, for she knew that her daughter was pregnant.[21] At last, she was brought to bed and gave birth to three children. The first of these was Manabozho, the second was a little wolf, Muh'wäse, and the last was a sharp flint stone. When the unfortunate mother gave issue to the rock, it cut her and she died. The old woman mourned her daughter greatly. In a paroxysm of rage and grief, she threw away the flint stone, but Manabozho * and Muh'wäse she cherished and cared for until they grew to be children.

B. Manabozho's Wolf Brother

(Menomini: Hoffman, *Report of the Bureau of American Ethnology*, xiv, 115)

When Manabozho had accomplished the works for which Kishä' Ma'nido [22] sent him down to the earth, he went far away and built his wigwam on the northeastern shore of a large lake, where he took up his abode. As he was alone, the good manidos concluded to give him for a companion his twin brother, whom they brought to life and called Naq'pote (which signifies an expert marksman). He was formed like a human being, but, being a manido, could assume the shape of a wolf, in which form he hunted for food. Manabozho was aware of the anger of the bad manidos who dwelt beneath the earth, and warned his brother, the Wolf, never to return home by crossing the lake, but always to go around along the shore. Once after the Wolf had been hunting all day long he found himself directly opposite his wigwam, and being tired, concluded to cross the lake. He had not gone halfway across when the ice broke, so the Wolf was seized by the bad manidos, and destroyed.[23]

Manabozho at once knew what had befallen his brother, and in his distress mourned for four days. Every time that Manabozho sighed the earth trembled, which caused the hills and ridges to form over its surface. Then the shade of Moquaio, the Wolf, appeared before Manabozho, and knowing that his brother could not be restored Manabozho told him to follow the path of the setting sun and become the chief of the shades in

---

* The hero's name appears in many forms. In this collection it is standardized.

the Hereafter where all would meet.[24] Manabozho then secreted himself in a large rock near Mackinaw. Here his uncles, the people, for many years visited Manabozho, and always built a long lodge, the mitä'wiko'mik, where they sang; so when Manabozho did not wish to see them in his human form he appeared to them in the form of a little white rabbit, with trembling ears, just as he had first appeared to Nokomis.

C. Manabozho plays Lacrosse [25]

(Menomini: Skinner and Satterlee, *Anthropological Papers of the American Museum of Natural History*, xiii, 255)

Now it happened that the beings above challenged the beings below to a mighty game of lacrosse. The beings below were not slow to accept the gage and the goals were chosen, one at Detroit and the other at Chicago. The center of the field was at a spot called Ke'sosasit ("where the sun is marked," [on the rocks]) near Sturgeon Bay on Lake Michigan. The above beings called their servants, the thunderers, the eagles, the geese, the ducks, the pigeons, and all the fowls of the air to play for them, and the great white underground bear called upon the fishes, the snakes, the otters, the deer, and all the beasts of the field to take the part of the powers below.

When everything was arranged, and the two sides were preparing, Manabozho happened along that way. As he strolled by he heard someone passing at a distance and whooping at the top of his voice. Curious to see who it was, Manabozho hastened over to the spot whence the noise emanated. Here he found a funny little fellow, like a tiny Indian, no other, however, than Nakuti, the sun fish. "What on earth is the matter with you?" queried Manabozho. "Why have n't you heard?" asked Sunfish, astonished; "to-morrow there is going to be a ball game, and fishes and the beasts of the field will take the part of the powers below against the thunderers and all the fowls, who are championing the powers above." "Oh ho!" said Manabozho, and the simple Nakuti departed, whooping with delight. "Well, well," thought Manabozho, "I must see this famous game, even if I was not invited."

The chiefs of the underworld left their homes in the waters and climbed high up on a great mountain where they could look over the whole field, and having chosen this spot they returned.

Manabozho soon found their tracks and followed them to the place of vantage which they had selected. He judged by its appearance that they had decided to stay there, so he concluded that he would not be far away when the game commenced. Early next morning, before daybreak, he went to the place, and, through his magic power he changed himself into a tall pine tree, burnt on one side.[26]

At dawn, he heard a great hubbub and whooping. From everywhere he heard derisive voices calling "Hau! Hau! Hau!" and "Hoo! hoo! hoo!" to urge on the enemy. Then appeared the deer, the mink, the otter, and all the land beings and the fishes in human form. They arrived at their side of the field and took their places and all became silent for a time. Suddenly the sky grew dark, and the rush of many wings made a thunderous rumbling, above which rose whoops, screams, screeches, cackling, calling, hooting, all in one terrific babel. Then the thunderers swooped down, and the golden eagles, and the bald eagles, and the buzzards, hawks, owls, pigeons, geese, ducks, and all manner of birds, and took the opposite end of the field. Then silence dropped down once more, and the sides lined up, the weakest near the goals, the strongest in the center. Someone tossed the ball high in the air and a pell mell mêlée followed, with deafening howling and whoopings. Back and forth surged the players, now one side gaining, now the other. At last one party wrested the ball through the other's ranks and sped it toward the Chicago goal. Down the field it went, and Manabozho strained his eyes to follow its course. It was nearly at the goal, the keepers were rushing to guard it and in the midst of the brandished clubs, legs, arms, and clouds of dust something notable was happening that Manabozho could not see. In his excitement he forgot where he was and changed back into a man.

Once in human shape he came to himself, and looking about, noted that the onlookers had not discovered him. Fired by his lust for revenge he promptly took his bow, which he had kept with him all the time, strung it, and fired twice at each of the underground gods as they sat on their mountain. His arrows sped true, and the gods rushed for the water, falling all over themselves as they scurried down hill. The impact of their diving caused great waves to roll down the lake towards the Chicago goal. Some of the players saw them coming, rolling high over the tree tops. "Manabozho, Manabozho!" they cried in breathless fright.

At once all the players on both sides rushed back to the center field to look. "What is the matter?" said everyone to everyone else. "Why it must have been Manabozho; he's done this; nobody else would dare to attack the underground gods." When the excited players reached the center of the field they found the culprit had vanished. "Let's all look for Manabozho," cried someone. "We will use the power of the water for our guide." So the players all waded into the water, and the water rose up and went ahead of them. It knew very well where Manabozho had gone.

In the meantime Manabozho was skipping away as fast as he could, for he was frightened at what the consequences of his rashness might be. All at once he happened to look back and saw the water flowing after him.[57] He ran faster and faster, but still it came. He strained himself to his utmost speed and it gained on him. On, on, led the chase, further, and further away.

"Oh dear! I believed that water will get me yet!" worried Manabozho. As he scampered he saw a high mountain, on the top of which grew a lofty pine. "I guess I'll go there and ask for help," thought Manabozho. So up the mountain side he raced, with the water swiftly rising behind him. "Hē′ē! Nasē′! Oh my dear little brother," gasped Manabozho to the pine tree, "won't you help me? Save me from the water! I am talking to you, pine tree." "How can I help you?" asked the pine deliberately. "You can let me climb on you, and every time I reach your top, you can grow another length," cried Manabozho anxiously, for the water was coming on.

"But I haven't so much power as all that; I can only grow four lengths." Oh, that will do anyway, I'll take that!" screamed Manabozho in terror, jumping into the branches just a few inches ahead of the water. With all his might and main Manabozho climbed, but the water wet his feet as it rose, rose, rose. He reached the top. "Oh, little brother, stretch yourself," he begged. The pine tree shot up one length,[199] and Manabozho climbed faster than ever, but still the water followed. "Oh, little brother, stretch yourself," he entreated. Up shot the pine tree, and up climbed Manabozho, but the water followed inexorably. When he reached the top, the tree shot up again, but still the water rose. "Stretch yourself, only once more, little brother, give me just one more length," prayed Manabozho, "maybe it will save me; if it does n't, why I'll be drowned." Up shot the pine tree for the fourth and last time. Manabozho climbed to the top, and the water followed. There it stopped. Manabozho clung to the tree with all his might, frightened half to death, but it rose no more.

V. THE WOMAN WHO FELL FROM THE SKY [27]

(SENECA: Curtin and Hewitt, *Report of the Bureau of American Ethnology*, xxxii, 460, No. 98)

A long time ago human beings lived high up in what is now called heaven. They had a great and illustrious chief.

It so happened that this chief's daughter was taken very ill with a strange affection. All the people were very anxious as to the outcome of her illness. Every known remedy was tried in an attempt to cure her, but none had any effect.

Near the lodge of this chief stood a great tree, which every year bore corn used for food. One of the friends of the chief had a dream, in which he was advised to tell the chief that in order to cure his daughter he must lay her beside this tree, and that he must have the tree dug up. This advice was carried out to the letter. While the people were at work and the young woman lay there, a young man came along. He was very angry and said: "It is not at all right to destroy this tree. Its fruit is all that we have to live on." With this remark he gave the young woman who lay there ill a shove with his foot, causing her to fall into the hole that had been dug.

Now, that hole opened into this world,[28] which was then all water,[29] on which floated waterfowl of many kinds. There was no land at that time. It came to pass that as these waterfowl saw this young woman falling they shouted, "Let us receive her," whereupon they, at least some of them, joined their bodies together, and the young woman fell on this platform of bodies. When these were wearied they asked, "Who will volunteer to care for this woman?" The great Turtle then took her, and when he got tired of holding her, he in turn asked who would take his place. At last the question arose as to what they should do to provide her with a permanent resting place in this world. Finally it was decided to prepare the earth, on which she would live in the future. To do this it was determined that soil from the bottom of the primal sea should be brought up and placed on the broad, firm carapace of the Turtle, where it would increase in size to such an extent that it would accommodate all the creatures that should be produced thereafter. After much discussion the toad was finally persuaded to dive to the bottom of the waters in search of soil. Bravely making the attempt, he succeeded in bringing up soil from the depths of the sea.[30] This was carefully spread over the carapace of the Turtle,[31] and at once both began to grow in size and depth.

After the young woman recovered from the illness from which she suffered when she was cast down from the upper world, she built herself a shelter, in which she lived quite contentedly. In the course of time she brought forth a girl baby, who grew rapidly in size and intelligence.

When the daughter had grown to young womanhood, the mother and she were accustomed to go out to dig wild potatoes.[32] Her mother had said to her that in doing this she must face the West at all times. Before long the young daughter gave signs that she was about to become a mother. Her mother reproved her, saying that she had violated the injunction not to face the east, as her condition showed that she had faced the wrong way while digging potatoes. It is said that the breath of the West Wind had entered her person, causing conception.[21] When the days of her delivery were at hand, she overheard twins within her body in a hot debate as to which should be born first and as to the proper place of exit, one declaring that he was going to emerge through the armpit of his mother, the other saying that he would emerge in the natural way.[33] The first one born, who was of a reddish color, was called Othagwenda; that is, Flint. The other, who was light in color, was called Djuskaha; that is, the Little Sprout.

The grandmother of the twins liked Djuskaha and hated the other; so they cast Othagwenda into a hollow tree some distance from the lodge.[34]

The boy that remained in the lodge grew very rapidly, and soon was able to make himself bows and arrows and to go out to hunt in the vicinity. Finally, for several days he returned home without his bow and arrows. At last he was asked why he had to have a new bow and arrows every morning. He re-

plied that there was a young boy in a hollow tree in the neighborhood who used them. The grandmother inquired where the
tree stood, and he told her; whereupon then they went there
and brought the other boy home again.

When the boys had grown to man's estate, they decided that
it was necessary for them to increase the size of their island,
so they agreed to start out together, afterward separating to
create forests and lakes and other things. They parted as
agreed, Othagwenda going westward and Djuskaha eastward.
In the course of time, on returning, they met in their shelter
or lodge at night, then agreeing to go the next day to see what
each had made. First they went west to see what Othagwenda
had made. It was found that he had made the country all
rocks and full of ledges, and also a mosquito which was very
large. Djuskaha asked the mosquito to run, in order that he
might see whether the insect could fight. The mosquito ran,
and sticking his bill through a sapling, thereby made it fall,
at which Djuskaha said, "That will not be right, for you would
kill the people who are about to come." So, seizing him, he
rubbed him down in his hands, causing him to become very
small[12]; then he blew on the mosquito, whereupon he flew away.
He also modified some of the other animals which his brother
had made. After returning to their lodge, they agreed to go
the next day to see what Djuskaha had fashioned. On visiting
the east the next day, they found that Djuskaha had made a
large number of animals which were so fat that they could
hardly move; that he had made the sugar-maple trees to drop
syrup; that he had made the sycamore tree to bear fine fruit;
that the rivers were so formed that half the water flowed up-
stream and the other half downstream. Then the reddish-
colored brother, Othagwenda, was greatly displeased with
what his brother had made, saying that the people who were
about to come would live too easily and be too happy. So he
shook violently the various animals — the bears, deer, and
turkeys — causing them to become small at once, a characteristic which attached itself to their descendants. He also caused
the sugar maple to drop sweetened water only, and the fruit
of the sycamore to become small and useless; and lastly he
caused the water of the rivers to flow in only one direction,
because the original plan would make it too easy for the human
beings who were about to come to navigate the streams.

The inspection of each other's work resulted in a deadly dis-agreement between the brothers,[35] who finally came to grips and blows, and Othagwenda was killed in the fierce struggle.

VI. THE BEGINNING OF NEWNESS [36]

(Zuñi: Cushing, *Report of the Bureau of American Ethnology*, xiii, 379)

Before the beginning of the new-making, Awonawilona (the Maker and Container of All, the All-father Father), solely had being. There was nothing else whatsoever throughout the great space of the ages save everywhere black darkness in it, and everywhere void desolation.

In the beginning of the new-made, Awonawilona conceived within himself and thought outward in space, whereby mists of increase, steams potent of growth, were evolved and uplifted. Thus, by means of his innate knowledge, the All-container made himself in person and form of the Sun whom we hold to be our father and who thus came to exist and appear. With his appearance came the brightening of the spaces with light, and with the brightening of the spaces the great mist-clouds were thickened together and fell, whereby was evolved water in water; yea, and the world-holding sea.

With his substance of flesh outdrawn from the surface of his person, the Sun-father formed the seed-stuff of twain worlds, impregnating therewith the great waters, and lo! in the heat of his light these waters of the sea grew green and scums rose upon them, waxing wide and weighty until, behold! they became Awitelin Tsita, the "Four-fold Containing Mother-earth," and Apoyan Tä'chu, the "All-covering Father-sky." [37]

From the lying together of these twain upon the great world-waters, so vitalizing, terrestrial life was conceived; whence began all beings of earth, men and the creatures, in the Four-fold womb of the World.

Thereupon the Earth-mother repulsed the Sky-father, growing big and sinking deep into the embrace of the waters below, thus separating from the Sky-father in the embrace of the waters above. As a woman forebodes evil for her first-born ere born, even so did the Earth-mother forebode, long withholding from birth her myriad progeny and meantime seeking counsel with the Sky-father. "How," said they to one another, "shall our children when brought forth, know one place from another, even by the white light of the Sun-father?"

Now like all the surpassing beings the Earth-mother and the Sky-father were changeable, even as smoke in the wind; transmutable at thought, manifesting themselves in any form at will, like as dancers may by mask-making.

Thus, as a man and woman, spake they, one to the other. "Behold!" said the Earth-mother as a great terraced bowl appeared at hand and within it water, "this is as upon me the homes of my tiny children shall be. On the rim of each world-country they wander in, terraced mountains shall stand, making in one region many, whereby country shall be known from country, and within each, place from place. Behold, again!" said she as she spat on the water and rapidly smote and stirred it with her fingers. Foam formed, gathering about the terraced rim, mounting higher and higher. "Yea," said she, "and from my bosom they shall draw nourishment, for in such as this shall they find the substance of life whence we were ourselves sustained, for see!" Then with her warm breath she blew across the terraces; white flecks of the foam broke away, and, floating over above the water, were shattered by the cold breath of the Sky-father attending, and forthwith shed downward abundantly fine mist and spray! "Even so, shall white clouds float up from the great waters at the borders of the world, and clustering about the mountain terraces of the horizons be borne aloft and abroad by the breaths of the surpassing of soul-beings, and of the children, and shall hardened and broken be by thy cold, shedding downward, in rain-spray, the water of life, even into the hollow places of my lap! For therein chiefly shall nestle our children mankind and creature-kind, for warmth in thy coldness."

Lo! even the trees on high mountains near the clouds and the Sky-father crouch low toward the Earth-mother for warmth and protection! Warm is the Earth-mother, cold the Sky-father, even as woman is the warm, man the cold being!

"Even so!" said the Sky-father; "Yet not alone shalt *thou* helpful be unto our children, for behold!" and he spread his hand abroad with the palm downward and into all the wrinkles and crevices thereof he set the semblance of shining yellow corn-grains; in the dark of the early world-dawn they gleamed like sparks of fire, and moved as his hand was moved over the bowl, shining up from and also moving in the depths of the water therein. "See!" said he, pointing to the seven grains clasped by his thumb and four fingers, "by such shall our children be guided; for behold, when the Sun-father is not nigh, and thy terraces are as the dark itself (being all hidden therein), then shall our children be guided by lights — like to these lights of all the six regions turning round the midmost one — as in and around the midmost place, where these our children shall abide, lie all the other regions of space! Yea! and even as these grains gleam up from the water, so shall seed-grains like to them, yet numberless, spring up from thy bosom when touched by my waters, to nourish our children." Thus and in other ways many devised they for their offspring.

VII. RAVEN'S ADVENTURES [38]

A. RAVEN BECOMES VORACIOUS [39]

(TSIMSHIAN: Boas, *Report of the Bureau of American Ethnology*, xxxi, 58)

At one time the whole world was covered with darkness. At the southern point of Queen Charlotte Islands there was a town in which the animals lived. Its name was Kungalas. A chief and his wife were living there, and with them a boy, their only child, who was loved very much by his parents. Therefore his father tried to keep him out of danger. He built for his son a bed above his own, in the rear of his large house. He washed him regularly, and the boy grew up to be a youth.

When he was quite large the youth became ill, and, being very sick, it was not long before he died. Therefore the hearts of his parents were very sad. They cried on account of their beloved child. The chief invited his tribe, and all the (animal) people [40] went to the chief's house and entered. Then the chief ordered the child's body to be laid out; and he said, "Take out his intestines." His attendants laid out the body of the chief's child, took out the intestines, burned them at the rear of the chief's house, and placed the body on the bed which his father had built for his son. The chief and the chieftainess wailed every morning under the corpse of their dead son, and his tribe cried with them. They did so every day after the young man's death.

One morning before daylight came, the chieftainess went again to wail. She arose, and looked up to where her son was lying. There she saw a youth, bright as fire, lying where the body of their son had been. Therefore she called her husband,

and said to him, "Our beloved child has come back to life."
Therefore the chief arose and went to the foot of the ladder
which reached to the place where the body had been. He went
up to his son, and said, "Is it you, my beloved son? Is it you?"
Then the shining youth said, "Yes, it is I." Then suddenly
gladness touched the hearts of the parents.

The tribe entered again to console their chief and their
chieftainess. When the people entered, they were much surprised to see the shining youth there. He spoke to them.
"Heaven was much annoyed by your constant wailing,⁴¹ so He
sent me down to comfort your minds." The great tribe of the
chief were very glad because the prince lived again among
them. His parents loved him more than ever.

The shining youth ate very little. He staid there a long time,
and he did not eat at all; he only chewed a little fat, but he
did not eat any. The chief had two great slaves — a miserable
man and his wife. The great slaves were called Mouth At
Each End. Every morning they brought all kinds of food into
the house. One day, when they came in from where they had
been, they brought a large cut of whale meat. They threw it
on the fire and ate it. They did this every time they came back
from hunting. Then the chieftainess tried to give food to her
son who had come back to life, but he declined it and lived without food. The chieftainess was very anxious to give her son
something to eat. She was afraid that her son would die again.
On the following day the shining youth took a walk to refresh
himself. As soon as he had gone out, the chief went up the ladder to where he thought his son had his bed. Behold, there was
the corpse of his own son! Nevertheless he loved his new child.

One day the chief and chieftainess went out to visit the tribe,
and the two great slaves entered, carrying a large piece of
whale meat. They threw the whale fat into the fire and ate of
it. Then the shining youth came toward them and questioned
the two great slaves, asking them, "What makes you so hungry?" The two great slaves replied, "We are hungry because
we have eaten scabs from our shin bones." Therefore the shining youth said to them, "Do you like what you eat?" Then
the slave-man said, "Yes, my dear!" Therefore the prince replied, "I will also try the scabs you speak about." Then the
slave-woman said, "No, my dear! Don't desire to be as we

are." The prince repeated, "I will just taste it and spit it out again." The male slave cut off a small piece of whale meat and put in a small scab. Then the female slave scolded her husband for what he was doing. "O bad man! what have you been doing to the poor prince?" The shining prince took up the piece of meat with the scab in it, put it into his mouth, tasted it, and spit it out again. Then he went back to his bed. When the chief and the chieftainess came back from their visit, the prince said to his mother, "Mother, I am very hungry." The chieftainess said at once, "Oh, dear, is it true, is it true?" She ordered her slaves to feed her beloved son with rich food. The slaves prepared rich food, and the youth ate it all. Again he was very hungry and ate everything, and the slaves gave him more to eat than before.

He did so for several days, and soon all the provisions in his father's house were at an end. Then the prince went to every house of his father's people and ate the provisions that were in the houses. This was because he had tasted the scabs of Mouth At Each End. Now the provisions were all used up. The chief knew that the provisions of his tribe were almost exhausted. Therefore the great chief felt sad and ashamed on account of what his son had done, for he had devoured almost all the provisions of his tribe.

Therefore the chief invited all the people in, and said, "I will send my child away before he eats all our provisions and we lack food." Then all the people agreed to what the chief had said. As soon as they had all agreed, the chief called his son. He told him to sit down in the rear of the house. As soon as he had sat down there, the chief spoke to his son, and said, "My dear son, I shall send you away inland to the other side of the ocean." He gave his son a small round stone and a raven blanket and a dried sea-lion bladder filled with all kinds of berries. The chief said to his son, "When you fly across the ocean and feel weary, drop this round stone on the sea, and you shall find rest on it; and when you reach the mainland, scatter the various kinds of fruit all over the land; and also scatter the salmon roe in all the rivers and brooks, and also the trout roe; so that you may not lack food as long as you live in this world." Then he started. His father named him Giant.

B. The Theft of Light [42]

(Tsimshian: Boas, *Report of the Bureau of American Ethnology*, xxxi, 60)

Giant flew inland (toward the east). He went on for a long time, and finally he was very tired, so he dropped down on the sea the little round stone which his father had given to him. It became a large rock way out at sea. Giant rested on it and refreshed himself, and took off the raven skin.

At that time there was always darkness. There was no daylight then. Again Giant put on the raven skin [132] and flew toward the east. Now, Giant reached the mainland and arrived at the mouth of Skeena River. There he stopped and scattered the salmon roe and trout roe. He said while he was scattering them, "Let every river and creek have all kinds of fish!" Then he took the dried sea-lion bladder and scattered the fruits all over the land, saying, "Let every mountain, hill, valley, plain, the whole land, be full of fruits!"

The whole world was still covered with darkness. When the sky was clear, the people would have a little light from the stars; and when clouds were in the sky, it was very dark all over the land. The people were distressed by this. Then Giant thought that it would be hard for him [43] to obtain his food if it were always dark. He remembered that there was light in heaven, whence he had come. Then he made up his mind to bring down the light to our world. On the following day Giant put on his raven skin, which his father the chief had given to him, and flew upward. Finally he found the hole in the sky,[28] and he flew through it. Giant reached the inside of the sky. He took off the raven skin and put it down near the hole of the sky. He went on, and came to a spring near the house of the chief of heaven. There he sat down and waited.

Then the chief's daughter came out, carrying a small bucket in which she was about to fetch water. She went down to the big spring in front of her father's house. When Giant saw her coming along, he transformed himself into the leaf of a cedar and floated on the water. The chief's daughter dipped it up in her bucket and drank it. Then she returned to her father's house and entered.

After a short time she was with child, and not long after she gave birth to a boy.[44] Then the chief and the chieftainess were very glad. They washed the boy regularly. He began to grow up. Now he was beginning to creep about. They washed him often, and the chief smoothed and cleaned the floor of the house. Now the child was strong and crept about every day. He began to cry, "Hama, hama!" He was crying all the time, and the great chief was troubled, and called in some of his slaves to carry about the boy. The slaves did so, but he would not sleep for several nights. He kept on crying, "Hama, hama!" Therefore the chief invited all his wise men, and said to them that he did not know what the boy wanted and why he was crying. He wanted the box that was hanging in the chief's house.

This box, in which the daylight was kept,[45] was hanging in one corner of the house. Its name was Mā. Giant had known it before he descended to our world. The child cried for it. The chief was annoyed, and the wise men listened to what the chief told them. When the wise men heard the child crying aloud, they did not know what he was saying. He was crying all the time, "Hama, hama, hama!"

One of the wise men, who understood him, said to the chief, "He is crying for the mā." Therefore the chief ordered it to be taken down. The man put it down. They put it down near the fire, and the boy sat down near it and ceased crying. He stopped crying, for he was glad. Then he rolled the mā about inside the house. He did so for four days. Sometimes he would carry it to the door. Now the great chief did not think of it. He had quite forgotten it. Then the boy really took up the mā, put it on his shoulders, and ran out with it. While he was running, some one said, "Giant is running away with the mā!" He ran away, and the hosts of heaven pursued him. They shouted that Giant was running away with the mā. He came to the hole of the sky, put on the skin of the raven, and flew down, carrying the mā. Then the hosts of heaven returned to their houses, and he flew down with it to our world.

At that time the world was still dark. He arrived farther up the river, and went down river. Giant had come down near the mouth of Nass River. He went to the mouth of Nass River. It was always dark, and he carried the mā about with him. He went on, and went up the river in the dark. A little farther up he heard the noise of the people, who were catching olachen in bag nets in their canoes. There was much noise out on the river, because they were working hard. Giant, who was sitting on the shore, said, "Throw ashore one of the things that you are catching, my dear people!" After a while, Giant said again, "Throw ashore one of the things you are catching!" Then those on the water scolded him. "Where did you come from, great liar, whom they call Txä′msem?" * The (animal) people knew that it was Giant. Therefore they made fun of him. Then Giant said again, "Throw ashore one of the things that you are catching, or I shall break the mā!" and all those who were on the water answered," "Where did you get what you are talking about, you liar?" Giant said once more, "Throw ashore one of the things that you are catching, my dear people, or I shall break the mā for you!" One person replied, scolding him.

Giant had repeated his request four times, but those on the water refused what he had asked for. Therefore Giant broke the mā. It broke, and it was daylight. The north wind began to blow hard; and all the fisherman, the Frogs, were driven away by the north wind. All the Frogs who had made fun of Giant were driven away down river until they arrived at one of the large mountainous islands. Here the Frogs tried to climb up the rock; but they stuck to the rock, being frozen by the north wind, and became stone. They are still on the rock.⁴⁶ The fishing frogs named him Txä′msem, and all the world had the daylight.

VIII. THE CREATION ⁴⁷

(MAIDU: Dixon, *Bulletin of the American Museum of Natural History*, xvii, 39, No. 1)

In the beginning there was no sun, no moon, no stars. All was dark, and everywhere there was only water.²⁹ A raft came floating on the water. It came from the north, and in it were two persons, — Turtle and Father-of-the-Secret-Society. The stream flowed very rapidly. Then from the sky a rope of feathers,⁴⁸ was let down, and down it came Earth-Initiate. When he reached the end of the rope, he tied it to the bow of the raft, and stepped in. His face was covered and was never seen, but his body shone like the sun. He sat down, and for a long time said nothing.

* Pronunciation approximately represented in English by "Chemsem."

At last Turtle said, "Where do you come from?" and Earth-Initiate answered, "I come from above." Then Turtle said, "Brother, can you not make for me some good dry land, so that I may sometimes come up out of the water?" Then he asked another time, "Are there going to be any people in the world?" Earth-Initiate thought awhile, then said, "Yes." Turtle asked, "How long before you are going to make people?" Earth-Initiate replied, "I don't know. You want to have some dry land: well, how am I going to get any earth to make it of?"

Turtle answered, "If you will tie a rock about my left arm, I'll dive for some." [30] Earth-Initiate did as Turtle asked, and then, reaching around, took the end of a rope from somewhere, and tied it to Turtle. When Earth-Initiate came to the raft, there was no rope there: he just reached out and found one. Turtle said, "If the rope is not long enough, I'll jerk it once, and you must haul me up; if it is long enough, I'll give two jerks, and then you must pull me up quickly, as I shall have all the earth that I can carry." Just as Turtle went over the side of the boat, Father-of-the-Secret-Society began to shout loudly.

Turtle was gone a long time. He was gone six years; and when he came up, he was covered with green slime, he had been down so long. When he reached the top of the water, the only earth he had was a very little under his nails: the rest had all washed away. Earth-Initiate took with his right hand a stone knife from under his left armpit, and carefully scraped the earth out from under Turtle's nails. He put the earth in the palm of his hand, and rolled it about till it was round; it was as large as a small pebble. He laid it on the stern of the raft. By and by he went to look at it: it had not grown at all. The third time that he went to look at it, it had grown so that it could be spanned by the arms. The fourth time he looked, it was as big as the world, the raft was aground, and all around were mountains as far as he could see. The raft came ashore at Ta'doikö, and the place can be seen to-day.

When the raft had come to land, Turtle said, "I can't stay in the dark all the time. Can't you make a light, so that I can see?" Earth-Initiate replied, "Let us get out of the raft, and then we will see what we can do." So all three got out. Then Earth-Initiate said, "Look that way, to the east! I am going to tell my sister to come up." Then it began to grow light, and day began to break; then Father-of-the-Secret-Society began to shout loudly, and the sun came up. Turtle said, "Which way is the sun going to travel?" Earth-Initiate answered, "I'll tell her to go this way, and go down there." After the sun went down, Father-of-the-Secret-Society began to cry and shout again, and it grew very dark. Earth-Initiate said, "I'll tell my brother to come up." Then the moon rose. Then Earth-Initiate asked Turtle and Father-of-the-Secret-Society, "How do you like it?" and they both answered, "It is very good." Then Turtle asked, "Is that all you are going to do for us?" and Earth-Initiate answered, "No, I am going to do more yet." Then he called the stars each by its name, and they came out. When this was done, Turtle asked, "Now what shall we do?" Earth-Initiate replied, "Wait, and I'll show you." Then he made a tree grow at Ta'doikö, — the tree called Hu'kīmtsa; and Earth-Initiate and Turtle and Father-of-the-Secret-Society sat in its shade for two days. The tree was very large, and had twelve different kinds of acorns growing on it.

After they had sat for two days under the tree, they all went off to see the world that Earth-Initiate had made. They started at sunrise, and were back by sunset. Earth-Initiate travelled so fast that all they could see was a ball of fire flashing about under the ground and the water. While they were gone, Coyote and his dog Rattlesnake came up out of the ground. It is said that Coyote could see Earth-Initiate's face. When Earth-Initiate and the others came back, they found Coyote at Ta'doikö. All five of them then built huts for themselves, and lived there at Ta'doikö, but no one could go inside of Earth-Initiate's house. Soon after the travellers came back, Earth-Initiate called the birds from the air, and made the trees and then the animals. He took some mud, and of this made first a deer; after that, he made all the other animals. Sometimes Turtle would say, "That does not look well: can't you make it some other way?"

Some time after this, Earth-Initiate and Coyote were at Marysville Buttes. Earth-Initiate said, "I am going to make people." In the middle of the afternoon he began, for he had returned to Ta'doikö. He took dark red earth, mixed it with water, and made two figures, — one a man, and one a woman.[49] He laid the man on his right side, and the woman on his left, inside his house. Then he lay down himself, flat on his back, with his arms stretched out. He lay thus and sweated all the afternoon and night. Early in the morning the woman began to tickle him in the side. He kept very still, did not laugh. By and by he got up, thrust a piece of pitch-wood into the ground, and fire burst out. The two people were very white. No one to-day is as white as they were. Their eyes were pink, their hair was black, their teeth shone brightly, and they were very handsome. It is said that Earth-Initiate did not finish the hands of the people, as he did not know how it would be best to do it. Coyote saw the people, and suggested that they ought to have hands like his. Earth-Initiate said, "No, their hands shall be like mine." Then he finished them. When Coyote asked why their hands were to be like that, Earth-Initiate answered, "So that, if they are chased by bears, they can climb trees." This first man was called Ku′ksū; and the woman, Morning-Star Woman.

When Coyote had seen the two people, he asked Earth-Initiate how he had made them. When he was told, he thought, "That is not difficult. I'll do it myself." He did just as Earth-Initiate had told him, but could not help laughing, when, early in the morning, the woman poked him in the ribs. As a result of his failing to keep still, the people were glass-eyed. Earth-Initiate said, "I told you not to laugh," but Coyote declared he had not. This was the first lie.

By and by there came to be a good many people. Earth-Initiate had wanted to have everything comfortable and easy for people, so that none of them should have to work. All fruits were easy to obtain, no one was ever to get sick and die. As the people grew numerous, Earth-Initiate did not come as often as formerly, he only came to see Ku′ksū in the night. One night he said to him, "To-morrow morning you must go to the little lake near here. Take all the people with you. I'll make you a very old man before you get to the lake." So in the morning Ku′ksū collected all the people, and went to the lake. By the time he had reached it, he was a very old man. He fell into the lake, and sank down out of sight. Pretty soon the ground began to shake, the waves overflowed the shore, and there was a great roaring under the water, like thunder. By and by Ku′ksū came up out of the water, but young again, just like a young man.[50] Then Earth-Initiate came and spoke to the people, and said, "If you do as I tell you, everything will be well. When any of you grow old, so old that you cannot walk, come to this lake, or get some one to bring you here. You must then go down into the water as you have seen Ku'ksū do, and you will come out young again." When he had said this, he went away. He left in the night, and went up above.

All this time food had been easy to get, as Earth-Initiate had wished. The women set out baskets at night, and in the morning they found them full of food, all ready to eat, and lukewarm. One day Coyote came along. He asked the people how they lived, and they told him that all they had to do was to eat and sleep. Coyote replied, "That is no way to do: I can show you something better." Then he told them how he and Earth-Initiate had had a discussion before men had been made; how Earth-Initiate wanted everything easy, and that there should be no sickness or death, but how he had thought it would be better to have people work, get sick, and die.[51] He said, "We'll have a burning." The people did not know what he meant; but Coyote said, "I'll show you. It is better to have a burning, for then the widows can be free." So he took all the baskets and things that the people had, hung them up on poles, made everything all ready. When all was prepared, Coyote said, "At this time you must always have games." So he fixed the moon during which these games were to be played.

Coyote told them to start the games with a foot-race, and every one got ready to run. Ku'ksū did not come, however. He sat in his hut alone, and was sad, for he knew what was going to occur. Just at this moment Rattlesnake came to Ku'ksū, and said, "What shall we do now? Everything is spoiled!" Ku'ksū did not answer, so Rattlesnake said, "Well, I'll do what I think is best." Then he went out and along the course that the racers were to go over, and hid himself, leaving his head just sticking out of a hole. By this time all the racers had started, and among them Coyote's son. He was Coyote's only child, and was very quick. He soon began to outstrip all the runners, and was in the lead. As he passed the spot where Rattlesnake had hidden himself, however, Rattlesnake raised his head and bit the boy in the ankle. In a minute the boy was dead.

Coyote was dancing about the home-stake. He was very happy, and was shouting at his son and praising him. When Rattlesnake bit the boy, and he fell dead, every one laughed at

Coyote, and said, "Your son has fallen down, and is so ashamed that he does not dare to get up." Coyote said, "No, that is not it. He is dead." This was the first death. The people, however, did not understand, and picked the boy up, and brought him to Coyote. Then Coyote began to cry,[52] and every one did the same. These were the first tears. Then Coyote took his son's body and carried it to the lake of which Earth-Initiate had told them, and threw the body in. But there was no noise, and nothing happened, and the body drifted about for four days on the surface, like a log. On the fifth day Coyote took four sacks of beads and brought them to Ku′ksū, begging him to restore his son to life. Ku′ksū did not answer. For five days Coyote begged, then Ku′ksū came out of his house bringing all his bead and bear-skins, and calling to all the people to come and watch him. He laid the body on a bear-skin, dressed it, and wrapped it up carefully. Then he dug a grave, put the body into it, and covered it up. Then he told the people, "From now on, this is what you must do. This is the way you must do till the world shall be made over."

About a year after this, in the spring, all was changed. Up to this time everybody spoke the same language. The people were having a burning, everything was ready for the next day, when in the night everybody suddenly began to speak a different language.[53] Each man and his wife, however, spoke the same. Earth-Initiate had come in the night to Ku′ksū, and had told him about it all, and given him instructions for the next day. So, when morning came, Ku′ksū called all the people together, for he was able to speak all the languages. He told them each the names of the different animals, etc., in their languages, taught them how to cook and to hunt, gave them all their laws, and set the time for all their dances and festivals. Then he called each tribe by name, and sent them off in different directions, telling them where they were to live.[54] He sent the warriors to the north, the singers to the west, the flute-players to the east, and the dancers to the south. So all the people went away, and left Ku′ksū and his wife alone at Ta′doikö. By and by his wife went away, leaving in the night, and going first to Marysville Buttes. Ku′ksū staid a little while longer, and then he also left. He too went to the Buttes, went into the spirit house, and sat down on the south side. He found Coyote's son there, sitting on the north side. The door was on the west.

Coyote had been trying to find out where Ku'ksū had gone, and where his own son had gone, and at last found the tracks, and followed them to the spirit house. Here he saw Ku'ksū and his son, the latter eating spirit food. Coyote wanted to go in, but Ku'ksū said, "No, wait there. You have just what you wanted, it is your own fault. Every man will now have all kinds of troubles and accidents, will have to work to get his food, and will die and be buried. This must go on till the time is out, and Earth-Initiate comes again,[55] and everything will be made over. You must go home, and tell all the people that you have seen your son, that he is not dead." Coyote said he would go, but that he was hungry, and wanted some of the food. Ku'ksū replied, "You cannot eat that. Only ghosts may eat that food." Then Coyote went away and told all the people, "I saw my son and Ku'ksū, and he told me to kill myself." So he climbed up to the top of a tall tree, jumped off, and was killed. Then he went to the spirit house, thinking he could now have some of the food; but there was no one there, nothing at all, and so he went out, and walked away to the west,[11] and was never seen again. Ku'ksū and Coyote's son, however, had gone up above.

IX. THE CREATION [47]

(KATO: Goddard, *University of California Publications in American Archaeology and Ethnology*, v, 184, No. 2)

The sandstone rock which formed the sky was old, they say. It thundered in the east; it thundered in the south; it thundered in the west; it thundered in the north. "The rock is old, we will fix it," he said. There were two, Nagaitcho and Thunder. "We will stretch it above far to the east," one of them said. They stretched it. They walked on the sky.

In the south he stood on end a large rock. In the west he stood on end a large rock. In the north he stood on end a large, tall rock. In the east he stood on end a large, tall rock.[56] He made everything properly. He made the roads. He made a road to the north (where the sun travels in summer).

"In the south there will be no trees but only many flowers," he said. "Where will there be a hole through?" he asked. At the north he made a hole through. East he made a large opening for the clouds. West he made an opening for the fog. "To the west the clouds shall go," he said.

He made a knife. He made it for splitting the rocks. He made the knife very strong.

"How will it be?" he considered. "You go north; I will go south," he said. "I have finished already," he said. "Stretch the rock in the north. You untie it in the west, I will untie it in the east."

"What will be clouds?" he asked. "Set fires about here," he told him. On the upland they burned to make clouds. Along the creek bottoms they burned to make mist. "It is good," he said. He made clouds so the heads of coming people would not ache.

There is another world above where Thunder lives. "You will live here near by," he told Nagaitcho.

"Put water on the fire, heat some water," he said. He made a person out of earth.[49] "Well, I will talk to him," he said. He made his right leg and his left leg. He made his right arm and his left arm. He pulled off some grass and wadded it up. He put some of it in place for his belly. He hung up some of it for his stomach. When he had slapped some of the grass he put it in for his heart. He used a round piece of clay for his liver. He put in more clay for his kidneys. He cut a piece into parts and put it in for his lungs. He pushed in a reed (for a trachea).

"What sort will blood be?" he enquired. He pounded up ochre. "Get water for the ochre," he said. He laid him down. He sprinkled him with water. He made his mouth, his nose, and two eyes. "How will it be?" he said. "Make him privates," he said. He made them. He took one of the legs, split it, and made woman of it.

Clouds arose in the east. Fog came up in the west. "Well, let it rain, let the wind blow," he said. "Up in the sky there will be none, there will be only gentle winds. Well, let it rain in the fog," he said. It rained. One could not see. It was hot in the sky. The sun came up now. "What will the sun be?" he said. "Make a fire so it will be hot. The moon will travel at night." The moon is cold.

He came down. "Who, I wonder, can kick open a rock?" he said. "Who can split a tree?" "Well, I will try," said Nagaitcho. He couldn't split the tree. "Who, I wonder, is the strongest?" said Thunder. Nagaitcho didn't break the rock. "Well, I will try," said Thunder. Thunder kicked the rock. He kicked it open. It broke to pieces. "Go look at the rock," he said. "He kicked the rock open," one reported. "Well, I will try a tree," he said. He kicked the tree open. The tree split to pieces.

Thunder and Nagaitcho came down. "Who can stand on the water? You step on the water," Thunder told Nagaitcho. "Yes, I will," Nagaitcho said. He stepped on the water and sank into the ocean. "I will try," said Thunder. He stepped on the water. He stood on it with one leg. "I have finished quickly," he said.

It was evening. It rained. It rained. Every day, every night it rained. "What will happen? It rains every day," they said. The fog spread out close to the ground. The clouds were thick. The people then had no fire. The fire became small. All the creeks were full. There was water in the valleys. The water encircled them.[57]

"Well, I have finished," he said. "Yes," Nagaitcho said. "Come, jump up. You must jump up to another sky," [58] he told him. "I, too, will do that." "At night when every kind of thing is asleep we will do it," he said.

Every day it rained, every night it rained. All the people slept. The sky fell. The land was not. For a very great distance there was no land. The waters of the oceans came together. Animals of all kinds drowned. Where the water went there were no trees. There was no land.

People became. Seal, sea-lion, and grizzly built a dance-house. They looked for a place in vain. At Usal they built it for there the ground was good. There are many sea-lions there. Whale became a human woman. That is why women are so fat. There were no grizzlies. There were no fish. Blue lizard was thrown into the water and became sucker.[4] Bull-snake was thrown into the water and became black salmon. Salamander was thrown into the water and became hook-bill salmon. Grass-snake was thrown into the water and became steel-head salmon. Lizard was thrown into the water and became trout.

Trout cried for his net. "My net, my net," he said. They offered him every kind of thing in vain. It was "My net" he said when he cried. They made a net and put him into it. He stopped crying. They threw the net and trout into the water. He became trout.

"What will grow in the water?" he asked. Seaweeds grew in the water. Abalones and mussels grew in the water. Two kinds of kelp grew in the ocean. Many different kinds grew there.

"What will be salt?" he asked. They tasted many things. The ocean foam became salt. The Indians tried their salt. They will eat their food with it. They will eat clover with it. It was good salt.

"How will the water of this ocean behave? What will be in front of it?" he asked. "The water will rise up in ridges. It will settle back again. There will be sand. On top of the sand it will glisten," he said. "Old kelp will float ashore. Old whales will float ashore.

"People will eat fish, big fish," he said. "Sea-lions will come ashore. They will eat them. They will be good. Devil-fish, although they are ugly looking, will be good. The people will eat them. The fish in the ocean will be fat. They will be good.

"There will be many different kinds in the ocean. There will be water-panther. There will be stone-fish. He will catch people. Long-tooth-fish will kill sea-lion. He will feel around in the water.

"Sea-lion will have no feet. He will have a tail. His teeth will be large. There will be no trees in the ocean. The water will be powerful in the ocean," he said.

He placed redwoods and firs along the shore. At the tail of the earth, at the north, he made them grow. He placed land in walls along in front of the ocean. From the north he put down rocks here and there. Over there the ocean beats against them. Far to the south he did that. He stood up pines along the way. He placed yellow pines. Far away he placed them. He placed mountains along in front of the water. He did not stop putting them up even way to the south.

Redwoods and various pines were growing. He looked back and saw them growing. The redwoods had become tall. He placed stones along. He made small creeks by dragging along his foot. "Wherever they flow this water will be good," he said. "They will drink this. Only the ocean they will not drink."

He made trees spring up. When he looked behind himself he saw they had grown. When he came near water-head-place (south) he said to himself, "It is good that they are growing up."

He made creeks along. "This water they will drink," he said. That is why all drink, many different kinds of animals. "Because the water is good, because it is not salt, deer, elk, panther, and fishers will drink of it," he said. He caused trees to grow up along. When he looked behind himself he saw they had grown up. "Birds will drink, squirrels will drink," he said. "Many different kinds will drink. I am placing good water along the way."

Many redwoods grew up. He placed water along toward the south. He kicked out springs. "There will be springs," he said. "These will belong to the deer," he said of the deer-licks.

He took along a dog. "Drink this water," he told his dog. He, himself, drank of it. "All, many different kinds of animals and birds, will drink of it," he said.

Tanbark oaks he made to spring up along the way. Many kinds, redwoods, firs, and pines he caused to grow. He placed water along. He made creeks with his foot. To make valleys for the streams he placed the land on edge. The mountains were large. They had grown.

"Let acorns grow," he said. He looked back at the ocean, and at the trees and rocks he had placed along. "The water is good, they will drink it," he said. He placed redwoods, firs, and tanbark oaks along the way. He stood up land and made the mountains. "They shall become large," he said of the redwoods.

He went around the earth, dragging his foot to make the streams and placing redwoods, firs, pines, oaks, and chestnut trees. When he looked back he saw the rocks had become large, and the mountains loomed up. He drank of the water and called it good. "I have arranged it that rocks shall be around the water," he said. "Drink," he told his dog. "Many animals will drink this good water." He placed rocks and banks. He put along the way small white stones. He stood up white and black oaks. Sugar-pines and firs he planted one in a place.

"I will try the water," he said. "Drink, my dog." The water was good. He dragged along his foot, making creeks. He placed the rocks along and turned to look at them. "Drink, my dog," he said. "I, too, will drink. Grizzlies, all kinds of animals, and human beings will drink the water which I have placed among the rocks." He stood up the mountains. He placed the trees along, the firs and the oaks. He caused the pines to grow up. He placed the redwoods one in a place.

He threw salamanders and turtles into the creeks. "Eels will live in this stream," he said. "Fish will come into it. Hook-bill and black salmon will run up this creek. Last of all steel-heads will swim in it. Crabs, small eels, and day-eels will come up."

"Grizzlies will live in large numbers on this mountain. On this mountain will be many deer. The people will eat them. Because they have no gall they may be eaten raw. Deer meat will be very sweet. Panthers will be numerous. There will be many jack-rabbits on this mountain," he said.

He did not like yellow-jackets. He nearly killed them. He made blue-flies and wasps.

His dog walked along with him. "There will be much water in this stream," he said. "This will be a small creek and the fish will run in it. The fish will be good. There will be many suckers and trout in this stream."

"There will be brush on this mountain," he said. He made manzanita and white-thorn grow there. "Here will be a valley. Here will be many deer. There will be many grizzlies at this place. Here a mountain will stand. Many rattlesnakes, bull-snakes, and water snakes will be in this place. Here will be good land. It shall be a valley."

He placed fir trees, yellow-pines, oaks, and redwoods one at a place along the way. He put down small grizzly bears. "The water will be bad. It will be black here," he said. "There will be many owls here, the barking-owl, the screech-owl, and the little owl. There shall be many bluejays, grouse, and quails. Here on this mountain will be many wood-rats. Here shall be many varied robins. There shall be many woodcocks, yellow-hammers, and sap-suckers. Here will be many mocking-birds and meadowlarks. Here will be herons and black-birds. There will be many turtle-doves and pigeons. The kingfishers will catch fish. There will be many buzzards and ravens. There will be many chicken-hawks. There will be many robins. On this high mountain there will be many deer," he said.

"Let there be a valley here," he said. "There will be fir trees, some small and some large. Let the rain fall. Let it snow. Let there be hail. Let the clouds come. When it rains let the streams increase, let the water be high, let it become muddy. When the rain stops let the water become good again," he said.

He came back. "Walk behind me, my dog," he said. "We will look at what has taken place." Trees had grown. Fish were in the streams. The rocks had become large. It was good.

He traveled fast. "Come, walk fast, my dog," he said. The land had become good. The valleys had become broad. All kinds of trees and plants had sprung up. Springs had become and the water was flowing. "Again I will try the water," he said. "You, too, drink." Brush had sprung up. He traveled fast.

"I have made a good earth, my dog," he said. "Walk fast, my dog." Acorns were on the trees. The chestnuts were ripe. The hazelnuts were ripe. The manzanita berries were getting white. All sorts of food had become good. The buckeyes were good. The peppernuts were black. The bunch grass was ripe. The grass-hoppers were growing. The clover was in bloom. The bear-clover was good. The mountains had grown. The rocks had grown. All kinds that are eaten had become good. "We made it good, my dog," he said. Fish for the people to eat had grown in the streams.

"We have come to south now," he said. All the different kinds were matured. They started back, he and his dog. "We will go back," he said. "The mountains have grown up quickly. The land has become flat. The trout have grown. Good water is flowing. Walk fast. All things have become good. We have made them good, my dog. It is warm. The land is good."

The brush had grown. Various things had sprung up. Grizzlies had increased in numbers. Birds had grown. The water had become good. The grass was grown. Many deer for the people to eat walked about. Many kinds of herbs had grown. Some kinds remained small.

Rattlesnakes had multiplied. Water-snakes had become numerous. Turtles had come out of the water and increased in numbers. Various things had grown. The mountains had grown. The valleys had become.

"Come fast. I will drink water. You, too, drink," he told his dog. "Now we are getting back, we are close home, my dog. Look here, the mountains have grown. The stones have grown.

Brush has come up. All kinds of animals are walking about. All kinds of things are grown.

"We are about to arrive. We are close home, my dog," he said. "I am about to get back north," he said to himself. "I am about to get back north. I am about to get back north. I am about to get back north," he said to himself.

That is all.

CHAPTER II

MYTHICAL INCIDENTS

X. THE LIZARD–HAND [59]

(Yokuts: Kroeber, *University of California Publications in American Archaeology and Ethnology*, iv, 231, No. 38)

IT was Coyote who brought it about that people die.[51] He made it thus because our hands are not closed like his. He wanted our hands to be like his, but a lizard said to him: "No, they must have my hand." He had five fingers and Coyote had only a fist. So now we have an open hand with five fingers. But then Coyote said: "Well, then they will have to die."

XI. DETERMINATION OF THE SEASONS [60]

(Tahltan: Teit, *Journal of American Folk-Lore*, xxxii, 226)

Once Porcupine and Beaver quarrelled about the seasons. Porcupine wanted five winter months. He held up one hand and showed his five fingers. He said, "Let the winter months be the same in number as the fingers on my hand." Beaver said, "No," and held up his tail, which had many cracks or scratches on it. He said, "Let the winter months be the same in number as the scratches on my tail." Now they quarrelled and argued. Porcupine got angry and bit off his thumb. Then, holding up his hand with the four fingers, he said emphatically, "There must be only four winter months." Beaver became a little afraid, and gave in. *For this reason porcupines have four claws on each foot now.*

Since Porcupine won, the winter remained four months in length, until later Raven changed it a little. Raven considered what Porcupine and Beaver had said about the winters, and decided that Porcupine had done right. He said, "Porcupine was right. If the winters were made too long, people could not live. *Henceforth the winters will be about this length*, but they will be variable. I will tell you of the *gaxewisa* month, when people will meet together and talk. At that time of the year people will ask questions (or propound riddles), and others will answer. If the riddle is answered correctly, then the person who propounded it must answer, "Fool-hen." Raven chose this word because the fool-hen has a shorter beak than any other game-bird. "If people guess riddles correctly at this time of year, then the winter will be short, and the spring come early."

XII. MARRIAGE OF THE NORTH AND THE SOUTH [61]

(CHEROKEE: Mooney, *Report of the Bureau of American Ethnology*, xix, 322, No. 70)

The North went traveling, and after going far and meeting many different tribes he finally fell in love with the daughter of the South and wanted to marry her. The girl was willing, but her parents objected and said, "Ever since you came, the weather has been cold, and if you stay here we may all freeze to death." The North pleaded hard, and said that if they would let him have their daughter he would take her back to his own country, so at last they consented. They were married and he took his bride to his own country, and when she arrived there she found the people all living in ice houses.

The next day, when the sun rose, the houses began to leak, and as it climbed higher they began to melt, and it grew warmer and warmer, until finally the people came to the young husband and told him he must send his wife home again, or the weather would get so warm that the whole settlement would be melted. He loved his wife and so held out as long as he could, but as the sun grew hotter the people were more urgent, and at last he had to send her home to her parents.

The people said that as she had been born in the South, and nourished all her life upon food that grew in the same climate, her whole nature was warm and unfit for the North.

XIII. DETERMINATION OF NIGHT AND DAY [62]

(IROQUOIS: Smith, *Report of the Bureau of American Ethnology*, ii, 80)

Once upon a time the porcupine was appointed to be the leader of all the animals. Soon after his appointment he called them all together and presented the question, "Shall we have night all the time and darkness, or daylight with its sunshine?"

This was a very important question, and a violent discussion arose, some wishing for daylight and the sun to rule, and others for continual night.

The chipmunk wished for night and day, weeks and months, and night to be separate from the day, so he began singing, "The light will come; we must have light," which he continued to repeat. Meanwhile the bear began singing, "Night is best; we must have darkness."

While the chipmunk was singing, the day began to dawn. Then the other party saw that the chipmunk was prevailing, and were very angry; and their leader, the bear, pursued the chipmunk, who managed to escape uninjured, the huge paw of the bear simply grazing his back as he entered his hole in a hollow tree, leaving its black imprint, which the chipmunk has ever since retained. But night and day have ever continued to alternate.

XIV. THE THEFT OF FIRE [63]

(MAIDU: Dixon, *Bulletin of the American Museum of Natural History*, xvii, 65, No. 5)

At one time the people had found fire, and were going to use it; but Thunder wanted to take it away from them, as he desired to be the only one who should have fire. He thought that if he could do this, he would be able to kill all the people. After a time he succeeded, and carried the fire home with him, far to the south. He put Woswosim (a small bird) to guard the fire, and see that no one should steal it. Thunder thought that people would die after he had stolen their fire, for they would not be able to cook their food; but the people managed to get along. They ate most of their food raw, and sometimes got Toyeskom (another small bird) to look for a long time at a piece of meat; and as he had a red eye, this after a long time would cook the meat almost as well as a fire. Only the chiefs had their food cooked in this way. All the people lived together in a big sweat-house. The house was as big as a mountain.

Among the people was Lizard and his brother; and they were always the first in the morning to go outside and sun themselves on the roof of the sweat-house. One morning as they lay there sunning themselves, they looked west, toward the Coast Range, and saw smoke. They called to all the other people, saying that they had seen smoke far away to the west. The people, however, would not believe them, and Coyote came out, and threw a lot of dirt and dust over the two. One of the people did not like this. He said to Coyote, "Why do you trouble people? Why don't you let others alone? Why don't you behave? You are always the first to start a quarrel. You always want to kill people without any reason." Then the other people felt sorry. They asked the two Lizards about what they had seen, and asked them to point out the smoke. The Lizards did so, and all could see the thin column rising up far to the west. One person said, "How shall we get that fire back? How shall we get it away from Thunder? He is a bad man. I don't know whether we had better try to get it or not." Then the chief said, "The best one among you had better try to get it. Even if Thunder is a bad man, we must try to get the fire. When we get there, I don't know how we shall get in but the one who is the best, who thinks he can get in, let him try." Mouse, Deer, Dog, and Coyote were the ones who were to try, but all the other people went too. They took a flute with them,[64] for they meant to put the fire in it.

They travelled a long time, and finally reached the place where the fire was. They were within a little distance of Thunder's house, when they all stopped to see what they would do. Woswosim, who was supposed to guard the fire in the house, began to sing, "I am the man who never sleeps. I am the man who never sleeps." Thunder had paid him for his work in beads, and he wore them about his neck and around his waist. He sat on the top of the sweat-house, by the smoke-hole.

After a while Mouse was sent up to try and see if he could get in. He crept up slowly till he got close to Woswosim, and then saw that his eyes were shut. He was asleep, in spite of the song that he sang. When Mouse saw that the watcher was asleep, he crawled to the opening and went in. Thunder had several daughters, and they were lying there asleep. Mouse stole up quietly, and untied the waist-string of each one's apron, so that should the alarm be given, and they jump up, these aprons or skirts would fall off, and they would have to stop to fix them. This done, Mouse took the flute, filled it with fire, then crept out, and rejoined the other people who were waiting outside.

Some of the fire was taken out and put in the Dog's ear, the remainder in the flute being given to the swiftest runner to carry. Deer, however, took a little, which he carried on the hock of his leg, where to-day there is a reddish spot. For a while all went well, but when they were about half-way back, Thunder woke up, suspected that something was wrong, and asked, "What is the matter with my fire?" Then he jumped up with a roar of thunder, and his daughters were thus awakened, and also jumped up; but their aprons fell off as they did so, and they had to sit down again to put them on. After they were all ready, they went out with Thunder to give chase. They carried with them a heavy wind and a great rain and a hailstorm, so that they might put out any fire the people had. Thunder and his daughters hurried along, and soon caught up with the fugitives, and were about to catch them, when Skunk shot at Thunder and killed him. Then Skunk called out, "After this you must never try to follow and kill people. You must stay up in the sky, and be the thunder. That is what you will be." The daughters of Thunder did not follow any farther; so the people went on safely, and got home with their fire, and people have had it ever since.

XV. THE SUN SNARER [65]

(MENOMINI: Hoffman, *Report of the Bureau of American Ethnology*, xiv, 181)

One day while two elder brothers were out hunting in the forest, the youngest went away to hide himself and to mourn because he was not permitted to join them. He had with him his bow and arrows and his beaver-skin robe; but when the Sun rose high in the sky he became tired and laid himself down to weep, covering himself entirely with his robe to keep out the Sun. When the Sun was directly overhead and saw the boy, it sent down a ray which burned spots upon the robe and made it shrink until it exposed the boy. Then the Sun smiled, while the boy wept more violently than before. He felt that he had been cruelly treated both by his brothers and now by the Sun. He said to the Sun, "You have treated me cruelly and burned my robe, when I did not deserve it. Why do you punish me like this?" The Sun merely continued to smile, but said nothing.

The boy then gathered up his bow and arrows, and taking his burnt robe, returned to the wigwam, where he lay down in a dark corner and again wept. His sister was outside of the wigwam when he returned, so she was not aware of his presence when she reëntered to attend to her work. Presently she heard someone crying, and going over to the place whence the sound came she found that it was her youngest brother who was in distress.

She said to him, "My brother, why are you weeping?" — to which he replied, "Look at me; I am sad because the Sun burned my beaver-skin robe; I have been cruelly treated this day." Then he turned his face away and continued to weep. Even in his sleep he sobbed, because of his distress.

When he awoke, he said to his sister, "My sister, give me a thread; I wish to use it."

She handed him a sinew thread, but he said to her, "No, that is not what I want: I want a hair thread." She said to him, "Take this; this is strong." "No," he replied, "that is not the kind of a thread I want; I want a hair thread."

She then understood his meaning, and plucking a single hair from her person handed it to him, when he said, "That is what I want," and taking it at both ends he began to pull it gently, smoothing it out as it continued to lengthen until it reached from the tips of the fingers of one hand to the ends of the fingers of the other.

Then he started out to where the Sun's path touched the earth. When he reached the place where the Sun was when it burned his robe, the little boy made a noose and stretched it across the path, and when the Sun came to that point the noose caught him around the neck and began to choke him until he almost lost his breath. It became dark, and the Sun called out to the ma'nidos, "Help me, my brothers, and cut this string before it kills me." The ma'nidos came, but the thread had so cut into the flesh of the Sun's neck that they could not sever it. When all but one had given up, the Sun called to the the Mouse to try to cut the string. The Mouse came up and gnawed at the string, but it was difficult work, because the string was hot and deeply embedded in the Sun's neck. After working at the string a good while, however, the Mouse succeeded in cutting it, when the Sun breathed again and the darkness disappeared. If the Mouse had not succeeded, the Sun would have died. Then the boy said to the Sun, "For your cruelty I have punished you; now you may go."

The boy then returned to his sister, satisfied with what he had done.

XVI. THE MAN WHO ACTED AS THE SUN [66]

(BELLA COOLA: Boas, *Jesup North Pacific
Expedition*, i, 95)

Once upon a time there lived a woman* some distance up Bella
Coola River. She refused the offer of marriage from the young
men of the tribe, because she desired to marry the Sun. She
left her village and went to seek the Sun. Finally she reached
his house, and married the Sun. After she had been there one
day,[116] she had a child. He grew very quickly, and on the second
day of his life he was able to walk and to talk.[112] After a short
time he said to his mother, "I should like to see your mother
and your father"; and he began to cry, making his mother
feel homesick. When the Sun saw that his wife felt downcast,
and that his son was longing to see his grandparents, he said,
"You may return to the earth to see your parents. Descend
along my eyelashes." His eyelashes [67] were the rays of the Sun,
which he extended down to his wife's home, where they lived
with the woman's parents.

The boy was playing with the children of the village, who
were teasing him, saying that he had no father. He began to
cry, and went to his mother, whom he asked for bow and arrows. His mother gave him what he requested. He went outside and began to shoot his arrows towards the sky. The first
arrow struck the sky and stuck in it; [68] the second arrow hit
the notch of the first one; and thus he continued until a chain
was formed, extending from the sky down to the place where he
was standing. Then he ascended the chain. He found the
house of the sun, which he entered. He told his father
that the boys had been teasing him, and he asked him to let
him carry the sun. But his father said, "You cannot do it. I
carry many torches. Early in the morning and late in the
evening I burn small torches, but at noon I burn the large ones."
The boy insisted on his request. Then his father gave him the
torches, warning him at the same time to observe carefully the
instructions that he was giving him in regard to their use.

Early the next morning, the young man started on the course
of the sun, carrying the torches. Soon he grew impatient, and
lighted all the torches at once. Then it grew very hot. The

---

* A number of Indian names have been omitted from this passage. They do not
affect the meaning.

trees began to burn, and many animals jumped into the water to save themselves, but the water began to boil. Then his mother covered the people with her blanket, and thus saved them. The animals hid under stones. The ermine crept into a hole, which, however, was not quite large enough, so that the tip of its tail protruded from the entrance. It was scorched, and since that time the tip of the ermine's tail has been black. The mountain-goat hid in a cave, hence its skin is perfectly white. All the animals that did not hide were scorched, and therefore have black skins, but the skin on their lower side remained lighter.[4] When the Sun saw what was happening, he said to his son, "Why do you do so? Do you think it is good that there are no people on the earth?"

The Sun took him and cast him down from the heavens, saying, "You shall be the mink, and future generations of man shall hunt you."

XVII. THE MAN IN THE MOON [69]

(LILLOOET: Teit, *Journal of American Folk-Lore*, xxv, 298, No. 3)

The three Frog sisters had a house in a swamp, where they lived together. Not very far away lived a number of people in another house. Among them were Snake and Beaver, who were friends. They were well-grown lads, and wished to marry the Frog girls.

One night Snake went to Frog's house, and, crawling up to one of the sisters, put his hand on her face. She awoke, and asked him who he was. Learning that he was Snake, she said she would not marry him, and told him to leave at once. She called him hard names, such as, "slimy-fellow," "small-eyes," etc. Snake returned, and told his friend of his failure.

Next night Beaver went to try, and, crawling up to one of the sisters, he put his hand on her face. She awoke, and, finding out who he was, she told him to be gone. She called him names, such as, "short-legs," "big-belly," "big-buttocks." Beaver felt hurt, and, going home, began to cry. His father asked him what the matter was, and the boy told him. He said, "That is nothing. Don't cry! It will rain too much." But young Beaver said, "I *will* cry."

As he continued to cry, much rain fell, and soon the swamp where the Frogs lived was flooded.[70] Their house was under the water, which covered the tops of the tall swamp-grass. The Frogs got cold, and went to Beaver's house, and said to him, "We wish to marry your sons." But old Beaver said, "No! You called us hard names."

The water was now running in a regular stream. So the Frogs swam away downstream until they reached a whirlpool, which sucked them in, and they descended to the house of the Moon. The latter invited them to warm themselves at the fire; but they said, "No. We do not wish to sit by the fire. We wish to sit there," pointing at him. He said, "Here?" at the same time pointing at his feet. They said, "No, not there." Then he pointed to one part of his body after another, until he reached his brow. When he said, "Will you sit here?" they all cried out, "Yes," and jumped on his face, thus spoiling his beauty. The Frog's sisters may be seen on the moon's face at the present day.

XVIII. ORIGIN OF THE PLEIADES [71]

(ONONDAGA: Beauchamp, *Journal of American Folk-Lore*, xiii, 281)

A long time ago a party of Indians went through the woods toward a good hunting-ground, which they had long known. They travelled several days through a very wild country, going on leisurely and camping by the way. At last they reached Kan-ya-ti-yo, "the beautiful lake," where the gray rocks were crowned with great forest trees. Fish swarmed in the waters, and at every jutting point the deer came down from the hills around to bathe or drink of the lake. On the hills and in the valleys were huge beech and chestnut trees, where squirrels chattered, and bears came to take their morning and evening meals.

The chief of the band was Hah-yah-no, "Tracks in the water," and he halted his party on the lake shore that he might return thanks to the Great Spirit for their safe arrival at this good hunting-ground. "Here will we build our lodges for the winter, and may the Great Spirit, who has prospered us on our way, send us plenty of game, and health and peace." The Indian is always thankful.

The pleasant autumn days passed on. The lodges had been built, and hunting had prospered, when the children took a fancy to dance for their own amusement. They were getting lonesome, having little to do, and so they met daily in a quiet spot by the lake to have what they called their jolly dance. They had done this a long time, when one day a very old man came to them. They had seen no one like him before. He was dressed in white feathers, and his white hair shone like silver. If his appearance was strange, his words were unpleasant as well. He told them they must stop their dancing, or evil would happen to them. Little did the children heed, for they were intent on their sport, and again and again the old man appeared, repeating his warning.

The mere dances did not afford all the enjoyment the children wished, and a little boy, who liked a good dinner, suggested a feast the next time they met. The food must come from their parents, and all these were asked when they returned home. "You will waste and spoil good victuals," said one. "You can eat at home as you should," said another, and so they got nothing at all. Sorry as they were for this, they met and danced as before. A little to eat after each dance would have made them happy indeed. Empty stomachs cause no joy.

One day, as they danced, they found themselves rising little by little into the air, their heads being light through hunger. How this happened they did not know, but one said, "Do not look back,[217] for something strange is taking place." A woman, too, saw them rise, and called them back, but with no effect, for they still rose slowly above the earth. She ran to the camp, and all rushed out with food of every kind, but the children would not return, though their parents called piteously after them. But one would even look back, and he became a falling star. The others reached the sky, and are now what we call the Pleiades, and the Onondagas Oot-kwa-tah. Every falling or shooting star recalls the story, but the seven stars shine on continuously, a pretty band of dancing children.[71a]

XIX. THE BAG OF WINDS [72]

(THOMPSON: Teit, *Memoirs of the American Folk-Lore Society*, vi, 87, No. 34)

Long ago the Wind did much damage, blowing violently over the country of the Indian. Moreover, it often killed many people and destroyed much property. At that time there was a man who lived near Spences Bridge, and who had three sons.

The youngest was very ambitious, and fond of trying to do wonderful things. One day he said to his father and brothers, "I will snare the Wind"; but they laughed at him, saying, "How can you do that? The Wind is unseen." However, he went out and set a snare.[73] He did not succeed for several nights, as his noose was too large. He made it smaller every night, and, on visiting his snare one morning, found he had caught the Wind. After great difficulty, he succeeded at last in getting it into his blanket, and made for home with it, where he put it down. He told his people that he had at last captured the Wind. They laughed at him. Then, to verify his statements, he opened one corner of the blanket, and immediately it began to blow fiercely, and the lodge itself was almost blown over. The people cried to him to stay the force of the Wind, which he did by again tying up the corner of the blanket. At last he released the Wind on the condition that he would never blow strongly enough to hurt people in the Indian country again, which promise he has kept.

XX. THE BIRD WHOSE WINGS MADE THE WIND [74]

(MICMAC: Rand, *Legends of the Micmacs*, p. 360, No. 68)

An Indian family resided on the sea-shore. They had two sons, the oldest of whom was married and had a family of small children. They lived principally by fishing, and their favorite food was eels.

Now it came to pass at a certain time that the weather was so stormy they could not fish. The wind blew fiercely night and day, and they were greatly reduced by hunger. Finally the old father told his boys to walk along the shore, and perhaps they might find a fish that had floated ashore, as sometimes happened. So one of the young men started off to try his luck in this line; when he reached a point where the wind blew so fiercely that he could hardly stand against it, he saw the cause of all the trouble. At the end of the point there was a ledge of rocks, called Rocky Point, extending far out; at low water the rocks were separated from one another by the shallow water, but were nearly all covered when the tide was in. On the farthest rock a large bird, the storm-king, was standing, flapping his wings and causing all the trouble by the wind he raised. The

Indian planned to outwit him. He called to the big bird, and addressing him as "my grandfather," said, "Are you cold?" He answered, "No." The man replied, "You are cold; let me carry you ashore on my back." "Do so," was the answer. So the man waded over to the rock on which the bird was sitting, took him on his back, and carefully carried him from rock to rock, wading over the intervening spaces of shoal water. In going down the last rock, he stumbled on purpose, but pretended that it was an accident; and the poor old bird fell and broke one of his wings. The man seemed very sorry, and immediately proceeded to set the bone and bind up the wing. He then directed the old fellow to keep quiet and not move his wings until the wounded one healed. He now inquired if it pained him much, and was told that it did not. "Remain there and I will visit you again soon, and bring you some food." He now returned home, and found that the wind had all died away; there was a dead calm, so that before long they were supplied with a great abundance of food, as the eels were plenty and easily taken. But there can be too much even of a good thing. Calm weather continued for a succession of days, causing the salt water to be covered with a sort of scum. The Indians say it is the result of sickness and vomiting among the larger fish; this scum prevents the fishermen from seeing into the water, and consequently is adverse to eel-spearing. This took place on the occasion referred to, and so they sought for a remedy. The big bird was visited and his wing examined. It was sufficiently recovered to admit of motion, and he was told to keep both his wings going, but that the motion must be steady and gentle. This produced the desired effect.

XXI. THE RELEASE OF THE WILD ANIMALS [75]

(COMANCHE: St. Clair, *Journal of American Folk-Lore*, xxii, 280, No. 17)

Long ago two persons owned all the buffalo. They were an old woman and her young cousin. They kept them penned up in the mountains, so that they could not get out. Coyote came to these people. He summoned the Indians to a council. "That old woman will not give us anything. When we come over there, we will plan how to release the buffalo." They all moved near the buffalo-inclosure. "After four nights," said Coyote, "we will again hold a council as to how we can release the buffalo. A very small animal shall go where the old woman draws her water. When the child gets water, it will take it home for a pet. The old woman will object; but the child will think so much of the animal, that it will begin to cry and will be allowed to keep it. The animal will run off at daybreak, and the buffalo will burst out of their pen and run away." The first animal they sent failed. Then they sent the Kill-dee.

When the boy went for water, he found the Kill-dee and took it home. "Look here!" he said to his cousin, "this animal of mine is very good." The old woman replied, "Oh, it is good for nothing! There is nothing living on the earth that is not a rascal or schemer." The child paid no attention to her. "Take it back where you got it," said the woman. He obeyed. The Kill-dee returned.

The people had another council. "Well, she has got the better of these two. They have failed," said Coyote; "but that makes no difference. Perhaps we may release them, perhaps we shall fail. This is the third time now. We will send a small animal over there. If the old woman agrees to take it, it will liberate those buffalo; it is a great schemer." So they sent the third animal. Coyote said, "If she rejects this one, we shall surely be unable to liberate the game." The animal went to the spring and was picked up by the boy, who took a great liking to it. "Look here! What a nice pet I have!" The old woman replied, "Oh, how foolish you are! It is a good for nothing. All the animals in the world are schemers. I'll kill it with a club." The boy took it in his arms and ran away crying. He thought too much of his pet. "No! this animal is too small," he cried. When the animal had not returned by nightfall, Coyote went among the people, saying, "Well, this animal has not returned yet; I dare say the old woman has consented to keep it. Don't be uneasy, our buffalo will be freed." Then he bade all the people get ready just at daybreak. "Our buffalo will be released. Do all of you mount your horses." In the mean time the animal, following its instructions, slipped over to the pen, and began to howl. The buffalo heard it, and were terrified. They ran towards the gate, broke it down, and escaped. The old woman, hearing the noise, woke up. The child asked, "Where is my pet?" He did not find it. The old woman said, "I told you so. Now you see the animal is bad, it has deprived us of our game." She vainly tried to hold the buffalo back. At daybreak all the Indians got on their horses, for they had confidence in Coyote. Thus the buffalo came to live on this earth. Coyote was a great schemer.

XXII. THE EMPOUNDED WATER [76]

(MALECITE: Speck, *Journal of American Folk-Lore*, xxx, 480, No. 2)

Aglabem kept back all the water in the world; so that rivers stopped flowing, and lakes dried up, and the people everywhere began dying of thirst. As a last resort, they sent a messenger to him to ask him to give the people water; but he refused, and gave the messenger only a drink from the water in which he washed. But this was not enough to satisfy even the thirst of one. Then the people began complaining, some saying, "I'm as dry as a fish," "I'm as dry as a frog," "I'm as dry as a turtle," "I'm as dry as a beaver," and the like, as they were on the verge of dying of thirst.

At last a great man was sent to Aglabem to beg him to release the water for the people. Aglabem refused, saying that he needed it himself to lie in. Then the messenger felled a tree, so that it fell on top of the monster and killed him. The body of this tree became the main river (St. John's River), and the branches became the tributary branches of the river, while the leaves became the ponds at the heads of these streams. As the waters flowed down to the villages of the people again, they plunged in to drink, and became transformed into the animals to which they had likened themselves when formerly complaining of their thirst.[4]

XXIII. THE ORIGIN OF CORN [77]

(ABANAKI: Brown, *Journal of American Folk-Lore*, iii, 214)

A long time ago, when Indians were first made, there lived one alone, far, far from any others. He knew not of fire, and subsisted on roots, barks, and nuts. This Indian became very lonesome for company. He grew tired of digging roots, lost his appetite, and for several days lay dreaming in the sunshine; when he awoke he saw something standing near, at which, at first, he was very much frightened. But when it spoke, his heart was glad, for it was a beautiful woman with long *light* hair, very unlike any Indian. He asked her to come to him, but she would not, and if he tried to approach her she seemed to go farther away; he sang to her of his loneliness and besought her not to leave him; at last she told him, if he would do just as she should say, he would always have her with him. He promised that he would.

She led him to where there was some very dry grass, told him to get two very dry sticks, rub them together quickly, holding them in the grass. Soon a spark flew out; the grass caught it, and quick as an arrow the ground was burned over. Then she said, "When the sun sets, take me by the hair and drag me over the burned ground." He did not like to do this, but she told him that wherever he dragged her something like grass would spring up, and he would see her hair coming from between the leaves; then the seeds would be ready for his use. He did as she said, and to this day, when they see the silk (hair) on the cornstalk, the Indians know she has not forgotten them.

CHAPTER III

TRICKSTER TALES [78]

XXIV. MANABOZHO'S ADVENTURES [79]

(Episodes A and B, OJIBWA: Radin, *Memoirs of the Geological Survey of Canada; Anthropological Series*, ii, 2–3. — Episodes C and D, MENOMINI: Hoffman, *Report of the Bureau of American Ethnology*, xiv, 203. — Episodes E and F, TIMAGAMI OJIBWA: Speck, *Memoirs of the Geological Survey of Canada: Anthropological Series*, ix, 33)

A

AT Lake St. Clair, Manabozho saw a number of ducks, and he thought to himself, "Just how am I going to kill them?" After a while, he took out one of his pails and started to drum and sing at the same time. The words of the song he sang were:

I am bringing new songs.

When the ducks saw Manabozho standing near the shore, they swam toward him and as soon as he saw this, he sent his grandmother ahead to build a little lodge, where they could live. In the meantime, he killed a few of the ducks, so, while his grandmother started out to build a shelter, Manabozho went towards the lake where the ducks and geese were floating around and around. Manabozho jumped into a sack and then dived into the water. The ducks and geese were quite surprised to see that he was such an excellent diver, and came closer and closer. Then Manabozho challenged them to a contest at diving. He said that he could beat them all. The ducks all accepted the challenge, but Manabozho beat them. Then he went after the geese and beat them too. For a time he was alternately diving and rising to the surface, all around. Finally he dived under the geese and started to tie their legs together with some basswood bark. When the geese noticed this, they tried to rise and fly away, but they were unable to do so, for Manabozho was hanging on to the other end of the string. The geese, nevertheless, managed to rise, gradually dragging Manabozho along with them. They finally emerged

from the water and rose higher and higher into the air. Manabozho, however, hung on, and would not let go, until his hand was cut and the string broke.[80]

B

While walking along the river he saw some berries in the water. He dived down for them, but was stunned when he unexpectedly struck the bottom. There he lay for quite a while, and when he recovered consciousness and looked up, he saw the berries hanging on a tree just above him.[81]

C

While Manabozho was once walking along a lake shore, tired and hungry, he observed a long, narrow sandbar, which extended far out into the water, around which were myriads of waterfowl, so Manabozho decided to have a feast. He had with him only his medicine bag; so he entered the brush and hung it upon a tree, now called "Manabozho tree," and procured a quantity of bark, which he rolled into a bundle and placing it upon his back, returned to the shore, where he pretended to pass slowly by in sight of the birds. Some of the Swans and Ducks, however, recognizing Manabozho and becoming frightened, moved away from the shore.

One of the Swans called out, "Ho! Manabozho, where are you going?" To this Manabozho replied, "I am going to have a song. As you may see, I have all my songs with me." Manabozho then called out to the birds, "Come to me, my brothers, and let us sing and dance." The birds assented and returned to the shore, when all retreated a short distance away from the lake to an open space where they might dance. Manabozho removed the bundle of bark from his back and placed it on the ground, got out his singing-sticks, and said to the birds, "Now, all of you dance around me as I drum; sing as loudly as you can, and keep your eyes closed. The first one to open his eyes will forever have them red and sore."

Manabozho began to beat time upon his bundle of bark, while the birds, with eyes closed, circled around him singing as loudly as they could. Keeping time with one hand, Manabozho suddenly grasped the neck of a Swan, which he broke; but before he had killed the bird it screamed out, whereupon Manabozho said, "That's right, brothers, sing as loudly as you can." Soon another Swan fell a victim; then a Goose, and so on until the number of birds was greatly reduced. Then the "Hell-diver," opening his eyes to see why there was less singing than at first, and beholding Manabozho and the heap of victims, cried out, "Manabozho is killing us! Manabozho is killing us!" and immediately ran to the water, followed by the remainder of the birds.[82]

As the "Hell-diver" was a poor runner, Manabozho soon overtook him, and said, "I won't kill you, but you shall always have red eyes and be the laughing-stock of all the birds." With this he gave the bird a kick, sending him far out into the lake and knocking off his tail, so that the "Hell-diver" is red-eyed and tailless to this day.[4]

D

Manabozho then gathered up his birds, and taking them out upon the sandbar buried them — some with their heads protruding, others with the feet sticking out of the sand. He then built a fire to cook the game, but as this would require some time, and as Manabozho was tired after his exertion, he stretched himself on the ground to sleep. In order to be informed if anyone approached, he slapped his thigh and said to it,[83] "You watch the birds, and awaken me if anyone should come near them." Then, with his back to the fire, he fell asleep.

After awhile a party of Indians came along in their canoes, and seeing the feast in store, went to the sandbar and pulled out every bird which Manabozho had so carefully placed there, but put back the heads and feet in such a way that there was no indication that the bodies had been disturbed. When the Indians had finished eating they departed, taking with them all the food that remained from the feast.[84]

Some time afterward, Manabozho awoke, and, being very hungry, bethought himself to enjoy the fruits of his strategem. In attempting to pull a baked swan from the sand he found nothing but the head and neck, which he held in his hand. Then he tried another, and found the body of that bird also gone. So he tried another, and then another, but each time met with disappointment. Who could have robbed him? he thought. He struck his thigh and asked, "Who has been here to rob me of my feast; did I not command you to watch while

I slept?" His thigh responded, "I also fell asleep, as I was very tired; but I see some people moving rapidly away in their canoes; perhaps they were the thieves. I see also they are very dirty and poorly dressed." Then Manabozho ran out to the point of the sandbar, and beheld the people in their canoes, just disappearing around a point of land. Then he called to them and reviled them, calling them "Winnibe′go! Winnibe′go!" And by this term the Menomini have ever since designated their thievish neighbors.[4]

E

After this Manabozho began travelling again. One time he feasted a lot of animals. He had killed a big bear, which was very fat and he began cooking it, having made a fire with his bow-drill. When he was ready to spread his meat, he heard two trees scraping together, swayed by the wind. He didn't like this noise while he was having his feast and he thought he could stop it. He climbed up one of the trees and when he reached the spot where the two trees were scraping, his foot got caught in a crack between the trees and he could not free himself.[85]

When the first animal guest came along and saw Manabozho in the tree, he, the Beaver, said "Come on to the feast, Manabozho is caught and can't stop us." And then the other animals came. The Beaver jumped into the grease and ate it, and the Otter did the same, and that is why they are so fat in the belly. The Beaver scooped up the grease and smeared it on himself, and that is the reason why he is so fat now. All the small animals came and got fat for themselves. Last of all the animals came the Rabbit, when nearly all the grease was gone — only a little left. So he put some on the nape of his neck and some on his groin and for this reason he has only a little fat in those places.[4] So all the animals got their fat except Rabbit. Then they all went, and poor Manabozho got free at last. He looked around and found a bear's skull that was all cleaned except for the brain, and there was only a little of that left, but he couldn't get at it. Then he wished himself to be changed into an ant in order to get into the skull and get enough to eat, for there was only about an ant's meal left.

F

Then he became an ant and entered the skull. When he had enough he turned back into a man, but he had his head inside the skull; this allowed him to walk but not to see.[86] On account of this he had no idea where he was. Then he felt the trees. He said to one, "What are you?" It answered, "Cedar." He kept doing this with all the trees in order to keep his course. When he got too near the shore, he knew it by the kind of trees he met. So he kept on walking and the only tree that did not answer promptly was the black spruce, and that said "I'm Se'segandak" (black spruce). Then Manabozho knew he was on low ground. He came to a lake, but he did not know how large it was, as he could n't see. He started to swim across. An Ojibwa was paddling on the lake with his family and he heard someone calling, "Hey! There's a bear swimming across the lake." Manabozho became frightened at this and the Ojibwa then said, "He's getting near the shore now." So Manabozho swam faster, and as he could understand the Ojibwa language, he guided himself by the cries. He landed on a smooth rock, slipped and broke the bear's skull, which fell off his head. Then the Ojibwa cried out, "That's no bear! That's Manabozho!" Manabozho was all right, now that he could see, so he ran off, as he did n't want to stay with these people.

XXV. THE TRICKSTER'S GREAT FALL AND HIS REVENGE [87]

(Menomini: Hoffman, *Report of the Bureau of American Ethnology*, xiv, 202)

Once while the Buzzard was soaring away through the air he saw Manabozho walking along. He flew a little toward the ground, with his wings outspread, and heard Manabozho say to him, "Buzzard, you must be very happy up there where you can soar through the air and see what is transpiring in the world beneath. Take me on your back so that I may ascend with you and see how it appears down here from where you live." The Buzzard came down, and said, "Manabozho, get on my back and I will take you up into the sky to let you see how the world appears from my abode." Manabozho approached the Buzzard, but seeing how smooth his back appeared said, "Buzzard, I am afraid you will let me slide from your back, so you must be careful not to sweep around too rapidly, that I may retain my place upon your back." The Buzzard told Manabozho that he would be careful, although the bird was determined to play a trick on him if possible. Manabozho mounted the Buzzard and held on to his feathers as well as he could. The Buzzard took a short run, leaped from the ground, spread his wings and rose into the air. Manabozho felt rather timid as the Buzzard swept through the air, and as he circled around his body leaned so much that Manabozho could scarcely retain his position, and he was afraid of slipping off. Presently, as Manabozho was looking down upon the broad earth below, the Buzzard made a sharp curve to one side so that his body leaned more than ever. Manabozho, losing his grasp, slipped off and dropped to earth like an arrow. He struck the ground with such force as to knock him senseless. The Buzzard returned to his place in the sky, but hovered around to see what would become of Manabozho.

Manabozho lay a long time like one dead. When he recovered he saw something close to and apparently staring him in the face. He could not at first recognize it, but when he put his hands against the object he found that it was his own buttocks, because he had been all doubled up. He arose and prepared to go on his way, when he espied the Buzzard above him, laughing at his own trickery.

Manabozho then said, "Buzzard, you have played a trick on me by letting me fall, but as I am more powerful than you I shall revenge myself." The Buzzard then replied, "No, Manabozho, you will not do anything of the kind, because you cannot deceive me. I shall watch you."

Manabozho kept on, and the Buzzard, not noticing anything peculiar in the movements of Manabozho, flew on his way through the air. Manabozho then decided to transform himself into a dead deer, because he knew the Buzzard had chosen to subsist on dead animals and fish. Manabozho then went to a place visible from a great distance and from many directions, where he laid himself down and changed himself into the carcass of a deer.[88] Soon the various birds and beasts and crawling things that subsist on such food began to congregate about the dead deer. The Buzzard saw the birds flying toward the place where the body lay, and joined them. He flew around several times to see if it was Manabozho trying to deceive him, then thought to himself, "No, that is not Manabozho; it is truly a dead deer." He then approached the body and began to pick a hole into the fleshy part of the thigh. Deeper and deeper into the flesh the Buzzard picked until his head and neck was buried each time he reached in to pluck the fat from the intestines. Without warning, while the Buzzard had his head completely hidden in the carcass of the deer, the deer jumped up and pinched together his flesh, thus firmly grasping the head and neck of the Buzzard. Then Manabozho said, "Aha! Buzzard, I did catch you after all, as I told you I would. Now pull out your head." The Buzzard with great difficulty withdrew his head from the cavity in which it had been inclosed, but the feathers were all pulled off, leaving his scalp and neck covered with nothing but red skin. Then Manabozho said to the bird, "Thus do I punish you for your deceitfulness; henceforth you will go through the world without feathers on your head and neck, and you shall always stink because of the food you will be obliged to eat." That is why the buzzard is such a bad-smelling fellow, and why his head and neck are featherless.[4]

XXVI. THE DECEIVED BLIND MEN [89]

(MENOMINI: Hoffman, *Report of the Bureau of American Ethnology*, xiv, 211)

There was a large settlement on the shore of a lake, and among its people were two very old blind men. It was decided to re-move these men to the opposite side of the lake, where they might live in safety, as the settlement was exposed to the attack of enemies, when they might easily be captured and killed. So the relations of the old men got a canoe, some food, a kettle, and a bowl and started across the lake, where they built for them a wigwam in a grove some distance from the water. A line was stretched from the door of the wigwam to a post in the water, so that they would have no difficulty in help-ing themselves. The food and vessels were put into the wig-wam, and after the relations of the old men promised them that they would call often and keep them provided with everything that was needful, they returned to their settlement.

The two old blind men now began to take care of them-selves. On one day one of them would do the cooking while the other went for water, and on the next day they would change about in their work, so that their labors were evenly divided. As they knew just how much food they required for each meal, the quantity prepared was equally divided, but was eaten out of the one bowl which they had.

Here they lived in contentment for several years; but one day a Raccoon, which was following the water's edge looking for crawfish, came to the line which had been stretched from the lake to the wigwam. The Raccoon thought it rather curious to find a cord where he had not before observed one, and wondered to himself, "What is this? I think I shall follow this cord to see where it leads." So he followed the path along which the cord was stretched until he came to the wigwam. Approaching very cautiously, he went up to the entrance, where he saw the two old men asleep on the ground, their heads at the door and their feet directed toward the heap of hot coals within. The Raccoon sniffed about and soon found there was something good to eat within the wigwam; but he decided not to enter at once for fear of waking the old men; so he retired a short distance to hide himself and to see what they would do.

Presently the old men awoke, and one said to the other, "My friend, I am getting hungry; let us prepare some food." "Very well," replied his companion, "you go down to the lake and fetch some water while I get the fire started."

The Raccoon heard this conversation, and, wishing to deceive the old man, immediately ran to the water, untied the cord from the post, and carried it to a clump of bushes, where he tied it. When the old man came along with his kettle to get water, he stumbled around the brush until he found the end of the cord; then he began to dip his kettle down upon the ground for water. Not finding any, he slowly returned and said to his companion, "We shall surely die, because the lake is dried up and the brush is grown where we used to get water. What shall we do?"

"That can not be," responded his companion, "for we have not been asleep long enough for the brush to grow upon the lake bed. Let me go out to try if I can not get some water." So taking the kettle from his friend he started off.

So soon as the first old man had returned to the wigwam, the Raccoon took the cord back and tied it where he had found it, then waited to see the result.

The second old man now came along, entered the lake, and getting his kettle full of water returned to the wigwam, saying as he entered, "My friend, you told me what was not true. There is water enough; for here, you see, I have our kettle full." The other could not understand this at all, and wondered what had caused the deception.

The Raccoon approached the wigwam and entered to await the cooking of the food. When it was ready, the pieces of meat, for there were eight of them, were put into the bowl and the old men sat down on the ground facing each other, with the bowl between them. Each took a piece of meat, and they began to talk of various things and were enjoying themselves.

The Raccoon now quietly removed four pieces of meat from the bowl and began to eat them, enjoying the feast even more than the old blind men. Presently one of them reached into the bowl to get another piece of meat, and finding that only two pieces remained, said, "My friend, you must be very hungry to eat so rapidly; I have had but one piece, and there are but two pieces left."

The other replied, "I have not taken them, but suspect you have eaten them yourself"; whereupon the other replied more angrily than before. Thus they argued, and the Raccoon, desiring to have more sport, tapped each of them on the face. The old men, each believing the other had struck him, began to fight, rolling over the floor of the wigwam, upsetting the bowl and the kettle, and causing the fire to be scattered. The Raccoon then took the two remaining pieces of meat and made his exit from the wigwam, laughing ha, ha, ha, ha; whereupon the old men instantly ceased their strife, for they now knew they had been deceived. The Raccoon then remarked to them, "I have played a nice trick on you; you should not find fault with each other so easily." Then the Raccoon continued his crawfish-hunting along the lake shore.

XXVII. THE TRICKSTER'S RACE [90]

(BLACKFOOT: Wissler and Duvall, *Anthropological Papers of the American Museum of Natural History*, ii, 27, No. 11)

Now Old Man went on and came to a place where deer and elk were playing a game called "Follow your leader." Old Man watched the game a while. Then he asked permission to play. He took the lead, sang a song, and ran about this way and that, and finally led them up to the edge of a cliff. Old Man jumped down and was knocked senseless. After a while he got up and called to the rest to follow. "No, we might hurt ourselves." "Oh!" said Old Man, "it is nice and soft here, and I had to sleep a while." Then the elk all jumped down and were killed.[91] Then Old Man said to the deer, "Now, you jump." "No," said the deer, "we shall not jump down, because the elk are all killed." "No," said Old Man, "they are only laughing." So the deer jumped down and were all killed. Now, when the elk were about to jump over, there was a female elk about to become a mother, and she begged Old Man not to make her jump, so he let her go. A few of the deer were also let go for the same reason. If he had not done this, all the elk and deer would have been killed.

Old Man was now busy butchering the animals that had been killed by falling over the cliff. When he was through butchering, he went out and found a place to camp. Then he carried his meat there and hung it up to dry. When he was all alone, a Coyote came to him. This Coyote had a shell on his neck, and one leg was tied up as if badly hurt. The Coyote said to Old Man, "Give me something to eat."

Old Man said to him, "Give me that shell on your neck to skim the soup, and I will give you something to eat." "No," said Coyote, "that shell is my medicine." Then Old Man noticed that the Coyote had his leg tied up, and said, "Well, brother, I will run you a race for a meal." "Well," said Coyote, "I am hurt. I cannot run." "That makes no difference," said Old Man, "run anyway." "Well," said Coyote, "I will run for a short distance." "No," said Old Man, "you have to run a long distance." Finally Coyote agreed. They were to run to a distant point, then back again. Coyote started out very slow, and kept crying for Old Man to wait, to wait. At last Coyote and Old Man came to the turning-point. Then Coyote took the bandage off his leg, began to run fast, and soon left Old Man far behind. He began to call out to all the coyotes, the animals, and mice, and they all came rushing up to Old Man's camp and began to eat his meat. It was a long time before Old Man reached the camp; but he kept calling out, "Leave me some meat, leave me some meat."

XXVIII. THE EYE–JUGGLER [92]

(CHEYENNE: Kroeber, *Journal of American Folk-Lore*, xiii, 168, No. 11)

There was a man that could send his eyes out of his head, on the limb of a tree, and call them back again, by saying "Eyes hang upon a branch." White-man saw him doing this, and came to him crying; he wanted to learn this too. The man taught him, but warned him not to do it more than four times in one day. [93] White-man went off along the river. When he came to the highest tree he could see, he sent his eyes to the top. Then he called them back. He thought he could do this as often as he wished, disregarding the warning.

The fifth time his eyes remained fastened to the limb. All day he called, but the eyes began to swell and spoil, and flies gathered on them. White-man grew tired and lay down, facing his eyes, still calling for them, though they never came; and he cried. At night he was half asleep, when a mouse ran over him. He closed his lids that the mice would not see he was blind, and lay still, in order to catch one.

At last one sat on his breast. He kept quiet to let it become used to him, and the mouse went on his face, trying to cut his hair for its nest. Then it licked his tears, but let its tail hang in his mouth. He closed it, and caught the mouse. He seized it tightly, and made it guide him, telling him of his misfortune. The mouse said it could see the eyes, and they had swelled to an enormous size. It offered to climb the tree and get them for him, but White-man would not let it go. It tried to wriggle free, but he held it fast. Then the mouse asked on what condition he would release it, and White-man said, only if it gave him one of its eyes. [94] So it gave him one, and he could see again, and let the mouse go. But the small eye was far back in his socket, and he could not see very well with it.

A buffalo was grazing near by, and as White-man stood near him crying, he looked on and wondered. White-man said: "Here is a buffalo, who has the power to help me in my trouble." So the Buffalo asked him what he wanted. White-man told him he had lost his eye and needed one. The buffalo took out one of his and put it in White-man's head. Now White-man could see far again. But the eye did not fit the socket; most of it was outside. The other was far inside. Thus he remained.

XXIX. THE SHARPENED LEG.[95]

(CHEYENNE: Kroeber, *Journal of American Folk-Lore*, xiii, 169, No. 12)

There was a man whose leg was pointed, so that by running and jumping against trees he could stick in them. By saying 'naiwatoutawa,' he brought himself back to the ground. On a hot day he would stick himself against a tree for greater shade and coolness. However, he could not do this trick more than four times.[93] Once while he was doing this, White-man came to him, crying, and said: "Brother, sharpen my leg!" The man replied: "That is not very hard. I can sharpen your leg." White-man stood on a large log, and the other, with an axe, sharpened his leg, telling him to hold still bravely.[271b] The pain caused the tears to come from his eyes.

When the man had sharpened his leg, he told him to do the trick only four times a day, and to keep count in order not to exceed this number. White-man went down toward the river, singing. Near the bank was a large tree; toward this he ran, then jumped and stuck in it. Then he called himself back to the ground. Again he jumped, this time against another tree; but now he counted one, thinking in this way to get the better of the other man. The third time, he counted two. The fourth time, birds and animals stood by, and he was proud to show his ability, and jumped high, and pushed his leg in up to the knee. Then coyotes, wolves, and other animals came to see him; some of them asked how he came to know the trick, and begged him to teach it to them, so they could stick to trees at night.

He was still prouder now, and for the fifth time he ran and jumped as high as he could, and half his thigh entered the tree. Then he counted four. Then he called to get to the ground again. But he stuck. He called out all day; he tried to send the animals to the man who had taught him. He was fast in the tree for many days, until he starved to death.

XXX. THE OFFENDED ROLLING STONE [96]

(PAWNEE: Dorsey, *Publications of the Carnegie Institution*, lix, 446, No. 126)

Coyote was going along, and as he had not had anything to eat for some time he was very hungry. In the evening he went to a high hill and sat down. Early the next morning he started again. He came to a big round stone. He took out his knife and said: "Grandfather, this knife I give to you as a present. I want you to help me to get something to eat."

Coyote went over a hill, and there in the bottom was a village of people. He went into the village and he could see meat hanging on poles everywhere in the camp. He went into one of the tipis and the people in the tipi roasted a piece of meat for him. Just as he was about to taste of the meat he thought of his knife and said: "Why did I give my knife to that stone? I should have kept it and then I should have been able to cut the meat without having to pull it with my hands." He asked to be excused and went out. He went to where the stone was. He said: "Grandfather, I will have to take back this knife, for I have found a village of people with plenty of meat." He went over the hills and into the bottom, but there was no village there. Coyote went back and returned the knife to the stone. He went back over the hills and there saw the village and he entered one of the tipis. They placed before him some meat. He began to chew the meat. He thought of his knife. He went back to the stone, and as he took the knife the stone said: "Why do you take the knife away from me? I am now going to kill you."

Then the stone ran after the Coyote. Coyote ran and came to a den of Bears. He told the Bears that a person was running after him and he asked them to help him. The Bears said that they were not afraid of anything. They asked what the thing was, and he said it was the stone. The Bears said: "Keep on running. We can not do anything with the stone." The stone was close to Coyote when he came up to another den of Mountain-Lions. They also told Coyote to pass on, as they could not do anything for him. After a while Coyote came to a Buffalo standing all alone, but when the Buffalo found out that it was the stone running after Coyote he told him to pass on.

At last Coyote came to a place where the Bull-Bats stayed. Coyote said: "Grandchildren, there is a person running after me." The Bull-Bats then said: "Enter our lodge and remain there." [146] When the stone came rolling up it said: "Where is that person who came here?" The Bull-Bats did not reply and the stone became angry. Then the Bull-Bats said: "He is here and we are going to protect him." The Bull-Bats flew up and then down, and they expelled flatus on the stone. Every time they did this a piece broke off from the stone. The largest Bull-Bat came down and expelled flatus right on the center and broke the stone into pieces. Then the Coyote was told to come out and go on his way.

Coyote started off, and when he got over the hills he turned around and yelled at the Bull-Bats and said: "All you big-nosed funny things, how you did behave to that stone." The Bull-Bats heard it and did not pay any attention, but he kept on making fun of them. Then the Bull-Bats flew up in a group, and came down, and with their wings they got the stones together again and started it to rolling, and said: "Go and kill that fellow." The stone then ran after Coyote and Coyote tried to get away, but he could not. At last he gave out. He jumped over a steep bank and the stone was right behind him. As Coyote struck the bottom, the stone fell on him and killed him. This is why we used to find dead coyotes in the hills and valleys.

XXXI. THE TRICKSTER KILLS THE CHILDREN [97]

(ARAPAHO: Dorsey and Kroeber, *Field Museum: Anthropological Series*, v, 101, No. 49)

Nihansan was travelling down a stream. As he walked along on the bank he saw something red in the water. They were red plums. He wanted them badly. Taking off his clothes, he dived in and felt over the bottom with his hands; but he could find nothing, and the current carried him down-stream and to the surface again. He thought. He took stones and tied them to his wrists and ankles so that they should weigh him down in the water. Then he dived again; he felt over the bottom, but could find nothing. When his breath gave out he tried to come up, but could not. He was nearly dead, when at last the stones on one side fell off and he barely rose to the surface sideways and got a little air. As he revived, floating on his back, he saw the plums hanging on the tree above him. He said to himself: "You fool!" He scolded himself a long time. Then he got up, took off the stones, threw them away, and went and ate the plums. He also filled his robe with them.

Then he went on down the river. He came to a tent. He saw a bear-woman come out and go in again. Going close to the tent, he threw a plum so that it dropped in through the top of the tent. When it fell inside, the bear-women and children all scrambled for it. Then he threw another and another. At last one of the women said to her child: "Go out and see if that is not your uncle Nihansan." The child went out, came back, and said: "Yes, it is my uncle Nihansan." Then Nihansan came in.. He gave them the plums, and said: "I wonder that you never get plums, they grow so near you!" The bear-women wanted to get some at once. He said: "Go up the river a little way; it is not far. Take all your children with you that are old enough to pick. Leave the babies here and I will watch them." They all went.

Then he cut all the babies' heads off. He put the heads back into the cradles; the bodies he put into a large kettle and cooked. When the bear-women came back, he said to them: "Have you never been to that hill here? There were many young wolves there." "In that little hill here?" they asked. "Yes. While you were gone I dug the young wolves out and cooked them." Then they were all pleased. They sat down and began to eat.[98] One of the children said: "This tastes like my little sister." "Hush!" said her mother, "don't say that." Nihansan became uneasy. "It is too hot here," he said, and took some plums and went off a little distance; there he sat down and ate. When he had finished, he shouted: "Ho! Ho! bear-women, you have eaten your own children."

All the bears ran to their cradles and found only the heads of the children. At once they pursued him. They began to come near him. Nihansan said: "I wish there were a hole that I could hide in." When they had nearly caught him he came to a hole and threw himself into it.

The hole extended through the hill, and he came out on the other side while the bear-women were still standing before the entrance. He painted himself with white paint to look like a different person, took a willow stick, put feathers on it, and laid it across his arm. Then he went to the women. "What are you crying about?" he asked them. They told him. He said: "I will go into the hole for you," and crawled in. Soon he cried as if hurt, and scratched his shoulders. Then he came out, saying: "Nihansan is too strong for me. Go into the hole yourselves; he is not very far in." They all went in, but soon came out again and said: "We cannot find him."

Nihansan entered once more, scratched himself bloody, bit himself, and cried out. He said: "He has long finger nails with which he scratches me. I cannot drag him out. But he is at the end of the hole. He cannot go back farther. If you go in, you can drag him out. He is only a little farther than you went last time."

They all went into the hole. Nihansan got brush and grass and made a fire at the entrance. "That sounds like flint striking," said one of the women. "The flint birds are flying," Nihansan said. "That sounds like fire," said another woman. "The fire birds are flying about; they will soon be gone by." "That is just like smoke," called a woman. "The smoke birds are passing. Go on, he is only a little farther, you will catch him soon," said Nihansan. Then the heat followed the smoke into the hole. The bear-women began to shout. "Now the heat birds are flying," said Nihansan.

Then the bears were all killed. Nihansan put out the fire and dragged them out. "Thus one obtains food when he is hungry," he said. He cut up the meat, ate some of it, and hung the rest on branches to dry. Then he went to sleep.

XXXII. WILDCAT GETS A NEW FACE [99]

(UINTAH UTE: Mason, *Journal of American Folk-Lore*, xxiii, 301, No. 3)

Long ago Wildcat had a long nose and tail. One day he was sleeping on a rock when Coyote came along. He pushed Wildcat's nose and tail in, and then went home. At noon Wildcat woke up, and noticed his short nose and tail. "What's the matter with me?" he asked. Then he guessed the cause. "Oh! Coyote did that," he said, and he hunted for him.

Now, Coyote was sleepy and had lain down. Wildcat came and sat down beside him. He pulled out Coyote's nose and tail and made them long. They were short before. Then he ran off. After a while Coyote woke up and saw his long nose and tail.

XXXIII. THE TRICKSTER BECOMES A DISH [100]

(LILLOOET: Teit, *Journal of American Folk-Lore*, xxv, 303, No. 7)

Two brothers lived at the very head waters of the Upper Lillooet River, and spent most of their time training themselves in the neighboring mountains, for they wished to become great. One of them became ill, and had to remain at home. After four years' illness, he became weak, and so thin that he seemed nothing but skin and bones. His brother grew anxious about him, and stopped his training. He hunted, and brought in rabbits, squirrel, and all kinds of meat, for his sick brother. He also threw small pieces of stick into the water, making them turn into fish.[101] Then he caught them and gave them to his brother to eat. But no kind of food seemed to agree with the invalid, for he rapidly grew weaker and thinner.

When the youth saw that no food did his brother good, he made up his mind to take him away to some other place to be cured. They embarked in a canoe, and proceeded down the Lillooet River, giving names to all the places as they passed along. They came to a place they called Ilamux. Here there was a rock which dammed the river. They made a hole through it to allow their canoe to pass. Even at the present day it appears like a stone bridge across the river. Proceeding, they came to a place they called Komelux. Here two creeks, running from opposite directions, met each other with very great force. They made the water smooth enough to be safe for a canoe to pass. Proceeding, they came to a place they named Kulexwin. Here there was a steep, rocky mountain close to the river. They threw their medicine-mat at it, and it became flat like a mat.

Thus they proceeded down to Big and Little Lillooet Lakes and the Lower Lillooet River, until they reached Harrison Lake. All the way along they gave names to the places, made the waters navigable, and changed many features of the country.[46] They reached Fraser River, went down to its mouth, and proceeded out to sea to the land of the salmon. When they arrived there, the strong brother hid himself, while the sick man transformed himself into a wooden dish, nicely painted and carved; and in this form he floated against the dam inside of which the people kept the salmon. A man found the dish, and took it to his daughter, who admired it very much, and used it to eat from. Whatever salmon she left in the dish over night always disappeared; but she did not care, because salmon were plentiful.

The dish ate the salmon, or, rather, the sick brother in dish form; and soon he became fat and well again. The other brother left his hiding-place every night to see the invalid, and to eat salmon out of the basket into which the people threw their leavings. He was glad to see his brother getting well so rapidly. When he had become very fat, his brother told him it was time they departed: so one night he broke the dam, and let the salmon out. Then they embarked in their canoe, and led the salmon toward the mouth of the Fraser River.

The salmon travelled very fast, and by the next morning they had reached the river. As they ascended, they took pieces of salmon from their basket, and threw them into the different creeks and rivers. Wherever they threw pieces of salmon, some of the fish followed. Thus they introduced the salmon into the streams of the interior. "Henceforth," said they, "salmon shall run at this time each year, and the people shall become acquainted with them and eat them." Then the brothers returned to their home at the head of the Upper Lillooet River, and they made near their house the hot springs called Tcîq, which they used for cooking their food.

XXXIV. COYOTE PROVES HIMSELF A CANNIBAL [102]

(JICARILLA APACHE: Goddard, *Anthropological Papers of the American Museum of Natural History*, viii, 225, No. 27)

Owl was the one who had arrows. He had a club also with which he killed men whom he ate. "Up at the low gap I am watching for men, wū hwū wō," he sang. Coyote came walking along in front of him. "Wū hwū wū," sang Owl, "I am looking for men in the low gap." The two came face to face there. "Now," said Owl, "the one who vomits human flesh will kill men." "Very well," said Coyote, "shut your eyes." Owl shut his eyes. When he vomited, Coyote put his hand under and took the meat. The grasshoppers which Coyote vomited he put in Owl's hand.

"Now open your eyes," said Coyote. Owl looked and saw the grasshoppers lying in his hand. Coyote showed him the meat. "What did I tell you," said Coyote, "this is the meat I threw up." "Where did I drink in the grasshoppers?" said Owl.

Coyote ran all around Owl. "Because I run fast like this I eat people," said Coyote. "These legs of yours are too large,

I will fix them for you. Shut your eyes." Coyote cut Owl's leg, trimming away the meat. He broke his leg with a stone and took the arrows away leaving him only the club.

Coyote ran around Owl who threw his club at him. He would say, "Come back, my club," and it would come back to him. He threw it again. "Come here, my club," he called. He hit him with it. Coyote said, "Wherever a stick falls when one throws it there it will lie." The club did not return to Owl.

"Now you will live right here in the canyon where many arrows will be in front of you. Somebody might kill you," Coyote told him. Owl hitched himself along into the canyon. "Arrows painted black may kill you," said Coyote. Coyote went around in front of him and shot him with his own (Owl's) arrows.

After that everybody was afraid of Coyote, who went around killing off the people.

XXXV. THE BUNGLING HOST [103]

(THOMPSON: Teit, *Memoirs of the American Folk-Lore Society*, vi, 40)

The Black Bear invited the Coyote to her underground lodge. He went the next morning, and on arriving was kindly treated by the Bear. She gave him berries and other food to eat, which was very acceptable to him, as he was almost famishing. Before long the Black Bear put more wood on the fire, and placed a dish down by the side of the fire. Then she held her hands, fingers turned downward, in front of the blaze. Before long melted fat commenced to drip from her finger-tips into the dish below, which in a short time became quite full. She took the dish and placed it in front of the Coyote, asking him to partake of the fat, which he did, eating as much as he was able. After finishing his repast, the Coyote said that he would now go home. At the same time he invited the Black Bear to his house on the morrow, when he said he would return her dish, which in the mean time he would borrow so as to take home the rest of the fat for his wife.

In due course the Black Bear arrived at the Coyote's house, where she was treated to some offal which the Coyote had found, but which he told her was fresh, as he had been out hunting and had just brought it in. After a while the Coyote told his wife to stir the fire, because he wanted to get some fat to give to his guest. He then set the dish down close to the fire, and holding up his paws in front of the blaze, exactly as the Black Bear had done, he awaited results. As there was no sign of any fat coming, he placed his paws still nearer to the flame, and held them there until they commenced to shrivel and curl up with the heat, and still there were no signs of any grease dripping down. His paws had now almost shrunk up into a ball. He was unable to endure the pain any longer, withdrew his hands from the fire, and ran around the house, howling with pain. The Black bear then said to him, "What a fool you are! Poor fellow! Watch me how I do it." She then held up her paws in front of the fire, as she had done on the previous day, and before long the dish was full of grease. She then made the Coyote a present of the grease, and told him never to try and do what was beyond his power.

Sometime afterwards the Coyote felt hungry and thought he would pay a visit to Tsalas, who lived in an underground lodge some little distance away. Upon entering, Tsalas treated him kindly, telling him that he would go and get some fresh fish for him to eat. He went outside, took a withe from some neighboring bushes, and went down to the river, where he made a small hole in the ice, and commenced to dive for fish. The Coyote, meanwhile, watched all his movements from the top of the ladder. Before long, Tsalas had caught a goodly number of fish, which he strung on the withe, and returning home, cooked some of them for the Coyote, who soon ate his fill.

On leaving, the Coyote invited Tsalas to visit him at his house on the morrow. Accordingly, the next day, Tsalas repaired to the Coyote's house, where he was offered old meat; but, unlike the Black Bear, he was not fond of such food. Therefore the Coyote proposed to go and get some fresh fish for him. The Coyote left the house, took a withe, and after making a hole in the ice put his head down the hole in order to look for the fish before diving. But in trying to get his head out again he found that he could not. Wondering at this long absence, Tsalas went to look for his friend, and found him with his head stuck down in the ice-hole. He pulled him out, more dead than alive, and addressing him, said, "Poor fellow! Why should you make yourself worse off than you already are? You are very foolish to try to do things that are beyond your powers. Now look at me!" Tsalas then put his head down in the hole and soon commenced to toss plenty of fish out on the ice. He made a present of them to the Coyote, and went home, leaving the Coyote in anything but a pleasant mood.

Some time afterwards the Coyote went to the mountains to watch the Magpie and learn his methods of hunting. The latter had set a net-snare close by his underground lodge. He went up the mountains, singled out a large buck deer, which he teased, and called names, such as "big posterior," "hairy posterior," "short-tail." The buck at last grew angry and charged the Magpie, who ran away. He just kept a little ahead of the buck, so as to encourage him, and led him right into the snare, in which his antlers stuck fast, whilst the Magpie jumped over it, and turning round, stabbed the entangled buck to death. The Coyote made up his mind that he would do as the Magpie had done. So he placed a net-snare close by his house, and, going up the mountains, soon fell in with a buck deer, whom he commenced to belittle and slander, calling him all kinds of nasty names, just as the Magpie had done. The buck grew angry, charged the Coyote, who made for home, where his snare was, with the buck close after him. On reaching the net, the Coyote tried to jump over it, but failed to so so. He fell into the net and became entangled in it. Then the buck began to prod him with his antlers, and would have killed him if the people had not run out and prevented it by killing the buck.

XXXVI. COYOTE AND PORCUPINE [104]

(NEZ PERCÉ: Spinden, *Journal of American Folk-Lore*, xxi, 21, No. 9)

Once Porcupine was going along the river bank looking for food. Soon he saw some fine, fat buffalo, ten of them, just across the river. Then Porcupine wanted to get across the river, but could not. After some thought he called to the buffalo to stand in line. This was so that he could tell which one was the fattest. Then he picked out the fattest one and told him to swim across the river. When this buffalo came up to Porcupine, he asked Porcupine where he wanted to sit, on his back or on his tail. Porcupine answered, "I would rather be under your forelegs, so I shall not drown."

The buffalo agreed. When they were nearly across, Porcupine struck the buffalo under the foreleg with a large knife. So he killed that buffalo, but the others ran away.

Porcupine was looking for something with which to sharpen his knife. He was singing, "I wish I could find something with which to sharpen my knife, for I have n't had any fat buffalo yet." Now, Coyote happened to be going by and he heard Porcupine singing. Coyote came up to him and Porcupine was afraid. Coyote asked him what he was singing, and Porcupine answered, "I was not singing anything, I was just saying I wish I had some string for my moccasin." Coyote said, "No, you did not say that; I heard what you said." Porcupine said nothing more; so Coyote told him what he had killed. Coyote said, "Now, I have a sharp knife, so I can help you." Then Coyote said, "Let us try jumping over the buffalo; the one who jumps over may have it all. I'll try first." Coyote succeeded, but Porcupine did not, so Coyote got all the meat. Then Coyote took his sharp knife and cut Porcupine's head, but did not kill him.

Now, Coyote had some children: one of them was with him, and the rest were at home. Coyote said to his child, "I am going after the other children. You watch the old Porcupine, and if he gets up you call me and I will come back and kill him." When Coyote was gone, Porcupine got up. The young Coyote cried, "Father, Porcupine is up." Then Coyote hurried back and asked his baby what the matter was. The child said, "He was trying to take some of the buffalo meat, but now he is quiet again." Coyote started off a second time. When he was a great way off Porcupine got up. The child called his father, but this time in vain. Porcupine struck the young Coyote with a stone and killed him. Then he set the child up under a tree and stuffed his mouth full of buffalo fat.[105] Then Porcupine took all the meat to the top of a tree and watched for Coyote and his family to come.

When Coyote with his wife and children had come up close, Coyote said to the children, "Look at your brother; he is eating and having a great time." But when they arrived they saw that the baby was killed and had his mouth stuffed with fat. Then Coyote was very angry. He wondered where Porcupine had gone. When Coyote looked up he saw Porcupine sitting in a tall tree laughing. Coyote said, "Please come down"; but Porcupine answered, "I do not like you because you are trying to cheat me out of my buffalo meat." Coyote said, "Just give us a little piece of fat or meat." Then Por-

cupine told Coyote and his family to all stand together under
the tree. They did this. Then Porcupine dropped the buffalo
head down on them and they were all killed.

XXXVII. BEAVER AND PORCUPINE [106]

(TLINGIT: Swanton, *Bulletin of the Bureau of American Ethnology*,
xxxix, 220, No. 63)

The beaver and the porcupine were great friends and went
about everywhere together. The porcupine often visited the
beaver's house, but the latter did not like to have him come
because he left quills there. One time, when the porcupine
said that he wanted to go out to the beaver's house, the beaver
said, "All right, I will take you out on my back." He started,
but instead of going to his house he took him to a stump in
the very middle of the lake. Then he said to him, "This is my
house," left him there, and went ashore.

While the porcupine was upon this stump he began singing
a song, "Let it become frozen.[107] Let it become frozen so that
I can cross to Wolverine-man's place." He meant that he
wanted to walk ashore on the ice. So the surface of the lake
froze, and he walked home.

Some time after this, when the two friends were again playing together, the porcupine said, "You come now. It is my
turn to carry you on my back." Then the beaver got on the
porcupine's back, and the porcupine took him to the top of
a very high tree, after which he came down and left him. For
a long time the beaver did not know how to get down, but
finally he climbed down, and they say that this is what gives
the broken appearance to tree bark.[4]

XXXVIII. THE BIG TURTLE'S WAR PARTY [108]

(SKIDI PAWNEE: Dorsey, *Memoirs of the American Folk-Lore
Society*, viii, 274, No. 74)

A turtle went on the warpath, and as he went along, he met
Coyote, who said: "And where are you going, grandson?"
The turtle said: "I am on the warpath." Coyote said: "Where
are you going?" "I am going to a camp where there are many
people," said the turtle. "Let me see you run," the turtle
said. Coyote ran. The turtle said: "You cannot run fast; I
do not want you."

The turtle went on, and he met a fox. "Well, brother," said the fox, "where are you going?" "I am going on the warpath," said the turtle. "Where are you going?" said the fox. "I am going where there are many people," said the turtle. "Can I go with you?" said the fox. The turtle said: "Let me see you run." The fox ran, and he went so fast that the turtle could hardly see him. The turtle said: "You cannot run fast; I do not want you."

The turtle then went on, and a hawk flew by him, and the hawk heard the turtle say: "I am on the warpath, I am looking for people to join me." The hawk said: "Brother, what did you say?" "I am on the warpath," said the turtle. "Can I join you?" said the hawk. "Let me see you fly your best," said the turtle. The hawk flew so fast that the turtle could not see him for a while. When the hawk came back, the turtle said: "You cannot fly fast; I do not want you."

Again the turtle went on, and kept on saying: "I am on the warpath, I am looking for people to join me." A rabbit jumped up and said: "Can I go along?" "Let me see you run," said the turtle. The rabbit ran, and ran fast. The turtle said: "You cannot run fast; I do not want you."

The turtle went on, saying: "I am looking for people to join me." Up jumped a flint knife and said: "Brother, can I join you?" "You may if you can run fast," said the turtle; "let me see you run." The knife tried to run, and could not. "You will do," said the turtle; "come with me."

They went on, and the turtle was saying: "I am looking for people to go on the warpath with me." Up jumped a hairbrush. "What did you say?" said the brush. "I am on the warpath," said the turtle. "Can I go along?" said the brush. The turtle said: "Let me see you run." The brush tried to run, but could not. The turtle said: "You will do; come with us."

They went on, and the turtle was saying: "I am on the warpath, I am looking for people to join me." Up jumped an awl, and it said: "Can I join you?" The turtle said: "Let me see you run." The awl tried to run, but could not. "You will do," said the turtle; "come with us."

So the four went on, and they came to a big camp, and the turtle sent the knife into camp. The knife went into camp, and one man found it, took it home, and while trying to cut meat the man cut his fingers, and threw the knife at the doorway. The knife went back to the turtle and said: "I was picked up, and while the man was trying to cut meat, I cut his hand and he threw me at the doorway, so I came back."

The turtle said: "Very well. Now, Brush, you go and see what you can do." So the brush went into camp, and a young girl picked it up and commenced to brush her hair. The brush pulled the girl's hair out, so that the girl threw the brush at the doorway, and it came back. It said: "Brother Turtle, there is a young girl who has lovely hair. She used me on her head, and I pulled on her hair, so that she threw me away. See I have her hair here." "Well done," said the turtle.

"Now, Awl, go and be brave," said the turtle. The awl went into camp, and an old woman picked it up. She began to sew her moccasins, and all at once she stuck the awl in one of her fingers. The woman threw it away, and it came back and said: "Brother Turtle, I hurt a woman badly. She was using me while she was sewing her moccasins, and I stuck one of her fingers; she threw me away." "Well done, brothers, now it is my turn," said the turtle.

The turtle went into camp, and people saw him and said: "What does this mean? Look at Turtle; he is on the warpath. Let us kill him." So they took him, and people said: "Let us spread hot coals and put him in there." "All right," said the turtle, "that will suit me for I will spread out my legs and burn some of you." People said: "True, let us then put a kettle over the fire, and when the water boils let us put him in." The turtle said: "Good! Put me in, and I will scald some of you." People said: "True! Let us throw him into the stream." The turtle said: "No, do not do that. I am afraid, I am afraid!" People said: "He is afraid of water; let us throw him in there." But the turtle hallooed the more: "I am afraid! Do not throw me in the water!" So the people threw the turtle in the water. The turtle came up to the surface and said: "I am a cheat. Heyru! Heyru!" poking his tongue out.

The people picked up the knife, awl, and brush and used them. The turtle stayed in the water, and every time the people went to the water, Turtle would say: "I cheated you; water is my home." People would throw stones at it, and it would dive.[109]

CHAPTER IV

HERO TALES[110]

XXXIX. THE SUN TESTS HIS SON–IN–LAW [111]

(BELLA COOLA: Boas, *Jesup North Pacific Expedition*, i, 73)

IN a place on Bella Coola River, there used to be a salmon-weir. A chief and his wife lived at this place. One day the wife was cutting salmon on the bank of the river. When she opened the last salmon, she found a small boy in it. She took him out and washed him in the river. She placed him near by, entered the house, and said to the people, "Come and see what I have found in my salmon!" She had a child in her house, which was still in the cradle. The little boy whom she had found was half as long as her fore-arm. She carried him into the house, and the people advised her to take good care of him. She nursed him with her own baby. When the people were talking in the house, the baby looked around as though he understood what they were saying. On the following day the people were surprised to see how much he had grown, and in a few days he was as tall as any ordinary child.[112] Her own baby also grew up with marvelous rapidity. She gave each of them one breast. After a few days they were able to walk and to talk.

   .   .   .   .

[When they mature, the boys go on adventures.]

The two young men were passing by the houses, and looked into the doorways. There was a house in the centre of this town; there they saw a beautiful girl sitting in the middle of the house. Her hair was red, and reached down to the floor. She was very white. Her eyes were large, and as clear as rock crystal. The boy fell in love with the girl. They went on, but his thoughts were with her. The Salmon boy said, "I am going to enter this house. You must watch closely what I do, and imitate me. The Door of this house tries to bite every one who enters." The Door opened, and the Salmon jumped into the house. Then the Door snapped,[113] but missed him. When it opened again, the boy jumped into the house. They found a number of people inside, who invited them to sit down. They spread food before them, but the boy did not like their food. It had a very strong smell, and looked rather curious. It consisted of algae that grow on logs that lie in the river.

When the boy did not touch it, one of the men said to him, "Maybe you want to eat those two children. Take them down to the river and throw them into the water, but do not look." The two children arose, and he took them down to the river. Then he threw them into the water without looking at them. At the place where he had thrown them down, he found a male and a female Salmon. He took them up to the house and roasted them. The people told him to preserve the intestines and the bones carefully. After he had eaten, one of the men told him to carry the intestines and the bones to the same place where he had thrown the children into the water. He carried them in his hands, and threw them into the river without looking. When he entered the house, he heard the children following him. The girl was covering one of her eyes with her hands. The boy was limping, because he had lost one of his bones. Then the people looked at the place where the boy had been sitting, and they found the eye, and a bone from the head of the male salmon. They ordered the boy to throw these into the water. He took the children and the eye and the bone, and threw them into the river. Then the children were hale and well.[114]

After a while the youth said to his Salmon brother, "I wish to go to the other house where I saw the beautiful girl." They went there, and he said to his Salmon brother, "Let us enter. I should like to see her face well." They went in. Then the man arose, and spread a caribou blanket for them to sit on, and the people gave them food. Then he whispered to his brother, "Tell the girl I want to marry her." The Salmon boy told the girl, who smiled, and said, "He must not marry me. Whoever marries me must die. I like him, and I do not wish to kill him; but if he wishes to die, let him marry me.[115]

.   .   .   .

The woman was the Salmon-berry Bird. After one day she gave birth to a boy, and on the following day she gave birth to a girl.[116] She was the daughter of the Spring Salmon.

After a while the girl's father said, "Let us launch our canoe, and let us carry the young man back to his own people." He sent a messenger to call all the people of the village; and they all made themselves ready, and early the next morning they started in their canoes. The young man went in the canoe of the Spring Salmon, which was the fastest. The canoe of the Sock-eye Salmon came next. The people in the canoe of the Calico Salmon were laughing all the time. They went up the river; and a short distance below the village of the young man's father they landed, and made fast their canoes. Then they sent two messengers up the river to see if the people had finished their salmon-weir. Soon they returned with information that the weir had been finished. Then they sent the young man and his wife, and they gave them a great many presents for the young man's father.

The watchman who was stationed at the salmon-weir saw two beautiful salmon entering the trap. They were actually the canoes of the salmon; but they looked to him like two salmon. Then the watchman put the traps down over the weir, and he saw a great many fish entering them. He raised the trap when it was full, and took the fish out. The young man thought, "I wish he would treat me and my wife carefully"; and his wish came true. The man broke the heads of the other salmon, but he saved the young man and his wife. Then he carried the fish up to the house, and hung them over a pole.

During the night the young man and his wife resumed their human shape.[117] The youth entered his father's house. His head was covered with eagle-down. He said to his father, "I am the fish whom you caught yesterday. Do you remember the time when you lost me? I have lived in the country of the Salmon.[236] The Salmon accompanied me here. They are staying a little farther down the river. It pleases the Salmon to see the people eating fish." And, turning to his mother, he continued, "You must be careful when cutting Salmon. Never break any of their bones, but preserve them, and throw them into the water." The two children of the young man had also entered into the salmon-trap. He put some leaves on the ground, placed red and white cedar-bark over them, and covered them with eagle-down, and he told his mother to place the Salmon upon these.

As soon as he had given these instructions, the Salmon began to come up the river. They crossed the weir and entered the traps. They went up the river as far as Stuick, and the people dried the Salmon according to his instructions. They threw the bones into the water, and the Salmon returned to life, and went back to their own country, leaving their meat behind. The Cohoes Salmon had the slowest canoe, and therefore he was the last to reach the villages. He gave many presents to the Indians. He gave them many-colored leaves, and thus caused the leaves of the trees to change color in the autumn.

Now all the Salmon had returned. The Salmon-berry Bird and her children had returned with them. Then the young man made up his mind to build a small hut, from which he intended to catch eagles. He used a long pole, to which a noose was attached. The eagles were baited by means of Salmon. He spread a mat in his little house, and when he had caught an eagle he pulled out its down. He accumulated a vast amount of down. Then he went back to his house and asked his younger brother to accompany him. When they came to the hut which he had used for catching eagles, he gave the boy a small staff. Then he said to him, "Do not be sorry when I leave you. I am going to visit the Sun. I am not going to stay away a long time. I staid long in the country of the Salmon, but I shall not stay long in heaven. I am going to lie down on this mat. Cover me with this down, and then begin to beat time with your staff. You will see a large feather flying upward, then stop." The boy obeyed, and everything happened as he had said. The boy saw the feather flying in wide circles. When it reached a great height, it began to soar in large circles, and finally disappeared in the sky.[118] Then the boy cried, and went back to his mother.

The young man who had ascended to heaven found there a large house. It was the House of Myths.[119] There he resumed his human shape, and peeped in at the door. Inside he saw a number of people who were turning their faces toward the wall. They were sitting on a low platform in the rear of the house. In the right-hand corner of the house he saw a large fire, and women sitting around it. He leaned forward and looked into the house. An old woman discovered him, and beckoned him to come to her. He stepped up to her, and she warned him by signs not to go to the rear of the house. She said, "Be careful!

The men in the rear of the house intend to harm you." She opened a small box, and gave him the bladder of a mountain-goat, which contained the cold wind.[72] She told him to open the bladder if they should attempt to harm him. She said that if he opened it, no fire could burn him. She told him that the men were going to place him near the fire, in order to burn him; that one of them would wipe his face, then fire would come forth from the floor, scorching everything. The old woman told him everything that the people were going to do.[171] Now the man in the rear of the house turned round. He was the Sun himself. He was going to try the strength of the visitor. When he saw the young man, he said to the old woman, "Did anybody come to visit you? Let the young man come up to me. I wish him to sit down near me." The young man stepped up to the Sun, and as soon as he had sat down, the Sun wiped his face and looked at the young man (he had turned his face while he was wiping it). Then the young man felt very hot. He tied his blanket tightly round his body, and opened the bladder which the woman had given him. Then the cold wind that blows down the mountains in the winter was liberated, and he felt cool and comfortable. The Sun had not been able to do him any harm. The old man did not say anything, but looked at his visitor.

After a while he said, "I wish to show you a little under-ground house that stands behind this house." They both rose and went outside. The small house had no door. Access was had to it by an opening in the centre of the roof, through which a ladder led down to the floor. Not a breath of air entered this house. It was made of stone. When they had entered, the Sun made a small fire in the middle of the house; then he climbed up the ladder and closed the door, leaving his visitor inside. The Sun pulled up the ladder, in order to make escape impossible. Then the house began to grow very hot.[120] When the boy felt that he could not stand the heat any longer, he opened the bladder, and the cold wind came out; snow began to fall on the fire, which was extinguished; icicles began to form on the roof, and it was cool and comfortable inside. After a while the Sun said to his four daughters, "Go to the little underground house that stands behind our house, and sweep it," meaning that they were to remove the remains of the young man whom he believed to be burned. They obeyed at once, each being eager to be the first to enter. When they opened the house, they were much surprised to find icicles hanging down from the roof.

When they were climbing down the ladder, the youth arose and scratched them. The youngest girl was the last to step down. The girls cried when the youth touched them, and ran away. The Sun heard their screams, and asked the reason. He was much surprised and annoyed to hear that the young man was still alive. Then he devised another way of killing his visitor. He told his daughters to call him into his house. They went, and the young man re-entered the House of Myths. In the evening he lay down to sleep. Then the Sun said to his daughters, "Early to-morrow morning climb the mountain behind our house. I shall tell the boy to follow you." The girls started while the visitor was still asleep. The girls climbed up to a small meadow which was near a precipice. They had taken the form of mountain-goats. When the Sun saw his daughters on the meadow, he called to his visitor, saying, "See those mountain-goats!" The young man arose when he saw the mountain-goats. He wished to kill them. The Sun advised him to walk up the right-hand side of the mountain, saying that the left-hand side was dangerous. The young man carried his bow and arrow. The Sun said, "Do not use your own arrows! Mine are much better." Then they exchanged arrows, the Sun giving him four arrows of his own. The points of these arrows were made of coal.[121]

Now the young man began to climb the mountain. When he came up to the goats, he took one of the arrows, aimed it, and shot. It struck the animals, but fell down without killing it. The same happened with the other arrows. When he had spent all his arrows, they rushed up to him from the four sides, intending to kill him. His only way of escape was in the direction of the precipice.[122] They rushed up to him, and pushed him down the steep mountain. He fell headlong, but when he was halfway down he transformed himself into a ball of bird's down.[117a] He alighted gently on a place covered with many stones. There he resumed the shape of a man, arose, and ran into the house of the Sun to get his own arrows. He took them, climbed the mountain again, and found the mountain-goats on the same meadow. He shot them and killed them, and threw them down the precipice; then he returned. He found the goats at the foot of the precipice, and cut off their feet. He took them home. He found the Sun sitting in front of the house. He offered him the feet, saying, "Count them, and see how many I have killed." The Sun counted them and now he knew that all his children were dead. Then he cried, "You killed my children!" Then the youth took the bodies of the goats, fitted the feet on, and threw the bodies into a little river that was running past the place where they had fallen down. Thus they were restored to life.[114] He had learned this art in the country of the Salmon. Then he said to the girls, "Now run to see your father! He is wailing for you." They gave him a new name, saying, "He has restored us to life." The boy followed them. Then the Sun said, when he entered, "You shall marry my two eldest daughters."

On the next morning the people arose. Then the Sun said to them, "What shall I do to my son-in-law?" [123] He called him, and said, "Let us raise the trap of my salmon-weir." They went up to the river in the Sun's canoe. The water of the river was boiling. The youth was in the bow of the canoe, while the Sun was steering. He caused the canoe to rock, intending to throw the young man into the water. The water formed a small cascade, running down over the weir. He told the young man to walk over the top of the weir in order to reach the trap. He did so, walking over the top beam of the weir. When he reached the baskets, the beam fell over, and he himself fell into the water.[124] The Sun saw him rise twice in the whirlpool just below the weir. When he did not see him rise again, he turned his canoe, and thought, "Now the boy has certainly gone to Nuskyakek." The Sun returned to his house, and said to his daughters, "I lost my son-in-law in the river. I was not able to find him." Then his daughters were very sad.

When the boy disappeared in the water, he was carried to Nuskyakek; and he resumed the shape of a salmon while in the water, and as soon as he landed he resumed human shape and returned to his wife. The Sun saw him coming, and was much surprised. In the evening they went to sleep. On the following morning the Sun thought, "How can I kill my son-in-law?" After a while he said to him, "Arise! We will go and split wood for fuel." He took his tools. They launched their canoe, and went down the river to the sea. When they reached there, it was perfectly calm. There were many snags embedded in the mud in the mouth of the river, some of which were only half submerged. They selected one of these snags a long distance from the shore, and began to split it. Then the Sun intentionally dropped his hammer into the water, and thought at the same time, "Do not fall straight down, but fall sideways, so that he will have much difficulty in finding you." Then he sat down in his canoe, and said, "Oh! I lost my old hammer. I had it at the time when the Sun was created." He looked down into the water, and did not say a word. After a while he said to the young man, "Do you know how to dive? [125] Can you get my hammer? The water is not very deep here." The young man did not reply. Then the Sun continued, "I will not go back without my hammer." Then the boy said, "I know how to dive. If you so wish, I will try to get it." The Sun promised to give him supernatural power if he was able to bring the hammer back. The youth jumped into the water, and then the Sun ordered the sea to rise, and he called the cold wind to make the water freeze. It grew so cold that a sheet of ice a fathom thick was formed at once on top of the sea. "Now," he thought, "I certainly have killed you!" He left his canoe frozen up in the ice, and went home. He said to his daughters, "I have lost my son-in-law. He drifted away when the cold winds began to blow down the mountains. I have also lost my little hammer." But when he mentioned his hammer, his daughters knew at once what had happened. The young man found the hammer, and after he had obtained it he was going to return to the canoe, but he struck his head against the ice, and was unable to get out. He tried everywhere to find a crack. Finally he found a very narrow one. He transformed himself into a fish, and came out of the crack. He jumped about on the ice in the form of a fish, and finally resumed his own shape.

He went back to the Sun's house, carrying the hammer. The Sun was sitting in front of the fire, his knees drawn up, and his legs apart. His eyes were closed, and he was warming himself. The young man took his hammer and threw it right against his stomach, saying, "Now take better care of your treasures." The young man scolded the Sun, saying, "Now stop trying to kill me. If you try again, I shall kill you. Do you think I am an ordinary man? You cannot conquer me." The Sun did not reply.

In the evening he said to his son-in-law, "I hear a bird singing, which I should like very much to have." [126] The young man asked, "What bird is it?" The Sun replied, "I do not know it. Watch it early to-morrow morning." The young man resolved to catch the bird. Very early in the morning he arose, then he heard the bird singing outside. He knew at once that it was the ptarmigan. He left the house, and thought, "I wish you would come down!" Then the bird came down, and when it was quite near by he shot it. He hit one of its wings, intending to catch it alive. He waited for the Sun to arise. The bird understood what the young man said, who thus spoke: "The chief here wishes to see you. Do not be afraid, I am not going to kill you. The chief has often tried to kill me, but he has been unable to do so. You do not need to be afraid." The young man continued, "When it is dark I shall tell the Sun to ask you to sit near him, and when he is asleep I want you to peck out his eyes." When the Sun arose, the youth went into the house carrying the bird, saying, "I have caught the bird; now I hope you will treat it kindly. It will awaken us when it is time to arise. When you lie down, let it sit down near you, then it will call you in the morning."

In the evening the Sun asked the bird to sit down next to his face. When he was asleep, the bird pecked out his eyes without his knowing it. Early in the morning he heard the bird singing. He was going to open his eyes, but he was not able to do so. Then he called his son, saying, "The bird has blinded me." The young man jumped up and went to his father-in-law, and said, "Why did you wish for the bird? Do you think it is good? It is a bad bird. It has pecked out your eyes." He took the bird and carried it outside, and thanked it for having done as it was bidden. Then the bird flew away.

When it was time for the Sun to start on his daily course, he said, "I am afraid I might fall, because I cannot see my way." For four days he staid in his house. He did not eat, he was very sad. Then his son-in-law made up his mind to cure him. He did not do so before, because he wanted to punish him for his badness. He took some water, and said to his father-in-law, "I will try to restore your eyesight." He threw the water upon his eyes, and at once his eyes were healed and well.[279] He said, "Now you can see what power I have. The water with which I have washed my face has the power to heal

diseases. While I was in the country of the Salmon, I bathed in
the water in which the old Salmon bathed, in order to regain
youth, therefore the water in which I wash makes everything
young and well." [50] From this time on, the Sun did not try
to do any harm to the young man.

Finally he wished to return to his father's village. He left
the house, and jumped down through the hole in heaven. His
wife saw him being transformed into a ball of eagle-down,
which floated down gently. Then her father told her to climb
as quickly as she could down his eyelashes. She did so, and
reached the ground at the same time as her husband. He met
his younger brother, who did not recognize him. He had been
in heaven for one year.

XL. THE JEALOUS UNCLE [127]

(KODIAK: Golder, *Journal of American Folk-Lore*, xvi, 90, No. 8)

In a village lived a man, known to his neighbors as "Unnatural Uncle." When his nephews became a few years old,
he would kill them. Two had already suffered death at his
hands. After the second had disappeared, his wife went to
the mother of the boys, and said: "Should another boy be
born to you, let us conceal the fact from my husband, and make
him believe the child a girl. In that case he will not harm him,
and we may succeed in bringing him up."

Not long after the above conversation another nephew was
born. Unnatural Uncle, hearing that a child was born, sent
his wife to ascertain the sex of the child. She, as had been
agreed upon, reported the child a girl. "Let her live," he said. [128]

The two women tended and dressed the boy as if he were a
girl. When he grew older, they told him to play with the
girls, and impressed upon him that he should at all times imitate the ways, attitudes, and postures of the girls, especially
when attending to the calls of nature. Unnatural Uncle watched
the boy as he was growing up, and often wondered at his boyish
looks. One day the boy, not knowing that his uncle was about
and observing him, raised up his parka, and so exposed his
body. "Ah," said Unnatural Uncle to his wife, on reaching
home, "this is the way you have fooled me. But I know everything now. Go and tell my nephew I wish to see him." With
tears in her eyes the poor woman delivered the message to the

nephew, told him of the disappearance of his brothers, and of his probable fate. The father and mother of the boy wept bitterly, for they were certain he would never return. The boy himself, although frightened, assured his parents to the contrary, and begged them not to worry, for he would come back safe and sound.

"Did my brothers have any playthings?" he asked before going.

He was shown to a box where their things were kept. In it he found a piece of a knife, some eagle-down, and a sour cranberry. These he hid about his person, and went to meet his uncle. The latter greeted him, and said: "Nephew, let us go and fetch some wood."

When they came to a large forest, the boy remarked: "Here is good wood; let us take some of it, and go back."

"Oh, no! There is better wood farther on," said the uncle.

From the forest they stepped into a bare plain. "Let us go back. There is no wood here," called the boy. But the uncle motioned to him to come on, telling him that they would soon find better wood. A little later they came to a big log. "Here is what I want," exclaimed the uncle, and began splitting it. "Here, nephew, jump in, and get that wedge out," called the uncle to the boy, as one of the wedges fell in. When the boy did so, the man knocked out the other wedges; the log closed in on the boy, and held him fast. "Stay there!" said Unnatural Uncle, and walked off.[129]

For some time the boy remained in this helpless condition, planning a means of escape. At last he thought of his sour cranberry, and, taking it in his hand, he rubbed with it the interior of the log from edge to edge. The sourness of the berry caused the log to open its mouth, thus freeing him.

On his way back to the village, he gathered a bundle of wood, which he left at his uncle's door, announcing the fact to him: "Here, uncle, I have brought you the wood." The latter was both surprised and vexed at his failure, and determined more than ever to kill the boy. His wife, however, warned him: "You had better not harm the boy; you have killed his brothers, and if you hurt him, you will come to grief."

"I will kill him, too," he savagely replied.

When the boy reached his father's home, he found them weeping and mourning. "Don't weep!" he pleaded. "He cannot hurt me; no matter where he takes me, I will always come back." In the morning he was again summoned to appear at his uncle's. Before going, he entreated his parents not to feel uneasy, assuring them that no harm would befall him, and that he would be back. The uncle called the boy to go with him after some ducks and eggs. They passed several places abounding in ducks and eggs, and each time that the boy suggested, "Let us take these and go back," the uncle replied: "Oh, no! There are better ducks and eggs farther on." At last they came to a steep bluff, and, looking down, saw a great many ducks and eggs. "Go down carefully, nephew, and gather those ducks and eggs. Be quick, and come back as soon as you can."

The boy saw the trap at a glance, and prepared for it by taking the eagle-down in each hand, between thumb and finger. As the boy took a step or two downward, the uncle gave him a push, causing him to lose his footing.[122] "He will never come back alive from here," smiled the uncle to himself, as he walked back. If he had remained awhile longer and looked down before going, he would have seen the boy descending gently instead of falling. The eagle-down kept him up in the air, and he lighted at his own pleasure safe and sound. After gathering all the ducks and eggs he wanted, he ascended by holding up the down, as before, and blowing under it. Up, up he went, and in a short time stood on the summit. It was night before he sighted his uncle's home. At the door he deposited the birds and eggs, and shouted: "Here, uncle, are the ducks and eggs."

"What! back again!" exclaimed the man very much mortified. His wife again pleaded with him to leave the boy in peace. "You will come to grief, if you don't," she said. "No; he cannot hurt me," he replied angrily, and spent the remainder of the night thinking and planning.

Although he assured them that he would return, the boy's parents did not have much faith in it; for he found them on his return weeping for him. This grieved him. "Why do you weep?" he said. "Did n't I say I would come back? He can take me to no place from which I cannot come back."

In the evening of the third day the aunt appeared and said that her husband wished the boy. He told his parents not to be disturbed, and promised to come back soon. This time the uncle invited him to go with him after clams. The clams were very large, large enough to inclose a man.[130] It was ebb tide, and they found plenty of clams not far from the beach. The boy suggested that they take these and go back, but the uncle put him off with, "There are better clams farther out." They waded into the water, and then the man noticed an extraordinarily large clam. "Take him," he said, but when the boy bent over, the clam took him in. So confident was Unnatural Uncle of his success this time that he uttered not a word, but with a triumphant grin on his face and a wave of his hand he walked away. The boy tried to force the valves apart, but not succeeding, he cut the ligament with his piece of a knife, compelling the clam to open up little by little until he was able to hop out. He gathered some clams, and left them at his uncle's door as if nothing had happened. The man, on hearing the boy's voice outside, was almost beside himself with rage. His wife did not attempt to pacify him. "I will say nothing more," she said. "I have warned you, and if you persist in your ways, you will suffer."

The next day Unnatural Uncle was busy making a box.

"What is it for?" asked his wife.

"A plaything for our nephew," he replied.

In the evening the boy was sent for. On leaving his parents he said: "Do not feel uneasy about my absence. This time I may be away a long time, but I will come back nevertheless."

"Nephew, here is something to amuse you," said his uncle. "Get inside of it, so that I may see whether it fits you." It fitted him; so did the lid the box; and the rope the lid. He felt himself borne along, and from the noise of the waves he knew it was to the sea. The box was lowered, and with a shove it was set adrift.[131] It was stormy, the waves beat over the box, and several times he gave himself up as lost. How long he drifted he had no idea; but at last he heard the waves dashing against the beach, and his heart rejoiced. Louder, and louder did the joyful peal sound. He gathered himself together for the sudden stop which soon came, only to feel himself afloat again the next moment. This experience he went through several times, before the box finally stopped and he realized he was on land once more.

As he lay there, many thoughts passed through his mind; where was he? was any one living there? would he be saved?

or would the flood tide set him adrift again? what were his people at home doing? These, and many other thoughts passed through his brain, when he was startled by hearing voices, which he recognized, a little later, as women's. This is what he heard:

"I saw the box first," said one.

"No, I saw it first," said the other.

"I am sure I saw it before you," said the first speaker again, "and, therefore, it is mine."

"Well, you may have the box, but its contents shall belong to me," replied the other.

They picked up the box, and began to carry it, but finding it somewhat heavy and being anxious to know what it contained, they stopped to untie it.

"If there are many things in there, I shall have some of them," said the first speaker, who rued her bargain. The other one said nothing. Great was their surprise on beholding him. He was in turn surprised to see two such beautiful girls, the large village, the numerous people, and their peculiar appearance, for he was among the Eagle people in Eagle land.[253a] The full grown people, like the full grown eagles, had white faces and heads, while those of the young people, like those of young eagles, were dark. Eagle skins were hanging about all over the village; and it amused him to watch some of the people put on their eagle skins and change to eagles, and after flying around, take them off and become human beings again.

The girls, being the daughters of the village chief, led the boy to their father, each claiming him. When he had heard them both, the chief gave the boy to the older girl (the second speaker). With her he lived happily, but his thoughts would very often wander back to his former home, the people there, his parents; and the thought of his uncle's cruelty to them would make his heart ache. His wife noted these spells of depression, and questioned him about them until he told her of his parents and uncle. She, like a good wife, bade him cheer up, and then went to have a talk with her father. He sent for his son-in-law, and advised him to put on his (chief's) eagle skin,[117] soar up high until he could see his village, fly over there, visit his parents, and bring them back with him. He did as he was told, and in a short time found himself in the village. Although he could see all other people, his parents were not in sight.

This was in the evening. During the night he went out to sea, brought back a large whale, and placed it on the beach, knowing that all the villagers would come out for the meat. The first person to come to the village beach in the morning was Unnatural Uncle; and when he saw the whale, he aroused the village, and a little later all, except the boy's father and mother, were there, cutting and storing up the whale. His parents were not permitted to come near the whale, and when some of the neighbors left some meat at their house, Unnatural Uncle scolded, and forbade it being done again. "I can forgive him the killing of my brothers, the attempts on my life, but I will revenge his treatment of my parents." With these thoughts in his mind, the eagle left his perch, and flew over to the crowd. He circled over its head a little while, and then made a swoop at his uncle. "Ah, he knows that I am chief, and the whale is mine, and he asks me for a piece of meat." Saying this, he threw a piece of meat at the eagle. The second time the eagle descended it was still nearer the man's head, but he tried to laugh it off, and turn it to his glory. The people, however, did not see it that way, and warned him to keep out of the eagle's clutches, for the eagle meant mischief. When the eagle dropped the third time, it was so near his head that he fell on his face. The fourth time the eagle swooped him, and flew off with him.

Not far from the shore was a high and steep rock, and on its summit the eagle put down the man, placing himself opposite. When he had taken off the skin, and disclosed himself, he said to his trembling uncle: "I could have forgiven you the death of my brothers, the four attempts on my life, but for the cruel treatment of my parents you shall pay. The whale I brought was for my parents and others, and not for you alone; but you took entire possession of it, and would not allow them even to approach it. I will not kill you without giving you a chance for your life. Swim back to the shore, and you shall be spared." As he could not swim, Unnatural Uncle supplicated his nephew to take him back, but the latter, putting on the eagle skin,[132] and hardening his eagle heart, clutched him, and from a dizzy height in the air dropped him into the sea.

From the beach the crowd watched the fatal act, understood and appreciated it, and, till it was dark, continued observing, from the distance, the eagle. When all had retired, he pulled

off the skin, and set out for his father's barrabara. He related
to his parents his adventures, and invited them to accompany
him to his adopted land, to which they gladly consented. Early
in the morning he put on again his skin, and, taking a parent
in each claw, flew with them to Eagle land, and there they are
living now.

XLI. BLUEJAY AND HIS COMPANIONS [133]

(Quinault: Farrand, *Jesup North Pacific Expedition*, ii, 102, No. 3)

Bluejay and his chief, with Land Otter, Beaver, and another
man, used to go out seal-hunting together. In the same house
with them, but at the other end, lived Grouse, who was a wid-
ower with a lot of children, and he spent most of his time in the
woods building a canoe. Every trip that the five men made,
they caught five seals, very fat ones; but they gave nothing but
the poor, lean parts to Grouse. Bluejay was at the bottom of
this, and kept saying that fat was too good for Grouse; and
he poked fun at him and sneered at him whenever he was about.
Grouse never said a word, but took what was given him without complaining.

One day Grouse made a wooden seal, carving it out of cedar,
and burning it until it was black. Then he talked to the seal,
and told it what it was to do; and it dived down into the water
and went out to sea.

Next day before daylight, the five men started out, and
about sunrise came upon a big seal, and speared it.[134] The seal
dived, and swam to the westward, dragging the canoe after it
until they were out of sight of land. The spearman tried to get
rid of it, but could not; and when night came they were still
rushing westward, and when they waked in the morning they
were still going, but not so fast. Not long afterward the line
slackened, and they heard something butting against the canoe.
Bluejay looked over, and saw a wooden seal with the harpoon
sticking into it just behind the flipper. Then his chief began
to scold Bluejay, and said, "I know this is Grouse's work. He
is angry because we gave him no fat, and because you talked
to him so much." Bluejay could only hang his head and say
nothing.

They cut the line and began to paddle back, but had no idea
where they were going. Three days and two nights they pad-

dled, and the third night they all fell asleep from exhaustion. When they waked in the morning, the canoe was stuck fast and they thought they were ashore, and one of them, the fifth man, jumped out, but he sank and was drowned; and, then they saw that they were not ashore, but that the seaweed was so thick that they had stuck fast in it. So now there were only four of them, and they paddled on. On the fourth night they did not feel like sleeping, for they thought they could see the hills back of Quinault. In the morning they could discern the coast plainly, and after paddling all day they reached the shore, and landed at a place quite strange to them. Next morning they went on again in what they thought was a southerly direction, and suddenly, as they rounded a point, came upon a village. Several canoes came out through the surf and helped them ashore, and they were taken up to the village.

In the centre of the village was a tall smooth pole which the people said was Squirrel's pole, which he used for climbing; and they said that Squirrel would like to have a climbing-match [135] with Bluejay. Bluejay's master said to him, "Now don't get frightened, but go in and do your best. You know you can climb well, and if you are beaten we may all be killed." Then both Squirrel and Bluejay took sharp bones, so that if one got ahead he could hit the one behind on the head; and they started to climb. All the people crowded around to see the contest, for the pole was high and the two were well matched. At last the people saw them reach the top, and saw one of them strike the other on the head so that he came tumbling down; and all the people shouted, for they thought it was Bluejay. But when he reached the ground, they found it was Squirrel who had lost. So now, since Bluejay had beaten their best climber, they let him and his companions go.

They paddled on down the coast, and after some time they rounded a point, and come upon another village, much like the first. Here Hair-seal challenged Bluejay to a diving-match,[136] and Bluejay found himself in a difficult position, for he was no diver at all. But his master turned the canoe over and washed it out, leaving the brush from the bottom floating about it on the water. Then he told Bluejay to accept the challenge and dive, but to come up under the brush and lie there concealed, and not to show himself. So both Bluejay and Hair-seal dived; and Bluejay came up immediately under the brush, and floated there where no one could see him. He waited until he shivered so with the cold that the brush moved with his shaking, and his master began to be afraid the people would notice it: so he rocked the canoe and made waves to conceal the motion of the brush, and no one suspected that Bluejay was hidden there. Now, they had agreed, that, when the sun had passed from one tree to another not far off, each was to have the right to hit the other in the head with a sharp bone. So, when Bluejay saw that the sun had reached the second tree, he dived down, and found Hair-seal lying with his head down close to the bottom. Bluejay jabbed him with the bone before Hair-seal knew what was happening, and Hair-seal came floating up to the surface. All the people shouted, "Bluejay's up!" But it turned out to be Hair-seal, while Bluejay went back under the brush without showing himself. There he waited about half an hour longer, and then came out shouting and laughing, and saying that he felt splendidly and not tired at all. In that way Hair-seal was beaten, and the people let Bluejay and his party go on again.

They paddled on as before until they came to another village, and there the people challenged the four wanderers to go into a sweat-house with four of their people and see which could stand the most heat. So four of the village people went into one corner of the sweat-house, and the four travelers into the other. Then the door was closed so that it was pitch dark, and soon it became very hot.[120] But Beaver and Land Otter began to dig, and in a very short time they had tunnelled to the river. Then all four got into the water and were as comfortable as could be, while the four men from the village were nearly baked. When the time was up, Bluejay and his friends came back into the sweat-house, and when the door was opened they all jumped out. Bluejay and his friends were as fresh as possible, while the four men from the village were nearly cooked, and their eyes were all white from the heat. So, having beaten the people at their own game, they were allowed to go on, and, paddling as hard as they could, before they knew it they had rounded another point, and come upon a village as before. They ran the canoe clear up on the beach and tied it, and, taking their paddles, went into one of the houses.

The people immediately challenged the new arrivals to sit up five days and five nights without sleeping,[137] against four of their own number. The friends were afraid not to accept, so they started the match. One party sat on one side of the house and the other on the other. The men from the village had spears, and when any one of them was falling asleep, they would prod him with a spear and wake him. They kept calling out to each other all night, "Are you awake? Are you still awake?" And they reviled each other constantly. Bluejay did all the talking for his side, and was hardly quiet a minute. All the next day they jeered at each other, and so they did the next night. Bluejay and the spokesman of the other side kept talking back and forth the whole time. The next day they did the same thing, and so on the third night; and the fourth day and the fourth night it was still the same. On that night the men from the village nearly went to sleep; but Bluejay's men were all right as yet. Bluejay himself was almost done up; but his master would pull his ears and kept him awake, for Bluejay's master was the best man of them all. The fifth night the men of the village went to sleep, and Bluejay's master told Land Otter and Beaver to dig so that they could get out. They did so, and fetched four pieces of old wood with phosphorescent spots on them; and they placed the pieces where they had been sitting,²⁸² one piece for each man; and the spots looked like eyes. Then, while the other crowd was still sleeping, they got out, and, taking everything they could lay their hands on, they stole away in the canoe. Just before daylight one of the other four waked, and called Bluejay several times, but got no answer. So he waked the others, and, taking their spears, they speared what they thought were their rivals. But when daylight came, they saw that they had been fooled, and that their spears were sticking into wood.

There was great excitement, and the people decided to give chase, and, making ready their canoes, they started after the fugitives. Along in the afternoon, Bluejay's master said, "I feel sure some one is following us," and, looking back, they saw a lot of canoes in pursuit. Then they paddled with all their might; and Bluejay's master paddled so hard that at every stroke he broke a paddle, until he had broken all they had, and they floated helpless. Then the others turned to Bluejay and said, "You are always talking about your tamanous. Make use of him now, if you have one, for we are in a bad fix." But Bluejay could only hang his head, for he had no tamanous.

Then Land Otter called on his tamanous, and a little wind arose.[138] Then Beaver called upon his, and the wind became a little stronger; but all the time the other canoes were drawing closer. Then Bluejay's master called upon his tamanous, and there swept down a great storm and a fog. The storm lasted only a short time, and when it had passed, they looked about them and saw hundreds of capsized canoes, but not a man living; for all the people had been drowned. They went around and gathered up all the paddles they wanted, and went on, and at last reached the Quinault country, and were among good people. The people who had pursued them were probably Makahs, for they are a bad lot. Finally they reached their home near Damon's Point, and after that, whenever they came in from sealing, they were careful to give Grouse the biggest and fattest seal.

XLII. DUG–FROM–GROUND [139]

(HUPA: Goddard, *University of California Publications in American Archæology and Ethnology*, i, 146, No. 2)

An old woman was living with her granddaughter, a virgin. The girl used to go to dig roots and her grandmother used to say to her, "You must not dig those with two stocks." The girl wondered why she was always told that. One morning she thought, "I am going to dig one," so she went across the river and began digging. She thought, "I am going to take out one with a double stock." When she had dug it out she heard a baby cry. She ran back to the river, and when she got there she heard someone crying "mother" after her. She jumped into the boat and pushed it across. When she got across, the baby had tumbled down to the other shore. She ran up to the house and there she heard it crying on that side. She ran into the house, then she heard it crying back of the house. At once she sat down and then she heard it tumble on the roof of the house. The baby tumbled through the smoke-hole and then rolled about on the floor. The old woman jumped up and put it in a baby basket. The young woman sat with her back to the fire and never looked at the child.

The old woman took care of the baby alone. After a time it commenced to sit up and finally to walk. When he was big enough to shoot, the old woman made a bow and he began to kill birds. Afterward he killed all kinds of game; and, because his mother never looked at him, he gave whatever he killed to his grandmother. Finally he became a man. The young woman had been in the habit of going out at dawn and not returning until dark. She brought back with her acorns as long as her finger. One time the young man thought "I am going to watch and see where she goes." The young woman had always said to herself, "If he will bring acorns from the place I bring them, and if he will kill a white deer, I will call him my son." Early one morning the son saw his mother come out of the house and start up the ridge. He followed her and saw her go along until she came to a dry tree. She climbed this and it grew with her to the sky. The young man then returned saying, "Tomorrow I am going up there." The woman came home at night with the usual load of long acorns.

The next morning the man went the way his mother had gone, climbed the tree as he had seen her do, and it grew with him to the sky.[199] When he arrived there he saw a road. He followed that until he came to an oak, which he climbed, and waited to see what would happen. Soon he heard laughing girls approaching. They came to the tree and began to pick acorns from allotted spaces under it. The young man began to throw down acorns. "That's right, Bluejay," said one of the girls. Then another said, "It might be Dug-from-the-ground. You can hardly look at him, they say, he is so handsome." Two others said, "Oh, I can look at him, I always look at this walking one (pointing to the sun); that is the one you can hardly look at." He came down from the tree and passed between the girls. The two who had boasted they could look at him, turned their faces to the ground. The other two who had thought they could not look him in the face were able to do so.[18a]

The young man killed the deer, the killing of which the mother had made the second condition for his recognition as a son. He then filled the basket from his mother's place under the tree and went home. When the woman saw him with the acorns as long as one's finger, she called him her son.

After a time he said, "I am going visiting." "All right," said the grandmother, and then she made for him a bow and arrows of blue-stone, and a shinny stick and sweat-house wood of the same material. These he took and concealed by putting them under the muscles of his forearm. He dressed himself for the journey and set out. He went to the home of the immortals at the edge of the world toward the east. When he got down to the shore on this side they saw him. One of them took out the canoe of red obsidian and stretched it until it was the proper size.[140] He launched it and came across for him. When he had landed, the young man placed his hand on the bow and as he did so, the boat gave a creak, he was so strong. When they had crossed he went to the village. In the middle of it he saw a house of blue-stone with a pavement in front of black obsidian. He went in and heard one say, "It is my son-in-law for whom I had expected to be a long time looking."

When the sun had set there came back from different places ten brothers. Some had been playing kiñ, some had been playing shinny, some had been hunting, some spearing salmon, and others had been shooting at a mark. Eagle and Panther were both married to daughters of the family. They said to him, "You here, brother-in-law?" "Yes," he said, "I came a little while ago." When it was supper time they put in front of him a basket of money's meat, which mortal man cannot swallow.[140] He ate two baskets of it and they thought he must be a smart man. After they had finished supper they all went to the sweat-house to spend the night. At midnight the young man went to the river to swim. There he heard a voice say, "The sweat-house wood is all gone." Then Mink told him that men could not find sweat-house wood near by, but that some was to be found to the southeast. They called to him for wood from ten sweat-houses and he said "Yes" to all. Mink told him about everything they would ask him to do. He went back to the sweat-house and went in. When the east whitened with the dawn, he went for sweat-house wood as they had told him. He came to the place where the trail forks and one of them turns to the northeast and the other to the southeast. There he drew out from his arm the wood his grandmother had provided him with and split it fine. He made this into ten bundles and carried them back to the village. When he got there he put them down carefully but the whole earth shook with the shock. He carried a bundle to each sweat-house. They all sweated themselves. He spent the day there and at evening went again to the sweat-house. When he went to the river to swim, Mink met him again and told him that the next day they would play shinny.

After they were through breakfast the next morning, they said, "Come, brother-in-law, let us go to the place where they play shinny." [141] They all went and after placing their bets began to play. Twice they were beaten. Then they said, "Come, brother-in-law, play." They passed him a stick. He pressed down on it and broke it. "Let me pick up something," he said. He turned about and drew out his concealed shinny stick and the balls. Then he stepped out to play and Wildcat came to play against him. The visitor made the stroke and the balls fell very near the goal. Then he caught Wildcat, smashing his face into its present shape,[99] and threw the ball over the line. He played again, this time with Fox. Again he made the stroke and when he caught Fox he pinched his face out long as it has been ever since. He then struck the ball over the line and won. The next time he played against Earthquake. The ground opened up a chasm but he jumped over it. Earthquake threw up a wall of blue-stone but he threw the ball through it. "Dol" it rang as it went through. Then he played with Thunder. It rained and there was thunder. It was the running of that one which made the noise. It was then night and he had won back all they had lost. There were ten strings of money, besides otterskins, fisherskins, and blankets.

The next day they went to shoot at the white bird which Indians can never hit.[142] The others commenced to shoot and then they said to their guest, "Come, you better shoot." They gave him a bow, which broke when he drew it. Then he pulled out his own and said, "I will shoot with this although the nock has been cut down and it is not very good." They thought, "He can't hit anything with that." He shot and hit the bird, and dentalia fell all about. They gathered up the money and carried it home.

The Hupa man went home to his grandmother. As many nights as it seemed to him he had spent, so many years he had really been away.[143] He found his grandmother lying by the fire. Both of the women had been worried about him. He said to them, "I have come back for you." "Yes," they said, "we will go." Then he repaired the house, tying it up anew with hazel withes. He poked a stick under it and away it went to the end of the world toward the east, where he had married. They are living there yet.

XLIII. THE ATTACK ON THE GIANT ELK [144]

(JICARILLA APACHE: Russell, *Journal of American Folk-Lore*, xi, 255)

In the early days, animals and birds of monstrous size preyed upon the people; the giant Elk, the Eagle, and others devoured men, women, and children, until the gods were petitioned for relief. A deliverer was sent to them in the person of Jonayaíyin, the son of the old woman who lives in the West, and the second wife of the Sun. She divided her time between the Sun and the Water-fall, and by the latter bore a second son, named Kobachíschini, who remained with his mother while his brother went forth to battle with the enemies of mankind. In four days Jonayaíyin grew to manhood,[112] then he asked his mother where the Elk lived. She told him that the Elk was in a great desert far to the southward. She gave him arrows with which to kill the Elk. In four steps [145] he reached the distant desert where the Elk was lying.

Jonayaíyin cautiously observed the position of the Elk from behind a hill. The Elk was lying on an open plain, where no trees or bushes were to be found that might serve to shelter Jonayaíyin from view while he approached. While he was looking at the Elk, with dried grass before his face, the Lizard said to him, "What are you doing, my friend?" [146] Jonayaíyin explained his mission, whereupon the Lizard suggested that he clothe himself in the garments of the Lizard, in which he could approach the Elk in safety. Jonayaíyin tried four times before he succeeded in getting into the coat of the Lizard. Next the Gopher came to him with the question, "What are you doing here, my friend?" When Jonayaíyin told the Gopher of his intention, the latter promised to aid him.[147] The Gopher thought it advisable to reconnoitre by burrowing his way underground to the Elk. Jonayaíyin watched the progress of the Gopher as that animal threw out fresh heaps of earth on his way.

At length the Gopher came to the surface underneath the Elk, whose giant heart was beating like a mighty hammer. He then proceeded to gnaw the hair from about the heart of the Elk. "What are you doing?" said the Elk. "I am cutting a few hairs for my little ones; they are now lying on the bare ground," replied the Gopher, who continued until the magic coat of the Elk was all cut away from about the heart of the

Elk. Then he returned to Jonayaíyin, and told the latter to go through the hole which he had made and shoot the Elk.

Four times the Son of the Sun tried to enter the hole before he succeeded. When he reached the Elk, he saw the great heart beating above him, and easily pierced it with his arrows; four times his bow was drawn before he turned to escape through the tunnel which the Gopher had been preparing for him. This hole extended far to the eastward, but the Elk soon discovered it, and thrusting his antler into it, followed in pursuit. The Elk ploughed up the earth with such violence that the present mountains were formed, which extend from east to west.[46] The black spider closed the hole with a strong web, but the Elk broke through it and ran southward, forming the mountain chains which trend north and south. In the south the Elk was checked by the web of the blue spider,[148] in the west by that of the yellow spider, while in the north the web of the many-colored spider resisted his attacks until he fell dying from exhaustion and wounds. Jonayaíyin made a coat from the hide of the Elk, gave the front quarters to the Gopher, the hind quarters to the Lizard, and carried home the antlers. He found that the results of his adventures were not unknown to his mother, who had spent the time during his absence in singing, and watching a roll of cedar bark which sank into the earth or rose in the air as danger approached or receded from Jonayaíyin, her son.[149]

Jonayaíyin next desired to kill the great Eagle, I-tsa. His mother directed him to seek the Eagle in the West. In four strides he reached the home of the Eagle, an inaccessible rock, on which was the nest, containing two young eaglets. His ear [150] told him to stand facing the east when the next morning the Eagle swooped down upon him and tried to carry him off.[151] The talons of the Eagle failed to penetrate the hard elk-skin by which he was covered. "Turn to the south," said the ear, and again the Eagle came, and was again unsuccessful. Jonayaíyin faced each of the four points in this manner, and again faced toward the east; whereupon the Eagle succeeded in fastening its talons in the lacing on the front of the coat of the supposed man, who was carried to the nest above and thrown down before the young eagles, with the invitation to pick his eyes out. As they were about to do this, Jonayaíyin gave a warning hiss, at which the young ones cried, "He is living yet." "Oh, no," replied the old Eagle; "that is only the rush of air from his body through the holes made by my talons." Without stopping to verify this, the Eagle flew away.

Jonayaíyin threw some of the blood of the Elk which he had brought with him to the young ones, and asked them when their mother returned. "In the afternoon when it rains," they answered. When the mother Eagle came with the shower of rain in the afternoon, he stood in readiness with one of the Elk antlers in his hand. As the bird alighted with a man in her talons, Jonayaíyin struck her upon the back with the antler, killing her instantly. Going back to the nest, he asked the young eagles when their father returned. "Our father comes home when the wind blows and brings rain just before sunset," they said. The male Eagle came at the appointed time, carrying a woman with a crying infant upon her back. Mother and babe were dropped from a height upon the rock and killed. With the second antler of the Elk, Jonayaíyin avenged their death, and ended the career of the eagles by striking the Eagle upon the back and killing him. The wing of this eagle was of enormous size; the bones were as large as a man's arm; fragments of this wing are still preserved at Taos. Jonayaíyin struck the young eagles upon the head, saying, "You shall never grow any larger." Thus deprived of their strength and power to injure mankind, the eagles relinquished their sovereignty with the parting curse of rheumatism, which they bestowed upon the human race.

Jonayaíyin could discover no way by which he could descend from the rock, until at length he saw an old female Bat on the plain below. At first she pretended not to hear his calls for help; then she flew up with the inquiry, "How did you get here?" Jonayaíyin told how he had killed the eagles. "I will give you all the feathers you may desire if you will help me to escape," concluded he. The old Bat carried her basket by a slender spider's thread. He was afraid to trust himself in such a small basket suspended by a thread, but she reassured him, saying: "I have packed mountain sheep in this basket, and the strap has never broken. Do not look while we are descending; keep your eyes shut as tight as you can." [217] He began to open his eyes once during the descent, but she warned him in time to avoid mishap. They went to the foot of the rock where the old Eagles lay. Jonayaíyin filled her basket with feathers, but told her not to go out on the plains, where there are many small birds. Forgetting this admonition, she was soon among the small birds, who robbed the old Bat of all her feathers. This accounts for the plumage of the small bird klokin, which somewhat resembles the color of the tail and wing feathers of the bald eagle. The Bat returned four times for a supply of feathers, but the fifth time she asked to have her basket filled, Jonayaíyin was vexed. "You cannot take care of your feathers, so you shall never have any. This old skin on your basket is good enough for you." "Very well," said the Bat, resignedly, "I deserve to lose them, for I never could take care of those feathers."

XLIV. LODGE–BOY AND THROWN–AWAY[152]

(CROW: Simms, *Field Museum: Anthropological Series*, ii, 303, No. 19)

Once upon a time there lived a couple, the woman being pregnant. The man went hunting one day, and in his absence a certain wicked woman named Red-Woman came to the tipi and killed his wife and cut her open and found boy twins. She threw one behind the tipi curtain, and the other she threw into a spring. She then put a stick inside the woman and stuck one end in the ground, to give her the appearance of a live person, and burned her upper lip, giving her the appearance as though laughing.[105]

When her husband came home, tired from carrying the deer he had killed, he saw his wife standing near the door of the tipi, looking as though she were laughing at him, and he said: "I am tired and hungry, why do you laugh at me?" and pushed her. As she fell backwards, her stomach opened, and he caught hold of her and discovered she was dead. He knew at once that Red-Woman had killed his wife.

While the man was eating supper alone one night a voice said, "Father, give me some of your supper." As no one was in sight, he resumed eating and again the voice asked for supper. The man said, "Whoever you are, you may come and eat with me, for I am poor and alone." A young boy came from behind the curtain, and said his name was "Thrown-behind-the-Curtain." During the day, while the man went hunting, the boy stayed home. One day the boy said, "Father, make me two bows and the arrows for them." His father asked him why he wanted two bows. The boy said, "I want them to change about." His father made them for him, but surmised the boy had other reasons, and concluded he would watch the boy, and on one day, earlier than usual, he left his tipi and hid upon a hill overlooking his tipi, and while there, he saw two boys of about the same age shooting arrows.

That evening when he returned home, he asked his son, "Is there not another little boy of your age about here?" His son said, "Yes, and he lives in the spring." His father said, "You should bring him out and make him live with us." The son said, "I cannot make him, because he has sharp teeth like an otter, but if you will make me a suit of rawhide, I will try and catch him."

One day, arrangements were made to catch the boy. The father said, "I will stay here in the tipi and you tell him I have gone out." So Thrown-behind-the-Curtain said to Thrown-in-Spring. "Come out and play arrows." Thrown-in-Spring came out just a little, and said, "I smell something." Thrown-behind-the-Curtain said, "No, you don't, my father is not home," and after insisting, Thrown-in-Spring came out, and both boys began to play. While they were playing, Thrown-behind-the-Curtain disputed a point of their game, and as Thrown-in-Spring stooped over to see how close his arrow came, Thrown-behind-the-Curtain grabbed him from behind and held his arms close to his sides and Thrown-in-Spring turned and attempted to bite him, but his teeth could not penetrate the rawhide suit. The father came to the assistance of Thrown-behind-the-Curtain and the water of the spring rushed out to help Thrown-in-Spring; but Thrown-in-Spring was dragged to a high hill where the water could not reach him, and there they burned incense under his nose, and he became human. The three of them lived together.

One day one of the boys said, "Let us go and wake up mother." They went to the mother's grave and one said, "Mother, your stone pot is dropping," and she moved.[153] The other boy said, "Mother, your hide dresser is falling," and she sat up. Then one of them said, "Mother, your bone crusher is falling," and she began to arrange her hair, which had begun to fall off. The mother said, "I have been asleep a long time."[154] She accompanied the boys home.

The boys[155] were forbidden by their father to go to the river bend above their tipi;[156] for an old woman lived there who had a boiling pot, and every time she saw any living object, she tilted the kettle toward it [157] and the object was drawn into the pot and boiled for her to eat. The boys went one day to see the old woman, and they found her asleep and they stole up and got her pot and awakened the old woman and said to her, "Grandmother, why have you this here?" at the same time tilting the pot towards her, by which she was drowned and boiled to death. They took the pot home and gave it to their mother for her own protection.

Their father told them not to disobey him again and said, "There is something over the hill I do not want you to go near." They were very anxious to find out what this thing was, and they went over to the hill and as they poked their heads over the hilltop, the thing began to draw in air,[158] and the boys were drawn in also; and as they went in, they saw people and animals, some dead and others dying. The thing proved to be an immense alligator-like serpent. One of the boys touched the kidneys of the thing and asked what they were. The alligator said, "That is my medicine, do not touch it." And the boy reached up and touched its heart and asked what it was, and the serpent grunted and said, "This is where I make my plans." One of the boys said, "You do make plans, do you?" and he cut the heart off and it died.[159] They made their escape by cutting between the ribs and liberated the living ones and took a piece of the heart home to their father.

After the father had administered another scolding, he told the boys not to go near the three trees standing in a triangular shaped piece of ground; for if anything went under them they would bend to the ground suddenly, killing everything in their way.[160] One day the boys went towards these trees, running swiftly and then stopping suddenly near the trees, which bent violently and struck the ground without hitting them. They jumped over the trees, breaking the branches and they could not rise after the branches were broken.

Once more the boys were scolded and told not to go near a tipi over the hill; for it was inhabited by snakes, and they would approach anyone asleep and enter his body through the rectum.[161] Again the boys did as they were told not to do and went to the tipi, and the snakes invited them in. They went in and carried flat pieces of stone with them and as they sat down they placed the flat pieces of stones under their rectums.

After they had been in the tipi a short while, the snakes began putting their heads over the poles around the fireplace and the snakes began to relate stories, and one of them said, "When there is a drizzling rain, and when we are under cover, it is nice to sleep." One of the boys said, "When we are lying down under the pine trees and the wind blows softly through them and has a weird sound, it is nice to sleep." [162] All but one of the snakes went to sleep, and that one tried to enter the rectum of each of the boys and failed, on account of the flat stone. The boys killed all of the other snakes but that one, and they took that one and rubbed its head against the side of a cliff, and that is the reason why snakes have flattened heads.[4]

Again the boys were scolded by their father, who said, "There is a man living on the steep cut bank, with deep water under it, and if you go near it he will push you over the bank into the water for his father in the water to eat." [163] The boys went to the place, but before going, they fixed their headdresses with dried grass. Upon their arrival at the edge of the bank, one said to the other, "Just as he is about to push you over, lie down quickly." The man from his hiding place suddenly rushed out to push the boys over, and just as he was about to do it, the boys threw themselves quickly upon the ground, and the man went over their heads, pulling their headdress with him, and his father in the water ate him.

Upon the boys' return, and after telling what they had done, their father scolded them and told them, "There is a man who wears moccasins of fire,[164] and when he wants anything, he goes around it and it is burned up." The boys ascertained where this man lived and stole upon him one day when he was sleeping under a tree and each one of the boys took off a moccasin and put it on and they awoke him and ran about him and he was burned and went up in smoke. They took the moccasins home.

Their father told them that something would yet happen to them; for they had killed so many bad things. One day while walking the valley they were lifted from the earth and after travelling in mid air for some time, they were placed on top of a peak in a rough high mountain with a big lake surrounding it and the Thunder-Bird said to them, "I want you to kill a long otter that lives in the lake; he eats all the young ones that I produce and I cannot make him stop." So the boys began to make arrows, and they gathered dry pine sticks and began to heat rocks, and the long otter came towards them. As it opened its mouth the boys shot arrows into it; and as that did not stop it from drawing nearer, they threw the hot rocks down its throat, and it curled up and died afterwards. They were taken up and carried through the air [145d] and gently placed upon the ground near their homes, where they lived for many years.

XLV. BLOOD–CLOT–BOY [165]

(BLACKFOOT: Wissler and Duvall, *Anthropological Papers American Museum of Natural History*, ii, 53)

Once there was an old man and woman whose three daughters married a young man. The old people lived in a lodge by themselves. The young man was supposed to hunt buffalo, and feed them all. Early in the morning the young man invited his father-in-law to go out with him to kill buffalo. The old man was then directed to drive the buffalo through a gap where the young man stationed himself to kill them as they went by. As soon as the buffalo were killed, the young man requested his father-in-law to go home. He said, "You are old. You need not stay here. Your daughters can bring you some meat." Now the young man lied to his father-in-law; for when the meat was brought to his lodge, he ordered his wives not to give meat to the old folks. Yet one of the daughters took pity on her parents, and stole meat for them. The way in which she did this was to take a piece of meat in her robe, and as she went for water drop it in front of her father's lodge.

Now every morning the young man invited his father-in-law to hunt buffalo; and, as before, sent him away and refused to permit his daughters to furnish meat for the old people. On the fourth day, as the old man was returning, he saw a clot of blood in the trail, and said to himself, "Here at least is something from which we can make soup." In order that he might not be seen by his son-in-law, he stumbled, and spilt the arrows out of his quiver. Now, as he picked up the arrows, he put the clot of blood into the quiver. Just then the young man came up and demanded to know what it was he picked up. The old man explained that he had just stumbled, and was picking up his arrows. So the old man took the clot of blood home and requested his wife to make blood-soup. When the pot began to boil, the old woman heard a child crying. She looked all around, but saw nothing. Then she heard it again. This time it seemed to be in the pot. She looked in quickly, and saw a boy baby: [166] so she lifted the pot from the fire, took the baby out and wrapped it up.

Now the young man, sitting in his lodge, heard a baby crying, and said, "Well, the old woman must have a baby." Then he sent his oldest wife over to see the old woman's baby, saying, "If it is a boy, I will kill it." The woman came in to look at the baby, but the old woman told her it was a girl.[128] When the young man heard this, he did not believe it. So he sent each wife in turn; but they all came back with the same report. Now the young man was greatly pleased, because he could look forward to another wife. So he sent over some old bones, that soup might be made for the baby. Now, all this happened in the morning. That night the baby spoke to the old man, saying, "You take me up and hold me against each lodge-pole in succession." So the old man took up the baby, and, beginning at the door, went around in the direction of the sun, and each time that he touched a pole the baby became larger.[112] When halfway around, the baby was so heavy that the old man could hold him no longer. So he put the baby down in the middle of the lodge, and, taking hold of his head, moved it toward each of the poles in succession, and, when the last pole was reached, the baby had become a very fine young man. Then this young man went out, got some black flint [obsidian] and, when he got to the lodge, he said to the old man, "I am the Smoking-Star. I came down to help you. When I have done this, I shall return."

Now, when morning came, Blood-Clot (the name his father gave him) arose and took his father out to hunt. They had not gone very far when they killed a scabby cow. Then Blood-Clot lay down behind the cow and requested his father to wait until the son-in-law came to join him. He also requested that he stand his ground and talk back to the son-in-law. Now, at the usual time in the morning, the son-in-law called at the lodge of the old man, but was told that he had gone out to hunt. This made him very angry, and he struck at the old woman, saying, "I have a notion to kill you." So the son-in-law went out.

Now Blood-Clot had directed his father to be eating a kidney when the son-in-law approached. When the son-in-law came up and saw all this, he was very angry. He said to the old man, "Now you shall die for all this." "Well," said the old man, "you must die too, for all that you have done." Then the son-in-law began to shoot arrows at the old man, and the latter becoming frightened called on Blood-Clot for help. Then Blood-Clot sprang up and upbraided the son-in-law for his cruelty. "Oh," said the son-in-law, "I was just fooling." At this Blood-Clot shot the son-in-law through and through. Then Blood-Clot said to his father, "We will leave this meat here: it is not good. Your son-in-law's house is full of dried meat. Which one of your daughters helped you?" The old man told him that it was the youngest. Then Blood-Clot went to the lodge, killed the two older women, brought up the body of the son-in-law, and burned them together. Then he requested the younger daughter to take care of her old parents, to be kind to them, etc. "Now," said Blood-Clot, "I shall go to visit the other Indians."

So he started out, and finally came to a camp. He went into the lodge of some old women, who were very much surprised to see such a fine young man. They said, "Why do you come here among such old women as we? Why don't you go where there are young people?" "Well," said Blood-Clot, "give me some dried meat." Then the old women gave him some meat, but no fat. "Well," said Blood-Clot, "you did not give me the fat to eat with my dried meat." "Hush!" said the old women. "You must not speak so loud. There are bears here that take all the fat and give us the lean, and they will kill you, if they hear you." "Well," said Blood-Clot, "I will go out to-morrow, do some butchering, and get some fat." Then he went out through the camp, telling all the people to make ready in the morning, for he intended to drive the buffalo over [the drive].

Now there were some bears who ruled over this camp. They lived in a bear-lodge [painted lodge], and were very cruel. When Blood-Clot had driven the buffalo over, he noticed among them a scabby cow. He said, "I shall save this for the old women." Then the people laughed, and said, "Do you mean to save that poor old beast? It is too poor to have fat." However, when it was cut open it was found to be very fat. Now, when the bears heard the buffalo go over the drive, they as usual sent out two bears to cut off the best meat, especially all the fat; but Blood-Clot had already butchered the buffalo, putting the fat upon sticks. He hid it as the bears came up. Also he had heated some stones in a fire. When they told him what they wanted, he ordered them to go back. Now the bears were very angry, and the chief bear and his wife came up to fight, but Blood-Clot killed them by throwing hot stones down their throats.[167]

Then he went down to the lodge of the bears and killed all, except one female who was about to become a mother. She pleaded so pitifully for her life, that he spared her. If he had not done this, there would have been no more bears in the world.[4] The lodge of the bears was filled with dried meat and other property. Also all the young women of the camp were confined there. Blood-Clot gave all the property to the old women, and set free all the young women. The bears' lodge he gave to the old women. It was a bear painted lodge.

"Now," said Blood-Clot, "I must go on my travels." He came to a camp and entered the lodge of some old women. When these women saw what a fine young man he was, they said, "Why do you come here, among such old women? Why do you not go where there are younger people?" "Well," said he, "give me some meat." The old women gave him some dried meat, but no fat. Then he said, "Why do you not give me some fat with my meat?" "Hush!" said the women, "you must not speak so loud. There is a snake-lodge [painted lodge] here, and the snakes take everything. They leave no fat for the people." "Well," said Blood-Clot, "I will go over to the snake-lodge to eat." "No, you must not do that," said the old women. "It is dangerous. They will surely kill you." "Well," said he, "I must have some fat with my meat, even if they do kill me."

Then he entered the snake-lodge. He had his white rock knife ready. Now the snake, who was the head man in this lodge, had one horn on his head. He was lying with his head in the lap of a beautiful woman. He was asleep. By the fire was a bowl of berry-soup ready for the snake when he should wake. Blood-Clot seized the bowl and drank the soup. Then the women warned him in whispers, "You must go away: you must not stay here." But he said, "I want to smoke." So he took out his knife and cut off the head of the snake, saying as he did so, "Wake up! light a pipe! I want to smoke." Then with his knife he began to kill all the snakes. At last there was one snake who was about to become a mother, and she pleaded so pitifully for her life that she was allowed to go. From her descended all the snakes that are in the world. Now the lodge of the snakes was filled up with dried meat of every kind, fat, etc. Blood-Clot turned all this over to the people, the lodge and everything it contained. Then he said, "I must go away and visit other people."

So he started out. Some old women advised him to keep on the south side of the road, because it was dangerous the other way.[156] But Blood-Clot paid no attention to their warning. As he was going along, a great windstorm struck him and at last carried him into the mouth of a great fish. This was a sucker-fish and the wind was its sucking.[158] When he got into the stomach of the fish, he saw a great many people. Many of them were dead, but some were still alive. He said to the people, "Ah, there must be a heart somewhere here. We will have a dance." So he painted his face white, his eyes and mouth with black circles, and tied a white rock knife on his head, so that the point stuck up. Some rattles made of hoofs were also brought. Then the people started in to dance. For a while Blood-Clot sat making wing-motions with his hands, and singing songs. Then he stood up and danced, jumping up and down until the knife on his head struck the heart. Then he cut the heart down. Next he cut through between the ribs of the fish, and let all the people out.[159]

Again Blood-Clot said he must go on his travels. Before starting, the people warned him, saying that after a while he would see a woman who was always challenging people to wrestle with her, but that he must not speak to her. He gave no heed to what they said, and, after he had gone a little way, he saw a woman who called him to come over. "No," said Blood-Clot. "I am in a hurry." However, at the fourth time the woman asked him to come over, he said, "Yes, but you must wait a little while, for I am tired. I wish to rest. When I have rested, I will come over and wrestle with you." Now, while he was resting, he saw many large knives sticking up from the ground almost hidden by straw.[168] Then he knew that the woman killed the people she wrestled with by throwing them down on the knives. When he was rested, he went over. The woman asked him to stand up in the place where he had seen the knives; but he said, "No, I am not quite ready. Let us play a little, before we begin." So he began to play with the woman, but quickly caught hold of her, threw her upon the knives, and cut her in two.

Blood-Clot took up his travels again, and after a while came to a camp where there were some old women. The old women told him that a little farther on he would come to a woman with a swing,[169] but on no account must he ride with her. After a time he came to a place where he saw a swing on the bank of a swift stream. There was a woman swinging on it. He watched her a while, and saw that she killed people by swinging them out and dropping them into the water. When he found this out, he came up to the woman. "You have a swing here; let me see you swing," he said. "No," said the woman, "I want to see you swing." "Well," said Blood-Clot, "but you must swing first." "Well," said the woman, "Now I shall swing. Watch me. Then I shall see you do it." So the woman swung out over the stream. As she did this, he saw how it worked. Then he said to the woman, "You swing again while I am getting ready"; but as the woman swung out this time, he cut the vine and let her drop into the water. This happened on Cut Bank Creek.

"Now," said Blood-Clot, "I have rid the world of all the monsters,[12] I will go back to my old father and mother." So he climbed a high ridge, and returned to the lodge of the old couple. One day he said to them, "I shall go back to the place from whence I came. If you find that I have been killed, you must not be sorry, for then I shall go up into the sky and become the Smoking-Star." Then he went on and on, until he was killed by some Crow Indians on the war-path. His body was never found; but the moment he was killed, the Smoking-Star appeared in the sky, where we see it now.[71]

XLVI. THE SON–IN–LAW TESTS [170]
(TIMAGAMI OJIBWA: Speck, *Memoirs of the Geological Survey of Canada: Anthropological Series*, ix, 44)

Wemicus [the animal-trickster] had a son-in-law who was a man. This man's wife, the daughter of Wemicus, had had a great many husbands, because Wemicus had put them to so many different tests that they had been all killed off except this one. He, however, had succeeded in outwitting Wemicus in every scheme that he tried on him. Wemicus and this man hunted beaver in the spring of the year by driving them all day with dogs.

The man's wife warned him [171] before they started out to hunt, saying, "Look out for my father; he might burn your moccasins in camp. That's what he did to my other husbands." That night in camp Wemicus said, "I did n't tell you the name of this lake. It is called 'Burnt moccasins lake.'" When the man heard this, he thought that Wemicus was up to some sort of mischief and was going to burn his moccasins. Their moccasins were hanging up before a fire to dry and, while Wemicus was not looking, the man changed the places of Wemicus' moccasins and his own, and then went to sleep. Soon the man awoke and saw Wemicus get up and throw his own moccasins into the fire. Wemicus then said, "Say! something is burning; it is your moccasins." Then the man answered, "No, not mine, but yours." So Wemicus had no moccasins, and the ground was covered with snow. After this had happened the man slept with his moccasins on. [172]

The next morning the man started on and left Wemicus there with no shoes. Wemicus started to work. He got a big boulder, made a fire, and placed the boulder in it until it became red hot. He then wrapped his feet with spruce boughs and pushed the boulder ahead of him in order to melt the snow. In this way he managed to walk on the boughs. Then he began to sing, "Spruce is warm, spruce is warm." When the man reached home he told his wife what had happened. "I hope Wemicus will die," she said. A little while after this they heard Wemicus coming along singing, "Spruce is warm, spruce is warm." He came into the wigwam and as he was the head man, they were obliged to get his meal ready.

The ice was getting bad by this time, so they stayed in camp a while. Soon Wemicus told his son-in-law, "We'd better go sliding." He then went to a hill where there were some very poisonous snakes. The man's wife warned her husband of these snakes and gave him a split stick holding a certain kind of magic tobacco, which she told him to hold in front of him so that the snakes would not hurt him. Then the two men went sliding. At the top of the hill Wemicus said, "Follow me," for he intended to pass close by the snakes' lair. So when they slid, Wemicus passed safely and the man held his stick with the tobacco in it in front of him, thus preventing the snakes from biting him. The man then told Wemicus that he enjoyed the sliding.[173]

The following day Wemicus said to his son-in-law, "We had better go to another place." When she heard this, the wife told her husband that, as it was getting summer, Wemicus had in his head many poisonous lizards instead of lice. She said, "He will tell you to pick lice from his head and crack them in your teeth. But take low-bush cranberries and crack them instead." So the man took cranberries along with him. Wemicus took his son-in-law to a valley with a great ravine in it. He said, "I wonder if anybody can jump across this?" "Surely," said the young man, "I can." Then the young man said, "Closer," and the ravine narrowed and he jumped across easily. When Wemicus tried, the young man said, "Widen," and Wemicus fell into the ravine. But it did not kill him, and when he made his way to the top again, he said, "You have beaten me." Then they went on.

They came to a place of hot sand and Wemicus said, "You must look for lice in my head."[174] "All right father," replied the son-in-law. So Wemicus lay down and the man started to pick the lice. He took the cranberries from inside his shirt and each time he pretended to catch a louse, he cracked a cranberry and threw it on the ground, and so Wemicus got fooled a second time that day. Then they went home and Wemicus said to his son-in-law, "There are a whole lot of eggs on that rocky island where the gulls are. We will go get the eggs, come back, and have an egg supper." As Wemicus was the head man, his son-in-law had to obey him.

So they started out in their canoe and soon came to the rocky island. Wemicus stayed in the canoe and told the man to go ashore and to bring the eggs back with him and fill the canoe. When the man reached the shore, Wemicus told him to go farther back on the island,[175] saying, "That's where the former husbands got their eggs, there are their bones." He then started the canoe off in the water by singing, without using his paddle.[14a] Then Wemicus told the gulls to eat the man, saying to them, "I give you him to eat." The gulls started to fly about the man, but the man had his paddle with him and he killed one of the gulls with it. He then took the gulls' wings and fastened them on himself, filled his shirt with eggs, and started flying over the lake by the aid of the wings.[176]

When he reached the middle of the lake, he saw Wemicus going along and singing to himself. Wemicus, looking up, saw his son-in-law but mistook him for a gull. The man flew back to camp and told his wife to cook the eggs, and he told his children to play with the wings. When Wemicus reached the camp, he saw the children playing with the wings and said, "Where did you get those wings?" "From father," was the reply. "Your father? Why the gulls ate him!" Then he went to the wigwam and there he saw the man smoking. Then Wemicus thought it very strange how the man could have gotten home, but no one told him how it had been done. Thought he, "I must try another scheme to do away with him."

One day Wemicus said to his son-in-law, "We'd better make two canoes of birch-bark, one for you and one for me. We'd better get bark." So they started off for birch-bark. They cut a tree almost through and Wemicus said to his son-in-law, "You sit on that side and I'll sit on this." He wanted the tree to fall on him and kill him. Wemicus said, "You say, 'Fall on my father-in-law,' and I'll say, 'Fall on my son-in-law,' and whoever says it too slowly or makes a mistake will be the one on whom it will fall." But Wemicus made the first mistake, and the tree fell on him and crushed him. However, Wemicus was a manitu and was not hurt. They went home with the bark and made the two canoes. After they were made, Wemicus said to his son-in-law, "Well, we'll have a race in our two canoes, a sailing race." Wemicus made a big bark sail, but the man did not make any, as he was afraid of upsetting. They started the race. Wemicus went very fast and the man called after him, "Oh, you are beating me." He kept on fooling and encouraging Wemicus, until the wind upset Wemicus' canoe and that was the end of Wemicus. When the man sailed over the spot where Wemicus had upset, he saw a big pike there, into which Wemicus had been transformed when the canoe upset. This is the origin of the pike.[4]

XLVII. THE JEALOUS FATHER [177]

(CREE: Skinner, *Anthropological Papers of the American Museum of Natural History*, ix, 92)

Once there was an old man named Aioswé who had two wives. When his son by one of these women began to grow up, Aioswé became jealous of him. One day, he went off to hunt and when he came back, found marks on one of the women (the co-wife with his son's mother) which proved to him that his son had been on terms of intimacy with her.[178]

One day the old man and the boy went to a rocky island to hunt for eggs.[175] Wishing to get rid of his son, the old man persuaded him to gather eggs farther and farther away from the shore. The young man did not suspect anything until he looked up and saw his father paddling off in the canoe. "Why are you deserting me, father?" he cried. "Because you have played tricks on your stepmother," answered the old man.

When the boy found that he was really left behind, he sat there crying hour after hour. At last, Walrus appeared. He came near the island and stuck his head above the water. "What are you crying for, my son?" said Walrus. "My father has deserted me on this island and I want to get home to the mainland. Will you not help me to get ashore?" the boy replied. Walrus said that he would do so willingly.[179] "Get on my back," said Walrus, "and I will take you to the mainland." Then Walrus asked Aioswé's son if the sky was clear. The boy replied that it was, but this was a lie, for he saw many clouds. Aioswé's son said this because he was afraid that Walrus would desert him if he knew it was cloudy. Walrus said, "If you think I am not going fast enough, strike on my horns [tusks] and let me know when you think it is shallow enough for you to get ashore, then you can jump off my back and walk to the land."

As they went along, Walrus said to the boy, "Now my son, you must let me know if you hear it thunder, because as soon as it thunders, I must go right under the water." The boy promised to let Walrus know. They had not gone far, when there came a peal of thunder. Walrus said, "My son, I hear thunder." "Oh, no, you are mistaken," said the boy who feared to be drowned, "what you think is thunder is only the noise your body makes going so quickly through the water." Walrus believed the boy and thought he must have been wrong. Some time later, there came another peal of thunder and this time, Walrus knew he was not mistaken, he was sure it was thunder. He was very angry and said he would drop Aioswé's son there, whether the water was shallow or not. He did so but the lad had duped Walrus with his lies so that he came where the water was very shallow and the boy escaped, but Walrus was killed by lightning before he could reach water deep enough to dive in. This thunderstorm was sent to destroy Walrus by Aioswé's father, who conjured for it. Walrus, on the other hand, was the result of conjuring by his mother, who wished to save her son's life.[182]

When Aioswé's son reached the shore, he started for home, but he had not gone far before he met an old woman,[180] who had been sent as the result of a wish for his safety by his mother (or was a wish for his safety on his mother's part, personified). The old woman instructed the lad how to conduct himself if he ever expected to reach his home and mother again. "Now you have come ashore there is still a lot of trouble for you to go through before you reach home," said she, and she gave him the stuffed skin of an ermine (weasel in white winter coat). "This will be one of your weapons to use to protect yourself," were her words as she tendered him this gift, and she told him what dangers he would encounter and what to do in each case.

Then the son of Aioswé started for his home once more. As he journeyed through the forest he came upon a solitary wigwam inhabited by two old blind hags, who were the result of an adverse conjuration by his father. Both of these old women had sharp bones like daggers protruding from the lower arm at the elbow.[181] They were very savage and used to kill everybody they met. When Aioswé's son approached the tent, although the witches could not see him, they knew from their magic powers that he was near. They asked him to come in and sit down, but he was suspicious, for he did not like the looks of their elbows.

He thought of a plan by which he might dupe the old women into killing each other. Instead of going himself and sitting between them he got a large parchment and fixing it to the end of a pole, he poked it in between them. The old women heard it rattle and thought it was the boy himself coming to sit between them. Then they both turned their backs to the skin and began to hit away at it with their elbows. Every time they stabbed the skin, they cried out, "I am hitting the son of Aioswé! I've hit him! I've hit him!" At last, they got so near each other that they began to hit one another, calling out all the time, "I am hitting the son of Aioswé!" They finally stabbed each other to death and the son of Aioswé escaped this danger also.

When the young man had vanquished the two old women he proceeded on his journey. He had not gone very far when he came to a row of dried human bones hung across the path so that no one could pass by without making them rattle. Not far away, there was a tent full of people and big dogs. Whenever they heard anyone disturb the bones, they would set upon him and kill him. The old woman who had advised Aioswé's son told him that when he came to this place he could escape by digging a tunnel in the path under the bones. When he arrived at the spot he began to follow her advice and burrow under. He was careless and when he was very nearly done and completely out of sight, he managed to rattle the bones. At once, the dogs heard and they cried out, "That must be Aioswé's son." All the people ran out at once, but since Aioswé's son was under ground in the tunnel they could not see him, so after they had searched for a while they returned. The dogs said, "We are sure this is the son of Aioswé," and they continued to search.

At length, they found the mouth of the hole Aioswé's son had dug. The dogs came to the edge and began to bark till all the people ran out again with their weapons. Then Aioswé's son took the stuffed ermine skin and poked its head up. All the people saw it and thought it was really ermine. Then they were angry and killed the dogs for lying.

Aioswé's son escaped again and this time he got home. When he drew near his father's wigwam, he could hear his mother crying, and as he approached still closer he saw her. She looked up and saw him coming. She cried out to her husband and co-wife, "My son has come home again." The old man did not believe it. "It is not possible," he cried. But his wife insisted on it. Then the old man came out and when he saw it was really his son, he was very much frightened for his own safety. He called out to his other wife, "Bring some caribou skins and spread them out for my son to walk on." But the boy kicked them away. "I have come a long way," said he, "with only my bare feet to walk on."

That night, the boy sang a song about the burning of the world and the old man sang against him [182] but he was not strong enough. "I am going to set the world on fire," said the boy to his father, "I shall make all the lakes and rivers boil."

He took up an arrow and said, "I am going to shoot this arrow into the woods; see if I don't set them on fire." He shot his arrow into the bush and a great blaze sprang up and all the woods began to burn.

"The forest is now on fire," said the old man, "but the water is not yet burning." "I'll show you how I can make the water boil also," said his son. He shot another arrow into the water, and it immediately began to boil. Then the old man who wished to escape said to his son, "How shall we escape?" The old man had been a great bear hunter and had a large quantity of bear's grease preserved in a bark basket. "Go into your fat basket," said his son, "you will be perfectly safe there." Then he drew a circle on the ground and placed his mother there. The ground enclosed by the circle was not even scorched, but the wicked old man who had believed he would be safe in the grease baskets, was burned to death.

Aioswé's son said to his mother, "Let us become birds. What will you be?" "I'll be a robin," said she. "I'll be a whisky jack (Canada jay)," he replied. They flew off together.[4]

XLVIII. DIRTY-BOY [183]

(OKANAGON: Teit, *Memoirs of the American Folk-Lore Society*, xi, 85, No. 6)

The people of a certain region were living together in a very large camp. Their chief had two beautiful daughters of marriageable age. Many young men had proposed to them, but all had been refused. The chief said, "Whom do my daughters wish to marry? They have refused all the men." Sun and Star, who were brother and sister,[184] lived in the sky, and had seen all that had happened. Sun said to his sister, "The chief's daughters have rejected the suits of all our friends. Let us go down and arrange this matter! Let us try these girls!" They made clothes, and at night they descended to earth.

During the darkness they erected a lodge on the outskirts of the camp. It had the appearance of being very old, and of belonging to poor people. The poles were old and badly selected. The covering was tattered and patched, and made of tule mats. The floor was strewn with old dried brush and grass, and the beds were of the same material. Their blankets consisted of old mats and pieces of old robes; and their kettles and cups

were of bark, poorly made. Star had assumed the form of a
decrepit old woman dressed in rags; and Sun, that of a dirty
boy with sore eyes.[185]

On the following morning the women of the camp saw the
lodge, and peered in. When they returned, they reported,
"Some very poor people arrived during the night, and are
camped in an old mat lodge. We saw two persons inside, —
a dirty, sore-eyed boy; and his grandmother, a very old woman
in ragged clothes."

Now, the chief resolved to find husbands for his daughters.
He sent out his speaker to announce that in four days there
would be a shooting-contest [142] open to all the men, and the
best marksman would get his daughters for wives.[186] The
young men could not sleep for eagerness. On the third day the
chief's speaker announced, "To-morrow morning every one
shall shoot. Each one will have two shots. An eagle will perch
on the tall tree yonder; and whoever kills it shall have the
chief's daughters." Coyote was there and felt happy. He
thought he would win the prize. On the following morning an
eagle was seen soaring in the air, and there was much excitement as it began to descend. It alighted on a tree which grew
near one end of the camp. Then the young men tried to shoot
it. Each man had two arrows. The previous evening Sun had
said to Star, "Grandmother, make a bow and arrows for me."
She said, "What is the use? You cannot shoot. You never
used bow and arrows." He replied, "I am going to try. I shall
take part in the contest to-morrow. I heard what the chief
said." She took pity on him, and went to a red willow-bush,
cut a branch for a bow, and some twigs for arrows. She strung
the bow with a poor string, and did not feather the arrows.

Coyote, who was afraid some one else might hit the bird,
shouted, "I will shoot first. Watch me hit the eagle." His
arrow struck the lowest branch of the tree and fell down, and
the people laughed. He said, "I made a mistake. That was a
bad arrow. This one will kill the eagle." He shot, and the
arrow fell short of the first one. He became angry, and pulled
other arrows from his quiver. He wanted to shoot them all.
The people seized him, and took away his arrows, saying, "You
are allowed to shoot twice only." All the people shot and
missed. When the last one had shot, Sun said, "Grandmother,
lift the door of the lodge a little, so that I can shoot." She said,

"First get out of bed." She pulled the lodge mat aside a little, and he shot. The arrow hit the tail of the eagle. The people saw and heard the arrow coming from Dirty-Boy's lodge, but saw no one shooting it. They wondered. He shot the second arrow, which pierced the eagle's heart.

Now, Wolf and others were standing near Dirty-Boy's lodge, and Wolf desired much to claim the prize. He shouted, "I shot the bird from the lodge-door!" and ran to pick it up; but the old woman Star ran faster than he, picked up the bird, and carried it to the chief. She claimed his daughters for her grandson. All the people gathered around, and made fun of Dirty-Boy. They said, "He is bedridden. He is lousy, sore-eyed, and scabby-faced." The chief was loath to give his daughters to such a person. He knew that Dirty-Boy could not walk. Therefore he said, "To-morrow there shall be another contest. This will be the last one, I cannot break my word. Whoever wins this time shall have my daughters."

He announced that on the morrow each man should set two traps for fishers,[187] an animal very scarce at the place where the camp was located. If any one should catch a fisher one night, then he was to stay in the mountains another day to catch a second one. After that he had to come back. Those who caught nothing the first night had to come home at once. Only two traps were allowed to each man; and two fishers had to be caught, — one a light one, and one a dark one, — and both prime skins. When all the men had gone to the mountains, Sun said to his sister, "Grandmother, make two traps for me." She answered, "First get out of bed!" However, she had pity on him, and made two deadfalls of willow sticks. She asked him where she should set them; and he said, "One on each side of the lodge-door."

On the following morning all the men returned by noon; not one of them had caught a fisher. When Star went out, she found two fine fishers in the traps. Now the chief assembled the men to see if any one had caught the fishers. He was glad, because he knew that Dirty-Boy could not walk; and unless he went to the mountains, he had no chance to kill fishers. Just then the old grandmother appeared, dragging the fishers. She said, "I hear you asked for two fishers; here are two that my grandson caught." She handed them over to him, and then left.

Coyote had boasted that he would certainly catch the fishers. When he went up the mountain, he carried ten traps instead of two. He said, "Whoever heard of setting only two traps? I shall set ten." He set them all, remained out two nights, but got nothing.

The chief said to his daughters, "You must become the wives of Dirty-Boy. I tried to save you by having two contests; but since I am a great chief, I cannot break my word. Go now, and take up your abode with your husband." They put on their best clothes and went. On the way they had to pass Raven's house, and heard the Ravens laughing inside, because the girls had to marry Dirty-Boy. The elder sister said, "Let us go in and see what they are laughing about!" The younger one said, "No, our father told us to go straight to our husband." The elder one went in, and sat down beside Raven's eldest son. She became his wife. Like all the other Ravens, he was ugly, and had a big head; but she thought it better to marry him than to become the wife of a dirty, sickly boy.

The younger one went on, entered Dirty-Boy's lodge, and sat down by his side. The old woman asked her who she was, and why she had come. When the old woman had been told, she said, "Your husband is sick, and soon he will die. He stinks too much. You must not sleep with him. Go back to your father's lodge every evening; but come here in the daytime, and watch him and attend him."

Now, the Raven family that lived close by laughed much at the younger daughter of the chief. They were angry because she had not entered their house and married there, as her elder sister had done. To hurt her feelings, they dressed their new daughter-in-law in the finest clothes they had. Her dress was covered with beads, shells, elk's teeth, and quill-work. They gave her necklaces, and her mother-in-law gave her a finely polished celt of green stone (jade) to hang at her belt. The younger sister paid no attention to this, but returned every morning to help her grandmother-in-law to gather fire-wood, and to attend to her sick husband.

For three days matters remained this way. In the evening of the third day Sun said to his sister, "We will resume our true forms to-night, so that people may see us to-morrow." That night they transformed themselves.[188] The old mat lodge became a fine new skin lodge, surpassing those of the Blackfeet and other tribes, richly decorated with ornaments, and with streamers tied to the top and painted. The old bark kettle became a bright copper kettle; and new pretty woven baskets, and embroidered and painted bags, were in the house. The old woman became a fine-looking person of tall figure, with clothes covered with shining stars. Dirty-Boy became a young, handsome man of light complexion. His clothes were covered with shining copper. His hair reached to the ground and shone like the rays of the sun. In the morning the people saw the new lodge, and said, "Some rich chief has arrived, and has camped where the poor people were. He has thrown them out."

When the girl arrived, she was much surprised to see the transformation. She saw a woman in the door, wearing a long skin dress covered with star pendants, with bright stars in her hair. She addressed her in a familiar voice, saying, "Come in and sit with your husband!" The girl then knew who she was. When she entered, she saw a handsome man reclining, with his head on a beautiful parfleche. His garments and hair were decorated with bright suns. The girl did not recognize him, and looked around. The woman said, "That is your husband; go and sit beside him." Then she was glad.

Sun took his wife to the copper kettle which stood at the door. It contained a shining liquid. He pushed her head into it, and when the liquid ran down over her hair and body, lines of sparkling small stars formed on her. He told her to empty the kettle. When she did so, the liquid ran to the chief's lodge, forming a path, as of gold-dust. He said, "This will be your trail when you go to see your father."

XLIX. THE FALSE BRIDEGROOM [189]

(GROS VENTRE: Kroeber, *Anthropological Papers American Museum of Natural History*, i, 108, No. 28)

There were two girls, sisters. The older sister said, "We will go to look for Shell-Spitter." There was a man who was poor and who lived alone with his old mother. He was the Loon and his mother was Badger-Woman. He heard that two girls were looking for Shell-Spitter. He went to the children of the camp, and took their shells away from them. The girls arrived, and asked for Shell-Spitter's tent. It was shown them, and they went to it. There stood the Loon. "What are you girls looking for?" he said. "We are looking for Shell-Spitter." "I am he." "Let us see you spit shells."

He had filled his mouth with shells, and now spit them out. The two girls stooped, and hastily picked them up, each trying to snatch them before the other. Then he took them to his tent. His tent was old and poor. His mother was gray-headed. He said to them, "I have another tent. It is fine and large. I have brought you here because there is more room to sleep." The girls went inside.

Soon some one called to the Loon, "Come over! they are making the sun-dance!" "Oh!" he said. "Now I have to sit in the middle again, and give away presents. I am tired of it. For once they ought to get some one else. I am to sit on the chief's bed in the middle of the lodge."

He told his mother, "Do not let these women go out." Then he went out, and the old woman guarded the door. When she was asleep, one of the girls said, "I will go out to look." She stepped over the old woman, and went to the dance-lodge. Looking in, she saw the people dancing on the Loon's rump. On the bed in the middle sat a fine man. Whenever he spit, he spit shells.[190] The ground all around him was covered with them.

Then the girl went back, and called to her sister, "Come out! They are dancing on this man; but the one who spits shells sits in the middle of the lodge." Then they both went to the lodge. They went inside and sat down behind Shell-Spitter.

Then the man on the ground, on whom the people were dancing, saw them. He jumped up. He killed Shell-Spitter, and ran out. He said to his mother, "I told you to watch, and not to let those women out." Then he told her, "Dig a hole quickly!" She quickly dug a hole inside the tent. He entered it, and then she followed him. The people came, but could do nothing. When they stopped trying to shoot, Badger-Woman came out of the hole, singing in ridicule of Shell-Spitter's death. Before the people could reach her she dropped into the hole again. She did this repeatedly.[191]

CHAPTER V

JOURNEYS TO THE OTHER WORLD [192]

L. THE STAR HUSBAND [193]

TYPE I: THE WISH TO MARRY A STAR

(TIMAGAMI OJIBWA: Speck, *Memoirs of the Geological Survey of Canada:
Anthropological Series*, ix, 47)

AT the time of which my story speaks people were camping
just as we are here. In the winter time they used birch
bark wigwams. All the animals could then talk together. Two
girls, who were very foolish, talked foolishly and were in no
respect like the other girls of their tribe, made their bed out-of-
doors, and slept right out under the stars. The very fact that
they slept outside during the winter proves how foolish they
were.

One of these girls asked the other, "With what star would
you like to sleep, the white one or the red one?" The other girl
answered, "I'd like to sleep with the red star." "Oh, that's
all right," said the first one, "I would like to sleep with the
white star. He's the younger; the red is the older." Then
the two girls fell asleep. When they awoke, they found themselves in another world, the star world. There were four of
them there, the two girls and the two stars who had become men.
The white star was very, very old and was grey-headed, while
the younger was red-headed. He was the red star. The girls
stayed a long time in this star world, and the one who had
chosen the white star was very sorry, for he was so old.

There was an old woman up in this world who sat over a hole
in the sky,[28] and, whenever she moved, she showed them the hole
and said, "That's where you came from." They looked down
through and saw their people playing down below, and then the
girls grew very sorry and very homesick. One evening, near
sunset, the old woman moved a little way from the hole.

The younger girl heard the noise of the *mitewin* down below.
When it was almost daylight, the old woman sat over the hole

again and the noise of *mitewin* stopped; it was her spirit that made the noise. She was the guardian of the *mitewin*.

One morning the old woman told the girls, "If you want to go down where you came from, we will let you down, but get to work and gather roots to make a string-made rope, twisted. The two of you make coils of rope as high as your heads when you are sitting. Two coils will be enough." The girls worked for days until they had accomplished this. They made plenty of rope and tied it to a big basket.[194] They then got into the basket and the people of the star world lowered them down. They descended right into an Eagle's nest, but the people above thought the girls were on the ground and stopped lowering them. They were obliged to stay in the nest, because they could do nothing to help themselves.

Said one, "We'll have to stay here until some one comes to get us." Bear passed by. The girls cried out, "Bear, come and get us. You are going to get married sometime. Now is your chance!" Bear thought, "They are not very good-looking women." He pretended to climb up and then said, "I can't climb up any further." And he went away, for the girls did n't suit him. Next came Lynx. The girls cried out again, "Lynx, come up and get us. You will go after women some day!" Lynx answered, "I can't, for I have no claws," and he went away. Then an ugly-looking man, Wolverine, passed and the girls spoke to him. "Hey, wolverine, come and get us." Wolverine started to climb up, for he thought it a very fortunate thing to have these women and was very glad. When he reached them, they placed their hair ribbons in the nest.[195] Then Wolverine agreed to take one girl at a time, so he took the first one down and went back for the next. Then Wolverine went away with his two wives and enjoyed himself greatly, as he was ugly and nobody else would have him. They went far into the woods, and then they sat down and began to talk. "Oh!" cried one of the girls, "I forgot my hair ribbon." Then Wolverine said, "I will run back for it." And he started off to get the hair ribbons. Then the girls hid and told the trees, whenever Wolverine should come back and whistle for them, to answer him by whistling.[196] Wolverine soon returned and began to whistle for his wives, and the trees all around him whistled in answer. Wolverine, realizing that he had been tricked, gave up the search and departed very angry.

LI. THE STAR HUSBAND [193]

TYPE II: THE GIRL ENTICED TO THE SKY

(ARAPAHO: Dorsey and Kroeber, *Field Museum: Anthropological Series*, v, 330, No. 135)

There was a camp-circle. A party of women went out after some wood for the fire. One of them saw a porcupine near a cottonwood tree and informed her companions of the fact. The porcupine ran around the tree, finally climbing it, whereupon the woman tried to hit the animal, but he dodged from one side of the trunk of the tree to the other, for protection. At length one of the women started to climb the tree to catch the porcupine, but it ever stopped just beyond her reach. She even tried to reach it with a stick, but with each effort it went a little higher. "Well!" said she, "I am climbing to catch the porcupine, for I want those quills, and if necessary I will go to the top."

When porcupine had reached the top of the tree the woman was still climbing, although the cottonwood was dangerous and the branches were waving to and fro; but as she approached the top and was about to lay hands upon the porcupine, the tree suddenly lengthened,[200] when the porcupine resumed his climbing. Looking down, she saw her friends looking up at her, and beckoning her to come down; but having passed under the influence of the porcupine and fearful for the great distance between herself and the ground, she continued to climb, until she became the merest speck to those looking up from below, and with the porcupine she finally reached the sky.[118]

The porcupine took the woman into the camp-circle where his father and mother lived. The folks welcomed her arrival and furnished her with the very best kind of accommodation. The lodge was then put up for them to live in. The porcupine was very industrious and of course the old folks were well supplied with hides and food.

One day she decided to save all the sinew from the buffalo, at the same time doing work on buffalo robes and other things with it, in order to avoid all suspicion on the part of her husband and the old folks, as to why she was saving the sinew. Thus she continued to save a portion of the sinew from each beef brought in by her husband, until she had a supply suitable for her purpose. One day her husband cautioned her, that while in search of roots, wild turnips and other herbs, she should not dig[197] and that should she use the digging stick, she should not dig too deep, and that she should go home early when out for a walk. The husband was constantly bringing in the beef and hide, in order that he might keep his wife at work at home all the time. But she was a good worker and soon finished what was required for them.

Seeing that she had done considerable work, one day she started out in search of hog potatoes, and carried with her the digging stick. She ran to a thick patch and kept digging away to fill her bag. She accidentally struck a hole,[28] which surprised her very much, and so she stooped down and looked in and through the hole, seeing below, a green earth with a camp-circle on it. After questioning herself and recognizing the camp-circle below, she carefully covered the spot and marked it. She took the bag and went to her own tipi, giving the folks some of the hog potatoes. The old folks were pleased and ate the hog potatoes to satisfy their daughter-in-law. The husband returned home too, bringing in beef and hides.

Early one morning the husband started off for more beef and hides, telling his wife to be careful about herself. After he was gone, she took the digging stick and the sinew she had to the place where she struck the hole. When she got to the hole, she sat down and began tying string, so as to make the sinew long enough to reach the bottom. She then opened the hole and laid the digging stick across the hole which she had dug, and tied one of the sinew strings in the center of this stick, and then also fastened herself to the end of the lariat.[194] She gradually loosened the sinew lariat as she let herself down, finally finding herself suspended above the top of the tree which she had climbed, but not near enough so that she could possibly reach it.

When the husband missed her, he scolded the old people for not watching their daughter-in-law. He began to look for her in the direction in which she usually started off, but found no fresh tracks, though he kept traveling until he tracked her to the digging stick which was lying across the hole. The husband stooped down and looked into this hole and saw his wife suspended from this stick by means of a sinew lariat or string. "Well, the only way to do is to see her touch the bottom," said he. So he looked around and found a circular stone two or three inches thick, and brought it to the place. Again he continued, "I want this stone to light right on top of her head," and he dropped the stone carefully along the sinew string, and it struck the top of her head and broke her off and landed her safe on the ground. She took up the stone and went to the camp-circle. This is the way the woman returned.[198]

LII. THE STRETCHING TREE [199]

(CHILCOTIN: Farrand, *Jesup North Pacific Expedition*, ii, 29, No. 13)

Once an old man and a young man and two women lived together. The two women were the young man's wives. Now, the young man needed some feathers for his arrows; and one day, seeing a hawk's nest in a high tree, he started to climb to it to get the hawk-feathers. Now, the old man was jealous of the young man, and had followed him. And when he saw him climbing the tree, he used his magic and made the tree grow higher and higher,[200] and at the same time peeled off all the bark so that the trunk was slippery; and as the young man was naked, he could not come down, but had to remain in the top of the tree. When the young man failed to appear that night, the old man said he wished to move camp, and that the women were to come with him. And the next morning they started. Now, one of the women liked the old man; but the other one, who had a baby, disliked him, and when they camped for the night, she would take her baby, and make a fire for herself outside the camp and away from the old man. So they went on for several days.

All this time the young man staid up in the tree; and as it was cold and he had no clothes, he took his hair, which was very long, and wove feathers in it, and so made a blanket to protect himself. The little birds who built their nests in the sticks of the hawk's nest tried their best to carry him down to the ground, but could not lift him, and so he staid on.

Finally one day he saw coming, a long way off, an old woman bent over, and with a stick in each hand. She came to the bottom of the tree where the young man was, and began to climb, and climbed until she reached the young man, and then she turned out to be Spider. Then Spider spun a web for him,[201] and of the web the young man made a rope and so reached the ground.

When he came back to his camp, he found it deserted, but discovered the trail of the fugitives, and started to follow. He trailed them a long time, and finally saw them in the distance. Now, the woman who did not like the old man was following behind with her little boy; and the child, looking back, saw his father and cried out, "Why, there is my father!" But the mother replied, "What do you mean? Your father has been dead a long time." But looking back herself, she saw her husband, and waited for him to come up, and they stopped together.

Then she told her husband all that had happened, how the old man had wished to take both his wives, and how she would not have him, but how the other one took him. Now, the woman was carrying a large basket, and she put her husband into it and covered him up. When they reached the old man's camp she put the basket down close to the fire; but the old man took it and placed it some distance away. The woman brought it back and as she did so the young man sprang out and struck the old man and killed him. Then he killed his faithless wife; and taking the other woman, who was true, and the little boy, they went back to their old home together.

LIII. THE ARROW CHAIN [202]

(TLINGIT: Swanton, *Bulletin of the Bureau of American Ethnology*, xxxix, 209, No. 56)

Two very high-caste boys were chums. The father of one was town chief and had his house in the middle of the village, but the house of the other boy's father stood at one end. These boys would go alternately to each other's houses and make great quantities of arrows which they would play with until all were broken up.

One time both of the boys made a great quantity of arrows to see which could have the more. Just back of their village was a hill on the top of which was a smooth grassy place claimed by the boys as their playground, and on a certain fine, moonlight night they started thither. As they were going along the lesser chief's son, who was ahead, said, "Look here, friend. Look at that moon. Don't you think that the shape of that moon is the same as that of my mother's labret and that the size is the same, too?" The other answered, "Don't: You must not talk that way of the moon."

Then suddenly it became very dark about them and presently the head chief's son saw a ring about them just like a rainbow. When it disappeared his companion was gone. He called and called to him but did not get any answer and did not see him. He thought, "He must have run up the hill to get away from that rainbow." He looked up and saw the moon in the sky. Then he climbed the hill, and looked about, but his friend was not there. Now he thought, "Well! the moon must have gone up with him. That circular rainbow must have been the moon."

The boy thus left alone sat down and cried, after which he began to try the bows. He put strings on them one after the other and tried them, but every one broke. He broke all of his own bows and all of his his chum's except one which was made of very hard wood. He thought, "Now I am going to shoot that star next to the moon." In that spot was a large and very bright one. He shot an arrow at this star and sat down to watch, when, sure enough, the star darkened. Now he began shooting at that star from the big piles of arrows he and his chum had made, and he was encouraged by seeing that the arrows did not come back. After he had shot for some time he saw something hanging down very near him and, when he shot up another arrow, it stuck to this. The next did likewise, and at last the chain of arrows [203] reached him. He put a last one on to complete it.

Now the youth felt badly for the loss of his friend and, lying down under the arrow chain, he went to sleep. After a while he awoke, found himself sleeping on that hill, remembered the arrows he had shot away, and looked up. Instead of the arrows there was a long ladder [204] reaching right down to him. He arose and looked so as to make sure. Then he determined to ascend. First, however, he took various kinds of bushes and stuck them into the knot of hair he wore on his head. He climbed up his ladder all day and camped at nightfall upon it, resuming his journey the following morning. When he awoke early on the second morning his head felt very heavy. Then he seized the salmon berry bush that was in his hair, pulled it out, and found it was loaded with berries. After he had eaten the berries off, he stuck the branch back into his hair and felt very much strengthened. About noon of the same day he again felt hungry, and again his head was heavy, so he pulled out a bush from the other side of his head and it was loaded with blue huckleberries. It was already summer there in the sky. That was why he was getting berries. When he resumed his journey next morning his head did not feel heavy until noon. At that time he pulled out the bush at the back of his head and found it loaded with red huckleberries.

By the time he had reached the top [118] the boy was very tired. He looked round and saw a large lake. Then he gathered some soft brush and some moss and lay down to sleep. But, while he slept, some person came to him and shook him saying, "Get up. I am after you." He awoke and looked around but saw no one. Then he rolled over and pretended to go to sleep again but looked out through his eyelashes. By and by he saw a very small but handsome girl coming along. Her skin clothes were very clean and neat, and her leggings were ornamented with porcupine quills. Just as she reached out to shake him he said, "I have seen you already."

Now the girl stood still and said, "I have come after you. My grandmother has sent me to bring you to her house." So he went with her, and they came to a very small house in which was an old woman. The old woman said, "What is it you came way up here after, my grandson?" and the boy answered, "On account of my playmate who was taken up hither." "Oh!" answered the old woman, "He is next door, only a short distance away. I can hear him crying every day. He is in the moon's house."

Then the old woman began to give him food. She would put her hand up to her mouth, and a salmon or whatever she was going to give would make its appearance. After the salmon she gave him berries and then meat, for she knew that he was hungry from his long journey. After that she gave him a spruce cone, a rose bush, a piece of devil's club, and a small piece of whetstone to take along.

As the boy was going toward the moon's house with all of these things he heard his playmate screaming with pain. He had been put up on a high place near the smoke hole, so, when his rescuer came to it, he climbed on top, and, reaching down through the smoke hole, pulled him out. He said, "My friend, come. I am here to help you." Putting the spruce cone down where the boy had been, he told it to imitate his cries, and he and his chum ran away.[196]

After a while, however, the cone dropped from the place where it has been put, and the people discovered that their captive had escaped. Then the moon started in pursuit. When the head chief's son discovered this, he threw behind them the devil's club he had received from the old woman, and a patch of devil's club arose which the moon had so much trouble in getting through that they gained rapidly on him.[205] When the moon again approached, the head chief's son threw back the rose bushes, and such a thicket of roses grew there that the moon was again delayed. When he approached them once more, they threw back the grindstone, and it became a high cliff from which the moon kept rolling back. It is on account of this cliff that people can say things about the moon nowadays with impunity. When the boys reached the old woman's house they were very glad to see each other, for before this they had not had time to speak.

The old woman gave them something to eat, and, when they were through, she said to the rescuer, "Go and lie down at the place where you lay when you first came up. Don't think of anything but the playground you used to have." They went there and lay down, but after some time the boy who had first been captured thought of the old woman's house and immediately they found themselves there. Then the old woman said, "Go back and do not think of me any more. Lie there and think of nothing but the place where you used to play." They did so, and, when they awoke, they were lying on their playground at the foot of the ladder.

As the boys lay in that place they heard a drum beating in the head chief's house, where a death feast was being held for them, and the head chief's son said, "Let us go," but the other answered, "No, let us wait here until that feast is over." Afterward the boys went down and watched the people come out with their faces all blackened. They stood at a corner, but, as this dance is always given in the evening, they were not seen.

Then the head chief's son thought, "I wish my younger brother would come out," and sure enough, after all of the other people had gone, his younger brother came out. He called to his brother saying, "Come here. It is I," but the child was afraid and ran into the house instead. Then the child said to his mother, "My brother and his friend are out here." "Why do you talk like that?" asked his mother. "Don't you know that your brother died some time ago?" And she became very angry. The child, however, persisted, saying, "I know his voice, and I know him." His mother was now very much disturbed, so the boy said, "I am going to go out and bring in a piece of his shirt." "Go and do so," said his mother. "Then I will believe you."

When the boy at last brought in a piece of his brother's shirt his mother was convinced, and they sent word into all of the houses, first of all into that of the second boy's parents, but they kept both with them so that his parents could come there and rejoice over him. All of the other people in that village also came to see them.

LIV. MUDJIKIWIS [206]

(PLAINS CREE: Skinner, *Journal of American Folk-Lore*, xxix, 353, No. 3)

ONCE upon a time the Indians were camping. They had ten lodges. There were ten of them; and the eldest brother, Mudjikiwis, was sitting in the doorway. It was winter, and all the Indians had their side-bags on; and every day they went off and hunted in the direction which they faced as they sat. Mudjikiwis always took the lead, and the others followed. Once when he came home to his camp, he saw smoke just as he crossed the last hill. When he approached the lodge, he saw a pile of wood neatly stacked by the door. He himself had always cooked the dinner; and when he saw it ready, he was very glad. "There is surely a girl here!" he thought. "There must be some one who has done this." [207]

He had many brothers younger than himself. "Maybe some one is trying to marry them, or some girl wants me!"

When he arrived at the lodge, he saw a girl's pigeon-toed tracks, and he was delighted. "It *is* a girl!" he cried, and he rushed in to see her, but there was no one there. The fire was just started, the meat cooked and ready, and water had been drawn. Some one had just finished work when he came. There were even ten pairs of moccasins hanging up. "Now, at last, there is some one to sew for us! Surely one of us will get married!" he thought, and he also thought that he would be the fortunate one. He did not touch anything, but left everything as he had found it for his brothers to see.

After a while the brother next to him in age came in. He looked up and saw all the moccasins, and he too was very glad. Then Mudjikiwis said, "I do not know which of us is going to be married. A girl has just left here, but I cannot tell who she is, and there are ten of us. One of us is loved by some one!" They soon were joined by the third, and then by the fourth brother, and the fire was out by that time. The youngest brother was the most handsome one of the family. "If one of us should marry, Mudjikiwis, we shall have to hunt hard and not let our sister-in-law hunger or be in need," he said. "I shall be very glad if we have a sister-in-law. Don't let her chop wood; she cannot attend to all of us. We just want her to cook and mend our clothes."

At night they were all crying, "*He, he, he!*" until dark came, because they were so glad. "I cannot attend to all my brothers, and I do not need to do so any more!" cried Mudjikiwis.

The next day nine went off, and left the youngest brother on guard to see the girl. Mudjikiwis came back first, and found that the tenth boy had not been taken. "Oh, well! leave our ninth brother next time," he said. "Then we will try it once more with our eighth brother."

Three of them then kept house in succession, but the woman did not come. They then left the fifth one, and said, "If no one comes, make dinner for us yourself." Soon after they had left, some one came along making a noise like a rattle, for she had bells on her leggings.

"Oh, she shall not know me!" said the youth. "I shall be a bit of eagle-down," [208] and he flew up between the canvas and the poles of the lodge. Presently the girl entered. She had very long hair, and was very pretty. She took the axe and went out to cut wood, and soon brought in four armfuls. Then she made the fire, took down the kettles, and prepared dinner. When she had done so she melted some snow, took another armful of wood, and started another fire. After she had finished she called to the youth to come down from his hiding-place. "Maybe you think I don't know you are up there," she said. So he came down and took a seat with her by the fire.

When Mudjikiwis came home, he saw another big pile of wood. When he came near, he cried, "*He, he, he!*" to show that he was well pleased. "I could not attend to the needs of my brothers," he shouted, "I could not cook for them, and I could not provide my relatives with moccasins!" He entered the door and bent down, for Mudjikiwis had on a fisher-skin head-band with an eagle-quill thrust in behind. As he came in, he saw a pretty girl sitting there. When he sat down, he said, "*Hai, hai, hai!* The girl is sitting like her mother." He pulled off his shoes and threw them to his youngest brother, and received a fine pair of moccasins from his sister-in-law. He was delighted, and cried, "*Hai, hai, hai!*" Soon all the other brothers came back, all nine of them, and each received new moccasins.

Mudjikiwis said, "I have already advised you. Do not let our sister-in-law chop wood or do any hard work. Hunt well, and do not let her be hungry." Morning came, and Mudjikiwis was already half in love with his sister-in-law. He started out, pretending that he was going to hunt, but he only went over a hill and stopped there. Then he wrapped his blanket around himself. It was winter, and he took some mud from under the snow and rubbed it over his forehead and on his hat-band. He had his ball-headed club with him, which had two eyes that winked constantly. Soon he saw his sister-in-law, who came out to chop wood. He went to speak to her, but the girl had disappeared. Soon she came back. There was one pile of wood here, and one there. Mudjikiwis stopped at the one to the west. He had his bow, his arrows, and his club with him. He held his club on the left arm, and his bow and arrow on the right arm, folded his arms across his breast, and was smiling at her when she came up. "O my brother-in-law! I don't want to do that," she cried.

Then Mudjikiwis was angry because she scorned him. He took an arrow and shot her in the leg, and fled off to hunt. That night he returned late, last of all. As he came close to the lodge, he called out, "*Yoha, yoha!* what is wrong with you? You have done some kind of mischief. Why is there no wood for our sister-in-law?" He went in. "What is wrong with our sister-in-law, that she is not home?" he demanded. His brother then said, "Why are you so late? You used to be the first one here."

Mudjikiwis would not speak in reply. The married brother came in last. The young brother was tired of waiting, and asked each, "You did not see your sister-in-law, did you?" The others replied, "Mudjikiwis came very late. He never did so before."

"I shall track my wife," said the husband. So he set off in pursuit of her. He tracked her, and found that she had brought one load of wood. Her second trail ended at a little lodge of willows that she had made, and where she was. She cried to him, "Do not come here! Your brother Mudjikiwis has shot me. I told him I did not want to receive him, and then he shot me down. Do not come here. You will see me on the fourth night. If you want to give me food, put it outside the door and go away, and I shall get it."

Her husband went home, as she commanded. After that the youth would bring her food, after hunting, every night. "It is well. Even though our brother shot my wife, I shall forgive him, if I can only see her after four nights," he said. The third night he could hardly stay away, he wanted to see her so badly. The fourth day at dawn he went to the lodge; and as he drew near, she cried, "Do not come!" but he went in, anyway, and saw her there. "I told you not to come, but you could not restrain yourself.²⁰⁹ When your brothers could not attend to themselves, I wished to help them," she cried. So he went home satisfied, since he had seen her. They breakfasted, and he started out again with food for her. She had gone out, for he found her tracks, little steps, dabbled with blood. Then he went back home, and said to his brothers, "My brothers, I am going to go after my wife."

He dressed, and followed her footprints. Sometimes he ran, and at sunset he wanted to camp. So he killed a rabbit; and as he came out of the brush, he saw a lodge. "*He*, my grandchild!" called a voice, "You are thinking of following your wife. She passed here at dawn. Come in and sit down! Here is where she sat before you." He entered, and found an old woman, who told him to sit in the same place where his wife had sat. He gave her the rabbit he had shot, as he was really hungry. "Oh, my grandchild must be very hungry!" she cried, "so I shall cook for him," said the old crone. Her kettle was no larger than a thimble. She put in one morsel of meat and one little berry. The youth thought that was a very small allowance, when he was really hungry.

"O my grandchild!" the old woman said aloud in answer to his thoughts, "no one has ever eaten all my kettle holds. You are wrong if you think you won't get enough of this."

But he still thought so, and did not believe her. After the food was cooked, she said, "Eat, *nosis!*" and gave him a spoon. He took out the piece of meat and the berry; but when he had eaten it, the kettle was still full.[210] He did this many times over. When he had finished, he had not eaten it all, yet he had enough. Then the grandmother told him that he had married one of ten sisters.

"They are not real people," she said, "they are from way up in the skies. They have ten brothers. There are three more of your grandmothers on the road where you are going. Each will tell you to go back, as I advised you; but if you insist, I will give you two bones to help you climb over the mountains."

Now, this old woman was really a moose, and not a human grandmother at all.[40] "If you get into difficulties, you must cry, 'Where is my grandmother?' and use these two front shin-bones of the moose that I gave you." He slept there, and in the morning she gave him breakfast from the same kettle. When he was through she said, "Do not walk fast. Even if you rest on the way, you will reach your next grandmother in the evening. If you walk as fast as you can, you will get there at night."

He followed the trail as fast as he could, for he did not believe his grandmother. In the evening he killed a rabbit; and when he came out of the brush, there stood another lonely lodge, as before.

"O my grandchild! there is room in here for you to come in," cried a voice. "Your wife passed here early yesterday morning." Yet he had travelled two days. "She came in here!"

The old woman cooked for him in the same way as his other grandmother had done.[211] Again he did not believe in her kettle, for he had already forgotten about his first grandmother. This grandmother was older than the first one whom he had left, and who was the youngest of the four grandmothers he was to meet. They were all sisters. "Why did you not believe my sister when she told you to go slowly? When you go fast, you make the trail longer. *Hau, nosis!* it is a difficult country where you are going," she cried. She gave him a squirrel-skin, saying, "Use this, *nosis*, whenever you are in difficulties. 'Where is my grandmother?' you shall say. This is what makes everything easy. You will cry, and you will throw it away. You will not leave me till the morning."

So very early next day he started off. He went very slowly; and in a few minutes it was night, and he killed another rabbit. When he came out of the brush, he saw another lodge, a little nearer than the others, and less ragged. The old woman said to him, "Your wife passed here the same morning that she left up there"; and this grandmother made supper for him, as the others had done. This time the food was corn. "*Nosis*, your last grandmother, who is my sister, will give you good advice. Your wife has had a child already. Go very slowly, and you will reach there at night; it is not far from here. It is a very difficult country where you are going. Maybe you will not be able to get there." She gave him a stuffed frog and some glue. "Whenever the mountains are too steep for you to climb, cry, 'Where is my grandmother?' put glue on your hands, and climb, and you will stick to the rocks. When you reach your next grandmother, she will advise you well. Your child is a little boy."

In the morning he had breakfast, and continued on the trail. He went on slowly, and it was soon night, and he killed another rabbit. When he reached the next lodge, nearer than all the rest, his grandmother said, "They have been saying you would be here after your wife; she passed here four days ago at dawn."

The youth entered the tent, and found that this grandmother was a fine young girl in appearance. She said, "To-morrow at noon your wife is going to be married, and the young men will all sit in a circle and pass your child around. The man upon whom he urinates will be known as his father,[212] and she will marry him." The old woman took off her belt, rolled it up nicely, and gave it to him. "This is the last one that you will use," she said, "When you are in trouble, cry out, 'Where is my grandmother?' and throw the belt out, and it will stick up there, so you can climb up to the top. Before noon you will reach a perpendicular precipice like a wall. Your wife is not of our people. She is one of the Thunderers."[213]

That night the youth camped there. In the morning he had food. "If you manage to climb the mountain somehow," his grandmother said to him before he started, "you will cross the hill and see a steep slope, and there you will find a nest. There is one egg in it. That is a Thunderer's nest. As you come down, you will strike the last difficult place. There is a large log across a river. The river is very deep, and the log revolves constantly. There you will find a big camp, headed by your father-in-law, who owns everything there. There is one old woman just on this side. She is one of us sisters; she is the second oldest of us. You will see bones strewn about when you get there. Many young men go there when they are looking for their wives, and their bones you will see lying about. The Thunderer destroys everything. Some have been cut in halves when they tried to get over the cut-knife mountain."

When the youth came to the mountain, he took first the two bones, and cried, "O grandmother! where are you?" and as he cried, she called from far off, "*He, nosis*, do not get into trouble!" He drove the bones into the mountain and climbed up hand over hand, driving them in as he climbed. The bones pierced the rock. When he looked back, he saw that he was far up. He continued until the bones began to grow short, and at last he had to stop. Then he took out the squirrel-hide, called upon his grandmother for help, and threw the skin ahead. He went up in the air following it. All at once he stopped, and his nails wore out on the rock as he slipped back. Then he took the glue out of its bundle. He cried for his grandmother, and heard her answer. She had told him that he would find a hollow at one place, and there he rested on a ledge when his glue gave out. Then he called for his next grandmother, heard her answer, and cast out his belt, unrolling it. Then he climbed up the sharp summit. He felt of the edge, which was very sharp indeed. Then he became a piece of eagle-down. "The eagle-down loved me once. I shall be it, and blow over the ledge," he cried.

When he got across, he saw the Thunderer's nest and the two Thunderers and their egg. He found a trail from there on, until he came to the rolling log that lay across the deep river. Then he became down again, and blew across; and though many others had been drowned there, he crossed alive. He went on, and at last saw a small, low lodge with a little stone beside it. His last grandmother had told him to enter, as this was the abode of one of her sisters. So he went in.

"*Ha, ha, ha, nosis!*" she cried, "They said a long time ago that you were following your wife. She is to be married right now." — "Yes," he said. The marriage was to be in a lodge. He went there, peeped in, and a man saw him, who said, "Are you coming in? Our chief says he will pass the child about, and he on whose breast it urinates shall marry its mother."

So he went in. The girl saw him, and told her mother. "Oh, that is the one I married."

When he arrived there, Mudjikiwis (not the youth's brother, but another one, a Thunderer) was there too. They took the child, and one man passed it. Mudjikiwis, the Thunderer, held some water in his mouth. He seized the child, crying, "Come here, *nosis!*" and spat the water over himself; but, when he tried to claim the child, all the others laughed, as they had seen his trick. When the child's real father took it up, it urinated on him. Then all went out. The chief said, "Do not let my son-in-law walk about, because he is really tired. He shall not walk for ten days."

His father-in-law would go off all day. Hanging in the lodge the youth saw his brother's arrow, with which his wife had been shot. The father-in-law would burn sweet-grass for the arrow at the rare intervals when he came back, for he would be off for days at a time. On the fifth night the youth felt rested, and could walk a little. Then he asked his wife, "Why does your father smoke that arrow?" and she answered, "Oh, we never see those things up here. It is from below, and he thinks highly of it; therefore he does so."

On the sixth night he was able to walk around in the brush; and he came to a spring, where he found, on the surface of the water, a rusty stain with which he painted his face. He returned, and, as he was entering, his father-in-law cried, "Oh, that is why I want a son-in-law that is a human being! Where did he kill that bear? He is covered with blood. Go and dress it," he ordered. The youth was frightened, as he had not seen any bear at all. "You people that live below," his wife said, "call them Giant Panthers. Show your brothers-in-law where it is." The youth took his brother-in-law to the spring. "Here is where I found the Panther," he said.

The ten Thunderers came up and struck the spring, and killed something there. After that the youth looked for springs all the time, and it came to pass that he found a number. One day he asked his wife, "Why does your father go away for whole days at a time?" and his wife said, "There is a large lake up here, and he hunts for fish there. He kills one every day, seldom two. He is the only one that can kill them."

The next morning the youth went to the lake, and found his father-in-law sitting by the shore fishing. The old man had a peculiar spear, which was forked at the end. The youth took it, and put barbs on it, so that the old man was able to catch a number of fish quickly. Then they went home. When they arrived, his father-in-law said, "My son-in-law has taken many of them. I myself can only kill one, and sometimes two."

So he told all the people to go and get fish and eat them freely. On the following day, the young man, according to his mother-in-law's wish, took his wife to fish. They took many fish, and carried them home. The father-in-law knew, before they returned, that they had caught many.

The old man had had a dream. When he saw how the youth prepared the spear which his daughter had given him, he said, referring to his dream, "My dream was wrong, I thought the youngest of the ten liked me the best. I made the spear in the way I saw it, not as this one has shown me. It is due to my dream that it is wrong. Your nine brothers are having a hard time. Now, my sons, your sisters are going away soon to be married."

For nine nights the youth saw a dim light at a distance. The father-in-law said to him, "Do not go there, for a powerful being lives there." The tenth night, however, the youth disobeyed this injunction. When he reached there, he saw a tall tree, and a huge porcupine that was burrowing at the foot of the tree. The porcupine struck the tree, and tried to kill it by shooting its quills into it. After the porcupine had shot off all its quills, the youth knocked it on the head, took two long quills from the tree, and carried them home. Even before he got there, his father-in-law knew what had happened. They were delighted, for they said that the porcupine would kill the Thunderers when they tried to attack it. The father-in-law went out, and called to his sons to go and dress the porcupine that the youth had killed. The latter gave the two quills to his wife, though his father-in-law wanted them. The father-in-law said, "My children, this porcupine killed all our friends when they went to war against it. My sons-in-law below are miserable and lonely."

The eldest of the daughters, who was called Mudjikiskwe'wic, was delighted at the news. "You will marry the oldest one, Mudjikiwis," she was told. They were all to be married in order, the eldest girl to the eldest brother, the youngest to the youngest one. The old man said, "Mudjikiskwe'wic shall take her brother-in-law with her when she goes down to the earth." The young women went down. Sh-swsh! went Mudjikiskwe'wic (the girl) with her dress. They reached the steep place, and the married woman said to her husband that they would fly around. "If you do not catch me when I fly past, you will be killed here." The women went off a little ways, and a heavy thunderstorm arose, big black clouds and lightning, yet he saw Mudjikiskwe'-wic in it. She was green, and so was the sun; and as they passed she shouted once, then again a little nearer, and again close by. Then he jumped off and caught her by the back. He closed his eyes [217] as he did so, and did not open them until the Thunderer wife said, "Now let go!" Then he found himself at home. He left the girls behind, and went to the lodge and opened the door a little.

As soon as he was inside, he said, "My brothers, I am here!" They were lying in the ashes around the fire. "The Canada Jays always make me angry when they say that," they retorted, and they threw a handful of ashes towards the door. "My brothers, I am coming!" he said again. "Ah! that is what the Crows say to make us angry," retorted the rest, and they threw ashes towards the door. "My brothers, I am coming!" he declared. "Ah! that is what the Chickadees say to make us angry," cried they, and threw ashes once more. Then for the fourth time, he cried, "My brothers, get up!" Then Mudjikiwis cried, "Look up! See who it is! They never say that four times!"

They looked up and their eyes were swollen from weeping on account of their brother. They were covered with ashes. When they opened their eyes, they saw their fifth brother restored. "Arise, wash your faces, and fix camp!" said he. "I have brought sisters-in-law with me."

Mudjikiwis was glad to hear this, and he and the others began to decorate themselves. They took white earth from crawfish-holes, and painted their faces with it. Mudjikiwis seized his winking war-club,[214] and they made the lodge larger by spreading the poles. Then the fifth brother called the sisters-in-law, and they all came in. The fifth son told Mudjikiskwe'-wic that the youngest of the sisters should come in first, she herself last, although it would have been proper for the eldest brother to receive his wife first. "Do not come in till I call you, saying, 'Now, come! my brothers are tired waiting.'" Mudjikiskwe'wic promised to obey.

Mudjikiwis sat with his head in his hands, and peeped at each girl. He saw them sit by his brothers, until every one but he was furnished with a wife. Then there was a pause. Mudjikiwis began to weep, and he sniffed audibly. At last the fifth brother had pity on him, and called the girl in. She came in with a swishing sound of rustling clothing. Then Mudjikiwis was very glad.

"What shall we feed them on?" said one. "Let me see!" said Mudjikiwis, and he took his winking club and went out, and clubbed a bear right there. "O wife! we shall have a meal of bear-meat!" he cried. Mudjikiskwe'wic replied, "Oh, you are hunting my younger brother!" — "Oh, I did not mean to kill my brother-in-law," retorted the other.

And they are married today, and live where the sun does not shine.

LV. ORPHEUS [215]

(Cherokee: Mooney, *Report of the Bureau of American Ethnology,*
xix, 252, No. 5)

The Sun lived on the other side of the sky vault, but her daughter lived in the middle of the sky, directly above the earth, and every day as the Sun was climbing along the sky arch to the west she used to stop at her daughter's house for dinner.

Now, the Sun hated the people on the earth, because they could never look straight at her without screwing up their faces. She said to her brother, the Moon,[6] "My grandchildren are ugly; they grin all over their faces when they look at me." But the Moon said, "I like my younger brothers; I think they are very handsome" — because they always smiled pleasantly when they saw him in the sky at night, for his rays were milder.

The Sun was jealous and planned to kill all the people; so every day when she got near her daughter's house she sent down such sultry rays that there was a great fever and the people died by hundreds, until everyone had lost some friend and there was fear that no one would be left. They went for help to the Little Men, who said the only way to save themselves was to kill the Sun.

The Little Men made medicine and changed two men to snakes, the Spreading-adder and the Copperhead, and sent them to watch near the door of the daughter of the Sun to bite the old Sun when she came next day. They went together and hid near the house until the Sun came, but when the Spreading-adder was about to spring, the bright light blinded him and he could only spit out yellow slime, as he does to this day when he tries to bite. She called him a nasty thing and went by into the house, and the Copperhead crawled off without trying to do anything.

So the people still died from the heat, and they went to the Little Men a second time for help. The Little Men made medicine again and changed one man into a great Uktena and another into the Rattlesnake and sent them to watch near the house and kill the old Sun when she came for dinner. They make the Uktena very large, with horns on his head, and every-one thought he would be sure to do the work, but the Rattle-snake was so quick and eager that he got ahead and coiled up just outside the house, and when the Sun's daughter opened the door to look out for her mother, he sprang up and bit her and she fell dead in the doorway. He forgot to wait for the old Sun, but went back to the people, and the Uktena was so very angry that he went back, too. Since then we pray to the rattlesnake and do not kill him, because he is kind and never tries to bite if we do not disturb him. The Uktena grew angrier all the time and very dangerous, so that if he even looked at a man, that man's family would die. After a long time the people held a council and decided that he was too dangerous to be with them, so they sent him up to Galunlati, and he is there now. The Spreading-adder, the Copperhead, the Rattlesnake, and the Uktena were all men.

When the Sun found her daughter dead, she went into the house and grieved, and the people did not die any more, but now the world was dark all the time, because the Sun would not come out. They went again to the Little Men, and these told them that if they wanted the Sun to come out again they must bring back her daughter from Tsusginai, the Ghost country, in Usunhiyi, the Darkening land in the west. They chose seven men to go, and gave each a sourwood rod a hand-breadth long. The Little Men told them they must take a box with them, and when they got to Tsusginai they would find all the ghosts at a dance. They must stand outside the circle, and when the young woman passed in the dance they must strike her with the rods and she would fall to the ground. Then they must put her into the box and bring her back to her mother, but they must be very sure not to open the box, even a little way, until they were home again.

They took the rods and a box and traveled seven days to the west until they came to the Darkening land.[216] There were a great many people there, and they were having a dance just as if they were at home in the settlements. The young woman was in the outside circle, and as she swung around to where the seven men were standing, one struck her with his rod and she turned her head and saw him. As she came around the second time another touched her with his rod, and then another and another, until at the seventh round she fell out of the ring, and they put her into the box and closed the lid fast. The other ghosts seemed never to notice what had happened.

They took up the box and started home toward the east. In a little while the girl came to life again and begged to be let out of the box, but they made no answer and went on. Soon she called again and she said she was hungry, but still they made no answer and went on. After another while she spoke again and called for a drink and pleaded so that it was very hard to listen to her, but the men who carried the box said nothing and still went on. When at last they were very near home, she called again and begged them to raise the lid just a little, because she was smothering. They were afraid she was really dying now, so they lifted the lid a little to give her air, but as they did so there was a fluttering sound inside and something flew past them into the thicket and they heard a redbird cry, "kwish! kwish! kwish!" in the bushes. They shut down the lid and went on again to the settlements, but when they got there and opened the box it was empty.

So we know the Redbird is the daughter of the Sun, and if the men had kept the box closed, as the Little Men told them to do, they would have brought her home safely,[217] and we could bring back our other friends also from the Ghost country, but now when they die we can never bring them back.[51]

The Sun had been glad when they started to the Ghost country, but when they came back without her daughter she grieved and cried, "My daughter, my daughter," and wept until her tears made a flood upon the earth,[218] and the people were afraid the world would be drowned. They held another council, and sent their handsomest young men and women to amuse her so that she would stop crying. They danced before the Sun and sang their best songs, but for a long time she kept her face covered and paid no attention, until at last the drummer suddenly changed the song, when she lifted up her face, and was so pleased at the sight that she forgot her grief and smiled.

LVI. THE VISIT TO CHIEF ECHO [219]

(TSIMSHIAN: Boas, *Report of the Bureau of American Ethnology*, xxxi, 85)

Txä'msem * remained sitting there, thinking quietly how many hard things he had done among men; still his needs were not satisfied. At last he made up his mind to try to go again to the people in order to get something to eat, for he was a great eater. [220] He went to a lonely place, and was very anxious to find some people in the woods. Soon he came to a great plain. No trees were to be seen, just grass and flowers.

At a distance he beheld a large house, and inside the large house with carved front he heard many people singing. He saw sparks flying up from the smoke hole, and he knew that it must be the house of a great chief. When he came near the house, he heard something saying with a loud voice, "A stranger is coming, a chief is coming!" and he knew that they meant him. So he went in, but he saw nobody. Still he heard the voices. [221] He saw a great fire in the center, and a good new mat was spread out for him alongside the fire. Then he heard a voice which called to him, "Sit down on the mat! This way, great chief! This way, great chief! This way!" He walked proudly toward the mat. Then Txä'msen sat down on it. This was the house of Chief Echo. Then Txä'msem heard the chief speak to his slaves and tell them to roast a dried salmon; and he saw a carved box open itself and dried salmon come out of it. Then he saw a nice dish walk toward the fire all by itself.

Txä'msem was scared and astonished to see these things. When the dried salmon was roasted and cut into pieces of the right length, the pieces went into the dish all by themselves. The dish laid itself down in front of Txä'msem, and he thought while he was eating, what strange things he was seeing now. When he had finished, a horn dipper came forward filled with water. He took it by its handle and drank. Then he saw a large dish full of crabapples mixed with grease, and a black

* Pronunciation approximately represented in English by "Chemsem."

horn spoon, come forward by themselves. Txä'msem took the handle and ate all he could. Before he emptied his dish, he looked around, and, behold! mountain-goat fat was hanging on one side of the house. He thought, "I will take down one of these large pieces of fat." Thus Txä'msem thought while he was eating.

Then he heard many women laughing in one corner of the house, "Ha, ha! Txä'msem thinks he will take down one of those large pieces of mountain-goat fat!" Then Txä'msem was ashamed on acount of what the women were saying. He ate all the crabapples, and another dish came forward filled with cranberries mixed with grease and with water. Txä'msem ate again, and, behold! he saw dried mountain-sheep fat hanging in one corner of the large house. He thought again, "I will take down one of these pieces of mountain-sheep fat, and I will run out with it." Again he heard many women laughing, "Ha, ha! Txä'msem is thinking he will take down a piece of the mountain-sheep fat and will run out with it." Txä'msem was much troubled on account of what he heard the women saying, and when he heard them laughing in the corner of the house. He arose, ran out, and snatched one of the pieces of mountain-goat meat and of mountain-sheep fat; but when he came to the door, a large stone hammer beat him on the ankle, and he fell to the ground badly hurt. He lost the meat and fat, and some one dragged him along and cast him out. He lay there a while and began to cry, for he was very hungry, and his foot very sore. On the following day, when he was a little better, he took a stick and tried to walk away.

CHAPTER VI

ANIMAL WIVES AND HUSBANDS [3]

LVII. THE PIQUED BUFFALO–WIFE [222]

(BLACKFOOT: Wissler and Duvall, *Anthropological Papers of the American Museum of Natural History*, ii, 117, No. 28)

ONCE a young man went out and came to a buffalo-cow fast in the mire. He took advantage of her situation. After a time she gave birth to a boy. When he could run about, this boy would go into the Indian camps and join in the games of the children, but would always mysteriously disappear in the evening. One day this boy told his mother that he intended to search among the camps for his father. Not long after this he was playing with the children in the camps as usual, and went into the lodge of a head man in company with a boy of the family. He told this head man that his father lived somewhere in the camp, and that he was anxious to find him. The head man took pity on the boy, and sent out a messenger to call into his lodge all the old men in the camp.

When these were all assembled and standing around the lodge, the head man requested the boy to pick out his father. The boy looked them over, and then told the head man that his father was not among them. Then the head man sent out a messager to call in all the men next in age; but, when these were assembled, the boy said that his father was not among them. Again the head man sent out the messenger to call in all the men of the next rank in age. When they were assembled, the boy looked them over as before, and announced that his father was not among them. So once again the head man sent out his messenger to call in all the young unmarried men of the camp. As they were coming into the head man's lodge, the boy ran to one of them, and, embracing his, said, "Here is my father." [212]

After a time the boy told his father that he wished to take him to see his mother. The boy said, "When we come near her, she will run at you and hook four times, but you are to stand perfectly still." The next day the boy and his father started out on their journey. As they were going along they saw a buffalo-cow, which immediately ran at them as the boy had predicted. The man stood perfectly still, and at the fourth time, as the cow was running forward to hook at him, she became a woman.[40] Then she went home with her husband and child. One day shortly after their return, she warned her husband that whatever he might do he must never strike at her with fire.[223] They lived together happily for many years. She was a remarkably good woman. One evening when the husband had invited some guests, and the woman expressed a dislike to prepare food for them, he became very angry, and, catching up a stick from the fire, struck at her. As he did so, the woman and her child vanished, and the people saw a buffalo cow and calf running from the camp.

Now the husband was very sorry and mourned for his wife and child. After a time he went out to search for them. In order that he might approach the buffalo without being discovered, he rubbed himself with filth from a buffalo-wallow. In the course of time he came to a place where some buffalo were dancing. He could hear them from a distance. As he was approaching, he met his son, who was now, as before, a buffalo-calf. The father explained to the boy that he was mourning for him and his mother and that he had come to take them home. The calf-boy explained that this would be very difficult, for his father would be required to pass through an ordeal. The calf-boy explained to him that, when he arrived among the buffalo and inquired for his wife and son, the chief of the buffalo would order that he select his child from among all the buffalo-calves in the herd. Now the calf-boy wished to assist his father, and told him that he would know his child by a sign, because, when the calves appeared before him, his own child would hold up its tail.[224] Then the man proceeded until he came to the place where the buffalo were dancing. Immediately he was taken before the chief of the buffalo-herd. The chief required that he first prove his relationship to the child by picking him out from among all the other calves of the herd. The man agreed to this and the calves were brought up. He readily picked out his own child by the sign.

The chief of the buffalo, however, was not satisfied with this proof, and said that the father could not have the child until he identified him four times. While the preparations were being made for another test, the calf-boy came to his father and explained that he would be known this time by closing one eye. When the time arrived, the calves were brought as before, and the chief of the buffalo directed the father to identify his child, which he did by the sign. Before the next trial the calf-boy explained to his father that the sign would be one ear hanging down. Accordingly, when the calves were brought up for the father to choose, he again identified his child. Now, before the last trial, the boy came again to his father and notified him that the sign by which he was to be known was dancing and holding up one leg. Now the calf-boy had a chum among the buffalo-calves, and when the calves were called up before the chief so that the father might select his child, the chum saw the calf-boy beginning to dance holding up one leg, and he thought to himself, "He is doing some fancy dancing." So he, also, danced in the same way. Now the father observed that there were two calves giving the sign, and realized that he must make a guess. He did so, but the guess was wrong. Immediately the herd rushed upon the man and trampled him into the dust. Then they all ran away except the calf-boy, his mother, and an old bull.

These three mourned together for the fate of the unfortunate man. After a time the old bull requested that they examine the ground to see if they could find a piece of bone. After long and careful search they succeeded in finding one small piece that had not been trampled by the buffalo. The bull took this piece, made a sweat-house, and finally restored the man to life.[225] When the man was restored, the bull explained to him that he and his family would receive some power, some head-dresses, some songs, and some crooked sticks, such as he had seen the buffalo carry in the dance at the time when he attempted to pick out his son.

The calf-boy and his mother then became human beings, and returned with the man. It was this man who started the Bull and the Horn Societies, and it was his wife who started the Matoki.

LVIII. BEAR–WOMAN AND DEER–WOMAN [226]

(LASSIK: Goddard, *Journal of American Folk-Lore*, xix, 135, No. 2)

Grizzly Bear and Doe, the two wives of Chickenhawk, were pounding acorns. When they had finished, one of them said, "Let us go down to the creek and leach the meal." While they were waiting for the meal to soak, they agreed to hunt one another's heads for lice.[174] Doe looked first in Grizzly's hair. "You have no lice," she said. "Well then," said Grizzly, "I will look in yours." When in her search she reached the Doe's neck she sprinkled in some sand. "You have many lice," she said, "I will chew them." "Ukka! ukka!" cried Doe, "hold on there." Biting her head off, she killed her. Taking Doe's head and both lots of acorn meal she went back to the house. She put the head in the fire and when the eyes burst with the heat she told the children it was only the white oak log cracking in the fire. "I think it is our mother's head," said one of the Doe's children. "Go a long way off and play," said Grizzly. "You won't be permitted to live long," they heard their mother's hair [150] say to them.

The two bear children and the two fawns went out to play. "Let us play smoke-each-other-out in this hollow log," suggested the fawns. The bears agreed and the fawns went in first. "That's enough, that's enough," they cried. "Now you go in," they told the bears. The fawns fanned the smoke into the log until the bears were smothered. Going back to the house, one of them held out what she had in her hand and said, "Here is a skunk we killed in a log." "Very well," said the bear mother. Then the other fawn held out hers and said, "Here is a skunk we killed in a log." "Thank you, my niece; after a while I will make a meal upon them," replied Grizzly.[98]

"She is eating her children," she heard some one say. "What did you say?" she asked. "First you killed a person, and now you are eating your own children's hands." She ran after the children who had been taunting her. When she came near them she called in a pleasant voice, "Well, come home." They ran up on a ridge and barely escaped being caught. Finally they came to a place where Crane was fishing by the river. "Grandfather, put your neck across and let us go over on it. An old woman is after us. Put your neck across." [227]

They crossed over safely and running to the top of a ridge hid in a hole in a rock. When Grizzly came, Crane put his neck across again for a bridge, but when she was half way over he gave it a sudden twist. She went floating down the middle of the stream.

LIX. SPLINTER–FOOT–GIRL[228]

(ARAPAHO: Dorsey and Kroeber, *Anthropological Papers of the Field Museum*, v, 153, No. 81)

It was in winter and a large party was on the war-path. Some of them became tired and went home, but seven continued on their way. Coming to a river, they made camp on account of one of them who was weary and nearly exhausted. They found that he was unable to go farther. Then they made a good brush hut in order that they might winter there. From this place they went out and looked for buffalo and hunted them wherever they thought they might find them.

During the hunting one of them ran against a thorny plant and became unable to hunt for some time. His leg swelled very much in consequence of the wound, and finally suddenly opened. Then a child issued from the leg.[229] The young men took from their own clothes what they could spare and used it for wrapping for the child. They made a panther skin answer as a cradle. They passed the child around from one to the other, like people smoking a pipe. They were glad to have another person with them and they were very fond of the child.

While they lived there they killed very many elk and saved the teeth. From the skins they made a dress for the child, which was then old enough to run about. The dress was a girl's, entirely covered with elk teeth. They also made a belt for her. She was very beautiful. Her name was Foot-stuck-child.

A buffalo bull called Bone-bull heard that these young men had had a daughter born to them. As is the custom, he sent the magpie to go to these people to ask for the girl in marriage. The magpie came to the young men and told them what the Bone-bull wished; but he did not meet with any success. The young men said, "We will not do it. We love our daughter. She is so young that it will not be well to let her go." The magpie returned and told the Bone-bull what the young men had said. He advised the bull to get a certain small bird which was very clever and would perhaps persuade the young men to consent to the girl's marriage with him.

So the small bird was sent out by the bull. It reached the place where the people lived and lighted on the top of the brush house. In a gentle voice it said to the men, "I am sent by Bone-bull to ask for your daughter." The young men still refused, giving the same answer as before. The bird flew back and told the bull of the result. The bull said to it, "Go back and tell them that I mean what I ask. I shall come myself later." It was known that the bull was very powerful and hard to overcome or escape from. The bird went again and fulfilled the bull's instruction, but again returned unsuccessfully. It told the bull: "They are at last making preparations for the marriage. They are dressing the girl finely." But the bull did not believe it.

Then, in order to free itself from the unpleasant task, the bird advised him to procure the services of some one who could do better than itself; some one that had a sweet juicy tongue. So the bull sent another bird, called "fire-owner," which has red on its head and reddish wings. This bird took the message to the young men. Now at last they consented.

.   .   .   .

So the girl went to the bull and was received by him and lived with him for some time.[3] She wore a painted buffalo robe. At certain times the bull got up in order to lead the herd to water. At such times he touched his wife, who, wearing her robe, was sitting in the same position as all the rest, as a sign for her to go too.

The young men were lonely and thought how they might recover their daughter. It was a year since she had left them. They sent out flies,[146] but when the flies came near the bull he bellowed to drive them away. The flies were so much afraid of him that they did not approach him. Then the magpie was sent, and came and alighted at a distance; but when the bull saw him he said, "Go away! I do not want you about."

. . . [Then] they sent the blackbird, which lit on his back and began to sing. But the bull said to it also: "Go away, I do not want you about." The blackbird flew back to the men and said, "I can do nothing to help you to get your daughter back, but I will tell you of two animals that work unseen, and are very cunning: they are the mole and the badger. If you get their help you will surely recover the girl."

Then the young men got the mole and the badger,[147] and they started at night, taking arrows with them. They went underground, the mole going ahead. The badger followed and made the hole larger. They came under the place where the girl was sitting and the mole emerged under her blanket. He gave her the arrows which he had brought and she stuck them into the ground and rested her robe on them and then the badger came under this too. The two animals said to her, "We have come to take you back." She said, "I am afraid," but they urged her to flee.

Finally she consented, and leaving her robe in the position in which she always sat, went back through the hole with the mole and the badger to the house of the young men.

When she arrived they started to flee. The girl had become tired, when they came to the stone and asked it to help them. The stone said, "I can do nothing for you, the bull is too powerful to contend with." They rested by the side of the stone; then they continued on their way, one of them carrying the girl. But they went more slowly on account of her. They crossed a river, went through the timber, and on the prairie the girl walked again for a distance. In front of them they saw a lone immense cottonwood tree. They said to it: "We are pursued by a powerful animal and come to you for help." The tree told them, "Run around me four times," and they did this. The tree had seven large branches, the lowest of them high enough to be out of the reach of the buffalo, and at the top was a fork in which was a nest. They climbed the tree,[230] each of the men sitting on one of the branches, and the girl getting into the nest. So they waited for the bull who would pursue them.

When the bull touched his wife in order to go to water, she did not move. He spoke to her angrily and touched her again. The third time he tried to hook her with his horn, but tossed the empty robe away. "They cannot escape me," he said. He noticed the fresh ground which the badger had thrown up in order to close the hole. He hooked the ground and threw it to one side, and the other bulls got up and did the same, throwing the ground as if they were making a ditch and following the course of the underground passage until they came to the place where the people had lived. The camp was already broken up, but they followed the people's trail.

Coming to the stone, the bull asked, "Have you hidden the people or done anything to help them?" The stone said: "I have not helped them for fear of you." But the bull insisted: "Tell me where you hid them. I know that they reached you and are somewhere about." "No, I did not hide them; they reached this place but went on," said the stone. "Yes, you have hidden them; I can smell them and see their tracks about here." "The girl rested here a short time; that is what you smell," said the stone.

Then the buffalo followed the trail again and crossed the river, the bull leading. One calf which was becoming very tired tried hard to keep up with the rest. It became exhausted at the lone cottonwood tree and stopped to rest. But the herd went on, not having seen the people in the tree. They went far on. The girl was so tired that she had a slight hemorrhage. Then she spat down. As the calf was resting in the shade below, the bloody spittle fell down before it. The calf smelled it, knew it, got up, and went after the rest of the buffalo. Coming near the herd, it cried out to the bull: "Stop! I have found a girl in the top of a tree. She is the one who is your wife." Then the whole herd turned back to the tree.

When they reached it, the bull said: "We will surely get you." The tree said: "You have four parts of strength. I give you a chance to do something to me." Then the buffalo began to attack the tree; those with least strength began. They butted it until its thick bark was peeled off. Meanwhile the young men were shooting them from the tree. The tree said: "Let some of them break their horns." Then came the large bulls, who split the wood of the tree; but some stuck fast, and others broke their horns or lost the covering.

The bull said, "I will be the last one and will make the tree fall." At last he came on, charging against the tree from the southeast, striking it, and making a big gash. Then, coming from the southwest, he made a larger hole. Going to the northwest, he charged from there, and again cut deeper, but broke his right horn. Going then to the northeast, he charged the tree with his left horn and made a still larger hole. The fifth time he went straight east, intending to strike the tree in the center and break it down. He pranced about, raising the dust; but the tree said to him: "You can do nothing. So come on quickly." This made him angry and he charged. The tree said: "This time you will stick fast," and he ran his left horn far into the middle of the wood and stuck fast. Then the tree told the young men to shoot him in the soft part of his neck and sides, for he could not get loose or injure them. Then they shot him and killed him, so that he hung there. Then they cut him loose.

The tree told them to gather all the chips and pieces of wood that had been knocked off and cover the bull with them, and they did so. All the buffalo that had not been killed went away. The tree said to them: "Hereafter you will be overcome by human beings. You will have horns, but when they come to hunt you, you will be afraid. You will be killed and eaten by them and they will use your skins." Then the buffalo scattered over the land with half-broken, short horns.[4]

After the people had descended from the tree, they went on their way. The magpie came to them as messenger sent by Merciless-man to ask the young men for their daughter in marriage. He was a round rock. The magpie knew what this rock had done and warned the men not to consent to the marriage. He said, "Do not have anything to do with him, since he is not a good man. Your daughter is beautiful, and I do not like to see her married to the rock. He has married the prettiest girls he could hear of, obtaining them somehow. But his wives are crippled, one-armed, or one-legged, or much bruised. I will tell the rock to get the hummingbird for a messenger because that bird is swift and can escape him if he should pursue." So the magpie returned and said that the young men refused the marriage. But the rock sent him back to say: "Tell them that the girl must marry me nevertheless." The magpie persuaded him to send the hummingbird as messenger instead of himself.

Then the hummingbird went to carry the message to the young men; but, on reaching them, told them instead: "He is merciless, and not the right man to marry this girl. He has treated his wives very badly. You had better leave this place." So he went back without having tried to help the rock. He told the rock that he had seen neither camp nor people. "Yes you saw them," said the rock; "you are trying to help them instead of helping me. Therefore you try to pretend that you did not see them. Go back and tell them that I want the girl. If they refuse, say that I shall be there soon." The hummingbird went again to the men and told them what the rock wished, and said: "He is powerful. Perhaps it is best if you let your daughter go. But there are two animals that can surely help you. They can bring her back before he injures her. They are the mole and the badger." "Yes," they said, now having confidence in these animals. So the hummingbird took the girl to the rock. He reached his tent, which was large and fine, but full of crippled wives. "I have your wife here," he said. "Very well," said the rock, "let her come in. I am pleased that you brought her; she is pretty enough for me."

Soon after the hummingbird had left with the girl, the mole and the badger [147] started underground and made their way to the rock's tent. In the morning the rock always went buzzing out through the top of the tent; in the evening he came back home in the same way. While he was away, the two animals arrived. The girl was sitting with both feet outstretched. They said to her, "Remain sitting thus until your husband returns." Then they made a hole large enough for the rock to fall into and covered it lightly. In the evening the rock was heard coming. As he was entering above, the girl got up, and the rock dropped into the hole while she ran out of the tent saying: "Let the hole be closed." "Let the earth be covered again," said the mole and the badger. They heard the rock inside the earth, tossing about, buzzing, and angry. The girl returned to her fathers.

They traveled all night, fleeing. In the morning the rock overtook them. As they were going, they wished a canyon with steep cliffs to be behind them. The rock went down the precipice, and while he tried to climb up again, the others went on. It became night again and in the morning the rock was near them once more. Then the girl said: "This time it shall happen. I am tired and weary from running, my fathers." She was carrying a ball, and, saying: "First for my father," she threw it up and as it came down kicked it upwards, and her father rose up. Then she did the same for the others until all had gone up. When she came to do it for herself the rock was near. She threw the ball, kicked it, and she too rose up. She said, "We have passed through dangers on my account; I think this is the best place for us to go. It is a good place where we are. I shall provide the means of living for you." To the rock she said. "You shall remain where you overtook us. You shall not trouble people any longer, but be found wherever there are hills." She and her fathers reached the sky in one place. They live in a tent covered with stars.[71]

LX. THE EAGLE AND WHALE HUSBANDS [231]

(GREENLAND ESKIMO: Rink, *Tales and Traditions of
the Eskimo*, p. 127, No. 8)

Two little girls were playing with some small bones on the beach; the one with eagle-bones, the other with whale-bones. Suddenly an eagle came soaring through the air above them, and one of the girls said, "I will have an eagle for my husband"; and the other replied, "Thou mayst rejoice that thou hast already got a husband; I will have a whale for mine." Instantly a whale was seen to spout out at sea.[217a]

And the eagle took one girl up and flew away with her, and the whale took the other down to the bottom of the sea, having first made her eyes and ears impenetrable, so that the water could not enter. The eagle carried his bride to the top of a steep cliff, and brought her different sorts of little birds for food; but she gathered all the sinews of the birds' wings, and knotted them together, in order to make a string of them. One day, when the eagle was away, she tried the length of it, and found that it reached down to the level of the sea. Another day she saw a kayaker rowing along the shore; and when he came just below, she called out to him to send a boat to rescue her.

Soon afterwards the boat appeared, and she went sliding down by her string of sinews, and got back to her parents. But the eagle, who missed his mate, soared above the houses beating his wings; and one of the inhabitants of the place cried out to him, "If thou wantest to show thou hast married into our family, spread out thy wings"; but when the eagle did so they shot him through the body.

The other girl who had been stolen by the whale was secured to the bottom of the sea by a rope; and when he was at home, she had nothing to do but to sit picking the lice from off his body.[174] She had two brothers living close by, and both set about building a boat of immense swiftness, in which they intended to deliver their sister; but when the boat was finished it could not match a bird in speed, and was therefore broken to pieces, and another begun. This boat proved a match for a flying bird, but was nevertheless discarded, and they again built a new one, in which they tried to overtake a gull; and on finding that this one even outdid the bird, they started from home to fetch back their sister. On becoming aware of their approach she loosened the cord that held her, and twisting it round the stone, she left with the boat.

When the whale on his return drew the cord to get hold of her, and discovered that she was gone, he hurried after her. But when he came quite close to the boat she threw her outer jacket into the water to him.[232] Having snapped at it he let it go, and again pursued her; and when he had got quite close up with them, she flung her inner jacket at him, which again detained the whale; but he soon reached them for the third time. Then she threw her long jacket, and before he could overtake them again they had already landed; but when the whale reached the shore he was transformed into a piece of whale-bone.

LXI. THE FOX–WOMAN [233]

(LABRADOR ESKIMO: Turner, *Report of the Bureau of American Ethnology*, xi, 264)

A hunter who lived by himself found when he returned to the place after an absence that it had been visited and everything put in order as a dutiful wife should do. This happened so often with no visible signs of tracks that the man determined to watch and see who would scrape his skin clothing and boots, hang them out to dry, and cook nice hot food ready to be eaten when he returned.[207] One day he went away as though going off on a hunt, but secreted himself so as to observe the entrance of anything into the house.

After a while he saw a fox enter. He suspected that the fox was after food. He quietly slipped up to the house and on entering saw a most beautiful woman dressed in skin clothing of wondrous make. Within the house, on a line, hung the skin of a fox. The man inquired if it was she who had done these things. She replied that she was his wife and it was her duty to do them, hoping that she had performed her labor in a manner satisfactory to him.

After they had lived together a short time the husband detected a musky odor about the house and inquired of her what it was.[234] She replied that she emitted the odor and if he was going to find fault with her for it she would leave.[223] She dashed off her clothing and, resuming the skin of the fox,[132] slipped quietly away and has never been disposed to visit a man since that time.

LXII. THE WOMAN STOLEN BY KILLER-WHALES [235]

(TAHLTAN: Teit, *Journal of American Folk-Lore*, xxxiv, 228, No. 35)

A man was out fishing and drying halibut, and his wife helped him. One day he felt something very heavy on his hook, and could not pull it up. He tied the line to the thwart of the canoe, and paddled ashore. With much trouble he managed to land the fish on the beach. He called on his wife to kill it quickly, and she despatched it with her knife. She cut it up and hung it up to dry, as is done with halibut. They did not know what kind of a fish it was. It was quite strange to them, but they thought it might be good food. When the woman had finished her work, she went to the edge of the water to wash her hands.

As soon as she put her hands into the water, something seized them and pulled her underneath the sea. She had been taken by the Killer-Whales, who had come to have revenge on the man for killing their friend.

The man followed the trail of his wife and her captors under the sea. He came to the house of the Fish chief,[236] and asked him if he knew where his wife was. The chief said, "Yes, the Killer-Whales have taken her to be their slave." The man asked the chief if any fish of his company would care to help him get back his wife. The chief asked the fishes if any of them would volunteer, and Shark [146] said he would go. Shark went ahead to Killer-Whale's house, and hid the man outside the door. He went in, and saw that the Killer-Whales were about to eat their evening meal. Their chief said, "Make the fire blaze, that we may see well!" Shark was standing next to the fire. He jumped up quickly and put much wood on the fire, so that it blazed up. The chief then said, "Some one fetch water!" Shark seized the buckets and ran out to draw water. As he came in and was passing the fire, he stumbled purposely, and upset the buckets in the fire, thus causing a dense cloud of ashes and steam to arise.[237] Quickly he caught up the woman, pushed her out into

the arms of her husband, who was waiting, and followed them.
Shark kept in the rear, and said to the man, "Keep a-going!
If they overtake us, I shall fight them." When the man and
woman were nearly home, they looked back, and saw a severe
fight in progress. Shark was fighting all the Killer-Whales,
biting them with his sharp teeth, and tearing them with his
rough skin.

LXIII. THE ROLLING HEAD [238]

(CHEYENNE: Kroeber, *Journal of American Folk-Lore*, xiii, 184, No. 22)

In a solitary tent lived a lone family, — a man, his wife, and
two children. When the man went out hunting, he always
painted his wife's face and body before he started in the morning. His wife went for water to a lake near by. She always
went to the same place; and when she came to the lake, she took
off her clothes, as if to bathe. Then a large snake [239] rose out
of the lake, after the woman had spoken to it and told it to appear. The snake asked her to come out to him, since her husband had gone away hunting. The woman did as the snake
said. Every morning she went to the lake.

Her husband brought back meat, and she and the children
were glad. The man did not know what happened. He did
not know that his wife went after water to the lake and met a
large snake. But one day he asked her what made the paint
come off her. She said that she took a bath. Next morning he
started as if to hunt; but dug a hiding-place near the lake to
see what his wife did. She came to the shore and called to the
snake: "Come, I am waiting." Then he saw a big old snake
rise from the water, and ask her if her husband had gone
hunting. She answered: "Yes, I am coming." She took off
her clothes and entered the lake, and the snake was soon
around her.

The man had watched them, and now, leaving his hiding-
place, he jumped on the snake, and with a large knife cut it in
pieces and at last killed it. Then he caught his wife and killed
her.[240] He cut her up [241] and took her meat home and gave it
to his children. He cooked his wife, and the children unknow-
ingly ate their mother.[98]

Then the man said to them: "Tell your mother when she
comes home that I went to get more meat which I left hanging

on a tree so that the wolves cannot reach it." And he went away. The younger child said: "Our mother is merely teasing us by staying away." But the older girl answered: "Do not say anything against our mother." Then their mother's head came rolling to them; and it said: "I am very sorry that my children have eaten me up."

The two children ran away, but the head pursued them. At last they were worn out, but their mother's head still rolled after them. Then the older girl drew a line or mark on the ground and so deep a hole opened [205] that the head could not cross. The younger girl was very hungry. She said to her sister: "Look at that deer." The older girl looked at the deer, and it fell down dead as if shot.[242] So they ate of it. Then some one was kind to them and helped them, and they lived in a large lodge and had much food of various kinds to eat. Two large panthers and two large black bears guarded them against all wild animals and persons.

A camp of people was starving.[243] Neither buffalo nor smaller game could be found. The people heard that the children had abundance of food of all kinds, and they all moved to them. When they arrived the children invited them, and the various companies came and ate with them. Finally they all went out again; only the children's father now stayed with them again. But they regretted what he had done to them. So they caused the lions to jump upon their father, and he was killed.

LXIV. THE BEAR–WOMAN [244]

(BLACKFOOT: Wissler and Duvall, *Anthropological Papers of the American Museum of Natural History*, ii, 68, No. 6)

Once there was a young woman with many suitors; but she refused to marry. She had seven brothers and one little sister. Their mother had been dead many years and they had no relatives, but lived alone with their father. Every day the six brothers went out hunting with their father. It seems that the young woman had a bear for her lover,[245] and, as she did not want any one to know this, she would meet him when she went out after wood. She always went after wood as soon as her father and brothers went out to hunt, leaving her little sister alone in the lodge. As soon as she was out of sight in the brush, she would run to the place where the bear lived.

As the little sister grew older, she began to be curious as to why her older sister spent so much time getting wood. So one day she followed her. She saw the young woman meet the bear and saw that they were lovers. When she found this out, she ran home as quickly as she could, and when her father returned she told him what she had seen. When he heard the story he said, "So, my elder daughter has a bear for a husband. Now I know why she does not want to marry." Then he went about the camp, telling all his people that they had a bear for a brother-in-law, and that he wished all the men to go out with him to kill this bear. So they went, found the bear, and killed him.

When the young woman found out what had been done, and that her little sister had told on her, she was very angry. She scolded her little sister vigorously, then ordered her to go out to the dead bear, and bring some flesh from his paws. The little sister began to cry, and said she was afraid to go out of the lodge, because a dog with young pups had tried to bite her. "Oh, do not be afraid!" said the young woman. "I will paint your face like that of a bear, with black marks across the eyes and at the corners of the mouth; then no one will touch you." So she went for the meat. Now the older sister was a powerful medicine-woman. She could tan hides in a new way. She could take up a hide, strike it four times with her skin-scraper and it would be tanned.

The little sister had a younger brother that she carried on her back. As their mother was dead, she took care of him. One day the little sister said to the older sister, "Now you be a bear and we will go out into the brush to play." The older sister agreed to this, but said, "Little sister, you must not touch me over my kidneys." So the big sister acted as a bear, and they played in the brush. While they were playing, the little sister forgot what she had been told, and touched her older sister in the wrong place. At once she turned into a real bear, ran into the camp, and killed many of the people. After she had killed a large number, she turned back into her former self. Now, when the little sister saw the older run away as a real bear, she became frightened, took up her little brother, and ran into their lodge. Here they waited, badly frightened, but were very glad to see their older sister return after a time as her true self.

Now the older brothers were out hunting, as usual. As the little sister was going down for water with her little brother on her back, she met her six brothers returning. The brothers noted how quiet and deserted the camp seemed to be. So they said to their little sister, "Where are all our people?" Then the little sister explained how she and her sister were playing, when the elder turned into a bear, ran through the camp, and killed many people. She told her brothers that they were in great danger, as their sister would surely kill them when they came home. So the six brothers decided to go into the brush. One of them had killed a jack-rabbit. He said to the little sister, "You take this rabbit home with you. When it is dark, we will scatter prickly-pears all around the lodge, except in one place. When you come out, you must look for that place, and pass through."

When the little sister came back to the lodge, the elder sister said, "Where have you been all this time?" "Oh, my little brother mussed himself and I had to clean him," replied the little sister. "Where did you get that rabbit?" she asked. "I killed it with a sharp stick," said the little sister. "That is a lie. Let me see you do it," said the older sister. Then the little sister took up a stick lying near her, threw it at the rabbit, and it stuck in the wound in his body. "Well, all right," said the elder sister. Then the little sister dressed the rabbit and cooked it. She offered some of it to her older sister, but it was refused: so the little sister and her brother ate all of it. When the elder sister saw that the rabbit had all been eaten, she became very angry, and said, "Now I have a mind to kill you." So the little sister arose quickly, took her little brother on her back, and said, "I am going out to look for wood." As she went out, she followed the narrow trail through the prickly-pears and met her six brothers in the brush. Then they decided to leave the country, and started off as fast as they could go.

The older sister, being a powerful medicine-woman, knew at once what they were doing. She became very angry and turned herself into a bear to pursue them. Soon she was about to overtake them, when one of the boys tried his power. He took a little water in the hollow of his hand and sprinkled it around. At once it became a great lake between them and the bear. Then the children hurried on while the bear went around. After a while the bear caught up with them again, when another brother threw a porcupine-tail (a hairbrush) on the ground. This became a great thicket; but the bear forced its way through, and again overtook the children. This time they all climbed a high tree. The bear came to the foot of the tree, and, looking up at them, said, "Now I shall kill you all." So she took a stick from the ground, threw it into the tree and knocked down four of the brothers. While she was doing this, a little bird flew around the tree, calling out to the children, "Shoot her in the head! Shoot her in the head!" [246] Then one of the boys shot an arrow into the head of the bear, and at once she fell dead. Then they came down from the tree.

Now the four brothers were dead. The little brother took an arrow, shot it straight up into the air, and when it fell one of the dead brothers came to life. This he repeated until all were alive again. Then they held a council, and said to each other, "Where shall we go? Our people have all been killed, and we are a long way from home. We have no relatives living in the world." Finally they decided that they preferred to live in the sky. Then the little brother said, "Shut your eyes." As they did so, they all went up. Now you can see them every night. The little brother is the North Star (?). The six brothers and the little sister are seen in the Great Dipper. The little sister and eldest brother are in a line with the North Star, the little sister being nearest it because she used to carry her little brother on her back. The other brothers are arranged in order of their age, beginning with the eldest. This is how the seven stars [Ursa major] came to be.

LXV. THE DOG–HUSBAND [247]

(QUINAULT: Farrand, *Jesup North Pacific Expedition*, ii, 127, No. 17)

A long time ago, in a certain village there lived a young girl who had a dog of which she was very fond. She took the dog with her wherever she went; and at night, as was a common custom at that time with young girls, the dog slept at the foot of the bed. Every night he would change into human form and lie with the girl, and in the morning, before it was light, would turn back again into his dog shape: [248] so no one knew anything about it. After a time she became pregnant; and when her parents found it out and knew that the dog was the cause [3] they were greatly ashamed, and calling the people together they tore down the house, put out all the fires, and moved away from the place, leaving the girl to die.

But Crow had pity on her, and, taking some coals, she placed them between two clam-shells, and told the girl secretly that after a time she would hear a crackling, and to go to the spot and she would find fire. So the girl was left alone, for the people had all gone a long way across the water. She sat still for a long time, listening for the crackling, and when she finally heard it she went to the place and found the fire as Crow had said.

Not long after this she gave birth to five dog pups, but as her father had killed the dog, her lover, she had to look after them by herself, and the only way she could live and care for them was to gather clams and other shellfish on the beach. There were four male pups and one female, and with the care their mother gave them, they grew very fast. Soon she noticed that whenever she went out, she heard a noise of singing and dancing, which seemed to come from the house, and she wondered greatly. Four times she heard the noise and wondered, and when, on going out again, she heard it for the fifth time, she took her clam-digger and stuck it in the sand, and put her clothes on it to make it look as if she were busy gathering clams. Then she stole back by a roundabout way, and creeping close to the house peeped in through a crack to see what the noise might be. There she saw four boys dancing and singing, and a little girl watching the place where the mother was supposed to be digging clams. The mother waited a moment and watched, and then coming in she caught them in human form, and scolded them, saying that they ought to have had that form in the first place, for on their account she had been brought to shame before the people. At this the children sat down and were ashamed. And the mother tore down the dog blankets which were hanging about, and threw them into the fire.[249]

So they remained in human form after this; and as soon as they were old enough she made little bows and arrows for the boys, and taught them how to shoot birds, beginning with the wren, and working up to the largest. Then she taught them to make large bows and arrows, and how to shoot fur animals, and then larger game, up to the elk. And she made them bathe every day to try to get tamanous for catching whales, and after that they hunted the hair-seal to make floats of its skin.

And the mother made harpoons for them of Elk-bone, and lines of twisted sinews and cedar, and at the end of the line she fastened the sealskin floats. And when everything was ready, the boys went out whaling and were very successful, and brought in so many whales that the whole beach stank with them.

Now, Crow noticed one day, from far across the water, a great smoke rising from where the old village had stood, and that night she came over secretly to see what it all meant. And before she neared the beach, she smelled the dead whales, and when she came up she saw the carcasses lying all about, and there were so many that some of them had not yet been cut up. When she reached the house, she found the children grown up; and they welcomed her and gave her food, all she could eat, but gave her nothing to take back, telling her to come over again if she wanted more.

When Crow started back, the girl told her that when she reached home, she was to weep so that the people would believe they were dead. But Crow, on getting home, instead of doing as she was told, described how the beach was covered with sea gulls feeding on the whales that had been killed by the boys.

Now, Crow had brought with her secretly a piece of whale-meat for her children,[250] and after putting out the light she fed it to them; and one of them ate so fast that she choked, and coughed a piece of the meat out on the ground. And some of the people saw it, and then believed what Crow had told them, as they had not done before.[251] Then the people talked it all over, and decided to go back; and they loaded their canoes and moved to the old village. And the boys became the chiefs of the village, and always kept the people supplied with whales.

LXVI. THE YOUTH WHO JOINED THE DEER [252]

(THOMPSON: Teit, *Memoirs of the American Folk-Lore Society*, xi, 40, No. 24)

There was a man who was a great deer-hunter. He was constantly hunting, and was very successful. He thought continually of the deer, and dreamed of them. They were as friends to him. Probably they were his manitou. He had two wives, one of whom had borne him no children, while the other one had borne a male child.

One day while hunting, he came on the fresh tracks of a doe and fawn, which he followed. They led to a knoll on which he saw a young woman and child sitting. The tracks led directly to them. He was surprised, and asked the woman if she had seen any deer pass. She answered, "No." He walked on, but could not find the tracks. On his return, he said to the woman, "You must have seen the deer; the tracks seem to disappear where you are, and they are very fresh." The woman laughed, and said, "You need not trouble yourself about the tracks. For a long time I have loved you and longed for you. Now you shall go with me to my house." They walked on together; and the hunter could not resist the attraction of the woman, nor help following her. As he went along, he thought, "It is not well that I am acting thus. My wives and my child are at home awaiting me." The woman knew his thoughts at once, and said, "You must not worry or think that you are doing wrong. You shall be my husband, and you will never regret it."

After the two had travelled a long way, they reached a hilly country. Then the man saw an entrance which seemed to lead underground.[253] When they had gone some distance underground, they found themselves in a large house full of people who were just like Indians. They were of both sexes and all ages. They were well dressed in clothes of dressed skin, and wore deer-skin robes. They seemed to be very amiable and happy. As the travellers entered, some of the people said, "Our daughter has brought her husband." That night the woman said to the hunter, "You are my husband, and will sleep with me. You may embrace me, but you must not try to have intercourse with me. You must not do so before the rutting-season. Then you may also go with my sisters. Our season comes but once a year, and lasts about a month. During the rest of the year we have no sexual connections." The hunter slept with his new wife.

On the following day the people said, "Let our son-in-law hunt. He is a great hunter. Let him get meat for us. We have no more meat." The hunter took his bow and arrows and went hunting. Two young deer, his brothers-in-law, ran ahead and stood on a knoll. Presently the hunter saw them, and killed both of them. He cut them up and carried them home, leaving nothing but their manure. The chief had told him in the morning to be careful and not to throw away any part of the game.

Now the people ate and were glad. They saved all the bones and put them away in one place. They said to the hunter, "We always save every bone." When the deer were eaten, the bones were wrapped in bundles, and the chief sent a man to throw them into the water. He carried the bones of the two deer that the hunter had killed, and of another one that the people were eating when the hunter first arrived. The hunter had missed his two brothers-in-law, and thought they were away hunting. When the man who had carried the bones away returned, the two brothers-in-law and another man were with him. They had all come to life when their bones were thrown into the water.[114a] Thus these Deer people lived by hunting and killing each other and then reviving. The hunter lived with his wife and her people, and hunted whenever meat was required. He never failed to kill deer, for some of the young deer were always anxious to be killed for the benefit of the people.

At last the rutting-season came on, and the chief put the body of a large old buck on the hunter, and so transformed him into a buck. He went out with his wife and felt happy. Some other younger bucks came and beat him off and took his wife. He did not like others to have his wife; therefore he went home and felt downcast. That night the people said, "What is the matter with our son-in-law, that he does not speak?" Some one said, "He is downcast because a young man took his wife." The chief said, "Do not feel sad. We shall give you ornaments to-morrow which will make you strong, and then nobody can take your wife away from you." On the following morning he put large antlers on him, and gave him the body of a buck in its prime. That day the hunter beat off all the rival bucks, and kept his wife and also all her sisters and cousins for himself. He hurt many of his brothers-in-law in fighting. The Deer people had shamans who healed the wounds of those hurt in battle, and they were busy throughout the rutting-season.

In this way they acted until the end of the rut, and the hunter was the champion during the whole season. In due time his wife gave birth to a son. When the latter was growing up, she said, "It is not fair to your people that you live entirely with my people. We should live with them for a while." She reduced a large quantity of deer-fat to the size of a handful. She did the same with a large quantity of dried venison, deer-skins, and dressed buckskins.[210a]

Now she started with her child and her husband, who hunted on the way, and killed one of his brothers-in-law whenever they required food. He put the bones into the water, and they revived. They travelled along as people do; but the woman thought this too slow; therefore they transformed themselves into deer. Now they went fast, and soon reached the country where her husband's people lived. She said to her husband, "Do not approach the people at once, or you will die. For eight days you must prepare yourself by washing in decoctions of herbs."

Presently they saw a young woman some distance away from the lodges. The hunter recognized her as his sister, showed himself, and called, "O sister! I have come back, but no one must come near me for eight days. After that I shall visit you; but you must clean your houses, so that there may be in them nothing old and no bad smell." The people thought him dead, and his childless wife had married again. After the hunter had become like other people, he entered his lodge with his new wife and his son. His wife pulled out the deer-fat from under her arm, and threw it down on long feast-mats that had been spread out by the people. It assumed its proper dimensions and covered all the mats. She did the same with the dried meat and the deer-skins, which almost filled a lodge. Now the people had a feast, and felt happy and pleased. The hunter staid with his people for a considerable time. Whenever they wanted fresh meat, he gave his bow and arrows to his son and told him to hunt. The youth always took with him his half-brother, the son of his father by his Indian wife. They killed deer, for the deer were the boy's relatives and were willing to be killed. They threw the bones into the water, and the deer came back to life. The Deer-Boy taught his half-brother how to hunt and shoot deer, how to hold his bow and arrows so that he would not miss, how to cut up and preserve the meat; and he admonished him always to throw the bones into the water, so that the deer might revive.

Finally the Deer-Woman said to her husband, "We have been here now for a long time. Let us return to my people." She invited the people to accompany them, but they said they had not a sufficient number of moccasins to undertake the long journey. The woman then pulled out a parcel of dressed skins, threw it on the ground, and it became a heap of fine skins for shoes. All the women worked night and day making moccasins, and soon they were ready to start. The first day of the journey the hunter said to his wife, "Let us send our son out, and I will shoot him." He hunted, and brought home a young deer, which the people ate. They missed the Deer-Boy, and wondered where he had gone. At night the hunter threw the bones into the water, and the boy came to life. On the next day the hunter's wife went out, and he killed her and fed the people. They missed her, and wondered where she had gone. At night he threw the bones into the water, and she came to life. She told her husband it would be better not to continue to do this, because the people were becoming suspicious and would soon discover what they were doing. She said, "After this kill your brothers-in-law." The people travelled slowly, for there were many, and the hunter killed deer for them every day.

After many days they reached the Deer people's house. They were well received. After a time they made up their minds to return; and the Deer-Boy said he would return with his half-brother's people, and hunt for them on the way, so that they might not starve. He accompanied them to their country, and never returned. He became an Indian and a great hunter. From him the people learned how to treat deer. He said to them, "When you kill deer, always see to it that the bones are not lost. Throw them into the water. Then the deer will come to life. A hunter who does this pleases the deer. They have affection for him, are not afraid of him, and do not keep out of his way, for they know that they will return to life whenever they give themselves into his power. The deer will always remain plentiful, because they are not really killed. If it is impossible to throw the bones into water, then burn them. Then the deer will really die, but they will not find fault with you. If a man throws deer-bones about, and takes no care of them, if he lets the dogs eat them, and people step on them, then the deer will be offended and will help him no more. They will withhold themselves, and the hunter will have no luck in hunting. He will become poor and starve." The hunter never returned to the people. He became a deer.[254]

CHAPTER VII

MISCELLANEOUS TALES

LXVII. THE DESERTED CHILDREN [255]

(Gros Ventre: Kroeber, *Anthropological Papers of the American Museum of Natural History*, i, 102, No. 26)

THERE was a camp. All the children went off to play. They went to some distance. Then one man said, "Let us abandon the children. Lift the ends of your tent-poles and travois when you go, so that there will be no trail." Then the people went off. After a time the oldest girl amongst the children sent the others back to the camp to get something to eat. The children found the camp gone, the fires out, and only ashes about. They cried, and wandered about at random. The oldest girl said, "Let us go toward the river."

They found a trail leading across the river, and forded the river there. Then one of the girls found a tent-pole. As they went along, she cried, "My mother, here is your tent-pole." "Bring my tent-pole here!" shouted an old woman loudly from out of the timber. The children went towards her.

They found that she was an old woman who lived alone. They entered her tent. At night they were tired. The old woman told them all to sleep with their heads toward the fire. Only one little girl who had a small brother pretended to sleep, but did not. The old woman watched if all were asleep. Then she put her foot in the fire. It became red hot. Then she pressed it down on the throat of one of the children, and burned through the child's throat. Then she killed the next one and the next one.

The little girl jumped up, saying, "My grandmother, let me live with you and work for you. I will bring wood and water for you." Then the old woman allowed her and her little brother to live. "Take these out," she said.

Then the little girl, carrying her brother on her back, dragged out the bodies of the other children. Then the old woman sent her to get wood. The little girl brought back a load of cotton-wood. When she brought it, the old woman said, "That is not the kind of wood I use. Throw it out. Bring another load." The little girl went out and got willow-wood. She came back, and said, "My grandmother, I have a load of wood." "Throw it in," said the old woman. The little girl threw the wood into the tent. The old woman said, "That is not the kind of wood I use. Throw it outside. Now go get wood for me." Then the little girl brought birch-wood, then cherry, then sagebrush; but the old woman always said, "That is not the kind of wood I use," and sent her out again. The little girl went. She cried and cried. Then a bird came to her and told her, "Bring her ghost-ropes for she is a ghost." Then the little girl brought some of these plants, which grow on willows. The old woman said, "Throw in the wood which you have brought." The little girl threw it in. Then the old woman was glad. "You are my good grand-daughter," she said.

Then the old woman sent the little girl to get water. The little girl brought her river-water, then rain-water, then spring-water; but the old woman always told her, "That is not the kind of water I use. Spill it!" Then the bird told the little girl, "Bring her foul, stagnant water, which is muddy and full of worms. That is the only kind she drinks." The little girl got the water, and when she brought it the old woman was glad.

Then the little boy said that he needed to go out doors. "Well, then, go out with your brother, but let half of your robe remain inside of the tent while you hold him." Then the girl took her little brother out, leaving half of her robe inside the tent. When she was outside, she stuck an awl in the ground. She hung her robe on this, and, taking her little brother, fled. The old woman called, "Hurry!" Then the awl answered,[196] "My grandmother, my little brother is not yet ready." Again the old woman said, "Now hurry!" Then the awl answered again, "My little brother is not ready." Then the old woman said, "Come in now; else I will go outside and kill you." She started to go out, and stepped on the awl.

The little girl and her brother fled, and came to a large river. An animal with two horns lay there. It said, "Louse me." The little boy loused it. Its lice were frogs. "Catch four, and crack them with your teeth," said the Water-monster. The boy had on a necklace of plum-seeds. Four times the girl cracked a seed.[174] She made the monster think that her brother had cracked one of its lice. Then the Water-monster said, "Go between my horns, and do not open your eyes until we have crossed." [179] Then he went under the surface of the water. He came up on the other side. The children got off and went on.

The old woman was pursuing the children, saying, "I will kill you. You cannot escape me by going to the sky or by entering the ground." She came to the river. The monster had returned, and was lying at the edge of the water. "Louse me," it said. The old woman found a frog. "These dirty lice! I will not put them into my mouth!" she said, and threw it into the river. She found three more, and threw them away. Then she went on the Water-monster.[227] He went under the surface of the water, remained there, drowned her, and ate her. The children went on.

At last they came to the camp of the people who had deserted them. They came to their parents' tent. "My mother, here is your little son," the girl said. "I did not know that I had a son," their mother said. They went to their father, their uncle, and their grandfather. They all said, "I did not know I had a son," "I did not know I had a nephew," "I did not know I had a grandson." Then a man said, "Let us tie them face to face, and hang them in a tree and leave them."

Then they tied them together, hung them in a tree, put out all the fires, and left them. A small dog with sores all over his body, his mouth, and his eyes, pretended to be sick and unable to move, and lay on the ground. He kept a little fire between his legs, and had hidden a knife. The people left the dog lying. When they had all gone off, the dog went to the children, climbed the tree, cut the ropes, and freed them. The little boy cried and cried. He felt bad about what the people had done.

Then many buffalo came near them. "Look at the buffalo, my brother," said the girl. The boy looked at the buffalo, and they fell dead.[242] The girl wondered how they might cut them up. "Look at the meat, my younger brother," she said. The boy looked at the dead buffalo, and the meat was all cut up. Then she told him to look at the meat, and when he looked at it, the meat was dried. Then they had much to eat, and the dog became well again. The girl sat down on the pile of buffalo-skins, and they were all dressed. She folded them together, sat on them, and there was a tent. Then she went out with the dog and looked for sticks. She brought dead branches, broken tent-poles, and rotten wood. "Look at the tent-poles," she said to her brother. When he looked, there were large straight tent-poles, smooth and good. Then the girl tied three together at the top, and stood them up, and told her brother to look at the tent. He looked, and a large fine tent stood there. Then she told him to go inside and look about him. He went in and looked. Then the tent was filled with property, and there were beds for them, and a bed also for the dog. The dog was an old man. Then the girl said, "Look at the antelopes running, my brother." The boy looked, and the antelopes fell dead. He looked at them again, and the meat was cut up and the skins taken off.

Then the girl made fine dresses of the skins for her brother and herself and the dog. Then she called as if she were calling for dogs, and four bears came loping to her. "You watch that pile of meat, and you this one," she said to each one of the bears. The bears went to the meat and watched it. Then the boy looked at the woods and there was a corral full of fine painted horses. Then the children lived at this place, the same place where they had been tied and abandoned. They had very much food and much property.

Then a man came and saw their tent and the abundance they had, and went back and told the people. Then the people were told, "Break camp and move to the children for we are without food." Then they broke camp and travelled, and came to the children. The women went to take meat, but the bears drove them away. The girl and her brother would not come out of the tent. Not even the dog would come out. Then the girl said, "I will go out and bring a wife for you, my brother, and for the dog, and a husband for myself." Then she went out, and went to the camp and selected two pretty girls and one good-looking young man, and told them to come with her. She took them into the tent, and the girls sat down by the boy and the old man, and the man by her. Then they gave them fine clothing, and married them. Then the sister told her brother, "Go outside and look at the camp." The boy went out and looked at the people, and they all fell dead.

LXVIII. THE PRINCESS WHO REJECTED
HER COUSIN [256]

(TSIMSHIAN: Boas, *Report of the Bureau of American Ethnology*,
xxxi, 185, No. 25)

There was a custom among our people that the nephew of the
chief had to marry the chief's daughter, because the tribe of
the chief wanted the chief's nephew to be the heir of his uncle
and to inherit his place after his death. This custom has gone
on, generation after generation, all along until now, and the
places of the head men have thus been inherited. So it is with
this story.

A very long time ago there was a great village with many
people. They had only one chief. There was also his sister.
They were the only two chiefs in the large town. The chief also
had a beautiful daughter, and the chief's sister had a fine son.
All the people of the village were glad to see the young prince
and the young princess growing up, and they expected that
these two would soon marry. Therefore the relatives of the
prince went and talked with the father of the princess, and they
also went to the uncles of the princess and talked to them.

Now, the relatives of the girl accepted, but the girl rejected
the proposal and said that she would not marry him; but the
young prince loved her very much, and still she refused him.
The young man loved her still more, and he was always true
to her. Moreover, he was very anxious to speak to her, but
the young woman rejected him.

Now, the princess wanted to make a fool of her cousin. One
day she dressed herself up and went to the end of the village
to take some fresh air. The young man saw her pass by his
door, and he went after her. Soon he saw her sitting under a
large tree, and went up to her, and the girl was very kind to
him. She smiled when she saw him coming. Then the young
man sat down by her side under the tree as gently as he could.
He asked her if she did not want to marry him. The girl said,
"If you make a deep cut in your cheek, then you may marry
me." Therefore the handsome young man took his knife and
cut down his right cheek. The girls laughed at him, and they
went home.

When the cheek of the young man was healed, the princess
put on her finest dress, passed the door of her cousin, and the

young man saw her pass by. He followed her, and saw her sit at the same place where he had met her before. He went to her; and she stretched out her hands to greet him, put her arms around him, and kissed him once, since her cousin wanted to marry her. Then the young man loved her still more because she had kissed him the first time ever since he had loved her; and when the young man was overflowing with love, she said, "If you love me so much, show your love and make a cut down your left cheek; then I shall know that you really love me." The young man did not like to do it. However, he wanted to marry her, and so he took his knife and made a cut down his left cheek. They went home, and the young man was always thinking of her.

Soon his wounded cheek was healed. He did not mind his foolish acts. On the following day he saw her passing his door. The young man followed her, and she was sitting under the tree. She smiled at him when he was coming to her, and said, "Do you come to me again, my beloved one?" and he replied, "Yes, I come to marry you." Then he put his arms around her, and she kissed him again. He asked her, "Do you love me, my dear cousin?" and she replied, "Yes, you know how much I love you," and the princess asked him, "Do you also love me, cousin?" and he replied, "Indeed, I love you very much." Thus said the young man, for he wanted to marry her. Then the princess said to him, "Now, show me your love. Cut off your hair; then you may marry me." So the young prince took his knife and cut off his beautiful yellow hair. (In those days the young men and the old men wore their hair as long as women's hair, and it was considered dishonorable to cut a man's hair as we do it now.)

They went home, and on the following day the young man sent some one to her, saying that he wanted to marry her now. Therefore the messenger went to her and told her what her cousin had said; but the woman replied, "Tell him that I do not want to marry a bad-looking person like him, ugly as he is"; and she gave him the nickname Mountain With Two Rock Slides, as he had a scar down each cheek. She laughed at him and scorned him, saying, "I do not want to marry a man who cut his hair like a slave."

The young man's messengers came back to him and told him what she had said. Therefore the youth was very much ashamed. He remembered that he also was a prince, and he cried because his own cousin had mocked him.

Now, he decided to leave his father's house and his uncle's house, for he was ashamed before his fellows of the scars which he had made on his own cheeks by order of his beloved one. He went about, not knowing which way to go. Day by day he went, and he came to a narrow trail. He walked along it, and saw a small hut away off. He went toward it. Before it was evening he reached there; and when he was near, he walked up to it quietly. He stood outside and looked through a small hole. Behold! a woman was sitting there by the side of a fireplace. She said, "Come in, dear prince, if it is you who was rejected by his own cousin!" So the young man went in, and the woman made him sit down on the other side of the fire. She gave him to eat. When he started from home, four young men, his own friends, had accompanied him on his way; but three of them had gone back home, and only one, his dearest friend, followed him all along the way until they came to the little hut.

After the old woman had given them to eat, she said to the young man, "Soon you will arrive at the large house of Chief Pestilence, which is just across the little brook yonder. Leave your companion at this side of the brook, and you yourself go to the large house. When you get there, push open the large door, then say this: 'I come to be made beautiful in the house of Pestilence!' Shout this as loud as you can. Then you will see that the house on both sides is full of maimed persons. They will call you to come to their sides; but do not go there, because they will make you like one of them. When they stop calling you, then Chief Pestilence will call you to the rear of the house. Follow his calling. He will make you beautiful." Thus said the old woman to him. On the following day, after they had had their breakfast, they started. As soon as they crossed the brook, the prince said to his companion, "Stay here, and I will go on alone. Wait until I come back to you!" So the companion staid there.

Now he went on alone. Soon he saw a large house in the distance, and went as quickly as he could. He pushed open the door, ran in, and shouted at the top of his voice, "I came to be made beautiful, Chief Pestilence!" Then all the maimed people on both sides of the house beckoned to him and shouted. Those on one side would say, "Come this way, come this way!" and those on the other side said, "Come, come, come!" The prince remained standing in the doorway. There were many good-looking women among these maimed persons. They shouted and called him; but he stood still, waiting until Chief Pestilence should come forth from his room in the rear of the large house.

Soon the noise of the maimed people ceased. Then the door of the chief's room was opened, and, behold! Chief Pestilence came forth with his beautiful daughter. He said, "Dear prince, come this way!" Then the young man went to him and sat down on his right side.

Then Chief Pestilence ordered his attendants to bring his bathtub. They brought him a large tub full of hot water. Then the chief took the young man, put him into this tub, and, as soon as he was in the tub,[257] the water began to boil and the water boiled over the tub, boiling of its own accord. When the dross was all off, the chief took the bare bones of the young man, put them on a wide board, joining them together, and after he had done so, he called to his young daughter, who leaped over the bones. Then the young man was alive again.[258] His features were changed, and his body was as white as snow.[259]

Then the chief said, "Bring me a nice comb!" and his attendants brought him a comb of crystal. The chief took it and combed the prince's hair down to his loins. His hair was red, like tongues of fire. He was the most beautiful of all.

The chief did not want to let him go at once, but kept him in his house for two days. The young man thought he had been there two days, but in reality two years had passed.[143] Then the young man remembered his friend whom he had left by the brook before he enterd the house of Chief Pestilence. Now, the prince told the young woman that he loved his friend by the brook; therefore the young woman said, "Let us go to see him!" They went together; and when they came to the place, they found the man's bare bones heaped up there. Therefore the young prince wept, but the young woman commanded him to take the bare bones to her father's house. The young man did what the young woman had told him, and took the bare bones to the chief. The chief ordered his attendants to bring his bathtub. They brought it to him, and he put the bare bones into the tub. Then the water began to boil, and the dross of the bare bones boiled over the tub. Thus the young man saw what the Chief Pestilence had done to him.

Then the chief took out the bones and placed them on a wide board and joined them together;[260] and the young woman leaped over them four times,[261] and the young man was alive again.

Next the chief asked for his own comb. They brought it to him, and the chief asked what color of hair he wanted. The man said, "Dark-yellow hair." He also asked him how long he wanted it; and the man said, "Right down to the knee." So the chief combed his hair down to his knees; and this man was lighter color than the other. Now they started for home. It was not many days before they arrived at their home. The prince looked like a supernatural being, and his friend too was handsomer than any of the other people. They came and visited them; and all the people talked about these two men who had just come back from the house of Chief Pestilence, who had transformed them and given them great beauty.

The young people coveted their beauty, and they questioned them one day to know how far the house of Chief Pestilence was from their village. Then the prince's friend told them that it was not very far away.

Now, let us go back to the princess who years ago had refused to marry her own cousin. She was very anxious to see her cousin who had just come home from the house of Chief Pestilence. People were talking about it, that he was more beautiful than any other person in the village; and she heard the people say that he looked like a supernatural being. Therefore the young woman tried hard to see him. One day the chief, the father of the princess, invited his nephew to his house. The prince went with some of the chief's head men; and as soon as the prince entered his uncle's house, the young princess looked at him. Oh, how fine he looked! and more beautiful than any of the people. Then she tried to make her rejected cousin turn and look at her, but the young man took no notice of her courting. His hair was like fire, and his face shone like the rays of the sun.

Now, the young woman came down from her room, and walked to and fro behind the guests, laughing and talking, trying to make the beautiful prince look at her; but he took no notice of her. As soon as the feasting was over, he arose and went home, and the young princess felt full of sorrow.

The following day she sent her maid to call the beautiful prince. When the girl came to him and told him what her mistress had said to the prince, he did not answer a word, and the maid went back to her mistress and told her that the prince would not answer her a word. She sent to him again; and when the girl came to him, she told him that her mistress wanted him to come and see her. But he said to the girl, "Go and tell her that she rejected me then, so I will not go to her now." Then the girl went and told her mistress what the prince had said. The princess sent her girl again. "Go and tell him that I will do whatever he desires me to do." She went and told him what her mistress had said: "My mistress says that whatever you desire her to do she will do." Then the prince said to the girl, "Go and tell her that I desire her to cut down her right cheek, and I will come and be her guest." Therefore the girl went and told her mistress what the prince had said. So the princess took her knife and cut down her right cheek. She said to her maid, "Go and tell him that I will do whatever he wants me to do." She went and told the prince what her mistress had done.

Again the beautiful prince said, "Just tell her to cut down her other cheek, and then I will come and see her." So she went and told her mistress, and thereupon the princess cut her left cheek. Again she sent her maid, who went to him and told him. This time he said, "Let her cut her hair, then I will go to her." She went and told her, and the princess took her knife and shaved off her hair, and she sent her hair to him. The maid took it to the prince; but when the prince saw the hair, he refused to accept it. "Don't bring it near me! It is too nasty! Take it back to your mistress and tell her that I don't want to see the ugly scars on her cheeks and her ugly shaved hair. It is too nasty for me." Then he left, and laughed louder and louder, mocking her; and the girl returned to her mistress very sad.

She came slowly; and her mistress asked her, "My dear, what tidings do you bring?" Then she told her mistress how scornfully he had spoken of the ugly scars on her cheeks, and of her shaving her hair, and that everybody had been laughing at her, and that every one had heard him mocking her. Then the young princess was very much ashamed. She set out with her maid, and walked along crying. She wanted to hang herself, but her maid talked to her and comforted her all the way. They went on and on, trying to go to the house of Chief Pestilence. Her heart took courage, for she hoped to get there and ask Chief

Pestilence to make her beautiful. They went on and on, and passed many mountains and rivers and valleys, and reached the edge of a large plain. There they met a man, who asked them which way they intended to go; and the princess told him that they intended to go to the house of Chief Pestilence. She passed by him, and did not look at him, for she was ashamed to let any one look at her.

Soon they saw a large house in the distance. They went toward it; and when they reached the door, they went right in and shouted as they stood in the doorway, "We come to the house of Chief Pestilence to be made beautiful!" Then all the maimed people on both sides of the house called to them, "Come, come, come!" and those on the other side shouted, "This way, this way, this way!" and the princess went to those who called her to come; and the other one went to those who shouted "This way!"

Then the maimed people fell on the princess, broke her backbone, and made her lame. They turned her head to one side, and broke one of her arms; and those on the other side plucked out one of the eyes of her maid, tore up one side of her mouth, and scratched the two women all over their bodies, and then threw them outside. There they lay wounded, and nobody came to help them. The princess was more severely injured than her maid.

When the maid felt a little better, she saw her mistress lying there with wounds all over her body. She went to her, and saw how she was bruised. They were both in great distress, and the princess was groaning. So her maid helped her up and led her home. They spent many days coming down, and finally arrived at their home. Then she lay in bed, and finally died.

LXIX. THE FATAL SWING [262]

(OSAGE: Dorsey, *Field Museum: Anthropological Series*, vii, 26, No. 22)

Once there was a man living by the big water. He was a deer hunter. He would go out and kill wild turkeys and bring them in. Finally his mother-in-law fell in love with him. There was a swing by the water, and the old woman and her daughter would swing across it and back. After a while, the old woman partially cut the rope, so that it would break. While the husband was out hunting one day the old woman said to her daughter, "Let us go to the swing, and have some fun." The old woman got in first, and swung across the water and back. Then the girl got in the swing and she swung across all right, but when she was half-way back, the rope broke in two, and the girl fell into the water and was drowned.

The old woman went home and got supper for her son-in-law. The man came in just at dark, and he missed his wife, and said, "Mother-in-law, where is my wife?" The old woman said, "She has gone to the swing, and has not yet returned." The old woman began to prepare supper for her son-in-law. The man said, "Do not give me any supper." So he started to cry. The old woman said, "Do not cry; she is dead, and we cannot help it. I will take care of the baby. Your wife got drowned, so she is lost entirely." The man cut off his hair and threw his leggings away and his shirt, and was mourning for his wife. He would go out, and stay a week at a time without eating. He became very poor. Finally he said he was going off to stay several days; that he could not help thinking of his wife. He went off and stayed several days, and when he came home he would cry all the time.

One time, when he was out mourning, a rain and thunderstorm came up, and lightning struck all around the tree he was sitting under. He went back home and saw his baby, but stayed out of his sight. Again he went out, and it rained and thundered, and he went up by a big tree and lightning struck a tree near by him. The Lightning left him a club, and said, "Man, I came here to tell you about your wife for whom you are mourning. You do not know where she is, or how she came to be missing. That old woman drowned her in the big water. The old woman broke the rope and the girl is drowned in the big water. This club you must keep in a safe place. I was sent here to you, and I will help you get your wife back, and you must not be afraid of the big water. Go ahead and try to get her, and the fourth day you will get her all right."

The man went to the big water, and he saw his wife out in the water, and she said, "I cannot get to you. I am tied here with chains. I am going to come up four times." The next time she came out half-way. She said, "Bring me the baby, and I will let her nurse." So the man took the baby to her mother and let her nurse.[263] The woman said, "They are pulling me, and I must go. But the next time you must get me." So she came out the third time up to her knees. The man took the baby to her and let it nurse again. The woman said, "I have got to go back. They are pulling me by the chains. I must go, but the next time will be the last. I want you to try your best to get me." The man said, "I am going to get you, without doubt." The woman came out the fourth time, and the man hit the chain with the club and it seemed as though lightning struck it, and broke it. He got his wife.

So they went home, and the old woman said, "My daughter, you have got home." But the woman said not a word. Then the man heated an arrow red-hot and put it through the old woman's ears.[264] So they killed the woman.

LXX. THE SKIN–SHIFTING OLD WOMAN [265]

(WICHITA: Dorsey, *Publications of the Carnegie Institution*, xxi, 124, No. 17)

In the story of Healthy-Flint-Stone-Man, it is told that he was a powerful man and lived in a village and was a chief of the place. He was not a man of heavy build, but was slim. Often when a man is of this type of build he is called "Healthy-Flint-Stone-Man," after the man in the story. Healthy-Flint-Stone-Man had parents, but at this time he had no wife. Soon afterwards he married, and his wife was the prettiest woman that ever lived in the village. When she married Healthy-Flint-Stone-Man they lived at his home. She was liked by his parents, for she was a good worker and kind-hearted. As was their custom, the men of the village came at night to visit Healthy-Flint-Stone-Man, and his wife did the cooking to feed them, so that he liked her all the more, and was kind to her.

Early in the morning a strange woman by the name of Little-Old-Woman came to their place and asked the wife to go with her to get wood. Out of kindness to Little-Old-Woman she went with her, leaving her husband at home. Little-Old-Woman knew where all the dry wood was to be found. When they reached the place where she thought there was plenty of wood they did not stop. They went on past, although there was plenty of good dry wood. The wife began to cut wood for the old woman and some for herself. When she had cut enough for both she fixed it into two bundles, one for each. Little-

Old-Woman knelt by her pile and waited for the wife to help her up. Little-Old-Woman then helped the wife in the same way, and they started toward their home. They talked on the way about their manner of life at home. Arrived at the village, the old woman went to her home. When the wife got home she began to do her work.

Again, the second time, the old woman came around and asked the wife to go with her to fetch wood. They started away together, and this time went farther than on the first time to get their wood, though they passed much good wood. The wife cut wood for both and arranged it in two piles, but this time she herself first knelt by her pile and asked the old woman to take hold of her hands and pull her up; then the wife helped the old woman with her load. They returned home, and on the way the old woman said to the wife, "If you will go with me to fetch wood for the fourth time I shall need no more help from you." They again went far beyond where any other women had gone to get wood. When they got to the village they parted. The wife wondered why the old woman came to her for help. She found the men passing the time talking of the past as usual. She kept on doing her duty day after day.

The third time the old woman came for the wife to ask her to help her fetch wood, as she was all out of it again. Again they went out, and this time they went still further for the wood, and now they were getting a long way from the village. The wife cut wood and arranged it in two bundles, one for each of them to carry. This time it was the old woman's turn first to be helped up with the wood. They helped each other, and on the way home the old woman told the wife that they had only once more to go for wood, and the work would all be done. She always seemed thankful for the help she received. They reached the village and went to their homes. The wife found her men as usual, and commenced to do her work. After the men were through eating they went home, though some stayed late in the night.

Finally the old woman came the fourth time [266] to ask the wife to go with her and help her fetch some wood. This time they went about twice as far as they had gone the third time from the village. When the old woman thought they were far enough they stopped, and the wife began cutting wood for both of them. When she had cut enough she arranged it in two bundles. Now it was the wife's turn to be helped up with the wood, but the old woman refused to do it as usual and told her to go ahead and kneel by the bundle of wood. The wife refused. Now, each tried to persuade the other to kneel first against the bundle of wood. The old woman finally prevailed, and the wife knelt against the wood, and as she put her robe around her neck the old woman seemed pleased to help her, but as the old woman was fixing the carrying ropes she tightened them, after slipping them around the wife's neck until the wife fell at full length, as though dying.

The old woman sat down to rest, as she was tired from choking the wife. Soon she got up and untied the wife. Now, they were in the thick timber, and there was flowing water through it. After the old woman had killed the wife she blew into the top of her head and blew the skin from her, hair and all.[267] This she did because she envied the wife her good looks, since the wife was the best-looking woman in the village, and her husband was good-looking and well thought of by all the prominent men, and the old woman wanted to be treated as well as the wife had been treated. Then the old woman began to put on the wife's skin, but the wife was a little smaller than the old woman, though the old woman managed to stretch the skin and drew it over her, fitting herself to it. Then she smoothed down the skin until it fitted her nicely. She took the wife's body to the flowing water and threw it in, having found a place that was never visited by anyone, and that had no trail leading to it. She then went to her pile of wood and took it to her home. She found the men visiting the chief.

The chief did not discover that she was not his wife. The old woman knew all about the former wife's ways, for she had talked much with her when they were coming home with the wood, and she had asked the wife all sorts of questions about her husband. She understood how the men carried on at the chief's place. The wife had told the chief that the old woman had said that they were to go for wood four different times, and the last time being the fourth time, he supposed it was all over and his wife had got through with the old woman. So, as the old woman was doing his wife's duty, he thought her to be his wife until the time came when the skin began to decay and the hair to come off. Still there were big crowds of men around, and the old woman began to be fearful lest they would find her out. So she made as if she were sick. The chief tried to get a man to doctor her, but she refused to be doctored. Finally he hired a servant to doctor her. This was the man who always sat right by the entrance, ready to do errands or carry announcements to the people. His name was Buffalo-Crow-Man. He had a dark complexion. The old woman began to rave at his medicine working. He began to tell who the old woman was, saying that there was no need of doctoring her; that she was a fraud and an evil spirit; and that she had become the wife of the chief through her bad deeds. The old woman told the chief not to believe the servant; and that he himself was a fraud and was trying to get her to do something wrong. The servant then stood at the feet of the old woman and began to sing.

Then over her body he went and jumped at her head. Then he commenced to sing again, first on her left side, then on her right. He sang the song* four times, and while he was doing this the decayed hide came off from her. The servant told the men to take her out and take her life for what she had done to the chief's wife, telling how she had fooled the chief. They did as they were told. The servant told the men he had suspected the old woman when she had come around to get the wife to go after wood with her; that when going after wood they always went a long distance, so that no one could observe them, but that he had always flown very high over them, so they could not see him, and had watched them; that on the fourth time they went for wood he had seen the old woman choke the wife with the wife's rope; how the old woman had secured the whole skin of the wife and had thrown her body into the flowing water. He told the men where the place was, and directed them there the next day. The men went to their homes, feeling very sad for the wicked thing the old woman had done.

On the next day the chief went as directed, and he came to a place where he found a pile of wood that belonged to his former wife. He went to the place where he supposed his wife to be. He sat down and commenced to weep. There he stayed all night and the next day. He returned to his home, but he could not forget the occurrence. So he went back again and stayed another night and again returned home. The chief was full of sorrow. He went back to the place the third time, and when he got there he sat down and commenced to weep. Again

---

* The song with its Indian words and music is given in the original text.

he stayed all night, and early next morning it was foggy and he could not see far. While he sat and wept he faced the east, and he was on the west side of the flowing waters, so that he also faced the flowing water wherein his wife's body was thrown.

He heard some one singing, but he was unable to catch the sound so that he could locate the place where the sound came from. He finally discovered that it came from the flowing water. He went toward the place and listened, and indeed it was his wife's voice, and this is what she sang:

> Woman-having-Powers-in-the-Water,
> Woman-having-Powers-in-the-Water,
> I am the one (you seek),
> I am here in the water.

As he went near the river he saw in the middle of the water his wife standing on the water. She told him to go back home and tell his parents to clean their grass-lodge and to purify the room by burning sage. She told her husband that he might then return and take her home; that he should tell his parents not to weep when she should return, but that they should rejoice at her return to life, and that after that he could take her home. So the man started to his home. After he arrived he told his mother to clean and purify the lodge; and that he had found his wife and that he was going back again to get her. He told her that neither she nor any of their friends should weep at sight of the woman. While his mother was doing this cleaning he went back to the river and stayed one more night, and early in the morning he heard the woman singing again. He knew that he was to bring his wife back to his home. When he heard her sing he went straight to her. She came out of the water and he met her. She began to tell her husband about her troubles — how she met troubles and how he was deceived. That day they went to their home, and Flint-Stone-Man's parents were glad to see his wife back once more. They lived together until long afterward.

LXXI. THE CHILD AND THE CANNIBAL [268]

(BELLA COOLA: Boas, *Jesup North Pacific Expedition*, i, 83)

Once upon a time there was a youth whose name was Anutkoats, who was playing with a number of girls behind the village. While they were playing, a noise like the cracking of twigs was heard in the woods. The noise came nearer and nearer. The youth hid behind a tree, and saw that a Snanaik was approaching. She was chewing gum, which caused the noise. He advised the children to run away, but they did not obey. When they saw the gum, they stepped up to the Snanaik and asked her to give them some. The Snanaik gave a piece of gum to all the children, and when she saw Anutkoats, who was advising the children to return home, she took him and threw him into the basket which she was carrying on her back. Then she took all the other children and threw them on top of him into her basket. After she had done so, she turned homeward. Then Anutkoats whispered to the girls to take off their cedar-bark blankets, and to escape through a hole that he was going to cut in the basket. He took his knife, cut a hole in the bottom of the basket, and fell down. The girls also fell down one by one until only one of them was left.

All the children returned home and told their parents what had happened. The mother of the girl who had not been able to escape began to cry, mourning for her daughter. She cried for four days and four nights. Then her nose began to swell, because she had been rubbing it all the time. She had thrown the mucus of her nose on the ground. Now when she looked down, she saw that something was moving at the place where it had fallen. She watched it from the corners of her eyes, and soon she discovered that her mucus was assuming the shape of a little child.[269] The next time she looked, the child had grown to the size of a new-born baby. Then the woman took it up, and the child began to cry. She carried it into the house, and washed the baby for four days. Then the child, who was very pretty and had red hair, began to speak,[112] and said, "My father, the Sun, sent me to ask you to stop crying. I shall go out into the woods, but pray don't cry, for I am sent to recover your daughter. I know where she is. Make a small salmon-spear for me, which I shall need." Thus spoke the boy.

Then the woman asked an old man to make a salmon-spear, which she gave to her son. His mother gave him ear-rings made of abalone shells, and the boy played about with his spear, and always wore his ear ornaments. One day when his mother was crying again, the boy said, "Mother, I ask you once more, don't cry, for my father the Sun sent me down to bring back your daughter. He will show me where she is. I shall start to-day to recover my sister from the Snanaik, who stole her. Don't worry about me." Then the boy went up the river. After he had gone some distance, he came to a tree which overhung the river. He climbed it, and looked down in order to see if there were any fish in the water. Soon he heard a noise some distance up the stream, and gradually it sounded nearer. Then he saw the Snanaik coming down the river. When she reached the tree, she stopped and looked down into the clear water. She saw the image of the boy, who was sitting on the tree, and thought it was her own reflection. She said, "How pretty I am!" and she brushed her hair back out of her face. When she did so, the boy imitated her movements in order to make her believe that she was looking at her own reflection. When she laughed, he laughed also, in order to deceive her. But at last the Snanaik looked upward, and saw the boy sitting in the tree.[270]

Then she addressed him with kindly words, and asked him to come down. She said, "What did your mother do in order to make you so pretty?" The boy replied, "You cannot endure the treatment I had to undergo in order to become as pretty as I am." The Snanaik begged, "Oh, come down and tell me. I am willing to stand even the greatest pain in order to become as pretty as you are. What are you doing up there?" Then the boy said, "I was watching for salmon, which I desire to harpoon with my salmon-spear." The Snanaik repeated, "Oh, come down, and do with me whatever you please in order to make me as pretty as you are." The boy replied, "I don't believe you can endure the wounds that I have to inflict upon you." She replied, "You may cut me as much as you please. I want to become as pretty as you are."[271] Then the boy climbed down the tree, and the Snanaik asked, "What must we do first?" He said, "We must go up this river to find two stone knives with which my mother used to cut off my head."

They walked up the river, and found the stone knives. Then the boy said to the Snanaik, "Now lie down on this stone. Put your neck on this knife." The Snanaik did as she was bidden. Then the boy took the other knife, told the Snanaik to shut her eyes, and cut off her head. The head jumped back to the body, and was about to unite with it,[272] when the boy passed his hands over the wound, and thus prevented the severed head from joining the body again. Thus he had killed her.

Then he went to the Snanaik's house. He found his sister whom the Snanaik had killed and smoked over her fire. He took the body down, and patted it all over with his hands. Thus he resuscitated the girl.[273] On looking around in the house, he found the dried bodies of other children, whom he also brought back to life. Then he took the girl and the other children home.

LXXII. THE CANNIBAL WHO WAS BURNED [274]

(HAIDA: Swanton, *Jesup North Pacific Expedition*, v, 265, No. 34)

Five brothers were always hunting. After a while an unknown man came in to them. He came in many times. Once when he was there, the eldest brother's child began to cry, and, after all of the brothers had tried to quiet it without success, he offered to do so; but when they gave it to him, he secretly sucked the child's brains out from one side if its head. When he handed it back, and they saw what he had done, they seized wood from the fire and beat the stranger. Then he became angry and killed all of the brothers but the youngest, whom he chased about in the house until morning. The boy ran out, and after a long run, still pursued by the ogre, crossed a high mountain. By and by he crossed another, and saw a lake beneath it. Running thither, he came to a log, composed of two trees growing together so as to make a fork, floating upon the water. Going out upon this, he threw himself into the crotch.

When the pursuer came up, he saw the man's shadow in the lake, and began jumping at it. Now the man began to sing a North Song, and the lake at once began to freeze over.[610] When all had frozen over except the small hole where the ogre was jumping, it froze so quickly after he had gone in, that he could not get out again when he came up. Then he saw the man on the tree, and asked him to pull him out; but the man only sang louder, so that the ogre was held fast. The man now began to cut some dry wood to build a fire over the ogre's head, telling him at the same time that he was going to save him. When the fire was lighted, the ashes flying up from the monster's head turned into mosquitoes.[275] That is how they started.

LXXIII. THE CONQUERING GAMBLER [276]

(CHILCOTIN: Farrand, *Jesup North Pacific Expedition*,
ii, 38, No. 23)

Once two men played lehal together, and one of them lost everything he had. Finally he bet his wife, but soon lost her too,[277] and went away sad and sorrowful. He went to a place near Tatlah Lake, and lay down under an overhanging rock, which covered him like a roof. As he lay there and wondered how he could get his property back, he heard some ducks flying over, and, looking up, found to his surprise that he could see the ducks straight through the rock. Then he took his lehal-bones and laid them on top of the rock, and looked to see if they were visible through it, and he found he could see which was the white and which was the black one. Then he was joyful once more, and went home. All that summer he spent alone in the snow mountains, hunting ground-hogs, and making blankets of their skins, and he made a great many.

About salmon time he came back for the fishing, and met the man who had won his wife, and said, "Come, let us play lehal again, for I have blankets to bet now." So they started in to play again, and this time the man could see right through the other's hands and see the lehal-bones, and so could not lose. However, he let the other man win a few times, just to make him rash. And the other man said, "I think I'm going to beat you this time, just as I did before." The man replied, "Yes, I'm afraid you will." However, he soon started in to win, and won everything back, until his rival had nothing left to play for, except the two women. Then the man said, "Now let us play for my wife again." But the other replied, "I'd rather not play for your wife, for I should like to keep her; but my own wife I'll bet, for I don't care for her." The man agreed, and soon won the woman, and then they started to play for his own wife. When he had won back half of her, the other man said "Let us stop for to-night, so that she can stay with me one night more." But the man answered, "I did n't talk that way the other time we played, and I don't want to stop now." So they played again, and the man won both the women, and thus had his revenge.

LXXIV. THE DECEIVED BLIND MAN [278]

(SMITH SOUND ESKIMO: Boas, *Journal of American
Folk-Lore*, xii, 169, No. 7)

There was a blind boy (or young man) who lived with his
mother and sister. They went to a place where there was no
one and lived alone. One day, when they were in their tent,
a bear came up to it. Though the boy was blind he had a bow,
and the woman aimed it at the bear for him. The arrow struck
the bear and killed it. The mother, however, deceived her son
and told him he had missed it. She cut it up and then cooked
it. The young man now smelled the bear-meat, and asked his
mother whether it was not bear he was smelling. She, however,
told him he was mistaken. Then she and her daughter ate it,
but she would give him nothing. His sister, however, put half
her food in her dress secretly, to give him later. When her
mother asked her why she was eating so much (noticing that
she seemed to eat an unusual quantity), the girl answered that
she was hungry. Later, when her mother was away, she gave
the meat to her brother. In this way he discovered that his
mother had deceived him. Then he wished for another chance
to kill something, when he might not be thus deceived by his
mother.

One day, when he was out of doors, a large loon came down
to him and told him to sit on its head. The loon then flew with
him toward its nest, and finally brought him to it, on a large
cliff. After they had reached this, it began to fly again, and
took him to a pond.[279] The loon then dived with him, in order
to make him recover his eyesight. It would dive and ask him
whether he was smothering; when he answered that he was,
it took him above the surface to regain his breath. Thus they
dived, until the blind boy could see again. His eyesight was
now very strong; he could see as far as the loon, and could
even see where his mother was, and what she was doing. Then
he returned. When he came back, his mother was afraid, and
tried to excuse herself, and treated him with much consideration.

LXXV. THE GIRL WHO MARRIED HER BROTHER [280]

(SHASTA: Farrand and Frachtenberg, *Journal of American Folk-Lore,*
xxviii, 212, No. 5)

A mother and her ten children were living together. The oldest
was a girl.* She was mean; and her mother had to hide from
her the youngest child, a boy. The girl was wont to ask her
mother, "Where is that child you bore some time ago?" to
which her mother would reply, "Oh, I lost him long ago."
Every morning the daughter saw her mother go down to the
spring. She followed her, and noticed that the water was
disturbed, as if some one had been swimming there.

One day she found a long hair in the water. She measured it
with the hair of her other brothers, and found it to be too long.
So she decided to learn whose hair it was. Every night she
camped at the spring, until one morning she saw a strange man
come down to bathe. Then she knew who had been disturbing
the water, and to whom the hair belonged.[281] It was her youngest
brother. She fell in love with him, and decided to marry him.
She went home and asked her mother to prepare some food for
her, as she was going away. Her mother gave her food, and
the girl asked, "Who wants to accompany me?" The oldest
brother said, "I." — "No," replied the girl, "not you." In
a similar manner she refused to go with any of her other
brothers. Finally she ran to the side of the house, put her hand
there, and said, "This is the one I want to take along." Then
the young brother came out from where he had been hidden
all these years, and said, "All right! I'll go with you."

They travelled all day. When night came, she said, "Let
us stop here!" So they stopped there, and the girl began to
prepare the bed. The boy suspected what she wanted of him,
but he said nothing. He only wished she might fall sound
asleep, so as to be able to run away from her. When she was
sound asleep, he put a log in his place and left her, returning to
the house.[282] He ran home, and shouted, "Let all get ready to
come with me!" They did so, and before departing cautioned
everything in the house not to tell his sister where they had
gone. But they omitted to tell Ashes.[196]

* This story has been sufficiently changed to avoid the use of some very difficult
personal names.

Early in the morning she woke up and began to speak to the log, thinking it to be her husband; but soon she found out the deception, jumped up in anger, and cried, "I'll kill you!"

In the meantime the brother and his family had entered a basket and were drawn up to the sky.[283] The sister came home, and inquired of everything in the house as to the whereabouts of her mother and brothers. No one would tell. Finally she asked Ashes, and was told that they had gone up to the sky. She looked up, and saw her family half-way up the sky. She began to weep, and called for them repeatedly to come down. But the boy had told them not to look back,[217] no matter how often she might call. Soon, however, the mother looked back, and the basket began to fall. The daughter was glad when she saw the basket coming down. She made a big fire, intending to kill her family as soon as the basket should fall into it. The basket came down; but, when the youth hit the ground, he flew right up and floated away. The girl thought she had killed them all, and was very glad.

After a while the brother came down on the ocean beach, where two Sea-Gull girls found him. At first the girls were afraid of him; but he assured them, saying, "Don't be afraid of me! Touch me, wash me, and you will find that I am all right!" The girls did as directed, and he married them. After a while his wives became pregnant and gave birth to a boy and girl. As soon as the children grew up, the father gave them a bow and arrow, and taught them how to shoot, saying, "When you grow up, I want you to go to my sister over yonder, and watch her secretly." The children grew up and went to their aunt's house, who scared them so, that they ran back in a hurry. Then he said to his children, "Let us all go and kill my sister! She is mean. She killed my family." The children promised to help him.

So they all went, and the young man began to fight with his sister; but he could not kill her, because the only vulnerable spot, her heart, was in the sole of her foot.[246] In vain he shot arrow after arrow at her. He could not kill her. His arrows were all gone, and he was almost exhausted, when Meadow-Lark came to his help. She told him to look at her heel. He did so, and saw something bright and shining. On Meadow-Lark's advice he directed an arrow at that spot, and thus succeeded in killing the terrible sister.

LXXVI. THE SWAN–MAIDENS [284]

(SMITH SOUND ESKIMO: Boas, *Journal of American Folk-Lore*, xii, 171, No. 7)

A man who was walking, once upon a time, came to a pond, where there were a number of geese. These geese had taken off their garments and had become women, and were now swimming in the pond. The man came up to them without being seen, and seized their feather-garments. He gave them all back but two, whereupon the women put them on and flew away.[132] Finally he gave one of the two remaining ones hers, whereupon she also flew off. The last woman, however, he kept with him, took to his house, and married. Soon she became pregnant and gave birth to two children.

One day, when her husband had gone away, she found some wings, which she took into the house, and hid behind the skin-coverings of the walls. When her husband again went away, she put these on herself and her two children, whereupon they turned to geese and flew away. When the husband returned, they were already far away. However, he decided to follow them, and set out. He walked along the beach, where the tide was low, and kept travelling in this manner a long time. Finally he came to a large pot, where it was hot, and he had (cooked) codfish to eat. He stepped over this, and went on his way once more. Then he came to a large man, who was chopping with an axe, making seals and walruses. He threw the chipped pieces into the water, saying to them, "Be a quajuvaq," and they would be hooded seals, or "Be an uxssung," and they would be ground-seals.[107] The man then offered to take him to his wife. He took him into his boat, but told him to keep his eyes closed,[217] and they started off. Soon the husband heard voices of people, and was preparing to look, when the large man forbade him. This happened several times until they reached the shore.

Meanwhile the two children had seen their father coming, and had gone indoors to inform their mother. She, however, said that they were mistaken, for they had gone entirely too far for him ever to come. The children then told her to come out and look for herself, but she was so certain that she did not even do this. Soon the children came in again, saying that their father was coming, and again she refused to believe them or to look. Then the man himself entered, and now she quickly feigned to be dead. Her husband took her up, carried her away, and buried her, covering her with stones. Then he went back and sat down, pulling his hood down as a sign of mourning. Meanwhile his wife arose again, and began walking about the tent in which her husband was. Then he took his spear and killed her. Thereupon a great many geese came, which he also killed, but the two boys went away.

LXXVII. THE DEATH OF PITCH [285]

(TSIMSHIAN: Boas, *Report of the Bureau of American Ethnology*, xxxi, 86)

Txämsem * went on, not knowing which way to go. He was very weak and hungry, and sore of foot. He went on and on in the woods until he saw a house far off. He went toward it, came near, and entered There were a man and his wife, a very pretty young woman, there. They permitted him to come in for they had pity on the poor man who had come to their house. They asked him if he wanted something to eat, and they gave him to eat. Then the young woman tried to cure his ankle, which was hurt by the stone in the house of the Chief Echo. He was now in the house of Little Pitch. He came in, and the people were very kind to him. The wife of Little Pitch put pitch on his sore ankle. After two days he was quite well, and he was very glad. The young woman gave him to eat every day. The house of Little Pitch was full of dried halibut and of all kinds of provisions. Txämsen made up his mind to kill his friend who had treated him so kindly.

On the following evening, after he had eaten his supper, he said to his friend that they would go out the next morning to catch halibut. Little Pitch was willing, and said to Txämsem, "It is not good for me if I go out fishing in the sun, because I am so weak. I must return home while it is still chilly." Txämsem replied, "I will do whatever you say, sir. I think we shall have plenty of time." Thus spoke Txämsem.

They started for the fishing-ground, and fished all night until daybreak. When the sun rose, Little Pitch wanted to go home; but Txämsem said, "I enjoy fishing. Lie down there in the bow of the canoe, and cover yourself with a mat." Little Pitch lay down, and Txämsem called him, "Little Pitch!" — "Hey!"

* Pronunciation approximately represented in English by "Chemsem."

he replied. After a while Txämsem called him again, "Little Pitch!" — "Hey!" he answered again with a loud voice. Txämsem called him once more, "Little Pitch!" Then he answered "Hey!" in a low voice. Txämsem called him still again. He answered, "Hey, hey!" with a very weak voice. "Now I will pull up my fishing-lines," said Txämsem; and after he had hauled his lines into the canoe, he paddled away home.

Txämsem paddled very hard. He called again, "Little Pitch!" but there was no answer; so he went to see what had happened to Little Pitch. As soon as he touched the mat that covered Little Pitch, behold! pitch was running out all over the halibut. Little Pitch was dead,[286] and melted pitch ran all over the halibut. Therefore the halibut is black on one side.[4]

Txämsem was very glad. He paddled along until he reached the shore in front of Little Pitch's house, expecting to get a good supper from Little Pitch's wife. He took the line, tied up his canoe, and went up, glad in his heart. He went on and on, but could not find any house. He searched everywhere, but could not find it. Only a little green spruce tree was standing there, with a drop of pitch upon one side. Finally Txämsem remembered that his canoe was full of halibut; so he went down to the beach, being very hungry, but he could not find his canoe. Only a spruce log with roots was there.[287]

CHAPTER VIII

TALES BORROWED FROM EUROPEANS [288]

*Well-established titles to European tales have been retained, even
though in some instances their appropriateness to the American
Indian borrowings is not immediately apparent.*

LXXVIII. THE SEVEN–HEADED DRAGON [289]

(OJIBWA: Skinner, *Journal of American Folk-Lore*, xxix, 330, No. 1)

THERE was once an old man living alone with his wife.
They had a horse and one dog, a spaniel. They hunted and
fished only in the big lake. Once upon a time they could not
get any fish in the nets, and they were very hungry. The man
went to look after his net in the morning, and found a jackfish
with a large head. As he was going to kill the fish, it said,
"Hold on, old man! Don't kill me right away!" The old man
stopped, and the fish told the old man to take all its scales off
and not to lose any, and to go and put these in the garden. It
also told him to cut off its fins and place them in the garden,
to cut its head off and give it to his wife to eat, half of its body
to be fed to the dog, and the other end to the horse. He told
the old man to shut the stable, but not to look at it for four
days and four nights, and not to look at the scales for four
days and four nights, but each morning after that he could
look. The old man then killed it and took it home. He told
his wife about it; and she asked, "Is that true?" — "Yes,"
answered the old man, and repeated all. "We will obey. We
are poor and hungry; maybe we shall have good luck." He
scaled and cut the fish and put it in the garden. He also fed
his wife, dog, and horse as he had been told, and shut the stable.
For four days and nights he could not sleep. His wife became
pregnant;[166h] and on the fourth morning she had two sons, and
the old man was glad. He ran to the stable, and found that
the mare had two foals, the dog two pups. He went to the
garden, and there was silver money where the scales had been
placed. There were two fine swords where the fins had been.
The old man ran in to tell his wife what had happened, and
they were delighted. After that the old man caught many fish.
Soon his boys grew up.

One time, when they were home in the evening, the elder boy said, "Are there any other people in the world?" — "Certainly, there are many people." — "Where can I find them?" — "You can find them anywhere." The youth said, "I will start to-morrow to try to visit some people." He left his sword, and told his brother, "I shall take yours, and leave mine hanging here. Do not touch it! If I have trouble or if I am killed, it will become rusty."[149] Then he went off. About dinner-time he dismounted and drank from a spring. He found silver water; and when he dipped his little finger into it, it became solid silver. He put some of the water on the horse's ears, and they became silver. He did the same to the dog's and also on his own hair. Then he started off.

When he came to a large town, he took off his clothes, found some old ones, and put rags around his finger and a handkerchief over his hair. He had a little box in which he put the horse and dog after making them small and hid them in a blacksmith's shop. The blacksmith looked at him. "Where are you from?" — "Is there a town here? I am very poor." — "Oh, come in!" The blacksmith fed him. The man said, "I can keep you here," and engaged him to do the chores in the house. He staid there a while, when one night the blacksmith came home and said, "The king of this town has a fine daughter, and she is going to be fed to the Windigo that has eight heads. He eats only people." — "When is she going to be taken there?" — "To-morrow morning."

The next day, after his work, the young man went out. He mounted his horse, took his dog, put on his own clothes, and rode out of the city. After a while he heard some one weeping in the woods. He turned in that direction, and found a young girl who was crying. She stopped when she saw him. The young man asked her, "Why are you crying?" — "There is no use telling you." — "Oh, no! tell me! Where are you going?" — "There is no use telling you." — "Oh, yes! you must tell me." Then the girl, seeing that he was a stranger, said, "I will tell you. I am going to yonder bluff. There is an eight-headed manitou there, and I am going to be eaten by him." — "Why?" — "He wants me." — "What if you do not go?" — "Then he would devour every one in the city. Therefore I must go."

Then the youth said, "I will go first. You can go when I come back." — "No, No! you must not go. I am not going

there for life, I am going there to die." — "If that is so, I must
see him first." — "Oh, no!" The young man said, "I will go
and come back. You stay here." — "Well, go on! but he will
kill you," and she gave the boy a ring. He then went to the
bluff, and saw that the trees were shaken by the breath of the
manitou. He stopped, and said to his horse and dog, "Try as
hard as you can to help me," and then he rode on. The horse
and dog sank deep into the soil. The boy took his sword and
cut off one head, which sprang back again. Then he told his
dog to catch it; and he hit the monster again, cutting off
another of his heads. The dog seized it and shook it. The
youth cut off another one, and the horse kicked it. When he
had cut off four heads, the manitou was not breathing very
strongly. Finally he killed him. He cut out all the tongues and
put them in a handkerchief. When he came back, he found
the girl waiting, and told her that he had killed the manitou.
He told the girl to go home and take the tongues with her, but
not to tell who killed the manitou. "Give the tongues to your
father, and say that a young fellow did it, but that you do not
know who."

The blacksmith was working at home. "Where are you going,
— home? No, you have to be eaten by the manitou." — "The
manitou has been killed." — "Nobody can kill him." The girl
showed him the tongues. Then the blacksmith believed her,
and asked her who had killed him. "I do not know, he is a
youth." — "Go home and tell your father that I killed him.
If you don't, I will kill you." The girl agreed, and he went
with her. Her father and mother asked her why she had come
back, and she told them that the blacksmith had killed the
manitou. She called him in, and they asked him, "How did
you do it?" — "I hit his tongues."

The king was very glad, and gave the girl to the blacksmith.
The youth went home, put his horse back into the box, and
dressed in his old clothes.

There was to be a four-days' dance before the wedding. After
three night's dance, the blacksmith was very glad, and told
the boy that this was the last night. Then the lad put on his
clothes. He came into the lodge and sat down by the door.
The girl knew him at once, and told her father secretly that
he had slain the monster. The king invited him to a better
place. The blacksmith wanted to go out, pretending that his

stomach pained him, but he was not allowed to leave. He was locked up, taken to the sea, and thrown in. The youth married the girl; and the king gave him half of the town, half of his money, and half of everything he owned, he was so glad that his daughter had been saved.

They went upstairs into their rooms. There was a window at the top on the east side of the house, and from there could be seen a blue fire at a distance.

"What kind of fire is that?" asked the youth.

"Do not ask about it," said the princess, "and never go near it."

On the next day he took his little horse and dog and went to the fire. There he saw an old, long house. He entered the first room, but there was no one there. After a while he heard some one. The door opened, and a white-headed old woman came in, and said, "Grandchild, hold your little dog, he will bite me. I am cold." — "Warm yourself, the dog will not touch you." — "You must tie him." — "I have nothing to tie him with." So the old lady gave him one hair, and said, "*Nosis*, tie him with that." The youth did so, and also tied the horse. The old woman had a cane. She touched him with it on the feet, and he died.

One morning the other youth, who had been left at home, saw rust on the sword. He said to his father, "I fear brother is dead somewhere, for his sword is rusty. I must go and try to find him." His father consented, and told him to be careful.

The next morning the elder brother left. About noon he found the same spring, and did as his brother had done. In the evening he came to the city and went to the chief's house. The girl came out and kissed him, and asked him where he had been, but he did not answer. They had supper, and he thought to himself, "That must be my brother's wife." At night he refused to go to bed. Through the window he saw the blue fires. He asked, "What kind of fires are those?" — "Why did you not go over to see?"

In the morning he went there. When he arrived there, he saw his brother's horse and dog tied with brass wire, lying down and frozen to death. He went into the lodge, and saw that his brother also lay dead by the fire. Soon he heard some one coming. An old woman appeared, and said, "I am cold." — "Warm yourself by the fire." — "First tie your little dog."

He refused to do so, and finally said, "Now, granny, make that man and horse and dog alive! If you do not do so at once, I shall send the dog after you." — "*Nosis*, I cannot bring a dead man to life." — "You have to." — "No."

Then he set his dog on her. The dog bit her, and the horse kicked her.

"Stop! I'll bring them to life." He stopped the animals, and the old woman walked forward. The youth kept away from her cane. She told him to take up a little bottle and put it on his frozen brother. As soon as he dropped some of the liquid from the bottle into his mouth, he came to. She did the same to the dog and to the horse. Then the brothers killed the old woman. They took the bottle away from her and went home. As they rode along together, the elder brother said, "You must be married. Yes. Your wife mistook me for you, but I only let her sleep with my arm. That's how I found out."

The younger brother, on hearing this, became jealous. He drew back and shot his brother with his revolver. He also shot his dog and horse. Then he went home, and his wife was glad to see him. She asked him why he refused to sleep with her last night. "You only let me have your hand." Then the brother began to sorrow for his brother. He took his horse and went back to the corpse. There he wept over his brother. His little dog ran around the dead body, and began to look inside the coat. There he found the old woman's little bottle. He put some of the liquid on the wound, and thus brought the brother back to life. Then he dropped some on the dog and the horse, and they all came to. They went home, put their horses and dogs away, entered the lodge, and sat down. The younger one's wife saw them, and was unable to tell them apart. On the following day they started to return to their parents. When they came to a forked road, they decided to go in different directions. The elder one took one road, and said, "I will go this way, and my name will be God." The other said, "I will follow the other, and I will be the Devil." That's the end of it.

LXXIX. JOHN THE BEAR [290]

(ASSINIBOIN: Lowie, *Anthropological Papers of the American Museum of Natural History*, iv, 147)

A man was living with his wife. It was summer. The woman was pregnant. One day, while she was picking berries, a big bear saw and abducted the woman, whom he kept in his cave. Before spring, the woman gave birth to a child begotten by her first husband, but with plenty of hair on his body, wherefore he was called Icmá (Plenty-of-Hair). In the spring the bear came out of his cave. The boy looked outside and told his mother, "We had better run away to where you first came from." But the bear had stopped up the entrance with a big rock, and the woman said, "We can't get out, the rock is too heavy." The boy tried it, and was able to lift it. They fled before the bear returned. They were already near the Indian camp when they heard the bear coming in pursuit. The woman was exhausted, but the boy packed her on his back and ran to the camp. At first, the woman went to a stranger's lodge. Then someone told her husband that his wife was back. The chief then took both her and his son home.

The boy used to play with other boys. Once he quarreled with one of them and killed him with a single blow. This happened again on another occasion. Then Icmá said to his father, "I don't like to kill any more boys; I'll go traveling." He started out and met two men, who became his comrades. One of them was called Wood-Twister, the other Timber-Hauler. They got to a good lodge, and decided to stay there together. On the first day, Icmá and Wood-Twister went hunting. They bade Timber-Hauler stay home and cook. While they were away, an ogre that lived in the lodge came out, threw Timber-Hauler on his back, and killed him. The two other men found him dead, but Icmá restored him to life. The next day Icmá said, "Wood-Twister, you stay home, I'll go hunting with Timber-Hauler." At sunset Wood-Twister began cutting firewood. He saw something coming out of the lodge that looked like a man, but wearing a beard down to its waist and with nails as long as bear-claws. It assaulted Wood-Twister, who was found dying by his friends, but was restored by Icmá. The next day Icmá said "You two go hunting, I will stay home." As he was beginning to chop wood, the monster appeared and challenged him to fight. Icmá seized its head, cut it off, and left the body in the lodge. When his comrades returned, Icmá asked them, "Why did not you kill him like this?" Then he said, "I don't like this house; let us go traveling."

They started out and got to a large camp. The chief said, "My three daughters have been stolen by a subterranean being. Whoever brings them back, may marry them all." Icmá told Timber-Hauler to get wood and ordered Wood-Twister to twist a rope of it. Then he made a hole in the ground and put in a box to lower himself in. He descended to the underground country and pulled the rope to inform his friends of his arrival. He found the three girls. The first one was guarded by a mountain-lion, the second by a big eagle, the third by giant cannibals. Icmá killed the lion. The girl said, "You had better turn back, the eagle will kill you." But he slew the eagle. Then the girl said, "The cannibals are bad men, you had better go home." "I'll wait for them." The twelve cannibals approached yelling; they were as big as trees. The girl said, "Run as fast as you can." But Icmá remained, and made two slings. With the first he hurled a stone that went clean through six of the men and killed them; and with the other sling he killed the remaining cannibals in the same way. One of the girls gave him a handkerchief, another one a tie, and the youngest one a ring. He took them to his box, and pulled the rope. His two comrades hoisted up the oldest one. Both wanted to marry her, but Icmá pulled the rope again, and they hauled up the second girl. Then Icmá sat down in the box with the youngest, and pulled the rope. As they were hauling them up, Wood-Twister said, "Let us cut the rope." The other man refused, but Wood-Twister cut the rope, and Icmá fell down. He stayed there a long time, while his companions took the girls to the chief.

At last Icmá begged a large bird to carry him above ground. The bird said he did not have enough to eat for such a trip. Then Icmá killed five moose, and having packed the meat on the bird's back, mounted with the third girl. Flying up, Icmá fed the bird with moose-meat, and when his supply was exhausted, he cut off his own flesh and gave it to the bird to eat. Icmá came up on the day when his false friends were going to marry the girls. All the people were gathered there. Icmá arrived. "I should like to go into the lodge before they get married." When he came in, Wood-Twister was frightened. "I should like to go out, I'll be back in a short time," he said. But he never returned. Then the chief asked, "Which of you three rescued the girls?" Then Icmá showed the handkerchief, the tie and the ring given him by the girls, and got all the three girls for his wives.

LXXX. THE ENCHANTED HORSE [291]

(MALECITE: Mechling, *Journal of American Folk-Lore*, xxvi, 247, No. 5)

There was once an old man that had a son named Louis who used to go hunting to support his parents, for they were very poor. One day while he was hunting, a gentleman came to visit his parents. This gentleman offered the old man a beaver hat full of gold for his son, and promised to take good care of the boy, whose only duties should be to tend the gentleman's horses.

"In about twenty years you will get your son back," said he.

The old man communicated the offer of the gentleman to his wife. She, however, was not anxious to accept it. Then the old man, goaded by the thoughts of their poverty, tried to persuade her, and he finally accepted the offer against his wife's inclinations. The gentleman waited for Louis to arrive, and then he took him away.

When he arrived at his home, he showed the boy over his house, and gave him permission to eat and drink whatever he cared to. He also showed him two pots, — one full of gold and the other full of silver, — which he told Louis not to touch. Later he took him to the stable where he kept the horses, and showed him a black horse in the farthest stall, telling him to be very particular about caring for that horse. Among other things, he gave him orders to wash him three times, and to take him to water three times every day. Then he pointed out to him a gray horse, and ordered him to beat him three times a day, to give him very little to eat, and to water him only once in twenty-four hours. Further, he told him never to take the bridle off that gray horse. After this, he told Louis that he was going on a journey, and would not return for a few weeks.

Louis carried out the gentleman's instructions, and, when two weeks had passed, the gentleman returned. The first thing he did was to go into the stable and examine his horses. He was well pleased with the looks of his black horse, and was also pleased to note that the gray one was looking very poorly. While they were returning to the house together, the gentleman began to play with Louis, who noted that he had a knife in his hand, and was not surprised when his finger was soon cut by it. The gentleman, however, apologized, and, taking a bottle out of his pocket, rubbed a little of the liquid on Louis' finger.

Louis was greatly surprised to find that his finger was at once entirely healed.

Later in the day, he told Louis that he was going away again (for a week, this time), and told him to be careful to treat the horses as he had done before. When he had gone, Louis' curiosity got the better of him. He took the cover off the pots, and dipped his finger into the golden liquid. When he pulled it out, lo, and behold! his finger was changed to gold. At once he saw that his master would know what he had done, and, to hide his finger, he wrapped it up in a piece of rag. In addition, Louis' pity overcame him, and he did not beat the gray horse.

At the end of the week, the gentleman returned and asked Louis how the horses were. He was well satisfied after his inspection of the stable. Again he began to play with Louis, his knife in his hand. While he was playing with him, he noticed that Louis' finger was wrapped up, and he inquired of Louis what was the matter with his finger. Louis replied that he had cut it. The gentleman pulled the rag off, and seeing that Louis' finger had turned to gold, he knew that Louis had been meddling with the pots. He became very angry, and grasped Louis' finger, twisted it, pulled it off, and threw it back into the pot, warning Louis not to touch the pots again. He played with him as before, and again cut him on the hand. A second time he applied the liquid, and again the boy's hand was healed immediately.

He again told Louis that he was going away, and would be gone for three weeks, and ordered him to beat the gray horse on this occasion five times each day.

That day Louis watered the horses, and, noticing that the gray horse could hardly drink any water with the bit in his mouth, he took pity on him, removed the bridle, and gave the horse a good drink. When the horse lifted his head from the brook and looked at Louis, he had a man's face on him and he spoke to Louis as follows: "You have saved me. If you do as I tell you, we both shall be saved. The master is not a man, but the Devil. He came to my parents as he did to yours, and bought me with a beaver hat full of money. Every time he comes and cuts you, he is trying you to see if you are fat enough to be killed. When he returns this time, he will again try you, and, if he finds that you are not fat enough, he will turn you into a horse. If you are fat enough, he will kill you. If you do as I tell you, Louis, we both shall be saved. Now feed me as well as you can for two weeks; put my bridle on the black horse, and beat him five times a day. In short, give him the treatment which was destined for me."

Louis did as the Gray Horse requested, and the animal began to recover his lost weight. The black horse lost weight rapidly. After the two weeks were up, the gray horse was in good condition; the black horse was very poorly.

"Now," said the Gray Horse, "the Devil suspects that things have not gone properly, and he is returning. Now we must prepare speedily to leave. Since his black horse is very swift, you must go and cut his legs off: cut the left foreleg off below the knee; cut the right fore-leg off away above the knee; cut the right hind-leg off below the knee; and the left hind-leg, away above the knee. He will not then be able to travel so fast, for his legs will be short and of different lengths."

When Louis had completed his task, the Gray Horse told him to go to the house and get the pots of silver and gold; and, on Louis' return with them, the Horse told Louis to dip his tail in the silver pot, and to dip his mane and ears in the gold one.

"And you dip your hair into the gold pot," said the Horse, "and stick your little fingers into the metal. Take the saddle and put it on me, but, before we start, go into the house and get three grains of black corn which he has upon his shelf, and take his flint, steel, and punk. Take, also, an awl, that round pebble which comes from the seashore, and then take that wisp of hay which is pointed."

Louis did as the Horse bade him, and then mounted on his back and rode away.

The Devil returned two days after they had started, and, when he saw that the gray horse had gone and the black horse was mutilated, he knew what had taken place. This enraged him very much, and he at once began to think how he could outwit the fugitives. Finally he set out in pursuit.

After Louis and the Gray Horse had been gone several days, the Gray Horse spoke to the boy, and said, "The Devil and the black horse are pretty close. You did not cut his legs short enough. Give me one of those grains of black corn, and I'll go a little faster."

Louis gave him one of the grains of black corn, and the Gray Horse traveled much faster. After a few days had passed, the Horse again said, "Louis, he is getting very close. You will have to give me another grain."

So Louis gave him a second grain, and the Gray Horse increased his speed. Three days later, the Gray Horse said to Louis, "Give the the last grain. He is getting very close."

After three more days, the Gray Horse again spoke, and said, "Louis, he is very close. Throw the awl behind you." [205]

Louis did as he was told, and the Horse said, "Now, that awl has made a great field of thorn-bushes grow, many miles in extent."

When the Devil rode up, he was going so fast that he rode right in among the thorns, and got his horse out only after a great deal of trouble. By the time he had extricated his horse and had ridden around the field, Louis had gained a great distance over him.

"Louis, he is getting very close," said the Horse some days later. "Throw back the flint."

Louis obeyed him, with the result that, when the Devil came up, he was confronted by a high wall of bare rock, which extended for miles. He was forced to go around this, and, when he once more took up the trail, Louis had gained many more miles on him. After a couple of days, the Gray Horse said, "Louis, we have only two things left, and I am afraid that we are going to have a hard time."

"I think," said Louis, "we had better throw the punk behind." With that he threw the punk behind him. When it struck the ground, it immediately burst into flame, starting a forest fire which extended many miles.

When the Devil arrived, he was going too fast to avoid riding into the fire, and this caused him great trouble. He had to go many miles out of his way to avoid the fire, and this delay enabled the fugitives to make a material gain in distance. In two or three days the Devil had regained the distance that he had lost.

The Gray Horse now said to Louis, "I am afraid that he is going to overtake us before we can reach the sea. He is gaining rapidly upon us, and is now very close. You had better throw the pebble behind you; it is the only chance left us."

Louis threw the pebble behind them; and the result was that a great lake appeared, which extended over many square miles. The Devil rode up to the lake, and, knowing whither they had gone, he travelled around it. This manœuvre cost the Devil the loss of many valuable miles, for Louis and the Gray Horse were by this time quite close to the sea.

"He is still gaining on us." said the Gray Horse. "I'm getting very tired."

Looking ahead, Louis could see the ocean, and turning around, he could see the Devil coming, gaining on them all the time.

"Louis, I am afraid he is going to overtake us," said the Horse.

Now, Louis did not understand what advantage it would be for them to arrive at the sea; but this was soon apparent. They did manage to reach the seashore ahead of the Devil, however, when the Gray Horse said, "Louis, throw out that wisp of hay."

Louis pushed it out, and, behold! as he thrust it, the wisp of hay was converted into a bridge. They immediately rode out upon this, and as they passed over it, the bridge folded up behind them! The Devil did not reach the sea until they were a safe distance from the shore.

"It was very lucky," the Devil said, "that you took my bridge with you, or I would have eaten you two for my dinner!"

Now, Louis and his horse continued to cross the bridge until they came to the land on the other side. While travelling along through this new country, they discovered a cave.

"Now," the Gray Horse said to Louis, "you stable me in here, and go up to the king's house and see if you cannot get work. Wrap up your head in order that your hair may not be seen, and do the same to your little fingers. When you arrive there, go and lie with your face down behind the kitchen, and wait until they throw out the dish-water. They will ask you what you want. Tell them that you desire work, and that you are a good gardener. Do not forget to comb your hair once a day in the garden, where they cannot see you."

The young man did all the Gray Horse suggested, and, when one of the maids threw out some dish-water behind the kitchen, she noticed him, and straightway notified the king. His Majesty ordered the youth to be brought before him, and, when

Louis had come, the king inquired into his identity and his desires. Louis told the king that he wanted work, and the king employed him as a gardener, because Louis claimed greater ability than the other gardeners. Every noon he would seclude himself to comb his hair, and then he would tie up his head again in the cloth. Although he was quite handsome, he did not look well with his head tied up in this manner. His work, moreover, was so excellent that the king soon noticed an improvement in the garden.

One day, while he was combing his hair, the princess looked out of her window, and saw Louis' hair. She noticed that the hair was all of gold; and the light from it shone into her room as it would if reflected from a mirror. Louis did not notice her, and, when he had completed his toilet, he wrapped up his head again and went away, leaving the princess enchanted by his looks.

During the same afternoon, while he was working near the palace, the princess dropped a note down to him. Louis did not see it, and therefore did not pay any attention to it. She then dropped several more, one after another; but he paid no attention to them.

The next day, he thought he would go down and see his horse. When he arrived at the cave, the Gray Horse inquired what had happened. Louis related the few events to him; but the Gray Horse told him that that was not all, for he had not noticed the princess looking at him when he was combing his hair.

"To-morrow," said the Horse, "the king will ask you if you are descended of royal blood. You tell him that you are the child of poor parents. There is a prince who wants to marry the princess; but she does not love him. When you go back to work in the garden, the princess will drop notes to you again, but don't touch them. Louis, in time you shall marry her, but don't forget me."

Louis returned, and the princess again dropped him notes; but he ignored them.

In the meantime the prince had come to see the princess, and he made arrangements with the king to marry his daughter. The princess, however, would not look at the prince. The king demanded of his daughter why she did not want to see the prince, and she told him that she desired to marry the gardener.

The king became very angry; he declared that she could not marry the poor beggar.

"Did you not always say that you would give me anything I wanted?" she asked of the king.

"Yes," answered he; "but you must marry a prince."

She again refused to marry the prince. At this, the king became very angry, and went out to tell his wife what the princess had said.

"I think the gardener is a prince in disguise," the queen said to the king.

The king summoned Louis into his presence; and the young man, obeying, came into the midst of the royalty and nobility of the palace, with his head still covered. The king asked him if he was of royal blood.

"No," he replied. "I am the son of poor parents."

The king then dismissed him.

The princess, however, contrived a means to marry Louis, and, when the ceremony was over, they went back to the king. She told her father what she had done, and asked for her dowry. He told her that her dowry should be the pig-pen in which he fattened his hogs; and he drove them from the palace with nothing more. The queen was in tears at the way the king treated their daughter; but he was obdurate.

The princess and Louis had to subsist on what little the queen could send them. Soon the princess said to Louis, "We had better go to the place where your parents live."

"No," said Louis, "we must go where the king sends us, for his will is my pleasure."

So they went to the pig-pen and fixed up a place to sleep. Every day the princess went to the palace, and the servants there would give her what was left from the table. This continued for several weeks, until, one day, Louis thought of his Horse. He went over to the cave to find out how he was doing.

"Well, Louis, I see that you are married, and that your father-in-law is treating you pretty badly," the Horse said to him. "Now you look in my left ear, and you will see a cloth folded up."

Louis did as directed; and the Gray Horse continued, "Take the cloth. At meal-time unfold it, and you will find inside all sorts of food of the finest kind. Come back and see me to-morrow."

Louis returned to his hog-pen, where his wife had the leavings from the palace table arranged for supper.

"Take this cloth and unfold it," said he.

And when she unfolded it, she was amazed to see delicious food and fine wines all ready to eat and drink. This was the first decent meal that they had eaten since they were married. The next day he again went back to see the Horse, who asked Louis if he had heard any news. Louis said that he had not.

"Well," said the Gray Horse, "I did. Your father-in-law is going to war to-morrow, because his daughter did not marry the prince to whom she was betrothed. Louis, you had better go too. Send your wife up to borrow a horse and arms, and you go with him."

On returning to his hog-pen, Louis told his wife what he had heard and what he wished her to do. So she went up to the castle to borrow a horse and armor. The king at first refused to give it; but the queen finally persuaded him to loan his son-in-law a horse. Thus Louis was equipped with a gray mare and an old sword. Louis accepted this; and the next morning, when the king started with his followers, Louis went forth mounted on the gray mare. He found, however, that she was too old to carry him: so he rode her down to the cave. There the Gray Horse told him to look in his right ear for a little box. Louis did so, and found the article. On opening this box, he found a ring inside it. The Horse told him that he could now get anything he wished for, and directed him to wish for arms and armor better than the king's own. Louis did so, and the armor immediately appeared. When Louis had donned it, the Gray Horse told him to comb his mane and tail; and after this was done, they started, quite resplendent. While they were passing the pig-pen, Louis' wife, mistaking him for a foreign king, begged him not to kill her father, and Louis promised not to hurt the old gentleman.

The fight was already raging when Louis arrived, and the enemy was pressing the king hard; but he came at just the right time, and turned the tide of the battle. Not recognizing him, the king thanked him (a strange prince, as he thought) for his assistance; and the two rode back together. On the way they began to race; for the king was proud of his steed, and was fond of showing him off. Louis, however, far out-distanced him, and rode on to the cave, where he unsaddled his horse, resumed his old clothes, and tied up his head.

Before he departed, the Gray Horse told him that the king would go to war again on the morrow, and that he, Louis, should once more borrow the horse and sword. He took the old gray mare and the sword back to the pig-pen. His wife inquired eagerly how her father had fared. Louis answered that the king had been successful, and told her to take the horse and the sword back to the palace.

When she arrived, she told her father that her husband wished her to thank him for the horse and the sword. Whereupon the king inquired if Louis had been present at the battle, for, he said, he had not seen him. The princess replied that he had indeed been there; and truly, if it had not been for Louis, the king would not have won the battle. The king replied that he was sure that Louis was not there, or else he would have seen him; and he persisted in this view.

The princess, being unable to convince her father, returned to the pig-pen.

When the princess had left, the queen said that Louis must have been in the fight, for, if he had not been there, he would not have known about it.

"Was there no stranger there?" she asked.

"Yes," returned the king. "There was a strange prince there, who helped me."

"Well," said the queen, "that must have been your son-in-law."

Back in the pig-pen, the princess told her husband that the king was saying that he had not been at the battle.

"If it had not been for me," Louis replied, "the king would not have won the battle." And so the matter was dropped.

The next morning he sent his wife up to borrow the horse and equipment again. The king gave his daughter the same outfit. Again Louis went to the cave, where he again changed horses and armor. Once more, when he passed his hovel, his wife did not recognize him. When Louis arrived, the battle was going against the king, as on the former occasion; but the young man a second time turned the tide in favor of his father-in-law.

After the battle was over, Louis and the king rode back together. The king wished to find out who this prince might be, and he determined to put a mark on him, so that he would recognize him again. He took out his sword to show how he had overcome one of his adversaries in battle, and stabbed his son-in-law in the leg. A piece of the king's sword had broken off, and was left in the wound. The king pretended to be very sorry, and tied up the wound. When they started off again, Louis put spurs to his horse, and when he reached the cave he again changed horses. Then he returned to the pig-pen with the old gray mare.

He was cut so badly, that he could walk only with difficulty. When his wife inquired if he had been wounded, he explained how her father had done it. Thereupon his wife took the handkerchief off, took out the piece of sword, and rebound the wound. Then she took the horse and sword, together with the broken piece of the king's sword and his handkerchief, to her father.

She told her father that her husband sent back the handkerchief and the piece of sword, and also his thanks for stabbing him after he had won the battle. The king was so much surprised that he almost fainted. The queen began to scold the king, saying, "Did I not tell you that he was a prince?"

The king sent his daughter to the pig-pen to get her husband, so that he could ask his forgiveness. Louis refused to go, saying that the king's word was law, and was not to be altered. He was confined to his bed on account of the wound which he had received. The princess returned, and told her father what her husband had said. He then sent down his chief men to coax Louis, but they were refused every time. Finally, the king and the queen themselves went down and asked Louis' forgiveness; but Louis repeated his refusal. The king rushed up, but he was mired in the mud which surrounded the pig-pen. The queen, however, was able to cross on top of the mud, leaving the king, who returned alone to his palace.

The same night, Louis took his ring and wished that he and his wife should wake in the morning in a beautiful castle and when the day came, lo, and behold! it was as he desired. In surprise, the king saw the castle, and sent Louis a note, saying that he desired to wage war with him. The young man sent a reply, that, by the time he fired his second shot, there would not be even a cat left in the king's city. This note he sent by his wife, and requested her to bring her mother back with her.

The king's daughter obeyed, and brought her mother back.

That afternoon, the king fired on his son-in-law's castle, but did no damage. Louis then warned the king that he was going to begin his cannonade, and straightway fired. His first shot carried away half of the city, and the second swept away all that was left of it.

LXXXI. LITTLE POUCET [292]
(THOMPSON: Teit, *Journal of American Folk-Lore*, xxix, 318, No. 11)

Jack and his elder brother lived with their parents, who had a cook. They were enormous eaters; and when food was put on the table, they rapidly ate it all up, so that their parents had not enough. As they grew, they ate more; and at meal-time, even when the table was loaded with food, their parents had eaten only a few mouthfuls before all the food was finished.

Their parents made up their minds to get rid of them. They told the cook to provide them with a large lunch each, take them to a rough part of the mountains, and leave them. Jack read his parents' minds, and told his elder brother what was proposed. That day he went to a wise and friendly old woman who lived near by, and asked her for advice. She gave him a large reel of thread and told him what to do. Next morning the cook provided them with packs of food, and told them he would take them to hunt grouse. They followed him; and as they went, Jack unrolled the thread unobserved by the cook. When the thread was almost all unrolled, the cook halted in a wild spot, saying, "We will camp here for to-night. I am going over yonder to shoot some grouse, and will be back before dusk."

As soon as he was out of sight, the lads followed the thread back to their home, and arrived there shortly after the cook, and just as their parents were going to eat. Having left their lunch in the mountains, they were very hungry, and ate up the supper almost before their parents had commenced.

Their parents told the cook to take them farther away next time. Jack knew what they had arranged, and went to see the old woman again. She gave him a sack full of fine powder, which shone both by day and by night, but was brightest at night, and she told him what to do. On the following morning the cook said he would take them hunting. As they followed the cook, Jack sprinkled the phosphorescent dust along the way. When the sack was about empty, the cook said, "We will camp here. I will go to yonder brush and shoot rabbits. Stay here until I return." As soon as he was out of sight, the boys

ran back along the sprinkled trail. When they were about half-
way back in a rough piece of country, they ran into a very large
flock of small birds, and chased them hither and thither, trying
to catch them.

In this way they lost their trail. They searched for a long
time, but could not find it. They wandered on, not knowing
where they were going. They descended from the mountains,
and came to a plain where they saw a butte with a very tall
pine-tree growing on top. They went there. The elder brother
tried to climb the tree, but he became dizzy and descended again.
Then Jack went up, reached the top, and looked around. Far
away he saw a column of smoke, and called to his brother to
turn his face the way he pointed. Jack descended, and they
travelled the way his brother was facing. At night they camped,
and sat facing the same way, so that they might not go astray.

The next day they reached a large underground lodge. They
were almost famished. Their shoes and clothes were in tatters.
They found an old woman within, who fed them and then hid
them in the cellar within the house. She told them that her
husband was a cannibal. The cannibal and his wife had two
children of the same size as Jack and his brother. Being young
cannibals, they sniffed around Jack and his brother, and, when
they were in the cellar, continued to sniff about, so that their
mother had to drive them away. Towards evening the cannibal approached the house, saying, "Nôm, nôm, nôm, where
can I get some meat?" On entering, he told his wife that he
smelled game within the house; and she, on being threatened
with a thrashing, disclosed the fact that the boys were hidden
in the cellar. Jack told his brother that he would influence the
cannibal's mind, so that they might be spared.

The cannibal pulled them out of the cellar, and was about
to eat them. Then he hesitated, and began to look them over.
He said, "They are too thin." He put them back into the cellar,
and told his wife to feed them well and give them a good place
to sleep, that they might get fat and tender quickly. The next
day the woman made a bed for them. After they had been in
the house for some time, the cannibal told his wife the boys were
now fit to eat, and he would kill them in the morning.

Jack knew his intention. He made the cannibal and his
family sleep very soundly that night. The lads arose, and placed
the cannibal's children in the bed in which they themselves had

been, and put logs of rotten wood in the bed of the cannibal's children. They took the cannibal's magic staff of gold, four stones which, as he learned afterwards, were gold nuggets, and the key of his door. When any one attempted to open the house-door except with the proper key, a bell would ring.

In the morning, when the cannibal awoke, he immediately went to the bed in which the boys used to sleep, and killed his own children, whom he mistook for the captive boys. When about to eat them, he noticed their fingers, and thus realized that he had killed his own children. He uncovered what seemed to be children in the other bed, and found the logs of rotten wood.

The cannibal gave chase to Jack and his brother, who by this time were far away. When the lads saw that they would be overtaken, they hid themselves in the roots of a patch of tall grass. The cannibal, who had lost track of the boys, returned in another direction. As soon as he was out of sight, the lads ran on. Then the cannibal found their tracks again. The boys had just reached a broad lake, when he hove in sight. Jack threw his staff down on the water, and they crossed it as on a bridge. When they reached the opposite shore, he lifted it up, and the cannibal could not cross. He shouted, "I will forgive you, I will not harm you, if you will only give me back my staff!" but Jack stuck the staff in the ground at the edge of the lake, and left the cannibal crying.

Not far from here they came to a large town of whites, where there was a chief and many soldiers, also many houses, stores, and farms. The cannibal used to prey on these people, who were much afraid of him. Here Jack and his brother separated, each getting work on a different farm.

Jack's brother became jealous of him, and sought to accomplish his death by putting him in danger. He told his master that Jack intended to steal the large bell belonging to the cannibal. Jack's master heard of this, and asked him if it were true, adding that his elder brother had said so. Jack said, "Very well. I will go and get the bell. You will all see it." The cannibal kept the bell on a wheeled vehicle alongside his house. It was very large. Jack went at night, and, crossing the lake by means of the staff, he soon reached the cannibal's house. He caused a deep sleep to fall on the cannibal, his wife, and the bell. This bell could hear a long way off, and warned the cannibal of danger by ringing. Jack ran off with the bell, hauling it in a wagon. Just as he had reached the opposite side of the lake, the cannibal arrived at the shore. Jack drew in the staff, and stuck it in the ground. The cannibal begged for the staff, saying, "You may keep the bell, but give me back my staff, with which I cross water." Jack left him crying, and proceeded to town, where he displayed the bell to all the people.

After this, Jack's brother circulated the story that Jack intended to steal the cannibal's light. His master asked him about it, and he said he would do it. He took with him three small sacks of salt. When he came to the cannibal's house, he looked down the smoke-hole. He saw the cannibal busy boiling a large kettle full of human flesh, which was now almost ready to be eaten. Jack emptied one sack full of salt into the kettle. The cannibal had a large spoon with which he was tasting the broth. When he took the next spoonful, he found the taste so agreeable that he forgot to eat any of the meat, and drank only of the soup. He said, "This must be delicious game I am boiling, to make the broth so nice." Jack wanted to make him go to drink, so that he could steal the light. He threw in the other sack of salt. The cannibal went to the creek to drink, but, instead of leaving the light, took it with him attached to his forehead. Jack ran down to the trail and hid. When the cannibal was returning, he suddenly jumped up, and threw the salt in the cannibal's face and on the light, so that neither of them could see. The cannibal was so much startled that he ran away, and in his hurry and blindness struck his toe on a tuft of grass and fell down heavily. The light rolled off his head. Jack seized it and ran off. This light could see a long way off, and told the cannibal what it saw. It saw farthest at night. The cannibal could not follow Jack, because it was very dark and he had no proper light. Jack carried the light to town, and displayed it to the people.

Next Jack's brother told that Jack was going to bring in the cannibal himself. His master asked him regarding it, and he said he would do it. He went to the blacksmith and had a large trunk made of iron, with a lid which shut with a spring. When it was finished, Jack went into it and tried it with all his strength. He found the box was too weak. Therefore he ordered the blacksmith to re-enforce it with heavy iron bands. He placed the trunk on a wagon, to which he harnessed a fine team, and drove to the cannibal's house, crossing the lake on the magic staff. The cannibal came out and admired the team, wagon, and trunk. He did not recognize Jack, and thought he would kill the visitor and take his wagon, trunk, and team. The cannibal admired the trunk, which was polished and looked like steel. Jack opened the lid to show him the inside, which was decorated with carvings, pictures in colors, and looking-glasses. Jack proposed to sell the trunk to the cannibal, and asked him to go in and try it. The cannibal told Jack to go in first. Jack went in, lay down at full length, and claimed that it was very comfortable. The cannibal then went in and Jack shut the lid on him.

The cannibal struggled to free himself, and at times nearly capsized the trunk; but Jack drove him into town, where he stopped in the square. The chief and soldiers and all the people flocked to see the cannibal who had been killing them. They lifted him off the wagon, and asked Jack to liberate him. Jack said if he liberated him, he would kill all the people, and proposed to them to light a fire, and to roast him to death in the trunk. Jack's brother asked him to open the trunk, but he would not consent. Jack's brother said, "There is no danger. See these hundreds of armed soldiers." Jack said, "It matters not, for neither arrows, nor bullets, nor knives, can penetrate him. He will kill everybody." His brother laughed. Jack said, "I will give you the key of the trunk, and you may open it in four hours from now." The whites wanted to have some fun with their enemy. When Jack had been gone four hours, and while he was sitting on the top of a distant hill overlooking the town, his brother opened the trunk. The cannibal, who was in a violent rage, killed every one of the people, including Jack's brother. There were none left. After this Jack travelled. Some say he turned foolish, and became Jack the Trickster.

LXXXII. THE WHITE CAT [293]

(CHILCOTIN: Farrand, *Jesup North Pacific Expedition*, ii, 26, No. 11)

Thunder was a great chief who lived in the sky, and he had three daughters, whom all the young men from the earth wished to marry, but could not get; for whenever a suitor came to ask Thunder for one of his daughters, Thunder would kill him.

He would tell the young man to go into the house to get food, and would open the door for him, and the young man would go inside; but the house was really a bear's den, and the bears would kill him. Finally there came a young man to try for one of the daughters; and as he came near the house, he saw a small lake in which the three women were bathing. The man hid himself, and stole over to where the women's clothes were lying, and sat down upon them; and the women were ashamed and would not come out. So they sat down in the water and began to parley. The oldest woman said he could have the youngest sister if he would give back the clothes; but the young man declined. Then she said he could have both her sisters; but the young man said he wanted her herself. So at last the woman said, "Well, I am a poor woman, but if you will give back our clothes, you may have me."

The young man agreed, and turned his back while they dressed. Then they started together for their father's house; and on the way the women told him of how Thunder killed men, and what he had to do to escape. When they came to the house, Thunder told the young man to go into the house and get some food. He went in just like the other suitors; but there was a door on the other side of the room, and he ran quickly across, and got out before the bears could catch him. His wife was waiting for him, and together they went to her house and spent the night. Early in the morning he rose and went to Thunder's house, and Thunder said to him, "My house is too old. If you will make me a new one, you can have my daughter." The young man sat down and covered his head and thought hard. Pretty soon he uncovered his head, and there was a fine house all built. But Thunder refused to give him the girl. Then Thunder said to him, "My garden is in very bad condition; it is full of stones and weeds. If you will clear it out, you can have my daughter." So the young man sat down and covered his head and thought, and in a little while he uncovered, and there was the garden all cleared. Still Thunder refused to give him his daughter.

Every night the young man went to the woman's house and slept with her, and she told him all the ways in which her father killed men, but all the time she feared that her husband would get caught. At last she proposed that they should run away together to his home. So they took all their clothes and goods and filled several houses; but the young man turned them all into a small roll and put it in his blanket, and they started for home. Next day Thunder discovered that the young man had stolen his daughter, and started in pursuit; and they heard him coming a long way off and were frightened.

They came to a great lake, and turned themselves into ducks and swam across. And when Thunder came to the lake, he saw nothing but two ducks, and went back home, while the young man and his wife turned back to their proper shapes on the other side and started on. Thunder came home and told his wife what had happened, and she laughed at him and told him that the ducks were the man and the woman. Then Thunder was angry, and started in pursuit again. Again the fugitives heard Thunder coming. The young man looked all about for a way of escape, and, seeing an owl, both he and the woman hid themselves under the owl's wing. When Thunder came up, he saw no traces of them. Then, seeing the owl, he caught it and felt it all over, and picked over all the feathers; but he forgot to look under the wing, and so failed to find them, and went back home, while the young man and his wife started on again.

Finally they came near home. When they were only a little way off, the woman said, "I will wait here while you go on and tell them we are coming." As soon as the young man had gone, the woman made four houses, and, pulling the roll from her blanket, she filled them all with clothes and goods. And one of the houses she made ready for the young man's mother. Not long after that, they heard Thunder hunting for them again; and when he came up, he was very angry, and wanted to kill all the people in the village. But his daughter made a great crack in the ground, and Thunder fell in up to his waist, and stuck fast. Then his daughter built a tent over his head, and used to feed him through a hole in the tent. There he staid for two years. But at last he grew tired, and told his daughter if she would let him out he would go home and not trouble them any more. So she freed him, and he went away; and after that the young man and his wife lived in peace.

LXXXIII. CINDERELLA[294]
(Zuñi: Cushing, *Zuñi Folk Tales*, p. 54*)

Long, long ago, our ancients had neither sheep nor horses nor cattle; yet they had domestic animals of various kinds — amongst them Turkeys.

In Mátsaki, or the Salt City, there dwelt at this time many very wealthy families, who possessed large flocks of these birds, which it was their custom to have their slaves or the poor people of the town herd in the plains round about Thunder Mountain, below which their town stood, and on the mesas beyond.

Now, in Mátsaki at this time there stood, away out near the border of the town, a little tumbledown, single-room house, wherein there lived alone a very poor girl, — so poor that her clothes were patched and tattered and dirty, and her person, on account of long neglect and ill fare, shameful to look upon, though she herself was not ugly, but had a winning face and bright eyes; that is, if the face had been more oval and the eyes less oppressed with care. So poor was she that she herded Turkeys for a living; and little was given to her except the food she subsisted on from day to day, and perhaps now and then a piece of old, worn-out clothing.

Like the extremely poor everywhere and at all times, she was humble, and by her longing for kindness, which she never received, she was made kind even to the creatures that depended upon her, and lavished this kindness upon the Turkeys she drove to and from the plains every day. Thus, the Turkeys, appreciating this, were very obedient. They loved their mistress so much that at her call they would unhesitatingly come, or at her behest go whithersoever and whensoever she wished.

One day, this poor girl driving her Turkeys down into the plains, passed near Old Zuñi, — the Middle Ant Hill of the World, as our ancients have taught us to call our home, — and as she went along, she heard the herald-priest proclaiming from the house-top that the Dance of the Sacred Bird (which is a very blessed and welcome festival to our people, especially to the youths and maidens who are permitted to join in the dance) would take place in four days.

* Reprinted by special arrangement with G. P. Putnam's Sons, the publishers.

Now, this poor girl had never been permitted to join in or even to watch the great festivities of our people or the people in the neighboring towns, and naturally she longed very much to see this dance. But she put aside her longing, because she reflected: "It is impossible that I should watch, much less join in the Dance of the Sacred Bird, ugly and ill-clad as I am." And thus musing to herself, and talking to her Turkeys, as was her custom, she drove them on, and at night returned them to their cages round the edges and in the plazas of the town.

Every day after that, until the day named for the dance, this poor girl, as she drove her Turkeys out in the morning, saw the people busy in cleaning and preparing their garments, cooking delicacies, and otherwise making ready for the festival to which they had been duly invited by the other villagers, and heard them talking and laughing merrily at the prospect of the coming holiday. So, as she went about with her Turkeys through the day, she would talk to them, though she never dreamed that they understood a word of what she was saying.

It seems that they did understand even more than she said to them, for on the fourth day, after the people of Mátsaki had all departed toward Zuñi and the girl was wandering around the plains alone with her Turkeys, one of the big Gobblers strutted up to her, and making a fan of his tail, and skirts, as it were, of his wings, blushed with pride and puffed with importance, stretched out his neck and said: "Maiden mother, we know what your thoughts are, and truly we pity you, and wish that, like the other people of Mátsaki, you might enjoy this holiday in the town below. We have said to ourselves at night, after you have placed us safely and comfortably in our cages: 'Truly our maiden mother is as worthy to enjoy these things as any one in Mátsaki, or even Zuñi.' Now, listen well, for I speak the speech of all the elders of my people: If you will drive us in early this afternoon, when the dance is most gay and the people are most happy, we will help you to make yourself so handsome and so prettily dressed that never a man, woman, or child amongst all those who are assembled at the dance will know you; but rather, especially the young men, will wonder whence you came, and long to lay hold of your hand in the circle that forms round the altar to dance. Maiden mother, would you like to go to see this dance, and even to join in it, and be merry with the best of your people?"

The poor girl was at first surprised. Then it seemed all so natural that the Turkeys should talk to her as she did to them, that she sat down on a little mound, and, leaning over, looked at them and said: "My beloved Turkeys, how glad I am that we may speak together! But why should you tell me of things that you full well know I so long to, but cannot by any possible means, do?"

"Trust in us," said the old Gobbler, "for I speak the speech of my people, and when we begin to call and call and gobble and gobble, and turn toward our home in Mátsaki, do you follow us, and we will show you what we can do for you. Only let me tell you one thing: No one knows how much happiness and good fortune may come to you if you but enjoy temperately the pleasures we enable you to participate in. But if, in the excess of your enjoyment, you should forget us, who are your friends, yet so much depend upon you, then we will think: 'Behold, this our maiden mother, though so humble and poor, deserves, forsooth, her hard life, because, were she more prosperous, she would be unto others as others now are unto her.'"

"Never fear, O my Turkeys," cried the maiden, — only half trusting that they could do so much for her, yet longing to try, — "never fear. In everything you direct me to do I will be obedient as you always have been to me."

The sun had scarce begun to decline, when the Turkeys of their own accord turned homeward, and the maiden followed them, light of heart. They knew their places well, and immediately ran to them. When all had entered, even their bare-legged children, the old Gobbler called to the maiden, saying: "Enter our house." She therefore went in. "Now, maiden, sit down," said he, "and give to me and my companions, one by one, your articles of clothing. We will see if we cannot renew them."

The maiden obediently drew off the ragged old mantle that covered her shoulders and cast it on the ground before the speaker. He seized it in his beak, and spread it out, and picked and picked at it; then he trod upon it, and lowering his wings, began to strut back and forth over it. Then taking it up in his beak, and continuing to strut, he puffed and puffed, and laid it down at the feet of the maiden, a beautiful white embroidered cotton mantle. Then another Gobbler came forth, and she gave him another article of dress, and then another and another,

until each garment the maiden had worn was new and as beautiful as any possessed by her mistresses in Mátsaki.

Before the maiden donned all these garments, the Turkeys
circled about her, singing and singing, and clucking and clucking, and brushing her with their wings, until her person was as
clean and her skin as smooth and bright as that of the fairest
maiden of the wealthiest home in Mátsaki. Her hair was soft
and wavy, instead of being an ugly, sun-burnt shock; her
cheeks were full and dimpled, and her eyes dancing with smiles,
— for she now saw how true had been the words of the Turkeys.

Finally, one old Turkey came forward and said: "Only the
rich ornaments worn by those who have many possessions are
lacking to thee, O maiden mother. Wait a moment. We have
keen eyes, and have gathered many valuable things, — as such
things, being small, though precious, are apt to be lost from
time to time by men and maidens."

Spreading his wings, he trod round and round upon the
ground, throwing his head back, and laying his wattled beard
on his neck; and, presently beginning to cough, he produced
in his beak a beautiful necklace; another Turkey brought forth
earrings, and so on, until all the proper ornaments appeared,
befitting a well-clad maiden of the olden days, and were laid
at the feet of the poor Turkey girl.

With these beautiful things she decorated herself, and, thank-
ing the Turkeys over and over, she started to go, and they called
out: "O maiden mother, leave open the wicket, for who knows
whether you will remember your Turkeys or not when your
fortunes are changed, and if you will not grow ashamed that
you have been the maiden mother of Turkeys? But we love
you, and would bring you to good fortune. Therefore, remember our words of advice, and do not tarry too long."

"I will surely remember, O my Turkeys!" answered the
maiden.

Hastily she sped away down the river path toward Zuñi.
When she arrived there, she went in at the western side of the
town and through one of the long covered ways that lead into
the dance court. When she came just inside of the court, behold, every one began to look at her, and many murmurs ran
through the crowd, — murmurs of astonishment at her beauty
and the richness of her dress, — and the people were all asking
one another, "Whence comes this beautiful maiden?"

Not long did she stand there neglected. The chiefs of the dance, all gorgeous in their holiday attire, hastily came to her, and, with apologies for the incompleteness of their arrangements, — though these arrangements were as complete as they possibly could be, — invited her to join the youths and maidens dancing round the musicians and the altar in the center of the plaza.

With a blush and a smile and a toss of her hair over her eyes, the maiden stepped into the circle, and the finest youths among the dancers vied with one another for her hand. Her heart became light and her feet merry, and the music sped her breath to rapid coming and going, and the warmth swept over her face, and she danced and danced until the sun sank low in the west.

But, alas! in the excess of her enjoyment, she thought not of her Turkeys, or, if she thought of them, she said to herself, "How is this, that I should go away from the most precious consideration to my flock of gobbling Turkeys? I will stay a while longer, and just before the sun sets I will run back to them, that these people may not see who I am, and that I may have the joy of hearing them talk day after day and wonder who the girl was who joined in their dance."

So the time sped on, and another dance was called, and another, and never a moment did the people let her rest; but they would have her in every dance as they moved around the musicians and the altar in the center of the plaza.

At last the sun set, and the dance was well-nigh over, when suddenly breaking away, the girl ran out, and, being swift of foot, — more so than most of the people of her village, — she sped up the river path before any one could follow the course she had taken.

Meantime, as it grew late, the Turkeys began to wonder and wonder that their maiden mother did not return to them. At last a gray old Gobbler mournfully exclaimed, "It is as we might have expected. She has forgotten us; therefore is she not worthy of better things than those she has been accustomed to. Let us go forth to the mountains and endure no more of this irksome captivity, inasmuch as we may no longer think our maiden mother as good and true as once we thought her."

So, calling and calling to one another in loud voices, they trooped out of their cage and ran up toward the Cañon of the Cottonwoods, and then round behind Thunder Mountain, through the Gateway of Zuñi, and so on up the valley.

All breathless, the maiden arrived at the open wicket and looked in. Behold, not a Turkey was there! Trailing them, she ran and she ran up the valley to overtake them; but they were far ahead, and it was only after a long time that she came within the sound of their voices, and then, redoubling her speed, well-nigh overtook them, when she heard them singing this song:

> K'yaanaa, to! to!
> K'yaanaa, to! to!
>   Ye ye!
> K'yaanaa, to! to!
> K'yaanaa, to! to!
>   Yee huli huli!
>
> Hon awen Tsita
> Itiwanakwīn
>   Otakyaan aaa kyaa;
> Lesna Akyaaa
> Shoya-k'oskwi
> Teyäthltokwīn
>   Hon aawani!
>
> Ye yee huli huli,
> Tot-tot, tot-tot, tot-tot,
>   Huli huli! *
>
> Up the river, to! to!
> Up the river, to! to!
>   Sing ye ye!
> Up the river, to! to!
> Up the river, to! to!
>   Sing ye huli huli!
>
> Oh, our maiden mother
> To the middle place
>   To dance went away;
> Therefore as she lingers,
> To the Cañon Mesa
> And the plains above it
>   We all run away!
>
> Sing ye ye huli huli,
> Tot-tot, tot-tot, tot-tot,
>   Huli huli!
> Tot-tot, tot-tot, tot-tot,
>   Huli huli!

* This, like all the folk-songs, is difficult of translation; and that which is given is only approximate. [Cushing's note.]

Hearing this, the maiden called to her Turkeys; called and called in vain. They only quickened their steps, spreading their wings to help them along, singing the song over and over until, indeed, they came to the base of the Cañon Mesa, at the borders of the Zuñi Mountains. Then singing once more their song in full chorus, they spread wide their wings, and thlakwa-a-a, thlakwa-a-a, they fluttered away over the plains above.

The poor Turkey girl threw her hands up and looked down at her dress. With dust and sweat, behold! it was changed to what it had been, and she was the same poor Turkey girl that she was before. Weary, grieving, and despairing, she returned to Mátsaki.

Thus it was in the days of the ancients. Therefore, where you see the rocks leading up to the top of Cañon Mesa, there are the tracks of turkeys and other figures to be seen. The latter are the song that the Turkeys sang, graven in the rocks; and all over the plains along the borders of Zuñi Mountains since that day turkeys have been more abundant than in any other place.

After all, the gods dispose of men according as men are fitted; and if the poor be poor in heart and spirit as well as in appearance, how will they be aught but poor to the end of their days?

Thus shortens my story.

LXXXIV. THE TRUE BRIDE [295]

(THOMPSON: Teit, *Journal of American Folk-Lore*, xxix, 301, No. 1)

There was a white man who had a wife and daughter. The wife died, and he married another woman, who also bore him a daughter. The step-mother was always angry with her step-daughter, and accused her of being lazy. One day in the winter-time, when there was much snow on the ground, she told her to go and pick berries. The girl knew that no berries could be found at that season; but she was so hurt by the nagging of her step-mother, that she said she would go. She put some food in her basket and wandered off, saying to herself, "I will continue wandering around until I die."

After a time she saw the smoke of a lodge, which she approached and entered. Four young men lived there, who were her relatives, but she did not know it. They gave her food to eat, and asked her why she travelled in the snow. She answered that she had a bad step-mother, who always scolded her, and had sent her out to pick berries in the snow. They gave her a snow-shovel, or scraper of some kind, and told her to go up on the roof of the house and dig away the snow. When she had removed the snow from the roof of the house, she saw that it was covered with earth, in which grew many strawberries of large size. The men passed up her basket, and she soon filled it with the finest strawberries.

When she had come down and was about to leave, the men said, "What shall we do for our sister?" She answered, "If by any means you can help me, I shall be glad. I am very poor, and have only rags to wear." Now, the youngest brother told her to spit; and when she spat, the spittle became a nugget of gold. The next brother made shoes for her of very fine material, which fitted her perfectly, and would never wear out. The third brother made a dress for her in the same way. The eldest brother said, "I will make a robe for her which will always look well and new, and will never wear out." As the brothers in succession made their awards, each article in turn appeared on her person, while her old clothes disappeared. She returned home with the basketful of strawberries, and delivered them to her step-mother, who was much surprised. She noticed that the clothes of the girl were all changed and of very fine material, and that she had the power of spitting gold, which she would gather up and put in a sack. This made her angry.

She said to her own daughter, "You see what your elder sister has brought us. She managed to find some berries. Go and get some too." She told her secretly to follow the tracks of her sister. She would then be sure of reaching the same place, and learn how she had obtained the strawberries, the fine clothes, and the power of spitting gold. The girl took her basket and departed. When she arrived at the house of the four brothers, they gave her food to eat, and asked her why she was travelling at that time of year. She answered, "My mother ordered me to go and gather strawberries, although it is winter-time and no berries are to be found. However, my sister found some, and my mother said I could get some at the same place."

The men directed her as they had her sister; and after removing the snow from the roof, she found strawberries grow-

ing profusely underneath. When she had filled her basket and
was about to return, the brothers said, "What shall we do for
our sister?" The youngest man asked her to spit, but she felt
insulted at the request. She was vain and haughty. She
thought they were fooling her. They intended to help her, but
became disgusted on account of her vanity, and decided to give
her nothing good. At last she spat, and the spittle turned into
a toe-nail and smelled like toe-nails. The other brothers refused to help her in any way. She returned with the strawberries, and gave them to her mother. The latter noticed that
she had no new clothes, and felt disappointed. She asked her
to spit, but instead of gold she spat a bad-smelling toe-nail.
She told her not to spit again.

One day the chief's son was passing, and saw the elder girl
busy washing clothes. He liked her looks and her dress. His
father, whom he told of his admiration for the girl, encouraged
him to visit her and make her acquaintance. He said, "You
may change your mind when you see her again." The young
man visited the girl and held some conversation with her, during which she coughed and spat on the ground several times.
He returned and told his father that the girl he fancied could
spit gold nuggets. His father would not believe it, and went
to see for himself. During his conversation with her, she spat
repeatedly, and picked up the gold nuggets and put them in a
sack she carried. He asked her to spit again. He picked up the
spittle and satisfied himself that it was really gold. Then he
advised his son to marry her, saying, "She is a valuable woman, she is worth many."

Now, it was reported that the chief's son was to marry the
girl who could spit gold. All the white people came to the great
wedding. At the end of the wedding feast the bride spat out
much gold, so the wedding guests carried away some to their
homes. Thus the bride provided them all with presents, and
became renowned, and well liked by all.

In due time She-who-spat-Gold became pregnant. When she
was about to be delivered, her husband was called away to an
important meeting in a distant place, from which he could not
return for a month. The chieftainess asked her husband to
request his mother to attend her when her time came, as she
had no faith in her step-mother, who might use the opportunity
to do her harm. Her husband, however, assuaged her misgiv-

ings, and insisted that her step-mother, who was an expert midwife, and her half-sister, should assist her.

When she was about to give birth, her step-mother made a hole in the floor, placed the young woman over it, and, when the child was born, she cut the navel-string and let the infant fall through the hole. Then she put a cat in its place; and when the mother sat up and asked for her child the step-mother put the cat in her arms. The woman said, "It is strange that I should give birth to a cat!" The step-mother said, "Odd people have odd children." The young woman reared the cat as if it were her own child.

Her husband was disappointed when he returned but said nothing. Again the woman became pregnant, and again her husband was called away about the time of her delivery. She was again attended by her step-mother, who dropped the child through a hole in the floor. This time she gave the woman a snake, telling her that she had given birth to it. She added, "How strange are the children to which you give birth!" On the return of the husband, the step-mother told him that he ought to kill his wife, because she was giving birth to cats and snakes. She told him that he ought to marry her own daughter, who was a good woman, and would give birth to proper children. The chief and all the people held a meeting, and decided that his wife should be killed. They bound her with iron, took her in a canoe to the middle of the lake, and cast her overboard.

Now, the four brothers knew what was happening, and were there under the water to intercept her, and prevent her from drowning. They untied her, and after telling her that her real children were alive, and that things would come well in the end, they transformed her into a goose, and she swam about on the lake. The chief's son did not like his new wife, because she was disgusting and smelled nasty.

Now, She-who-spat-Gold had a favorite dog called "Spiŏla," which she had not seen since the time of the birth of her first child. He lived or slept underneath the house; and when the step-mother dropped the baby through the hole, he had taken charge of it. He licked off the blood, got some white cloth to make a bed for it and to cover it. He had gone to town and got milk to feed it. Later he gathered other kinds of food and fed it, thus rearing the boy successfully. He had done the same with the younger boy. When the boys were large enough to run about, they came out of their house, and often played near the lake, watching the goose, which frequently approached them, crying. Spiŏla had to go on trips to gather food, and always warned them not to go too far away during his absence, or let any one see them.

One day, however, the old step-mother noticed them, and tried to capture them; but they disappeared in a small hole under the house, and blocked it with a stone from the inside. She made up her mind to poison them. She scattered some fine food, which the children ate and then died. When Spiŏla came home, he missed the boys. After a while he took their scent, found them, and carried their bodies into his house.

As he could not resuscitate them, he started off to the Sun to seek help. He ran continually day and night, for Sun lived a long way off. On the way he passed an old horse, who asked him where he was going. He answered, "To the Sun," but did not stop or look around. The horse shouted, "Ask the Sun why I am growing old!"

At another place he passed an apple-tree, which in like manner addressed him, and called on him to ask Sun what made it dry up and its wood turn dead.

Again he passed a spring of water, which also called on him to ask the Sun why it was drying up. After running many days and nights, he came to the edge of the earth. There he saw a stretch of water, and on the other side the house of the Sun. He jumped into the water and swam across. He was almost exhausted before he reached the opposite shore, and his body was reduced to almost nothing but bones, owing to his arduous journey.

When he arrived at the Sun's house, an old woman, the mother of the Sun, met him, and asked him why he had come there. She said, "No one comes to see us unless he is in great trouble and requires help and wisdom." Spiola told her that his two foster-children were dead, and he had come to ask help, so that they might be restored. He told her all that had happened. She fed him, and he immediately began to gain strength on the good food used by the Sun people.

The old woman advised him what to do. He must watch the Sun when he spat. He would spit twice, — the first time for the elder boy, and the second time for the younger one. Spiŏla must carefully gather up the spittle, and keep the one apart from the other. The questions he wished to ask in behalf of the people he had passed on the road, she would ask the Sun herself, and Spiŏla would hear the answers.

The Sun spoke of the dead children, and spat twice on the ground. Spiŏla gathered up the spittle carefully, and wrapped each separately in thin bark. Sun said the children would become quite well if treated within four days; but after that it would be too late, for their bodies would begin to decompose.

Now, the old woman asked Sun the questions. She said, "A horse wants to know why he is growing old." Sun answered, "Because he is lazy. He feeds too much in one place. He is too lazy to search for good nutritious grass, and he is too lazy to go to water regularly. He will stand for days in one place rather than go any distance to get water." She said, "The apple-tree wants to know why it is drying up." Sun answered, "Because it is too lazy, and because it has a nail in its trunk. If it removes the nail, and loosens the ground around its roots and spreads them out to gather moisture, and prunes off the dead and useless wood, then it will retain its youth; but it is too lazy to do this." She said, "The little spring wants to know why it is drying up." Sun answered, "Because it is too lazy. If it removes all the dead twigs and leaves which choke it up, if it makes a clean channel for itself to run in, and drains the neighboring moist places into itself, it will always run and be healthy."

Spiŏla was in despair when he learned that he had to be back in four days to save the lives of the two children. It had taken him more than double that time to reach the abode of the Sun. The old woman consoled him, and told him he could reach home in time by taking another route. She said, "You will start early to-morrow morning, and follow the Sun on his journey. You must travel as fast as you can. The way he takes is a very straight and short course, and you may reach home in one day."

Spiŏla started the following morning, and, following the Sun's tracks, he arrived at home about nightfall. As he passed the small spring, the apple-tree, and the old horse, he informed them without stopping what the Sun had said.

Now, Spiŏla rubbed the spittle on the mouths of the children, and at once they returned to life. It was the same as if their breath had come back. When they became alive, each boy showed a luminous spot on the forehead; on the forehead of one shone a sun, and on that of the other a bright moon. Both were beautiful to behold.

Spiŏla told their mother the Goose that he was now going on another journey to see the wise Bird, and she must warn her children of approaching danger. He told the boys, "When you hear the Goose on the lake calling loudly, you must go home at once and hide, for the people may see you and kill you again." Spiŏla ran with all swiftness to the house of the Bird who talked all languages, knew the future, and never told a lie. He dwelt on the top of a pinnacle of clear ice in a snowy region. Spiola rushed at the cliff, and just managed to climb to the top of the ice before his claws had worn off. He told the Bird what he had come for, and asked his help, for every one believed what he said. The Bird answered, "I know your need is great, and I pity you." Spiŏla put the Bird under his robe, and slid down the ice. He brought him to the children, and the Bird seemed to be very glad to see them.

The day after the Bird had arrived, the father of the boys heard talking underneath the house, and resolved to investigate its cause. Some of the voices were like those of children. He found the entrance to their abode, but was unable to throw down the stone which blocked it. Spiŏla removed the stone, and asked him to come in. He said, "The passage is too small. I cannot pass through." Spiŏla replied, "If you try, you will manage it." He squeezed through, and was surprised to find himself in a large room, well kept and clean, and full of many kinds of food. When he saw the Bird there, he knew something important was going to happen, for he never came excepting when required to settle a serious difficulty which the chief himself and people could not decide properly. When Spiŏla told all that had happened, the chief's son became exceedingly sorry that he had killed his first wife, and had believed her step-mother. He told his father what he had learned, and a meeting was called for a certain day to inquire into the truth of the matter. Meanwhile the chief gave orders that the toe-nail woman, or She-who-spits-Toe-Nails, should be kept a prisoner in her house with her mother. The doors and windows of the house were all battened and nailed up. Now, Spiŏla went to the lake, and called the Goose, whom he shook until her goose-skin fell off. She-who-spits-Gold was restored to her natural form. She and her sons, the wise Bird, and Spiŏla, all attended the meeting when the people were gathered. The Bird told the true story in all its details, and every one believed him. He praised Spiŏla for his courage in running to the house of the Sun for the breath of the children. The chief ordered the two women to be taken out and hanged publicly. This the people did. The chief's son took back his wife, and they lived thenceforth in a great house, which was richly ornamented with gold by his wife. He became chief after his father, and his son became chief after him.

LXXXV. THE MAGIC APPLES [296]

(PENOBSCOT: Speck, *Journal of American Folk-Lore*, xxviii, 56, No. 4)

There was a soldier in the army whose name was Jack. One day he deserted, ran down the road, and left his horse and uniform. The general sent a captain and a corporal after him to capture him; but when they overtook him, Jack said, "Sit down here, and we will talk it over." Then he asked them if they were satisfied with their job, getting only a shilling a week, and he coaxed them to start in the world with him to seek their fortunes.

At last they agreed, and all three started out on the road in search of adventure. Soon they struck into a big woods, and at night saw lights shining in the windows of a wonderful palace. When they entered, they found it completely furnished, but without occupants. A fine meal was spread on the table, and three beds were found made up. The only living things they saw were three cats. After eating and smoking, three beautiful maidens appeared and told the men that they would like them to stay and live with them. That night they all slept together; and the next morning found everything as before, but the beautiful women had turned back into cats. For three nights they staid in this way; and the last night the captain's girl told him that if he would live with her, she would make him a present of a tablecloth which would always supply itself with whatever food he wished. The corporal's girl told him the same, and offered a wallet which should always be full of gold. Jack's girl made him an offer of a cap which would transport him wherever he wished. The men accepted the offer and received their presents. The next day, when the women had turned back into cats, the three men proposed to travel around and see the world; so they all put their heads together, and Jack pulled the cap over them and wished them to be in London.

They found themselves in London at once. Soon Jack became infatuated with a beautiful woman whom he wished to marry. She kept refusing him, however, and putting him off till the next day. He offered her a wonderful present. Then he went to the captain and borrowed his tablecloth. He gave her that, but still she put him off. Then he borrowed the corporal's wallet and gave her that, yet she put him off. At last he begged her to give him a kiss. She laughed and agreed. Then he slipped the cap over their heads and wished to be in the wild woods of America. Immediately they found themselves in the heart of the wild woods, with not a soul near them for miles.

She cried very hard, but soon begged Jack to go to sleep, and smoothed his forehead for him. Then, when he fell asleep, she took his cap and wished herself back in London again. When Jack woke up, he found himself alone in the wilderness, and he began wandering, and soon came to a great apple-tree with apples as big as pumpkins. He tasted one, and immediately a growing tree sprouted from his head, and he could not move. Near by, however, was another small apple-tree whose fruit he could just reach. He ate one of these small apples, and immediately the tree came off his head. So he gathered some of the big apples and the little ones, and wandered on.

Soon he came out upon a great headland overlooking the ocean, and there he saw a ship sailing by. He signalled to it, and at last the sailors came ashore to get him. He told them he was a great doctor who had been lost in the woods, and wanted to get back to the old country. Then they took him on board and started back to England. Halfway across the ocean the captain got terribly sick, and the sailors called upon Jack to try to help him. He went down and gave the captain a piece of one of the big apples to eat; and at once a growing tree sprang from his head, its branches reaching way up among the masts. When the sailors saw this, they were going to throw him overboard, but he told them to wait until he tried his other medicine. Then he gave the captain a piece of the small apple, and the tree came off his head. By this they knew Jack was a great doctor.

When they landed in England, Jack saw his two friends, the captain and the corporal, sawing wood at an inn to earn their living. He went to a town and built a shop, where he put his great apples up for sale, and many people came to see the wonderful fruit. In the meantime Jack's lover had built a great palace with the money from her wallet; and she heard of the wonderful doctor and his apples; so she went to see them. When she saw Jack, she did not know him because his beard had grown, and thought the apples were very wonderful. She bought one at the price of fifty dollars. When she took it home, Jack left his shop, and waited to see what would happen. Soon the word went around that the wealthiest woman in the kingdom had a tree growing from her head, which none of the doctors could take off. So Jack sent word to the woman that he was a great doctor and would guarantee to cure her.

So she sent for him, and he came. First, he told her that she had some great mystery in her life, that she had wronged somebody. He told her that before he could cure her, she would have to confess to him. Then she admitted that she had wronged a man, and had taken his things and left him. Then he told her that she would have to give up these things before he could cure her. So she gave him a little key, and told him to go in the cellar to a certain brick, behind which he would find the tablecloth, the wallet, and the cap.

When he got these things, he left the palace, and soon she died for her wrongs. He went back to his friends who were sawing wood, and gave them their things. Now, they all started back to the palace where the three cats were. When they arrived, they found the palace all neglected, and the three cats looked very old. That night they turned back into three old women, who complained bitterly of being neglected.

After they had eaten, however, the old women resumed their youth and beauty, and that night the youngest told Jack how they were bewitched by a great bull who lived near by. She told him that if the bull could be killed and his heart cut out, the spell would be removed, but that others had tried in vain. So the next morning Jack went down to his enclosure of stone and looked over. He saw a monster bull coursing around the inside. In the middle of the yard was a well, and a big rock standing at one side. When the bull was at the far end of the yard, Jack jumped the wall and ran for the well, followed by the bull. He had no sooner jumped into the well than the bull smashed against the rock and fell over dead. Then Jack climbed out and cut out his heart, which he took back with him. That night the three girls ate a piece of the heart, and the spell was removed. After that they all lived together in the palace.

LXXXVI. MAKING THE PRINCESS LAUGH [297]

(MICMAC: Rand, *Legends of the Micmacs*, p. 34, No. 6)

There was once a king who owned a large farm in the neighborhood of the town where he resided; the farm was cultivated by a man who paid rent for it to the king. This man had but one child, a son, who was considered only about half-witted; he was very stupid, and was continually doing silly things.

After a while his father died; but as he had left a large store of money, the rent was easily met for a year or two. Finally a pay-day approached when there was no cash. The mother consulted with her son as to what was to be done. "The king will call in a day or two for his money, and we have none for him. What can we do?" He replies, "I don't know." She concludes to select one of the finest cows, and send the boy off to market to sell it. He agrees to the proposal and starts with the cow to market.

As he drives his animal along, he passes a house standing near the road; there is a man on the steps who has come out to hail him. He inquires, "Where are you going with that cow?" "I am driving her to market," Jack answers. "Come in and rest yourself," says the man, pleasantly. Jack accepts the invitation, goes in, and sits down. "I want you to make me a present of that cow," says the man. "Can't do it," replies Jack; "but I will be glad to sell her to you, for we are in need of the money." The man replies that he will not buy the cow, but that he wants Jack to make him a present of her. This the boy refuses to do. The man asks if he will have something to eat. He answers in the affirmative, and on a tiny dish is set before him a very small piece of food. The boy looks at the food, and ventures to taste it. He finds it very palatable, and eats away, but does not diminish the amount. After a while the distension of his stomach indicates that he has eaten sufficiently; but his appetite is as keen as ever, and the morsel that lies on the tiny plate is not in the least diminished.[210] He endeavors to stop eating, but finds that he cannot do so. He has to keep on eating, whether he will or not. So he calls out to the man, "Take away your food." The man coolly answers, "Give me your cow, and I will." The boy answers indignantly, "I'll do no such thing; take your dish away." "Then eat on," quietly answers the man; and eat on he does, until he begins to think that his whole abdominal region will burst if he continues much longer. He gives over the contest, cries for quarter, and yields up the cow. In return he receives the little dish with the food undiminished in quantity or quality, remaining in it. He then returns home with the magical food in his pocket.

Arriving at his home, he is questioned as to the success of his mission. He relates his adventures and says, "I have been robbed of the cow." His mother calls him a thousand fools, upbraids him outrageously, and seizes the fire-shovel in order to knock him down. He dodges her, however, and taking a particle of the magical food on the tip of his finger, adroitly touches her mouth with it as he jumps by her. She stops instantly, charmed with the exquisite taste, and inquires, "What is this that tastes so delicious?" Thereupon he hands the dish over to her; and she falls to eating greedily, while he quietly looks on. But soon sensations and difficulties similar to those which he had himself experienced lead her to call out to him to remove the plate. "Will you beat me then?" he coolly asks. "I will," exclaims the mother, now more than ever enraged, finding herself thus caught in a trap. "Then you may eat away," says the boy. The indignant old lady eats on, until she can really stand the strain no longer, when she yields, and promises to lay aside the "rod of correction"; then he releases her by removing the tiny platter and its contents.

The next morning the old lady sends Jack off to market with another cow. Passing the same house, he is again accosted by the man, who is waiting on the door-step to meet him; in the same manner as on the former occasion, the man makes the modest request that Jack will give him the cow. Jack, however, has learned some wisdom by his late adventure, and has no idea of repeating the experiment. "Be off with you, you evil spirit," he exclaims. "You robbed me yesterday; you're not going to do it again today"; and he hurries on. The man takes off his belt, and throws it down in the middle of the road. Instantly the belt leaps up around both Jack and his cow, binds the animal's legs fast to her body, and lashes the boy to her side. There they lie, unable to stir. "Untie me!" shouts the struggling boy. "Give me your cow and I will," the man answers. "I won't do it," says Jack. "Then lie there!" is the answer. But the belt, like a huge boa-constrictor, begins to contract, and to press upon Jack and his cow, so that they can scarcely draw their breath. At length the poor fellow gives up the cow, is unfastened, receives the magic belt in return, and goes home. He informs his mother that the same man has again robbed him. The old woman is now more angry than ever. She calls him hard names, threatens to beat and even to kill him, and searches for a suitable weapon; then Jack unclasps his belt, casts it upon the floor, and instantly the poor woman is bound hand and foot, and calls lustily to be released. Jack looks on and says, "Will you beat me, then?" "Yes, I will," she screams; "untie me, you dog!" Jack pulls the magic cord a little tighter round her, and the violence of her wrath abates; she begins to gasp, and promises if he will let her go she will not beat him. Thereupon he unties her, and she keeps her word.

The difficulty still remains; the rent is not yet paid, and the mother determines to make one more attempt to sell a cow. Away goes the boy again towards the town, driving the third animal, when the same man again encounters him with the same proposal. "Give me your cow." "Give you my cow, indeed!" exclaims the boy in wrath. "I'll give a stone and hurl it at your head." He is about to suit the action to the word, when the man pulls out a tiny flute and begins to play on it. Jack's muscles instantly contract in different directions; the stone drops from his hand, and, literally charmed with the music, he begins to dance. The cow joins in the jig; and both dance away with all their might, unable to stop. "Hold! hold!" he exclaims at length; "stop your music! Let me get my breath!" "Give me your cow, and I will," answers the man. "I won't do it," Jack replies. "Then dance away!" is the answer; and the poor fellow dances until he is ready to drop from very weariness. He then yields, gives up the cow, receives the magic flute, and returns to his mother to report his ill success for the third time. This time the old woman's rage knows no bounds. She will kill him outright. But while she is in the act of springing upon him with some deadly weapon, he commences operations on his magical flute. The old lady is enchanted with the music, drops her weapon, and begins to dance, but retains her wrath, and long persists in her determination to deal summary vengeance upon the boy. Again and again she orders him to cease playing; but in answer to his interrogatory, "Will you beat me then?" she answers, "Indeed I will." Soon she becomes so weary that she can scarcely keep on her feet, but sways to and fro, almost sinking. Finally she falls and strikes her head with great force. She yields, and promises to let him alone, and he withdraws the enchantment of his music.

There was another effect produced by the magic flute when the man who met Jack commenced playing; no sooner had the boy and cow begun to dance, than they were joined by a great swarm of hornets. These hornets hovered over them, and danced in concert in the air; they followed the flute; whenever it played they came, but they were invisible to all eyes accept those of the musician, and his commands and wishes they implicitly obeyed.

The difficulty of paying the rent remains. The mother is still in trouble about it; but the boy quiets her fears, and undertakes to manage the affair. "To-day," she says, "the king will be here. What can we do?" He says to her, "I'll pay him; give yourself no uneasiness." He then takes a lot of earthen dishes and smashes them up fine, packs the pieces into a bag, and fills it so full that he can scarcely tie it up, then seals the strings with gum.

Presently a carriage containing the king himself and two servants drives up to the door. They have come to collect the rent. They enter the house, and the terrified old woman runs and hides. The boy, however, meets them at the door, and politely conducts them to a seat. They sit down and wait, and he immediately fetches them what seems to be a well-filled money-bag, and sets it down on the table, making it rattle and chink like a bag of money, as he sets it down.

He then produces his little magic platter and food, and gravely informs the king that his father, before he died, had given him instructions to set that before his Majesty as a portion of exquisitely delicious food. The king takes the bait and falls into the trap; he first tastes a morsel, then falls to eating, and the two servants join him. Meanwhile the boy seems to be very busy getting ready to count out the cash, bustling round, going into another room where he remains a good while, then coming out and lifting up the bag, and, as if having forgotten something, going back into some other apartment of the house.

Meanwhile the king and his servants become gorged with the food; but they can neither refrain from eating, nor push away from the enchanted platter. They call to the boy to come and remove his dish; but he is altogether too busy to hear or to notice them. Meanwhile their troubles increase. Their stomachs become distended beyond endurance, and they are glad to purchase a respite by giving up rent, house, stock, farm, and all. On these conditions the dish and food are removed, and the king and his retinue return to the palace, leaving the good people in quiet possession of everything.

After they have retired, the old woman, who has been watching the manœuvres from her hiding-place, comes out, and this time praises her boy for his adroitness. He makes over all the property to her, and starts off to seek his fortune and a wife, taking with him the enchanted dish, belt, and flute.

So he travels on, and finally arrives at a town where a king resides who has one beautiful daughter. She has many suitors, for the king has promised her hand to the first one who will make her laugh three times in succession. Now, it happens that our hero is very ill-shaped, ugly-looking, and awkward, and can, by a little affectation, make himself appear much more so than he really is. He strolls about the city, hears the current gossip, and learns about the domestic arrangements of the palace. So one day he strolls into the king's palace among the other suitors and visitors, and looks round at everything, and soon attracts the attention of the servants, who inquire what his business is there. At first he makes no reply. But he knows that, according to rule, unless he answers the third challenge, he will be summarily ejected. So he answers the second time. "Is it true, as I have heard, that the princess will marry the first man who can make her laugh three times in succession?" He is told that it is true, and he says he wishes to make the trial. So he is allowed to remain in the palace.

Being admitted into the apartment where the young lady is in waiting, surrounded by her suitors, who are to be umpires in the trial, he first brings out his magical dish with the enchanted food, and requests her to examine and taste it. She does this cautiously, following the bent of curiosity, and finds the taste so agreeable that she continues to eat, and offers it to the others, who also eat. To their astonishment the quantity of food does not diminish in the platter, nor does the taste become any less exquisite, although their distended stomachs protest against any further infliction. Finally the protestations of the gastric region overcome the clamors of the palate, and they attempt to stop eating and to push away the plate. But they can do neither the one nor the other, and so call upon the youth to take away his food. He will do so, but upon one condition: *the princess must laugh*. She hesitates; she had thought of laughing only from pleasure, not from pain. She refuses to comply, but he is inexorable; she may do what she pleases, — laugh, or continue to eat. Finally she can hold out no longer, and she laughs, saying to herself, "He'll not make me laugh a second time." As soon as he releases them from the enchantment of the food, they fly furiously at him to expel him from the palace. But they "reckon without their host." Quick as lightning he unclasps the magic belt, tosses it on the floor, and instantly they are all bound together in a bundle wound round from head to foot, and lie in a helpless heap before him. "Untie us," shouts the tortured and terrified princess. "Laugh, then," he coolly answers. But no, she will not laugh. But he knows how to bring her to terms. He has but to will it, and the obedient belt will tighten its embrace. When she and her guardians can endure the pressure no longer, she gives forth a forced and feeble laugh. Then they are all released. No sooner done, than the men draw their weapons and rush furiously at him. Before they reach the spot where he stands, however, he has the magic flute to his lips; their steps are arrested, and princess, suitors, umpires, guards, and all are wheeling in the mazy dance. They are charmed, not figuratively but literally, with the music of the tiny magic flute.

At length they grow tired of the exericse, and vainly endeavor to stop; but they cannot do it. "Stop your playing!" they shout. "I will," he answers, "when the princess laughs." But she determines that she will not laugh this time, come what may. But the stakes are for a princess and a kingdom, and he will not yield. She dances till she can no longer stand. She falls upon the floor, striking it heavily with her head. She then yields to her fate, performs her part nobly, and gives forth a hearty laugh. The music then ceases, the umpires are left to decide the case, and the young man walks away and leaves them.

The news of the affair reaches the ears of the king, and he commands that the young man shall be introduced into his presence. This is done; and the king is disgusted with the looks and manners of the young man, and declares the contract null and void. But the matter must be hushed up, and not allowed to get abroad. The "victor" is to be privately despatched, and another more suitable match substituted in his place. By the king's direction the stranger is seized, conveyed to the menagerie, and thrown in with the beasts. This is a large apartment surrounded by high walls. The ferocious animals rush upon him; but the magic belt is tossed down, and they are all tied up in a heap, their legs being bound fast to their bodies, while he sits quietly down awaiting the issue of events in one corner of the yard.

Meanwhile word is circulated that one of the suitors at the royal palace has won the princess's hand, and the wedding is to be celebrated that very evening. "All goes merrily as a marriage-bell," until the hour arrives for the bridegroom to be introduced into the bridal chamber. There the whole affair is quashed. Hosts of invisible foes are there who have entered at the key-hole, and are waiting to vindicate the innocent, defend his rights, and punish the intruder. The victorious Jack has taken his flute and called the troops of hornets to his aid; he bids them enter the key-hole and wait until his rival has unrobed, and then ply him with their tiny weapons about his lower extremities. This they do; and the poor fellow, unable to see the hornets, but fully able to feel their stinging, begins to jump and scream like a madman. The terrified princess rushes out of the room, and screams for help. The domestics run to her assistance, and she declares that the bridegroom is a maniac. They, hearing his screams and witnessing his contortions of countenance, and unable to learn the cause, come to the same conclusion, and hurry away from the palace. Another bridegroom is substituted, who shares the same fate. The king at length concludes that he is outgeneralled; that the young man who has won the hand of his daughter still lives; that he must be a remarkable personage, possessed of miraculous powers. He sends to the menagerie for him. The animals are all tied up; but a thick mist fills the place, and they cannot see the young man. They attempt to release the beasts, but find this impossible. They bring the report to the king. "Ay," said he, "it is just as I said; he is a necromancer, a remarkable man. Go again, seek him carefully, and if you can find him bring him in." This time they find him. They recognize him; but he is now transformed into a most lovely person. All admire his portly bearing and his polished manners. The wedding is consummated with great pomp. He builds a splendid palace, and, when the old king dies, is crowned in his place.

LXXXVII. THE CLEVER NUMSKULL [298]
(Micmac: Rand, *Legends of the Micmacs*, p. 326, No. 57)

Three brothers lived together. They had no sisters, and their mother was sick. The youngest was supposed to be a silly fellow, and was always doing outrageous things. One day they killed a pig. The two older brothers went to fetch salt, and told the youngest one to remain and watch the house, and take care of their mother and the pig. They said they were going to salt down the pork, and keep it for the long days. After they were gone, he went out and found some men at work, and told them that if there was a man there named Longdays, he had a pig for him. One of them declared that that was his name; forthwith the pig was delivered to him, and he carried it off. By and by the other brothers arrived, and wondered what had become of the pig. "Why, Longdays has been here and taken it away! Did not you say it was to be kept for Mr. Longdays?" "Oh, you blockhead! we told you it was to be kept for ourselves when the days become long next summer."

Some time after this, Coolnajoo was sent to buy a horse. He made the purchase, and brought the horse home. But there was a long avenue, lined by trees and bushes, extending from the highway down to the house; and when he came to the head of this lane, he gravely told the horse that this was the road, and bade him go on directly to the house. Saying this, he removed the halter; and the horse kicked up his heels and made for home. The boy arrived home, wondering at the stupidity of the horse; and on relating the case to his brothers, they wondered at his stupidity. "You numskull!" they exclaimed, "you can never do anything right. Why did you not ride him down the lane?" "Oh, I will do better next time," he promised.

So, as the old mother got no better, they sent him to find and bring home a woman to assist in nursing her and in taking care of the house. He took his bridle and started. He succeeded in his expedition, and the woman came with him all quiet and kindly till they reached the head of the lane; but there and then he made an attempt to put the bridle on her head, and assured her that she had to carry him on her back, and walk on all fours down to the house. Persisting in his determination, the terrified woman screamed, broke from her persecutor, and ran.

Chopfallen and sad, he went into the house. What was his trouble? they asked him. "Why! I attempted to bring her home in the way you directed; but she screamed and tore away from me, and crying went back, as hard as she could go." "Oh, you abominable fool!" they exclaimed; "was that the way to treat a woman? You should have taken her by the arm, and occasionally given her a kiss." "Ah, well!" he cried, "I shall know better next time."

The next time he was sent for a pig. He led the pig all right until he came to the lane. He then tried to make the pig walk on his hind legs; and when the terrified animal squealed and kicked, he attempted to conciliate it by kissing it; but he received such a return from the tusks of his captive as made the blood flow, and caused him to let go his grip, — and poor piggy went off home at the top of his speed.

Poor Coolnajoo returned crestfallen to his home, to relate his adventures, and to be blamed and lectured for the hundredth time for his outrageous stupidity.

His next expedition was for a tub of hog's-lard. This he purchased; but on his way home he passed over a portion of road that was dried and cracked by the sun. "Oh, my old grandfather!" he exclaimed, "what a terribly sore back you have got, — so naked and dry! You shall have my lard for salve, and I will rub it on." So saying, he began spreading the lard over the dry road; and when it was all gone, he went home. "Why have you not brought the lard?" "Oh, dear me! I came across a poor old man lying in the road with his back all sore and cracked; and I pitied him, and spread the lard over him." To this the brothers made no objection until they ascertained the truth of the case; when another attempt was made to teach him a lesson, and with the usual success.

His sixth expedition was in quest of a quantity of needles. These were purchased, but on his way home he passed a newly reaped field of grain. He looked at the stubble, and perceived the holes in the top; he was sure that when the rain should fall, the water would fill all those holes, and concluded that it would be a very benevolent act to stop them up. This would be a capital end to which to apply his needles. So he opened the packages, and carefully placed one in every straw; and when the supply was exhausted, many remained undoctored. "Alas, poor things!" he cried, "I cannot help you any more, as my stock is out." So he went home without his needles.

Afterward he was sent for some red flannel. Passing a graveyard on his way home, he looked at the crosses, and took them for poor old penitents kneeling in the cold with out-stretched arms, and carefully tore up his roll of red flannel and covered their poor shivering shoulders.

After this the two other brothers went together to town to make some purchases, and left him to take care of the sick mother. They charged him to give her drink, and especially to wash her face. He obeyed the directions, but supposed he must wash her face as he had seen her wash clothes, — by thrusting them into boiling water. So he set on the great pot; and when the water was boiling, he took up the old woman and thrust her head into it, and held her there. When he took her out, she was dead, and her lips were contracted to a grin, which he affected to mistake for laughter, and placed her back in the bed, and leaped and laughed at her quiet and pleasant counte-nance. He ran to meet his brothers, and told them that their mother had not been so quiet nor looked so well this long time. She had not stirred nor spoken, and she was laughing all the time. They went in, and were horror-stricken. "Oh, you out-rageous simpleton! what have you done? You have killed your mother. We shall all be executed for murder."

But now Coolnajoo began to exhibit his shrewdness, and soon became as clever as he had hitherto been simple. "Never you fear," said he; "we will turn the incident to good account, we will make some money out of it. Wait you here; I will run for the priest." So off he ran posthaste, and informed the priest that his mother was dying, and requested him to come with all haste, to perform over her the indispensable rite of extreme unction. The priest started immediately; but Coolnajoo outran him, and took his dead mother and placed her against the door, inside. The priest reached the house, burst the door open, and tumbled the old woman over. Coolnajoo sprang to raise her. Alas! she was dead. "Oh!" he exclaimed, wringing his hands and weeping, "you have killed our mother!" All three gathered round, and the horrified priest did not know what to do. They threatened to accuse him of the murder. He finally succeeded in pacifying them, and gave them a whole handful of money to hush up the matter and say nothing about it.

The development of his shrewdness proceeded. The two other brothers went away one day, and left the place in his charge. Among other occupations he had to tend the pigs. These he sold; but in order to cheat his brothers, he cut off their tails and took them down to a quagmire near the shore, and stuck them all up in the sand. When they came back and inquired for the pigs, he told them they had broken out of the pen and rushed down toward the shore, and had sunk in the quagmire. They went down to see; and sure enough, there they all were, just the tips of their tails sticking above the ground. They seized hold of the tails, and tried to draw up the porkers; but the tails broke, and down into the mire sank the bodies, as they believed, and could not be found.

Soon his pranks became unbearable, and the brothers resolved to make away with him. They concluded to drown him. So they tied him up in a bag, and took him down below high-water mark and buried him, — not deep, however, — and left him to be drowned when the tide came in. They returned; and he soon heard the "Uh! uh! uh!" of a drove of hogs, and called lustily for them to come to his aid. If they would uncover and untie him, he would lead them to a place where they could feast on chickweed to their hearts' content. The hogs, attracted by the noise, approached the spot. Their noses were soon thrust deep into the soft earth. The bag was soon reached, and instinct alone was sufficient to pull it out; and they soon removed the string, — when up jumped Coolnajoo, who seized one of his deliverers, transferred him to the bag, and the bag to the hole, drove the others away to the field of chickweed, where they were kept busy till the tide returned and covered the spot where he was supposed to lie.

In due time the tide receded, and compunction returned to the brothers' hearts; they repaired to the spot and dug up the bag, mournfully chanting, "Our poor brother is dead." Astonishment seized them when, on opening the bag, there, instead of the brother's corpse, was a dead pig. Meanwhile Coolnajoo had waited at a distance from the spot until his brothers went down to the shore to look for him. When they returned, he was astride the ridge-pole, laughing at them.

They made another attempt to kill him. This time they planned better; they would take him to a waterfall and toss him in above, and let him be dashed to pieces in going over the rapids. So they tied him up in a bag again, placed it across a pole, and started for the waterfall. They became hungry on the way, and placed him by the side of the road, and went to get some dinner. While they were gone, a drover came by; and seeing the bag, he went up and gave it a kick. "Halloa!" he exclaimed, "what is all this?" Coolnajoo replied, and informed the drover that he and his brothers were on a money-hunting expedition; concealed in this bag, so as not to excite suspicion, he was to be taken to a certain place where they would all make their fortunes. He gave such a glowing account of the matter, and with such apparent truthfulness and sincerity, that the drover was deceived, and offered him a whole drove of cattle and sheep for his chance in the money-hunting speculation. The bargain was struck, and the parties exchanged places. But Coolnajoo gave his substitute some cautions: "You must be cautious not to speak, or the cheat will be discovered; my brothers must not mistrust that it is not I. By and by you will hear the roar of a waterfall; do not be frightened. Before lowering you to the place where you are to find the money, they may give you two or three swings. You must keep still, and not speak; and after that you can have it all your own way." So saying, he went on to the market with the drove. The brothers came back to the bag. "Are you there?" they asked. No answer. But they saw that all was right, placed the bag on the pole, the pole on their shoulders, and moved on.

When they came to the waterfall, they approached as near as they could, and then gave him three swings in order to send him as far out as possible; and just as they let go, the terrified man sang out. They were startled at the voice; it sounded like a stranger's voice. They returned home, and shortly after their brother arrived with his pockets full of money, — the proceeds of his drove of cattle and sheep.

So they concluded to share the spoil and remain together. But one night a band of robbers was seen advancing upon them, and they ran for their lives. Coolnajoo was the last to leave the house and the others told him to "bring the door to after him," — meaning, of course, that he shall shut the door. He obeyed to the letter, — took the door off the hinges, and carefully brought it after him. They made for the woods, and took shelter in a tree, — Coolnajoo dragging the door up after him, and holding it carefully all the while. The robbers came up to the same tree, kindled a fire under it, cooked and ate their dinner, and then began counting and dividing their gold. While this process was going on, Coolnajoo got tired of holding the door, and dropped it down among them. It fell with a noise that terrified the robbers, who supposed that it had fallen from the sky; so they ran off as fast as their legs could carry them, and left everything behind, — gold, food, and dishes. Down scrambled our heroes, and gathered all up and ran; finally they came to a house, where they remained all night. They divided the money; but Coolnajoo claimed the largest share, as he declared that it was through his efforts that it had been obtained. The next night they called and stayed all night at another strange house. Coolnajoo became thirsty, and hunted around for a drink. Feeling carelessly about, he thrust his two hands into a pitcher, and could not withdraw them. He went out-of-doors, and looked around for something to strike the pitcher against, in order to break it. At length he saw what seemed in the darkness to be a white rock. He gave the pitcher a smart blow in order to free his hands; when, alas! he had struck a young woman in the head, and killed her with the blow. At the sight of what he had done, he was terribly frightened, and called up his brothers. He told them what had happened, and proposed immediate flight. They all departed; and his brothers, fearing that Coolnajoo would ultimately get them into difficulties from which they would be unable to extricate themselves, separated from him. By mutual consent the partnership was dissolved. They went each his own way.

Coolnajoo was bent on making money, and an opportunity occurred soon. He kept his eye on the robbers, and saw them

going out to bury a dead child; he watched to see where they
deposited the body, and also followed them unseen to their
retreat. When night came, he took up the corpse they had
buried, and went up to their house. The window was open,
and he looked in; they were busy counting and dividing their
ill-gotten booty. Piles of money covered the table, and he heard
all the accounts of their expeditions. All at once he sent the
dead baby flying in among them, — which so frightened them
that they took to their heels and left all behind. He leaped in,
gathered all the money, and left for home.

He now determined to settle, and to this end built a small
house. One day a heavy rain-storm came on; and just at nightfall two weary priests, wet to the skin, called and requested a
night's lodging. This he refused, as he had no accomodations
for strangers. They pleaded hard, and offered him a large re-
ward; this he accepted, and kept them until morning, but
managed to exact a still further contribution from them before
their departure.

LXXXVIII. THE FOX AND THE WOLF [299]

(MENOMINI: Skinner, *Journal of American Folk-Lore*, xxvi, 72, No. 2)

Very long ago there were two men living together, and making
maple-sugar. They made one *mokok* ("bark box") of sugar,
and then they cached it away, burying it, and said to each
other, "We will let it remain here until we are very hungry."

The younger man was a Fox, and he was a good hunter.
Every time he went out, he brought home chickens or small
wild game. The other man was a greedy Wolf, and he never
killed anything, or brought anything home: so Fox thought he
would play a trick on his chum for being lazy.

"You ought to go over to that house," said Fox to Wolf.
"Maybe they will give you something to eat. When I went
over there, they gave me a chicken."

So Wolf went over as he was told. When he got to the house,
he did not hide himself, but went in open sight. The owner of
the house saw the Wolf coming up; so he set his dogs on him
to drive him away; and Wolf escaped only by running into
the river.

"So it is this one that takes off our chickens!" said the man.

When Wolf arrived at his home, he told his younger brother,
Fox, "Why, I hardly escaped from that man!"

"Why!" said Fox to him. "They did not recognize you; that's why." But Wolf made no answer.

While they were in the house together, Fox went outside, and cried, "*He!*" to deceive Wolf.

"What's the matter with you?" asked Wolf.

"Oh! they have come after me to give a name to a child."

"Then you'd better go over. Maybe they will give you something to eat."

Instead of going, however, Fox went to their cache of maple-sugar, and ate some of it. When he returned, Wolf asked him, "What did you name the baby?"

"*Mokimon,*" replied Fox; and this word means to "reveal" or "dig out" something you have hidden.

At another time, while they were sitting together, Fox said, "*He!*" and "Oh, yes!"

"What's that?" inquired Wolf.

"Oh, I am called to give a name to a newborn baby."

"Well, then, go. Maybe they will give you something to eat." So Fox went and returned.

"What's the name of the child?" asked Wolf.

This time, Fox answered, "*Wapiton,*" and this word means "to commence to eat."

At another time, time, Fox cried out, "*He!*" and "All right!" as though some one had called to him, "I'll come."

"What's that?" asked Wolf.

"They want me to go over and name their child."

"Well, then, go," says Wolf. "You always get something to eat every time they want you."

So Fox went, and soon returned. Wolf asked him again, "What name did you give it?"

"*Hapata kiton,*" answered Fox; that is to say, "half eaten."

Then another time Fox cried "*He!*" as if in answer to some one speaking to him, and then, as though some one called from the distance, "*Hau!*"

Wolf, as he did not quite hear, asked Fox what the matter was.

"Oh, nothing!" replied Fox, "only they want me to come over and name their child."

"Well, then, you'd better go. Maybe you'll get a chance to eat; maybe you'll fetch me something too."

So Fox started out, and soon returned home.

"Well, what name did you give this time?" asked Wolf.

"*Noskwaton*," said Fox; and this means "all licked up."

Then Wolf caught on. "Maybe you are eating our stored maple-sugar!" he cried. But Fox sat still and laughed at him. Then Wolf went over and looked at their cache. Sure enough, he found the empty box with its contents all gone, and pretty well licked up. Meantime Fox skipped out, and soon found a large tree by the river, leaning out over the water. He climbed into its branches and hid there. Presently the angry Wolf returned home, and, not finding Fox, tracked him to the tree. Wolf climbed part way to Fox without seeing him, as he was on the branches. Then Wolf was afraid, and while he was hesitating, he happened to look at the water, and there he saw the reflection of Fox laughing at him on the surface.[270] The Wolf, in a fury, plunged into the bottom of the stream, but of course failed to catch Fox. He tried four times, and after the fourth attempt he was tired, and quit jumping in for a while. While he was resting, he looked up and saw Fox laughing at him. Then Wolf said to Fox, "Let's go home and make up"; for he thought in his heart that anyway Fox was feeding him all the time.

By and by it became winter. Fox frequently went out, and returned with abundance of fish.

"How do you manage to get so many?" asked Wolf.

"You'd better go out and try for yourself," said Fox. "The way I do, when I am fishing, is to cut a hole in the ice. I put my tail in, instead of a line, and I remain there until I feel bites. I move ahead a little to let the fish string on my tail; but I stay a long time, until I get a great many fish on my tail. When it feels pretty heavy, I jerk it out, and catch all I want."

Fox was in hopes that he could get Wolf frozen to death in the ice, and so avoid the necessity of feeding him any longer. So he took Wolf out, and cut five holes in the ice, — one for his tail, and one for each paw, — telling him he could catch more fish that way. Wolf staid there to fish all night. Every once in a while he would move his feet or tail a little, and they felt so heavy, he was sure he was getting a tremendous load; and he staid a little longer. In the mean time he was freezing fast in the ice. When he found out the predicament he was in, he jerked backwards and forwards again and again, until all the hair wore off his tail, and there he was. He thought he had let too many fish on his tail and feet to haul them out, and he worked hard to free himself. At last he wore his tail out at the surface of the ice, and pulled off his claws and the bottoms of his feet. Fox told him he had caught too many fish, and that they had bitten his tail and feet; and Wolf believed it.

Another time, Fox found a wasp's nest in a tree: so he went home and told Wolf that there was honey in it, and persuaded him to try and jump up and get it, on the plea that Wolf could jump higher than he could. As soon as Wolf set out to try, Fox ran away, and Wolf was nearly stung to death. Fox fled over a wagon-road to conceal his tracks, and as he travelled, he met a negro with a team, hauling a load of bread. Fox, cunning as he was, lay down on the side of the road and pretended that he was dead. The negro saw him lying there, and picked him up and put him in his wagon behind his load. Fox very presently came to, and, waiting for his chance, he would throw off a loaf of bread every now and then, till he had gotten rid of a good many. Then he jumped off, and carried the loaves to a secret place, where he built him a shelter, and prepared to live for a time.

In the mean time, Wolf came along, half starved, and crippled from his meddling with a live wasp's nest and from his fishing experiemce.

Fox fed him on his arrival, and said, "You ought to do the way I did. It's easy to get bread. I got mine by playing dead on the road. To-morrow the negro will pass by with another load; and you can watch for him and do as I did, and steal his bread."

Next morning, Wolf started out to watch the road and pretty soon he saw the negro coming with a big load of bread: so he lay down beside the road, where the darky could see him, and played dead. The darky did see him, sure enough; and he stopped his team, and got off and got a big stick, and knocked Wolf over the head, and killed him dead for sure.

"I will not get fooled this time!" he said, "for yesterday I lost too many loaves of bread for putting a dead Fox in my wagon without examining him!"

So he did take the Wolf home dead. That ended him, and since then Fox has eaten alone.

LXXXIX. THE TAR–BABY [300]

(CHEROKEE: Mooney, *Report of the Bureau of American Ethnology*, xix, 272)

Once upon a time there was such a severe drought that all streams of water and all lakes were dried up. In this emergency the beasts assembled together to devise means to procure water. It was proposed by one to dig a well. All agreed to do so except the hare. She refused because it would soil her tiny paws. The rest, however, dug their well and were fortunate enough to find water. The hare, beginning to suffer and thirst and having no right to the well, was thrown upon her wits to procure water. She determined, as the easiest way, to steal from the public well. The rest of the animals, surprised to find that the hare was so well supplied with water, asked her where she got it. She replied that she arose betimes in the morning and gathered the dewdrops. However the wolf and the fox suspected her of theft and hit on the following plan to detect her:

They made a wolf of tar and placed it near the well. On the following night the hare came as usual after her supply of water. On seeing the tar wolf she demanded who was there. Receiving no answer she repeated the demand, threatening to kick the wolf if he did not reply. She receiving no reply kicked the wolf, and by this means adhered to the tar and was caught. When the fox and wolf got hold of her they consulted what it was best to do with her. One proposed cutting her head off. This the hare protested would be useless, as it had often been tried without hurting her. Other methods were proposed for dispatching her, all of which she said would be useless. At last it was proposed to let her loose to perish in a thicket. Upon this the hare affected great uneasiness and pleaded hard for life. Her enemies, however, refused to listen and she was accordingly let loose. As soon, however, as she was out of reach of her enemies she gave a whoop, and bounding away she exclaimed: "This is where I live." [108]

XC. THE TURTLE'S RELAY RACE [301]

(ARIKARA: Dorsey, *Publications of the Carnegie Institution*, xvii, 143, No. 56)

One time a Coyote met a Turtle. The Coyote began to boast of his swiftness, and the Turtle said, "Why, I can beat you

running!" So the Coyote said, "We will run a race to-morrow."
That night they parted, and went to their homes, so that they
could get ready for the race the next morning. After the Turtle
reached home he began to worry, and he could not get to sleep,
for he knew that the Coyote could run fast. But the Turtle
said to himself: "I will take him up there and go to the other
Turtles, and ask them to assist me." So the Turtle went to
the other Turtles, and said: "I am about to run a race with
the Coyote. I want you to help me." He told them the place
where they were to run, and the distance they were to run. So
several Turtles volunteered to go and help the Turtle to beat
the Coyote.

All the Turtles went to the place. They placed one Turtle
at the end of the course; then they placed another one at a certain distance back of him; then another back of this one, and
so on, and finally the Turtle himself took his stand. Each Turtle carried a long pole, and hid in the ground.

The next morning the Turtle met the Coyote. The Coyote
began to run around and was happy, for he thought that he was
going to beat the Turtle. The Turtle and the Coyote got ready
to start. The Turtle gave the command to start. The Coyote
ran and the Turtle crawled into his hole. When he got over a
little ridge the Coyote saw the Turtle going ahead of him.
Coyote ran and caught up with the Turtle. The Turtle threw
his pole away and crawled into the ground. When the Coyote
got to another knoll, there was the Turtle ahead of him again.
The Coyote caught up with him. The Turtle crawled into the
ground. The Coyote ran, and when he got up to another hill,
there was the Turtle going ahead. The Coyote caught up with
and passed him. At the end, the Turtle was at the goal, and the
Coyote got up, and said, "You have beaten me." This fine
stretch of running killed the Coyote.

XCI. THE PEACE FABLE [302]

(WYANDOT: Barbeau, *Memoirs of the Geological Survey of Canada:
Anthropological Series*, xi, 210, No. 65)

As he was travelling one day, the Fox saw his cousin the Rooster
perched high upon a tree. "Come down, cousin!" exclaimed
the Fox, "let us have a chat!" The Rooster replied, "Oh, no!"
And the Fox went on saying, "We all live in peace now, and

have arranged not to slay each other any longer." The rooster then warned the Fox, "I hear something, cousin; I hear the hounds rushing this way." The Fox said, "Oh! I must be going!" But the Rooster objected, "No! You have just told me that we all live in peace now, and that we must not kill each other any longer!" The Fox explained, "I must be going! They have not yet received word as we have."

So the old Fox has been running ever since.

XCII. THE ANT AND THE GRASSHOPPER [303]
(SHUSWAP: Teit, *Jesup North Pacific Expedition*, ii, 655)

Grasshopper lived with the people who were busy catching and curing salmon. They said to him, "Come help us. It is the salmon season. We must all work, that we may have a plentiful store of salmon for the winter." Grasshopper answered, "No, I do not like to work. I like to amuse myself playing, jumping, and making a noise. I do not need salmon. I like to eat grass, of which there is great plenty all around here." Soon winter came, and the grass was all covered deep with snow. Then Grasshopper was cold and hungry. Finding nothing to eat, and being in a starving condition, he begged the people to give him some dried salmon. This they refused to do, telling him to go and play, and eat grass. When he was nearly dead, they transformed him, saying, "Henceforth you shall be the grasshopper and, as you were too lazy and thoughtless to catch salmon, you shall live on grass, and spend your time jumping around and making much noise."

CHAPTER IX

BIBLE STORIES [304]

XCIII. ADAM AND EVE [305]

(Thompson: Teit, *Jesup North Pacific Expedition*, viii, 399, No. 105)

WHEN this earth was very young, only two people lived on it, — a man called A'tām and a woman called Ĭm. The Chief (or God) lived in the upper world, and the Outcast (or Devil) lived in the lower world. They were enemies to each other, and tried to do each other harm, but God was the more powerful. He frequently visited the earth and talked with A'tām and Ĭm.

One day the Devil created an animal like a horse, and made it appear before the man and woman. When the latter saw it, she said, "That is God come to visit us"; but A'tām said it was not. At last, however, he believed it must be God, and they went and spoke with it. Soon afterwards God appeared, and then they recognized the difference. He was angry and said, "Why do you mistake the Devil for me and converse with him? Have I not told you he is evil, and will do you harm?" Then, looking at the animal, he said to the couple, "Well, since this beast is here, I will so transform him that he will be useful to you." He wetted both his thumbs, pressed them on the animal's front legs, and thus marked him, saying, "Henceforth you will be a horse and a servant and plaything of the people, who will ride you, and use you for many purposes. You will be a valuable slave of man."

Now the mosquitoes were tormenting the horse very much, so God plucked some long grass which grew near by, and threw it at the animal's backside, and it became a long tail. He also threw some on the horse's neck, and it became a mane. He said, "Henceforth you will be able to protect yourself from the mosquitoes." Then he plucked out more grass, and threw it ahead of the horse, saying, "That will be your food." It turned into bunch grass, which soon spread over the whole country.

Now God departed, telling the man and woman he would soon return and show them which trees bore the proper kinds of food to eat. Hitherto they had eaten no fruit, for they did not know the edible varieties. At that time all trees bore fruit, and the pines and firs in particular had large sweet fruit. Now the Devil appeared, and, pretending to be God, he took the large long fruit of the white pine, and gave it to Im. She thought he was God, ate the fruit as directed, and gave some to A'tām. Then the Devil disappeared; and all the fruit on the trees withered up, and became transformed into cones. Some kinds shrivelled up to a small size, and became berries. When God came and saw what had happened, he sent the woman to live with the Devil, and, taking A'tām, he broke off his lower rib, and made a woman out of it. This rib-woman became A'tām's wife, and bore many children to him.

XCIV. NOAH'S FLOOD [306]

(THOMPSON: Teit, *Jesup North Pacific Expedition*, viii, 400, No. 106)

God came down to the earth, and found it was very dirty, and full of bad things, bad people, mysteries, and cannibals. He thought he would make a flood to clean the earth, and drown all the bad people and monsters. The flood covered the tops of the mountains; and all the people were drowned, except one man and his two daughters, who escaped in a canoe. When the water receded, they came ashore and found that the earth was clean. They were starving, and looked for food, but nothing edible could they see. No plants grew near by, only some trees of several varieties. They crushed a piece of fir with stones, and soaked it in water. They tried to eat it, and to drink the decoction; but it was too nasty, and they threw it away. Thus they tried pine, alder, and other woods, and at last they tried service-berry wood, which tasted much better. The women drank the decoction, and found that it made them tipsy. They gave some to their father, and he became quite drunk. Now they thought to themselves, "How is the earth to be peopled!" And they each had connection with their father without his knowing it. As the water receded, they became able to get more and more food; but they still continued to drink the service-berry decoction, and, as their father was fond of it, they frequently made him drunk, and had connection with him. Thus they bore many children, and their father wondered how they became pregnant. These children, when they grew up, married one another, and thus was the earth repeopled. The animals and birds also became numerous again.

XCV. THE TOWER OF BABEL [307]

(CHOCTAW: Bushnell, *Bulletin of the Bureau of American Ethnology*, xlviii, 30)

Many generations ago Aba, the good spirit above, created many men, all Choctaw, who spoke the language of the Choctaw, and understood one another. These came from the bosom of the earth, being formed of yellow clay, and no men had ever lived before them. One day all came together and, looking upward, wondered what the clouds and the blue expanse above might be. They continued to wonder and talk among themselves and at last determined to endeavor to reach the sky. So they brought many rocks and began building a mound that was to have touched the heavens. That night, however, the wind blew strong from above and the rocks fell from the mound. The second morning they again began work on the mound, but as the men slept that night the rocks were again scattered by the winds. Once more, on the third morning, the builders set to their task. But once more, as the men lay near the mound that night, wrapped in slumber, the winds came with so great force that the rocks were hurled down on them.

The men were not killed, but when daylight came and they made their way from beneath the rocks and began to speak to one another, all were astounded as well as alarmed—they spoke various languages and could not understand one another. Some continued thenceforward to speak the original tongue, the language of the Choctaw, and from these sprung the Choctaw tribe. The others, who could not understand this language, began to fight among themselves. Finally they separated. The Choctaw remained the original people; the others scattered, some going north, some east, and others west, and formed various tribes. This explains why there are so many tribes throughout the country at the present time.

XCVI. CROSSING THE RED SEA [308]

(CHEYENNE: Dorsey, *Field Museum: Anthropological Series*, ix, 37, No. 15)

Many thousands of years ago the Cheyenne inhabited a country in the far north, across a great body of water. For two or three years they had been overpowered by an enemy that outnumbered them, and they were about to become the enemy's slaves, and they were filled with sorrow. Among their number was a great medicine-man who possessed a wooden hoop, like those used in the games of to-day. On one side of the hoop were tied magpie feathers, while opposite them, on the other side of the hoop, was a flint spear head, with the point projecting toward the center of the hoop. One night the great chief told the people to come to a certain place.

When they were assembled he led them away. He kept in advance of them all the time, and in his left hand he held a long staff, and in his right hand he held his hoop horizontally in front of him, with the spear head of the hoop pointing forward. No one was allowed to go in front of him. On the fourth night of their journey they saw, at some distance from the ground, and apparently not far in front of them, a bright light. As they advanced the light receded, and appeared always a little farther beyond. They traveled a few more nights, and the fire preceded them all the way, until they came to a large body of water. The medicine-man ordered the Cheyenne to form in a line along the edge of the water, and they obeyed. He then told them that he was going to take them across the water to another land, where they would live forever. As they stood facing the water the medicine-man asked them to sing four times with him, and he told them that as they sang the fourth time he would lead them across the water. As he sang the fourth time he began to walk forwards and backwards and the fourth time he walked directly into the water. All the people followed him. He commanded them not to look upward, but ever downward. As they went forward the waters separated, and they walked on dry ground, but the water was all around them. Finally, as they were being led by night the fire disappeared, but they continued to follow the medicine-man until daylight, when they found themselves walking in a beautiful country.

In the new country they found plenty of game to live on. The medicine-man taught the Cheyenne many things, but they seemed to be of weak minds, though they were physically strong. Out of these Cheyenne there sprang up men and women who were large, tall, strong, and fierce, and they increased in number until they numbered thousands. They were so strong that they could pick up and carry off on their backs the large animals that they killed. They tamed panther and bear and trained them to catch wild game for them to eat. They had bows and arrows, and were always dressed in furs and skins, and in their ignorance they roamed about like animals. In those days there were very large animals. One variety of these animals was of the form of a cow, though four times as large; by nature they were tame and grazed along the river banks; men milked them. Boys and men to the number of twenty could get upon their backs without disturbing them. Another variety of these large animals resembled in body the horse, and they had horns and long, sharp teeth. This was the most dangerous animal in the country. It ate man, had a mind like a human being, and could trail a human being through the rivers and tall grasses by means of its power of scent. Of these there were but few. In the rivers there were long snakes whose bodies were so large that a man could not jump over them.

The Cheyenne remained in the north a long time, but finally roamed southward, conveying their burdens by means of dogs. While they were traveling southward there came a great rain and flood all over the country. The rivers rose and overflowed, and still the rain kept falling. At last the high hills alone could be discerned. The people became frightened and confused. On a neighboring hill, and apart from the main body of the Cheyenne, were a few thousand of their number, who were out of view, and had been cut off from the main body by the rising water. When the rains ceased and the water subsided the part who were cut off looked for their tribesmen, but they found no sign of them; and it has ever since been a question among the Cheyenne whether this band of people was drowned, or whether it became a distinct tribe. Long afterward the Cheyenne met a tribe who used many of their words, and to-day they believe that a part of their people are still living in the north. Nearly all the animals were either drowned or starved to death. The trees and fruit upon which the people had formerly subsisted were destroyed. A few large gray wolves escaped with them, for they had crossed with the tame dogs. The dogs were so large that they could carry a child several miles in a day. After the flood had subsided the senses of the Cheyenne seemed to be awakened. They became strong in mind but weak in body, for now they had no game to subsist on. They lived on dried meat and mushrooms, which sustained them for a long time.

NOTES

ABBREVIATIONS USED IN THE NOTES
AND BIBLIOGRAPHY

THE following list of abbreviations conforms to the practice of the *Journal of American Folk-Lore* and the Bureau of American Ethnology.

AA ....*American Anthropologist.*

Alexander........H. B. Alexander, *The Mythology of all Races: North American.*

BAAS ....British Association for Advancement of Science, Reports.

BAM ....Bulletin of the American Museum of Natural History, New York.

BBAE ....Bulletin of the Bureau of American Ethnology.

Boas, *Sagen* .....Franz Boas, *Indianische Sagen von der Nord-Pacifischen Küste Amerikas.*

Bolte-Polívka....Bolte und Polívka, *Anmerkungen zu den Kinder- und Hausmärchen der Brüder Grimm.*

CColl ....Colorado College Publications, Language Series.

CI ....Publications of the Carnegie Institution.

CNAE..........Contributions to North American Ethnology (Smithsonian Institution).

CU............Columbia University Contributions to Anthropology.

Curtis ....E. S. Curtis, *The North American Indian.*

Cushing ....F. H. Cushing, *Zuñi Folk Tales.*

FL ....*Folklore* (London).

FLJ ....*Folk Lore Journal* (London).

FM ....Field Museum of Natural History, Anthropological Series.

GSCan ....Geological Survey of Canada, Anthropological Series.

JAFL ....*Journal of American Folk-Lore.*

JAI ....*Journal of the Anthropological Institute of Great Britain and Ireland.*

JE ....Publications of the Jesup North Pacific Expedition.

Leland.........C. G. Leland, *Algonquin Legends of New England.*

MAAA ....Memoirs of the American Anthropological Association.

MAFLS ......Memoirs of the American Folk-Lore Society.

OAR ....Ontario Archeological Report.

PaAM ....Anthropological Papers of the American Museum of Natural History, New York.

PAES ....Publications of the American Ethnological Society.

Petitot ....É. Petitot, *Traditions indiennes du Canada Nord-ouest* (1886 edition).

PFLS ....Publications of the Folklore Society (English).

Rand ....S. T. Rand, *Legends of the Micmacs*.

RBAE ....Report of the Bureau of American Ethnology.

Rink ....H. Rink, *Tales and Traditions of the Eskimo*.

Russell ....Frank Russell, *Explorations in the Far North*.

TCI ....Transactions of the Canadian Institute.

UCal ....University of California Publications in American Archaeology and Ethnology.

UPa ....University of Pennsylvania, The University Museum Anthropological Publications.

VKAWA........Verhandelingen der Koninklijke Akademie van Wetenschappen te Amsterdam.

The notes on each incident are arranged by culture areas as follows: ESK. (Eskimo); MACK. (Mackenzie River district); PLAT. (Plateau area); N.PAC. (North Pacific Coast from Alaska to California); CAL. (California); PLNS. (Plains area); WDL. CENT. (Central Woodland area); WDL. N.E. (Northeast Woodland area); WDL. IROQ. (Iroquois area); S.E. (Southeastern area); S.W. (Southwestern area).

The letter and number occurring immediately after the name of an incident indicates the place assigned to this incident in the editor's forthcoming work, *Motif-Index of Folk-Literature*. See note at end of p. 367.

COMPARATIVE NOTES

THE following comparative notes make no claim to completeness. Although the reading represented by them covers with insignificant exceptions all the American Indian tales at present in print, and although the editor made notes on all of them, it has happened in many cases that the significance of an incident has escaped him and that only later in his reading he has begun to make note of its occurrence. To go back over the entire reading to look for such incidents has been impossible.

During the last ten years many of the most representative motifs have been very completely studied, particularly by Professor Boas in his treatment of the Tsimshian (RBAE, vol. XXXI) and of the Kutenai (BBAE, vol. LIX), by Mr. Teit and Professor Boas in the former's study of the Tahltan (JAFL, vols. XXXII and XXXIV) and of the Kaska (JAFL, vol. XXX), by Dr. Lowie in his treatment of the test-theme (JAFL, vol. XXI) and Dr. Waterman in his investigation of the explanatory element in North American Indian tales (JAFL, vol. XXVII). There have been several thorough studies of single motifs, such as those of Miss Gladys Reichard (JAFL, vol. XXXIV). It has not been the purpose of the editor to duplicate any of this work. Hence, wherever possible, he has referred to these studies and has merely listed the tribes in which the incident is found. He has added to these references such further notes as he has accumulated.

The order of listing the tribes is geographical, the tribes being grouped in accordance with Dr. Wissler's arrangement (AA, new ser., XVI, 447 ff.) into nine culture areas. These are designated by abbreviations that will be sufficiently apparent. It is hoped that this arrangement will make the notes of value to the general reader who is unfamiliar with the tribes and their habitat. The distribution of a motif can be seen at a glance.

Even with the very effective work of collectors of tales during the past century and the laborious annotations of successive students, it is by no means safe to assume that a tale or a motif is actually not found in a tribe because it is not mentioned in the notes. Except among a dozen or two tribes the tales have not been collected with such exhaustiveness as to preclude the probability of new discoveries. And the eyes of annotators are not infallible. In general, however, the study of the better-known motifs is not likely to be affected materially by future collections or further comparisons.

With full appreciation of "the little done, the undone vast," the editor is encouraged to hope that some parts at least of his notes may prove of value to the future editor of the much-needed concordance of American Indian tales.

1. In this division on Mythological Stories, several typical mythological cycles are given in full. They are chosen to represent the different geographical divisions, and preference has been given those tales of most general currency. Most tribes possess something in the way of explanations of their beginnings and their religious ideas. In some tribes these are gathered together in relatively long mythologies; in others they appear in separate tales. Examples of the longer myths are given in this chapter; the shorter episodes form the following chapter. — For a somewhat systematic treatment of American Indian mythology, see H. B. Alexander's *The Mythology of All Races: North American.* — Good cosmogonic myths exist in many parts of America, and most of them are told with a considerable degree of interest. Some of the very best, such as the Creek, the Pawnee, and the Navaho, have been omitted from this collection only with the greatest reluctance. Their length has made inclusion impossible. — For lists of myths from those sections of the continent represented by mythologies in this chapter, see notes 5, 10, 20, 27, 36, 38, and 47. — For sections not covered by these notes, the following references may be useful: **MACK.** ANVIK: Chapman, PAES, vi, 8 ff.; Chapman, JAFL, xxv, 66. UPPER YUKON: Schmitter, p. 21. KASKA: Teit, JAFL, xxx, 429 ff. LOUCHEUX: Camsell-Barbeau, JAFL, xxviii, 249. DOG RIB: Petitot, p. 309. TS'ETS'AUT: Boas, JAFL, ix, 260. BEAVER: Goddard, PaAM, x, 232. — **PLAT.** SHUSWAP: Teit, JE, ii, 642 ff. THOMPSON: Teit, JE, viii, 320. OKANAGON: Teit, MAFLS, xi, 84. — **PLNS.** SOUTHERN UTE: Lowie, JAFL, xxxvii, 61, No. 33. WICHITA: Dorsey, JAFL, xv, 216; Dorsey, CI, xxi, 25 ff. ARAPAHO: Dorsey, FM, iv, 191 ff. CHEYENNE: Dorsey, FM, ix, 34 ff.; Kroeber, JAFL, xiii, 164. CROW: Simms, FM, ii, 281 ff.; Lowie, PaAM, xxv, 19. PAWNEE: Dorsey, CI, lix, 13 ff.; Dorsey, MAFLS, viii, 3 ff. DAKOTA: Wallis, JAFL, xxxvi, 36, 40. MANDAN: Will and Spinden, *Peabody Museum Papers*, iii, 138. ARIKARA: Dorsey, CI, xvii, 11 ff.; Hall, JAFL, xxii, 90; Grinnell, JAFL, vi, 123. BLACKFOOT: Maclean, JAFL, vi, 165; Wissler and Duvall, PaAM, ii, 19 ff. SARCEE: Simms, JAFL, xvii, 180. GROS VENTRE: Kroeber, PaAM, i, 59. ASSINIBOIN: Potts, JAFL, v, 72; Lowie, PaAM, iv, 100 ff. KIOWA: Gatschet, *Das Ausland*, Nov. 17, 1893. — **S.E.** CHEROKEE: Mooney, RBAE, xix, 239 ff. YUCHI: Speck, UPa, i, 138; Gatschet, AA, old ser., vi, 278. CREEK: Gatschet, *Migration Legends of the Creek Indians*, i, 247 ff.; Speck, MAAA, ii, 149 ff. CADDO: Dorsey, CI, xli, 7 ff. — For the other areas, see notes as follows: Eskimo, note 5; North Pacific, note 38; California, note 47; Central Woodland, note 20; Northeast Woodland, note 10; Iroquois, note 27; Southwest, note 36.

2. *I. Sedna, Mistress of the Underworld* (A315). A girl refuses suitors and marries a bird (or dog). The girl's father kills the bird and takes the daughter in his boat. On the return a storm comes up and the father throws her overboard. When she clings to the boat he cuts off her fingers, which become the various kinds of fish. Her animal children eat up her father. She is the deity of the lower world. — The story is told throughout the Eskimo region. For discussion, see Wardle, AA, new ser., ii, 568; Boas, RBAE, v, 583; Boas,

BAM, xv, 359. The story sometimes merges into that of the "Dog-Husband," tale No. LXV in this collection (see note 247). For the relation between the two, see Signe Rink, AA, old ser., XI (1898), 181 ff. and 209 ff. — **ESK.** EAST GREENLAND: Holm, p. 56. WEST GREENLAND: Rink, p. 471, No. 148. SMITH SOUND: Kroeber, JAFL, XII, 168, 179. BAFFIN LAND: Rink and Boas, JAFL, II, 124, 127; Boas, BAM, xv, 163, 165. LABRADOR: Turner, RBAE, XI, 261; Smith, JAFL, VII, 205, 207. WEST HUDṢON BAY: Boas, BAM, xv, 327; Boas, RBAE, VI, 583, 637. POINT BARROW: Murdoch, *American Naturalist* (1886), p. 594.

3. *Animal marriages* (B600). Marriages between human beings and animals are very common motifs in American Indian tales. See the whole of Chapter VI.

4. *Explanatory myths.* The explanatory element in Indian tales is discussed at length by Dr. Waterman in his "The Explanatory Element in the Folk-Tales of the North-American Indians," JAFL, XXVII, 1 ff. He shows that it is the least stable part of the tales, that it is more often than not an afterthought or at least an addition to the tale. The same tale may be used to introduce many different explanations.

5. *The Eskimo cosmogony.* For an account of Eskimo conceptions of the universe and of Eskimo mythology in general, see the following: Rink, pp. 35 ff.; Boas, RBAE, VI, 583 ff.; Boas, BAM, xv, 119 ff.; Turner, RBAE, XI, 193; Nelson, RBAE, XVIII, 421. — See also all references in notes 2 and 6.

6. *II. Sun Sister and Moon Brother.* A brother visits a sister secretly at night. She identifies him by painting his back with her hands. She then cuts off her breasts and gives them to him. She ascends to sky; he chases. They are sun and moon. — References: Boas, BAM, xv, 359. — **ESK.** EAST and WEST GREENLAND, SMITH SOUND, CUMBERLAND SOUND, LABRADOR, WEST HUDSON BAY, MACKENZIE RIVER, POINT BARROW, ST. MICHAEL: Boas, *loc. cit.* KODIAK: Golder, JAFL, XVIII, 227. — **MACK.** LOWER YUKON: Boas, *loc. cit.* ANVIK: Chapman, PAES, VI, 21, No. 4. — **S.E.** CADDO: Dorsey, CI, XLI, 11, No. 1. (The brother visits the sister as in this tale. She identifies him by smearing paint on his face. He is the man in the moon.) — For a discussion of related tales in Panama and Brazil see Hagar, *Boas Anniversary Volume*, p. 356. — In other contexts than that here given occurs:

(a) *The moon as wooer* (A753). — **ESK.** EAST and WEST GREENLAND, SMITH SOUND, CUMBERLAND SOUND: Boas, BAM, xv, 359. — **MACK.** ANVIK: Chapman, PAES, VI, 61, No. 9. — **CAL.** SINKYONE: Kroeber, JAFL, XXXII, 349, No. 9. — **PLNS.** CANADIAN DAKOTA: Wallis, JAFL, XXXVI, 43. — **WDL.N.E.** MONTAGNAIS: LeJeune, *Jes. Rel.*, VI (1634), 223.

7. *Tell-tale hand mark* (H58). Clandestine lover identified by paint marks left on his skin by his mistress. A motif not only in all versions of this tale (see note 6), but also frequently in "The Dog-Husband," No. LXV, and several other tales. — As introduction to "The Dog-Husband," see note 247 (THOMPSON RIVER, ARAPAHO, CHILCOTIN, NEZ PERCÉ, and BLACKFOOT references). — As introduction to "The Bear-Woman," No. LXIV, see **PLNS.** WICHITA: Dorsey, CI, XXI, 70, No. 9. ARAPAHO: Dorsey and Kroeber, FM, V, 189, No. 85. ATSINA: Curtis, V, 123. ASSINIBOIN: Lowie, PaAM, IV, 160. — As introduction to "The Deserted Children," No. LXVII, see **PLAT.** THOMPSON: Teit, JE, VIII, 287, No. 49. — See also: **ESK.** KODIAK: Golder, JAFL, XVIII,

227. Cf. ALEUT: Golder, JAFL, xx, 139.—PLAT. LILLOOET: Teit, JAFL, xxv, 340.—CAL. ATSUGEWI: Dixon, JAFL, xxi, 174.

8. *Brother and sister incest* (T415).— All references in note 6.—MACK. KASKA: Teit, JAFL, xxx, 464, No. 19, and 459, No. 14. TS'ETS'ÁUT: Boas, JAFL, ix, 257.—PLAT. LILLOOET: Teit, JAFL, xxv, 340. THOMPSON: Teit, MAFLS, xi, 47.—N. PAC. TAHLTAN: Teit, JAFL, xxxiv, 238, No. 44. TLINGIT: Krause, p. 270. SONGISH: Hill-Tout, JAI, xxxvii, 337.— CAL. WESTERN MONO: Gifford, JAFL, xxxvi, 344, No. 15. SHASTA: Dixon, JAFL, xxiii, 14. ATSUGEWI: Dixon, JAFL, xxi, 174. YANA: Sapir, UCal, ix, 103, No. 7; Curtin, *Creation Myths*, p. 407.—PLNS. WICHITA: Dorsey, CI, xxi, 70, No. 9. ARAPAHO: Dorsey and Kroeber, FM, v, 189, No. 85. ATSINA: Curtis, v, 123. ASSINIBOIN: Lowie, PaAM, iv, 160.—S.W. ZUÑI: Stevenson, RBAE, xiii, 32. ——— EASTERN SIBERIA: Jochelson, JE, vi, 376.

9. *Pursuit of sun by moon* (A735). Usually the moon is considered feminine, though in this tale it is masculine.— All references in note 6.—PLNS. BLACKFOOT: Grinnell, JAFL, vi, 47. SKIDI PAWNEE: Dorsey, MAFLS, viii, 4, No. 1.—WDL. CENT. OTTAWA: Schoolcraft, *Indian in his Wigwam*, p. 82. MENOMINI: Alexander, p. 25.— Cf. WDL. N.E. MONTAGNAIS: LeJeune, *Jes. Rel.*, vi (1634), 223 and xii (1637), 31, 73.

10. *III. Glooscap.* The hero myth containing the principal part of the mythology of the Northeast Woodland tribes. It has several elements in common with the Manabozho myth of the Central Woodland (see note 20). For a comparative study, see Dixon, "The Mythology of the Central and Eastern Algonkins," JAFL, xxii, 1 ff.—WDL. N.E. MONTAGNAIS: LeJeune, *Jes. Rel.*, vi (1634), 159 and v (1633), 157; Speck, JAFL, xxxviii, 12. MICMAC: Rand, pp. 228, 232, 253, 270, 284, 294, 339, Nos. 33, 35, 43, 46, 50, 51, 60; Hagar, JAFL, x, 101; Leland, pp. 15, 31, 50, 51, 59, 66, 74, 81, 92, 94, 98, 106, 114; Michelson, JAFL, xxxviii, 51, 54; Parsons, JAFL, xxxviii, 62, 85 ff.; Speck, JAFL, xxviii, 60. MALECITE: Jack, JAFL, viii, 193 ff.; Mechling, GSCan, iv, 1 ff. PASSAMAQUODDY: Leland, pp. 18, 28, 36, 44, 104, 110, 111, 114, 127, 130, 134; Prince, PAES, x, 49, No. 11. PENOBSCOT: Leland, pp. 65, 120, 122.

11. *Divinity's departure for the west* (A561).—N. PAC. TAHLTAN: Teit, JAFL, xxxii, 213.— CAL. MAIDU: Dixon, BAM, xvii, 45 (No. VIII in this volume, p. 24).— WDL. CENT. Fox: Jones, JAFL, xiv, 238. — WDL. N.E. MICMAC: Rand, p. 293, No. 50; Parsons, JAFL, xxxviii, 90, No. 19. — In several of the Glooscap or Manabozho myths is mentioned:

(a) *Divinity's expected return* (A580). It is also found sporadically in other areas. — PLAT. THOMPSON: Teit, MAFLS, vi, 49, and notes 157 and 159. —CAL. MAIDU: Dixon, BAM, xvii, 45.—WDL. CENT. OJIBWA: Laidlaw, OAR, xxvii, 85. Fox: Jones, JAFL, xiv, 238. Cf. MENOMINI: Hoffman, RBAE, xiv, 200. — WDL. N.E. MONTAGNAIS: Speck, JAFL, xxxviii, 12. MICMAC: Speck, JAFL, xxviii, 60; Jack, JAFL, viii, 193. PASSAMAQUODDY: Leland, p. 130; Prince, PAES, x, 49, No. 11.— S.W. SIA: Stevenson, RBAE, xi, 67.

12. *Divinity teaches arts and crafts* (A540). This is a prominent part of the work of the culture hero in all the North American mythologies. See note 1. In nearly all of them also occurs the related incident: *Culture hero pacifies monsters.*

13. *Creator's grandmother* (A31). A grandmother of the creator (or culture hero) is casually mentioned. Primarily an Algonquin motif, but with sporadic appearance in the West. — **CAL.** SHASTA: Farrand-Frachtenberg, JAFL, XXVIII, No. 9. HUPA: Goddard, UCal, I, 134, No. 1. WINTUN: Curtin, *Creation Myths*, p. 4. — **WDL. CENT.** Jones-Michelson, PAES, VII (I), 3. MENOMINI: Skinner and Satterlee, PaAM, XIII, 239, 305. FOX: Jones, JAFL, XXIV, 210. — **WDL. N.E.** MICMAC: Rand, p. 232, No. 35; Leland, p. 30; Parsons, JAFL, XXXVIII, 73, 86, Nos. 8, 18; Speck, JAFL, XXVIII, 60. MALECITE: Jack, JAFL, VIII, 193; Speck, JAFL, XXX, 479. PASSAMAQUODDY: Leland, p. 30. — **WDL. IROQ.** HURON-WYANDOT: Barbeau, GSCan, XI, 37, No. 1.

14. *Island canoe* (D1122.2). — **WDL. N.E.** MICMAC: Rand, p. 232, No. 35; Parsons, JAFL, XXXVIII, 81, No. 13; Speck, JAFL, XXX, 479, No. 1. MALECITE: Jack, JAFL, VIII, 197. — Related incidents are:

(*a*) *Magic self-moving boat* (D1121.2). — References: Boas, RBAE, XXXI, 832; Skinner, JAFL, XXVII, 97. — **ESK.** ALASKA: Golder, JAFL, XXII, 17 (submarine at will). — **PLAT.** LILLOOET: Boas, *loc. cit.* SECHELT: Hill-Tout, JAI, XXXIV, 56. — **N. PAC.** TLINGIT, TSIMSHIAN, NASS, BELLA BELLA, KWAKIUTL, NEWETTEE: Boas, *loc. cit.* LKUÑGEN (SONGISH): Hill-Tout, JAI, XXXVII, 334. — **WDL. CENT.** CREE, OJIBWA, MENOMINI: Skinner, JAFL, XXVII, 97. — **WDL. IROQ.** SENECA: Curtin-Hewitt, RBAE, XXXII, 146, 225, 291, 362.

(*b*) *Canoe created by magic* (D1122.1). — **WDL. IROQ.** SENECA: Curtin-Hewitt, RBAE, XXXII, 568, No. 116.

(*c*) *Compressible canoe* (D1122). — **WDL. IROQ.** SENECA: Curtin-Hewitt, RBAE, XXXII, 85, No. 3, and 363, No. 65 (= Curtin, *Seneca Indian Myths*, p. 453).

(*d*) *Magic airships* (D1118). — **WDL. IROQ.** SENECA: Curtin-Hewitt, RBAE, XXXII, 223, 224, No. 42 (= Curtin, *Seneca Indian Myths*, p. 185); 391, No. 70; 407, No. 73 (= Curtin, *op. cit.*, p. 300); Curtin, *op. cit.*, p. 130.

(*e*) *Magic hollow-log boat* (D1121.3). — **PLNS.** SOUTHERN UTE: Lowie, JAFL, XXXVII, 85, No. 56.

15. *Symplegades* (D931.3). Rocks or caves that alternately open and close. — References: Boas, RBAE, XXXI, 798. — **ESK.** GREENLAND: Rink, p. 158, No. 15. CUMBERLAND SOUND: Boas, BAM, XV, 180. — **N. PAC.** TLINGIT, HAIDA, TSIMSHIAN, BELLA COOLA, BELLA BELLA, KWAKIUTL, NEWETTEE, COMOX, TILLAMOOK: Boas, RBAE, XXXI, 798. TSIMSHIAN: Boas, PAES, III, 97, 99. PUYALLUP: Cùrtis, IX, 117 ff. SNUQUALMI: Haeberlin, JAFL, XXXVII, 372, 376. QUINAULT: Farrand, JE, II, 112, No. 8. — **CAL.** MIWOK: Gifford, UCal, XII, 308, No. 5. SOUTH SIERRA MIWOK: Barrett, UCal, XVI, 12, No. 7. CAHUILLA: Hooper, UCal, XVI, 321. — **PLNS.** SHOSHONI: Lowie, PaAM, II, 264. CROW: Simms, FM, II, 315, No. 25. ASSINIBOIN: Lowie, PaAM, IV, 151. — **WDL. IROQ.** SENECA: Curtin-Hewitt, RBAE, XXXII, 121, No. 18 (= Curtin, *Seneca Indian Myths*, p. 372). — **S.E.** CHEROKEE: Mooney, JAFL, I, 105; Mooney, RBAE, XIX, 256, No. 7. YUCHI: Speck, UPa, I, 145, No. 8. — **S.W.** NAVAHO: Matthews, MAFLS, V, 109. WHITE MOUNTAIN APACHE: Goddard, PaAM, XXIV, 116. — A special variety of the incident is:

(*a*) *Rising and falling sky* (F791). — For discussion, see J. O. Dorsey, "The Rising and Falling of the Sky in Siouan Mythology," AA, old ser., VI, 64.

— **MACK.** KASKA: Teit, JAFL, xxx, 453; cf. 445, No. 6. — **N. PAC.**
TAHLTAN: Teit, JAFL, xxxiv, 336, No. 58. — **PLNS.** PONCA: Dorsey,
CNAE, vi, 187. — **WDL. CENT.** Fox: Jones, JAFL, xxiv, 209. — **WDL.**
IROQ. SENECA: Curtin-Hewitt, RBAE, xxxii, 610, No. 119; Hewitt, AA,
old ser., v, 344. — **S.E.** LOUISIANA COAST: Swanton, JAFL, xx, 287. — **S.W.**
NAVAHO: Matthews, MAFLS, v, 71. — Compare also:

(b) *Magic parting of waters* (D1551). — **CAL.** PAVIOTSO: Lowie, JAFL,
xxxvii, 209, No. 2. — **PLNS.** CHEYENNE: Dorsey, FM, ix, 37, No. 15.

16. *Boneless man turned over to produce seasons* (A1152). — **WDL. N.E.**
MICMAC: Rand, p. 234, No. 35; Hagar, JAFL, x, 101. MALECITE: Jack,
JAFL, viii, 193. — See also, for the determination of seasons, note 60.

17. *Deity grants requests to visitors* (A575). Men go on a journey to the
divinity or culture hero and each requests one gift. — **PLNS.** PLAINS OJIBWA:
Skinner, JAFL, xxxii, 291. ASSINIBOIN: Lowie, PaAM, iv, 123. — **WDL.**
CENT. Fox: Jones, PAES, i, 333; Jones, JAFL, xxiv, 209. MENOMINI:
Hoffman, RBAE, xiv, 118, 206; Skinner and Satterlee, PaAM, xiii, 487.
OJIBWA: Schoolcraft, *Algic Researches*, ii, 51; Schoolcraft, *Hiawatha*, p. 51;
Laidlaw, OAR, xxvii, 82; Jones, JAFL, xxix, 389. — **WDL. N.E.** MICMAC:
Rand, p. 233, No. 35; p. 253, No. 43; p. 417, No. 79; Parsons, JAFL, xxxviii,
70, 71, 87, Nos. 7, 18; Leland, pp. 69, 94, 98. MALECITE: Jack, JAFL, viii,
193. PASSAMAQUODDY: Prince, PAES, x, 51, No. 11.

18. *Immoderate request punished* (Q339). In all the references given below
the request is for eternal life. The punishment is transformation to a tree or
a stone. — **PLNS.** PLAINS OJIBWA: Skinner, JAFL, xxxii, 290, 291. AS-
SINIBOIN: Lowie, PaAM, iv, 123. — **WDL. CENT.** OJIBWA: Jones, JAFL,
xxix, 389; Schoolcraft, *Hiawatha*, p. 51; Laidlaw, OAR, xxvii, 82. Fox:
Jones, PAES, i, 333. MENOMINI: Hoffman, RBAE, xiv, 119, 206; Skinner
and Satterlee, PaAM, xiii, 487. — **WDL. N.E.** MICMAC: Rand, p. 233, No.
35, and p. 256, No. 43; Leland, p. 98; Parsons, JAFL, xxxviii, 70 f., No. 7.
MALECITE: Jack, JAFL, viii, 193. — Closely related incidents are:

(a) *Modest choice rewarded* (L200). A fundamental idea in all the tales
cited in notes 17 and 18. — For analogous incidents, see **PLAT.** NEZ PERCÉ:
Spinden, JAFL, xxi, 156. SECHELT: Hill-Tout, JAI, xxxiv, 55. — **CAL.**
MODOC: Curtin, *Myths of the Modocs*, p. 82. — **PLNS.** ARIKARA: Dorsey,
CI, xvii, 62, No. 16. — **WDL. IROQ.** SENECA: Curtin-Hewitt, RBAE,
xxxii, 153, 247, Nos. 25, 47. — **S.W.** ZUÑI: Parsons, JAFL, xxxi, 245. SAN
CARLOS APACHE: Goddard, PaAM, xxiv, 23. — In a group of tales of the
Northwest Coast a supernatural being who claims arrows as his own rewards
those who acquiesce, and punishes others. — References: Boas, RBAE, xxxi,
716 (**N. PAC.** TSIMSHIAN, BELLA COOLA, NOOTKA, COWICHAN. — **PLAT.**
CHILCOTIN, NEZ PERCÉ. — **WDL. CENT.** OJIBWA).

(b) *Kind and unkind* (Q2). One person because of kindness or obedience
is helped; his follower because of his unkind actions or disobedience is punished. All the references to *Crane bridge*, note 227, involve this motif. — See
also: **N. PAC.** SKAGIT: Haeberlin, JAFL, xxxvii, 381. — **PLAT.** SAHAPTIN:
Farrand-Mayer, MAFLS, xi, 169. — **PLNS.** CANADIAN DAKOTA: Wallis,
JAFL, xxxvi, 89, No. 20. — **WDL. IROQ.** SENECA: Curtin-Hewitt, RBAE,
xxxii, 466, No. 100.

19. *Pandora's box* (C321). A box is given a mortal by the gods (or divinity) with injunctions against looking in it on the way home. The injunction

is broken, with disastrous results. — **CAL.** Wappo: Radin, UCal, xix, 67, No. 9. — **PLNS.** Southern Ute: Lowie, JAFL, xxxvii, 3, 4, No. 2. Southern Paiute (Shivwits): Lowie, JAFL, xxxvii, 103, No. 2. Southern Paiute (Maopa): Lowie, JAFL, xxxvii, 158, No. 1. — **WDL. N.E.** Montagnais: LeJeune, *Jes. Rel.*, vi (1634), 159. Micmac: Rand, pp. 235, 257, Nos. 35, 43; Leland, pp. 70, 95, 101. Cf. note 72, *Bag of Winds*. — A related incident is:

(*a*) *Love-compelling man sickens of bargain* (D1904). A man given by the divinity the power of attracting women finds that he has no control over the power, and is overcome by the women he attracts. — **PLNS.** Assiniboin: Lowie, PaAM, iv, 106 (remote parallel). — **WDL. CENT.** Cree: Skinner, PaAM, ix, 87 (like Assiniboin). — **WDL. N.E.** Micmac: Rand, p. 235, No. 35. Passamaquoddy: Fewkes, JAFL, iii, 274; Prince, PAES, x, 53, No. 11.

20. *IV. Manabozho.* This myth is common to the entire Central Woodland group of tribes. For full references covering Ojibwa, Menomini, Potawatomi, Ottawa, Missisauga, Kickapoo, Fox, and kindred tribes, see Thompson, *Publications of the Modern Language Association of America,* xxxvii, 130–132. The name of the hero appears in many different forms. In this volume the spelling has been standardized.

21. *Impregnation by wind* (T524). See tale No. v in this volume. — **WDL. CENT.** Ojibwa: Jones-Michelson, PAES, vii (1), 3; DeJong, *Original Odjibwe-Texts,* p. 5. Menomini: Skinner and Satterlee, PaAM, xiii, 240; Michelson, AA, new ser., xiii, 69. — **WDL. IROQ.** Seneca: Curtin-Hewitt, RBAE, xxxii, 461, No. 98. — Cf. Longfellow's treatment of the motif at the beginning of "Hiawatha." For the motif in general, see Hartland, *Primitive Paternity,* i, 22. — A related motif occurring in some of the versions of this tale is:

(*a*) *Impregnation from sunlight* (T521). — **PLNS.** Southern Paiute (Maopa): Lowie, JAFL, xxxvii, 190, No. 21. Southern Ute: Lowie, JAFL, xxxvii, 76, No. 48. Arapaho: Dorsey and Kroeber, FM, v, 151, No. 79. — **WDL. CENT.** Timagami Ojibwa: Speck, GSCan, ix, 29. — **S.W.** Navaho: Pepper, JAFL, xxi, 179; Matthews, MAFLS, v, 105. Jicarilla Apache: Mooney, AA, old ser., xi (1898), 200 (also by moonlight). White Mountain Apache: Goddard, PaAM, xxiv, 93, 116, 120. San Carlos Apache: *Ibid.*, p. 31. Mohave-Apache: N. Curtis, *Indian Book,* p. 331. Sia: Stevenson, RBAE, xi, 43. — World-wide distribution: Hartland, *Primitive Paternity,* i, 25 ff., 89 ff.; Bolte-Polívka, iii, 89. — Frequently associated with this motif is that of:

(*b*) *Imprisoned virgin (to avoid impregnation)* (T381). — **WDL. IROQ.** Seneca: Curtin-Hewitt, RBAE, xxxii, 510. — **S.W.** Zuñi: Cushing, p. 132. Somewhat parallel are: — **WDL. CENT.** Ottawa: Schoolcraft, *Hiawatha,* p. 213. — **ESK.** Kodiak: Golder, JAFL, xvi, 95. —— For references to Northeast Siberia, Mongol-Turk, Slav, etc., see Jochelson, JE, vi, 363. See also Hartland, *Legend of Perseus,* Chapter I.

22. *Kisha Manido.* For a discussion of the concept "manitou" see Jones, "The Algonkin Manitou," JAFL, xviii, 183.

23. *Hero drowned by water-spirits* (F420.1). — **PLNS.** Plains Ojibwa: Skinner, JAFL, xxxii, 284. — **WDL. CENT.** Ojibwa: Schoolcraft, *Hiawatha,* p. 35; DeJong, *Original Odjibwe-Texts,* p. 13; Carson, JAFL, xxx, 941; Jones-Michelson, PAES, vii (1), 89, 251, 389, Nos. 10, 31, 45. Menomini:

Hoffman, RBAE, xiv, 87, 115, 116; Skinner and Satterlee, PaAM, xiii, 253.
Fox: Jones, JAFL, xiv, 228; Jones, PAES, i, 341. — S.W. NAVAHO: Matthews, MAFLS, v, 168 ff.

24. *Chief of the lower world.* See notes 2 and 5.

25. Most of the incidents included in this section of the tale appear regularly as a sequel of the part given just before. The lacrosse game is peculiar to the Menomini version.

26. *Transformation to kill enemies* (D651). In tales of the Central Woodland area Manabozho transforms himself to a stump in order to deceive his enemies. In other areas the transformation differs in detail. — PLNS. SOUTHERN PAIUTE (SHIVWITS): Lowie, JAFL, xxxvii, 123, No. 10; (MAOPA): *Ibid.*, p. 189, No. 20. SHOSHONI: Lowie, PaAM, ii, 241. PONCA: Dorsey, CNAE, vi, 239. PLAINS OJIBWA: Skinner, JAFL, xxxii, 284. — WDL. CENT. OJIBWA: Schoolcraft, *Hiawatha*, pp. 38, 40; Radin, GSCan, ii, 20, 23; DeJong, *Original Odjibwe-Texts*, p. 14; Jones-Michelson, PAES, vii (1), 95, 257, 395, Nos. 10, 31, 45. CREE: Russell, p. 207; Skinner, PaAM, ix, 174. MENOMINI: Skinner and Satterlee, PaAM, xiii, 255, 260, 511, 520. OTTAWA: Blackbird, *Ottawa and Chippeway Indians*, p. 54. Fox: Jones, JAFL, xiv, 230; Jones, PAES, i, 353. The Shoshoni and Cree references are perhaps more properly considered as examples of the *Disguised flayer* (note 267).

27. *V. The Woman who fell from the Sky* (A21.1). The Iroquois origin myth. — WDL. IROQ. IROQUOIS: Smith, RBAE, ii, 76; Converse, p. 33. SENECA: Curtin-Hewitt, RBAE, xxxii, 165, 410, 460, Nos. 28, 74, 98. ONONDAGA: Hewitt, RBAE, xxi, 141 ff. MOHAWK: *Ibid.*, pp. 255 ff. HURON-WYANDOT: Barbeau, GSCan, xi, 37, 47, 50, Nos. 1, 2, 3; LeJeune, *Jes. Rel.*, viii (1634), 119, 147; Ragueneau, *Jes. Rel.*, xxx (1646), 61; Hale, JAFL, i, 180; Connelley, JAFL, xii, 120.

28. *Sky window* (F59). An opening in the sky gives admission to the upper world. — For a large number of references, see Reichard, JAFL, xxxiv, 271. — ESK. GREENLAND: Rink, p. 468. CUMBERLAND SOUND: Boas, BAM, xv, 339. BERING STRAIT: Nelson, RBAE, xviii, 458. — MACK. KASKA, TS'ETS'ÁUT: Reichard, *loc. cit.* — PLAT. KUTENAI, CHILCOTIN: *Ibid.* WASCO: Curtin, PAES, ii, 306. CHILCOTIN: Farrand, JE, ii, 29, No. 12. — N. PAC. TAHLTAN, SONGISH, QUINAULT: Reichard, *loc. cit.* BELLA COOLA: Boas, JE, i, 83. BELLA BELLA: Boas, *Sagen*, p. 237. TSIMSHIAN: Boas, *Sagen*, p. 279. PUYALLUP: Curtis, ix, 117. SNUQUALMI: Haeberlin, JAFL, xxxvii, 373, 376. SNOHOMISH: *Ibid.*, p. 412. KATHLAMET: Boas, BBAE, xxvi, 17. — CAL. MAIDU: Dixon, PAES, iv, 183, No. 10. ATSUGEWI: Dixon, JAFL, xxi, 170. WESTERN MONO: Gifford, JAFL, xxxvi, 326, No. 9. — PLNS. SHOSHONI, KIOWA, WICHITA, ARAPAHO, CHEYENNE, OTO, PAWNEE, CROW, DAKOTA, HIDATSA, MANDAN, ARIKARA, GROS VENTRE: Reichard, *loc. cit.* SOUTHERN PAIUTE: Lowie, JAFL, xxxvii, 112, No. 6. BLACKFOOT: Wissler and Duvall, PaAM, ii, 59; Curtis, vi, 62. — WDL. CENT. OJIBWA: Reichard, *loc. cit.* — WDL. N.E. PASSAMAQUODDY: Prince, PAES, x, 61, No. 12. — WDL. IROQ. SENECA: Curtin-Hewitt, RBAE, xxxii, 410, No. 74, and 460, No. 98 (= Curtin, *Seneca Indian Myths*, p. 193). MOHAWK: Hewitt, RBAE, xxi, 284. HURON-WYANDOT: Barbeau, GSCan, xi, 37, No. 1; Connelley, JAFL, xii, 120; Brébeuf, *Jes. Rel.*, x (1636), 125. (The SENECA, MOHAWK, and HURON-WYANDOT are versions of the tale here given). — S.E. CADDO: Dorsey, CI, xli, 27, No. 14, and 29, No. 15. — S.W. NAVAHO: Matthews, MAFLS, v,

65, 66, 76, 113, 200. WHITE MOUNTAIN APACHE: Goddard, PaAM, xxiv, 94.
—— For references to the Koryak and the Mongol Turks, see Jochelson, JE, vi, 371.

29. *Primeval water* (A810). Water originally covers the whole face of the world. See all the references to note 30, *Earth diver*, which involves the existence of primeval water. See in addition: — **N. PAC.** Coos: Frachtenberg, CU, i, 1. — **CAL.** JOSHUA: Farrand-Frachtenberg, JAFL, xxviii, 224, No. 16. COSTANOAN: Kroeber, UCal, iv, 199, No. 1. YUKI: Kroeber, UCal, iv, 184. DIEGUEÑO: DuBois, JAFL, xiv, 181, and xxi, 236; Waterman, AA, new ser., xi, 45. WESTERN MONO: Gifford, JAFL, xxxvi, 305, No. 1. — **PLNS.** SOUTHERN PAIUTE (MAOPA): Lowie, JAFL, xxxvii, 157, No. 1. CANADIAN DAKOTA: Wallis, JAFL, xxxvi, 59. BUNGEE (SWAMPY): Simms, JAFL, xix, 337. — **S.W.** JICARILLA APACHE: Mooney, AA, old ser., xi, 197. YUMA: N. Curtis, *Craftsman*, xvi, 559. MOHAVE-APACHE: N. Curtis, *Indian Book*, p. 330.

30. *Earth diver* (A812). From the surface of the primeval water the Creator sends down animals one after the other to try to reach bottom and bring back soil. One animal only (usually the muskrat) succeeds. — Extensive references: Teit, JAFL, xxx, 442; Reichard, JAFL, xxxiv, 305. — **MACK.** KASKA, LOUCHEUX, HARE, DOG RIB, CHIPEWYAN, BEAVER, CARRIER: Teit, *loc. cit.* UPPER YUKON: Schmitter, p. 21. — **N. PAC.** NEWETTE, KATHLAMET: Teit, *loc. cit.* — **CAL.** YOKUTS, MIWOK, MAIDU, SALINAN: *Ibid.* SOUTH SIERRA MIWOK: Barrett, UCal, xvi, 4, No. 1. WESTERN MONO: Gifford, JAFL, xxxvi, 305, No. 2. — **PLNS.** SHOSHONI, ARAPAHO, IOWA, HIDATSA, BLACKFOOT, SARCEE, GROS VENTRE, ASSINIBOIN: Teit, *loc. cit.* CROW, WAHPETON, ARIKARA: Reichard, *loc. cit.* GROS VENTRE: Curtis, v, 154. BLACKFOOT: Wissler and Duvall, PaAM, ii, 151; Grinnell, *Blackfoot Lodge Tales*, p. 272. CHEYENNE: Grinnell, JAFL, xx, 169. — **WDL. CENT.** CREE, OJIBWA, MISSISAUGA, OTTAWA, FOX: Teit, *loc. cit.* SAULTEAUX: Reichard, *loc. cit.* FOX: Jones, JAFL, xiv, 234. OJIBWA: Laidlaw, OAR, xxx, 89. — **WDL. N.E.** ALGONQUIN, DELAWARE: Teit, *loc. cit.* MONTAGNAIS: Reichard, *loc. cit.* — **WDL. IROQ.** SENECA, ONONDAGA, HURON-WYANDOT: Teit, *loc. cit.* SENECA: Curtin-Hewitt, RBAE, xxxii, 411, No. 74, and 461, No. 98 (= Curtin, *Seneca Indian Myths*, p. 194). — **S.E.** CHEROKEE, YUCHI: Teit, *loc. cit.* CREEK: Speck, MAAA, ii, 145; Tuggle, MS. cited in Mooney, RBAE, xix, 430.

31. *Earth from turtle's back* (A815). — Occurs in all references in note 27. — **WDL. N.E.** DELAWARE (LENAPE): Heckewelder "Indian Nations" in *Am. Philos. Soc. Proc.*, i (Philadelphia, 1819), 246; Brinton, *Lenape and their Legends*, p. 179; DeVries, *Journal* (cited in Skinner, PaAM, iii, 53). — **WDL. IROQ.** IROQUOIS: Cusick, *Ancient History of the Six Nations*, p. 13; HURON: Brébeuf, *Jes. Rel.*, x (1636), 129, and xxx (1646), 61.

32. Cf. the similar situation in "Manabozho," tale No. iv.

33. *Twins quarrel before birth* (T575). Twins quarrel as to the method of emerging from their mother. One bursts through her side. — **WDL. CENT.** OJIBWA: Jones-Michelson, PAES, vii (1), 3 ff.; Chamberlain, JAFL, iv, 206. OTTAWA: *Ibid.*, p. 204. MENOMINI: Skinner and Satterlee, PaAM, xiii, 241. — **WDL. N.E.** MICMAC: Rand, p. 339, No. 60; Leland, p. 15. MALECITE: Jack, JAFL, viii, 194. — **WDL. IROQ.** SENECA: Curtin-Hewitt, RBAE, xxxii, 412, No. 74, and 461, No. 98. ONONDAGA: Hewitt, RBAE,

xxi, 185. Huron-Wyandot: Barbeau, GSCan, xi, 37, No. 1; cf. Hale, JAFL, i, 180.

34. Cf. "Lodge-Boy and Thrown-Away," tale No. xliv in this volume.

35. For the relation of these brothers of Iroquois myth to the two friendly brothers of the Manabozho cycle of the Ojibwa, see Alexander p. 297. The idea of good and evil heroes appears more prominently perhaps than elsewhere in Iroquois myth, but it is not unknown elsewhere. See, for example, Yuma: N. Curtis, *Craftsman*, xvi, 559 (twin creators, good and evil). Discussion: Sapir, UPa, ii, 34.

36. *VI. The Beginning of Newness.* Typical in many ways of Pueblo myths in general, this particular form has no exact parallels outside the Zuñi tribe. A good study of this origin myth by Mrs. Parsons (JAFL, xxxvi, 131 ff.) finds the following incidents in the extended myth: *Heirarchy of worlds* (note 58), *origin of death* (note 51), *Lizard-hand* (note 59), *brother and sister incest* (note 8), *land of the dead* (note 216), *distribution of tribes* (note 54), *birth from foam, twins visit sun-father* (cf. note 118*b*). — A list of cosmogonic myths for the tribes of the Southwest area follows. Navaho: Matthews, MAFLS, v, 63; Packard, *Transactions Anthropological Soc. of Washington*, i, 84. Apache: Bourke, JAFL, iii, 209. Jicarilla Apache: Russell, JAFL, xi, 253; Goddard, PaAM, viii, 193; Mooney, AA, old ser., xi, 197 ff. San Carlos Apache: Goddard, PaAM, xxiv, 7, 26. White Mountain Apache: *Ibid.*, p. 93. Mohave-Apache: Gould, JAFL, xxxiv, 319. Mohave: Bourke, JAFL, ii, 169. Zuñi: Cushing, RBAE, xiii, 321 ff.; Cushing, JAFL, v, 49; Stevenson, RBAE, xxiii, 1 ff.; Parsons, JAFL, xxxvi, 131 ff. Hopi: Voth, FM, iii, 349 and viii, 1 ff. Oraibi: Cushing, JAFL, xxxvi, 163 ff. Pima: Azul, *Assembly Herald* (Philadelphia, 1909), xv, 70 (reviewed in JAFL, xxiii, 150); Russell, RBAE, xxvi, 206; Bancroft, *Native Races*, iii, 78; Lloyd, *Aw-aw-tam*, p. 27. Papago: Bancroft, *op. cit.*, iii, 75; Mason, JAFL, xxxiv, 254; Curtis, ii, 56. Sia: Stevenson, RBAE, xi, 26. Yuma: Harrington, JAFL, xxi, 324 ff. Walapai: James, *The Indians of the Painted Desert Region*, pp. 188 ff. — For comparison with other areas, see Boas, "Northern Elements in the Mythology of the Navaho," AA, old ser., x (1897), 371.

37. *World parents* (A625). Earth and sky, formerly joined, are the parents of man. — **CAL.** Luiseño: DuBois, JAFL, xvii, 185 and xix, 52; DuBois, UCal, viii, 128, 138; Kroeber, JAFL, xix, 312. Diegueño: DuBois, JAFL, xiv, 181. — **S.W.** Zuñi: Cushing, RBAE, xiii, 379. Pima: Curtis, ii, 56; Russell, RBAE, xxvi, 208. Mohave: Bourke, JAFL, ii, 179. Yuma: Curtis, ii, 73. — In some northwestern tribes occurs:

(*a*) *Earth mother* (A801). — **PLAT.** Thompson: Teit, MAFLS, xi, 48. Okanagon: Teit, MAFLS, xi, 80. — **N. PAC.** Tahltan: Teit, JAFL, xxxii, 227, Nos. 2, 3. Tlingit: Boas, RBAE, xxxi, 732.

38. *VII. Raven's Adventures.* — For references and full discussion, see Boas, RBAE, xxxi, 634, 636 (**N. PAC.** Tsimshian, Nass, Newettee, Tlingit, Haida). — The story is only an episode of the larger Raven cycle, the cosmogonic myth of the northern tribes of the North Pacific area. A list of origin myths for the whole North Pacific territory with an analysis into their incidents will be found in Boas, RBAE, xxxi, 567 ff. (for the northern tribes), 585 ff. (for the southern tribes), 618 (comparative study). — See also Tahltan: Teit, JAFL, xxxii, 198 ff. Quileute: Farrand-Mayer, JAFL, xxxii, 252, No. 1. Skagit: Haeberlin, JAFL, xxxvii, 392. Alsea: Frachten-

berg, BBAE, LXVII, 22 ff. Coos: Frachtenberg, CU, I, 5 ff. LOWER UMPQUA: Frachtenberg, CU, IV, 7 ff.

39. *Raven becomes voracious.* — **N. PAC.** TSIMSHIAN, NASS, NEWETTEE, TLINGIT, HAIDA: Boas, RBAE, XXXI, 636.

40. A point that strikes the most cursory reader of American Indian tales is the little difference made between animals and persons. It is impossible at times to tell which concept is in the mind of the teller. The characteristics seem generally to be transferable at a moment's notice. The same general way of thinking has produced our negro tales of "Brer Rabbit," and these seem to give even mature civilized persons little difficulty.

41. *Ghost summoned by weeping* (E381). The incident in this tale is rather closely paralleled by that of the ghost who returns to stop the inordinate weeping of his loved ones on earth. — **WDL. CENT.** OJIBWA: Drake, *Indian Tribes*, p. 57. MENOMINI: Hoffman, RBAE, XIV, 88, 115. Fox: Jones, JAFL, XIV, 228. —— Also European: Bolte-Polívka, II, 485.

42. *Theft of light* (A1411). A widespread motif. The details differ somewhat in the various areas. With many tribes the theft of light and the theft of fire (note 63) are confused. Even where they are not, many of the details are parallel. In some cases light is identified with the sun; in some it is joined to the idea of the summer weather. In others no such identification is made. — References: Boas, RBAE, XXXI, 567. — **ESK.** BERING STRAIT, ASIATIC: Boas, *loc. cit.* ALASKA: Boas, JAFL, VII 205. KODIAK: Golder, JAFL, XVI, 85. Cf. CHUCKCHEE (SIBERIA): Bogaras, AA, new ser., IV, 627. — **MACK.** ANVIK, TEN'A, LOUCHEUX, CARRIER: Boas, RBAE, XXXI, 567. ANVIK: Chapman, PAES, VI, 22, No. 5. UPPER YUKON: Schmitter, p. 26. LOUCHEUX: Camsell-Barbeau, JAFL, XXVIII, 254, No. 8. HARE: Bell, JAFL, XVI, 79. — **PLAT.** CHILCOTIN: Boas, RBAE, XXXI, 567. LILLOOET: Teit, JAFL, XXV, 300, No. 6. SALISH: Hill-Tout, *British North America*, p. 213: Boas, *Am. Philos. Soc. Proc.*, XXXIV, 43. — **N. PAC.** TAHLTAN, TLINGIT, HAIDA, TSIMSHIAN, NASS, BELLA COOLA, BELLA BELLA, NEWETTEE, RIVERS INLET, NOOTKA, COWICHAN, SQUAMISH, CHEHALIS: Boas, RBAE, XXXI, 567. KWAKIUTL: Boas and Hunt, JE, III, 393, No. 13; Boas, *Sagen*, p. 173; Boas, CU, II, 233. NANAIMO: Boas, AA, old ser., II (1889), 328, No. 2; Boas, *Sagen*, p. 55. TAHLTAN: Teit, JAFL, XXXII, 204. QUILEUTE: Farrand-Mayer, JAFL, XXXII, 254, No. 1. SKAGIT: Haeberlin, JAFL, XXXVII, 391 f. — **CAL.** POMO: Bartlett, JAFL, XIX, 37, No. 5. LASSIK: Goddard, JAFL, XIX, 136. KATO: Goddard, UCal, V, 96, 101, Nos. 3, 4. MEWAN: Merriam, pp. 34, 45, 153. SOUTH SIERRA MIWOK: Barrett, UCal, XVI, 19, No. 10. SINKYONE: Kroeber, JAFL, XXXII, 346, No. 3. YUKI: Kroeber, UCal, IV, 185. YOKUTS: *Ibid.*, p. 212, No. 18. — **WDL. IROQ.** ONONDAGA: Hewitt, RBAE, XXI, 202. — **S.W.** SAN CARLOS APACHE: Goddard, PaAM, XXIV, 43, 44. — For *theft of summer* see note 60.

43. "The identification of the trickster and transformer is a feature which deserves special notice. I have called attention to the fact — borne out by most of the mythologies in which trickster and culture-hero appear as one person — that the benefactions bestowed by the culture-hero are not given in an altruistic spirit, but that they are the means by which he supplies his own needs. Even in his heroic achievements he remains a trickster bent upon the satisfaction of his own desires. This feature may be observed distinctly in the Raven-cycle of the Northwest coast. He liberates the sun, not because he

pities mankind; but because he desires it. . . . He gets the fresh water because he is thirsty, and unwillingly spills it all over the world while he is making his escape." — Boas, JAFL, xxvii, 395.

44. *Theft of light by being swallowed and re-born* (A1411.2). In some cases
it is fire or other things that the hero steals. See in note 42 the references
here indicated. — **ESK.** BERING STRAIT, KODIAK. — **MACK.** ANVIK, UPPER
YUKON, LOUCHEUX, HARE. — **PLAT.** CHILCOTIN. — **N. PAC.** TAHLTAN,
TLINGIT, HAIDA, TSIMSHIAN, BELLA COOLA, BELLA BELLA, RIVERS INLET,
NOOTKA, QUILEUTE. — Some additional references are: **CAL.** MEWAN:
Merriam, p. 35. SOUTH SIERRA MIWOK: Barrett, UCal, xvi, 19, No. 10.
(In these two tales the hero transforms himself into a stick and enters the
chief's house to steal the sun.) PAVIOTSO: Lowie, JAFL, xxxvii, 236, No. 15.
— **WDL. CENT.** MENOMINI: Hoffman, RBAE, xiv, 126. — **WDL. IROQ.**
SENECA: Curtin-Hewitt, RBAE, xxxii, 80, No. 1; 151, No. 24; 445, No. 89.

45. *Light kept in box or basket* (A1411.1). — See references in note 42 for the
following tribes: **ESK.** BERING STRAIT, ALASKA, KODIAK. — **MACK.**
ANVIK, UPPER YUKON, LOUCHEUX, HARE. — **PLAT.** CHILCOTIN, LILLOOET.
— **N. PAC.** TAHLTAN, TLINGIT, TSIMSHIAN, HAIDA, BELLA COOLA, BELLA
BELLA, KWAKIUTL, NANAIMO, SQUAMISH, CHEHALIS, QUILEUTE. — For other
things kept in a box or basket (fire, summer, etc.) see: **MACK.** LOUCHEUX:
Barbeau, JAFL, xxviii, 254. DOG RIB: Petitot, p. 375. TS'ETS'ÁUT: Boas,
JAFL, ix, 260. SLAVEY: Bell, JAFL, xiv, 26. CHIPEWYAN: Petitot, p. 373.
— **PLNS.** BLACKFOOT: Maclean, JAFL, vi, 166.

46. Many myths of all the different areas explain physical features of the
country. The most usual form of the explanation is either that the culture
hero deliberately transformed persons into the present physical features or
that the many conflicts with the early monsters resulted in changing the face
of the country. The remarks made about the unstable nature of explanatory
myths (note 4) apply equally well to myths of this type. The stories seem
rarely to be made to fit the explanation, but the latter seems usually to be
little more than an afterthought. Some of the "Transformer" tales of the
North Pacific coast are probably exceptions to this statement, for without
the transformation there would be little point in the tale. For this group see
Boas, RBAE, xxxi, 586 ff.

47. *VIII and IX. California Creation Myths.* The myths of the whole
California area have many elements in common, most of which will be seen
in the two myths here given. These tales also appear among the tribes of
southern Oregon. The Kato myth has been chosen as an example of the rather
pointless and tedious myths so frequent in the California collections. A list
of California creation myths follows. KLAMATH: Gatschet, CNAE, ii, 103.
MODOC: Curtin, *Myths of the Modocs*, pp. 39, 51. KAROK: Powers, CNAE,
iii, 38. CHIMARIKO: Goddard, UCal, v, 349, No. 4. SHASTA: Kroeber, UCal,
iv, 180; Dixon, JAFL, xxiii, 13; Farrand-Frachtenberg, JAFL, xxviii,
209 ff. JOSHUA: Farrand-Frachtenberg, JAFL, xxviii, 224 ff. ACHOMAWI:
Powers, CNAE, iii, 200; Dixon, JAFL, xxi, 159. ATSUGEWI: *Ibid.*, p. 170.
YANA: Sapir, UCal, ix, 33; Dixon, UCal, ix, 209; Curtin, *Creation Myths*, pp.
365 ff. SALINAN: Mason, UCal, ix, 190. WISHOSK: Kroeber, JAFL, xviii,
97 ff. HUPA: Goddard, UCal, i, 123, No. 1. KATO: Goddard, UCal, v,
183 ff. LASSIK: Goddard, JAFL, xix, 136. SINKYONE: Kroeber, JAFL,
xxxii, 346, No. 3. YUKI: Kroeber, UCal, iv, 185. WINTUN: Curtin, *Crea-*

tion Myths, pp. 3 ff. MAIDU: Dixon, PAES, IV, 5, No. 1, and 59, No. 2; Dixon, BAM, XVII, 39 ff.; Powers, CNAE, III, 292, 339. SOUTH SIERRA MIWOK: Barrett, UCal, XVI, 2 ff. MEWAN: Merriam, pp. 33 ff.; Kroeber, UCal, IV, 202, Nos. 7, 8, and 203, No. 9. COSTANOAN: Kroeber, UCal, IV, 199, No. 1. YOKUTS: Kroeber, UCal, IV, 204, No. 11; 209, No. 15; 218, No. 25; 219, No. 26; Stewart, JAFL, XXI, 237; Powers, CNAE, III, 383. DIEGUEÑO: Waterman, AA, new ser., XI, 41; Waterman, UCal, VIII, 338; DuBois, AA, new ser., VII, 620; DuBois, *International Congress of Americanists*, XIII, 101; DuBois, JAFL, XIV, 181. LUISEÑO: DuBois, JAFL, XVII, 185 and XIX, 52; DuBois, UCal, VIII, 128, 138; Kroeber, JAFL, XIX, 312; James, JAFL, XV, 36. CAHUILLA: Hooper, UCal, XVI, 317. WESTERN MONO: Gifford, JAFL, XXXVI, 305.

48. *Sky rope* (F51). A rope is used for ascent to or descent from the sky. In most cases the motif of *Sky window* (note 28) occurs in connection with the sky rope. It appears in many of the versions of "The Star Husband," Nos. L and LI (note 193). — For a large number of references, see Reichard, JAFL, XXXIV, 271. — **MACK.** KASKA, TS'ETS'ÁUT: Reichard, *loc. cit.* CHIPEWYAN: Lowie, PaAM, X, 192. — **PLAT.** KUTENAI, CHILCOTIN: Reichard, *loc. cit.* CHILCOTIN: Farrand, JE, II, 29, No. 12, and 31, No. 13. LILLOOET: Teit, JAFL, XXV, 308. CŒUR D'ALÈNE: Teit, MAFLS, XI, 120, No. 3. SAHAPTIN: Farrand-Mayer, MAFLS, XI, 136. SHUSWAP: Teit, JE, II, 689, No. 26. WASCO: Curtin, PAES, II, 306. — **N. PAC.** TAHLTAN, SONGISH, QUINAULT: Reichard, *loc. cit.* PUYALLUP: Curtis, IX, 117. SNOHOMISH: Haeberlin, JAFL, XXXVII, 401. SNUQUALMI: Haeberlin, JAFL, XXXVII, 373, 376. CHEHALIS: Hill-Tout, JAI, XXXIV, 357. KATHLAMET: Boas, BBAE, XXVI, 17, 71. QUILEUTE: Farrand-Mayer, JAFL, XXXII, 267, No. 11. — **CAL.** MODOC: Curtin, *Myths of the Modocs*, p. 88. SHASTA: Dixon, JAFL, XXIII, 15, No. 4. POMO: Barrett, JAFL, XIX, 39. WISHOSK: Kroeber, JAFL, XVIII, 98, No. 8. YOKUTS: Kroeber, UCal, IV, 209, No. 14. — **PLNS.** SHOSHONI, KIOWA, WICHITA, ARAPAHO, CHEYENNE, OTO, PAWNEE, CROW, DAKOTA, HIDATSA, MANDAN, ARIKARA, GROS VENTRE: Reichard, *loc. cit.* — **WDL. CENT.** OJIBWA: *Ibid.* and Jones-Michelson, PAES, VII (II), 151, No. 13. — **S.E.** CADDO: Dorsey, CI, XLI, 27, No. 14, and 29, No. 15. — **S.W.** MOHAVE-APACHE: Gould, JAFL, XXXIV, 319. —— SIBERIA: Bogaras, AA, new ser., IV, 677.

49. *Creation of man* (A1200). Not all cosmogonic myths contain an account of the creation of man. The following list is but fragmentary. — **ESK.** LABRADOR: Turner, RBAE, XI, 338. BERING STRAIT: Nelson, RBAE, XVIII, 456. — **MACK.** ANVIK: Chapman, PAES, VI, 9, No. 1. TS'ETS'ÁUT: Boas, JAFL, IX, 260. DOG RIB: Petitot, p. 309. — **PLAT.** OKANAGON: Teit, MAFLS, XI, 81, 84. — **N. PAC.** QUILEUTE: Farrand-Mayer, JAFL, XXXII, 251, No. 1. — **CAL.** KAROK: Powers, CNAE, III, 35. JOSHUA: Farrand-Frachtenberg, JAFL, XXVIII, 225, No. 16. ACHOMAWI: Dixon, JAFL, XXI, 160. ATSUGEWI: *Ibid.*, p. 170. YANA: Dixon, UCal, IX, 209, No. 1. WISHOSK: Kroeber, JAFL, XVIII, 94, No. 1, and 98, No. 7. HUPA: Goddard, UCal, I, 132, No. 1. KATO: Goddard, UCal, V, 185, No. 2. YUKI: Kroeber, UCal, IV, 184. WAPPO: Radin, UCal, XIX, 45, No. 7. MAIDU: Powers, CNAE, III, 292; Dixon, BAM, XVII, 41, No. 1; Dixon, PAES, IV, 13, No. 1. MEWAN: Merriam, p. 159. YOKUTS: Stewart, JAFL, XIX, 322. DIEGUEÑO: DuBois, JAFL, XIV, 181 and XXI, 236; Waterman, AA, new ser., XI, 47; Waterman,

UCal, VIII, 339. LUISEÑO: DuBois, UCal, VIII, 129; Kroeber, JAFL, XIX, 313. CAHUILLA: Hooper, UCal, XVI, 319. — **PLNS.** SOUTHERN UTE: Lowie, JAFL, XXXVII, 3, No. 2. WICHITA: Dorsey, CI, XXI, 25, No. 1; Dorsey, JAFL, XV, 214. ARAPAHO: Dorsey and Kroeber, FM, V, 2, No. 1; Dorsey, FM, IV, 191. CHEYENNE: Dorsey, FM, IX, 34, No. 14. PAWNEE: Grinnell, JAFL, VI, 122; Dorsey, CI, LIX, 13, No. 1; Dorsey, MAFLS, VIII, 4, No. 1. CROW: Simms, FM, II, 281, No. 1; Lowie, PaAM, XXV, 16, 156. BLACKFOOT: Grinnell, *Blackfoot Lodge Tales*, p. 138. BUNGEE: Simms, JAFL, XIX, 338. — **WDL. CENT.** OJIBWA: Jones-Michelson, PAES, VII (II), 531, No. 62, and 553, No. 63; Laidlaw, OAR, XXVI, 77. MENOMINI: Skinner and Satterlee, PaAM, XIII, 305. SAUK and Fox: Jones, JAFL, XIV, 237. — **WDL. IROQ.** SENECA: Curtin-Hewitt, RBAE, XXXII, 168, No. 30, and 413, No. 74. MOHAWK: Hewitt, RBAE, XXI, 320. WYANDOT: Barbeau, GSCan, XI, 48, No. 2, and 50, No. 3. — **S.E.** SHAWNEE: Spencer, JAFL, XXII, 319. CHOCTAW: Bushnell, AA, new ser., XII, 527, No. 3. — **S.W.** NAVAHO: Matthews, MAFLS, V, 69, 137, 148; Stevenson, RBAE, VIII, 277. APACHE: Bourke, JAFL, III, 211; (SAN CARLOS): Goddard, PaAM, XXIV, 27. PAPAGO: H. R. Kroeber, JAFL, XXV, 96. PIMA: Bancroft, *Native Races*, III, 78; Lloyd, *Aw-aw-tam*, p. 28. HOPI: Voth, FM, VIII, 2, No. 1. SIA: Stevenson, RBAE, XI, 27. YUMA: Harrington, JAFL, XXI, 328.

50. *Rejuvenation* (D1880). A widespread motif. — A few references are: **CAL.** WISHOSK: Kroeber, JAFL, XVIII, 98. MAIDU: Dixon, PAES, IV, 66, No. 2; Dixon, BAM, XVI, 43. CAHUILLA: Hooper, UCal, XVI, 375. — **PLNS.** PAWNEE: Dorsey, CI, LIX, 32. CANADIAN DAKOTA: Wallis, JAFL, XXXVI, 41. — **WDL. CENT.** OJIBWA: Schoolcraft, *Hiawatha*, pp. 71 ff. — **WDL. N.E.** MALECITE: Stamp, JAFL, XXVIII, 247. PASSAMAQUODDY: Prince, PAES, X, 41, No. 9. — **WDL. IROQ.** ONONDAGA: Beauchamp, JAFL, II, 269; Hewitt, RBAE, XXI, 218. — A special variety of this motif is:

(*a*) *Fountain of youth* (D925, D1338.1). — **CAL.** WINTUN: Curtin, *Creation Myths*, pp. 162 ff. — **WDL. N.E.** MICMAC: Leland, p. 100. — Nearly always accompanying the motif of rejuvenation is that of:

(*b*) *Magic aging* (D1890). — **N. PAC.** TAKELMA: Sapir, UPa, II, 66, No. 4. — **CAL.** MODOC: Curtin, *Myths of the Modocs*, p. 126. MAIDU: Dixon, BAM, XVII, 42. CAHUILLA: Hooper, UCal, XVI, 374. — **PLNS.** CANADIAN DAKOTA: Wallis, JAFL, XXXVI, 42. PAWNEE: Dorsey, CI, LIX, 32, No. 5. — **WDL. CENT.** OJIBWA: Schoolcraft, *Hiawatha*, pp. 71 ff. Fox: Jones, PAES, I, 355. — **WDL. N.E.** PASSAMAQUODDY: Leland, p. 327. — **S.W.** HOPI: Voth, FM, III, 349.

51. *Origin of death* (A1335). It is first proposed that people shall not die. The culture hero, however, sometimes by divination, decides otherwise. — For full references, see Boas, JAFL, XXX, 486; Boas, RBAE, XXXI, 663; Boas, BBAE, LIX, 303. — **ESK.** GREENLAND: Boas, JAFL, XXX, 486. — **MACK.** KASKA, HARE, DOG RIB: *Ibid.* — **PLAT.** THOMPSON, KUTENAI, LILLOOET, SHUSWAP, SANPOIL, CŒUR D'ALÈNE, WISHRAM: *Ibid.* — **N. PAC.** TSIMSHIAN, NASS, TLINGIT, HAIDA: Boas, RBAE, XXXI, 663. QUINAULT, COOS, TAKELMA: Boas, JAFL, XXX, 486. TAHLTAN: Teit, JAFL, XXXII, 216; Emmons, UPa, IV, 119. LOWER UMPQUA: Frachtenberg, CU, IV, 40–43. KALAPUYA: *Ibid.* — **CAL.** KLAMATH, SHASTA, POMO, YANA, WISHOSK, HUPA, YUKI, WINTUN, MAIDU, MIWOK, YOKUTS, DIEGUEÑO, LUISEÑO: Boas, JAFL, XXX, 486. SINKYONE: Kroeber, JAFL, XXXII, 346, No. 1. — **PLNS.**

SHOSHONE, COMANCHE, ARAPAHO, CHEYENNE, BLACKFOOT, NORTH PIEGAN, PAWNEE: Boas, JAFL, xxx, 486. UTE: Lowie, JAFL, xxxvii, 3, 5, No. 2. CROW: Lowie, PaAM, xxv, 28. — **WDL. CENT.** OJIBWA: Jones-Michelson, PAES, vii (ii), 535, No. 62, and 555, No. 63. — **WDL. IROQ.** SENECA: Curtin-Hewitt, RBAE, xxxii, 697, No. 133. — **S.E.** CHEROKEE, CADDO: Boas, JAFL, xxx, 486. — **S.W.** NAVAHO, JICARILLA APACHE: *Ibid.* WHITE MOUNTAIN APACHE: Goddard, PaAM, xxiv, 138. MOHAVE-APACHE: Gould, JAFL, xxxiv, 320.

52. *Originator of death first sufferer* (K1681). After the culture hero has instituted death, his own child dies and he repents in vain. — The following references in note 51 contain this incident: **PLAT.** THOMPSON, KUTENAI, LILLOOET, SHUSWAP, SANPOIL. — **N. PAC.** COOS, TAKELMA, LOWER UMPQUA, KALAPUYA. — **CAL.** SHASTA, YANA, WISHOSK, WINTUN, MAIDU, MIWOK, SINKYONE. — **PLNS.** UTE (also BLACKFOOT: Grinnell, *Blackfoot Lodge Tales*, p. 139). — **WDL. CENT.** OJIBWA. — **S.W.** MOHAVE-APACHE, WHITE MOUNTAIN APACHE. — A related incident occurring in Southern California is:

(a) *Dying culture hero* (A565). The culture hero teaches people how to die by dying himself. — **CAL.** LUISEÑO, CAPISTRANO, MOHAVE: Waterman, AA, new ser., xi, 50.

53. *Confusion of tongues* (A1333). See tale No. xcv for the biblical parallels. The following tales seem to be quite independent of biblical influence. — References: Teit, JAFL, xxx, 443. — **MACK.** KASKA, CARRIER, TS'ETS'ÁUT: Teit, *loc. cit.* HARE: Petitot, p. 130. CHIPEWYAN: *Ibid.*, p. 383. — **PLAT.** THOMPSON, LILLOOET: Teit, *loc. cit.* SANPOIL: Gould, MAFLS, xi, 112, No. 14. — **N. PAC.** TSIMSHIAN, BELLA COOLA, COMOX, MAKA, SQUAMISH, TWANA: Teit, *loc. cit.* TAHLTAN: Teit, JAFL, xxxii, 234, No. 11. — **CAL.** JOSHUA: Farrand-Frachtenberg, JAFL, xxviii, 228, No. 16. HUPA: Goddard, UCal, i, 129. MAIDU: Dixon, BAM, xvii, 61. MEWAN: Merriam, p. 63. MAIDU: Dixon, BAM, xvii, 44, No. 1. — **PLNS.** SOUTHERN UTE: Lowie, JAFL, xxxvii, 3, No. 2. SOUTHERN PAIUTE (MAOPA): Lowie, JAFL, xxxvii, 159, No. 1. PAWNEE: Grinnell, JAFL, vi, 125. ARIKARA: Dorsey, CI, xvii, 21, No. 4. BLACKFOOT: Wissler and Duvall, PaAM, 1, 19. — **WDL. N.E.** MICMAC: Leland, p. 66. PASSAMAQUODDY: Prince, PAES, x, 49, No. 11. — **WDL. IROQ.** SENECA: Curtin-Hewitt, RBAE, xxxii, 538, No. 112.

54. *Distribution of tribes* (A1620). A large number of the cosmogonic myths account for the distribution of peoples. The following list is very fragmentary. — **PLAT.** THOMPSON: Teit, JE, viii, 254, 295, 314, 400, 401; Teit, MAFLS, xi, 12. SHUSWAP: Teit, JE, ii, 661, 662, 665–667. OKANAGON: Teit, MAFLS, xi, 82. KUTENAI: Boas, BBAE, lix, 83. CŒUR D'ALÈNE: Teit, MAFLS, xi, 122. SAHAPTIN: Farrand-Mayer, MAFLS, xi, 145. NEZ PERCÉ: *Ibid.*, p. 149. — **N. PAC.** KWAKIUTL: Boas and Hunt, JE, x, 28 ff. SNOHOMISH: Haeberlin, JAFL, xxxvii, 384. ALSEA: Frachtenberg, BBAE, lxvii, 111. — **CAL.** MODOC: Curtin, *Myths of the Modocs*, pp. 39 ff. KLAMATH: Gatschet, CNAE, ii, 103. YANA: Sapir, UCal, ix, 74, No. 5. COSTANOAN: Kroeber, UCal, iv, 200. CAHUILLA: Hooper, UCal, xvi, 324. — **PLNS.** SOUTHERN PAIUTE (MAOPA): Lowie, JAFL, xxxvii, 158, No. 1. NORTHERN PAIUTE (PAVIOTSO): *Ibid.*, pp. 200, 204, 205, No. 1. SOUTHERN UTE: *Ibid.*, pp. 3, 4, No. 1. CROW: Lowie, PaAM, xxv, 17, 30, 156. ARIKARA: Dorsey, CI, xvii, 23, No. 4.

55. See *Divinity's expected return*, note 11a.

56. *Four world-columns* (A841). The earth is represented as having four columns or barriers, one at each of the cardinal points. — **CAL.** Yuki: Kroeber, UCal, iv, 184. — **S.E.** Cherokee: Mooney, RBAE, xix, 239, No. 1. — **S.W.** San Carlos Apache: Goddard, PaAM, xxiv, 27. — Related motifs are:

(*a*) *World tree* (A652). A tree deeply rooted in earth brings forth all life, — See Parker, AA, new ser., xv, 608 ff. (**WDL. IROQ.** Seneca, Wyandot, Mohawk. — **WDL. N.E.** Delaware. — **S.E.** Cherokee).

(*b*) *Atlas* (A842). A person supports the earth. — **MACK.** Hare: Boas, RBAE, xxxi, 731. — **N. PAC.** Tlingit, Haida: *Ibid.* — **CAL.** Wishosk: Kroeber, JAFL, xviii, 99, No. 11. Yuki: Kroeber, UCal, iv, 186.

57. *Deluge* (A1010). A widespread motif. In some cases it is impossible to distinguish between this incident and that discussed in note 29 (*Primeval water*). In some tales the diving for earth (note 30, *Earth diver*) takes place in connection with a deluge. See, for example, tale No. iv in this volume: the selection here given is followed by the diving for earth. A few obvious borrowings of the story of "Noah's Flood" occur; see note 306. It is usually easy to distinguish between these borrowings and the native tales. — **ESK.** Bering Strait: Nelson, RBAE, xviii, 452; cf. Petitot, p. 6. — **MACK.** Loucheux: Camsell-Barbeau, JAFL, xxviii, 250, No. 2; Petitot, p. 30. Kaska: Teit, JAFL, xxx, 442, No. 3. Hare: Petitot, p. 141. Ts'ets'áut: Boas, JAFL, ix, 262. Chipewyan: Lowie, PaAM, x, 195; Petitot, pp. 373 ff. Carrier: Morice, TCI, v, 4. — **PLAT.** Thompson: Teit, MAFLS, xi, 13; Teit, JE, viii, 230; Hill-Tout, FL, x, 205; Hill-Tout, BAAS, lxix, p. 78. Lillooet: Teit, JAFL, xxv, 298. Sechelt: Hill-Tout, JAI, xxxiv, 37. — **N. PAC.** Tahltan, Bella Coola, Coast Salish, Comox: Teit, JAFL, xxxii, 232. Tsimshian: Teit, JAFL, xxxii, 232; Boas, BBAE, xxvii, 243. Kwakiutl: Boas and Hunt, JE, iii, 100, 318. Comox: Boas, *Sagen*, p. 79. Fraser Delta: *Ibid.*, p. 35. Lower Fraser: Teit, MAFLS, xi, 132, No. 5. Nootka: Sapir, JAFL, xxxii, 351 ff. Squamish: Hill-Tout, BAAS, lxx, 548. Kathlamet: Boas, BBAE, xxvi, 23. Alsea: Frachtenberg, BBAE, lxvii, 115, No. 7. Coos: Frachtenberg, CU, i, 45. Mollala: noted in Frachtenberg, JAFL, xxviii, 210. — **CAL.** Karok: Powers, CNAE, iii, 41. Shasta: Farrand-Frachtenberg, JAFL, xxviii, 210, No. 3; Dixon, JAFL, xxiii, 31. Achomawi: Powers, CNAE, iii, 200. Wishosk: Kroeber, JAFL, xviii, 96. Kato: Goddard, UCal, v, 186, No. 2. Sinkyone: Kroeber, JAFL, xxxii, 347, No. 5. Maidu: Powers, CNAE, iii, 290; Dixon, PAES, iv, 41, No. 2. Miwok: Gifford, UCal, xii, 310, No. 6. Western Mono: Gifford, JAFL, xxxvi, 306, No. 3, and 326, No. 9. Paviotso: Lowie, JAFL, xxxvii, 200, No. 1. — **PLNS.** Cheyenne: Dorsey, FM, ix, 35, No. 14. Skidi Pawnee: Dorsey, MAFLS, viii, 23, No. 4. Wichita: Dorsey, CI, xxi, 290, No. 55, and 294, No. 56. Arapaho: Dorsey and Kroeber, FM, v, 8, No. 5, and 13, No. 6. Crow: Lowie, PaAM, xxv, 16. Shoshoni: Lowie, PaAM, ii, 247, No. 5. Hidatsa: Curtis, iv, 184. Sarcee: Simms, JAFL, xvii, 180. Plains Cree: Skinner, JAFL, xxix, 346, 350. Plains Ojibwa: Skinner, JAFL, xxxii, 287. Bungee: Simms, JAFL, xix, 340. — **WDL. CENT.** Ojibwa: Radin, GSCan, ii, 20, 23; Schoolcraft, *Hiawatha*, p. 39; DeJong, *Original Odjibwe-Texts*, p. 14; Carson, JAFL, xxx, 491, No. 5; Jones-Michelson, PAES, vii (1), 151, 271, 403. Ottawa: Chamberlain, JAFL, iv, 204. Sauk and Fox: Jones, JAFL, xiv,

234. MENOMINI: Hoffman, RBAE, XIV, 133; Skinner and Satterlee, PaAM, XIII, 255, No. 6, and 260, No. 7. SAULTEAUX: Young, *Algonquin Indian Tales*, p. 182. — **WDL. N.E.** MONTAGNAIS: LeJeune, *Jes. Rel.*, V (1633), 155 and VI (1634), 159. ALGONQUIN: *Ibid.*, IX (1636), 127. — **WDL. IROQ.** SENECA: Curtin-Hewitt, RBAE, XXXII, 636, No. 121. — **S.E.** SHAWNEE: Spencer, JAFL, XXII, 319. CADDO: Dorsey, CI, XLI, 18, No. 8. — **S.W.** NAVAHO: Matthews, MAFLS, V, 74; Packard, *Anth. Soc. of Washington*, I, 84. SAN CARLOS APACHE: Goddard, PaAM, XXIV, 8, 29. MOHAVE-APACHE: Gould, JAFL, XXIV, 319. PIMA: Russell, RBAE, XXVI, 209, 211; Curtis, II, 18, 56; Lloyd, *Aw-aw-tam*, pp. 36 ff. — Some related motifs are:

(a) *Birds cling to sky in flood (cause of tail colors)* (A2211.7).— Fragmentary notes: **S.W.** NAVAHO: Matthews, MAFLS, V, 218, note 38; SAN CARLOS APACHE: Goddard, PaAM, XXIV, 29. JICARILLA APACHE: Russell, JAFL, XI, 254. SIA: Stevenson, RBAE, XI, 36. MOHAVE: Bourke, JAFL, II, 178.

(b) *Flood from tears* (A1012). The tears are usually those of a jealous suitor or deserted husband. — References: Teit, JAFL, XXV, 298. — **PLAT.** THOMPSON, LILLOOET, SECHELT: Teit, *loc. cit.* — **N. PAC.** FRASER DELTA, COMOX, KWAKIUTL, KATHLAMET: *Ibid.* — **S.W.** PIMA: Russell, RBAE, XXVI, 210; Azul, *Assembly Herald*, XV (Philadelphia, 1909), 70 f. PAPAGO: H. R. Kroeber, JAFL, XXV, 98.—— KORYAK (Northeast Siberia): Jochelson, JE, VI, 374.

(c) *Flood from belly* (A1013). A monster drinks up a lake, is killed, and causes a flood. — References: Teit, JAFL, XXX, 439. — **MACK.** BEAVER, KASKA: Teit, *loc. cit.* — **PLAT.** KUTENAI, THOMPSON, LILLOOET: *Ibid.* — **N. PAC.** TAHLTAN: Teit, JAFL, XXXII, 219; Emmons, UPa, IV, 23. — **CAL.** CHILULA, LUISEÑO: Teit, JAFL, XXX, 439. YUKI: Powers, CNAE, III, 144. — **WDL. N.E.** MICMAC: Teit, *loc. cit.* — **WDL. IROQ.** HURON: *Ibid.*

(d) *World fire* (A1030). A fire (or great heat) destroys life on the earth. — References: Teit, JAFL, XXX, 440, No. 1. — **MACK.** KASKA, TS'ETS'ÁUT: Teit, *loc. cit.* — **PLAT.** KUTENAI, SHUSWAP: *Ibid.*—**N. PAC.** BELLA COOLA, BELLA BELLA, KWAKIUTL, NEWETTEE, TSIMSHIAN, TAHLTAN: *Ibid.* — **CAL.** PATWIN: Powers, CNAE, III, 227. PAVIOTSO: Lowie, JAFL, XXXVII, 227, No. 15. — **PLNS.** SOUTHERN UTE: Lowie, JAFL, XXXVII, 61, No. 33. SOUTHERN PAIUTE: *Ibid.*, p. 146, No. 15. — **S.W.** NAVAHO: Parsons, JAFL, XXXVI, 370, No. 5.

58. *Hierarchy of worlds* (A651). A series of worlds, one above the other, is either expressed or implied in the myths and tales of most tribes. See notes to the following tales in this collection, all of which imply the existence of at least two such worlds: Nos. I, V, VI, VIII, IX, XV, XVI, XVIII, XXXIX, XL, L, LI, LII, LIII, LIV, LV, LVI, LXII, LXVI, LXVIII (?). Aside from these tales in which the idea is implied, the following are a few of the more striking accounts of the different worlds. — **N. PAC.** BELLA COOLA: Boas, JE, I, 28 ff. HAIDA: Swanton, JE, V, 13 ff. SNOHOMISH: Haeberlin, JAFL, XXXVII, 401. — **PLNS.** SOUTHERN PAIUTE: Lowie, JAFL, XXXVII, 165, No. 4. MANDAN: Will and Spinden, *Peabody Museum Papers*, III, 140.—**S.E.** CHOCTAW: Bushnell, AA, new ser., XII, 527, No. 2.—**S.W.** NAVAHO: Matthews, MAFLS, V, 64 ff. SAN CARLOS APACHE: Goddard, PaAM, XXIV, 28. JICARILLA APACHE: Mooney, AA, old ser., XI, 198. MOHAVE-APACHE: Gould, JAFL, XXIV, 319. ZUÑI: Stevenson, RBAE, XXIII, 24. HOPI: Voth, FM, VIII, 10 ff., Nos. 3, 4. PIMA: Russell, RBAE, XXVI, 226. SIA: Stevenson, RBAE, XI, 26 ff.—— SIBERIA: Bogaras, AA, new ser., IV, 590.

59. *X. The Lizard-Hand* (A1311.1). At first mankind had no fingers. The hand was then made on the model of the lizard's. — **CAL.** YANA: Sapir, UCal, IX, 88, No. 6; Curtin, *Creation Myths*, p. 479. YUKI: Kroeber, UCal, IV, 185. MAIDU: Dixon, BAM, XVI, 42. MEWAN: Merriam, pp. 55, 61. YOKUTS: Kroeber, UCal, IV, 231, No. 38. — A related motif is:

(*a*) *Misplaced genitalia* (A1313.3). The correcting of the location of the sexual organs or the method of giving birth appears in myths throughout the western half of the continent. — **ESK.** CUMBERLAND SOUND: Boas, BAM, XV, 168. — **PLAT.** CHILCOTIN, SHUSWAP, THOMPSON, LILLOOET: Boas, RBAE, XXXI, 609. THOMPSON: Teit, MAFLS, XI, 4. — **N. PAC.** TAHLTAN: Teit, JAFL, XXX, 207; CHEHALIS: Boas, *loc. cit.* — **CAL.** YANA: Sapir, UCal, IX, 88, No. 6. SALINAN: Mason, UCal, X, 190. HUPA: Goddard, UCal, I, 126, No. 1. COSTANOAN: Kroeber, UCal, IV, 199, No. 1. YOKUTS: *Ibid.*, p. 231, No. 37. MAIDU: Dixon, PAES, IV, 49 ff., No. 2. — **PLNS.** SHOSHONI: Lowie, PaAM, II, 239, No. 2. CROW: Simms, FM, II, 281, No. 1. ARIKARA: Dorsey, CI, XVII, 12, No. 2. BLACKFOOT: Maclean, JAFL, VI, 166. — **WDL. CENT.** FOX: Jones, PAES, I, 75. — **S.W.** NAVAHO: Matthews, MAFLS, V, 72 (unsuccessful attempt at universal celibacy). YUMA: Harrington, JAFL, XXI, 330. —— For KORYAK (Siberia), see Jochelson, JE, VI, 377. — Cf. *Vagina dentata*, note 115.

60. *XI. Determination of the Seasons* (A1150). — References: Boas, RBAE, XXXI, 728. — **MACK.** HARE: Boas, *loc. cit.* — **PLAT.** SHUSWAP: *Ibid.* — **N. PAC.** TLINGIT, HAIDA, TSIMSHIAN: *Ibid.* TAHLTAN: Teit, JAFL, XXXII, 226, 246. SKYKOMISH: Haeberlin, JAFL, XXXVII, 398. — **CAL.** MODOC: Curtin, *Myths of the Modocs*, p. 58. JOSHUA: Farrand-Frachtenberg, JAFL, XXVIII, 233, No. 17. ATSUGEWI: Dixon, JAFL, XXI, 170. PAVIOTSO: Lowie, JAFL, XXXVII, 222, No. 7, and 223, No. 8. — **PLNS.** COMANCHE: St. Clair, JAFL, XXII, 279. SOUTHERN UTE: Lowie, JAFL, XXXVII, 7, Nos. 4, 5. CROW: Lowie, PaAM, XXV, 28. ASSINIBOIN: Lowie, PaAM, IV, 101. BUNGEE: Simms, JAFL, XIX, 337. — **WDL. CENT.** FOX, OJIBWA: Boas, *loc. cit.* — **S.W.** ACOMA: Pradt, JAFL, XV, 88. — Cf. the following motifs:

(*a*) *Theft of the seasons* (A1151). Analogous to the *theft of light* (note 42) and the *theft of fire* (note 63). — References: Boas, BBAE, LIX, 301. — **MACK.** CHIPEWYAN: Boas, *loc. cit.* — **PLAT.** CHILCOTIN, SHUSWAP, THOMPSON: *Ibid.* — **CAL.** YANA: *Ibid.* — **PLNS.** SHOSHONI, CROW, GROS VENTRE, ASSINIBOIN: *Ibid.* BLACKFOOT: Maclean, JAFL, VI, 166. — **WDL. CENT.** OJIBWA: Boas, *loc. cit.*; DeJong, *Original Odjibwe-Texts*, pp. 6, 7. TIMAGAMI OJIBWA: Speck, GSCan, IX, 63. MENOMINI: Skinner and Satterlee, PaAM, XIII, 243; Hoffman, RBAE, XIV, 126. — **WDL. N.E.** MONTAGNAIS: Speck, JAFL, XXXVIII, 7. NASKAPI: Speck, JAFL, XXXVIII, 28. MICMAC: Parsons, JAFL, XXXVIII, 74, 75, No. 9.

(*b*) *Determination of the span of life* (A1320). — **CAL.** MAIDU: Dixon, PAES, IV, 14, No. 1.

61. *XII. Marriage of the North and the South* (A1153). — References: Boas, RBAE, XXXI, 732. — **PLAT.** SHUSWAP, THOMPSON, LILLOOET: Boas, *loc. cit.* — **N. PAC.** TLINGIT, HAIDA, TSIMSHIAN: *Ibid.* — **S.E.** CHEROKEE: Mooney, RBAE, XIX, 322, No. 70. — Related motifs are:

(*a*) *Weather contest* (D2159). A contest between heat and cold, sun and wind, or the like. — **PLAT.** SHUSWAP: Teit, JE, II, 671, No. 13, and 701, No. 32. THOMPSON: Teit, MAFLS, VI, 40, 55, and XI, 21, 61; Teit, JE,

VIII, 210; Hill-Tout, JAI, xxxv, 204. LILLOOET: Teit, JAFL, xxv, 292, 310. OKANAGON: Teit, MAFLS, xi, 74. SANPOIL: Gould, MAFLS, xi, 104. CŒUR D'ALÈNE: *Ibid.*, p. 124. SAHAPTIN: Farrand-Mayer, MAFLS, xi, 147. NEZ PERCÉ: Spinden, JAFL, xxi, 17. — **N. PAC.** TSIMSHIAN, HAIDA, NEW-ETTEE, KWAKIUTL, NOOTKA: Boas, RBAE, xxxi, 658. TAHLTAN: Teit, JAFL, xxxii, 224, 230. SKYKOMISH: Haeberlin, JAFL, 397. SNUQUALMI: *Ibid.*, p. 398. — **CAL.** MODOC: Curtin, *Myths of the Modocs,* pp. 76 ff. — **PLNS.** ARAPAHO: Dorsey and Kroeber, FM, v, 231, No. 101. EASTERN DAKOTA: Skinner and Satterlee, PaAM, xiii, 531. — **WDL. CENT.** OJIBWA: Jones-Michelson, PAES, vii (ii), 353, No. 45; Radin, GSCan, ii, 12; School-craft, *Indian in his Wigwam,* p. 85; Schoolcraft, *Hiawatha,* p. 97. MENOMINI: Skinner and Satterlee, PaAM, xiii, 430. — **WDL. N.E.** NASKAPI: Speck, JAFL, xxviii, 76. MICMAC: Rand, pp. 72, 99; Leland, pp. 74, 134. — **WDL. IROQ.** SENECA: Curtin, *Seneca Indian Myths,* p. 1; cf. Curtin-Hewitt, RBAE, xxxii, 356, No. 62. — **S.W.** ACOMA: Pradt, JAFL, xv, 58.

(*b*) *Magic storm* (D2150). Many of the stories cited in the preceding note (*weather contest*) contain magic storms. See also the next note (*local winter*). — **PLAT.** SECHELT: Hill-Tout, JAI, xxxiv, 37. — **N. PAC.** TAHLTAN: Teit, JAFL, xxxiv, 324 and xxxii, 212. SNOHOMISH: Haeberlin, JAFL, xxxvii, 411. — **CAL.** PAVIOTSO: Lowie, JAFL, xxxvii, 214, No. 3*a.* — **PLNS.** SOUTH-ERN PAIUTE (SHIVWITS): Lowie, JAFL, xxxvii, 100, No. 1; 107, No. 5; 151, No. 17; (MAOPA): *Ibid.*, p. 162, No. 3; p. 172, No. 8; p. 180, No. 15; p. 193, No. 22; p. 198, No. 29. CROW: Lowie, PaAM, xxv, 161, 168. — **WDL. IROQ.** SENECA: Curtin-Hewitt, RBAE, xxxii, 188, 306, 453, 548. — **S.W.** NAVAHO: Matthews, MAFLS, v, 108. —— SIBERIA: Jochelson, JE, ii, 375.

(*c*) *Local winter* (D2155.2). A magician causes winter to remain in one place while summer is all around. — References: Boas, RBAE, xxxi, 829. — **PLAT.** CHILCOTIN, SHUSWAP, WASCO: Boas, *loc. cit.* — **N. PAC.** TLINGIT, HAIDA, TSIMSHIAN, KATHLAMET: *Ibid.* TAHLTAN: Teit, JAFL, xxxiv, 234, No. 40. CHEHALIS: Hill-Tout, JAI, xxxiv, 361. — **CAL.** SHASTA: Farrand-Frachtenberg, JAFL, xxviii, 218, No. 9; Dixon, JAFL, xxiii, 27. JOSHUA: Farrand-Frachtenberg, JAFL, xxviii, 228, No. 17. — **WDL. CENT.** MENOM-INI: Skinner and Satterlee, PaAM, xiii, 426; Hoffman, RBAE, xiv, 210. WINNEBAGO: Radin, JAFL, xxii, 294. — Cf. note 107.

62. *XIII. Determination of Night and Day* (A1172). — **ESK.** BAFFIN LAND: Boas, BAM, xv, 306. — **PLNS.** CROW: Lowie, PaAM, xxv, 25. PAWNEE: Dorsey, CI, LIX, 44, No. 9. — **WDL. CENT.** MENOMINI: Skinner and Satterlee, PaAM, xiii, 408; Hoffman, RBAE, xiv, 200. CREE: Russell, p. 217. PEORIA: Michelson, JAFL, xxx, 495. — **WDL. IROQ.** IROQUOIS: Smith, RBAE, ii, 80. — **S.E.** CADDO: Dorsey, CI, XLI, 13, No. 2. — **S.W.** JICARILLA APACHE: Mooney, AA, old ser., xi, 198.

63. *XIV. The Theft of Fire* (A1415). Fire is stolen by the culture hero for the use of mankind. — References: Boas, RBAE, xxxi, 660. — **ESK.** LABRA-DOR: Turner, RBAE, xi, 340. — **MACK.** CARRIER: Boas, *loc. cit.* TS'ETS'ÁUT: Boas, JAFL, ix, 262. SLAVEY: Bell, JAFL, xiv, 26. KASKA: Teit, JAFL, xxx, 443, No. 4. — **PLAT.** CHILCOTIN, LILLOOET: Boas, RBAE, xxxi, 660. THOMPSON: Teit, MAFLS, vi, 56; Teit, JE, viii, 229, 378. SHUSWAP: Teit, JE, ii, 669. OKANAGON: Teit, MAFLS, xi, 92. SANPOIL: Gould, MAFLS, xi, 108. NEZ PERCÉ: Packard, JAFL, iv, 327. — **N. PAC.** TLINGIT, HAIDA, TSIMSHIAN, NASS, BELLA COOLA, BELLA BELLA, KWAKIUTL, NEWETTEE, RIVERS INLET,

Comox, Nootka, Squamish, Chehalis: Boas, RBAE, xxxi, 660. Fraser
Delta: Boas, *Sagen*, p. 42. Tahltan: Teit, JAFL, xxxii, 218. Skagit: Haeberlin, JAFL, xxxvii, 390. Snohomish: *Ibid.*, p. 412. Quileute: Farrand-
Mayer, JAFL, xxxii, 266, No. 10. Sinkiuse: Curtis, vii, 108. Coos: Frach-
tenberg, CU, i, 39, No. 4. Tututuni: Farrand-Frachtenberg, JAFL, xxviii,
242. — CAL. Modoc: Curtin, *Myths of the Modocs*, pp. 51–59. Shasta:
Farrand-Frachtenberg, JAFL, xxviii, 209, No. 2; Dixon, JAFL, xxiii, 8;
Kro-eber, UCal, iv, 180. Achomawi: Powers, CNAE, iii, 273; Dixon, JAFL,
xxi,165. Atsugewi: *Ibid.*, p. 174. Chimariko: Dixon, UCal, v, 353, No. 4.
Karok: Powers, CNAE, iii, 341. Yana: Curtin, *Creation Myths*, p. 365;
Sapir, UCal, ix, 23, No. 2, and 160, No. 13 (= Curtin, *loc. cit.*). Yurok:
Powers, CNAE, iii, 70. Kato: Goddard, UCal, v, 195, No. 5. Sinkyone:
Kroeber, JAFL, xxxii, 347, No. 4. Yuki: Kroeber, UCal, iv, 185. Maidu:
Dixon, PAES, iv, 163, No. 8; Dixon, BAM, xvii, 65, No. 5. Mewan:
Merriam, pp. 49, 61, 89, 139; Kroeber, UCal, iv, 202, No. 8. Miwok: Gifford,
UCal, xii, 284, No. 1, and 332, No. 12. Yokuts: Kroeber, UCal, iv, 211,
No. 16; Stewart, JAFL, xix, 322 and xxi, 237.—PLNS. Shoshoni: Lowie,
PaAM, ii, 244, No. 3. Paiute (Southern, Maopa): Lowie, JAFL, xxxvii,
159, No. 1; (Southern, Shivwits): *Ibid.*, p. 117, No. 8; (Northern,
Paviotso): *Ibid.*, p. 228, No. 5. Ute: Kroeber, JAFL, xv, 52; (Southern):
Lowie, JAFL, xxxvii, 6, No. 3. Swampy Cree: Cresswell, JAFL, xxxvi, 406.
—WDL. CENT. Ojibwa: Jones, PAES, vii (i), 7 ff.; (Western): DeJong,
Original Odjibwe-Texts, pp. 6, 7. Menomini: Skinner and Satterlee, PaAM,
xiii, 243. — S.E. Cherokee: Mooney, RBAE, xix, 240, No. 2. Creek:
Speck, *Southern Workman*, xxxviii, 9. Yuchi: Speck, UPa, i, 144, Nos. 6,
7. — S.W. Jicarilla Apache: Russell, JAFL, xi, 261; Goddard, PaAM,
viii, 208–209, Nos. 15, 16. San Carlos Apache: Goddard, PaAM, xxiv,
41, 43. Pima: Russell, RBAE, xxvi, 216; Lloyd, *Aw-aw-tam*, p. 103. Mohave:
Bourke, JAFL, ii, 188.

64. *Fire brought in flute* (A1415.1). Interesting because of the comparison
with the Greek account of the theft of fire in a flute by Prometheus are the
two California tales here cited. Maidu: Dixon, PAES, iv, 169. Miwok:
Gifford, UCal, xii, 284, No. 1, and 332, No. 12.

65. *XV. The Sun Snarer* (A728.1). A youth, angered because the sun
has burnt his robe, makes a snare (usually from his sister's pubic hair) and
catches the sun. Many animals try to release the sun. The mouse succeeds.
— MACK. Chipewyan: Lowie, PaAM, x, 184; Petitot, pp. 379, 411.
Beaver: Goddard, PaAM, x, 233. — PLAT. Chilcotin: Farrand, JE,
ii, 42, No. 28 (wind snared in similar fashion).—CAL. Yurok: Powers,
CNAE, iii, 60.—PLNS. Southern Paiute: Lowie, JAFL, xxxvii, 146,
198. Northern Paiute: *Ibid.*, p. 224. (These Paiute tales are not exact
parallels.) Omaha: Dorsey, CNAE, vi, 84. Assiniboin: Lowie, PaAM, iv,
140. Eastern Sioux: Schoolcraft, *Algic Researches*, i, 79. Bungee (Swampy):
Simms, JAFL, xix, 337; Cresswell, JAFL, xxxvi, 404. — WDL. CENT.
Eastern Cree: Skinner, PaAM, ix, 100, 102. Ojibwa: Jones-Michelson,
PAES, vii (ii), No. 46; Schoolcraft, *Hiawatha*, p. 239; Schoolcraft, *Indian
in his Wigwam*, p. 97; Jones, JAFL, xxix, 376. Timagami Ojibwa: Speck,
GSCan, ix, 69. Menomini: Skinner and Satterlee, PaAM, xiii, 357, 360;
Hoffman, RBAE, xiv, 181. Fox: Jones, PAES, i, 79. — WDL. N.E. Mon-
tagnais: Speck, JAFL, xxxviii, 3; LeJeune, *Jes. Rel.*, xii (1637), 35. Nas-
kapi: Speck, JAFL, xxxviii, 26 (moon snarer). — WDL. IROQ. Seneca:

Curtin-Hewitt, RBAE, XXXII, 353, No. 60 (= Curtin, *Seneca Indian Myths*, p. 172). (The sun is pushed back with a pole.)

66. *XVI. The Man who acted as the Sun* (A 724.1). The *Phaëton* motif. The Sun lets his son carry the sun (or act as the sun). The youth almost burns up the earth and has to be rescued. — **N. PAC.** BELLA COOLA, BELLA BELLA, KWAKIUTL, NEWETTEE, RIVERS INLET: Boas, RBAE, XXXI, 640. CHEHALIS: Hill-Tout, JAI, XXXIV, 345.

In another group of tales animals have a contest as to which shall act as the sun (and usually also as the moon). — **PLAT.** SHUSWAP, THOMPSON, OKANAGON, KUTENAI, WASCO, WISHRAM: Boas, RBAE, XXXI, 727. CŒUR D'ALÈNE: Teit, MAFLS, XI, 123, No. 8. LILLOOET: Teit, JAFL, XXV, 350.

In the following tales the hero is taken by the sun on a journey, and thus sees all that is going on in the world below. — **WDL. CENT.** OTTAWA: Schoolcraft, *Indian in his Wigwam*, p. 82. Cf. MENOMINI: Skinner and Satterlee, PaAM, XIII, 376. — **S.W.** ZUÑI: Cushing, p. 150. HOPI: Voth, FM, III, 349. NAVAHO: Matthews, MAFLS, V, 111 (a "bearer of the sun").

OJIBWA: Jones-Michelson, PAES, VII (1), 193 (Manabozho acts as the "fisher" constellation, breaks a tabu, and falls).

67. Cf. *Rainbow-bridge*, note 204.

68. Cf. "The Arrow Chain," tale LIII, notes 202, 203.

69. *XVII. The Man in the Moon* (A751). Most stories explaining the man in the moon are similar to the Lillooet version. — **PLAT.** SHUSWAP: Teit, JE, II, 653; Boas, *Sagen*, p. 15. THOMPSON: Teit, MAFLS, VI, 91; Teit, JE, VIII, 229, 230. LILLOOET: Teit, JAFL, XXV, 298, No. 3. SALISH: *Trans. Ethn. Soc. London* (1866), p. 304. KALISPEL: Curtis, VII, 97 ff. CŒUR D'ALÈNE: Teit, MAFLS, XI, 123, No. 9. NEZ PERCÉ: Spinden, MAFLS, XI, 195, No. 16. — **N. PAC.** TAHLTAN: Teit, JAFL, XXXII, 229, No. 7. SNUQUALMI: Haeberlin, JAFL, XXXVII, 377. COOS: St. Clair, JAFL, XXII, 40; Frachtenberg, CU, I, 133. — **CAL.** PAVIOTSO: Lowie, JAFL, XXXVII, 234, No. 12. — **PLNS.** SOUTHERN PAIUTE: Lowie, JAFL, XXXVII, 157, No. 19. SHOSHONI: St. Clair, JAFL, XXII, 275. CROW: Lowie, PaAM, XXV, 52. GROS VENTRE: Kroeber, PaAM, I, 90, No. 21. ARAPAHO: Dorsey, FM, IV, 214 ff. — **WDL. N.E.** MONTAGNAIS: Speck, JAFL, XXXVIII, 5; LeJeune, *Jes. Rel.*, VI (1634), 223. MICMAC: Parsons, JAFL, XXXVIII, 92, No. 22. — **WDL. IROQ.** SENECA: Curtin, *Seneca Indian Myths*, p. 508. — **S.W.** JICARILLA APACHE: Mooney, AA, old ser., XI, 209.

70. *Flood from tears of disappointed suitor.* See in note 57 (*Flood from tears*), the Koryak, Plateau, and North Pacific references.

71. *XVIII. Origin of the Pleiades* (A773). — **ESK.** Kroeber, JAFL, XIII, 182, 183. — **PLAT.** CHILCOTIN: *Ibid.* — **N. PAC.** TLINGIT: *Ibid.* — **CAL.** SHASTA: Farrand-Frachtenberg, JAFL, XXVIII, 221, No. 11. YOKUTS: Kroeber, UCal, IV, 213, No. 20. CAHUILLA: Hooper, UCal, XVI, 363, 366. Cf. LUISEÑO: DuBois, UCal, VIII, 163, 164. PAVIOTSO: Lowie, JAFL, XXXVII, 234, No. 12. — **PLNS.** CROW: Lowie, PaAM, XXV, 205. ARAPAHO: Dorsey and Kroeber, FM, V, 161, No. 82. CHEYENNE: Kroeber, JAFL, XIII, 182. PAWNEE: Dorsey, CI, LIX, 122, No. 30. Cf. BLACKFOOT: McClintock, p. 488; Wissler and Duvall, PaAM, II, 61. — **WDL. IROQ.** IROQUOIS: Smith, RBAE, II, 80. WYANDOT: Barbeau, GSCan, XI, 56, No. 6, and 58, No. 7. ONONDAGA: Beauchamp, JAFL, XIII, 281. — **S.E.** CHEROKEE: Mooney, RBAE, XIX, 258,

No. 10; Hagar, *Boas Anniversary Volume*, p. 357. — The central incident of the ascent to the stars occurs frequently in other connections.

(*a*) *Escape to the stars* (R321). In most cases the ascent to the stars is made by fugitives who rise in the air and become stars. — See all references to the Pleiades just given. For a general discussion, see Hagar, *Boas Anniversary Volume*, p. 358. — **ESK.** GREENLAND, SMITH SOUND, CUMBERLAND SOUND, POINT BARROW: Boas, BAM, xv, 360 (s.v. *Orion*). — **PLAT.** CHILCOTIN: Farrand, JE, II, 30, No. 14, and 31, No. 15. THOMPSON: Teit, MAFLS, XI, 26. CŒUR D'ALÈNE: *Ibid.*, pp. 125, 126. — **N. PAC.** TAHLTAN: Teit, JAFL, XXXII, 229, Nos. 5, 6. KATHLAMET: Boas, BBAE, XXVI, 71. COOS: St. Clair-Frachtenberg, JAFL, XXII, 40. — **CAL.** MODOC: Curtin, *Myths of the Modocs*, pp. 95 ff. YUKI: Kroeber, UCal, IV, 185. YOKUTS: *Ibid.*, p. 214, No. 21. — **PLNS.** UTE: Kroeber, JAFL, XIV, 268; (SOUTHERN): Lowie, JAFL, XXXVII, 30, No. 15. CROW: Lowie, PaAM, XXV, 210, 211; Curtis, IV, 117; Simms, FM, II, 309, No. 20, and 312, No. 21. WICHITA: Dorsey, CI, XXI, 73, No. 9; Dorsey, JAFL, XVI, 179. ARAPAHO: Dorsey and Kroeber, FM, V, 159, 239, Nos. 81, 105. CHEYENNE: Kroeber, JAFL, XIII, 182. PAWNEE: Dorsey, MAFLS, VIII, 51, No. 10. PONCA: Dorsey, CNAE, VI, 224. DAKOTA: Riggs, CNAE, IX, 115. CANADIAN DAKOTA: Wallis, JAFL, XXXVI, 44. BLACKFOOT: Wissler and Duvall, PaAM, II, 70. SARCEE: Simms, JAFL, XVII, 180. ASSINIBOIN: Lowie, PaAM, IV, 176–178, Nos. 19–22. GROS VENTRE: Kroeber, PaAM, I, 108, No. 27. — **WDL. CENT.** OJIBWA: Carson, JAFL, XXX, 493; Schoolcraft, *Hiawatha*, pp. 77 ff. MENOMINI: Skinner and Satterlee, PaAM, XIII, 456. FOX: Jones, PAES, I, 71 ff. — **WDL. N.E.** MICMAC: Hagar, JAFL, XIII, 92. — **WDL. IROQ.** IROQUOIS: Converse, pp. 53 ff. SENECA: Curtin-Hewitt, RBAE, XXXII, 277, No. 54 (= Curtin, *Seneca Indian Myths*, p. 503). — **S.E.** CADDO: Dorsey, CI, XLI, 25–27, Nos. 11–13. — **S.W.** HOPI: Voth, FM, VIII, 71, No. 14.

72. *XIX. The Bag of Winds* (C322). Cf. note 45, in which light is kept in a bag, box, or basket. The wind in the bag appears in the following: — **MACK.** YUKON: Schmitter, p. 21. TS'ETS'ÁUT: Boas, JAFL, IX, 260. — **PLAT.** CHILCOTIN: Farrand, JE, II, 42. THOMPSON: Teit, MAFLS, VI, 87. — **N. PAC.** BELLA COOLA: Boas, JE, I, 79. — **CAL.** MODOC: Curtin, *Myths of the Modocs*, pp. 83–87. MAIDU: Dixon, PAES, IV, 131 ff., No. 5. — **S.W.** ZUÑI: Cushing, p. 269.

73. Cf. *Sun snarer*, note 65. See for this incident with the wind: — **PLAT.** THOMPSON: Teit, JE, VIII, 330. CŒUR D'ALÈNE: Teit, MAFLS, XI, 124, No. 10.

74. *XX. The Bird whose Wings made the Wind* (A1127). The wind is caused by the flapping wings of a giant bird. The hero breaks the wing and tames the winds. — **WDL. N.E.** MICMAC: Rand, p. 360, No. 68. MALECITE: Mechling, GSCan, IV, 45, No. 5; Speck, JAFL, XXX, 480, No. 1. PASSAMAQUODDY: Prince, PAES, X, 47, No. 10; Leland, p. 111; Fewkes, JAFL, III, 266.

75. *XXI. The Release of the Wild Animals* (*hoarded game*) (A1421). All game is kept in one place. It is finally released by the culture hero. — References: Jochelson, JE, VI, 367, 372; Boas, RBAE, XXXI, 653, and BBAE, LIX, 303, note 3; Teit, MAFLS, XI, 139. — **ESK.** Jochelson, *op. cit.*, p. 367. — **MACK.** KASKA, BEAVER, CHIPEWYAN: Boas, BBAE, LIX, 303. HARE: Petitot, p. 154. LOUCHEUX: *Ibid.*, pp. 71 ff. — **PLAT.** THOMPSON, KUTENAI, NEZ PERCÉ: Boas,

BBAE, LIX, 303. THOMPSON, OKANAGON, SANPOIL, SAHAPTIN: Teit, *loc. cit.*
WISHRAM: Sapir, PAES, II, 5, No. I. — **N. PAC.** TLINGIT, TSIMSHIAN, BELLA
BELLA, HAIDA, NEWETTEE, TILLAMOOK: Boas, RBAE, XXXI, 653. Cf. TLINGIT,
TSIMSHIAN, HAIDA, KWAKIUTL, NEWETTEE, COMOX: Boas, RBAE, XXXI,
674. TAHLTAN: Teit, JAFL, XXXII, 203; Emmons, UPa, IV, 119. — **CAL.**
KAROK: Powers, CNAE, III, 37. HUPA: Goddard, UCal, I, 123, No. I.
YOKUTS: Kroeber, UCal, IV, 205, No. 14. YUKI: *Ibid.*, p. 185. — **PLNS.**
COMANCHE: St. Clair, JAFL, XXII, 280. SOUTHERN UTE: Lowie, JAFL,
XXXVII, 63, No. 34. WICHITA: Dorsey, CI, XXI, 191, No. 27. ARAPAHO:
Dorsey and Kroeber, FM, V, 275, No. 122. PAWNEE: Dorsey, CI, LIX, 42,
No. 8. BLACKFOOT: Wissler and Duvall, PaAM, II, 50 ff.; Grinnell, *Black-
foot Lodge Tales*, p. 145. GROS VENTRE: Kroeber, PaAM, I, 65, No. 4. —
WDL. N.E. MALECITE: Mechling, GSCan, IV, 3 ff., No. I. — **WDL. IROQ.**
IROQUOIS: Beauchamp, JAFL, IV, 298. SENECA: Curtin-Hewitt, RBAE,
XXXII, 525, No. 110. — **S.E.** CHEROKEE: Mooney, JAFL, I, 100. BILOXI:
Dorsey and Swanton, BBAE, XLVII, 54, No. 19. CADDO: Dorsey, CI, XLI, 10,
No. I. — **S.W.** JICARILLA APACHE: Goddard, PaAM, VIII, 212 ff.; Russell,
JAFL, XI, 259. WHITE MOUNTAIN APACHE: Goddard, PaAM, XXIV, 126.
ZUÑI: Cushing, p. 104.

In the following tales the hero secures vegetables, tobacco, or nuts, simi-
larly hoarded. — **WDL. CENT.** MENOMINI: Skinner and Satterlee, PaAM,
XIII, 247; Hoffman, RBAE, XIV, 205 (tobacco). — **WDL. N.E.** MICMAC:
Parsons, JAFL, XXXVIII, 82, No. 13 (plants). — **WDL. IROQ.** SENECA:
Curtin-Hewitt, RBAE, XXXII, 84, No. 2, and 509, No. 109 (tobacco, chest-
nuts). — **S.E.** CADDO: Dorsey, CI, XLI, 52, No. 27 (pecans). —— SIBERIA:
Jochelson, JE, VI, 367, 372. — Cf. note 42, *Theft of light* and 63, *Theft of
Fire.*

76. *XXII. The Empounded Water* (A1111). Similar to the last incident.
All the water is kept by a monster (often the frog) and is released by the hero.
— References: Boas, RBAE, XXXI, 651; Jochelson, JE, VI, 372 f. — **PLAT.**
NEZ PERCÉ: Spinden, MAFLS, XI, 187, No. 8. — **N. PAC.** TLINGIT, HAIDA,
NASS, BELLA BELLA, KWAKIUTL, NEWETTEE, RIVERS INLET, NOOTKA: Boas,
loc. cit. TAHLTAN: Teit, JAFL, XXXII, 201. — **WDL. N.E.** MICMAC: Speck,
JAFL, XXVIII, 62; Leland, pp. 114 ff.; Rand, p. 68, No. 8. MALECITE:
Speck, JAFL, XXX, 480, No. 2; Mechling, GSCan, IV, 46, 53; Stamp, JAFL,
XXVIII, 247. PASSAMAQUODDY: Leland, pp. 114 ff. —— SIBERIA: Jochelson,
JE, VI, 372 f. — An analogous motif is:

(*a*) *Origin of tides* (A913). The hero, in much the same way as in the ac-
quisition of fresh water, rescues the tides from the person who controls them,
so that they are now properly regulated. — **N. PAC.** TLINGIT, HAIDA, TSIM-
SHIAN, BELLA BELLA, RIVERS INLET, NEWETTEE, KWAKIUTL, NOOTKA: Boas,
RBAE, XXXI, 656. TAHLTAN: Teit, JAFL, XXXII, 201.

77. *XXIII. The Origin of Corn* (A2611.1). Analogous tales of the origin of
corn are: — **WDL. N.E.** PENOBSCOT: N. Curtis, *Indian Book*, p. 4. MALECITE:
Mechling, GSCan, IV, 87. — **WDL. IROQ.** IROQUOIS: Converse, pp. 63 ff.;
Smith, RBAE, II, 52. HURON: Hale, JAFL, I, 180. SENECA: Curtin-Hewitt,
RBAE, XXXII, 412, 636, 642, 649, 652. — **S.E.** CHEROKEE: Mooney, JAFL,
I, 98; Mooney, RBAE, XIX, 242. — Other accounts of the origin of corn are:
PLNS. SOUTHERN UTE: Lowie, JAFL, XXXVII, 86, No. 56. PAWNEE:
Grinnell, JAFL, VI, 122 ff.; Dorsey, MAFLS, VIII, 20, No. 3. ARIKARA:

Dorsey, CI, XVII, 12–32, Nos. 3–7. — **WDL. CENT.** MISSISAUGA: Chamberlain, JAFL, II, 142.

78. *Trickster Tales.* This series of adventures in which the culture hero appears as a dupe or trickster is found over a large part of the continent. The central character changes from one culture area to another and some of the adventures have a narrow distribution, but one cycle fades so imperceptibly into another, and so many motifs are common to several cycles, that it is impossible to arrange the adventures in definite groups. An exception to this statement is the three-fold cycle of the North Pacific Coast, containing the adventures of Raven, Bluejay, and Mink. These adventures merge so as to form a rather definite series. For comparative study, see Boas, RBAE, XXXI, 565 ff.

In other parts of the country as well it is possible to recognize certain rather vaguely defined cycles of tales. In nearly all cases the foolish adventures happen to the culture hero, who thus plays a double rôle in the mythology. Going from east to west, one may recognize the following heroes of trickster tales: Glooscap of the Northeast Algonquins; Flint and Sapling of the Iroquois; Manabozho or Wiskajak of the Central Woodland (corresponding in general with Iktomi of the Sioux); Rabbit of the Southeastern tribes; Coyote of the Plains, Plateau, and California tribes; Mink, Bluejay, and Raven of the North Pacific. Notes on the most prominent of the adventures follow. For an adequate consideration of the distribution, each incident must be treated separately.

79. *XXIV. Manabozho's Adventures.* Compare with these trickster adventures of Manabozho, the tales in which he appears as a culture hero. See note 20 and tale IV in this volume. For a general bibliography of these adventures, see Thompson, *Publications of the Modern Language Association of America*, XXXVII, 130–132.

80. *Trickster carried by birds and dropped (borrowed feathers)* (K1041). — **PLAT.** SAHAPTIN: Farrand-Mayer, MAFLS, XI, 146, No. 3. NEZ PERCÉ: Spinden, JAFL, XXI, 150. — **PLNS.** SOUTHERN UTE: JAFL, XXXVII, 53, No. 27. UINTAH UTE: Mason, JAFL, XXIII, 310. SOUTHERN PAIUTE (SHIVWITS): Lowie, JAFL, XXXVII, 124, No. 11; (MAOPA): *Ibid.*, p. 165, No. 5. SHOSHONI: Lowie, PaAM, II, 247, No. 5. PAWNEE: Dorsey, MAFLS, VIII, 251, No. 60; Dorsey, CI, LIX, 443, No. 124. PONCA: Dorsey, CNAE, VI, 77. CROW: Lowie, PaAM, XXV, 38, cf. 115, 160. EASTERN DAKOTA, IOWA: cited in Skinner and Satterlee, PaAM, XIII, 521, No. 17. MANDAN: Maximilian, II, 158. BLACKFOOT: McClintock, p. 343. ASSINIBOIN: Lowie, PaAM, IV, 108. PLAINS OJIBWA: Skinner, JAFL, XXXII, 282. PLAINS CREE: Skinner, JAFL, XXIX, 348. — **WDL. CENT.** OJIBWA: Jones-Michelson: PAES, VII (I), 127, 433, and (II), 267; Radin, GSCan, II, 2; (TIMAGAMI): Speck, GSCan, IX, 38. MENOMINI: Hoffman, RBAE, XIV, 165, 202; Skinner, and Satterlee, PaAM, XIII, 292. Fox: Jones, JAFL, XIV, 235. KICKAPOO: Jones, PAES, IX, 11, No. 2. PEORIA: Michelson, JAFL, XXX, 494. — **WDL. N.E.** MICMAC: Parsons, JAFL, XXXVIII, 68, 72. — **WDL. IROQ.** IROQUOIS: Smith, RBAE, II, 88. WYANDOT: Barbeau, GSCan, XI, 356. — **S.E.** CHEROKEE: Mooney, RBAE, XIX, 293. — **S.W.** NAVAHO: Matthews, MAFLS, V, 121. JICARILLA APACHE: Russell, JAFL, XI, 261. ZUÑI: Parsons, JAFL, XXXI, 218; Cushing, p. 237. LAGUNA: Parsons, JAFL, XXXI, 219. HOPI: Voth, FM, VIII, 197, 202. — See Thompson, CColl, II, 449 and Parsons, JAFL,

XXXI, 218, note 1, for foreign parallels. — For flight by putting on bird feathers, see: SAHAPTIN: Farrand-Mayer, MAFLS, XI, 176, No. 14. KATHLAMET: Boas, BBAE, XXVI, 142, 146. NOOTKA: Boas, *Sagen*, p. 109.

81. *Diving for reflected food* (J1792). — References: Boas, RBAE, XXXI, 699. — **PLAT.** SHUSWAP, LILLOOET, THOMPSON, KUTENAI, WASCO: Boas, *loc. cit.* SALISH: Hill-Tout, *British North America*, p. 220. — **N. PAC.** KWAKIUTL, NEWETTEE, QUINAULT: Boas, *loc. cit.* SHOALWATER BAY: Curtis, I, 125. — **CAL.** YOKUTS: Kroeber, UCal, IV, 238, No. 39. — **PLNS.** SHOSHONI, PONCA, ARAPAHO: Boas, *loc. cit.* SOUTHERN UTE: Lowie, JAFL, XXXVII, 55, No. 31, and 58, No. 32. OSAGE: Dorsey, FM, VII, 17, No. 13. DAKOTA: Meeker, JAFL, XIV, 161 and XV, 84. BLACKFOOT: Wissler and Duvall, PaAM, II, 29; McClintock, p. 345; Uhlenbeck, VKAWA, XII (1), 64. PLAINS OJIBWA: Skinner, JAFL, XXXII, 281. — **WDL. CENT.** FOX, KICKAPOO: Boas, *loc. cit.* CREE: Russell, p. 214. OJIBWA: Radin, GSCan, II, 3, 11; Jones-Michelson, PAES, VII (1), 117, 179. MENOMINI: Hoffman, RBAE, XIV, 165; Skinner and Satterlee, PaAM, XIII, 298. — **WDL. N.E.** MICMAC, PENOBSCOT: Boas, *loc. cit.* — **S.E.** CATAWBA: Radin, JAFL, XXIV, 325 (European?). — **S.W.** NAVAHO: Parsons, JAFL, XXXVI, 374, No. 14. KERES: Parsons and Boas, JAFL, XXXIII, 49. ZUÑI: JAFL, XXXI, 453. PIMA: Neff, JAFL, XXV, 55. — Also European: Thompson, CColl, II, 420 (incident D). Cf. note 270*a*.

82. *Hoodwinked dancers* (K826). Trickster induces ducks to dance with closed eyes and kills them. — References: Jones, PAES IX, 131. — **ESK.** LABRADOR: Turner, RBAE, XI, 327. — **MACK.** Beaver: Goddard, PaAM, X, 256. CHIPEWYAN: Lowie, PaAM, X, 199. — **PLAT.** SALISH (IDAHO): Hoffman, RBAE, XIV, 162, 204. — **PLNS.** SOUTHERN UTE: Lowie, JAFL, XXXVII, 18, No. 8, and 37, No. 21 (prairie dogs). SOUTHERN PAIUTE (MAOPA): *Ibid.*, p. 194, No. 23 (mountain sheep). COMANCHE: St. Clair, JAFL, XXII, 273. KIOWA: Mooney, RBAE, XIX, 449. OSAGE: Dorsey, FM, VII, 9, No. 2. ARAPAHO: Dorsey and Kroeber, FM, V, 59, No. 26, and 60, No. 27. CHEYENNE: Kroeber, JAFL, XIII, 165, 166. OMAHA: Dorsey, CNAE, VI, 362, 580. PONCA: *Ibid.*, p. 67. CROW: Lowie, PaAM, XXV, 34; Simms, FM, II, 288, No. 10. DAKOTA: Riggs, CNAE, IX, 110, 113; Wissler, JAFL, XX, 122; Zitkala-Ša, p. 3; Hoffman, RBAE, XIV, 162, 203. PAWNEE: Dorsey, MAFLS, VIII, 265, No. 65; Dorsey, CI, LIX, 91. IOWA: Skinner, MS. cited in Skinner aud Satterlee, PaAM, XIII, 520. BLACKFOOT: Grinnell, *Blackfoot Lodge Tales*, pp. 158, 171. PIEGAN: Michelson, JAFL, XXIV, 247. ATSINA (GROS VENTRE): Curtis, V, 134; Kroeber, PaAM, I, 71, No. 14. ASSINIBOIN: Lowie, PaAM, IV, 111, 112, Nos. 15, 16. PLAINS CREE: Skinner, JAFL, XXIX, 349, No. 5. PLAINS OJIBWA: Skinner, JAFL, XXXII, 280. SWAMPY CREE: Cresswell, JAFL, XXXVI, 405. — **WDL. CENT.** CREE: Skinner, PaAM, IX, 83; Russell, p. 212; Hamilton, JAFL, VII, 202; Young, *Algonquin Indian Tales*, p. 215. TIMISKAMING ALGONQUIN: Speck, GSCan, IX, 9. OJIBWA: Schoolcraft, *Hiawatha*, p. 30; Schoolcraft, *Algic Researches*, II, 119; Hoffman, RBAE, XIV, 203; Radin, GSCan, II, 2, 7, 21; Jones-Michelson, PAES, VII (1), 101, 169, 409; Laidlaw, OAR, XVII, 71, 86; DeJong, *Original Odjibwe-Texts*, p. 23. MENOMINI: Skinner and Satterlee, PaAM, XIII, 266; Hoffman, RBAE, XIV, 162, 204. Fox: Jones, PAES, I, 279. KICKAPOO: Jones, PAES, IX, 17. — **WDL. N.E.** MICMAC: Rand, p. 263; Leland, p. 186 (also PASSAMAQUODDY). — **WDL. IROQ.** HURON-WYANDOT: Barbeau, GSCan, XI, 180, No. 57, and 192, No. 58. — **S.E.** CHEROKEE: Mooney, RBAE, XIX, 269, 449. CREEK:

Ibid., p. 449. CADDO: Dorsey, CI, XLI, 86, No. 52. — **S.W.** JICARILLA APACHE: Russell, JAFL, XI, 264; Goddard, PaAM, VIII, 230, No. 34; Mooney, AA, old ser., XI, 203. The incident has not been reported from any part of the Pacific Coast. — A closely related incident is:

(a) *Birds enticed into bag* (K711). — **PLNS.** PAWNEE: Dorsey, CI, LIX, 458. PONCA: Dorsey, CNAE, VI, 580. — **WDL. CENT.** Fox: Jones, PAES, I, 289. — **S.E.** BILOXI: Dorsey and Swanton, BBAE, XLVII, 30. CADDO: Dorsey, CI, XLI, 102, No. 65.

83. *Buttocks watcher* (D999, D1317.3). A trickster commands his buttocks to act as watchman while he sleeps. The tale usually represents the buttocks as talking. This occurs in substantially all the tales cited under *Hoodwinked dancers* in note 82, and does not occur independently. — KICKAPOO, Fox, MENOMINI, CREE, DAKOTA, GROS VENTRE, ARAPAHO, SAULTEAUX, OJIBWA, ASSINIBOIN, BLACKFOOT: Jones, PAES, IX, 132. — A closely related incident is:

(a) *Talking privates* (D998, D1610.3). A man is given advice by his private parts. — **PLNS.** SHOSHONI: Lowie, PaAM, I, 244, No. 3. SOUTHERN PAIUTE (SHIVWITS): Lowie, JAFL, XXXVII, 94, 95, 98. — Special varieties of this motif are:

(b) *Mentula loquens* (D998, D1610.3, H451). A man's member speaks and can be silenced only by his mother-in-law. — **PLNS.** CROW, ASSINIBOIN, PAWNEE, KIOWA APACHE: Lowie, PaAM, XXV, 225.

(c) *Talking excrements* (D1002, D1312.1). A man is given advice by his excrements. — References: Boas, RBAE, XXXI, 705; Boas, BBAE, LIX, 294.— **MACK.** KASKA: Teit, JAFL, XXX, 444, No. 5. — **PLAT.** CHILCOTIN, SHUSWAP, THOMPSON, LILLOOET, OKANAGON, FLATHEAD, NEZ PERCÉ: Boas, BBAE, LIX, 294. WISHRAM: Sapir, PAES, II, 101, No. 6. WASCO: Curtin, *Ibid.*, p. 267. — **N. PAC.** BELLA COOLA, RIVERS INLET, NEWETTEE, NOOTKA, COMOX: Boas, RBAE, XXXI, 705. TAHLTAN, CHINOOK, KATHLAMET, TAKELMA: Boas, BBAE, LIX, 294. TAHLTAN: Teit, JAFL, XXXII, 206. SNUQUALMI: Haeberlin, JAFL, XXXVII, 377. SNOHOMISH: *Ibid.*, p. 403. — **CAL.** KATO: Goddard, UCal, V, 216, No. 10. MAIDU: Dixon, PAES, IV, 35, No. 2, and 115, No. 4; Dixon, BAM, XVII, 84 No. 10. — **PLNS.** SHOSHONI: St. Clair, JAFL, XXII, 266. SOUTHERN UTE: Lowie, JAFL, XXXVII, 32, No. 17. — **WDL. CENT.** OJIBWA: Jones, PAES, VII (I), 459. — PEQUOT-MOHEGAN: Speck, JAFL, XVI, 105 (speaking excrements like objects in note 196, below).

(d) *Talking privates betray unchastity* (H451). — **WDL. N.E.** ABANAKI, PASAMAQUODDY: Leland, p. 206. MALECITE: Mechling, GSCan, IV, 86.

Cf. notes: 150, *Bodily members as advisers;* 196, *Magic objects impersonate fugitives;* 286, *Trickster's false creations fail him.*

84. *Sleeping trickster's feast stolen* (J2194). A regular sequel to the *Hoodwinked dancers* motif. For references, see note 82. — See in addition: **N. PAC.** COMOX, BELLA BELLA, TLINGIT, TSIMSHIAN: Jochelson, JE, VI, 376. — **PLAT.** SHUSWAP: *Ibid.* SANPOIL: Gould, MAFLS, XI, 104. — **CAL.** YOKUTS: Kroeber, UCal, IV, 235, No. 39. — **PLNS.** SOUTHERN UTE: Lowie, JAFL, XXXVII, 37, No. 21; 51, No. 25; 64, No. 35. SOUTHERN PAIUTE (SHIVWITS): *Ibid.*, p. 155, No. 19. —— KORYAK (SIBERIA): Jochelson, JE, VI, 376. — In the following Plateau tales the trickster's feast is stolen, but not while

he is asleep. LILLOOET: Teit, JAFL, xxv, 307. THOMPSON: Teit, JE, VIII, 310; Teit, MAFLS, XI, 7. SHUSWAP: Teit, JE, II, 683. KUTENAI: Boas, BBAE, LIX, 15, 65.

85. *Creaking limbs* (J1872). A man hears limbs creaking and goes to the tree to help them. He is caught between the limbs. — **MACK.** Cf. CHIPE-WYAN: Lowie, PaAM, x, 196. — **PLNS.** ARAPAHO: Dorsey and Kroeber, FM, v, 57, No. 24. CHEYENNE: Kroeber, JAFL, XIII, 165. DAKOTA: Wissler, JAFL, xx, 122; Zitkala-Ša, p. 3. PAWNEE: Dorsey, CI, LIX, 441, 442. PONCA: Dorsey, CNAE, VI, 67. PLAINS CREE: Skinner, JAFL, XXIX, 347, No. 2. PLAINS OJIBWA: Skinner, JAFL, XXXII, 288. — **WDL. CENT.** SAUK, SAULTEAUX, MISSISAUGA, OJIBWA, CREE, KICKAPOO: Jones, PAES, IX, 131. OJIBWA: Jones-Michelson, PAES, VII (I), 121, 161, 417. TIMAGAMI OJIBWA: Speck, GSCan, IX, 33. TIMISKAMING ALGONQUIN: *Ibid.*, p. 5. MENOMINI: Skinner and Satterlee, PaAM, XIII, 297. — In a closely parallel tale the trickster's feast is stolen while he magically sticks to a stone. — References: Boas, BBAE, LIX, 295 (**PLAT.** KUTENAI, SHUSWAP, THOMPSON. — **PLNS.** ASSINIBOIN).

86. *Trickster puts on buffalo skull* (J2152). The trickster, in order to obtain food, transforms himself and enters a buffalo skull. Then he resumes his own form and is caught. He goes to a river, enquiring his direction of various trees he encounters. He falls into the river and at last succeeds in breaking the skull. — **PLAT.** THOMPSON: Teit, MAFLS, XI, 33, 34. — **PLNS.** ARAPAHO: Dorsey and Kroeber, FM, v, 107. CROW: Lowie, PaAM, xxv, 22. BLACKFOOT: Wissler and Duvall, PaAM, II, 32; McClintock, p. 341. GROS VENTRE: Kroeber, PaAM, I, 68. ASSINIBOIN: Lowie, PaAM, IV, 116. — **WDL. CENT.** TIMAGAMI OJIBWA: Speck, GSCan, IX, 33. TIMISKAMING ALGONQUIN: *Ibid.*, p. 6. MISSISAUGA: Chamberlain, JAFL, v, 291. WINNE-BAGO: N. Curtis, *Indian Book*, p. 245. — The last part of the incident appears independently:

(a) *Blinded trickster directed by trees* (D1313.4). — In addition to the references above: **WDL. CENT.** MENOMINI, FOX, EASTERN CREE: Skinner and Satterlee, PaAM, XIII, 531. — **PLNS.** PLAINS CREE: *Ibid.* — **CAL.** PAVIOTSO: Lowie, JAFL, XXXVII, 222, No. 6. — **PLNS.** SOUTHERN UTE: Lowie, JAFL, XXXVII, 30, No. 17. — Analogous motifs follow:

(b) *Advice from magic object* (D1312). Cf. note 83, *Buttocks watcher; 83c, Talking excrements;* and 150, *Bodily members as advisers.* — **ESK.** WEST HUDSON BAY: Boas, BAM, xv, 312. — **PLAT.** CHILCOTIN: Farrand, JE, II, 16, No. 4. NEZ PERCÉ: Spinden, JAFL, XXI, 18. — **N. PAC.** BELLA COOLA: Boas, JE, I, 98. — **WDL. CENT.** FOX: Owen, PFLS, LI, 92. — **WDL. N.E.** MICMAC: Parsons, JAFL, XXXVIII, 64, No. 4; Michelson, JAFL, XXXVIII, p. 53. — **WDL. IROQ.** SENECA: Curtin-Hewitt, RBAE, XXXII, 588, No. 118, and 379, No. 69 (= Curtin, *Seneca Indian Myths*, p. 233). — **S.W.** SAN CARLOS APACHE: Goddard, PaAM, xxiv, 68.

(c) *Magic objects point out road* (D1313). — **MACK.** KASKA: Teit, JAFL, xxx, 447, No. 7. — **N. PAC.** TAHLTAN: Teit, JAFL, xxxiv, 347, No. 69. HAIDA: Swanton, BBAE, xxix, 335. — **CAL.** MIWOK: Barrett, UCal, xvi, 10, No. 7. YOKUTS: Kroeber, UCal, IV, 242, No. 40. — **WDL. IROQ.** SENECA: Curtin-Hewitt, RBAE, xxxii, 110, No. 12; Curtin, *Seneca Indian Myths*, p. 130. — **S.W.** NAVAHO: Matthews, MAFLS, v, 101.

87. *XXV. The Trickster's Great Fall and his Revenge.* The trickster is carried by birds and dropped. He then feigns death and catches the bird who has dropped him. For the first part, see note 80; for the second, note 88.

88. *Game caught by feigning death* (K751). — **ESK.** BERING STRAIT: Nelson, RBAE, xviii, 475. — **MACK.** KASKA: Teit, JAFL, xxx, 432, 441, No. 1. TS'ETS'ÁUT: Boas, JAFL, x, 45. — **PLAT.** SAHAPTIN: Farrand-Mayer, MAFLS, xi, 163, No. 9. — **N. PAC.** TAHLTAN: noted in Teit, JAFL, xxx, 432. SKAGIT: Haeberlin, JAFL, xxxvii, 390. — **CAL.** WISHOSK: Kroeber, JAFL, xviii, 103, No. 19. — **PLNS.** OMAHA, PLAINS OJIBWA, EASTERN DAKOTA, IOWA: Skinner and Satterlee, PaAM, xiii, 531. SOUTHERN UTE: Lowie, JAFL, xxxvii, 32, No. 18. KIOWA: Mooney, RBAE, xix, 449. OSAGE: Dorsey, FM, vii, 23, No. 18, and 24, No. 19. PAWNEE: Dorsey, CI, lix, 175, No. 46. SIOUX: Dorsey, *American Antiquarian* (1884), pp. 237 ff.; Emerson, *Indian Myths,* p. 411. CANADIAN DAKOTA: Wallis, JAFL, xxxvi, 87, No. 19. BLACKFOOT: Grinnell, *Blackfoot Lodge Tales,* p. 147. ASSINIBOIN: Lowie, PaAM, iv, 107, 146. PLAINS OJIBWA: Skinner, JAFL, xxxii, 282, 292. PLAINS CREE: Teit, JAFL, xxxiv, 321. — **WDL. CENT.** SAULTEAUX: Young, *Algonquin Indian Tales,* pp. 224 ff. OJIBWA: Radin, GSCan, ii, 19. MENOMINI: Skinner and Satterlee, PaAM, xiii, 421. MISSISAUGA: Chamberlain, JAFL, ii, 142. Fox: Jones, PAES, i, 131. KICKAPOO: Jones, PAES, ix, 11, No. 2. — **WDL. IROQ.** SENECA: Curtin-Hewitt, RBAE, xxxii, 229, No. 44 (= Curtin, *Seneca Indian Myths,* p. 243). HURON-WYANDOT: Barbeau, GSCan, xi, 193, No. 58. — **S.E.** CHEROKEE: Mooney, RBAE, xix, 293. YUCHI: Speck, UPa, i, 154, No. 21. CREEK: noted in Mooney, RBAE, xix, 449. — **S.W.** NAVAHO: Parsons, JAFL, xxxvi, 371, No. 8. SAN CARLOS APACHE: Goddard, PaAM, xxiv, 72 f. KERES: Parsons, JAFL, xxxvi, 230, No. 11. SIA: Stevenson, RBAE xi, 150.

89. *XXVI. The Deceived Blind Men* (K331.2). In many of the versions the blind persons who are deceived by the moving of the lines leading to the water are women. In some versions the hero causes them to fight by taking food from them and causing them to accuse each other. — **PLAT.** SECHELT, CHILCOTIN: Boas, RBAE, xxxi, 593. SHUSWAP: Teit, JE, ii, 711, No. 38. THOMPSON: Teit, MAFLS, vi, 23. WASCO: Curtin, PAES, ii, 294. — **N. PAC.** TSIMSHIAN, HAIDA, BELLA COOLA, KWAKIUTL, NOOTKA, COMOX, NANAIMO, CHEHALIS: Boas, *loc. cit.* TAKELMA: Sapir, UPa, ii, 38, No. 2. — **CAL.** PAVIOTSO: Lowie, JAFL, xxxvii, 238, No. 19. — **PLNS.** PONCA: Dorsey, CNAE, vi, 204. — **WDL. CENT.** OJIBWA: Radin, GSCan, ii, 80, No. 44. MENOMINI: Hoffman, RBAE, xiv, 211; Skinner and Satterlee, PaAM, xiii, 413. Fox: noted in *Ibid.,* p. 530. KICKAPOO: Jones, PAES, ix, 81, No. 10. WINNEBAGO: N. Curtis, *Indian Book,* p. 247. — **WDL. IROQ.** SENECA: Curtin-Hewitt, RBAE, xxxii, 448, No. 89.

90. *XXVII. The Trickster's Race* (K11.5). The trickster feigns lameness and receives handicap in a race. Then he returns and eats up the food which is the prize. — **PLNS.** SHOSHONI: Lowie, PaAM, ii, 274. CHEYENNE: Kroeber, JAFL, xiii, 168. BLACKFOOT: Grinnell, *Blackfoot Lodge Tales,* p. 156; Wissler and Duvall, PaAM, ii, 28; Maclean, JAFL, vi, 170. ATSINA: Curtis, v, 134. DAKOTA: Zitkala-Śa, p. 27. ASSINIBOIN: Lowie, PaAM, iv, 111 (notes to CREE). — **S.W.** SAN CARLOS APACHE: Goddard, PaAM, xxiv, 73. SIA: Stevenson, RBAE, xi, 149.

91. *Animals (or giants) enticed over precipice* (K894.1). — References: Boas, RBAE, xxxi, 704; Boas, BBAE, lix, 312. — **MACK.** Kaska: Teit, JAFL, xxx, 431. Ts'ets'ʌut: Boas, JAFL, x, 45. — **PLAT.** Kutenai: Boas, BBAE, lix, 269. Sanpoil: Gould, MAFLS, xi, 104. — **N. PAC.** Tlingit, Bella Coola, Rivers Inlet, Kwakiutl, Nootka, Comox: Boas, RBAE, xxxi, 704. Quileute: Farrand-Mayer, JAFL, xxxii, 271, No. 14. — **PLNS.** Shoshoni, Uintah Ute, Blackfoot: Boas, BBAE, lix, 312. Crow: Lowie, PaAM, xxv, 19; Simms, FM, ii, 27. Arapaho: Dorsey and Kroeber, FM, v, 61. Blackfoot: Wissler and Duvall, PaAM, ii, 27. Arikara: Dorsey, CI, xvii, 141, No. 54.

92. *XXVIII. The Eye-Juggler* (J2423). A trickster is given the power to throw his eyes into the air and replace them. He must not do this beyond a specified number of times. When he does so, he loses them. He usually gets animal eyes as substitutes. — References: Boas, BBAE, lix, 302, note 1. — **PLAT.** Shuswap, Thompson, Kutenai, Nez Percé: Boas, *loc. cit.* — **N. PAC.** Quileute: Farrand-Mayer, JAFL, xxxii, 265, No. 10. Snohomish: Haeberlin, JAFL, xxxvii, 407. — **CAL.** Paviotso: Lowie, JAFL, xxxvii, 221, No. 6. — **PLNS.** Shoshoni, Uintah Ute, Comanche, Arapaho, Cheyenne, Blackfoot, Gros Ventre, Assiniboin: Boas, *loc. cit.* Southern Ute: Lowie, JAFL, xxxvii, 26, No. 12. Southern Paiute (Shivwits): *Ibid.*, p. 108, No. 5. Dakota: Meeker, JAFL, xiv, 161. — **WDL. CENT.** Cree: Boas, *loc. cit.* Cf. Ojibwa: Hoffman, RBAE, vii, 280. — **WDL. N.E.** Montagnais: Speck, JAFL, xxxviii, 4 (substituted eyes). — **WDL. IROQ.** Seneca: Curtin-Hewitt, RBAE, xxxii, 81, No. 1 (substituted eyes). — **S.E.** Caddo: Dorsey, CI, xli, 103. — **S.W.** Navaho, Jicarilla Apache, Zuñi, Sia: Boas, *loc. cit.* San Carlos Apache: Goddard, PaAM, xxiv, 73. ——— Siberia: Jochelson, JE, vi, 375. South American Indian: Koch-Grünberg, No. 40.

93. *Tabu: using magic power too often* (C762.1). A frequent incident not only in connection with "The Eye-Juggler" but also with other tales, particularly with "The Sharpened Leg". See notes 92 and 95. — A few references are: **PLAT.** Thompson: Teit, MAFLS, xi, 6, No. 12. — **PLNS.** Pawnee: Grinnell, *Pawnee Hero Stories*, p. 93; Dorsey, CI, lix, 440, No. 124. Arapaho: Dorsey and Kroeber, FM, v, 111, No. 56. Piegan: Michelson, JAFL, xxix, 408. Plains Cree: Skinner, JAFL, xxix, 352. — **WDL. CENT.** Ojibwa: Jones-Michelson, PAES, vii (1), 49, 321; Carson, JAFL, xxx, 491, No. 3. — The well-known European motif of *Three wishes foolishly wasted* (J2071) appears in several Indian borrowings. See Thompson, CColl, ii, 454.

94. *Substituted eyes* (E781). In several of the references given in note 92 the central incident of the juggling with the eyes is lacking, but the use of substitute eyes appears. — See the following references in note 92: Quileute, Montagnais, Seneca, Siberia.

95. *XXIX. The Sharpened Leg* (J2424). Trickster is given the power of sharpening his leg without harm if he will use it but four times. He breaks the tabu and is left with his leg sticking in a tree. — **PLAT.** Thompson: Teit, MAFLS, xi, 46; Teit, JE, viii, 269. Shuswap: Boas, *Sagen*, p. 11. — **PLNS.** Arapaho: Dorsey and Kroeber, FM, v, 112, No. 57; 257, No. 108; 258, No. 109. Cheyenne: Kroeber, JAFL, xiii, 169. Blackfoot: Wissler and Duvall, PaAM, ii, 153, No. 9. Gros Ventre: Kroeber, PaAM, i, 87, No. 20. Assiniboin: Lowie, PaAM, iv, 118, 184, 186. — **WDL. IROQ.**

SENECA: Curtin-Hewitt, RBAE, XXXII, 283, No. 56. —— SOUTH AMERICA: Koch-Grünberg, p. 26, No. 7. SIBERIA (KORYAK): Jochelson, JE, VI, 375.

96. *XXX. The Offended Rolling Stone* (C61). A trickster gives his blanket to a stone. Later he goes back and takes the blanket. The stone is offended and chases him. At last, with the aid of helpful animals, the stone is destroyed. —References: Jones, PAES, IX, 130; Boas, BBAE, LIX, 295, note I.—In some of the variants the trickster offends the rock in other ways than by stealing the blanket.—ESK. LABRADOR: Turner, RBAE, XI, 337.—PLAT. THOMPSON, SHUSWAP, OKANAGON, NEZ PERCÉ: Boas, *loc. cit.* THOMPSON: Teit, MAFLS, XI, 10. FLATHEAD: McDermott, JAFL, XIV, 245.—PLNS. ASSINIBOIN, SHOSHONI: Boas, *loc. cit.* ARAPAHO, BLACKFOOT, GROS VENTRE, ARIKARA: Jones, *loc. cit.* SOUTHERN UTE: Lowie, JAFL, XXXVII, 25, No. 11. UINTAH UTE: Mason, JAFL, XXIII, 306, 307; Kroeber, JAFL, XIV, 261. CROW: Lowie, PaAM, XXV, 37. PAWNEE: Dorsey, CI, LIX, 446, No. 126; Dorsey, MAFLS, VIII, 260, No. 62. DAKOTA: Zitkala-Ša, p. 19.—WDL. CENT. CREE, KICKAPOO: Jones, *loc. cit.*—WDL. N.E. Cf. MICMAC: Rand, p. 316, No. 55. ABNAKI: Leland, p. 155.— S.W. NAVAHO: Matthews, MAFLS, V, 125. JICARILLA APACHE: Mooney, AA, old ser., XI, 197, 208. — Cf. note 238, *The Rolling Head.*

97. *XXXI. The Trickster kills the Children.* A trickster left at home by animals to guard their children kills the children and cooks them. When the mothers return they eat of their own children without knowing it. They chase the trickster, who escapes by a ruse. — PLNS. SHOSHONI: Lowie, PaAM, II, 248. SOUTHERN UTE: Lowie, JAFL, XXXVII, 56, No. 31. SOUTHERN PAIUTE: *Ibid.,* p. 169, No. 5a, and p. 171, No. 7. ARAPAHO: Dorsey and Kroeber, FM, V, 101, No. 49, and 103, No. 50. DAKOTA: Meeker, JAFL, XV, 84. BLACKFOOT: Wissler and Duvall, PaAM, II, 34. ASSINIBOIN: Lowie, PaAM, IV, 124, No. 36. GROS VENTRE: Kroeber, PaAM, I, 70. PONCA: Dorsey, CNAE, VI, 564. PLAINS OJIBWA: note in PaAM, XIII, 522. — WDL. CENT. WINNEBAGO, OJIBWA: Meeker, JAFL, XV, 84. MENOMINI: Skinner and Satterlee, PaAM, XIII, 298. — WDL. N.E. PASSAMAQUODDY: Prince, PAES, X, 79, No. 12.

98. *Relative's flesh unwittingly eaten* (G61). See all the references in note 97 and in note 226, *Bear-Woman and Deer-Woman.*—See also: ESK. GREENLAND: Holm, Nos. 43, 44. — MACK. KASKA: Teit, JAFL, XXX, 450, No. 8. — CAL. MIWOK: Gifford, UCal, XII, 298, No. 3.

99. *XXXII. Wildcat gets a New Face* (A2330.1). The trickster pushes in wildcat's face so that it is flat; hence all wildcats have flat faces. The story is given as an example of a purely explanatory tale. See note 4. — References: Boas, BBAE, LIX, 296, note 4.— MACK. CHIPEWYAN: Boas, *loc. cit.* — PLAT. SHUSWAP, THOMPSON, NEZ PERCÉ: *Ibid.* — N. PAC. TILLAMOOK: *Ibid.* — PLNS. SHOSHONI, UTE, BLACKFOOT: *Ibid.* SOUTHERN UTE: Lowie, JAFL, XXXVII, 38, No. 21. WICHITA: Dorsey, CI, XXI, 282. — S.W. NAVAHO: Parsons, JAFL, XXXVI, 369, No. 2.

100. *XXXIII. Trickster becomes a Dish* (D251). The hero transforms himself into a dish and thus secures part of the food placed on the dish. Later he assumes his own form and releases the salmon which have been kept from mankind. (For the latter incident, cf. note 44, *Theft of light by being swallowed and re-born,* and note 75, *Hoarded game.*) For the transformation to the dish to secure food, see:— PLAT. KUTENAI, SHUSWAP, THOMPSON,

OKANAGON, LILLOOET, SECHELT, SANPOIL, CŒUR D'ALÈNE, FLATHEAD, NEZ PERCÉ, WISHRAM: Boas, BBAE, LIX, 301.— **CAL.** HUPA: *Ibid.*— **S.E.** CADDO: *Ibid.*—**N. PAC.** SNOHOMISH: Haeberlin, JAFL, XXXVII, 403.

101. *Fish made from wood* (A2101). — References: Boas, RBAE, XXXI, 666, 822. — **ESK.** LABRADOR: Turner, RBAE, XI, 261. WEST HUDSON BAY: Boas, RBAE, V, 617. KODIAK: Golder, JAFL, XVI, 95. GREENLAND, POINT BARROW: noted in Boas, BAM, XV, 361. — **MACK.** KASKA: Teit, JAFL, XXX, 452, No. 10. — **PLAT.** THOMPSON: Teit, JE, VIII, 272. — **N. PAC.** BELLA COOLA, RIVERS INLET, NEWETTEE: Boas, RBAE, XXXI, 666 (salmon). HAIDA, NASS, TLINGIT, TSIMSHIAN, COMOX, LKUÑGEN, NEWETTEE, NISQUALLY, QUINAULT: *Ibid.*, p. 822 (whales). TAHLTAN: Teit, JAFL, XXXII, 236, No. 13.—**CAL.** KAROK: Powers, CNAE, III, 37.—— For Siberian comparisons, see Jochelson, JE, VI, 380.

102. *XXXIV. Coyote proves himself a Cannibal (Vomit-exchange)* (K1721). — **PLAT.** SHUSWAP: Boas, *Sagen*, p. 9; Dawson, *Trans. Royal Society of Canada* (1892), p. 29; Teit, JE, II, 632. THOMPSON: Teit, MAFLS, VI, 30; Teit, JE, VIII, 300); Hill-Tout, FL, X, 206.—**S.W.** NAVAHO: Matthews, MAFLS, V, 227. JICARILLA APACHE: Goddard, PaAM, VIII, 225, No. 27. —— SIBERIA: Jochelson, JE, VI, 368.

103. *XXXV. The Bungling Host* (J2425). The trickster visits various animals who display their peculiar powers in obtaining food. He returns the invitation and tries to provide food in similar ways. He fails and usually has a narrow escape from death. The incident has been studied with minute analysis by Boas, RBAE, XXXI, 694 ff. It appears in several types, each of which has a definite area of distribution. Professor Boas recognizes the following incidents: (*a*) the host lets oil drip out of his hands — **N. PAC., PLAT.**; (*b*) birds produce food by their song — **N. PAC., PLAT.**; (*c*) birds produce salmon eggs by striking the ankle — **N. PAC., PLAT.**; (*d*) an animal cuts its hands or feet — **PLAT., N. PAC., PLNS., WDL. CENT., WDL. N.E., S.E., S.W.**; (*e*) animals stab or shoot themselves — **PLAT., N. PAC., PLNS., WDL. CENT., S.E.**; (*f*) wood transformed into meat — **PLAT., N. PAC., PLNS., S.W.**; (*g*) the host obtains food by killing his children — **N. PAC., PLNS., WDL. CENT.**; (*h*) diving for fish — **PLAT., N. PAC., PLNS., WDL. CENT., WDL. N.E.**; (*i*) miscellaneous incidents scattered over the continent. — In the following tribal list the references, unless otherwise indicated, are to Boas, *loc. cit.*— **PLAT.** CHILCOTIN, SHUSWAP, THOMPSON, UTAMQT, LILLOOET, SECHELT, KUTENAI, WASCO, WISHRAM. NEZ PERCÉ: Farrand-Mayer, MAFLS, XI, 164; Spinden, MAFLS, XI 181. KUTENAI: Boas, BBAE, LIX, 8. — **N. PAC.** TLINGIT, HAIDA, TSIMSHIAN, NASS, BELLA COOLA, BELLA BELLA, KWAKIUTL, NEWETTEE, COMOX, NOOTKA, SQUAMISH, CHEHALIS, LKUÑGEN, CHINOOK, QUINAULT. QUILEUTE: Farrand-Mayer, JAFL, XXXII, 259, No. 6. TAHLTAN: Teit, JAFL, XXXII, 220. — **PLNS.** SHOSHONI, UTE, WICHITA, ARAPAHO, PONCA, CROW. SOUTHERN PAIUTE (MAOPA): Lowie, JAFL, XXXVII, 172, No. 8. SOUTHERN UTE: *Ibid.*, pp. 19, 20, 23, No. 9, and p. 56, No. 31. OSAGE: Dorsey, FM, VII, 13, 15. CROW: Lowie, PaAM, XXV, 38. CANADIAN DAKOTA: Wallis, JAFL, XXXVI, 90, No. 21. ASSINIBOIN: Lowie, PaAM, IV, 128. PIEGAN: Michelson, JAFL, XXX, 494. — **WDL. CENT.** OJIBWA, FOX, KICKAPOO. MENOMINI: Skinner and Satterlee, PaAM, XIII, 278, 282, 284, 286. WINNEBAGO: noted in *Ibid.*, p. 521. PEORIA: Michelson, JAFL, XXX, 494. — **WDL. N.E.** MICMAC,

PENOBSCOT. MICMAC: Parsons, JAFL, XXXVIII, 83, No. 15. MONTAGNAIS: Speck, JAFL, XXXVIII, 10.—**WDL. IROQ.** SENECA: noted in Skinner and Satterlee, PaAM, XIII, 521.—**S.E.** CHEROKEE, YUCHI, ALABAMA, NATCHEZ, HITCHITI, BILOXI, CADDO. CATAWBA: Radin, JAFL, XXIV, 321, No. 1.—**S.W.** NAVAHO, JICARILLA APACHE, HOPI, CORA. ZUÑI: Handy, JAFL, XXXI, 459. NAVAHO: Parsons, JAFL, XXXVI, 369, No. 2.——Siberian relations: Jochelson, JE, VI, 379 (and for incident *a*), 376.— Cf. note 271, *Death by foolish imitation.*

104. *XXXVI. Coyote and Porcupine.* The tale has two rather distinct parts: (*a*) Porcupine kills the buffalo by climbing into his paunch as they cross a stream (K952.1) and (*b*) Coyote cheats porcupine of his prize in a jumping game (K17); the latter retaliates by killing coyote's children.— References: Boas, BBAE, LIX, 305.—**PLAT.** SHUSWAP, THOMPSON, CHILCOTIN, OKANAGON, SANPOIL, NEZ PERCÉ, KUTENAI: Boas, *loc. cit.*—**CAL.** MODOC: Curtin, *Myths of the Modocs*, p. 272. MAIDU: Dixon, BAM, XVII, 83, No. 10. —**PLNS.** SHOSHONI, UTE, WICHITA, OSAGE, PAWNEE, ASSINIBOIN: Boas, *loc. cit.* SOUTHERN PAIUTE (SHIVWITS): Lowie, JAFL, XXXVII, 119, No. 9. SOUTHERN UTE: *Ibid.*, p. 30, No. 17. CROW: Lowie, PaAM, XXV, 34. DAKOTA: Zitkala-Ša, p. 103.—**S.W.** JICARILLA APACHE: Boas, *loc. cit.*—Cf. note 159, *Monster killed from within.*

105. *Unresponsive corpse* (K2152). The incident occurs in most tales of this type.— See also: **MACK.** ANVIK: Chapman, PAES, VI, 48, No. 6.— **WDL. CENT.** OJIBWA: Schoolcraft, *Hiawatha*, p. 246; Jones-Michelson, PAES, VII (II), 441, No. 51. — **WDL. N.E.** NASKAPI: Speck, JAFL, XXXVIII, 25.— **S.W.** ZUÑI: Cushing, p. 255.— Also European.

106. *XXXVII. Beaver and Porcupine* (K896). Beaver carries porcupine to the center of a lake and leaves him there. Porcupine causes the lake to freeze and escapes. He retaliates by taking beaver to the top of a tree. — **MACK.** TS'ETS'ÁUT, HARE: Boas, RBAE, XXXI, 724.—**PLAT.** SHUSWAP: *Ibid.*—**N. PAC.** TLINGIT, HAIDA, TSIMSHIAN, NASS: *Ibid.* TAHLTAN: Teit, JAFL, XXXII, 245, No. 26.—**S.W.** JICARILLA APACHE: Boas, *loc. cit.* NAVAHO: Parsons, JAFL, XXVI, 370, No. 4.

107. *Porcupine as controller of cold* (D2155.1). A central idea in all these tales. See Boas, RBAE, XXXI, 724.— For the same idea in a Northeastern tribe, see MICMAC: Speck, JAFL, XXVIII, 63.

108. *XXXVIII. Big Turtle's War Party.* Two distinct parts: (*a*) Turtle takes various unusual companions with him on the war-path and they get into trouble (F1027); (*b*) When caught, turtle professes to fear no punishment except drowning. The following contain both parts of the tale: — References: Jones, PAES, IX, 133; Skinner and Satterlee, PaAM, XIII, 529. — **PLNS.** OSAGE, ARAPAHO, SKIDI PAWNEE, PAWNEE, PONCA, CHEYENNE, BLACKFOOT, OGLALA: Jones, *loc. cit.* WICHITA, PLAINS OJIBWA: Skinner and Satterlee, *loc. cit.* DAKOTA: Wissler, JAFL, XX, 126; Zitkala-Ša, p. 159.—**WDL. CENT.** KICKAPOO, OJIBWA: Jones, *loc. cit.* MENOMINI: Skinner and Satterlee, *op. cit.*, p. 392. PEORIA: Michelson, JAFL, XXX, 495. — **WDL. IROQ.** IROQUOIS: Skinner and Satterlee, PaAM, XIII, 529. SENECA: Curtin-Hewitt, RBAE, XXXII, 92; Curtin, *Seneca Indian Myths*, p. 410.—**S.E.** CHEROKEE: Mooney, RBAE, XIX, 278.——The second part, *Drowning punishment for turtle* (K581), appears independently. — Aside from references given above, see: References: Boas, BBAE, LIX, 305, note 2.—**PLAT.** OKANAGON: Boas, *loc. cit.*—**N. PAC.**

TLINGIT: Swanton, BBAE, XXXIX, 251, No. 88. — **PLNS.** BLACKFOOT: Boas, *loc. cit.* — **WDL. N.E.** MICMAC, PASSAMAQUODDY: *Ibid.* PASSAMAQUODDY: Prince, PAES, X, 45, No. 9. MALECITE: Jack, JAFL, VIII, 197. — **S.E.** CHEROKEE, NATCHEZ, BILOXI: Boas, *loc. cit.* — **S.W.** HOPI, LAGUNA: *Ibid.* —— The second part has large foreign affinities. CELEBES, PHILIPPINE, VISAYAN, CEYLON, BURMESE, CHINESE, ANGOLA, NORTH AMERICAN NEGRO: Boas, *loc. cit.* — See also Thompson, CColl, II, 440; Dähnhardt, *Natursagen*, IV, 229.

109. Aside from the trickster incidents included in this volume the following are frequently met in American Indian tales:

(*a*) *Trickster pollutes nest and brood of bird* (K932). — **PLNS.** SOUTHERN UTE: Lowie, JAFL, XXXVII, 25, No. 11. PLAINS OJIBWA: Skinner, JAFL, XXXII, 281. — **WDL. CENT.** OJIBWA: Jones, PAES, VII (1), 41, 187; (TIMAGAMI): Speck, GSCan, IX, 33. TIMISKAMING ALGONQUIN: *Ibid.*, p. 13.

(*b*) *Trickster frightens people from food and eats it himself* (K335). — References: Boas, RBAE, XXXI, 941. — **PLAT.** LILLOOET: Boas, *loc. cit.* — **N. PAC.** TLINGIT, HAIDA, TSIMSHIAN, BELLA COOLA, RIVERS INLET, NEWETTEE, COMOX, NOOTKA: *Ibid.* KATHLAMET: Boas, BBAE, XXVI, 75. —— SIBERIA: Jochelson, JE, VI, 378.

(*c*) *Trickster poses as helper and eats women's stored provisions* (K1983). — References: Jochelson, JE, VI, 374; Boas, RBAE, XXXI, 705. — **PLAT.** LILLOOET: Boas, *loc. cit.* — **N. PAC.** BELLA COOLA, RIVERS INLET, NEWETTEE, NOOTKA, COMOX: *Ibid.* —— SIBERIA: Jochelson, *loc. cit.*

(*d*) *Trickster shams death and eats grave offerings* (K1867). — References: Boas, RBAE, XXXI, 706. — **PLAT.** CHILCOTIN: Boas, *loc. cit.* — **N. PAC.** KWAKIUTL, COMOX, CHEHALIS: *Ibid.* —— SIBERIA: Jochelson, JE, VI, 376.

(*e*) *Killed game revives and flees away from killers* (E161). — References: Jochelson, JE, VI, 378 (**MACK.** HARE, TS'ETS'ÁUT. — **PLAT.** CHILCOTIN. —— SIBERIA).

(*f*) *Person frightened into falling down cliff* (J2611). — References: Boas, BBAE, LIX, 293. — **PLAT.** SHUSWAP, LILLOOET, OKANAGON, PEND D'OREILLES, SANPOIL, KUTENAI: Boas, *loc. cit.* — **PLNS.** PAWNEE, ASSINIBOIN: *Ibid.* CROW: Lowie, PaAM, XXV, 48. CREE: Russell, p. 211. — **WDL. CENT.** OJIBWA: Boas, *loc. cit.*

(*g*) *Forgetting by stumbling* (D2006). Trickster stumbles and forgets what he was trying to remember. — **PLNS.** CROW: Lowie, PaAM, XXV, 125. — **WDL. IROQ.** SENECA: Curtin-Hewitt, RBAE, XXXII, 588, No. 118. — **S.E.** CHITIMACHA: Swanton, JAFL, XXX, 476. — **S.W.** ZUÑI: Parsons, JAFL, XXXI, 222, No. 6; Cushing, pp. 255 ff. ACOMA: Parsons, JAFL, XXXI, 225, No. 7. HOPI: Voth, FM, VIII, 67, 68; Lummis, *Pueblo Indian Folk-Stories*, pp. 84–86.

(*h*) *Trickster eats medicines that physic him* (J2153). — **PLNS.** CROW, WICHITA, PAWNEE, ARIKARA, ASSINIBOIN, EASTERN DAKOTA: Skinner and Satterlee, PaAM, XIII, 522. — **WDL. CENT.** MENOMINI, FOX: *Ibid.* OJIBWA: Jones, PAES, VII (1), 23, 113.

(*i*) *Magic self-returning robe* (D1052). Trickster steals a magic robe (or moccasins) that always returns to the owner. — **PLNS.** CROW: Lowie, PaAM, XXV, 21 (also KUTENAI noted). BLACKFOOT: Wissler and Duvall, PaAM, II, 31; McClintock, p. 347. — **WDL. CENT.** FOX: Jones, PAES, I, 309.

(*j*) *Trickster tells lies to fishes and causes them to fight* (K1084). — **PLNS.** ASSINIBOIN: Lowie, PaAM, IV, 110. — **WDL. CENT.** OJIBWA: Jones-Michelson, PAES, VII (II), 127, No. 9. MENOMINI: Skinner and Satterlee, PaAM, XIII, 405.

(*k*) *Trickster eats scratch-berries* (J2154). In spite of warning, trickster eats scratch-berries, which cause extraordinary itching. The incident is often followed by the next given. — References: Lowie, PaAM, XXV, 47. — **PLNS.** CROW, WICHITA, PAWNEE, ARIKARA, GROS VENTRE, ASSINIBOIN: Lowie, *loc. cit.* — **WDL. CENT.** CREE: *Ibid.* — **WDL. N.E.** PASSAMAQUODDY: Prince, PAES, X, 81, No. 12. ABNAKI: Leland, p. 85.

(*l*) *Trickster's burnt (or scratched) flesh becomes gum on trees* (A2731.1). — References: Lowie, PaAM, IV, 127. The parallels there cited are not all very close. — **MACK.** LOUCHEUX: Camsell-Barbeau, JAFL, XXXVIII, 256, No. 11. — **PLNS.** CROW, WICHITA, PAWNEE, ARAPAHO, CHEYENNE, GROS VENTRE, ASSINIBOIN: Lowie, *loc. cit.* — **WDL. CENT.** CREE, FOX: *Ibid.* OJIBWA: Laidlaw, OAR, XXVII, 87 and XXX, 89; Laidlaw, 1918 reprint OAR, p. 68; Radin, GSCan, II, 8. TIMISKAMING ALGONQUIN: Speck, GSCan, IX, 10.

(*m*) *Disintegration: a man eats himself up or dismembers himself* (F1035, G51.1). Usually the head retains the power of locomotion. Cf. note 238, *Rolling Head.* — References: Waterman, JAFL, XXVII, 44 (s.v., *Disintegration*). — **PLAT.** KUTENAI: Boas, BBAE, LIX, 26. WASCO: Curtin, PAES, II, 246. — **N. PAC.** BELLA COOLA, KWAKIUTL: Waterman, *loc. cit.* ALSEA: Frachtenberg, BBAE, LXVII, 191, No. 17. MOLALA: *Ibid.*, p. 190. TAKELMA: Sapir, UPa, II, 91. — **CAL.** YANA: Waterman, *loc. cit.* MAIDU: Dixon, PAES, IV, 189, No. 11; Dixon, BAM, XVII, 37. — **PLNS.** BLACKFOOT: Wissler and Duvall, PaAM, II, 143. — **WDL. CENT.** OJIBWA: Jones-Michelson, PAES, VII (II), 123, No. 7. — **WDL. IROQ.** SENECA: Curtin-Hewitt, RBAE, XXXII, 464, No. 100. The Ojibwa and Seneca tales have merely the eating of the person's own flesh, not the *disintegration* motif.

(*n*) *Trickster poses as woman and marries man* (K1321.1). — **ESK.** CUMBERLAND SOUND: Boas, BAM, XVII, 248 f. — **N. PAC.** TLINGIT, HAIDA, TSIMSHIAN: Boas, RBAE, XXXI, 692. CHEHALIS: Boas, *Sagen*, p. 28. COOS: Frachtenberg, CU, I, 153, No. 24. — **PLAT.** NEZ PERCÉ: Spinden, MAFLS, XI, 184, No. 3. OKANAGON: Teit, MAFLS, XI, 75. — **CAL.** WAPPO: Radin, UCal, XIX, 85, No. 10. WESTERN MONO: Gifford, JAFL, XXXVI, 344, No. 17. PAVIOTSO: Lowie, JAFL, XXXVII, 213, No. 3. — **PLNS.** ARAPAHO, DAKOTA: Dorsey and Kroeber, FM, V, 135. CROW: Lowie, PaAM, XXV, 142. SOUTHERN PAIUTE: Lowie, JAFL, XXXVII, 177. — **WDL. CENT.** OJIBWA: Jones-Michelson, PAES, VII (I), 139. MENOMINI: Skinner and Satterlee, PaAM, XIII, 263, 303. — **WDL. N.E.** MICMAC: Speck, JAFL, XXVIII, 67. PASSAMAQUODDY: Prince, PAES, X, 21, No. 2, and 75, No. 12. —— SIBERIA: Jochelson, JE, VI, 366, cf. 382.

(*o*) *Trickster has tree as wife* (T471). — **ESK.** Jochelson, JE, VI, 367. — **PLAT.** THOMPSON, UTAMQT, LILLOOET, SHUSWAP: Boas, RBAE, XXXI, 609. — **N. PAC.** CHEHALIS: *Ibid.* —— SIBERIA: Jochelson, *loc. cit.*

(*p*) *Lecherous father* (T411.1). A trickster seduces his own daughter by deception, usually by feigning death and returning in disguise. — **MACK.** HARE: Petitot, p. 219. — **PLAT.** CHILCOTIN: Farrand, JE, II, 17. SHUSWAP: Teit, JE, II, 639. OKANAGON: Teit, MAFLS, XI, 72. WISHRAM: Sapir, PAES, II, 105. — **N. PAC.** KWAKIUTL, COMOX, CHEHALIS: Boas, RBAE,

XXXI, 586, No. 28. — **CAL.** SINKYONE: Kroeber, JAFL, XXXII, 348, No. 8 (YUROK and KAROK references). MAIDU: Dixon, PAES, IV, 97, No. 3; Dixon, JAFL, XIII, 270. WESTERN MONO: Gifford, JAFL, XXXVI, 341 f., Nos. 13, 14. CAHUILLA: Hooper, UCal, XVI, 322.— **PLNS.** SHOSHONI, UTE, PAWNEE, GROS VENTRE, ASSINIBOIN: Lowie, PaAM, XXV, 41. ARAPAHO: Dorsey and Kroeber, FM, V, 82. SOUTHERN PAIUTE (MAOPA): Lowie, JAFL, XXXVII, 172. SOUTHERN UTE: *Ibid.*, p. 28, No. 15. PLAINS CREE: Skinner, JAFL, XXIX, 350. CANADIAN DAKOTA: Wallis, JAFL, XXXVI, 92, No. 23. — **WDL. CENT.** Cf. OJIBWA: Jones-Michelson PAES, VII (I), 279 ff. and (II), 463. PEORIA: Michelson, JAFL, XXX, 494. — **WDL. IROQ.** Cf. SENECA: Curtin-Hewitt, RBAE, XXXII, 285.

(*q*) *Lecherous brother* (T415.1). Seduces sister by suggesting deceptive remedy for burned groins, usually sitting on a certain plant. — **MACK.** LOUCHEUX: Boas, RBAE, XXXI, 706.— **PLAT.** CHILCOTIN: *Ibid.* — **N. PAC.** HAIDA, BELLA COOLA, RIVERS INLET, NEWETTEE, KWAKIUTL, NOOTKA, COMOX: *Ibid.* TAHLTAN: Teit, JAFL, XXXII, 207. — Closely related is:

(*r*) *Seduction by sham doctor* (K1315). — **PLAT.** THOMPSON, SHUSWAP, WISHRAM: Boas, RBAE, XXXI, 722.— **N. PAC.** TSIMSHIAN, KWAKIUTL, TILLAMOOK, CHEHALIS: *Ibid.*— **CAL.** MAIDU: Dixon, PAES, IV, 73, No. 3. ——SIBERIA: Jochelson, JE, VI, 373.

(*s*) *Lecherous son-in-law* (T417). Sleeps with mother-in-law by trickery, usually on a camping trip. — **CAL.** JOSHUA: Farrand-Frachtenberg, JAFL, XXVIII, 233, No. 18. MAIDU: Dixon, PAES, IV, 69, No. 3. YANA: Sapir, UCal, IX, 103, 112. — **PLNS.** SOUTHERN PAIUTE (MAOPA): Lowie, JAFL, XXXVII, 172, No. 9. CROW: Lowie, PaAM, XXV, 49. ARAPAHO: Dorsey and Kroeber, FM, V, 75, 77, Nos. 39, 40.

(*t*) *Death feigned to meet paramour* (K1539). A woman feigns death in order to meet paramour in the grave-box. In some cases the son of this union is the culture hero.— **PLAT.** WASCO: Curtin, PAES, II, 242.— **N. PAC.** TSIMSHIAN, NASS, TLINGIT, HAIDA: Boas, RBAE, XXXI, 781. TAHLTAN: Teit, JAFL, XXXIV, 243, No. 48.

(*u*) *Long-distance sexual intercourse* (K1391). A trickster has connection with a woman on the opposite side of a stream. — References: Teit, MAFLS, XI, 71. — **MACK.** KASKA: Teit, JAFL, XXX, 444, No. 5. — **PLAT.** SHUSWAP: Teit, JE, II, 741. THOMPSON: Teit, JE, VIII, 206. WISHRAM: Sapir, PAES, II, 11. OKANAGON: Teit, MAFLS, XI, 71. NEZ PERCÉ: Spinden, MAFLS, XI, 189.— **N. PAC.** FRASER: Boas, *Sagen*, p. 26. COMOX: *Ibid.*, p. 73. NOOTKA: *Ibid.*, p. 108. NEWETTEE: *Ibid.*, p. 172. TILLAMOOK: Boas, JAFL, XI, 140. SKAGIT: Haeberlin, JAFL, XXXVII, 393. ALSEA, MOLALA, KALAPUYA: noted in Frachtenberg, JAFL, XXVIII, 223. — **CAL.** SHASTA: Farrand-Frachtenberg, JAFL, XXVIII, 222, No. 15. TUTUTUNI: *Ibid.*, p. 242, No. 21. Cf. PAVIOTSO: Lowie, JAFL, XXXVII, 233, No. 12 (removable vulva). — **PLNS.** ARAPHO, BLACKFOOT, GROS VENTRE, ASSINIBOIN: Teit, MAFLS, XI, 71. CREE: Skinner, JAFL, XXIX, 351.— **WDL. CENT.** PEORIA, POTAWATOMI: Michelson, JAFL, XXX, 494. Cf. CHILCOTIN: Farrand, JE, II, 19, No. 7 (like PAVIOTSO).

(*v*) *Transformation to seduce women* (D658). — **PLAT.** SHUSWAP: Teit, JE, II, 734. CHILCOTIN: Farrand, JE, II, 17, No. 5. — **N. PAC.** HAIDA: Boas, RBAE, XXXI, 710, No. 42. TILLAMOOK: Boas, JAFL, XI, 145. — **CAL.** KATO: Goddard, UCal, V, 219, No. 15. MAIDU: Dixon, BAM, XVII, 89.

Yokuts: Kroeber, UCal, IV, 223, No. 31. — **PLNS.** Gros Ventre: Kroeber, PaAM, I, 68, No. 7.

(*w*) *Trickster and girls play obscene tricks on one another* (K1392). — **PLNS.** Crow: Lowie, PaAM, XXV, 43; Simms, FM, II, 284. Blackfoot: Wissler and Duvall, PaAM, II, 35.

(*x*) *The stolen harpoon* (D657.1). Trickster transforms himself into a fish in order to steal valuable harpoon or fishhook. — References: Boas, RBAE, XXXI, 606, No. 67.—**MACK.** Loucheux: Boas, *loc. cit.* Kaska: Teit, JAFL, XXX, 434, No. 1.—**PLAT.** Chilcotin, Shuswap, Thompson: Boas, *loc. cit.* —**N. PAC.** Tlingit, Haida, Bella Coola, Kwakiutl, Comox, Fraser Delta: *Ibid.* —— Siberia: Jochelson, JE, VI, 372.

(*y*) *Trickster caught on fishhook* (J2138). Trickster steals bait from fish-hooks and is caught and injured. — **N. PAC.** Tsimshian, Nass, Tlingit, Haida, Newettee: Boas, RBAE, XXXI, 684. Tahltan: Teit, JAFL, XXXI, 684. Cf. Quileute: Farrand-Mayer, JAFL, XXXII, 252, No. 1.—**MACK.** Loucheux: Russell, JAFL, XIII, 15. —— Siberia: Jochelson, JE, VI, 371.

(*z*) *Magic provider destroyed* (*goose that laid the golden egg*) (D876). References fragmentary. — **PLAT.** Sanpoil: Gould, MAFLS, XI, 103. Sahaptin: Farrand-Mayer, MAFLS, XI, 170. Nez Percé: Spinden, MAFLS, XI, 184.—**WDL. IROQ.** Seneca: Curtin-Hewitt, RBAE, XXXII, 149, No. 24, and 579, No. 117.

(*aa*) *Cormorant's tongue pulled out by putting louse on it* (K825).—**N. PAC.** Tsimshian, Nass, Tlingit, Haida, Bella Coola, Newettee, Kwakiutl, Nootka: Boas, RBAE, XXXI, 678. Tahltan: Teit, JAFL, XXXII, 223.—— Siberia: Boas, JAFL, XXXII, 679; Dähnhardt: *Natursagen*, III, 28.

(*bb*) *Coyote wears fox's rattle; caught in brush and injured* (J2155). — References: Teit, MAFLS, XI, 8 (**PLAT.** Thompson, Shuswap. — **CAL.** Maidu, Hupa.)

(*cc*) *False plea* (K550). A captive gets long respite by a false plea and escapes. A worldwide motif. — **ESK.** Cumberland Sound, West Hudson Bay, Norton Bay: Boas, BAM, XV, 360 (s.v., *Owl and Lemming*).— **MACK.** Lower Yukon: Chapman, JAFL, XVI, 181, No. 1. — **PLAT.** Sechelt: Farrand-Mayer, JAFL, XXXII, 254.— **N. PAC.** Kwakiutl, Nootka, Squamish, Comox, Quileute: *Ibid.* Nootka: Swan, *Smithsonian Contributions to Knowledge*, XIV, 65. — **S.E.** Catawba: Radin, JAFL, XXIV, 329, No. 3.— **S.W.** Navaho: Parsons, JAFL, XXXVI, 372. Keres: *Ibid.*, p. 230. San Carlos Apache: Goddard, PaAM, XXIV, 14. —— Siberia: Jochelson, JE, VI, 363.— Cf. tale No. LXXI in this collection.

(*dd*) *Trickster joins bulrushes in a dance* (J1883). He thinks waving bul-rushes are dancing, joins them, and dances until exhausted. — **PLNS.** Plains Ojibwa: Skinner, JAFL, XXXII, 289. — **WDL. CENT.** Ojibwa: Jones-Michelson, PAES, VII (1), 45.

(*ee*) *Scratching contest* (K83). — **PLNS.** Shoshoni: Lowie, PaAM, II, 258. Uintah Ute: Mason, JAFL, XXIII, 305. — **WDL. CENT.** Menomini: Skinner and Satterlee, PaAM, XIII, 407. — **S.W.** Navaho: Parsons, JAFL, XXXVI, 369, No. 3.

110. *Hero Tales.* For a general discussion of this well-defined series of tales, see Lowie, "The Test-theme in North American Mythology," JAFL, XXI, 97–148, and Boas, RBAE, XXXI, 794–816. Examples have been chosen with a view to illustrating the principal types. —— The cycle has affinities with

Asiatic and European tales. For references, see Lowie, JAFL, XXI, 147 (CHUCKCHEE, YUKAGHIR, KORYAK, JAPANESE, MONGOLIAN, FINNISH, SAMOAN, GERMAN). — Cf. tale LXXXII in this collection (note 293).

III. *XXXIX. The Sun tests his Son-in-law.* A youth goes to the land of the sun (or sky-chief) and marries the sun's daughter. He is submitted to tests by his father-in-law. General discussion: Boas, RBAE, XXXI, 797. For analysis, see the following notes.

112. *Supernatural growth* (T615). — **ESK.** SIBERIA: Jochelson, JE, VI, 364. — **MACK.** LOUCHEUX: Petitot, p. 16. CHIPEWYAN: Lowie, PaAM, X, 218. — **PLAT.** WISHRAM: Curtis, VIII, 116. WASCO: Curtin, PAES, II, 254. — **N. PAC.** BELLA COOLA: Boas, JE, I, 74, 95. KWAKIUTL: Boas and Hunt, JE, III, 180. HAIDA: Swanton, JE, V, 189. SNOHOMISH: Haeberlin, JAFL, XXXVII, 406. COOS: Frachtenberg, CU, I, 61. — **CAL.** MODOC: Curtin, *Myths of the Modocs,* pp. 17, 95 ff. YANA: Sapir, UCal, IX, 18, No. 1; Curtin, *Creation Myths,* p. 349. HUPA: Goddard, UCal, I, 188, No. 9. WAPPO: Radin, UCal, XIX, 133, No. 11; H. R. Kroeber, JAFL, XXI, 322. MAIDU: Powers, CNAE, III, 300. YOKUTS: Kroeber, UCal, IV, 207, No. 14. — **PLNS.** SOUTHERN PAIUTE (SHIVWITS): Lowie, JAFL, XXXVII, 125, No. 11, and 139, No. 14; (MAOPA): *Ibid.,* p. 185, No. 19, and p. 192, No. 22. WICHITA: Dorsey, JAFL, XV, 227. ARAPAHO: Dorsey and Swanton, FM, V, 14, No. 6. DAKOTA: Zitkala-Ša, p. 145. BLACKFOOT: Wissler and Duvall, PaAM, II, 121. GROS VENTRE: Kroeber, PaAM, I, 98, No. 23; Curtis, V, 127. ASSINIBOIN: Lowie, PaAM, IV, 136. — **WDL. CENT.** WINNEBAGO: Radin, JAFL, XXII, 295. — **WDL. N.E.** NASKAPI: Speck, JAFL, XXXVIII, 24. MALECITE: Mechling, GSCan, IV, 52, No. 8. — **WDL. IROQ.** ONONDAGA: Hewitt, RBAE, XXI, 186. MOHAWK: *Ibid.,* p. 297. Cf. SENECA: Curtin-Hewitt, RBAE, XXXII, 616, No. 119. — **S.W.** NAVAHO: Matthews, MAFLS, V, 70, 106. ZUÑI: Cushing, pp. 65, 134, 171.

113. *Snapping door* (K736). — **PLAT.** THOMPSON: Teit, MAFLS, XI, 22, No. 10, and VI, 46. — **N. PAC.** NASS, BELLA BELLA, BELLA COOLA, KWAKIUTL, NEWETTEE, RIVERS INLET, NOOTKA, COMOX, SQUAMISH, TILLAMOOK: Boas, RBAE, XXXI, 797. TSIMSHIAN: Boas, BBAE, XXVII, 129. — An analogous theme is:

(*a*) *Guardian animals evaded* (B576.1.1). Animals which act as guardians or sentinels are evaded by the hero. — **PLAT.** THOMPSON, UTAMQT: Boas, RBAE, XXXI, 798. — **N. PAC.** NOOTKA, CHEHALIS, CHINOOK: *Ibid.* SONGISH: Hill-Tout, JAI, XXXVII, 334. — **CAL.** WINTUN: Curtin, *Creation Myths,* pp. 131 ff., 430 ff. — **PLNS.** PAWNEE: Dorsey, MAFLS, VIII, 33, No. 6, and 40, No. 8; Dorsey, CI, LIX, 38. CROW: Lowie, PaAM, XXV, 127, 142. — **WDL. CENT.** MENOMINI: Skinner and Satterlee, PaAM, XIII, 319. CREE: Skinner, PaAM, IX, 92 ff. — **WDL. N.E.** NASKAPI: Speck, JAFL, XXVIII, 73. Cf. MICMAC: *Ibid,* p. 63. — **WDL. IROQ.** SENECA: Curtin-Hewitt, RBAE, XXXII, 670, No. 129; cf. 394, 404, 421. — **S.W.** NAVAHO: Matthews, MAFLS, V, 110. JICARILLA APACHE: Mooney, AA, old ser., XI, 203. SAN CAROLS APACHE: Goddard, PaAM, XXIV, 33, 34, 38. HOPI (TUSAYAN): Voth, FM, VIII, 31; Fewkes, *Jour. Am. Ethnology and Archaeology,* IV, 106. — Closely related is:

(*b*) *Path between monsters (Scylla and Charybdis)* (G333). — References fragmentary. — **ESK.** CUMBERLAND SOUND: Boas, BAM, XV, 179. — **MACK.** KASKA: Teit, JAFL, XXX, 435, No. 1. — **N. PAC.** KWAKIUTL:

Boas, CU, II, 63. — **WDL. CENT.** OJIBWA: Schoolcraft, *Hiawatha*, p. 28. — **WDL. N.E.** MICMAC: Rand, p. 233, No. 35, and p. 272, No. 46; Leland, p. 94. — **WDL. IROQ.** SENECA: Curtin-Hewitt, RBAE, XXXII, 82, No. 2; p. 201, No. 41 (= Curtin, *Seneca Indian Myths*, p. 329); p. 505, No. 109. Impossible to make clear division between this motif and the one immediately before it. — A special variety of the last two motifs is:

(c) *Sop to Cerberus* (B325.1, B576.1). Guardian monsters are placated by food or gifts. — **MACK.** KASKA: Teit, JAFL, xxx, 436, No. 1. — **WDL. IROQ.** SENECA: Curtin-Hewitt, RBAE, XXXII, 83, 149, 554, 571, 573, Nos. 2, 24, 114, 116.

(d) *Wild animals kept as dogs* (B575.1). — References: Jochelson, JE, VI, 374. — **MACK.** HARE: Petitot, p. 139. KASKA: Teit, JAFL, xxx, 446, No. 7. — **N. PAC.** COMOX, NOOTKA: Jochelson, *loc. cit.* SKAGIT: Haeberlin, JAFL, xxxVII, 386. — **PLNS.** SOUTHERN PAIUTE (MAOPA): Lowie, JAFL, xxxVII, 199, No. 32. —— SIBERIA: Jochelson, *loc. cit.*

114. *Resuscitation by assembling members* (E30). The members of a slain and dismembered person or animal are assembled and arranged. The person or animal comes to life. See also notes 114a, 114b, 153. — **ESK.** SMITH SOUND: Kroeber, JAFL, XII, 170, No. 6. — **PLAT.** Chilcotin, JE, II, 46, No. 30. SHUSWAP: Teit, JE, II, 677, No. 16. LILLOOET: Teit, JAFL, xxv, 370. WASCO: Curtin, PAES, II, 292. KUTENAI: Curtis, VII, 152. THOMPSON: Teit, JE, VIII, 243; Teit, MAFLS, VI, 79, No. 29. — **N. PAC.** TSIMSHIAN: Boas, BBAE, xxvII, 234; Boas, RBAE, xxxI, 127, 130. COWICHAN: Curtis, IX, 134. CHINOOK: Boas, BBAE, xx, 20. SONGISH: Hill-Tout, JAI, xxxvII, 336. SNUQUALMI: Haeberlin, JAFL, xxxvII, 427. SKAGIT: *Ibid.*, pp. 388, 389. TAKELMA: Sapir, UPa, II, No. 4. — **CAL.** MAIDU: Dixon, BAM, xvII, 76, No. 7; Dixon, PAES, IV, 129, No. 5. — **PLNS.** SOUTHERN PAIUTE (SHIVWITS): Lowie, JAFL, xxxvII, 147; (MAOPA): p. 187. UTE: Kroeber, JAFL, xIV, 280. PAWNEE: Grinnell, *Pawnee Hero Stories*, pp. 95, 124. PONCA: Dorsey, CNAE, VI, 18. BLACKFOOT: Grinnell, *Blackfoot Lodge Tales*, p. 106. ARIKARA: Dorsey, CI, xvII, 88, No. 25. ASSINIBOIN: Lowie, PaAM, IV, 169. PLAINS OJIBWA: Skinner, JAFL, xxxII, 340, No. 7. — **WDL. N.E.** MICMAC: Rand, p. 316, No. 55; Parsons, JAFL, xxxvIII, 68; Leland, p. 158. PASSAMAQUODDY: Fewkes, JAFL, III, 273; Prince, PAES, x, 71, No. 12. — **WDL. IROQ.** IROQUOIS: Smith, RBAE, II, 103. ONONDAGA: Beauchamp, JAFL, II, 261. SENECA: Curtin-Hewitt, RBAE, xxxII, 138, 160, 213, 217, 398, 404, 490, 586, 699; Curtin, *Seneca Indian Myths*, pp. 12, 46, 344, 486. — **S.W.** HOPI: Voth, FM, 139, No. 37. PIMA: Neff, JAFL, xxv, 58. —— SIBERIA: Jochelson, JE, VI, 374. — A special variety of this motif is:

(a) *Resuscitated eaten animal* (E32). An eaten animal is resuscitated by reassembling its members. — References: Boas, RBAE, xxxI, 698. — **PLAT.** THOMPSON: Teit, MAFLS, xI, 41, 42. — **N. PAC.** TLINGIT, HAIDA, TSIMSHIAN, KWAKIUTL, NEWETTEE, RIVERS INLET, CHEHALIS, SQUAMISH, NOOTKA, QUINAULT, CHINOOK: Boas, *loc. cit.* BELLA COOLA: Boas, JE, I, 76. — **PLNS.** SHOSHONI, PONCA: Boas, RBAE, xxxI, 698. — **WDL. CENT.** FOX, KICKAPOO: *Ibid.* OJIBWA: Jones, PAES, VII (II), 235. PEORIA: noted in Jones, PAES, IX, 129. —— SIBERIA: Jochelson, JE, VI, 374.

(b) *Resuscitation with missing member* (E33). In many tales of resuscitation by assembling members the failure to collect all the parts results in some missing member in the restored person or animal.— **MACK.** Loucheux: Petitot, p. 37.— **PLAT.** Chilcotin: Boas, RBAE, xxxi, 773. Lillooet: Hill-Tout, JAI, xxxv, 195. Sanpoil: Gould, MAFLS, xi, 108.— **N. PAC.** Kwakiutl, Rivers Inlet: Boas, *op. cit.*, p. 672. Tlingit, Haida, Bella Bella: *Ibid.*, p. 773. Bella Coola: Boas, JE, i, 76. Chehalis: Hill-Tout, JAI, xxxiv, 361. Tsimshian: Boas, RBAE, xxxi, 127, 195. Chinook: Boas, BBAE, xx, 20, No. 1.— **PLNS.** Osage: Dorsey, FM, vii, 13, No. 8.— **WDL. CENT.** Ojibwa: Jones-Michelson, PAES, vii (ii), 235, No. 20. Menomini: Skinner and Satterlee, PaAM, xiii, 380. —— Siberia: Jochelson, JE, vi, 376.

(*c*) *Resuscitation with misplaced head* (E34). Two or more persons are restored (as above), but the heads are mixed. — **MACK.** Loucheux, Hare: Petitot, pp. 36, 153.— **N. PAC.** Tsimshian: Boas, RBAE, xxxi, 127. Cowichan: Curtis, ix, 134.— **PLNS.** Pawnee: Grinnell, *Pawnee Hero Stories*, p. 154. — **WDL. IROQ.** Huron-Wyandot: Barbeau, GSCan, xi, 160, No. 48. Seneca: Curtin-Hewitt, RBAE, xxxii, 138, 213, 404, 586. — **S.W.** Hopi: Voth, FM, viii, 130, No. 35.

115. *Vagina dentata* (F547.1). At this point in the tale comes the adventure with the dangerous woman who killed all her husbands by means of her toothed vagina. The hero grinds off the teeth by means of a stone. — References: Boas, RBAE, xxxi, 604, No. 63; 614, No. 12; 809, No. 11; Waterman, JAFL, xxvii, 49. — **MACK.** Chipewyan: Lowie, PaAM, x, 47; Petitot, p. 356. Beaver: Goddard, PaAM, x, 235. Ts'ets'áut: Boas, JAFL, x, 48. Kaska: Teit, JAFL, xxx, 435, No. 1. — **PLAT.** Chilcotin, Thompson, Utamqt: Boas, *op. cit.*, p. 809. Shuswap, Thompson: *Ibid.*, p. 614. Lillooet: *Ibid.*, p. 604. Okanagon: Teit, MAFLS, xi, 71. Sahaptin: Farrand-Mayer, MAFLS, xi, 152. Wishram: Curtis, viii, 107 ff. — **N. PAC.** Haida, Bella Coola, Kwakiutl, Newettee, Comox, Chehalis: Boas, *op. cit.*, p. 809. Alsea: Frachtenberg, BBAE, lxvii, 101. Kalapuya, Molala: noted in *Ibid.*, p. 100. Takelma: Sapir, UPa, ii, 37, No. 2.— **CAL.** Maidu: Waterman, *loc. cit.* Wappo: Radin, UCal, xix, 93, No. 11. Yokuts: Kroeber, UCal, iv, 207, No. 14. Paviotso: Lowie, JAFL, xxxvii, 210, No. 2, and 216, No. 3.— **PLNS.** Wichita, Arapaho, Pawnee, Shoshoni, Dakota: Waterman, *loc. cit.* Southern Paiute (Shivwits): Lowie, JAFL, xxxvii, 103, No. 2, and 104, No. 3; (Maopa): *Ibid.*, p. 158, No. 1. Southern Ute: *Ibid.*, p. 10, No. 5. Plains Ojibwa: Skinner, JAFL, xxxii, 297, No. 6.— **WDL. N.E.** Naskapi: Speck, JAFL, xxviii, 73.— **WDL. IROQ.** Seneca: Curtin-Hewitt, RBAE, xxxii, 228, No. 43, and 270, No. 51.— **S.W.** San Carlos Apache: Goddard, PaAM, xxiv, 14. —— Siberia: Bogaras, AA, new ser., iv, 668.

For other private parts with teeth, see:— **PLAT.** Okanagon: Teit, MAFLS, xi, 71. Thompson: Teit, JE, viii, 298. — **N. PAC.** Tahltan: Teit, JAFL, xxxiv, 245, No. 50. Tillamook: Boas, JAFL, xi, 141. Lower Umpqua: Frachtenberg, CU, iv, 91, No. 19. —— Siberia: Jochelson, JE, vi, 377.

116. *Short pregnancy* (T571). A common motif. Usually accompanies the *supernatural growth* motif (note 112, *q.v.*). The following notes are very incomplete.— **N. PAC.** Chehalis, Nootka, Quinault: Jochelson, JE, vi, 375. Skykomish: Haeberlin, JAFL, xxxvii, 384.— **CAL.** Maidu: Dixon, PAES, iv, 71, 79, No. 3. Paviotso: Lowie, JAFL, xxxvii, 202, 203, 207, No. 1.

— **PLNS.** Arapaho: Dorsey and Kroeber, FM, v, 338, No. 144. — **S.W.** Navaho: Matthews, MAFLS, v, 70, 105. San Carlos Apache: Goddard, PaAM, xxiv, 93. —— Siberia: Jochelson, JE, vi, 375. — A related motif is: (*a*) *Many children at a birth* (T585). — **PLNS.** Southern Paiute (Shivwits): Lowie, JAFL, xxxvii, 108, No. 5. — **S.W.** Pima: Russell, RBAE, xxvi, 239.

117. *Transformation to reach difficult place* (D641). See notes 26, 44, 100, all of which involve this motif. — **PLAT.** Chilcotin: Farrand, JE, ii, 25, No. 10. Thompson: Teit, MAFLS, xi, 31, 37. Shuswap: Teit, JE, ii, 660, No. 6. Kutenai: Boas, BBAE, lix, 257. Nez Percé: Spinden, JAFL, xxi, 150. Wishram: Curtis, viii, 107. — **N. PAC.** Tsimshian: Boas, BBAE, xxvii, 126. Kwakiutl: Boas and Hunt, JE, iii, 335. Bella Coola: Boas, JE, i, 77. Tillamook: Boas, JAFL, xi, 138. Snuqualmi: Haeberlin, JAFL, xxxvii, 377. — **CAL.** Yana: Curtin, *Creation Myths*, p. 449. Hupa: Goddard, UCal, i, 125, No. 1. Lassik: Goddard, JAFL, xix, 136, No. 3. Mewan: Merriam, pp. 35, 45. Yuki: Kroeber, UCal, iv, 185. Cahuilla: Hooper, UCal, xvi, 368. — **PLNS.** Southern Ute: Lowie, JAFL, xxxvii, 29, No. 15. Crow: Lowie, PaAM, xxv, 142. Pawnee: Dorsey, CI, lix, 148, No. 39. Omaha: Dorsey, JAFL, i, 204. Dakota: Wissler, JAFL, xx, 130. Gros Ventre: Kroeber, PaAM, i, 85, 96, Nos. 20, 22. Assiniboin: Lowie, PaAM, iv, 196. — **WDL. CENT.** Ojibwa: Jones, PAES, vii (ii), 245, No. 22; Smith, JAFL, xix, 221. Fox: Owen, PFLS, li, 88. — **WDL. N.E.** Micmac: Hagar, AA, old ser., viii, 39. Naskapi: Speck, JAFL, xxviii, 70. — **WDL. IROQ.** Seneca: Curtin-Hewitt, RBAE, xxxii, 86, 160, 191, 209, 476 f. (transformation to snake for easy traveling, pp. 317, 323, 331). — **S.E.** Yuchi: Speck, UPa, i, 145, No. 8. Muskhogean: Swanton, JAFL, xxvi, 204. Caddo: Dorsey, CI, xli, 61, No. 33, and 108, No. 70. — **S.W.** Jicarilla Apache: Goddard, PaAM, viii, 213, No. 20. Navaho: Pepper, JAFL, xxi, 179. Zuñi: Cushing, p. 94. — Some analogous motifs are:

(*a*) *Transformation to feather to escape death* (D275, D642). — **MACK.** Kaska: Teit, JAFL, xxx, 468, No. 21. — **PLAT.** Chilcotin, Thompson: Teit, *loc. cit.* Nez Percé: Spinden, JAFL, xxi, 150. — **PLNS.** Southern Paiute (Maopa): Lowie, JAFL, xxxvii, 165, No. 4, and cf. 188, No. 19; (Shivwits): *Ibid.*, p. 113, No. 6. Gros Ventre: Kroeber, PaAM, i, 85 f. Plains Cree: Skinner, JAFL, xxix, 358, No. 3. Wichita: Dorsey, CI, xxi, 134. — **WDL. CENT.** Kickapoo: Jones, PAES, ix, 11, No. 2 (leaf). — **WDL. IROQ.** Seneca: Curtin-Hewitt, RBAE, xxxii, 555. — **S.W.** Navaho: Matthews, MAFLS, v, 119. San Carlos Apache: Goddard, PaAM, xxiv, 70. White Mountain Apache: *Ibid.*, pp. 97, 117.

(*b*) *Transformation (miscellaneous) to escape death* (D642). Many of the examples given in note 117 and all in 117*a* belong here. — **PLAT.** Sahaptin: Farrand-Mayer, MAFLS, xi, 176, No. 14. Okanagon: Gould, MAFLS, xi, 99. — **CAL.** Paviotso: Lowie, JAFL, xxxvii, 201. — **PLNS.** Crow: Lowie, PaAM, xxv, 163. — **WDL. IROQ.** Seneca: Curtin-Hewitt, RBAE, xxxii, 424, No. 79, and 352, No. 60.

(*c*) *Transformation to receive food* (D655). Besides the references in note 100, see:— **N. PAC.** Tsimshian, Tlingit, Haida: Boas, RBAE, xxxi, 692.— **PLNS.** Cheyenne: Campbell, JAFL, xxix, 407, No. 1.

(*d*) *Protean beggar* (D611). A trickster repeatedly asks for food in a different guise. — **CAL.** Wishosk: Kroeber, JAFL, xviii, 99, No. 12. — **PLNS.**

CROW: Simms, FM, II, 285, No. 6. Cf. ARAPAHO: Dorsey and Kroeber, FM, v, 101, No. 49, and 103, No. 50. Cf. BLACKFOOT: Wissler and Duvall, PaAM, II, 34.

(e) *Transformation combat* (D615). Combatants vie with each other in changing forms. — **MACK.** BEAVER: Goddard, PaAM, x, 258. — **PLAT.** SHUSWAP: Teit, JE, II, 700, No. 31. — **N. PAC.** Cf. BELLA COOLA: Boas, JE, I, 80 (this volume, p. 83). — **PLNS.** ARAPAHO: Dorsey and Kroeber, FM, v, 55 f., Nos. 20–23. PONCA: Dorsey, CNAE, VI, 612. BLACKFOOT: PaAM, II, 51. ARIKARA: Curtis, V, 86 ff. ASSINIBOIN: Lowie, PaAM, IV, 184. — **WDL. CENT.** OJIBWA: Smith, JAFL, XIX, 221. — **WDL. N.E.** MICMAC: Rand, p. 5, No. 1.

118. *Ascent to sky* (F10). A characteristic of several well-known tales. See numbers III, XV, XVI, XXXIX, L, LI, LII, LIII, LIV, LXXV, and notes 15a, 28, 48, 65, 66, 192, 193, 194, 199, 201, 202, 203, 204, 206, 280. — This incident presents special forms:

(a) *Ascent to sky on feather* (F61.2). In some cases the person is carried on the feather; in some, he adheres magically to the feather, which draws him to the sky. — References: **N. PAC.** TSIMSHIAN, NASS, TLINGIT, HAIDA: Boas, RBAE, XXXI, 734. — **PLAT.** CHILCOTIN: Farrand, JE, II, 25. — For other cases of *magic adhesion*, see Boas, BBAE, LIX, 295 (**PLAT.** KUTENAI, SHUSWAP, THOMPSON. — **PLNS.** ASSINIBOIN).

(b) *Visit to the land of the sun* (F17). — References: Boas, RBAE, XXXI, 850. — **MACK.** KASKA: Teit, JAFL, XXX, 441, No. 1. — **PLAT.** CHILCOTIN: Farrand, JE, II, 25, No. 10. WASCO: Curtin, PAES, II, 303. — **N. PAC.** TLINGIT, HAIDA, TSIMSHIAN, NASS: Boas, *loc. cit.* BELLA COOLA: Boas, JE, I, 79, 95 (tales XVI and XXXIX in this volume). KATHLAMET: Boas, BBAE, XXVI, 16, 26. — **CAL.** YANA: Curtin, *Creation Myths*, pp. 287 ff., 430 ff. — **PLNS.** SOUTHERN UTE: Lowie, JAFL, XXXVII, 76, No. 48. BLACKFOOT: Wissler and Duvall, PaAM, II, 61; Grinnell, *Blackfoot Lodge Tales*, p. 95. CROW: Lowie, PaAM, XXV, 156. GROS VENTRE: Kroeber, PaAM, I, 90, No. 21. — **WDL. CENT.** FOX: Jones, JAFL, XIV, 235. — **S.W.** NAVAHO: Matthews, MAFLS, V, 110 ff., 127. WHITE MOUNTAIN APACHE: Goddard, PaAM, XXIV, 94, 116. SAN CARLOS APACHE: *Ibid.*, pp. 9, 36. SIA: Stevenson, RBAE, XI, 43 ff. TUSAYAN: Fewkes, JAFL, VIII, 132–137. — See also note 66.

(c) *Visit to land of stars* (F15). See references to note 193, *Star Husband.* — **PLNS.** PAWNEE: Dorsey, MAFLS, VIII, 32; Dorsey, CI, LIX, 38. For *Visit to the land of the thunders*, see note 213.

119. *House of Myths.* An interesting aspect of Bella Coola cosmogony. They have an upper and a lower heaven. The *House of Myths* is the house of the gods, and stands in the middle of the lower heaven. The master of the house is the Sun. It is to him and not to the deity of the upper heaven that the Bella Coola pray. See Boas, JE, I, 28 f.

120. *Heat test; burning magically evaded* (H1511, D1841.3). — References: Boas, RBAE, XXXI, 806. — **MACK.** TS'ETS'ÁUT: Boas, *loc. cit.* KASKA: Teit, JAFL, XXX, 463, No. 1. — **PLAT.** CHILCOTIN, THOMPSON, UTAMQT, LIL-LOOET, WISHRAM: Boas, *loc. cit.* — **N. PAC.** TLINGIT, HAIDA, TSIMSHIAN, NASS, KWAKIUTL, NEWETTEE, NOOTKA, QUINAULT, CHINOOK, TILLAMOOK: *Ibid.* — **CAL.** WINTUN: Curtin, *Creation Myths*, pp. 121 ff. LUISEÑO: DuBois, UCal, VIII, 150. — **PLNS.** SOUTHERN UTE: Lowie, JAFL, XXXVII,

77, No. 48. Uintah Ute: Mason, JAFL, xxiii, 326. Wichita: Dorsey, CI, xxi, 96 (evaded by trickery). Assiniboin: Lowie, PaAM, iv, 211. — **WDL. CENT.** Menomini: Hoffman, RBAE, xiv, 227. — **WDL. N.E.** Micmac: Rand, p. 71. — **WDL. IROQ.** Seneca: Curtin-Hewitt, RBAE, xxxi, 428, No. 79, and 604, No. 118. — **S.E.** Cherokee: Mooney, JAFL, i, 105; Mooney, RBAE, xix, 312, No. 63. — **S.W.** Navaho: Matthews, MAFLS, v, 112. Jicarilla Apache: Goddard PaAM, viii, 197, No. 3; Mooney, AA, old ser., xi, 201. White Mountain Apache: Goddard, PaAM, xxiv, 97, 117. San Carlos Apache: *Ibid.*, p. 11. Tusayan: Fewkes, JAFL, viii, 132, 136. Sia: Stevenson, RBAE, xi, 44. —— Siberia: Jochelson, JE, vi, 379. — Similar tests are:

(*a*) *Smoke test* (H1511.3). Attempt is made to kill the hero by smoke. — References: Boas, RBAE, xxxi, 808 (**PLAT.** Thompson, Wishram. — **N. PAC.** Chinook).

(*b*) *Burning food test* (H1511.2). — **N. PAC.** Haida: Boas, RBAE, xxxi, 809.

(*c*) *Swallowing red-hot stones* (H1511.1). — **N. PAC.** Haida, Comox: Boas, RBAE, xxxi, 809. Cf. notes 167, 274.

121. *Substituted arrows* (K1617). In the attempt to kill the hero, the persecutor substitutes arrows with soft points when he sends him against dangerous foes. — **PLAT.** Chilcotin, Okanagon, Shuswap, Utamqt, Wasco: Boas, RBAE, xxxi, 742. Kaska: Teit, JAFL, xxx, 439. — **N. PAC.** Tsimshian, Tlingit, Bella Coola: Boas, *loc. cit.*

122. *Precipice test* (H1535). The hero is pushed over a precipice. — Boas, RBAE, xxxi, 803 (**ESK.** Kodiak. — **PLAT.** Chilcotin, Lillooet. — **N. PAC.** Tlingit, Haida, Bella Coola, Newettee).

123. *Sun father-in-law* (A226). — **MACK.** Ts'ets'áut: Boas, RBAE, xxxi, 771, 797. — **PLAT.** Chilcotin: *Ibid.* — **N. PAC.** Tsimshian, Bella Coola, Newettee, Comox, Nootka, Squamish, Chehalis: *Ibid.* Skagit: Haeberlin, JAFL, xxxvii, 431.

124. *Drowning test* (H1538). Vain attempts to drown hero. — **PLAT.** Thompson, Utamqt, Lillooet: Boas, RBAE, xxxi, 804. — **N. PAC.** Nass, Tlingit, Bella Coola, Comox, Squamish, Kathlamet: *Ibid.* Tahltan: Teit, JAFL, xxxii, 200.

125. *Diving test* (K16). See note 136.

126. *Quest for dangerous animals* (H1360). The hero is sent to kill or capture dangerous animals. — References: Boas, RBAE, xxxi, 804–806. — **ESK.** Kodiak: Boas, *loc. cit.* Greenland: Rink, *International Congress of Americanists*, xiii, 284. — **MACK.** Kaska: Teit, JAFL, xxx, 438, No. 1. Beaver: Goddard, PaAM, x, 235. — **PLAT.** Wishram: Boas, *loc. cit.* Okanagon: Gatschet, *Globus*, lii, 137. — **N. PAC.** Tlingit, Haida, Newettee, Bella Coola, Kwakiutl, Comox, Chehalis, Quinault, Chinook, Kathlamet: Boas, *loc. cit.* — **CAL.** Maidu: Dixon, BAM, xvii, 70. Yana: Curtin, *Creation Myths*, pp. 430 ff. — **PLNS.** Kiowa: Mooney, RBAE, xvii, 239. Pawnee: Dorsey, MAFLS, viii, 33, 40, 63, 91; Dorsey, CI, lix, 38, 143, 493, 494. Ponca: Dorsey, CNAE, vi, 215. Crow: Lowie, PaAM, xxv, 141. Gros Ventre: Kroeber, PaAM, i, 88. — **WDL. CENT.** Sauk and Fox: Lasley, JAFL, xv, 177. — **WDL. IROQ.** Iroquois: Smith, RBAE, ii, 84. — **S.E.** Cherokee: Mooney, RBAE, xix, 242 ff., 312 ff., 345 ff. Biloxi: Dorsey and Swanton, BBAE, xlvii, 99. — **S.W.** Navaho: Matthews, MAFLS, v,

186. Zuñi: Cushing, pp. 65 ff., 288 ff., 424 ff. Sia: Stevenson, RBAE, xi, 43 ff. Hopi: Voth, FM, viii, 81 ff.— Closely related incidents are:

(a) *Captured animals avenge themselves* (Q385). The captured animals or persons take vengeance on the man who sent the hero to capture them. — **N. PAC.** Tlingit, Bella Coola, Kwakiutl, Comox, Chehalis: Boas, RBAE, xxxi, 810.

(b) *Impossible quests* (H1371, H1375). — **PLNS.** Arapaho: Dorsey and Kroeber, FM, v, 294 ff. Cheyenne: Kroeber, JAFL, xiii, 177. Gros Ventre: Kroeber, PaAM, i, 88 ff. Wichita: Dorsey, CI, xxi, 130 ff. — **S.E.** Biloxi: Dorsey and Swanton, BBAE, xlvii, 99 ff.

(c) *Quest for berries in winter* (H1001). — **N. PAC.** Kwakiutl, Comox, Squamish: Boas, RBAE, xxxi, 806. — **PLNS.** Pawnee: Dorsey, CI, lix, 289, No. 80.— European borrowing: **PLAT.** Thompson: Teit, JAFL, xxix, 301; Thompson, CColl, ii, 386 f.

127. XL. *The Jealous Uncle* (S71). An uncle tries to make away with his nephews. — **ESK.** Kodiak: Rink, *International Congress of Americanists*, xiii, 284; Boas, RBAE, xxxi, 796.—**N. PAC.** Tlingit, Haida, Bella Coola, Newettee: Boas, *loc. cit.* Tahltan: Teit, JAFL, xxxii, 199. — **WDL. IROQ.** Seneca: Curtin-Hewitt, RBAE, xxxii,586, No. 118, and 744, No. 137.—**S.E.** Biloxi: Dorsey and Swanton, BBAE, xlvii, 99.

128. *Boy passes as girl to avoid decree of death on males* (K514).—**PLAT.** Kutenai: Boas, BBAE, lix, 28. — **N. PAC.** Tsimshian, Haida, Tlingit, Kwakiutl, Songish, Kathlamet: Boas, RBAE, xxxi, 622, 857. — **PLNS.** Southern Paiute (Maopa): Lowie, JAFL, xxxvii, 190, No. 21.

129. *Wedge test* (H1532). The hero is caught in the cleft of a tree. — **ESK.** Kodiak: Boas, RBAE, xxxi, 801. — **MACK.** Kaska: Teit, JAFL, xxx, 437, No. 1.—**PLAT.** Chilcotin, Thompson, Utamqt, Lillooet: Boas, *loc. cit.* — **N. PAC.** Nass, Tlingit, Haida, Bella Coola, Newettee, Kwakiutl, Nootka, Comox, Chehalis, Squamish, Chinook, Coos: *Ibid.* Alsea: Frachtenberg, BBAE, lxvii, 119, No. 9.

130. *Clam test* (H1521). The hero is sent to capture a giant clam. — Boas, RBAE, xxxi, 805 (**ESK.** Kodiak. — **N. PAC.** Haida, Tlingit, Newettee).

131. *Abandonment in boat* (S141). — **ESK.** Kodiak: Boas, RBAE, xxxi, 810.—**PLAT.** Sechelt, Lillooet: *Ibid.*—**N. PAC.** Tlingit, Haida, Newettee, Rivers Inlet: *Ibid.* Clallam: Curtis, ix, 161 ff. Chinook: Boas, BBAE, xx, No. 4. Alsea: Frachtenberg, BBAE, lxvii, 121.

132. *Transformation by putting on skin* (D531). A person is transformed by putting on the skin or feathers of an animal or bird. — Cf. note 250, *Disenchantment by destroying animal skin;* 247, *The Dog-Husband;* 233, *The Fox-Woman;* and 284, *The Swan-Maidens.* In addition see:—**ESK.** Alaska: Golder, JAFL, xvi, 95. — **PLAT.** Sechelt: Hill-Tout, JAI, xxxiv, 55. — **N. PAC.** Tsimshian: Boas, BBAE, xxvii, 10, 151. Kwakiutl: Boas and Hunt, JE, iii, 15. — **WDL. IROQ.** Seneca: Curtin-Hewitt, RBAE, xxxii, 128, 136, 267; Curtin, *Seneca Indian Myths,* p. 474.— An analogous motif is:

(a) *Transformation by eating or drinking* (D550). — References: Lowie, PaAM, xxv, 214.— **ESK.** Greenland: Rink, p. 173. — **N. PAC.** Tsimshian: Boas, BBAE, xxvii, 234. Kathlamet: Boas, BBAE, xxvi, 228. — **PLNS.** Arapaho, Crow, Omaha, Hidatsa, Mandan, Gros Ventre, Ari-

KARA: Lowie, *loc. cit.* SKIDI PAWNEE: Dorsey, MAFLS, VIII, 293, No. 80. ASSINIBOIN: Lowie, PaAM, IV, 121.—**WDL. CENT.** CREE: Bell, JAFL, X, 1.

133. *XLI. Bluejay and his Companions.* The tale of the traveling companions who engage in dangerous contests occurs primarily among the Columbia River and neighboring tribes.—**N. PAC.** CHINOOK, QUINAULT, KATHLAMET, TILLAMOOK: Boas, RBAE, XXXI, 816.—**PLAT.** WISHRAM: *Ibid.*—**PLAT.** KUTENAI: Boas, BBAE, LIX, 297.

134. *Harpooning contest* (K33). A contest in harpooning a whale. Hero succeeds.—Boas, BBAE, LIX, 297 (**N. PAC.** CHINOOK, TILLAMOOK.—**CAL.** YANA).

135. *Climbing match* (K15).—Boas, BBAE, LIX, 297 (**PLAT.** SHUSWAP, NEZ PERCÉ, WISHRAM. — **N. PAC.** QUINAULT, CHINOOK, COOS. — **CAL.** LUISEÑO).

136. *Diving match* (K16). In most cases the hero wins by trickery, coming up for breath under brush without being discovered.—**PLAT.** KUTENAI, NEZ PERCÉ: Boas, BBAE, LIX, 297.—**N. PAC.** COMOX, CHINOOK, ALSEA: *Ibid.* BELLA COOLA: Boas, JE, I, 81.—**PLNS.** SHOSHONI, PAWNEE: Boas, BBAE, LIX, 297. — **WDL. IROQ.** SENECA: Curtin-Hewitt, RBAE, XXXII, 708, No. 135.

137. *Waking contest* (D1997). — Boas, BBAE, LIX, 297 (**N. PAC.** KATHLAMET, QUINAULT.—**CAL.** LUISEÑO).—**S.E.** CHEROKEE: Mooney, RBAE, XIX, 240, No. 1.—Other similar contests are:

(a) *Wrestling contest* (K12).—Boas, BBAE, LIX, 297 (**PLAT.** WISHRAM. —**PLNS.** SHOSHONI. Cf. **PLAT.** THOMPSON, LILLOOET. — **N. PAC.** KATHLAMET).

(b) *Eating contest* (K81).— Boas, BBAE, LIX, 297 (**PLAT.** KUTENAI. — **CAL.** LUISEÑO.—**PLNS.** SHOSHONI).

138. Cf. *Magic storm,* note 61b.

139. *XLII. Dug-from-Ground.* A California type. A woman digs up a root and it turns to a child (T545). When grown, the hero goes on adventures. He climbs a stretching tree, goes to the sky, and kills a deer. Other adventures: a shinny contest, eating test, heat test, shooting contest. — **CAL.** YANA: Sapir, UCal, IX, 21 f.; Curtin, *Creation Myths,* pp. 309 f. HUPA: Goddard, UCal, I, 146, No. 2. WINTUN: Curtin, *op. cit.,* pp. 131 ff. MAIDU: Dixon, BAM, XVII, 67. — For the *birth from ground* alone, see **WDL. N.E.** MICMAC: Rand, p. 280, No. 48.

140. *Poisoned food test* (H1515). Hero is fed poisoned food. Through magic power or trickery he escapes harm.—**N. PAC.** HAIDA, KWAKIUTL, CHINOOK: Boas, RBAE, XXXI, 809, 816.—**PLAT.** WISHRAM: *Ibid.,* p. 816.—**CAL.** HUPA: Goddard, UCal, I, 148, No. 2.—**S.W.** NAVAHO: Matthews, MAFLS, V, 179.

141. *Shinny match* (K19).—**PLNS.** WICHITA: Dorsey, CI, XXI, 248, No. 39.—Cf. the lacrosse game in tale IV.

142. *Shooting contest* (K31).—**N. PAC.** TLINGIT, NOOTKA, CHINOOK, KATHLAMET: Boas, BBAE, LIX, 279.—**CAL.** HUPA: Goddard, UCal, I, 149, No. 2.—**PLAT.** and **PLNS.** See references in note 183, *Dirty-Boy,* the central incident of which is a shooting contest.

143. *Rip Van Winkle (years thought days)* (D1991.1).—**MACK.** ANVIK: Chapman, PAES, VI, 56, No. 7.—**N. PAC.** BELLA COOLA: Boas, JE, I, 54. TILLAMOOK: Boas, JAFL, XI, 26. — **CAL.** HUPA: Goddard, UCal, I, 149,

No. 2, and 168, No. 5. — **PLNS.** Skidi Pawnee: Dorsey, MAFLS, viii, 22, No. 3. Assiniboin: Lowie, PaAM, iv, 124. — **WDL. CENT.** Fox, Menomini, Ojibwa: Lowie, *loc. cit.* Ojibwa: Jones, PAES, vii (i), 501. — **WDL. N.E.** Montagnais: Lowie, *loc. cit.* Micmac: Rand, p. 95, No. 10. Passamaquoddy: Leland, p. 261. — **WDL. IROQ.** Seneca: Curtin-Hewitt, RBAE, xxxi, 255, No. 48 (= Curtin, *Seneca Indian Myths,* p. 87), and 629, No. 119. — **S.E.** Cherokee: Mooney, RBAE, xix, 324, No. 73, and 347, No. 84.

144. *XLIII. The Attack on the Giant Elk.* A hero attacks a giant elk with the help of a rodent ally; later he attacks a giant eagle. For parallels to the second part, see note 151. Some examples of the first part are: — **MACK.** Kaska: Teit, JAFL, xxx, 438. Beaver: Goddard, PaAM, x, 236. — **PLAT.** Kutenai: Boas, BBAE, lix, 105. Pend d'Oreille: Teit, MAFLS, xi, 117. — **PLNS.** Southern Paiute (Shivwits): Lowie, JAFL, xxxvii, 123, No. 10. — **S.W.** Navaho: Matthews, MAFLS, v, 117. Jicarilla Apache: Russell, JAFL, xi, 255; Mooney, AA, old ser., xi, 204; Goddard, PaAM, viii, 197. San Carlos Apache: Goddard, PaAM, xxiv, 15, 34. Mohave-Apache: Gould, JAFL, xxxiv, 319.

145. *Magic journey: hundred-league stride* (D1065, D1521, D2121.3). In just the form found in this story, not usual in American Indian tales. Cf., however, Seneca: Curtin-Hewitt, RBAE, xxxii, 585, No. 117. The magic journey ordinarily appears as:

(*a*) *Magic arrow flight* (D1092, D1526.1). Hero magically keeps ahead of the arrow which he shoots. — **MACK.** Beaver: Goddard, PaAM, x, 234. Chipewyan: Lowie, PaAM, x, 190; Goddard, PaAM, x, 46. — **CAL.** Hupa: Goddard, UCal, i, 205, No. 15, and 212, No. 16. — **PLNS.** Southern Paiute (Maopa): Lowie, JAFL, xxxvii, 168, No. 5a. Pawnee: Dorsey, CI, lix, 72, No. 18, and 159, No. 43. Wichita: Dorsey, CI, xxi, 217, No. 31, and 145, No. 19. Hidatsa: Matthews, *U. S. Geol. and Geog. Survey, Misc. Pub.,* vii, 63 ff. Crow: Lowie, PaAM, xxv, 125. Plains Ojibwa: Skinner, JAFL, xxxii, 293, No. 4. — **WDL. CENT.** Ojibwa: Jones-Michelson, PAES, vii (ii), 233, No. 20. — **WDL. N.E.** Montagnais: Speck, JAFL, xxxviii, 13. Micmac: Rand, p. 7, No. 2. — **WDL. IROQ.** Seneca: Curtin-Hewitt, RBAE, xxxii, 172, 271, 287, 337, 470; Curtin, *Seneca Indian Myths,* pp. 309, 423. — In the Beaver and Chipewyan tales the hero follows an arrow to the sky (cf. note 203, *Arrow chain*). In the Seneca tales the hero is made small and placed in the head of a magic arrow.

(*b*) *Magic ball flight* (D1256, D1526.2). A magic ball carries its owner with it. — **PLNS.** Arapaho: Dorsey and Kroeber, FM, v, 159, No. 81. Skidi Pawnee: Dorsey, MAFLS, viii, 25, No. 5. — **WDL. CENT.** Menomini: Skinner and Satterlee, PaAM, xiii, 311. — **WDL. N.E.** Delaware: *Ibid.,* p. 523.

(*c*) *Magic contraction of road* (D2121.4). — **ESK.** Greenland, West Hudson Bay: Boas, BAM, xv, 361. — **MACK.** Cf. Kaska: Teit, JAFL, xxx, 476. — **PLAT.** Lillooet: Hill-Tout, JAI, xxxv, 188. — **N. PAC.** Tahltan: Teit, JAFL, xxxiv, 230, No. 37; cf. p. 222. — **CAL.** Joshua: Farrand-Frachtenberg, JAFL, xxviii, 229, No. 17. — **WDL. IROQ.** Seneca: Curtin-Hewitt, RBAE, xxxii, 289, No. 57 (= Curtin, *Seneca Indian Myths,* p. 311). — **N. PAC.** Chehalis: Hill-Tout, JAI, xxxiv, 342 (magic lengthening of trail).

(d) *Magic journey through air* (D2135). A common motif. A few references are: — **PLNS.** CROW: Lowie, PaAM, xxv, 128. SOUTHERN PAIUTE: (MAOPA): Lowie, JAFL, xxxvii, 191, No. 21; (SHIVWITS): *Ibid.*, p.130, No. 12. — **WDL. N.E.** MICMAC: Michelson, JAFL, xxxviii, 43. — **WDL. IROQ.** SENECA: Curtin-Hewitt, RBAE, xxxii, 225, 340, 408, 470, 476.

(e) *Magic underground journey* (D2131). Fragmentary references: — **CAL.** MAIDU: Dixon, PAES, iv, 231 ff., No. 17. — **PLNS.** SOUTHERN PAIUTE (SHIVWITS): Lowie, JAFL, xxxvii, 131, 132, No. 12. — **WDL. IROQ.** SENECA: Curtin-Hewitt, RBAE, xxxii, 298, 349.

146. *Helpful animals* (B300). Fragmentary references: — **ESK.** EAST GREENLAND, SMITH SOUND, CUMBERLAND SOUND, WEST HUDSON BAY: Boas, BAM, xv, 360. GREENLAND: Rink, pp. 101, 270, 462. — **MACK.** BEAVER: Goddard, PaAM, x, 260. HARE: Petitot, p. 248. — **PLAT.** SHUSWAP: Teit, JE, ii, 726, No. 48. LILLOOET: Boas, JAFL, xxv, 360, No. 46. — **N. PAC.** TSIMSHIAN, HAIDA, RIVERS INLET, NASS: Boas, RBAE, xxxi, 784 f., 842, 955. SKAGIT: Haeberlin, JAFL, xxxvii, 438. — **CAL.** PAVIOTSO: Lowie, JAFL, xxxvii, 229, 231, No. 11. — **PLNS.** SHOSHONI: St. Clair, JAFL, xxii, 271. SOUTHERN UTE: Lowie, JAFL, xxxvii, 85, No. 56. WICHITA: Dorsey, CI, xxi, 221, No. 32. ARAPAHO: Dorsey and Kroeber, FM, v, 238, No. 105. CHEYENNE: Kroeber, JAFL, xiii, 177, No. 16. CROW: Lowie, PaAM, xxv, 162, 165, 169, 183, 190, 204; Simms, FM, ii, 310, No. 21. TETON: J. O. Dorsey, JAFL, ii, 133. PAWNEE: Dorsey, MAFLS, viii, 21, No. 3; 125, No. 33; 257, No. 61; Dorsey, CI, lix, 81, No. 18; 207, No. 59; 288, No. 80; 313, No. 86; 323, No. 88; Grinnell, *Pawnee Hero Stories*, p. 104. BLACKFOOT: Wissler and Duvall PaAM, ii, 78, 92, 149; Grinnell, *Blackfoot Lodge Tales*, p. 68; McClintock, pp. 468 ff. MANDAN: Will, JAFL, xxvi, 333. ARIKARA: Dorsey, CI, xvii, 75, No. 21. ASSINIBOIN: Lowie, PaAM, iv, 187. PLAINS CREE: Skinner, JAFL, xxix, 356 f., No. 3. PLAINS OJIBWA: Skinner, JAFL, xxxii, 294, No. 4. — **WDL. CENT.** CENTRAL ALGONQUIN (general): Skinner, JAFL, xxvii, 99. CREE: Bell, JAFL, x, 1. SAC and FOX: Lasley, JAFL, xv, 176; Jones, JAFL, xiv, 229. OJIBWA: Hoffman, RBAE, vii, 280. MENOMINI: Hoffman, RBAE, xiv, 183; Skinner, JAFL, xxvi, 76. — **WDL. N.E.** MICMAC: Rand, p. 270, No. 46. PASSAMA-QUODDY: Fewkes, JAFL, iii, 269; Leland, p. 230. — **WDL. IROQ.** IROQUOIS: Smith, RBAE, ii, 84. SENECA: Curtin-Hewitt, RBAE, 120, 161, 162, 189, 366 f., 442; Curtin, *Seneca Indian Myths*, pp. 3, 438. — **S.E.** CHOCTAW: Bushnell, AA, new ser., xii, 530. — **S.W.** NAVAHO: Matthews, MAFLS, v, 171 ff. JICARILLA APACHE: Russell, JAFL, xi, 268; Goddard, PaAM, viii, 215, No. 22, and 218, No. 23. ZUÑI: Cushing, pp. 124, 189, 444; Parsons, JAFL, xxxi, 235, 245. HOPI: Fewkes, JAFL, viii, 133; Voth, FM, viii, 30, No. 6; 150, No. 41; 168, No. 50. See also references in notes 65, 96, 147, 176, 179, 227, 249, 279. — Special varieties of *helpful animal* motifs follow:

(a) *Grateful animals* (B350). See references in note above to the following tribes: — **ESK.** EAST GREENLAND, SMITH SOUND, CUMBERLAND SOUND, WEST HUDSON BAY. — **N. PAC.** All references. — **CAL.** PAVIOTSO.

(b) *Animal nurse* (B535). An animal adopts an infant and suckles it (or at least rears it). — References not otherwise indicated are the same as in the note on *Helpful animals*. — **MACK.** HARE: Petitot, p. 164. BEAVER. — **PLNS.** CROW: Lowie, PaAM, xxv, pp. 162, 165, 169. BLACKFOOT, ASSINI-BOIN. PAWNEE: Dorsey, MAFLS, 99, No. 27, and 178, No. 45. — **WDL.**

CENT. CREE. SAC and Fox: Lasley, JAFL, xv, 176. CENTRAL ALGONQUIN. OJIBWA: Jones-Michelson, PAES, vii (ii), 271. MENOMINI: Skinner and Satterlee, PaAM, xiii, 331. — **WDL. IROQ.** IROQUOIS, SENECA (RBAE, xxxii, 366, 368, 442, 658). — **S.E.** CHOCTAW.

(*c*) *Helpful animals give magic power to hero* (B500). See following references in note on *Helpful animals*: — **PLNS.** CROW: Lowie, PaAM, xxv, 183. PLAINS CREE. PLAINS OJIBWA. — **WDL. IROQ.** SENECA: Curtin-Hewitt, RBAE, xxxii, 120, 162; Curtin, *Seneca Indian Myths*, pp. 3, 371.

147. *Rodent ally* (B431). The help of a rodent is regular in this tale and also in tale LIX, "Splinter-Foot-Girl" (note 228). See the latter for additional references. In nearly all cases the rodent burrows under the animal and makes its capture possible. In tale xv, "The Sun Snarer," the rodent gnaws the snare loose for the sun. See the references under note 65. — **MACK.** YUKON: Schmitter, p. 22. BEAVER: Goddard, PaAM, x, 236. — **PLAT.** SECHELT: Hill-Tout, JAI, xxxiv, 55, 57. FLATHEAD: McDermott, JAFL, xiv, 242. — **CAL.** JOSHUA: Farrand-Frachtenberg, JAFL, xxviii, 231, No. 17. SINKYONE: Kroeber, JAFL, xxxii, 347, No. 6. KATO: Goddard, UCal, v, 223, No. 20. MIWOK: Gifford, UCal, xii, 309, No. 5. PAVIOTSO: Lowie, JAFL, xxxvii, 231, and 232, No. 11. — **PLNS.** SOUTHERN UTE: Lowie, JAFL, xxxvii, 36, No. 20. ARAPAHO: Dorsey and Kroeber, FM, v, 35, No. 12; Voth, JAFL, xxv, 44, No. 3. CROW: Lowie, PaAM, xxv, 121 f.; Curtis, iv, 117 ff.; Simms, FM, ii, 302, No. 18. GROS VENTRE: Kroeber, PaAM, i, 101, No. 24, and 102, No. 25. PLAINS OJIBWA: Skinner, JAFL, xxxii, 290, No. 1 (11). PLAINS CREE: Skinner, JAFL, xxix, 341, 350, No. 7. — **WDL. CENT.** OJIBWA: Jones-Michelson, PAES, vii (i), 201, and (ii), 391; Schoolcraft, *Hiawatha*, p. 274; Radin, GSCan, ii, 66, No. 33. — **WDL. IROQ.** SENECA: Curtin-Hewitt, RBAE, xxxii, 417 (regular) (in *Ibid.*, pp. 79, 83, 150, 189, 205, 208, 217, 350, 356, 448, 486, 554; Curtin, *Seneca Indian Myths*, pp. 15, 31, 169, 337, 344, boys are carried inside a mole; cf. CROW: Simms, FM, ii, 302). — **S.W.** NAVAHO: Matthews, MAFLS, v, 84, 117. JICARILLA APACHE: Mooney, AA, old ser., xi, 204; Russell, JAFL, xi, 255; Goddard, PaAM, viii, 197. SAN CARLOS APACHE: Goddard, PaAM, xxiv, 24. ZUÑI: Cushing, pp. 80, 124. TUSAYAN: Fewkes, JAFL, viii, 135.

148. All the tribes of the Southwest have somewhat elaborate color symbolism. There are usually colors referring to the four cardinal points, and among some tribes, e.g., the Zuñi, to the center, the zenith, and the nadir. See the collections of tales referred to in note 36. For a fuller account of some of the ceremonials of the Southwest, see the series of studies published by the Field Columbian Museum giving the results of the Stanley McCormick Hopi Expedition.

149. *Life-token* (E761). A magic object indicates the safety or danger of a person at a distance. A world-wide motif. — **MACK.** KASKA: Teit, JAFL, xxx, 448, No. 7. HARE: Petitot, p. 138. TS'ETS'ÁUT: Boas, JAFL, x, 44, No. 14. — **PLAT.** SHUSWAP: Teit, JE, ii, 708, No. 34. THOMPSON: Teit, MAFLS, vi, 34. NEZ PERCÉ: Spinden, JAFL, xxi, 149. — **N. PAC.** SNOHOMISH: Haeberlin, JAFL, xxxvii, 422. SKAGIT: *Ibid.*, p. 388. COOS: St. Clair-Frachtenberg, JAFL, xxii, 35. TAKELMA: Sapir, UPa, ii, Nos. 4, 13. — **CAL.** MODOC: Curtin, *Myths of the Modocs*, p. 26. MEWAN: Merriam, p. 79. MAIDU: Dixon, BAM, xvii, 104, No. 21. YOKUTS: Kroeber, UCal, iv, 242, No. 40. DIEGUEÑO: DuBois, JAFL, xvii, 234. — **PLNS.** SOUTHERN

Ute: Lowie, JAFL, xxxvii, 55, No. 30. Shoshoni: Lowie, PaAM, ii, 248, No. 6, and 285, No. 26. Wichita: Dorsey, CI, xxi, 129, No. 18; 210, No. 30; 215, No. 31. Skidi Pawnee: Dorsey, MAFLS, viii, 29, No. 5. Blackfoot: Wissler and Duvall, PaAM, ii, 68, No. 5. Canadian Dakota: Wallis, JAFL, xxxvi, 85, No. 19. — **WDL. CENT.** Menomini: Skinner and Satterlee, PaAM, xiii, 306. — **WDL. N.E.** Micmac: Rand, p. 86, No. 9. Malecite: Mechling, GSCan, iv, 51, No. 8; Stamp, JAFL, xxviii, 244. — **WDL. IROQ.** Iroquois: Smith, RBAE, ii, 92. Seneca: Curtin-Hewitt, RBAE, xxxii, 103, 399, 403, 504, 581. — **S.W.** Navaho: Matthews, MAFLS, v, 117, 122. Jicarilla Apache: Russell, JAFL, xi, 257. ——— Siberian and Asiatic relations: Jochelson, JE, vi, 367. European: Bolte-Polívka, i, 528.

150. *Bodily members as advisers* (D990, D1312.2). Just in the form found in this story, not a common motif. The usual form is that discussed in notes 83, 83a, and 83c.

151. *Roc* (*giant bird*) (B31.1). The hero is carried to a cliff by a giant bird. Here, with the aid of the young birds, he kills the giant bird. With the help of bat he reaches ground. This compound motif is common in the Southwest, on the plains, and the plateaus. — References: Boas, BBAE, lix, 286, note 1. — **MACK.** Beaver, Hare, Chipewyan, Kaska, Dog Rib: Boas, *loc. cit.* — **PLAT.** Chilcotin, Shuswap, Thompson, Okanagon, Sanpoil, Kutenai: *Ibid.* — **PLNS.** Shoshoni, Uintah Ute, Arapaho, Ponca, Gros Ventre, Assiniboin: *Ibid.* Crow: Lowie, PaAM, xxv, 9, 26, 36, 144, 147 (notes to Hidatsa and Arikara). Southern Paiute (Maopa): Lowie, JAFL, xxxvii, 187, No. 19, and 164, No. 4; (Shivwits): *Ibid.*, p. 112, No. 6. — **S.W.** Sia, Jicarilla Apache: Boas, *loc. cit.* Navaho: Matthews, MAFLS, v, 119. San Carlos Apache: Goddard, PaAM, xxiv, 17, 40. White Mountain Apache: *Ibid.*, p. 132. Zuñi: Cushing, p. 83. — Separate parts of this complex follow:

(a) *Roc* (motif alone). — **CAL.** Mewan: Merriam, pp. 67 ff. South Sierra Miwok: Barrett, UCal, xvi, 3, No. 1. Yokuts: Kroeber, UCal, iv, 208, No. 14. — **WDL. N.E.** Micmac: Hagar, AA, old ser., viii, 41. Montagnais: Speck, JAFL, xxxviii, 9. Passamaquoddy: Prince, PAES, x, 71, No. 12. — See also note 151c, *Thunderbird.*

(b) *Bat rescue from height: spider-web basket* (B542.1.2). Occurs in most versions of the *Roc* story.— In addition see: **PLNS.** Southern Paiute (Maopa): Lowie, JAFL, xxxvii, 187, No. 19. Southern Ute: Lowie, JAFL, xxxvii, 53, No. 28. — **WDL. IROQ.** Seneca: Curtin-Hewitt, RBAE, xxxi, 130, 426; Curtin, *Seneca Indian Myths*, pp. 119, 477. — **S.W.** Acoma: Parsons, JAFL, xxxi, 220, No. 4. Cf. note 283, *Sky basket.*

(c) *Thunderbird* (A284.2). It is impossible to separate with any degree of precision this motif from that of *Roc*, for stories of the adventure with the *Roc* are told of the thunderbird, but many other forms of the visit to the thunderbird appear. For this giant bird that produces the thunder, see Boas, RBAE, xxxi, 708, 712. — **MACK.** Ts'ets'áut: Boas, JAFL, ix, 261. Carrier: Morice, TCI, v, 6. — **N. PAC.** Haida, Bella Bella, Rivers Inlet: Boas, *op. cit.*, p. 708. Bella Bella, Rivers Inlet, Newettee, Kwakiutl, Nootka, Comox, Chehalis: Boas, *op. cit.*, p. 712.— **PLNS.** Wichita: Dorsey, CI, xxi, 102, No. 13, and 120, No. 16. Gros Ventre: Kroeber, PaAM, i, 88. — **WDL. CENT.** Ojibwa: Smith, JAFL, xix, 219; Laidlaw, OAR, xxvii, 72, and xxviii, 90; Laidlaw, OAR, reprint 1918, p. 60; Jones-Michelson, PAES, VII (II), 191, No. 18; Schoolcraft, *Hiawatha*, p. 205. CREE: Russell, p. 203. WINNEBAGO: Radin, JAFL, xxII, 288, No. 1. MENOMINI: Skinner and Satterlee, PaAM, xIII, 488.—**WDL. N.E.** PASSAMAQUODDY: Fewkes, JAFL, III, 265; Leland, pp. 263, 266.—**WDL. IROQ.** SENECA: Curtin-Hewitt, RBAE, xxxII, 177, No. 34. HURON: LeJeune, *Jes. Rel.*, VI, 225.—**S.E.** CHEROKEE: Mooney, RBAE, xIX, 312 ff. References fragmentary. IROQUOIS, OMAHA, ZUÑI, NAVAHO: Cf. Alexander, pp. 287.

152. *XLIV. Lodge-Boy and Thrown-Away.* In her husband's absence, a pregnant woman is killed by a man and twins taken from her body (T581). One is thrown in the lodge and the other is thrown away. Lodge-Boy is reared by his father. He discovers Thrown-Away, who has to be captured. The twins go on adventures.— Definitive study: Reichard, JAFL, xxxiv, 272, 306. Unless otherwise indicated, references are to her study.— **N. PAC.** TSIMSHIAN, KWAKIUTL.— **PLNS.** SHOSHONI, WICHITA, ARAPAHO, OMAHA, PAWNEE, CROW, HIDATSA, BLACKFOOT, GROS VENTRE, ASSINIBOIN. Add OGLALA, CREE: Jones, PAES, IX, 134. Cf. PAWNEE: Dorsey, CI, LIX, 142, 156, Nos. 39, 40, 41.— **WDL. CENT.** OJIBWA, MENOMINI, SAUK and FOX, KICKAPOO. — **WDL. N.E.** MICMAC: Reichard, *loc. cit.*; Parsons, JAFL, xxxviii, 55, No. 1; Speck, *International Journ. for American Linguistics*, I, 200.— **WDL. IROQ.** ONONDAGA, IROQUOIS (cf. SENECA: Curtin-Hewitt, RBAE, xxxII, 176, No. 34, and 461, No. 98).— **S.E.** CHEROKEE. Add CADDO: Dorsey, CI, xLI, 31, No. 17.

153. *Resuscitation by frightening dead* (E25). Usually combined with *resuscitation by assembling members* (note 114). The hero, after assembling the members, threatens them with a falling tree or frightens them into life in some other manner.— **PLNS.** SOUTHERN PAIUTE (MAOPA): Lowie, JAFL, xxxvii, 165, No. 4, and 188, No. 19. CROW: Lowie, PaAM, xxv, 66. PLAINS OJIBWA: Skinner, JAFL, xxxII, 340, No. 7.— **WDL. CENT.** OJIBWA: Schoolcraft, *Algic Researches*, I, 204; Jones-Michelson, PAES, VII (II), 244, No. 21. MENOMINI: Hoffman, RBAE, xIV, 232; Skinner and Satterlee, PaAM, xIII, 308.— **WDL. IROQ.** SENECA: Curtin-Hewitt, RBAE, xxxII, 138, 212, 217, 398, 404, 490, 586, 699. — Some closely related motifs are:

(*a*) *Resuscitation by breathing on corpse* (E66). In most cases a clear example of sympathetic magic. — **PLNS.** SOUTHERN PAIUTE (SHIVWITS): Lowie, JAFL, xxxvii, 131, No. 12, and 148, No. 16. — **WDL. CENT.** OJIBWA: Jones-Michelson, PAES, VII (II), 109, 367. — **WDL. IROQ.** SENECA: Curtin-Hewitt, RBAE, xxxI, 308, No. 58.

(*b*) *Resuscitation by music* (E55). — **N. PAC.** KWAKIUTL: Boas, CU, II, 465 (a rattle). — **CAL.** MIWOK: Gifford, UCal, xII, 312, No. 7. — **PLNS.** BLACKFOOT: Grinnell, *Blackfoot Lodge Tales*, p. 106. PLAINS OJIBWA: Skinner, JAFL, xxxII, 301, No. 7. — **WDL. N.E.** MICMAC: Leland, p. 61; Parsons, JAFL, xxxviii, 72, No. 7. — **WDL. IROQ.** SENECA: Curtin-Hewitt, RBAE, xxxII, 275, No. 53. — **S.W.** ZUÑI: Handy, JAFL, xxxI, 471, No. 19. HOPI: Voth, FM, VIII, 208, No. 76.

154. *Death thought sleep* (E175). A resuscitated person thinks he has been sleeping. — **MACK.** KASKA: Teit, JAFL, xxx, 440, No. 1. — **PLAT.** THOMPSON: Teit, MAFLS, VI, 79, No. 29. FLATHEAD: McDermott, JAFL, xIV, 244, No. 5. PEND D'OREILLE (KALISPEL): Teit, MAFLS, xI, 114, No. 1, and 116, No. 3; Curtis, VII, 104. — **N. PAC.** RIVERS INLET, NEWETTEE,

KWAKIUTL: Boas, RBAE, XXXI, 667. KWAKIUTL: Boas, CU, II, 63, 111, 199.
COWICHAN: Curtis, IX, 134. CHEHALIS: Hill-Tout, JAI, XXXIV, 359. SKAGIT:
Haeberlin, JAFL, XXXVII, 389. KATHLAMET: Boas, BBAE, XXVI, 108. Coos:
Frachtenberg, CU, I, 121, No. 18. — CAL. MODOC: Curtin, *Myths of the
Modocs*, p. 207. JOSHUA: Farrand-Frachtenberg, JAFL, XXVIII, 230. WAPPO:
Radin, UCal, XIX, 59, No. 9. — PLNS. CROW: Simms, FM, II, 304, No. 19.
SKIDI PAWNEE: Dorsey, MAFLS, VIII, 93, No. 25. — WDL. CENT. OTTAWA:
Schoolcraft, *Hiawatha*, pp. 158 ff. — WDL. N.E. MICMAC: Rand, p. 275,
No. 46; Leland, p. 108.

155. *Twin adventurers* (Z420). Belongs regularly to the tales listed in note
152. See also note 33, *Twins quarrel before birth*. In addition, see: — CAL.
MAIDU: Dixon, BAM, XVII, 54, No. 3. YUKI: Kroeber, UCal, IV, 186.
DIEGUEÑO: DuBois, JAFL, XVII, 217 ff. — PLNS. WICHITA: Dorsey, CI,
XXI, No. 12. ARAPAHO: Dorsey and Kroeber, FM, V, 343, No. 139. PAWNEE:
Dorsey, MAFLS, VIII, 39, No. 8, and 89, No. 25; Dorsey, CI, LIX, 57, No. 13,
and 143, No. 39. PONCA: Dorsey, CNAE, VI, 215. CROW: Simms, FM, II,
303, No. 19. HIDATSA: Matthews, *U. S. Geol. and Geog. Survey, Misc. Pub.*,
VII, 63. GROS VENTRE: Kroeber, PaAM, I, 79, No. 19. — WDL. CENT.
FOX: Owen, PFLS, LI, 93; Lasley, JAFL, XV, 177. — WDL. N.E. MICMAC:
Rand, p. 71, No. 8. — WDL. IROQ. SENECA: Curtin-Hewitt, RBAE, XXXI,
79, No. 1, and 629, No. 119 (sworn brotherhood). — S.E. CHEROKEE:
Mooney, RBAE, XIX, 242, No. 3. — S.W. NAVAHO: Matthews, MAFLS,
V, 108 ff., 115 ff. JICARILLA APACHE: Mooney, AA, old ser., XI, 201; Russell, JAFL, XI, 255. WHITE MOUNTAIN APACHE: Goddard, PaAM, XXIV,
93 ff. ZUÑI: Parsons, JAFL, XXXVI, 143. SIA: Stevenson, RBAE, XI, 43,
44.

156. *Dreadnaughts* (Z411). Hero goes repeatedly on adventures in spite
of warning against them. Most of the tales of *Lodge-Boy and Thrown-Away*
(note 152), of *Blood-Clot-Boy* (note 165), of *The Attack on the Giant Elk* have
this incident. — ESK. KODIAK: Golder, JAFL, XVI, 95 and XXII, 17. —
PLAT. WASCO: Curtin, PAES, II, 276. — N. PAC. CHEHALIS: Hill-Tout,
JAI, XXXIV, 360.—CAL. WINTUN: Curtin, *Creation Myths*, pp. 121 ff. MODOC:
Curtin, *Myths of the Modocs*, pp. 95 ff., 161 ff. YUKI: Kroeber, UCal, IV, 186.
YANA: Sapir, UCal, IX, 17, No. 1. MAIDU: Dixon, BAM, XVII, 51, No. 3,
and 59, No. 4; Powers, CNAE, III, 294. MIWOK: cf. Kroeber, UCal, IV,
203, No. 10. — PLNS. SHOSHONI: St. Clair, JAFL, XXII, 267. SOUTHERN
PAIUTE (MAOPA): Lowie, JAFL, XXXVII, 187, No. 19, and 189, No. 20.
WICHITA: Dorsey, CI, XXI, 88, No. 12. ARAPAHO: Dorsey and Kroeber,
FM, V, 341–388, Nos. 139–143. PAWNEE: Dorsey, MAFLS, VI, 91, No. 25;
Dorsey, CI, LIX, 59, No. 13, and 143, No. 39; Grinnell, *Pawnee Hero Stories*,
p. 197. OMAHA: Dorsey, JAFL, I, 76. PONCA: Dorsey, CNAE, VI, 215.
BLACKFOOT: Wissler and Duvall, PaAM, II, 61. GROS VENTRE: Kroeber,
PaAM, I, 90, No. 21. CROW: Simms, FM, II, 303. DAKOTA: Riggs, CNAE,
IX, 91. ASSINIBOIN: Lowie, PaAM, IV, 142, No. 4. — WDL. CENT. SAUK
and FOX: Lasley, JAFL, XV, 177. — WDL. IROQ. SENECA: Curtin-Hewitt,
RBAE, XXXII, 79, 81, 150, 177, 183, 187, 203, 342, 348, 354, 373, 424, 446,
520, 565. IROQUOIS: Smith, RBAE, II, 86. — S.E. MUSKHOGEAN: Swan-
ton, JAFL, XXVI, 204. — S.W. NAVAHO: Matthews, MAFLS, VI, 106 ff.
JICARILLA APACHE: Goddard, PaAM, VIII, 196, No. 3; Mooney, AA, old ser.,
XI, 201. SAN CARLOS APACHE: Goddard, PaAM, XXIV, 9 ff., 26 ff., 36 ff.

MOHAVE-APACHE: Gould, JAFL, XXIV, 319. ZUÑI: Cushing, p. 65. PIMA: Russell, RBAE, XXVI, 246.

157. *Pot-tilter* (G331). Old woman has a pot that sucks people in as she points it at them. The hero succeeds in turning it on her and destroying her. — **PLNS.** CROW, HIDATSA: Reichard, JAFL, XXXIV, 270, 273. GROS VENTRE: Kroeber, PaAM, I, 85, No. 20.

158. *Sucking monster* (G332). Giant (sometimes represented as giant hall or cave) sucks in victims. — References: Reichard, JAFL, XXXIV, 270, 273. — **PLAT.** and **N. PAC.** See note 159. — **PLNS.** CHEYENNE [?], CROW: Reichard, *op. cit.*, p. 271. CROW, HIDATSA, WICHITA, PAWNEE: *Ibid.*, p. 273. BLACK-FOOT: Grinnell, *Blackfoot Lodge Tales*, p. 36; Uhlenbeck, VKAWA, XII, 47; Wissler and Duvall, PaAM, II, 57. GROS VENTRE: Kroeber, PaAM, I, 85, No. 20. — **WDL. IROQ.** SENECA: Curtin-Hewitt, RBAE, XXXII, 182, No. 35. — **S.W.** JICARILLA APACHE: Mooney, AA, old ser., XI, 202; Voth, FM, VIII, 217, No. 83. — Practically all examples of this motif contain the incidents handled in the next note (159) and will be found listed there.

159. *Monster killed from within* (K952). — References: Boas, RBAE, XXXI, 611, 659, 718, 868. — **ESK.** GREENLAND: Rink, p. 438, No. 89. BAFFIN LAND: Boas, BAM, XV, 538. ALASKA: Nelson, RBAE, XVIII, 465. — **MACK.** ANVIK: Chapman, PAES, VI, 98, No. 24. LOUCHEUX: Camsell-Barbeau, JAFL, XXVIII, 257, No. 13. — **PLAT.** CHILCOTIN, SHUSWAP, THOMPSON, UTAMQT, WISHRAM, WASCO: Boas, RBAE, XXXI, 611. SHUSWAP, THOMPSON, LILLOOET: Boas, *op. cit.*, pp. 718, 719. PEND D'OREILLE: Teit, MAFLS, XI, 116, No. 2; Curtis, VII, 103. FLATHEAD: McDermott, JAFL, XIV, 240 f. NEZ PERCÉ: Spinden, JAFL, XXI, 14; Curtis, VIII, 162. KUTENAI: Boas, BBAE, LIX, 45, 77, 87. CŒUR D'ALÈNE, THOMPSON, SAHAPTIN: Teit, JAFL, XXXII, 221. — **N. PAC.** TLINGIT, HAIDA, BELLA COOLA, RIVERS INLET, CHINOOK, COOS: Boas, RBAE, XXXI, 718 f. NASS: *Ibid.*, p. 868. TA-KELMA: *Ibid.*, pp. 611, 612. TAHLTAN: Teit, JAFL, XXXII, 221 and XXXIV, 235, 237. TSIMSHIAN: Boas, BBAE, XXVII, 118. SONGISH: Hill-Tout, JAI, XXXVII, 348. — **CAL.** SHASTA: Farrand-Frachtenberg, JAFL, XXVIII, 215, No. 6. JOSHUA: Frachtenberg, JAFL, XXVIII, 236. ACHOMAWI: Dixon, JAFL, XXI, 169. — **PLNS.** UINTAH UTE: Mason, JAFL, XXIII, 335. OSAGE: Dorsey, FM, VII, 42, No. 34. PONCA: Dorsey, CNAE, VI, 30, 34. DAKOTA: Riggs, CNAE, IX, 91, 140. PAWNEE: Dorsey, CI, LIX, 493 f., Nos. 40–41. GROS VENTRE: Kroeber, PaAM, I, 85, No. 20. — **WDL. CENT.** OJIBWA: Schoolcraft, *Hiawatha*, pp. 21, 23; Carson, JAFL, XXX, 492; DeJong, *Original Odjibwe-Texts*, pp. 10, 11; Jones-Michelson, PAES, VII (1), 201, 207, 467. MENOMINI: Skinner and Satterlee, PaAM, XIII, 272; Hoffman, RBAE, XIV, 89, 125. OTTAWA: Blackbird, p. 55. CREE: Skinner, PaAM, IX, 101; Russell, p. 312. SAULTEAUX: Young, *Algonquin Indian Tales*, p. 169. WINNE-BAGO: N. Curtis, *Indian Book*, p. 248. — **S.E.** CHEROKEE: Mooney, RBAE, XIX, 320. — **S.W.** NAVAHO: Parsons, JAFL, XXXVI, 368, No. 1. HOPI: Voth, FM, VIII, 83, No. 19. PIMA: Russell, RBAE, XXVI, 246. ⸺ SIBERIA: Joch-elson, JE, VI, 368; Bogaras, AA, new ser., IV, 645. — EUROPEAN: Parsons, MAFLS, XIII, 8, note 3 (references). — A related motif is:

(a) *Victims rescued when swallower is killed* (F913). — **ESK.** SMITH SOUND: Boas, JAFL, XII, 175. — **MACK.** DOG RIB: Petitot, p. 319. — **PLAT.** CHILCOTIN: Farrand, JE, II, 46, No. 30. WISHRAM: Curtis, VIII, 139 ff. — **N. PAC.** TLINGIT, HAIDA, NEWETTEE, NOOTKA, COMOX: Boas,

RBAE, xxxi, 687–688. Chinook: Boas, BBAE, xx, No. 1. Kathlamet: Boas, BBAE, xxvi, 108. Quinault: Farrand, JE, ii, 84, No. 1. — CAL. Kato: Goddard, UCal, v, 224, No. 20. — PLNS. Osage: Dorsey, FM, vii, 30, No. 24. Arapaho: Dorsey and Kroeber, FM, v, 10, No. 5, and 87, No. 44. Ponca: Dorsey, CNAE, vi, 30, 34. Atsina: Curtis, v, 129 ff. Arikara: Dorsey, CI, xvii, 77, No. 21. Dakota: Zitkala-Ša, p. 141. — WDL. CENT. Timagami Ojibwa: Speck, GSCan, ix, 65. Cree: Cresswell, JAFL, xxxvi, 404. Menomini: Hoffman, RBAE, xiv, 231. — WDL. IROQ. Iroquois: Smith, RBAE, ii, 91. Seneca: Curtin-Hewitt, RBAE, xxxii, 183, No. 35, and 483, No. 104. —— Siberia: Bogaras, AA, new ser., iv, 645. — Also European: Bolte-Polívka, i, 40. — An interesting related motif is: (b) *Swallowed person becomes bald* (F921). — N. PAC. Cowichan, Comox, Nootka: Boas, RBAE, xxxi, 688 —— Siberia:Jochelson, JE, vi, 375.

160. *Killing trees threaten hero* (H1522). — PLNS. Crow: Lowie, PaAM, xxv, 299 ff., 303 ff. It appears in this tribe as a part of two different tales (our Nos. xliv and li).

161. *Rectum snakes* (G328). Snakes enter hero's rectum and kill him. — References: Reichard, JAFL, xxxiv, 270, 273. — PLNS. Arapaho, Hidatsa, Pawnee, Arikara: Reichard, *op. cit.*, p. 270. Crow, Blackfoot, Arapaho, Pawnee: *Ibid.*, p. 273. Gros Ventre: Kroeber, PaAM, i, 93, No. 21. A number of stories tell of the entrance into a body through the rectum, though they are not exactly parallel to the incident under discussion. See tale xxxvi (note 104), "Coyote and Porcupine," and references in Jochelson, JE, vi, 377 (Siberia, Chehalis, Tsimshian, Hare).

162. *Lulling to sleep by "sleepy" stories* (D1963). In the several versions of the *Rectum snakes* incident there is a contest between the hero and the snakes in lulling one another to sleep by stories. — References: Lowie, PaAM, xxv, 36 (PLNS. Crow, Arapaho, Gros Ventre, Assiniboin, Arikara).

163. *Cliff ogre* (G321). A monster kicks people over a cliff, where they are eaten by her brood. — References: Waterman, JAFL, xxvii, 43. — MACK. Kaska: Teit, JAFL, xxx, 430. Beaver: Goddard, PaAM, x, 236. — PLAT. Chilcotin, Pend d'Oreille, Sahaptin: Teit, JAFL, xxx, 430. — N. PAC. Chinook: Waterman, *loc. cit.* — CAL. Wintun: *Ibid.* — PLNS. Shoshoni, Arapaho: *Ibid.* Blackfoot: Grinnell, *Blackfoot Lodge Tales*, p. 37. Crow: Simms, FM, ii, 306, No. 19, and 310, No. 21; Curtis, iv, 117 ff. — WDL. N.E. Micmac: cf. Rand, p. 90, No. 9. — S.W. Navaho: Matthews, MAFLS, v, 107, 122. Jicarilla Apache: Goddard, PaAM, viii, 203. San Carlos Apache: Goddard, PaAM, xxiv, 12, 34. Sia: Stevenson, RBAE, xi, 46.

164. *Fire-moccasins* (G345). An ogre has moccasins that set fire to everything he walks around. — References: Reichard, JAFL, xxxiv, 271, 273, 306 f. (PLNS. Crow, Hidatsa).

165. *XLV. Blood-Clot-Boy* (T541.1). Old man abused by son-in-law brings in a clot of blood, from which a child is born. The blood-clot boy avenges the old man and also goes on adventures. — PLNS. Southern Ute: Lowie, JAFL, xxxvii, 39, 44, 46, No. 22. Arapaho: Dorsey and Kroeber, FM, v, 298–309, Nos. 130, 131, cf. 310 ff., Nos. 132, 133. Ponca: Dorsey, CNAE, vi, 48. Pawnee: Dorsey, MAFLS, viii, 80, No. 24. Dakota: Zitkala-Ša, pp. 61, 77; Curtis, iii, 111; Riggs, CNAE, ix, 101. Blackfoot: Uhlenbeck, VKAWA, xii, 34; Maclean, JAFL, vi, 167; Grinnell, *Blackfoot Lodge Tales*, p. 29; Wissler and Duvall, PaAM, ii, 53. Gros Ventre: Kroeber, PaAM,

1, 82, No. 20. Canadian Dakota: Wallis, JAFL, xxxvi, 75.—Cf. the following fairly close parallels: **CAL.** Maidu: Dixon, BAM, xvii, 59. Yokuts: Kroeber, UCal, iv, 225, No. 34.—**WDL. CENT.** Winnebago: Radin, JAFL, xxii, 288 ff.—**WDL. N.E.** Micmac: Rand, p. 280, No. 48.—**S.E.** Texas Coast: Hilder, AA, new ser., i, 592.

166. *Miraculous birth.* (T540). Stories of miraculous birth are very widespread among the American Indians. In addition to the references given below, see the following notes: 21, *Impregnation by wind, Impregnation from sunlight;* 44, *Theft of light by being swallowed and re-born;* 116, *Short pregnancy;* 139, *Dug-from-Ground;* 152, *Lodge-Boy and Thrown-Away;* 165, *Blood-Clot-Boy;* 229, *Birth from wound;* 265, *Birth from mucus;* and the various subdivisions of this note.—References: Boas, RBAE, xxxi, 708, 734.—Only a few miscellaneous types are given here; for detailed treatment, see the subdivisions of this note.—**MACK.** Beaver: Goddard, PaAM, x, 240 (from scrapings of buffalo hide).—**PLAT.** Lillooet: Hill-Tout, JAI, xxxv, 185 (from salmonroe).—**N. PAC.** Chehalis, Chinook, Tillamook, Coos: Boas, RBAE, xxxi, 735 (fish-roe, branches, arrowhead, hammer).—**WDL. N.E.** Passamaquoddy: Leland, p. 255 (child of a mountain).

(a) *Birth from tears* (T543).—**N. PAC.** Tsimshian, Haida, Kwakiutl, Nootka, Comox, Songish: Boas, RBAE, xxxi, 734.

(b) *Birth from secretions of body* (T542).—**N. PAC.** Haida, Rivers Inlet, Newettee, Kwakiutl: Boas, RBAE, xxxi, 734.

(c) *Child born in jug* (T561).—**CAL.** Paviotso: Lowie, JAFL, xxxvii, 200, No. 1, and 211, No. 2.—**S.W.** Hopi: Voth, FM, viii, 155, No. 46.

(d) *Pregnant man* (T578.)—Cf. **MACK.** Kaska: Teit, JAFL, xxx, 472, No. 25.—**PLNS.** Southern Paiute: Lowie, JAFL, xxxvii, 125, 137, 166 (man suckles child). Pawnee: Dorsey, CI, lix, 313, No. 86.——Siberia: Jochelson, JE, vi, 365.

(e) *Immaculate conception* (T510). No reason assigned for virgin's pregnancy.—**CAL.** Hupa: Goddard, UCal, i, 193, No. 10.—**PLNS.** Pawnee: Dorsey, MAFLS, viii, 178, No. 45. Cheyenne: Kroeber, JAFL, xiii, 187 (through imagination).—**WDL. CENT.** Fox: Jones, PAES, i, 19.—**S.E.** Caddo: Dorsey, CI, xli, 43, No. 20.

(f) *Pregnancy from casual contact with man* (T531). General references: Hartland, *Primitive Paternity,* i, 18, 26.—**PLAT.** Shuswap: Jochelson, JE, vi, 380 f.—**N. PAC.** Comox, Nootka, Kwakiutl, Rivers Inlet, Quinault: *Ibid.*—**PLNS.** Wichita: Dorsey, CI, xxi, 172, No. 24. Osage: Dorsey, FM, vii, 43, No. 36. Assiniboin: Lowie, PaAM, iv, 136. —— Siberia: Jochelson, JE, vi, 380 f.

(g) *Conception from rain* (T522).—General references: Hartland, *Primitive Paternity,* i, 24.—**S.W.** San Carlos Apache: Goddard, PaAM, xxiv, 8, 30. White Mountain Apache: *Ibid.*, p. 93. Cf. **PLNS.** Wichita: Dorsey, CI, xxi, 249, No. 39 (bathing).

(h) *Conception from eating* (T511).—References: Jochelson, JE, vi, 380 f.—**ESK.** Greenland: Rink, p. 437, No. 87. Bering Strait: Nelson, RBAE, xviii, 461. Kodiak: Golder, JAFL, xvi, 85.—**MACK.** Chipewyan: Goddard, PaAM, x, 58, No. 8.—**PLAT.** Shuswap: Jochelson, *loc. cit.*—**N. PAC.** Comox, Nootka, Kwakiutl, Newettee, Rivers Inlet, Tsimshian, Tlingit, Quinault, Chinook: *Ibid.* Tlingit, Haida: Boas, RBAE, xxxi, 734. Takelma: Sapir, UPa, ii, 18, No. 1.—**PLNS.** Arapaho: Dorsey and Kroeber, FM, v, 185, No. 85. CROW: Lowie, PaAM, xxv, 129. MANDAN: Will and Spinden, *Peabody Museum Papers*, III, 138; Curtis, v, 39 ff. DAKOTA: Wissler, JAFL, xx, 201. GROS VENTRE: Kroeber, PaAM, I, 98, No. 23. (In all the Plains versions the object swallowed is a stone). — **WDL. N.E.** PASSAMAQUODDY: Fewkes, JAFL, III, 273; Leland, p. 277.— General references: Hartland, *Primitive Paternity*, I, 4 ff.

(i) *Child removed from dead mother* (T581). See all references in note 152, *Lodge-Boy and Thrown-Away.* — See also: **PLNS.** SOUTHERN UTE: Lowie, JAFL, xxxvII, 53, No. 27. SOUTHERN PAIUTE (SHIVWITS): *Ibid.*, p. 108, No. 5, and p. 125, No. 11; (MAOPA): *Ibid.*, p. 166, No. 5, and p. 192, No. 22. — **WDL. IROQ.** SENECA: Curtin-Hewitt, RBAE, xxxII, 372, No. 68.

167. *Monster killed by throwing hot stones into throat* (K951).— References: Boas, RBAE, xxxi, 681 f.— **PLAT.** WISHRAM: Boas, *loc. cit.* — **N. PAC.** TSIMSHIAN, NASS, TLINGIT, HAIDA, COMOX, QUINAULT, KATHLAMET: *Ibid.* — **PLNS.** BLACKFOOT: Wissler and Duvall, PaAM, II, 55.——SIBERIA: Jochelson, JE, vi, 376. — Cf. note 274.

168. *Spine test* (H1531). Attempt is made to kill the hero by throwing him on a sharp spine or spike.— References: Teit, JAFL, xxx, 430; Boas, RBAE, xxxi, 799.— **MACK.** LOUCHEUX, KASKA, TS'ETS'ÁUT: Teit, *loc. cit.* — **N. PAC.** NASS, TLINGIT, NEWETTEE, KWAKIUTL, NOOTKA, COMOX, CHEHALIS, SQUAMISH: Boas, *loc. cit.* — **S.E.** CHEROKEE: Mooney, RBAE, xix, 312, No. 63, and 346, No. 84.— **S.W.** NAVAHO: Matthews, MAFLS, v, 111. WHITE MOUNTAIN APACHE: Goddard, PaAM, xxiv, 96, 97.

169. *Swinging contest* (K1618). — References: Boas, BBAE, LIX, 307 (**PLAT.** THOMPSON, LILLOOET, KUTENAI, SECHELT. — **N. PAC.** CHINOOK, QUINAULT. — **CAL.** MODOC, YANA, HUPA. — **PLNS.** SHOSHONI, OSAGE, PONCA, PAWNEE, ARAPAHO, GROS VENTRE, BLACKFOOT, ASSINIBOIN. — **WDL. CENT.** CREE, Fox). Add **CAL.** WESTERN MONO: Gifford, JAFL, xxxvi, 348, No. 18.— **WDL. N.E.** MONTAGNAIS: Speck, JAFL, xxxviii, 15.

170. *XLVI. The Son-in-law Tests* (H310). The testing of a son-in-law by a father-in-law is one of the commonest forms of the test theme. It has been met already in tale XXXIX, "The Sun Tests his Son-in-law" (note 111). — References: Boas, RBAE, xxxi, 797.— **ESK.** KODIAK: Golder, JAFL, xvi, 95. — **MACK.** TS'ETS'ÁUT: Boas, *loc. cit.* KASKA: Teit, JAFL, xxx, 436, No. 1. CARRIER: Morice, TCI, v, 7. ANVIK: Chapman, PAES, vi, 20, No. 3.— **PLAT.** THOMPSON, UTAMQT, LILLOOET, WISHRAM: Boas, *loc. cit.* OKANAGON: Teit, MAFLS, xi, 79; Teit, JAI, xli, 150.— **N. PAC.** TSIMSHIAN, NASS, HAIDA, BELLA COOLA, NEWETTEE, KWAKIUTL, COMOX, NOOTKA, SQUAMISH, CHEHALIS, KATHLAMET, QUINAULT, CHINOOK, TILLAMOOK: Boas, *loc. cit.* TAHLTAN: Teit, JAFL, xxxiv, 235, No. 41. QUILEUTE: Farrand-Mayer, JAFL, xxxii, 262, No. 9. ALSEA: Frachtenberg, BBAE, LXVII, 119, No. 9. COOS: Frachtenberg, CU, I, 27. KALAPUYA: noted in Farrand-Frachtenberg, JAFL, xxviii, 211.— **CAL.** MODOC: Curtin, *Creation Myths*, p. xxix. SHASTA: Farrand-Frachtenberg, JAFL, xxviii, 211, No. 4. YANA: Curtin, *op. cit.*, pp. 281, 430. HUPA: Goddard, UCal, I, 146, No. 2. WAPPO: Radin, UCal, xix, 99, No. 11. WINTUN: Curtin, *op. cit.*, pp. 134 ff. MAIDU: Dixon, BAM, xvii, 67. WESTERN MONO: Gifford, JAFL, xxxvi, 338, No. 11. — **PLNS.** UINTAH UTE: Mason, JAFL, xxiii, 322. WICHITA: Dorsey, CI, xxi, 130, No. 19. PAWNEE: Dorsey, MAFLS, viii, 30, No. 6; Dorsey, CI, LIX, 38, No. 6. CROW: Simms, FM, II, 297, No. 15; Lowie, PaAM, xxv,

149. CHEYENNE: Kroeber, JAFL, XIII, 177, No. 16. ARAPAHO: Dorsey and Kroeber, FM, V, 294, No. 129. GROS VENTRE: Kroeber, PaAM, I, 88; Curtis, V, 129. ASSINIBOIN: Lowie, PaAM, IV, 154, No. 8. — **WDL. CENT.** OJIBWA: Schoolcraft, *Indian in his Wigwam*, p. 106; Schoolcraft, *Hiawatha*, p. 202; Jones, JAFL, XXIX, 376; Radin, GSCan, II, 53–56, Nos. 27, 28; Jones-Michelson, PAES VII (II), 65, 179. TIMAGAMI OJIBWA: Speck, GSCan, IX, 44, 61. MENOMINI: Skinner and Satterlee, PaAM, XIII, 366; Hoffman, RBAE, XIV, 169, 187, 233. CREE: Swindlehurst, JAFL, XVIII, 140, 143; Skinner, PaAM, IX, 92; Skinner, JAFL, XXIX, 353; Russell, p. 205. SAULTEAUX: Skinner, PaAM, IX, 168. MISSISAUGA: Chamberlain, JAFL, III, 151. — **WDL. N.E.** MONTAGNAIS: Speck, JAFL, XXXVIII, 16. NASKAPI: Speck, JAFL, XXVIII, 70. MICMAC: Speck, JAFL, XXVIII, 64. — **WDL. IROQ.** IRO-QUOIS: Smith, RBAE, II, 100. HURON-WYANDOT: Barbeau, GSCan, XI, 154, No. 48. SENECA: Curtin-Hewitt, RBAE, XXXII, 85, No. 3; 394, No. 70; 404, No. 71; 427, No. 79; 467, No. 100. — **S.W.** NAVAHO: Matthews, MAFLS, V, 177. JICARILLA APACHE: Mooney, AA, old ser., XI, 201. ZUÑI: Parsons, JAFL, XXXI, 240, No. 16. —— SIBERIA: Jochelson, JE, VI, 373. SOUTH AMERICA: Koch-Grünberg, Nos. 2, 13, 14, 38, 64, 115. — For European forms of the theme, see tale LXXXII, "The White Cat," (note 293).

171. *Help from ogre's child (or wife)* (G532). In a large number of tales of the test theme the hero is helped by the child or the wife of the tester. In the son-in-law type it is naturally the daughter. The help from children also appears in the *Roc* motif. See all the references in note 151. It also occurs in most versions of tale LVII, "The Piqued Buffalo-Wife." See all references in note 224. — **PLAT.** THOMPSON: Teit, MAFLS, VI, 35, and 93, No. 38. SHUSWAP: Teit, JE, II, 736, No. 52, and 757, No. 65. CHILCOTIN: Farrand, JE, II, 27, No. 11. — **N. PAC.** BELLA COOLA: Boas, JE, I, 58, 89. KWAKIUTL: Boas and Hunt, JE, III, 354. CHINOOK: Boas, BBAE, XX, No. 1. KATHLA-MET: Boas, BBAE, XXVI, 10. TAKELMA: Sapir, UPa, II, 125, No. 14. — **CAL.** MODOC: Curtin, *Myths of the Modocs*, p. 73. HUPA: Goddard, UCal, I, 213. PAVIOTSO: Lowie, JAFL, XXXVII, 206, No. 1*e*. — **PLNS.** SOUTHERN UTE: *Ibid.*, p. 77, No. 48. ARAPAHO: Dorsey and Kroeber, FM, V, 391, No. 144. PAWNEE: Dorsey, CI, LIX, 31, No. 5. PONCA: Dorsey, CNAE, VI, 284. WICHITA: Dorsey, CI, XXI, 63, No. 8. — **WDL. CENT.** OJIBWA: Schoolcraft, *Hiawatha*, pp. 202 ff.; Speck, GSCan, IX, 44; information from Laidlaw. MENOMINI: Skinner, JAFL, XXVI, 71 (European?); Hoffman, RBAE, XIV, 223 ff. — **WDL. N.E.** MICMAC: Rand, p. 9, No. 2. MONTAGNAIS: Speck, JAFL, XXXVIII, 14. — **WDL. IROQ.** IROQUOIS: Smith, RBAE, II, 101. HURON-WYANDOT: Barbeau, GSCan, XI, 65, No. 12. — **S.E.** BILOXI: Dorsey and Swanton, BBAE, XLVII, 103. — **S.W.** JICARILLA APACHE: Goddard, PaAM, VIII, 210, No. 18.

172. *Ogre's own moccasins burned* (K1615). Ogre plans to burn hero's moccasins while they are camping together. Hero exchanges the moccasins and ogre burns his own. — **MACK.** KASKA: Teit, JAFL, XXX, 441, No. 1. BEAVER: Goddard, PaAM, X, 233. — **N. PAC.** TAHLTAN: Teit, JAFL, XXXII, 228, No. 5. — **PLNS.** PLAINS CREE: Skinner, JAFL, XXIX, 353, No. 2. — **WDL. CENT.** CREE: Skinner PaAM, IX, 88. OJIBWA: Schoolcraft, *Hiawatha*, p. 209. TIMAGAMI OJIBWA: Speck, GSCan, IX, 45. MISSISAUGA: Chamberlain, JAFL, III, 151. — **WDL. N.E.** MONTAGNAIS: Speck, JAFL, XXXVIII, 16. — **S.W.** NAVAHO: Matthews, MAFLS, V, 190.

173. *Toboggan test* (H1536). — **WDL. CENT.** OJIBWA: Jones-Michelson, PAES, VII (II), 99, 185, 639, No. 67. TIMAGAMI OJIBWA: Speck, GSCan, IX, 45.

174. *Lousing* (D1962). Lousing of the head occurs in tales scattered over the continent. In some cases it is done to put the victim to sleep; in others it is a service demanded by an ogre of the hero, who deceives him, as in our tale, by cracking cranberries to make the ogre think the hero is cracking the lice (really frogs or large vermin) in his teeth. References fragmentary. — **MACK.** KASKA: Teit, JAFL, XXX, 449, No. 8, and 459, No. 14. — **PLAT.** SHUSWAP: Teit, JE, II, 751, No. 60. — **N. PAC.** KWAKIUTL: Boas and Hunt, JE, III, 121, 293. CHINOOK: Boas, BBAE, XX, Nos. 1, 9. — **CAL.** LASSIK: Goddard, JAFL, XIX, 135, No. 2. — **PLNS.** ARAPAHO: Dorsey and Kroeber, FM, V, 132, No. 69; 135, No. 70; 345, No. 139; 381, No. 142. CROW: Lowie, PaAM, XXV, 143. CHEYENNE: Campbell, JAFL, XXIX, 408. BLACKFOOT: Wissler and Duvall, PaAM, II, 139. PAWNEE: Dorsey, CI, LIX, 33, No. 5. — **WDL. CENT.** OJIBWA: Jones-Michelson, PAES, VII (II), 639, No. 67. TIMAGAMI OJIBWA: Speck, GSCan, IX, 44. MENOMINI: Skinner and Satterlee, PaAM, XIII, 365. — **WDL. N.E.** MICMAC: Rand, p. 285, No. 50. PASSAMAQUODDY: Leland, p. 38. — **WDL. IROQ.** SENECA: Curtin-Hewitt, RBAE, XXXII, 84, 191, 753.

175. *Marooned egg-gatherer* (K1616). The father-in-law has the youth hunt eggs on an island and deserts him. On the Pacific Coast a parallel incident is that of a marooned hunter. — **MACK.** KASKA: Teit, JAFL, XXX, 451, No. 10. — **N. PAC.** HAIDA, RIVERS INLET, TLINGIT, TSIMSHIAN: Teit, *loc. cit.* — **PLNS.** DAKOTA: Riggs, CNAE, IX, 139. — **WDL. CENT.** OJIBWA: Schoolcraft, *Hiawatha*, p. 205. TIMAGAMI OJIBWA: Speck, GSCan, IX, 46. MENOMINI: Skinner and Satterlee, PaAM, XIII, 368. CREE: Skinner, PaAM, IX, 92; Russell, p. 204; Petitot, p. 452. MISSISAUGA: Chamberlain, JAFL, III, 151. — **WDL. N.E.** NASKAPI: Speck, JAFL, XXVIII, 71. MICMAC: Rand, p. 79. PASSAMAQUODDY: Prince, PAES, X, 21, No. 2. — **WDL. IROQ.** SENECA: Curtin-Hewitt, RBAE, XXXII, 218, No. 41 (= Curtin, *Seneca Indian Myths*, p. 347). —— SIBERIA: Bogaras, AA, new ser., IV, 664.

176. Cf. note 80.

177. *XLVII. The Jealous Father* (S11). A father, jealous of his son, seeks the son's life. Exact parallels are few. — **PLNS.** CANADIAN DAKOTA: Wallis, JAFL, XXXVI, 78. — **WDL. CENT.** CREE: Skinner, PaAM, IX, 92. OJIBWA: Jones, PAES, VII (II), 381, No. 47. — **WDL. N.E.** NASKAPI: Speck, JAFL, XXVIII, 71.

178. *Potiphar's wife* (K2111). A woman makes vain overtures to a man and then accuses him of attempting to force her. — **ESK.** WEST HUDSON BAY: Boas, BAM, XV, 329. — **PLAT.** SAHAPTIN: Farrand-Mayer, MAFLS, XI, 158. — **N. PAC.** TSIMSHIAN, HAIDA: Boas, RBAE, XXXI, 782. — **PLNS.** OMAHA: Wissler, JAFL, XX, 196, No. 7. ARAPAHO: Dorsey and Kroeber, FM, V, 190, No. 86; 193, No. 87; 200, No. 88. DAKOTA: Riggs, CNAE, IX, 139. BLACKFOOT: Grinnell, *Blackfoot Lodge Tales*, p. 24. GROS VENTRE: Kroeber, PaAM, I, 118, No. 44, and 119, No. 45. ASSINIBOIN: Lowie, PaAM, IV, 150. — **WDL. CENT.** CREE: Skinner, PaAM, IX, 92. OJIBWA: Radin, GSCan, II, 28, No. 14, and 30, No. 15. KICKAPOO: Jones, PAES, IX, 77, No. 10. — **WDL. N.E.** NASKAPI: Speck, JAFL, XXVIII, 70, No. 1. — **WDL. IROQ.**

SENECA: Curtin-Hewitt, RBAE, xxxii, 545, No. 114. — **S.E.** BILOXI: Dorsey and Swanton, BBAE, xlvii, 99. —— Also EUROPEAN.

179. *Whale-boat* (R245). A man is carried across the water on a whale (or fish). In most cases he deceives the whale as to the nearness to the shore or as to hearing thunder. — **N. PAC.** CHINOOK: Boas, BBAE, xx, Nos. 4, 10. — **PLNS.** DAKOTA: Wissler, JAFL, xx, 197; Riggs, CNAE, ix, 139; Wallis, JAFL, xxxvi, 78. ARIKARA: Dorsey, CI, xvii, 77, No. 21. — **WDL. CENT.** OJIBWA: Schoolcraft, *Hiawatha*, p. 207. TIMAGAMI OJIBWA: Speck, GSCan, ix, 71. KICKAPOO: Jones, PAES, ix, 85, No. 10. — **WDL. N.E.** NASKAPI: Speck, JAFL, xxviii, 72. MICMAC: Parsons, JAFL, xxxviii, 63, No. 4; Rand, p. 229, No. 33; Leland, p. 35; Michelson, JAFL, xxxviii, 52. MALECITE: Mechling, GSCan, iv, 60, No. 4. PASSAMAQUODDY: Fewkes, JAFL, iii, 266; Prince, PAES, x, 21, No. 2; 29, No. 4; 81, No. 12. — **WDL. IROQ.** HURON-WYANDOT: Barbeau, GSCan, xi, 102, No. 27. —— Siberian parallels: Jochelson, JE, vi, 379.

180. *Old woman adviser* (N825). Often the old woman is not to be distinguished from an animal adviser. See, for an example of this merging, tale LIV, "Mudjikiwis." — References: Teit, JAFL, xxx, 435 (**MACK.** KASKA. — **PLAT.** THOMPSON. — **N. PAC.** TAHLTAN, TSIMSHIAN, TLINGIT, KWAKIUTL). — **WDL. CENT.** MENOMINI: Skinner and Satterlee, PaAM, xiii, 313.

181. *Sharp-elbowed women* (G341). Women with sharp elbows kill victims. At last they are deceived into stabbing one another. — **N. PAC.** TAHLTAN: Teit, JAFL, xxxiv. — **PLNS.** SHOSHONI: St. Clair, JAFL, xxii, 267, No. 4. ASSINIBOIN: Lowie, PaAM, iv, 183. DAKOTA: Riggs, CNAE, ix, 140. — **WDL. CENT.** CREE: Skinner, PaAM, ix, 92. OJIBWA: Jones-Michelson, PAES, vii (ii), 391, No. 47; (TIMAGAMI): Speck, GSCan, ix, 62. MENOMINI: Skinner and Satterlee, PaAM, xiii, 314; Skinner, JAFL, xxvi, 64. — **WDL. N.E.** MICMAC: Michelson, JAFL, xxxviii, 52. — **WDL. IROQ.** SENECA: Curtin-Hewitt, RBAE, xxxii, 554, No. 114.

182. *Contest in magic* (D1701.1). For other contests in magic, see note 61*a*, *Weather contest*; 117*e*, *Transformation combat*. — See also: **WDL. IROQ.** SENECA: Curtin-Hewitt, RBAE, xxxii, 127, 184, 587.

183. *XLVIII. Dirty-Boy* (L113, K1932). A supernatural being assumes a humble disguise. In a contest for the chief's daughter he wins the girl. Impostor who claims prize is unmasked. Loathly bridegroom assumes original form. — References: Boas, BBAE, lix, 292. — **PLAT.** SHUSWAP, OKANAGON, KUTENAI, NEZ PERCÉ: Boas, *loc. cit.* — **PLNS.** SHOSHONI, OMAHA, PAWNEE, ARAPAHO, CHEYENNE, BLACKFOOT, CROW, HIDATSA, TETON, ASSINIBOIN: *Ibid.* GROS VENTRE: Kroeber, PaAM, i, 105, No. 28.

184. Cf. note 6, *Sun sister and moon brother*.

185. *Male Cinderella* (L11, L100). An unpromising (abused or youngest son) hero achieves unexpected success. — **ESK.** GREENLAND: Rink, p. 93, No. 1; p. 281, No. 47; p. 438, No. 88. SMITH SOUND: Kroeber, JAFL, xii, 178. BAFFIN LAND: Boas, RBAE, v, 630. CUMBERLAND SOUND: Boas, BAM, xv, 186. LABRADOR: Turner, RBAE, xi, 265. WEST HUDSON BAY: BAM, xv, 309. KODIAK: Golder, JAFL, xvi, 16. — **PLAT.** OKANAGON: Teit, MAFLS, xi, 79, 85. LILLOOET: Teit, JAFL, xxv, 327. — **N. PAC.** TSIMSHIAN, NASS, HAIDA, TLINGIT: Boas, RBAE, xxxi, 729. QUINAULT: Farrand, JE,

II, 114, No. 10. CHINOOK: Boas, BBAE, xx, Nos. 2, 4. KATHLAMET: Boas, BBAE, xxvi, 175. SONGISH: Hill-Tout, JAI, xxxvii, 335, 341. QUILEUTE: Farrand-Mayer, JAFL, xxxii, 257, No. 4. — CAL. SHASTA: Farrand-Frachtenberg, JAFL, xxviii, 214, No. 6; Kroeber, UCal, iv, 186; Dixon, JAFL, xxiii, 18. HUPA: Goddard, UCal, i, 212, No. 16. WISHOSK: Kroeber, JAFL, xviii, 104, 105. YUKI: Kroeber, UCal, iv, 186. — PLNS. PONCA: Dorsey, CNAE, vi, 604; Dorsey, JAFL, i, 74. WICHITA: Dorsey, CI, xxi, 106, No. 14; 114, No. 15; 257, No. 41; Dorsey, JAFL, xvi, 160. PAWNEE: Dorsey, CI, lix, 68, No. 17; 156, No. 42; 164, No. 44; 206, No. 59; Dorsey, MAFLS, viii, 30, No. 6; 44, No. 9; 191, No. 49; 239, No. 60. ARIKARA: Dorsey, CI, xvii, 65, No. 17; 69, No. 18; 106, No. 32; 109, No. 33; 129, No. 47. ARAPAHO: Dorsey and Kroeber, FM, v, 23, No. 10; 29, No. 11; 267, No. 119; 311, No. 133. CROW: Lowie, PaAM, xxv, 133, 136, 191. CHEY-ENNE: Kroeber, JAFL, xiii, 170. BLACKFOOT: Grinnell, *Blackfoot Lodge Tales*, pp. 93, 117; McClintock, p. 491. HIDATSA: Curtis, iv, 165. ASSINIBOIN: Lowie, PaAM, iv, 134, 138. GROS VENTRE: Kroeber, PaAM, i, 81, 105. DAKOTA: Curtis, iii, 117. — WDL. CENT. CREE: Lowie, PaAM, iv, 139. OJIBWA: Schoolcraft, *Hiawatha*, p. 72. FOX: Jones, PAES, i, 79. MENOMINI: Skinner and Satterlee, PaAM, xiii, 327. — WDL. N.E. MICMAC: Michelson, JAFL, xxxviii, 45. — WDL. IROQ. SENECA: Curtin-Hewitt, RBAE, xxxii, 130, No. 20; 342, No. 59; 379, No. 69; 417, No. 76; 486, No. 105; 519, No. 110; 525, No. 111; 565, No. 116; Curtin, *Seneca Indian Myths*, pp. 232, 477. — S.W. MOQUI: Stephens, JAFL, i, 109. ZUÑI: Cushing, pp. 1, 113, 288, 310. —— SIBERIA: Jochelson, JE, vi, 380. — See also the following notes: 188, *Loathly bridegroom;* 189, *The False Bridegroom;* 290, *John the Bear.*

186. *Suitor contests: bride offered as prize* (H310). — ESK. KODIAK: Golder, JAFL, xvi, 16. — PLAT. CHILCOTIN: Farrand, JE, ii, 43, No. 28 (European ?). SAHAPTIN: Farrand-Mayer, MAFLS, xi, 160, No. 9. SALISH: Hill-Tout, *British North America*, p. 228. SHUSWAP: Teit, JE, ii, 684, No. 22. THOMPSON: Teit, MAFLS, vi, 36. — N. PAC. TSIMSHIAN: Boas, BBAE, xxvii, 137. CHINOOK: Boas, BBAE, xx, No. 4. SKYKOMISH: Haeberlin, JAFL, xxxvii, 384. SNOHOMISH: *Ibid.*, p. 383. — CAL. ACHOMAWI: Curtin, JAFL, xxii, 284. PAVIOTSO: Lowie, JAFL, xxxvii, 237, No. 18. — PLNS. Cf. OSAGE: Dorsey, FM, vii, 42, No. 34. CROW: Lowie, PaAM, xxv, 141; Lowie, FM, ii, 292, No. 13. OMAHA: Dorsey, CNAE, vi, 604. WICHITA: Dorsey, CI, xxi, 172, No. 24. PAWNEE: Grinnell, *Pawnee Hero Stories*, p. 87; Dorsey, CI, lix, 164, No. 44, and 281, No. 80; Dorsey, MAFLS, viii, 30, No. 6; 114, No. 31; 179, No. 45; 239, No. 60. ARAPAHO: Dorsey and Kroeber, FM, v, 106, No. 51. DAKOTA: Zitkala-Ša, pp. 77 ff.; Curtis, iii, 111; Wissler, JAFL, xx, 128. GROS VENTRE: Kroeber, PaAM, i, 80, No. 19, and 105, No. 28. — WDL. CENT. OJIBWA: Jones-Michelson, PAES, vii (i), 133. MENOMINI: Skinner and Satterlee, PaAM, xiii, 396. — WDL. IROQ. IROQUOIS: Smith, RBAE, ii, 90–91. SENECA: Curtin-Hewitt, RBAE, xxxii, 140, No. 22; 318, No. 58; 513, No. 109; 567, No. 116; Curtin, *Seneca Indian Myths*, pp. 27, 383. — S.W. NAVAHO: Matthews, MAFLS, v, 92. ZUÑI: Cushing, pp. 1, 107, 185, 288; Parsons, JAFL, xxxi, 240. —— For European parallels, see tales LXXVIII, "The Seven-headed Dragon," (note 289) and LXXXVI, "Making the Princess laugh," (note 297).

187. *Trapping contest* (K32). An incident in several of the tales of this type.

188. *The loathly bridegroom* (D733). A loathsome man becomes handsome when the woman of his choice submits herself to his embraces. — **ESK.** KODIAK: Golder, JAFL, xvi, 16. — **PLAT.** THOMPSON: Teit, JE, viii, 265, No. 33, and 373, No. 86. LILLOOET: Teit, JAFL, xxv, 344. SAHAPTIN: Farrand-Mayer, MAFLS, xi, 161, No. 9. — **N. PAC.** TSIMSHIAN: Boas, RBAE, xxxi, 344. CHINOOK: Boas, BBAE, xx, No. 4. CHEHALIS: Hill-Tout, JAI, xxxiv, 349. — **PLNS.** ARAPAHO: Dorsey and Kroeber, FM, v, 341–388, Nos. 139–143. CHEYENNE: Kroeber, JAFL, xiii, 170. PAWNEE: Dorsey, MAFLS, viii, 174, No. 44. BLACKFOOT: Grinnell, *Blackfoot Lodge Tales*, pp. 93, 117. — **WDL. CENT.** OJIBWA: Schoolcraft, *Hiawatha*, p. 71. — **WDL. N.E.** MALECITE: Mechling, GSCan, iv, 55, No. 9. — **WDL. IROQ.** IROQUOIS: Canfield, p. 155. — **S.E.** CHEROKEE: Mooney, RBAE, xix, 337, No. 81. — **S.W.** HOPI: Voth, FM, viii, 131, No. 36. — See also references given in note 183, *Dirty-Boy*, and 185, *Male Cinderella.* — Cf. the European motif, *The Loathly Lady* (Bolte-Polívka, ii, 30, 466).

189. XLIX. *The False Bridegroom* (K1915). Trickster poses as a man of magic power, usually the power of producing magic treasure. He marries girls under this pretence. He is unmasked at a dance, where girls learn of the real situation. — **MACK.** HARE: Bell, JAFL, xvi, 73. LOUCHEUX: Camsell-Barbeau, JAFL, xxviii, 251, No. 6. — **CAL.** ACHOMAWI: Dixon, JAFL, xxi, 163, No. 3. — **PLNS.** SOUTHERN UTE: Lowie, JAFL, xxxvii, 12, No. 5, and 37, No. 22*b*. ARAPAHO: Dorsey and Kroeber, FM, v, 203, No. 89, and 272, No. 121. GROS VENTRE: Kroeber, PaAM, i, 108, No. 28. — **WDL. CENT.** MENOMINI: Skinner and Satterlee, PaAM, xiii, 408, cf. p. 324. OJIBWA: Jones-Michelson, PAES, vii (ii), 157, No. 13, and 679, No. 69. — **WDL. IROQ.** SENECA: Curtin-Hewitt, RBAE, xxxii, 196, No. 39, cf. pp. 115, 132, 142, 143, 167, 264. HURON-WYANDOT: Barbeau, GSCan, xi, 203, No. 61. — **S.E.** Cf. CHEROKEE: Mooney, RBAE, xix, 397, No. 114. MUSKHOGEAN: Swanton, JAFL, xxvi, 201. CADDO: Dorsey, CI, xli, 67, No. 40. — **S.W.** Cf. JICARILLA APACHE: Goddard, PaAM, viii, 235, No. 42. NAVAHO: Matthews, MAFLS, v, 88.

190. *Jewels from spittle* (D1001, D1456). — **PLAT.** KUTENAI: Boas, BBAE, lix, 203. — **PLNS.** GROS VENTRE: Kroeber, PaAM, i, 108, No. 28. DAKOTA: Riggs, CNAE, ix, 148. — **WDL. CENT.** MENOMINI, Fox: Skinner and Satterlee, PaAM, xiii, 530, No. 33*b*. — **WDL. IROQ.** SENECA: Curtin-Hewitt, RBAE, xxxii, 97, 133, 140, 263, 516. — **S.E.** CREEK: Skinner and Satterlee, *loc. cit.* — Two related motifs are:

(a) *Jewels from excrements* (D1002, D1458). — **N. PAC.** COMOX: Boas, Sagen, p. 73. RIVERS INLET: *Ibid.*, p. 226. — **CAL.** ACHOMAWI: Dixon, JAFL, xxi, 163, No. 3. — **PLNS.** ASSINIBOIN: Lowie, PaAM, iv, 142. — **WDL. IROQ.** SENECA: Curtin-Hewitt, RBAE, xxxii, 158. —— SIBERIA and MONGOLIA: Jochelson, JE, vi, 367.

(b) *Jewels from tears* (D1004, D1457). — **WDL. IROQ.** SENECA: Curtin-Hewitt, RBAE, xxxii, 186, 208, 226, 320, 408, 755.

191. In other hero stories than those given here occur the following motifs:
(a) *Sham blood and brains* (K522.1). In the *Wedge test* (note 129) the hero usually feigns death and by the use of juice, or the like, convinces the ogre that blood and brains are issuing from the tree. The same idea occurs in other connections in various parts of the continent. — **MACK.** KASKA: Teit, JAFL, xxx, 430, 449. — **PLAT.** THOMPSON, SHUSWAP, LILLOOET: Teit, JAFL,

xxv, 370.—**N. PAC.** Nass, Kwakiutl, Comox, Nootka, Chehalis: see note 129.—**WDL. CENT.** Menomini: Skinner and Satterlee, PaAM, xiii, 409.—**WDL. N.E.** Malecite: Speck, JAFL, xxx, 484, No. 8 (European). —**S.W.** Navaho: Matthews, MAFLS, v, 119. Jicarilla Apache: Mooney, AA, old ser., xi, 206; Goddard, PaAM, viii, 198, No. 4. San Carlos Apache: Goddard, PaAM, xxiv, 17, 40. Zuñi: Cushing, p. 65.

(*b*) *Sham eating* (K81). Cf. notes 137*b*, 140. Hero avoids eating poisoned food or human flesh. In many cases the food is dropped into a hidden bag. —**ESK.** Greenland: Rink, p. 108, No. 3. Baffin Land: Boas, RBAE, vi, 627; Boas, BAM, xv, 313.—**PLAT.** Wishram: Curtis, viii, 139 ff.— **N. PAC.** Quinault, Chinook, Nootka: Jochelson, JE, vi, 366. Snohomish: Haeberlin, JAFL, xxxvii, 437. Bella Coola: Boas, JE, i, 58. Kathlamet: Boas, BBAE, xxvi, 149. —**CAL.** Miwok: Gifford, UCal, xii, 293, No. 3.— **PLNS.** Southern Ute: Lowie, JAFL, xxxvii, 73, No. 45. Assiniboin: Lowie, PaAM, iv, 158.—**WDL. N.E.** Cf. Malecite: Mechling, GSCan, iv, 33. Micmac: Rand, p. 71, No. 8. Mohegan: Speck, JAFL, xvii, 183. — **WLD. IROQ.** Seneca: Curtin-Hewitt, RBAE, xxxii, 178, 393; Curtin, *Seneca Indian Myths*, p. 40.——European: see Thompson, CColl, ii, 432.

(*c*) *Substitute smoker* (K528.1). Hero is compelled to smoke a fatal pipe, but a helpful insect which he carries on his head smokes the pipe for him. — **CAL.** Wintun: Curtin, *Creation Myths*, p. 137. Yana: Dixon, UCal, ix, 233, No. 13. — **S.W.** Navaho: Matthews, MAFLS, v, 112. Hopi: Voth, FM, viii, 31, No. 6; Fewkes, *Journal of Am. Ethnology and Archeology*, iv, 106. Cf. San Carlos Apache: Goddard, PaAM, xxiv, 11, 35. White Mountain Apache: *Ibid.*, p. 94.

(*d*) *Smoking test* (H1511). See all references in the last note. The fatal pipe is escaped in various ways. —**WDL. N.E.** Malecite: Mechling, GSCan, iv, 33. Passamaquoddy: Prince, PAES, x, 35, No. 6, and 37, No. 7. — **S.W.** Navaho: Matthews, MAFLS, v, 177. San Carlos Apache: Goddard, PaAM, xxiv, 10, 37. White Mountain Apache: *Ibid.*, p. 117.

(*e*) *Burr-woman* (G311). Hero takes old woman on his back and she sticks there magically. — **PLNS.** Wichita: Dorsey, CI, xxi, 188, No. 26. Skidi Pawnee: Dorsey, MAFLS, viii, 87, No. 24. Ponca: Dorsey, CNAE, vi, 217. — **WDL. CENT.** Sauk and Fox: Lasley, JAFL, xv, 177.—**WDL. IROQ.** Seneca: Curtin-Hewitt, RBAE, xxxii, 481, No. 104; 369, No. 67; 677, No. 129.— Related motif: *Magic adhesion to turtle* (D1661.8.1).—**PLNS.** Crow: Lowie, PaAM, xxv, 220, 221; Simms, FM, ii, 314. Cheyenne: Kroeber, JAFL, xiii, 184. Pawnee: Dorsey, CI, 426, No. 116. Sioux: McLaughlin, p. 24. Cf. Southern Paiute (Shivwits): Lowie, JAFL, xxxvii, 102, No. 1.

(*f*) *Tree-pulling contest* (K46).—**CAL.** Wintun: Curtin, *Creation Myths*, p. 152. Yana: *Ibid.*, p. 292.

(*g*) *Feigned dream to send hero on dangerous quests* (H1212.1). —**WDL. IROQ.** Seneca: Curtin-Hewitt, RBAE, xxxi, 85, 394, 404, 427.

192. *Journeys to the Other World* (F0–F199). Besides the stories given below, see also note 118, *Ascent to sky*.

193. *L* and *LI. The Star Husband.* Regular motifs are: *wish for star husband* (C15); *digging tabu* (C523); and *sky rope* (see note 48). For a thorough analysis of the various types of this tale, see Reichard, JAFL, xxxiv, 271, 307.— **MACK.** Kaska, Ts'ets'áut. — **PLAT.** Chilcotin, Shuswap,

THOMPSON, KUTENAI. — **N. PAC.** TAHLTAN, TLINGIT, SONGISH, QUILEUTE, QUINAULT. — **CAL.** WASHO. — **PLNS.** SHOSHONI, KIOWA, WICHITA, ARA- PAHO, CHEYENNE, OTO, PAWNEE, CROW, DAKOTA, ARIKARA, BLACKFOOT, GROS VENTRE, ASSINIBOIN. — **WDL. CENT.** OJIBWA, CREE. — **WDL. N.E.** MICMAC, PASSAMAQUODDY. — **S.E.** NATCHEZ, KOASATI: Reichard, *loc. cit.* Add: — **N. PAC.** PUYALLUP: Curtis, IX, 117. SNUQUALMI: Haeberlin, JAFL, XXXVII, 373, 375. — **PLNS.** CANADIAN DAKOTA: Wallis, JAFL, XXXVI, 85, No. 19. — **WDL. CENT.** TIMAGAMI OJIBWA: Speck, GSCan, IX, 48. — **WDL. N.E.** PASSAMAQUODDY: Prince, PAES, X, 61, No. 12. MICMAC: Parsons, JAFL, XXXVIII, 65, No. 5.

194. *Sky rope.* See note 48.

195. *Lecherous trickster seduces women from tree and loses them* (K1387). A regular feature of one type of the *Star Husband.* See Reichard, JAFL, XXXIV, 271, 307 (**MACK.** KASKA, TS'ETS'ÁUT. — **PLAT.** CHILCOTIN, SHUSWAP. — **N. PAC.** TAHLTAN. — **PLNS.** ASSINIBOIN. — **WDL. CENT.** OJIBWA. — **WDL. N.E.** MICMAC, PASSAMAQUODDY).

196. *Magic objects talk and delay pursuer* (D1611). A fugitive leaves be- hind him magic objects which talk and delay the pursuer, who is deceived by the impersonation. — **ESK.** CUMBERLAND SOUND: Boas, BAM, XV, 194. WEST HUDSON BAY: *Ibid.*, p. 318. Cf. CENTRAL: Boas, RBAE, VI, 634. — **MACK.** TS'ETS'ÁUT: Boas, JAFL, X, 41. — **PLAT.** LILLOOET: Teit, JAFL, XXV, 297, No. 2; cf. p. 317, No. 16. THOMPSON: Teit, JE, VIII, 231, No. 19, and 367, No. 80. SHUSWAP: Teit, JE, II, 709, No. 36. KALISPEL: Curtis, VI, 97 ff. — **N. PAC.** TLINGIT: Swanton, BBAE, XXIX, 211. No. 56. CHEHALIS: Hill-Tout, JAI, XXXIV, 347. — **CAL.** MODOC: Curtin, *Myths of the Modocs,* pp. 95 ff. YANA: Sapir, UCal, IX, 155, No. 12 (putrid food instructed not to smell and betray fugitive). MEWAN: Merriam, p. 107. CAHUILLA: Hooper, UCal, XVI, 375. — **PLNS.** OSAGE: Dorsey, FM, VII, 18, No. 15, and 23, No. 17. ARAPAHO: Dorsey and Kroeber, FM, V, 9, No. 5; 13, No. 6; 36, No. 12; 281, No. 124. PONCA: Dorsey, CNAE, VI, 20. PAWNEE: Dorsey, CI, LIX, 116, No. 29. — **WDL. CENT.** TIMAGAMI OJIBWA: Speck, GSCan, IX, 48. — **WDL. N.E.** MOHEGAN: Speck, JAFL, XVI, 104. — **WDL. IROQ.** SENECA: Curtin-Hewitt, RBAE, XXXII, 77, No. 1; 105, No. 10; 119, No. 18; 470, No. 101. — **S.W.** JICARILLA APACHE: Goddard, PaAM, VIII, 210, No. 17. —— SIBERIA: Jochelson, JE, VI, 365. SOUTH AMERICA: Koch-Grün- berg, Nos. 10, 47, 68. EUROPEAN: cf. note 282. — Related motifs are:

(*a*) *Spittle impersonates fugitive* (D1001, D1611.1). A variety of the pre- ceding. See the following references in that note: — **PLAT.** SHUSWAP, THOMPSON, KALISPEL. — **CAL.** MEWAN.

(*b*) *Magic objects betray fugitives* (D1320, D1612). — References: Jochelson, JE, VI, 374. — **N. PAC.** BELLA COOLA, NOOTKA, NEWETTEE, RIVERS INLET, BELLA BELLA: Jochelson, *loc. cit.* TSIMSHIAN: Boas, BBAE, XXVII, 235. SONGISH: Hill-Tout, JAI, XXXVII, 346. Cf. KWAKIUTL: Boas and Hunt, JE, X, 60 ff. — **CAL.** SHASTA: Farrand-Frachtenberg, JAFL, XXVIII, 214, No. 5, and 221, No. 11. YANA: Sapir, UCal, IX, 208, No. 24. — **WDL. CENT.** OJIBWA: information from Laidlaw. — **WDL. N.E.** MICMAC: Rand, p. 239, No. 36. NASKAPI: Speck, JAFL, XXXVIII, 25. — **WDL. IROQ.** SENECA: Curtin-Hewitt, RBAE, XXXII, 290, No. 57 (= Curtin, *Seneca Indian Myths,* p. 312); 82, No. 2; 506, No. 109; 523, No. 110; 553, No. 114. — **S.W.** JICARILLA APACHE: Russell, JAFL, XI, 360.

197. *Digging tabu* (C523). A regular incident in the *Star Husband* story. See in note 193, references to the following tribes: — **MACK.** KASKA. — **PLAT.** KUTENAI. — **N. PAC.** PUYALLUP, SNUQUALMI. — **PLNS.** SHOSHONI, KĪOWA, WICHITA, ARAPAHO, CHEYENNE, OTO, PAWNEE, CROW, DAKOTA, ARIKARA, BLACKFOOT, GROS VENTRE, ASSINIBOIN. — **WDL. CENT.** TIMAGAMI OJIBWA. — **WDL. N.E.** MICMAC. — See also **WDL. IROQ.** SENECA: Curtin-Hewitt, RBAE, XXXII, 410, No. 74, and 460, No. 98 (= Curtin, *Seneca Indian Myths*, p. 193). — Cf. notes 194, *Sky rope* and 28, *Sky window*.

198. At this point in a number of versions begins the tale of "Star-Boy." For an analysis of that tale (a typical hero-adventure story similar to "Blood-Clot-Boy"), see Lowie, JAFL, XXI, 144; Reichard, JAFL, XXXIV, 271.

199. *LII. The Stretching Tree* (D482). A father, jealous of his son, sends him up a tree which magically stretches to the upper world. With the help he receives in the upper world, the son returns and takes revenge on his father. — References: Teit, MAFLS, XI, 120. — **PLAT.** THOMPSON, SHUSWAP, LILLOOET, CŒUR D'ALÈNE, NEZ PERCÉ, SAHAPTIN, WASCO: Teit, *loc. cit.* SECHELT: Hill-Tout, JAI, XXXIV, 43. CHILCOTIN: Farrand, JE, II, 29, No. 13. — **N. PAC.** SNOHOMISH: Haeberlin, JAFL, XXXVII, 400. ALSEA: Frachtenberg, BBAE, LXVII, 79. COOS: Frachtenberg, CU, I, 21. Cf. TAKELMA: Sapir, UPa, II, 83. — **CAL.** MODOC: Curtin, *Myths of the Modocs*, p. 13. KLAMATH: Gatschet, CNAE, II, 94, 100. Cf. HUPA: Goddard, UCal, I, 146. SHASTA: Farrand-Frachtenberg, JAFL, XXVIII, 212. — **PLNS.** UINTAH UTE; cf. BLACKFOOT, CROW, KIOWA: Teit, *loc. cit.* Cf. CANADIAN DAKOTA: Wallis, JAFL, XXXVI, 86, No. 19. — **WDL. IROQ.** Cf. SENECA: Curtin-Hewitt, RBAE, XXXII, 425, No. 79 (abandonment on cliff).

200. *Tree to upper world* (F54). — See all references in note 199, *The Stretching Tree*, and in note 193, *Star Husband*, the following references: — **PLNS.** KIOWA, ARAPAHO, CROW, HIDATSA, GROS VENTRE, ARIKARA. — See in addition: **MACK.** CHIPEWYAN: Bell, JAFL, XVI, 83; Goddard, PaAM, X, 46, No. 1; Petitot, pp. 352 ff.; Lowie, PaAM, X, 190. — **PLAT.** SHUSWAP: Teit, JE, II, 694, No. 28. — **N. PAC.** HAIDA: Swanton, BBAE, XXIX, 266. TAKELMA: Sapir, UPa, II, 83, No. 5. — **CAL.** HUPA: Goddard, UCal, I, 147, No. 2. WESTERN MONO: Gifford, JAFL, XXXVI, 347, No. 18. — **PLNS.** PONCA: Dorsey, CNAE, VI, 607. PIEGAN: Michelson, JAFL, XXIX, 409 (European). — **WDL. CENT.** MENOMINI, OJIBWA: Skinner and Satterlee, PaAM, XIII, 520. — **WDL. N.E.** MONTAGNAIS: LeJeune, *Jes. Rel.*, XII, 33. — **WDL. IROQ.** SENECA: Curtin-Hewitt, RBAE, XXXII, 403, No. 71. — **S.E.** CADDO: Dorsey, CI, XLI, 34, No. 17. — **S.W.** NAVAHO: Matthews, MAFLS, V, 74. JICARILLA APACHE: Mooney, AA, old ser., XI, 198 f. SAN CARLOS APACHE: Goddard, PaAM, XXIV, 28. HOPI: Voth, FM, VIII, 10, No. 3, and 16, No. 4. —— SIBERIA: Jochelson, VI, 376. In several of the references just given, a seed is planted which in a single night grows to the upper world (PIEGAN, NAVAHO, HOPI, CADDO). This is, of course, the *Jack-and-the-Beanstalk* motif (A515.1).

201. *Spider-web sky rope* (F51.1). A frequent form of the *sky-rope* motif. See note 194. Cf. also note 151, *Roc*. In that incident the hero is usually helped down from the eagle's nest in a basket by a bat or by a rope made by a spider. — See also **S.W.** SIA: Stevenson, RBAE, XI, 43. NAVAHO: Matthews, MAFLS, V, 109. SAN CARLOS APACHE: Goddard, PaAM, XXIV, 9.

202. *LIII. The Arrow Chain* (tale). Hero and his company ascend to upper world on chain of arrows. They make war on the sky-people and escape with difficulty.— **PLAT.**. KUTENAI, OKANAGON, PEND D'OREILLE, SHUSWAP, THOMPSON; cf. SANPOIL: Boas, BBAE, LIX, 288. — **N. PAC.** TAHLTAN: Teit, JAFL, XXIV, 337, No. 58. SKAGIT: Haeberlin, JAFL, XXXVII, 390.

203. *Ascent to upper world on arrow chain* (F53).—References: Boas, RBAE, XXXI, 863 ff. — **PLAT.** THOMPSON, UTAMQT, LILLOOET, SHUSWAP, KUTENAI, OKANAGON, WISHRAM, WASCO: Boas, *loc. cit.* CŒUR D'ALÈNE: Teit, MAFLS, XI, 126, No. 16. SANPOIL: *Ibid.*, p. 107. PEND D'OREILLE: Gould, MAFLS, XI, 118.— **N. PAC.** TLINGIT, NASS, HAIDA, BELLA COOLA, BELLA BELLA, RIVERS INLET, KWAKIUTL, TSIMSHIAN, NEWETTEE, NOOTKA, NITINATH, COMOX, CHEHALIS, SQUAMISH, QUINAULT, KATHLAMET, TILLAMOOK, COOS: Boas, *loc. cit.* QUILEUTE: Farrand-Mayer, JAFL, XXXII, 264, No. 10. ALSEA: Frachtenberg, BBAE, LXVII, 129, No. 10, and 139, No. 11. SKAGIT: Haeberlin: JAFL, XXXVII, 389. Cf. note 145a, *Magic arrow flight.* —— SIBERIA: Jochelson, JE, VI, 377. MELANESIA: Codrington, *Melanesian Anthropology and Folk-Lore*, p. 397; Boas, JAFL, XXVII, 384. BOLIVIA: Koch-Grünberg, No. 104. — General treatment: R. Pettazzoni, "The chain of arrows: the diffusion of a mythical motive," FL, XXXV, 151.

204. *Ladder to upper world* (F52). Except in this version, not a common form for the *arrow-chain* motif. — A realted motif, much more widespread is:

(*a*) *Rainbow-bridge to other world* (F152).— **MACK.** TS'ETS'ÁUT: Boas, JAFL, IX, 268. — **N. PAC.** BELLA COOLA: Boas, JE, I, 95 (rays of sun).— **CAL.** ACHOMAWI: Curtin, JAFL, XXII, 283, No. 1. MAIDU: Dixon, BAM, XVII, 60.— **WDL. IROQ.** HURON-WYANDOT: Barbeau, GSCan, XI, 42, No. 1; Connelley, JAFL, XII, 123; Connelley, *Wyandot Folklore*, p. 78. — **S.W.** NAVAHO: Matthews, MAFLS, V, 96, 113, 115, 149. SAN CARLOS APACHE: Goddard, PaAM, XXIV, 37. SIA: Stevenson, RBAE, XI, 56. HOPI: Voth, FM, VIII, 31, No. 6, and 137, No. 37.

205. *Obstacle flight* (D672). A fugitive throws behind him objects which magically become obstacles in the path of the pursuer. One of the most widely distributed motifs in folk-lore. For general distribution, see Bolte-Polívka, II, 140. Professor Boas sees in the American Indian versions two different currents of transmission: "an ancient one, coming from Siberia by way of Bering Strait; a recent one arising in Spain and passing into Latin America and gradually extending northward until the two meet in California." — JAFL, XXVII, 386.— References: Teit, JAFL, XXXIV, 236.— **ESK.** Cf. CUMBERLAND SOUND: Boas, BAM, XV, 177. — **MACK.** TS'ETS'ÁUT: Teit, *loc. cit.* DOG RIB: Bell, JAFL, XVI, 81. — **PLAT.** SHUSWAP: Teit, JE, II, 636, 641, 688, No. 25; 729, No. 49; 757, No. 65. THOMPSON: Teit, MAFLS, VI, 92, No. 37. NEZ PERCÉ: Spinden, JAFL, XXI, 157.— **N. PAC.** BELLA BELLA, BELLA COOLA, KWAKIUTL, QUINAULT, RIVERS INLET, CHINOOK: Teit, *loc. cit.* TLINGIT: Swanton, BBAE, XXXIX, 127, No. 31, and 211, No. 56. HAIDA: Swanton, BBAE, XXIX, 337. Cf. KATHLAMET: Boas, BBAE, XXVI, 123. ALSEA: Frachtenberg, BBAE, LXVII, 75 (note to MOLALA). QUILEUTE: Farrand-Mayer, JAFL, XXXII, 254, No. 1. TAHLTAN: Teit, JAFL, XXXIV, 236, No. 41, and 240 f., Nos. 45a, 45b.— **CAL.** MAIDU: Dixon, BAM, XVII, 77, No. 8. — **PLNS.** OSAGE, PAWNEE, CHEYENNE: Teit, JAFL, XXXIV, 236. SOUTHERN PAIUTE (SHIVWITS): Lowie, JAFL, XXXVII, 131, No. 12. SOUTHERN

Ute: *Ibid.*, pp. 65, 67, No. 36. Shoshoni: St. Clair, JAFL, xxII, 271, No. 8. Wichita: Dorsey, CI, xxI, 70, No. 9, and 238, No. 35. Osage: Dorsey, FM, vII, 18, No. 15. Arapaho: Dorsey and Kroeber, FM, v, 71, No. 35, and 281, No. 124. Cheyenne: Grinnell, JAFL, xvi, 108; Kroeber, JAFL, xIII, 185, No. 22. Crow: Lowie, PaAM, xxv, 122, 205; Curtis, iv, 117. Pawnee: Dorsey, CI, lix, 120, No. 30, and 448, No. 127; cf. Teit, MAFLS, viii, 117, No. 32. Dakota: Wissler, JAFL, xx, 195, No. 6. Blackfoot: Wissler and Duvall, PaAM, II, 70. Gros Ventre: Kroeber, PaAM, i, 62, No. 3. Plains Cree: Skinner, JAFL, xxIX, 343. Assiniboin: Lowie, PaAM, iv, 178. — WDL. CENT. Saulteaux: Teit, JAFL, xxxIV, 236. Ojibwa: Schoolcraft, *Indian in his Wigwam*, p. 109; Schoolcraft, *Hiawatha*, pp. 196, 246; Jones, JAFL, xxIX, 380; Smith, JAFL, xIX, 220; Laidlaw, OAR, xxvII, 74. — Cree: Skinner, PaAM, ix, 88; Skinner, JAFL, xxIX, 343. Menomini: Hoffman, RBAE, xiv, 196; Skinner and Satterlee, PaAM, xIII, 364, 371. — WDL. N.E. Mohegan: Speck, JAFL, xvi, 105. — WDL. IROQ. Seneca: Curtin-Hewitt, RBAE, xxxII, 120, 173, 271, 675; cf. 78. Huron-Wyandot: Barbeau, GSCan, xI, 213, No. 66. — S.E. Creek: Speck, *Southern Workman*, xxxvIII, 9. — S.W. Navaho: Matthews, MAFLS, v, 102. — Siberia: Jochelson, JE, vi, 364, 370; Bogaras, AA, new ser., iv, 626. South American Indian: Koch-Grünberg, p. 329, Nos. 75, 83. — In European borrowings among North America: Thompson, CColl, II, 349, 369. — Related motifs are:

(*a*) *Reversed obstacle flight* (D673). Pursuer throws obstacles in front of the fugitive. — PLAT. Nez Percé: Spinden, JAFL, xxI, 156. Wasco: Curtin, PAES, II, 275. Twana: Curtis, ix, 166 ff. — N. PAC. Tsimshian: Boas, BBAE, xxvII, 235. — PLNS. Pawnee: Dorsey, CI, lix, 39, No. 6. — S.E. Cherokee: Mooney, RBAE, xix, 259, No. 12.

(*b*) *Transformation flight* (*transformed fugitives*) (D671). Fugitives transform themselves so as to deceive pursuer. — PLAT. Shuswap: Teit, JE, II, 733, No. 51. Thompson: Teit, MAFLS, xI, 60. Nez Percé: Spinden, JAFL, xxI, 18, No. 6. — CAL. Modoc: Curtin, *Myths of the Modocs*, pp. 17 ff. — PLNS. Southern Paiute (Shivwits): Lowie, JAFL, xxxvII, 100, No. 1; cf. 130, No. 12. Wichita: Dorsey, CI, xxI, 130, No. 18. Ponca: Dorsey, CNAE, vi, 285; Dorsey, JAFL, i, 204. Pawnee: Dorsey, CI, lix, 429, No. 117. — WDL. CENT. Kickapoo: Jones, PAES, ix, 23, No. 4. — WDL. N.E. Penobscot: Speck, JAFL, xxvIII, 53, 54. Micmac: *Ibid.*, p. 65. — WDL. IROQ. Seneca: Curtin-Hewitt, RBAE, xxxII, 105, No. 10; No. 18; 271, No. 52. — S.E. Cf. Biloxi: Dorsey and Swanton, BBAE, xlviI, 80. — S.W. San Carlos Apache: Goddard, PaAM, xxiv, 84. — European borrowings by American Indians: Thompson, CColl, II, 366 ff. — Opposite of this motif (*transformed pursuer*) appears in Siberian tales: Jochelson, JE, vi, 363.

206. *LIV. Mudjikiwis.* Ten brothers return from hunt and find house put in order by mysterious housekeeper. Take turns in remaining at home to investigate. One brother succeeds and marries the girl. Eldest jealous, courts girl, and shoots her when she rejects him. She is supernatural. Tells husband to seek her after ten days. He comes in eight days and she becomes bird and flies away. Husband goes on quest for her. Sent from one informant to another. Transformed to butterfly, etc. Reaches upper world (world of thunders). Suitor contest. Hero wins wife. Takes her nine sisters for his brothers. —PLNS. Plains Cree: Skinner, JAFL, xxIX, 353, No. 3.

PLAINS OJIBWA: Skinner, JAFL, xxxii, 293, No. 4. SWAMPY CREE: Cresswell, JAFL, xxxvi, 405. — **WDL. CENT.** OJIBWA: Jones, JAFL, xxix, 372, No. 19; Schoolcraft, *Hiawatha*, p. 194; Jones-Michelson, PAES, vii (ii), 133, No. 12. Cf. Fox: Jones, PAES, i, 79, No. 7. — Is probably related to the European "Swan-Maiden" tale; see Aarne-Thompson, *Types of the Folk-tale*, type 400.

207. *Mysterious housekeeper* (N831). Men find their house put in order by a mysterious housekeeper. See all references in note 206, *Mudjikiwis*, and note 233, *The Fox-Woman*. — See also: **ESK.** KODIAK: Golder, JAFL, xvi, 88, No. 7. — **PLAT.** LILLOOET: Teit, JAFL, xxv, 310, No. 9. — **N. PAC.** KWAKIUTL: Boas and Hunt, JE, iii, 122. — **WDL. IROQ.** IROQUOIS: Smith, RBAE, ii, 104. SENECA: Curtin-Hewitt, RBAE, xxxii, 361, No. 65 (= Curtin, *Seneca Indian Myths*, p. 452).

208. *Transformation to feather*. See notes 117a, 118a.

209. *Nuptial tabu* (C117). A man is forbidden cohabitation with his wife for a definite period. — See in note 215, *Orpheus*, the following references: **PLAT. SALISH. — PLNS.** WICHITA. — **WDL. IROQ.** IROQUOIS. — **S.W.** ZUÑI (?). — See also **PLAT.** NEZ PERCÉ: Spinden, MAFLS, xi, 191, No. 11. — **N. PAC.** TAHLTAN: Teit, JAFL, xxxiv, 344, No. 66. — **PLNS.** SOUTHERN UTE: Lowie, JAFL, xxxvii, 34, No. 19. — Plains Cree: Skinner, JAFL, xxix, 355. — **WDL. CENT.** MENOMINI: Skinner and Satterlee, PaAM, xiii, 302. — **WDL. IROQ.** SENECA: Curtin-Hewitt, RBAE, xxxii, 363, No. 65 (= Curtin, *Seneca Indian Myths*, p. 455); cf. 112. — A closely related motif is:

(*a*) *Tabu: incontinence* (C111). — **PLAT.** Cf. SHUSWAP: Teit, JE, ii, 712, No. 38. — **N. PAC.** KWAKIUTL: Boas and Hunt, JE, iii, 25. — **PLNS.** WICHITA: Dorsey, CI, xxi, 35, No. 2; 186, No. 25; 256, No. 40; 313, No. 60. PAWNEE: Dorsey, CI, lix, 178, No. 47; Dorsey, MAFLS, viii, 67, No. 17.

210. *Inexhaustible food-supply* (D1031). Sometimes this motif appears in the form of an inexhaustible cup or kettle, sometimes as a bone or nut that supplies unlimited quantities of food. — References: Teit, JAFL, xxx, 436. — **MACK.** KASKA, CHIPEWYAN: Teit, *loc. cit.* — **PLAT.** SHUSWAP, THOMPSON, LILLOOET: Teit, *loc. cit.* KALISPEL: Curtis, vii, 105 ff. THOMPSON: Teit, MAFLS, xi, 37, 41. LILLOOET: Teit, JAFL, xxv, 357; Hill-Tout, JAI, xxxv, 200. SAHAPTIN: Farrand-Mayer, MAFLS, xi, 147. — **N. PAC.** BELLA BELLA, KWAKIUTL, NEWETTEE, NOOTKA, TAHLTAN, KATHLAMET: Teit, JAFL, xxx, 436. TAHLTAN: Teit, JAFL, xxxiv, 349, No. 69. BELLA COOLA: Boas, JE, i, 54. QUINAULT: Farrand, JE, ii, 86, No. 2. TWANA: Curtis, ix, 166 ff. — **CAL.** MODOC: Curtin, *Myths of the Modocs*, p. 219. SHASTA: Farrand-Frachtenberg, JAFL, xxviii, 220, No. 10. YANA: Curtin, *Creation Myths*, p. 425. YOKUTS: Kroeber, UCal, iv, 228, No. 35. CAHUILLA: Hooper, UCal, xvi, 368. — **PLNS.** PONCA: Teit, JAFL, xxx, 436. SOUTHERN PAIUTE (SHIVWITS): Lowie, JAFL, xxxvii, 123, No. 10; 106, No. 5; 132, No. 12; 152, No. 18. SOUTHERN UTE: *Ibid.*, p. 67. WICHITA: Dorsey, JAFL, xv, 216; Dorsey, CI, xxi, 181, No. 25. PAWNEE: Dorsey, MAFLS, viii, 133, No. 34. ARAPAHO: Dorsey and Kroeber, FM, v, 397, No. 145. CHEYENNE: Dorsey, FM, ix, 40, No. 16. CROW: Lowie, PaAM, xxv, 157, 203. MANDAN: Will and Spinden, *Peabody Museum Papers*, iii, 141. PLAINS CREE: Skinner, JAFL, xxix, 356. PLAINS OJIBWA: Skinner, JAFL, xxxii, 293, No. 4. — **WDL. CENT.** CENTRAL ALGONQUIN: Skinner, JAFL, xxvii, 98. OJIBWA: Radin, GSCan, ii, 54, 55; Laidlaw, OAR, xxvii, 82; Jones-Michelson, PAES, vii (ii), 199,

No. 19, and 387, No. 47. MENOMINI: Hoffman, RBAE, XIV, 182; Skinner and Satterlee, PaAM, XIII, 313. FOX: Jones, PAES, I, 317. — **WDL. N.E.** MICMAC: Rand, p. 24, No. 4; p. 35, No. 6; p. 114, No. 13.—**WDL. IROQ.** SENECA: Curtin-Hewitt, RBAE, XXXII, 148, 187, 199, 376, 502, 638; Curtin, *Seneca Indian Myths*, pp. 8, 18, 328. HURON-WYANDOT: Barbeau, GSCan, XI, 175, No. 56. — **S.E.** YUCHI: Speck, UPa, I, 145, No. 8. — **S.W.** NAVAHO: Matthews, MAFLS, V, 165, 199. SAN CARLOS APACHE: Goddard, PaAM, XXIV, 19. ZUÑI: Parsons, JAFL, XXXI, 245.— A related motif is:

(a) *Compressible objects* (D490). Objects are made large or small at will. In some cases the object is a dog, in some it is slaughtered game, in some it is food, as in the preceding note. — **PLAT.** CHILCOTIN: Farrand, JE, II, 34, No. 19. SHUSWAP: Teit, JE, II, 689, No. 25; 690, No. 26; 691, No. 27; 707, No. 33; 712, No. 38. KUTENAI: Boas, BBAE, LIX, 139.—**N. PAC.** TSIMSHIAN, NASS, KWAKIUTL: Boas, RBAE, XXXI, 742, 793. TLINGIT: Swanton, BBAE, XXXIX, 223. — **CAL.** MODOC: Curtin, *Myths of the Modocs*, p. 25. YANA: Curtin, *Creation Myths*, p. 344. WINTUN: *Ibid.*, p. 189.—**PLNS.** TETON: Dorsey, JAFL, II, 139. — **WDL. CENT.** OJIBWA: Jones-Michelson, PAES, VII (II), 173, No. 15; Laidlaw, OAR, XXVII, 84; Radin, GSCan, II, 29, 31, 69. OTTAWA: Schoolcraft, *Hiawatha*, p. 149. — **WDL. N.E.** MICMAC: Rand, p. 5, No. 1, and p. 273, No. 46. PASSAMAQUODDY: Leland, pp. 29, 228. MALECITE: Mechling, GSCan, IV, 73. — **WDL. IROQ.** IROQUOIS: Smith, RBAE, II, 90, 96, 97. SENECA: Curtin-Hewitt, RBAE, XXXII, 143, 158, 169, 486, 672, 679. HURON-WYANDOT: Barbeau, GSCan, XI, 239, No. 70.—**S.W.** NAVAHO: Matthews, MAFLS, V, 97.

211. *Succession of helpers* (H1235). Hero is sent continually from one helper to another. See references to note 206.—See also **PLNS.** BLACKFOOT: Grinnell, *Blackfoot Lodge Tales*, p. 96. CROW: Lowie, PaAM, XXV, 108, 141, 167, 192. CANADIAN DAKOTA: Wallis, JAFL, XXXVI, 80. — **WDL. CENT.** OJIBWA: Jones-Michelson, PAES, VII (II), 199, No. 19. References fragmentary.

212. *Father test* (H481). A child magically picks out his unknown father. — References: Boas, BBAE, LIX, 287, note 2. —**MACK.** BEAVER: Goddard, PaAM, X, 239, 243.—**PLAT.** SHUSWAP, THOMPSON, LILLOOET, KUTENAI: Boas, *loc. cit.* SHUSWAP: Teit, JE, II, 684.—**N. PAC.** NOOTKA: Boas, *loc. cit.* TLINGIT: Swanton, BBAE, XXXIX, 239, No. 78. TAHLTAN: Teit, JAFL, XXXIV, 236, No. 42 (modified). SNOHOMISH: Haeberlin, JAFL, XXXVII, 414. SKAGIT: *Ibid.*, p. 394. QUINAULT: Farrand, JE, II, 125, No. 14. CHINOOK: Boas, BBAE, XX, No. 4. TILLAMOOK: Boas, JAFL, XI, 27. — **CAL.** YANA: cf. Sapir, UCal, IX, 22, No. 1. — **PLNS.** WICHITA: Dorsey, CI, XXI, 172, No. 24. SKIDI PAWNEE: Dorsey, MAFLS, VIII, 307, No. 89. ASSINIBOIN: Lowie, PaAM, IV, 136 (note to JAMES BAY CREE). PLAINS CREE: Skinner, JAFL, XXIX, 357, No. 3. CANADIAN DAKOTA: Wallis, JAFL, XXXVI, 94, No. 24. — **WDL. CENT.** OJIBWA: Jones-Michelson, PAES, VII (II), 719, No. 72. CREE: Skinner, PaAM, IX, 104. — For the incident in a European borrowing, see Mechling, JAFL, XXVI, 219 ff. (MALECITE).

213. *Thunders.* Usually, but not always, conceived of as "thunderbirds." See note 151c.

214. *Winking club* (F835). A club that has opening and shutting eyes. ("Peculiar to the Plains Cree." — Skinner, JAFL, XXVII, 98.) PLAINS CREE:

Skinner, JAFL, xxix, 361, No. 3. — Live headdresses, pouches, or furs occur in Seneca tales: Curtin-Hewitt, RBAE, xxxii, 115, 140, 263; Curtin, *Seneca Indian Myths*, p. 28.

215. *LV. Orpheus* (F81.1). An interesting parallel to the classical story of Orpheus and Eurydice occurs in all parts of North America. The story consists of the following parts: (*a*) journey to the land of the dead to bring back a wife (sweetheart, etc.), (*b*) permission obtained, (*c*) prohibition against looking at wife on way out (or other tabu), (*d*) tabu broken and wife lost. — The following versions have all four parts: **ESK.** GREENLAND: Rink, p. 298, No. 51. — **PLAT.** SALISH: Hill-Tout, *British North America*, p. 214. KALISPEL: Curtis, vii, 95. SAHAPTIN: Farrand-Mayer, MAFLS, xi, 178, No. 16. — **N. PAC.** TLINGIT: Swanton, BBAE, xxxix, 249, No. 87. KWAKIUTL: Boas and Hunt, JE, iii, 104–106; Boas, CU, ii, 447. CHINOOK: Boas, BBAE, xx, No. 15. — **CAL.** YOKUTS: Kroeber, UCal, iv, 216, No. 24, and 228, No. 35. WESTERN MONO: Gifford, JAFL, xxxvi, 340, No. 12. — **PLNS.** WICHITA: Dorsey, CI, xxi, 300, No. 58, and 306, No. 59. PAWNEE: Dorsey, CI, lix, 126, No. 34; Dorsey, MAFLS, viii, 74, No. 21. BLACKFOOT: Grinnell, *Blackfoot Lodge Tales*, p. 127. — **WDL. N.E.** MALECITE: Mechling, GSCan, iv, 88, No. 25. MICMAC: LeClercq, *New Relation of Gaspesia* (Champlain Society, v) p. 209. — **WDL. IROQ.** HURON-WYANDOT: Brébeuf, *Jes Rel.*, x, 149–153. — **S.E.** CHEROKEE: Mooney, RBAE, xix, 252, No. 5. YUCHI: Speck, UPa, i, 144, No. 8. — **S.W.** ZUÑI: Cushing, p. 18. — Fragmentary versions are: **PLAT.** WARMSPRING: Lewis, *Southern Workman*, xxxix, 94. — **N. PAC.** TAHLTAN: Teit, JAFL, xxxiv, 337, No. 58. TLINGIT: Swanton, BBAE, xxxix, 181, No. 41, and 250, No. 88. — **CAL.** MODOC: Curtin, *Myths of the Modocs*, p. 39. MAIDU: Powers, CNAE, iii, 339. SHASTA: Dixon, JAFL, xxiii, 21. — **PLNS.** PAWNEE: Dorsey, MAFLS, viii, 71, No. 20; Grinnell, *Pawnee Hero Stories*, p. 129. — **WDL. IROQ.** SENECA: Curtin-Hewitt, RBAE, xxxii, 570, No. 116. IROQUOIS: Smith, RBAE, ii, 103. — **S.E.** SHAWNEE: Gregg, *Commerce of the Prairies*, ii, 239. — A curious similarity exists between the Iroquois tale and the Tlingit, No. 41, cited above. In both, the bereaved husband makes an image of his wife, and this image comes to life.

216. *Visit to the land of the dead* (F81). See in the preceding note, all references except IROQUOIS, PAWNEE (Grinnell), and TLINGIT, No. 41. — See also: **MACK.** ANVIK: Chapman, JAFL, xxv, 67; Chapman, PAES, vi, 14, No. 2. — **PLAT.** THOMPSON: Teit, JE, viii, 379. SANPOIL: Gould, MAFLS, xi, 113, No. 16. — **N. PAC.** QUINAULT: Farrand, JE, ii, 109, No. 6. NISQUALLI: Curtis, ix, 129. TWANA: *Ibid.*, p. 163. COOS: Frachtenberg, CU, i, 139, No. 23 (= JAFL, xxii, 37, No. 10). TAKELMA: Sapir, UPa, ii, 97, No. 8. — **CAL.** MAIDU: Powers, CNAE, iii, 339. MEWAN: Merriam, p. 195. LUISEÑO: DuBois, UCal, viii, 155. CAHUILLA: Hooper, UCal, xvi, 321. — **PLNS.** ARIKARA: Dorsey, CI, xvii, 152, No. 63. — **WDL. CENT.** OJIBWA: Knight, JAFL, xxvi, 92; Jones-Michelson, PAES, vii (ii), 3, 312, 537. FOX: Jones, PAES, i, 207. — **S.W.** HOPI: Voth, FM, viii, 109, No. 28, and 114, No. 29. — A related motif is:

(*a*) *Metempsychosis* (E600). Return to life in another form. — **ESK.** GREENLAND, EAST GREENLAND, CUMBERLAND SOUND, WEST HUDSON BAY: Boas, BAM, xv, 359. — **PLAT.** LILLOOET: Hill-Tout, JAI, xxxv, 204. — **N. PAC.** TAHLTAN: Teit, JAFL, xxxii, 240, No. 18. — **CAL.** KATO: God-

dard, UCal, v, 219.—**PLNS.** PAWNEE: Dorsey, MAFLS, VIII, 185, No. 47.—
WDL. CENT. Fox: Owen, PFLS, LI, 89.

217. *Looking tabu* (C300). In nearly all cases the prohibition against looking is during a magic journey to a high place, through the air from a cliff, or
to or from the other world. See the following references in note 215, *Orpheus:*
ESKIMO, KALISPEL, KWAKIUTL, TLINGIT (No. 87), BLACKFOOT, MALECITE,
CHEROKEE, YUCHI.— References: Boas, RBAE, XXXI, 850 f.—See also
references in note 151, *Roc.* In these tales the hero is carried from a cliff with
the injunction against opening his eyes on the way.—**ESK.** CUMBERLAND
SOUND: Boas, BAM, XV, 181. BERING STRAIT: Nelson, RBAE, XVIII, 458.
—**MACK.** LOUCHEUX: Camsell-Barbeau, JAFL, XXVIII, 250, No. 5.
ANVIK: Chapman, PAES, VI, 73, No. 12.—**PLAT.** SHUSWAP: Dawson,
p. 31; Teit, JE, II, 645, No. 3. THOMPSON: Teit, MAFLS, VI, 43.—**N.
PAC.** TSIMSHIAN, NASS, TLINGIT, HAIDA: Boas, *loc. cit.* CHEHALIS: Hill-
Tout, JAI, XXXIV, 357. SKAGIT: Haeberlin, JAFL, XXXVII, 380. COOS: St.
Clair-Frachtenberg, JAFL, XXII, 30; Frachtenberg, CU, I, 127, No. 19, and
187, No. 32. LOWER UMPQUA: Frachtenberg, CU, IV, 105, No. 23. TAKELMA:
Sapir, UPa, II, 67, No. 4.—**CAL.** MODOC: Curtin, *Myths of the Modocs*, p. 157.
See note 280, *The Girl who married her Brother* (MAIDU, SHASTA, ACHOMAWI,
YANA). HUPA: Goddard, UCal, I, 239. MAIDU: Dixon, PAES, IV, 123.
ATSUGEWI: Dixon, JAFL, XXI, 174. SINKYONE: Kroeber, JAFL, XXXII, 347,
No. 6. PAVIOTSO: Lowie, JAFL, XXXVII, 212, No. 3.—**PLNS.** SOUTHERN
PAIUTE (SHIVWITS): Lowie, JAFL, XXXVII, 97, No. 1, 106, No. 5; (MAOPA):
162, No. 3. SOUTHERN UTE: *Ibid.*, p. 66, No. 36, and p. 77, No. 48. OSAGE:
Dorsey, FM, VII, 49, No. 40. BLACKFOOT: McClintock, p. 344. CROW:
Lowie, PaAM, XXV, 154. PLAINS CREE: Skinner, JAFL, XXIX, 360, No. 3.
SWAMPY CREE: Cresswell, JAFL, XXXVI, 404. CANADIAN DAKOTA: Wallis,
JAFL, XXXVI, 88, No.·20.—**WDL. CENT.** OJIBWA: Jones-Michelson, PAES,
VII (I), 129, 435. TIMAGAMI OJIBWA: Speck, GSCan, IX, 57. MENOMINI:
Skinner and Satterlee, PaAM, XIII, 290.—**WDL. IROQ.** SENECA: Curtin-
Hewitt, RBAE, XXXII, 263, 267, No. 50, and 354, No. 60 (= Curtin, *Seneca
Indian Myths*, p. 174).—**S. W.** NAVAHO: Matthews, MAFLS, V, 121, 164.
JICARILLA APACHE: Mooney, AA, old ser., XI, 207; Goddard, PaAM, VIII,
199, No. 4. SAN CARLOS APACHE: Goddard, PaAM, XXIV, 41. ACOMA: Par-
sons, JAFL, XXXI, 220, No. 4. ZUÑI: Parsons, JAFL, XXX, 239, No. 15.——
SIBERIA: Jochelson, JE, VI, 381.— Notes on some other tabu-motifs follow:

   (*a*) *Tabu: profanely calling on spirit* (C10). — References: Boas, RBAE,
XXXI, 749.—**ESK.** GREENLAND: *Grønlandske Folkesagn*, No. 3.—**PLAT.**
SHUSWAP: Teit, JE, II, 657.—**N. PAC.** TSIMSHIAN, TLINGIT, HAIDA: Boas,
loc. cit. BELLA COOLA: Boas, JE, I, 89. CHINOOK: Boas, BBAE, XX, 31,
No. 2.—**PLNS.** ARAPAHO: Dorsey and Kroeber, FM, V, 239, No. 106.

   (*b*) *Tabu: drinking* (C250). — References: Boas, BBAE, LIX, 290, note 1
(**PLAT.** KUTENAI, SHUSWAP.—**N. PAC.** TAKELMA.—**PLNS.** BLACKFOOT,
HIDATSA).—**WDL. IROQ.** SENECA: Curtin-Hewitt, RBAE, XXXII, 129,
No. 20.

   (*c*) *Tabu: eating in other world* (C211).—**N. PAC.** TSIMSHIAN, HAIDA,
KWAKIUTL: Boas, RBAE, XXXI, 862.—**MACK.** ANVIK: Chapman, PAES,
VI, 69, No. 11.—**PLNS.** Cf. PAWNEE: Grinnell, *Pawnee Hero Stories*,
pp. 171 ff.—**S.E.** CHEROKEE: Mooney, RBAE, XIX, 350, No. 86.

   218. *Flood from tears.* See note 57*b.*

219. *LVI. The Visit to Chief Echo.* The hero visits the land of shadows and echoes. — References: Boas, RBAE, xxxi, 702. — **PLAT.** Shuswap: Boas, *loc. cit.* Thompson: Teit, MAFLS, xi, 4, No. 8. — **N. PAC.** Tsimshian, Nass, Tlingit, Haida, Bella Coola, Chinook, Tillamook, Takelma: Boas, *loc. cit.*

220. Cf. note 39, *Raven becomes voracious.*

221. *Shadow people* (E481). Invisible people; they live on the odors of food, etc. — In addition to references in note 219, see: **MACK.** Anvik: Chapman, JAFL, xxv, 66; Chapman, PAES, vi, 14, No. 2. Hare: Petitot, p. 121. Ts'ets'áut: Boas, JAFL, ix, 265. — **N. PAC.** Tahltan: Teit, JAFL, xxxii, 225, 239. Quileute: Farrand-Mayer, JAFL, xxxii, 274, No. 16. — **PLNS.** Southern Ute: Lowie, JAFL, xxxvii, 73, No. 45. Cf. Teton: Dorsey, AA, old ser., ii, 148, 151. — **WDL. CENT.** Menomini: Skinner and Satterlee, PaAM, xiii, 447. — **WDL. IROQ.** Seneca: Curtin-Hewitt, RBAE, xxxii, 580, 616. — **S.W.** Zuñi: Cushing, pp. 47 ff. —— Siberia: Jochelson, JE, vi, 377 f. — Two related motifs are:

(*a*) *Cloak (or cap) of invisibility* (D1053, D1067, D1361). — **PLNS.** Uintah Ute: Mason, JAFL, xxiii, 322 (cloak). Omaha: Dorsey, JAFL, i, 76 (cap). Skidi Pawnee: Dorsey, MAFLS, viii, 226, No. 58 (feather). — **WDL. CENT.** Sauk and Fox: Jones, JAFL, xiv, 230 (spider thread). — **WDL. N.E.** Micmac: Rand, p. 16, No. 3 (coat). — **S.W.** Zuñi: Parsons, JAFL, xxxi, 241 (hat) (European). — Cf. Klamath: Gatschet, CNAE, ii, 109 (hat acts as enchanting spell).

(*b*) *Mist of invisibility* (D902, D1361.4). — **PLAT.** Thompson: Teit, MAFLS, vi, 37. Shuswap: Teit, JE, ii, 684, No. 22 (note); Boas, *Sagen*, p. 9. Salish: Hill-Tout, *British North America*, p. 228. — **PLNS.** Pawnee: Dorsey, MAFLS, viii, 220, No. 57.

222. *LVII. The Piqued Buffalo-Wife.* Man marries buffalo, who becomes a woman. They have child. Man's second wife refers to buffalo-wife's origin, or, as in this version, he offends her in some other way. She and her child return to buffalo herd and become buffalo. Husband goes in search of them. Is compelled by old buffalo to pick his wife and child from herd. With help of child he succeeds. — References: Lowie, PaAM, xxv, 115. — **PLNS.** Omaha, Pawnee, Cheyenne, Arapaho, Crow, Blackfoot, Arikara, Assiniboin: Lowie, *loc. cit.* Ponca: Dorsey, CNAE, vi, 140 ff. Wichita: Dorsey, CI, xxi, 94, No. 29. Crow: Simms, FM, ii, 319, No. 12. Arikara: Curtis, v, 93. Mandan: Curtis, v, 50. — **S.W.** Jicarilla Apache: Goddard, PaAM, viii, 229, No. 25.

223. *Tabu: offending animal wife* (C35). An animal wife is easily offended. See all references in notes 222 and 233. — References: Boas, RBAE, xxxi, 670, 743, 939. — **ESK.** Greenland: Rink, p. 145, No. 12. Baffin Land: Boas, RBAE, vi, 616. — **MACK.** Ts'ets'áut: Boas, JAFL, ix, 263. — **PLAT.** Shuswap: Boas, RBAE, xxxi, 670, 939. — **N. PAC.** Tsimshian, Nass, Haida, Bella Coola, Rivers Inlet, Newettee, Kwakiutl: *Ibid.* — **PLNS.** Southern Ute: Lowie, JAFL, xxxvii, 46, No. 22 (piqued husband). Pawnee: Dorsey, CI, lix, 185, No. 50. Ponca: Dorsey, JAFL, i, 76. — **WDL. CENT.** Ojibwa: Jones-Michelson, PAES, vii (ii), 225, No. 20. — **WDL. N.E.** Malecite: Mechling, GSCan, iv, 95. — **WDL. IROQ.** Seneca: Curtin-Hewitt, RBAE, xxxii, 76, No. 1. — **S.W.** Zuñi: Cushing, pp. 150 ff.; Parsons, JAFL, xxxi, 245. —— Siberia: Jochelson, JE, vi, 378.

(a) *Offended supernatural wife* (C31). Supernatural wives of all kinds are easily offended and leave on the slighest provocation. — **MACK.** Anvik: Chapman, PAES, vi, 58, No. 7. Ts'ets'áut: Boas, JAFL, ix, 265. — Lillooet: Teit, JAFL, xxv, 329. — **N. PAC.** Songish: Hill-Tout, JAI, xxxvii, 336. — **CAL.** Luiseño: DuBois, UCal, viii, 153. — **PLNS.** Southern Ute: Lowie, JAFL, xxxvii, 34, No. 19. Pawnee: Dorsey, CI, lix, 126, No. 34. Blackfoot: Wissler and Duvall, PaAM, ii, 154. Plains Cree: Skinner, JAFL, xxix, 355, No. 3. — **WDL. CENT.** Menomini: Skinner and Satterlee, PaAM, xiii, 376. Ojibwa: Jones-Michelson PAES, vii (i), 133. — **WDL. IROQ.** Seneca: Curtin-Hewitt, RBAE, xxxii, 639, No. 121.

224. *Picking out transformed wife and child from identical companions (prearranged signal)* (H161). An interesting parallel to a European tale. There the hero is made to pick out his fiancée from her sisters, who have been made magically to look alike. There is a prearranged signal, as in this tale. The European motif usually occurs in the tale of "The White Cat" (No. lxxxii in this volume) though not in the version here given. A version containing the motif among the American Indians is found in Teit, MAFLS, xi, 60 (Thompson). The picking out of the wife and child from the buffalo occurs regularly in "The Piqued Buffalo-Wife" (note 222). See also Seneca: Curtin-Hewitt, RBAE, xxxii, 119, No. 18.

225. *Resuscitation by sweating* (E15.2). — **CAL.** Wappo: Radin, UCal, xix, 59, No. 9. — **PLNS.** Southern Paiute (Shivwits): Lowie, JAFL, xxxvii, 108, No. 5. Crow: Lowie, PaAM, xxv, 126, 163. Blackfoot: Wissler and Duvall, PaAM, ii, 119, No. 28. — **WDL. CENT.** Ojibwa: Jones, PAES, vii (ii), 201.

226. *LVIII. Bear-Woman and Deer-Woman.* Bear-Woman and Deer-Woman have their children play together. Bear kills deer. In revenge deer's children kill bear's children in her absence and cook them. When she returns she eats the cooked children (G61), and then, discovering the truth, she pursues deer's children. They are helped across a river by a crane, and escape. — **PLAT.** Thompson: Boas, *Sagen*, p. 16; Hill-Tout, FL, x, 195; Teit, JE, viii, 218; Teit, MAFLS, vi, 69, No. 22. Shuswap: Teit, JE, ii, 681. — **N. PAC.** Kwakiutl: Boas, *Sagen*, p. 168; Boas and Hunt, JE, x, 15. Chehalis: Hill-Tout, JAI, xxxiv, 360. Comox: Boas, *Sagen*, p. 81. Snohomish: Haeberlin, JAFL, xxxvii, 422. Kathlamet: Boas, BBAE, xxvi, 118. Takelma: Sapir, UPa, ii, 117, No. 13. — **CAL.** Klamath: Gatschet, CNAE, ii, 118. Yana: Curtin, *Creation Myths*, p. 456; Sapir, UCal, ix, 207, No. 24. Kato: Goddard, UCal, v, 221, No. 17. Lassik: Goddard, JAFL, xix, 135. Sinkyone: Kroeber, JAFL, xxxii, 349, No. 11. Wappo: Radin, UCal, xix, 47, No. 8. Maidu: Dixon, BAM, xvii, 79, No. 9; Powers, CNAE, iii, 341. Miwok: Gifford, UCal, xii, 286, No. 2, and 333, No. 13; Merriam, p. 103; Kroeber, UCal, iv, 203, No. 10. — **PLNS.** Shoshoni: Lowie, PaAM, ii, 253, No. 9.

227. *Crane bridge* (R246). Fugitives are helped across a stream by a crane who lets them cross on his leg. The pursuer is either refused assistance or drowned by the crane. Occurs regularly in "Bear-Woman and Deer-Woman" (note 226) and frequently in "The Bear-Woman" (note 244, tale lxiv). See all references in preceding note. — References: Waterman, JAFL, xxvii, 43. — **MACK.** Kaska: Teit, JAFL, xxx, 458, No. 13. — **PLAT.** Chilcotin, Shuswap: Waterman, *loc. cit.* Sahaptin: Farrand-Mayer, MAFLS, xi, 177,

No. 14. THOMPSON: Teit, MAFLS, XI, 25. WASCO: Curtin, PAES, II, 278. WISHRAM: Sapir, PAES, II, 171.—**N. PAC.** QUINAULT, KATHLAMET: Waterman, *loc. cit.* CHINOOK: Boas, BBAE, XX, 32, No. 2. SNOHOMISH: Haeberlin, JAFL, XXXVII, 423, 425.—**CAL.** MODOC: Curtin, *Myths of the Modocs*, p. 241.—**PLNS.** DAKOTA, PAWNEE, ASSINIBOIN: Waterman, *loc. cit.* OSAGE: Dorsey, FM, VII, 39, No. 31. BLACKFOOT: Uhlenbeck, VKAWA, XIII, 130.— **WDL. CENT.** CREE: Maclean, *Canadian Savage Folk*, p. 71. MENOMINI: Skinner and Satterlee, PaAM, XIII, 366. OJIBWA: Jones-Michelson, PAES, VII (1), 287; Schoolcraft, *Indian in his Wigwam*, p. 109; Schoolcraft, *Hiawatha*, p. 267; Laidlaw, OAR, XXVII, 74.—**WDL. N.E.** MICMAC: Rand, p. 164, No. 20; Speck, JAFL, XXVIII, 68; Parsons, JAFL, XXXVIII, 67, No. 5, and 68, No. 9. PASSAMAQUODDY: Prince, PAES, X, 67, No. 12.—**WDL. IROQ.** SENECA: Curtin-Hewitt, RBAE, XXXII, 465, No. 100 (modified).—**S.W.** SAN CARLOS APACHE: Goddard, PaAM, XXIV, 70.

228. *LIX. Splinter-Foot-Girl.* Young men live alone. Girl born from splinter wound kept as foster sister. Girl is carried off by buffalo bull (R11.1), who has demanded her in marriage. Young men, with help of mole and badger (cf. note 147), rescue girl and flee with her. Take refuge in tree (R301) which buffalo tries in vain to break down. Same experience with round rock who demands girl in marriage.—**PLNS.** ARAPAHO: Dorsey and Kroeber, FM, V, 31, No. 12, and 153 ff., Nos. 81–84; Voth, JAFL, XXV, 44. GROS VENTRE: Kroeber, PaAM, I, 100, No. 24, and 101, No. 25. CHEYENNE: Kroeber, JAFL, XIII, 182. PONCA: Dorsey, CNAE, VI, 224. OMAHA: Dorsey, JAFL, I, 77. DAKOTA: Riggs, CNAE, IX, 121. OSAGE: Dorsey, FM, VII, 49, No. 40. CROW: Simms, FM, II, 301, No. 18.—**WDL. CENT.** OJIBWA: Schoolcraft, *Hiawatha*, p. 274. The Arapaho (No. 12 and Voth, p. 44) and Crow references lack the initial incident of the birth from the splinter wound.—Closely related in many of its incidents is the tale:

(*a*) *The Buffalo Husband.* A girl abducted by a buffalo (R11.1) is transformed into a ring (D263). With the help of animals (B550) the hero rescues and disenchants her. The incidents are sometimes confused with those in "Splinter-Foot-Girl".—**PLNS.** CROW, SHOSHONI, BLACKFOOT, ASSINIBOIN: Lowie, PaAM, XXV, 308. PONCA: Dorsey, CNAE, VI, 82. PAWNEE: Dorsey, CI, LIX, 228, No. 70: Dorsey, MAFLS, VIII, 254, No. 61. DAKOTA: Riggs, CNAE, IX, 115. BLACKFOOT: Grinnell, *Blackfoot Lodge Tales*, p. 104.— **WDL. CENT.** Cf. OJIBWA: Jones-Michelson, PAES, VII (1), 291.—**S.W.** ZUÑI: Parsons, JAFL, XXXI, 235, No. 15.

229. *Birth from wound* (T541).—See in addition to references in note 228, Boas, RBAE, XXXI, 735 (**N. PAC.** TLINGIT, KWAKIUTL, NEWETTEE, HAIDA).

230. *Tree refuge* (R301).—References: Waterman, JAFL, XXVII, 50.— **PLAT.** SHUSWAP: Teit, JE, II, 636. THOMPSON: Teit, MAFLS, XI, 32.— **N. PAC.** SKYKOMISH: Haeberlin, JAFL, XXXVII, 385. SKAGIT: *Ibid.*, p. 387. TAKELMA: Sapir, UPa, II, 53.—**PLNS.** BLACKFOOT, ARAPAHO, PAWNEE, SHOSHONI, GROS VENTRE: Waterman, *loc. cit.*—**WDL. CENT.** OJIBWA: Jones-Michelson, PAES, VII (II), 207, No. 20.—**S.E.** CADDO: Waterman, *loc. cit.* —**S.W.** ZUÑI: *Ibid.*—Special discussion in Parsons, *Zeitschrift für Ethnologie*, LIV, 1–29; Parsons, MAFLS, XIII, 66, note 2; Boas, BBAE, LIX, 309, note 1; Boas, JAFL, XXV, 259.—Cf. note 270a.

231. *LX. The Eagle and Whale Husbands* (C26, R11.1). Girls wish for eagle and whale respectively as husbands. Their wished-for husbands appear

and take them off. They escape with difficulty. — References: Boas, BAM, xv, 360 (under heading, "A Tale about Two Girls"). — **ESK.** East Green-land, Greenland, Smith Sound, Cumberland Sound, Labrador, West Hudson Bay: Boas, *loc. cit.* —— Siberia: Bogaras, AA, new ser., IV, 607.

232. *Obstacle flight: Atalanta type* (R231). Treasure, or the like, is thrown back to tempt pursuer to delay. — **ESK.** See references in note 231. — **N. PAC.** Tsimshian: Boas, RBAE, xxvii, 92. Cf. Rivers Inlet: Boas, *Sagen*, p. 210. — **PLNS.** Osage: Dorsey, FM, vii, 20, No. 17. Omaha: Kercheval, JAFL, vi, 202. Pawnee: Dorsey, CI, lix, 34, No. 5. Arapaho: Dorsey and Kroeber, FM, v, 243, No. 106. Crow: Lowie, PaAM, xxv, 209. — **WDL. CENT.** Menomini: Skinner and Satterlee, PaAM, xiii, 372. Fox: Jones, PAES, i, 99. — **WDL. N.E.** Micmac: Rand, p. 56, No. 7; Parsons, JAFL, xxxviii, 62. — **WDL. IROQ.** Seneca: Curtin-Hewitt, RBAE, xxxii, 463, No. 99; Curtin, *Seneca Indian Myths*, p. 53. —— Siberia: Jochelson, JE, vi, 369.

233. *LXI. The Fox-Woman* (B651). Man finds house put in order by mysterious housekeeper (see note 207) and finds that it is a fox-woman. They marry. When her origin is suggested on one occasion she leaves. — **ESK.** Greenland, Cumberland Sound, Labrador: Boas, BAM, xv, 360 (under heading, "The Faithless Wife"). —— Siberia: Jochelson, JE, vi, 364.

234. *Origin tabu* (C441). The origin of a supernatural being must not be mentioned. See all references in note 233. — **MACK.** Hare: Petitot, pp. 120 ff. Ts'ets'áut: Boas, JAFL, ix, 265. — **N. PAC.** Kwakiutl: Boas and Hunt, JE, iii, 67. Chinook: Boas, BBAE, xx, 190, No. 17. — **CAL.** Mewan: Merriam, p. 132. — **PLNS.** Southern Ute: Lowie, JAFL, xxxvii, 48, No. 22*b*. Shoshoni: Lowie, PaAM, ii, 300, 301, Nos. 38*a*, 38*c*. Pawnee: Dorsey, CI, lix, 132, No. 34; Grinnell, *Pawnee Hero Stories*, p. 129. — **WDL. CENT.** Menomini: Skinner and Satterlee, PaAM, xiii, 377. — **WDL. N.E.** Malecite: Speck, JAFL, xxx, 482, No. 6. Passamaquoddy: Leland, p. 256.

235. *LXII. The Woman Stolen by Killer-Whales.* A woman is stolen by a whale (or other sea-beast) (R11.1) and taken to the whale-kingdom. Her husband (R125), with the aid of helpful animals (B550), rescues her. — References: Boas, RBAE, xxxi, 840. — **PLAT.** Sechelt: Boas, *loc. cit.* — **N. PAC.** Tsimshian, Tlingit, Haida, Bella Coola, Rivers Inlet, Nass: *Ibid.* Nanaimo: Boas, AA, old ser., ii, 326, No. 1. Lower Fraser: Teit, MAFLS, xi, 131, No. 3. Tahltan: Teit, JAFL, xxxiv, 228, No. 35. Coos: Frachtenberg, CU, i, 55, No. 10. —— Siberia: Jochelson, JE, vi, 365. Cf. Coos: Frachtenberg, CU, i, 157, No. 25 (= JAFL, xxii, 27). — In the following tales the woman is stolen by a bear and rescued by her husband, who follows directions he has received in a dream. — **PLAT.** Okanagon: Teit, MAFLS, xi, 90. Thompson: *Ibid.*, p. 46. Sanpoil: Gould, MAFLS, xi, p. 109. Sahaptin: Farrand-Mayer, MAFLS, xi, p. 175. Nez Percé: Spinden, MAFLS, xi, 188. — **N. PAC.** Cf. Tahltan: Teit, JAFL, xxxiv, 337, No. 59, and 338, No. 60. — In the following, she offends a bear and is taken off to marry the bear's son; after adventures she escapes. — References: **N. PAC.** Tsimshian, Tlingit, Haida, Bella Coola, Rivers Inlet: Boas, RBAE, xxxi, 836.

236. *Kingdom of fishes* (B223). Cf. note 253, *Underground animal kingdom.* See all references from Boas, RBAE, xxxi, 840, cited in note 235. — In addition: **MACK.** Beaver: Goddard, PaAM, x, 252. Kaska: Teit, JAFL,

xxx, 452, No. 10. — **N. PAC.** BELLA COOLA: Boas, RBAE, xxxi, 668. BELLA COOLA, RIVERS INLET: *Ibid.*, p. 671. TAHLTAN: Teit, JAFL, xxxii, 235, 236 and xxxiv, 342. NANAIMO: Boas, AA, old ser., ii, 327. QUILEUTE: Farrand-Mayer, JAFL, xxxii, 266, 276. — **PLNS.** CROW: Lowie, PaAM, xxv, 178. — A related motif is:

(a) *Under-water world* (F111). The three following references, all telling substantially the same story, deal with the world of the beavers. A man marries a beaver and lives in the beaver world. — **ESK.** LABRADOR: Turner, RBAE, xi, 339. — **WDL. CENT.** OJIBWA: Jones-Michelson, PAES, vii (ii), 251. — **WDL. N.E.** MICMAC: Michelson, JAFL, xxxviii, 34.

237. *Light extinguished and woman stolen* (R31). — References: Jochelson, JE, vi, 379. — **N. PAC.** TSIMSHIAN, BELLA COOLA, CHEHALIS, SQUAMISH: Jochelson, *loc. cit.* TAHLTAN: Teit, JAFL, xxxiv, 228. —— SIBERIA: Jochelson, *loc. cit.*

238. *LXIII. The Rolling Head.* A woman commits adultery with a snake. Her husband kills the snake (and, in some versions, serves the snake, or the snake's privates, to the wife to eat). He kills the wife and cuts off her head. The head pursues the family. In many of the versions of the Plateau and North Pacific areas, the story stops with the serving of the snake to the woman. — References: Boas, BBAE, lix, 304, note 1. — **MACK.** CHIPEWYAN, TS'ETS'ÁUT: Boas, *loc. cit.* CARRIER: Morice, TCI, v, 4 f., 22 f. — **PLAT.** SHUSWAP, LILLOOET, THOMPSON: Boas, *loc. cit.* — **N. PAC.** BELLA COOLA: *Ibid.* TAHLTAN: Teit, JAFL, xxxiv, 239, No. 45a, and 242, Nos. 47a, 47b. — **CAL.** Cf. YANA: *Ibid.* — **PLNS.** CHEYENNE, ASSINIBOIN, SIOUX: *Ibid.* CHEYENNE: Grinnell, JAFL, xvi, 108. BLACKFOOT: DeJong, VKAWA, xiv, 32; Knox, JAFL, xxxvi, 401; Wissler and Duvall, PaAM, ii, 68; Grinnell, JAFL, vi, 44. ARAPAHO: Voth, JAFL, xxv, 48, No. 12. OSAGE: Dorsey, FM, vii, 21, No. 17. PLAINS OJIBWA: Skinner, JAFL, xxxii, 291, No. 2. — **WDL. CENT.** CREE, OJIBWA: Boas, *loc. cit.* CREE: Maclean, *Canadian Savage Folk*, p. 71. OJIBWA: Jones-Michelson, PAES, vii (ii), 45, No. 3, and 405, No. 49; Laidlaw, OAR, xxvii, 74. — **WDL. N.E.** PASSAMAQUODDY: Boas, *loc. cit.* — **S.E.** CADDO: *Ibid.* —— SIBERIA: *Ibid.* — The central incident occurs in other contexts:

(a) *Pursuit by rolling head* (R261). Occurs in the following versions of the tale under discussion: — **MACK.** CARRIER. — **PLNS.** BLACKFOOT, OSAGE, PAWNEE, CHEYENNE, SIOUX, ARAPAHO. — **WDL. CENT.** CREE, OJIBWA. — See also **ESK.** BAFFIN LAND: Boas, BAM, xv, 255. — **MACK.** CHIPEWYAN: Petitot, pp. 405, 407. — **PLAT.** THOMPSON: Teit, MAFLS, xi, 25. CŒUR D'ALÈNE: *Ibid.*, p. 128, No. 21. WASCO: Curtin, PAES, ii, 246. — **N. PAC.** TAKELMA: Sapir, UPa, ii, No. 23. — **CAL.** MODOC: Curtin, *Myths of the Modocs*, p. 333. MAIDU: Dixon, BAM, xvii, 97, No. 14. YANA: Sapir, UCal, ix, 123, No. 9, and 202, No. 23; Curtin, *Creation Myths*, p. 327. PAVIOTSO: Lowie, JAFL, xxxvii, 201, 203, 206, No. 1. — **PLNS.** OMAHA: Kercheval, JAFL, vi, 201. GROS VENTRE: Kroeber, PaAM, i, 65, No. 4. ARAPAHO: Dorsey and Kroeber, FM, v, 278, No. 124. — **WDL. CENT.** FOX: Jones, PAES, i, 93. MENOMINI: Skinner and Satterlee, PaAM, xiii, 429. — **WDL. N.E.** PENOBSCOT: Leland, p. 126. PASSAMAQUODDY: Prince, PAES, x, 35, No. 6. — **WDL. IROQ.** SENECA: Curtin-Hewitt, RBAE, xxxii, 487, No. 105 (= Curtin, *Seneca Indian Myths*, p. 485). Cf. Curtin-Hewitt, *op. cit.*, pp. 262, 291 (flying head). An interesting parallel to this motif is that of the animal-head ball. It is a ball which snaps at people at which it is thrown. This occurs among the Central Algonquins. See Skinner, JAFL, xxvii, 98.

239. *Snake paramour* (B613.1). In addition to the references in note 238 (most of which have to do with a snake paramour), see **CAL.** MAIDU: Dixon, PAES, iv, 197, No. 13.

240. *Adultery revenged* (Q241). See references in the following notes: 178, *Potiphar's wife;* 238, *The Rolling Head;* 241, *Eaten heart;* 244, *The Bear-Woman.* — References: Boas, RBAE, xxxi, 634, 710, 847. — **ESK.** KODIAK: Golder, JAFL, xviii, 215. ALEUT: *Ibid.,* xxii, 10–16, *passim.* — **MACK.** CHIPEWYAN: Boas, *op. cit.,* p. 857. ANVIK: Chapman, PAES, vi, 42, No. 6. — **PLAT.** CHILCOTIN: Boas, *op. cit.,* p. 847. LILLOOET: Teit, JAFL, xxv, 320. SHUSWAP: Teit, JE, ii, 724, No. 46. — **N. PAC.** TSIMSHIAN, NASS, NEWETTEE: Boas, *op. cit.,* p. 634. HAIDA: *Ibid.,* p. 710. TSIMSHIAN, NASS, HAIDA, BELLA BELLA, BELLA COOLA, RIVERS INLET, KWAKIUTL: *Ibid.,* p. 847. — **CAL.** MEWAN: Merriam, p. 127. — **PLNS.** SKIDI PAWNEE: Dorsey, MAFLS, viii, 294, No. 81. WICHITA: Dorsey, CI, xxi, 151, No. 20, and 157, No. 21. ARIKARA: Dorsey, CI, xvii, 126, No. 44, and 155, No. 67. ARAPAHO: Dorsey and Kroeber, FM, v, 252, No. 107, and 271, No. 120. BLACKFOOT: Wissler and Duvall, PaAM, ii, 147. ASSINIBOIN: Lowie, PaAM, iv, 224, Nos. 59, 60. — **WDL. CENT.** CREE: Skinner, PaAM, ix, 92. — **WDL. IROQ.** IROQUOIS: Smith, RBAE, ii, 90. — **S.E.** CADDO: Dorsey, CI, xli, 79, No. 46. — **S.W.** HOPI: Voth, FM, viii, 69, No. 14.

241. *Eaten heart* (Q478). In some versions the well-known motif of the *Eaten heart* occurs at this point in the story. Instead of the mother being cut up and fed to the children, the father kills the mother's paramour and serves the paramour's genitals or his heart to the adulterous wife, who eats it unwittingly. Cf. note 98, *Relative's flesh unwittingly eaten.* — **ESK.** CUMBERLAND SOUND: Boas, BAM, xv, 223, No. 42. — **MACK.** TS'ETS'ÁUT: Boas, JAFL, ix, 260, No. 2. — **PLAT.** CHILCOTIN: Farrand, JE, ii, 45, No. 30. THOMPSON: Teit, JE, viii, 372; Teit, MAFLS, vi, 83, and xi, 46. SALISHAN: Boas, *Am. Philos. Soc. Proc.,* xxxiv, 38. LILLOOET: Boas, JAFL, xxv, 336, No. 30. SHUSWAP: Teit, JE, ii, 725, No. 47. — **N. PAC.** TAHLTAN: Teit, JAFL, xxxiv, 239, No. 45*a* and 242, Nos. 47*a* and *b.* HAIDA: Swanton, BBAE, xxix, 286. COMOX: Boas, *Sagen,* p. 74. — **PLNS.** BLACKFOOT: Wissler and Duvall, PaAM, ii, 116. — **WDL. CENT.** FOX: Jones, PAES, i, 147, 161. CREE: Russell, p. 202. MENOMINI: Skinner and Satterlee, PaAM, xiii, 453; Hoffman, RBAE, xiv, 175. — **WDL. N.E.** MALECITE: Mechling, GSCan, iv, 84; Stamp, JAFL, xxviii, 244. — **WDL. IROQ.** SENECA: Curtin-Hewitt, RBAE, xxxii, 102, No. 9. — **S.E.** CADDO: Dorsey, CI, xli, 67, No. 39. —— SIBERIA: Jochelson, JE, vi, 365. — Also European.

242. *Death-giving glance* (D2064). — References: Teit, JAFL, xxxii, 218. — **MACK.** KASKA, TS'ETS'ÁUT: Teit, *loc. cit.* — **PLAT.** THOMPSON, SHUSWAP: *Ibid.* — **N. PAC.** TAHLTAN: *Ibid.* TUALATI: Gatschet, JAFL, iv, 141. — **CAL.** HUPA: Goddard, UCal, i, 178, No. 7. PAVIOTSO: Lowie, JAFL, xxxvii, 202, No. 1*c.* — **PLNS.** ARAPAHO: Dorsey and Kroeber, FM, v, 289, No. 127. CHEYENNE: Kroeber, JAFL, xiii, 185, No. 22. GROS VENTRE (ATSINA): Curtis, v, 127; Kroeber, PaAM, i, 104, No. 26. Cf. PAWNEE: Dorsey, CI, lix, 155, No. 39. — **S.W.** SAN CARLOS APACHE: Goddard, PaAM, xxiv, 13, 33. NAVAHO: Matthews, MAFLS, v, 108, 123. PIMA:

Russell, RBAE, xxvi, 241. The incident is usually a part of the tale of "The Deserted Children" (No. LXVII, note 254).— A closely related motif is: (a) *Death by pointing* (D2062).— References: Teit, JAFL, xxxII, 249. — **PLAT.** THOMPSON, LILLOOET: Teit, *loc. cit.* CHILCOTIN: Farrand, JE, II, 44, No. 30. — **N. PAC.** TAHLTAN: Teit, *loc. cit.* TLINGIT: Swanton, BBAE, xxxIX, 35, No. 8. — **CAL.** MAIDU: Powers, CNAE, III, 291. WINTUN: Curtin, *Creation Myths*, p. 4.— **PLNS.** Cf. SOUTHERN UTE: Lowie, JAFL, xxxvII, 15, 16, No. 7 (game killed by uttering formula). — **WDL. N.E.** MICMAC: Parsons, JAFL, xxxvIII, 60, No. 7. PASSAMAQUODDY: Leland, p. 255. — **WDL. IROQ.** SENECA: Curtin-Hewitt, RBAE, xxxII, 122, No. 19, cf. 317, No. 58; 535, No. 111; 566, 567, No. 116. — **S.E.** CADDO: Dorsey, CI, xli, 17, No. 6.

243. The story goes at this point into that of "The Deserted Children" (No. LXVII).

244. *LXIV. The Bear-Woman.* A woman commits adultery with a bear. When the bear is killed, the woman turns into a bear and attacks her family. Invulnerable except in one spot. Obstacle flight. Cf. tale LXIII, "The Rolling Head." The introduction to the tale varies: (a) adultery with bear (most of the versions); (b) woman kidnapped by bear (Plateau versions); (c) a brother and sister commit incest; when the girl is scolded, she turns into a bear. The attack on the family, the invulnerability, and usually the obstacle flight are regular in all types. — **PLAT.** SHUSWAP: Teit, JE, II, 715, No. 41. CHILCOTIN: Farrand, JE, II, 17, No. 8. — **N. PAC.** BELLA COOLA: Boas, JE, I, 111 (type b). Coos: Frachtenberg, CU, I, 181, No. 30 (= JAFL, xxII, 32). — **CAL.** SHASTA: Kroeber, UCal, IV, 181. — **PLNS.** WICHITA: Dorsey, CI, xxi, 69, No. 9 (type c). PONCA: Dorsey, CNAE, VI, 292, cf. 19. ARAPAHO: Dorsey and Kroeber, FM, v, 238, No. 105. BLACK-FOOT: Wissler and Duvall, PaAM, II, 68; McClintock, p. 488. PIEGAN: Michelson, JAFL, xxiv, 244. GROS VENTRE (ATSINA): Kroeber, PaAM, I, 105, No. 27; Curtis, v, 123 (type c). CROW: Lowie, PaAM, xxv, 206. AS-SINIBOIN: Lowie, PaAM, IV, 179. — **WDL. CENT.** MENOMINI: Skinner and Satterlee, PaAM, xIII, 305, No. 2. OJIBWA: Jones-Michelson, PAES, VII (II), 399, No. 48. — **WDL. IROQ.** SENECA: Curtin-Hewitt, RBAE, xxxII, 180, No. 35. — **S.W.** NAVAHO: Matthews, MAFLS, v, 100.

245. *Bear paramour* (B611.1).— See the following references in note 244: **PLAT.** SHUSWAP, CHILCOTIN. — **N. PAC.** BELLA COOLA. — **PLNS.** PONCA, BLACKFOOT, PIEGAN, GROS VENTRE (Kroeber), CROW, ASSINIBOIN. — **WDL. CENT.** MENOMINI, OJIBWA. — **WDL. IROQ.** SENECA. — See also **N. PAC.** TSIMSHIAN, TLINGIT, HAIDA, BELLA COOLA, RIVERS INLET: Boas, RBAE, xxxI, 836. TAHLTAN: Teit, JAFL, xxxiv, 339, No. 61. ALSEA: Frachtenberg, BBAE, lxvii, 185, No. 16. — **PLNS.** ARAPAHO: Dorsey and Kroeber, FM, v, 227, No. 94. — **WDL. CENT.** MENOMINI: Hoffman, RBAE, xiv, 174; Skinner and Satterlee, PaAM, xIII, 249, 305. Fox: Jones, PAES, I, 161. KICKAPOO: Jones, PAES, IX, 67. OJIBWA: Jones-Michelson, PAES, VII (I), 397; Jones, JAFL, xxix, 379, 381, 387. SAULTEAUX: Skinner, PaAM, IX, 168. — **WDL. IROQ.** SENECA: Curtin-Hewitt, RBAE, xxxII, 102, No. 9.

246. *Achilles' heel* (Z311). A person is vulnerable in one place alone.— See the following references in note 244: **PLAT.** SHUSWAP, CHILCOTIN.— **N. PAC.**

BELLA COOLA. — **PLNS.** WICHITA, BLACKFOOT, GROS VENTRE. — See in
addition: **PLAT.** SAHAPTIN: Farrand-Mayer, MAFLS, XI, 147. — **N. PAC.**
TLINGIT: Swanton, BBAE, XXXIX, 93, No. 31. SNOHOMISH: Haeberlin,
JAFL, XXXVII, 405. KATHLAMET: Boas, BBAE, XXVI, 10. TILLAMOOK:
Boas, JAFL, XI, 38. — **CAL.** MODOC: Curtin, *Myths of the Modocs*, p. 75.
SHASTA: Farrand-Frachtenberg, JAFL, XXVIII, 214, No. 5. KATO: Goddard,
UCal, V, 225, No. 24. YANA: Curtin, *Creation Myths*, p. 318. MAIDU:
Dixon, BAM, XVII, 71, No. 6, and 92, No. 10 (11). MEWAN: Merriam, pp.
76, 81. CHILULA: Goddard, UCal, X, 353, 367. SOUTH SIERRA MIWOK:
Barrett, UCal, XVI, 2, No. 1, and 7, No. 3. — **PLNS.** CROW (APSAROKE):
Lowie, PaAM, XXV, 126, 128, 163; Curtis, IV, 17. DAKOTA: Wissler, JAFL,
XX, 200. ARAPAHO: Dorsey and Kroeber, FM, V, 153, No. 80. — **WDL.**
CENT. OJIBWA: Schoolcraft, *Hiawatha*, pp. 29, 77 ff., 202 ff.; Jones-
Michelson, PAES, VII (I), 15, 491, and (II), 403; Michelson, JAFL, XXIV, 250. —
WDL. N.E. PASSAMAQUODDY: Prince, PAES, X, 71, No. 12. — **WDL. IROQ.**
IROQUOIS: Smith, BBAE, II, 63. SENECA: Curtin-Hewitt, RBAE, XXXII,
169, No. 31; 250, No. 47; 259, No. 48. — **S.E.** CHEROKEE: Mooney,
RBAE, XIX, 319, No. 66; Ten Kate, JAFL, II, 54; Terrill, JAFL, V, 125.
CREEK: Speck, *Southern Workman*, XXXVIII, 9. MUSKHOGEAN: Swanton,
JAFL, XXVI, 197, No. 4. CADDO: Dorsey, CI, XLI, 19, No. 9. — **S.W.**
NAVAHO: Matthews, MAFLS, V, 91. JICARILLA APACHE: Mooney, AA, old
ser., XI, 208. — Motifs very closely related are:

(*a*) *External soul* (E700). A person's life (or soul) exists somewhere out-
side his body. — **PLAT.** CHILCOTIN: Farrand, JE, II, 21, No. 8. SAHAPTIN:
Farrand-Mayer, MAFLS, XI, 151, No. 5. WISHRAM: Sapir, PAES, II, 41.
— **N. PAC.** KWAKIUTL: Boas and Hunt, JE, III, 354 f. BELLA COOLA:
Boas, *Sagen*, p. 242. SKAGIT: Haeberlin, JAFL, XXXVII, 388. KATHLAMET:
Boas, BBAE, XXVI, 11. TILLAMOOK: Boas, JAFL, VI, 38. COOS: Frachten-
berg, CU, I, 73, No. 12. TAKELMA: Sapir, UPa, II, 141. — **CAL.** MODOC:
Curtin, *Creation Myths*, p. xxix; Curtin, *Myths of the Modocs*, pp. 4, 325.
HUPA: Goddard, UCal, I, 168, No. 5. KATO: Goddard, JAFL, XIX, 138, No. 5.
PAVIOTSO: Lowie, JAFL, XXXVII, 226, No. 10. — **PLNS.** SOUTHERN PAIUTE
SHIVWITS): *Ibid.*, p. 107, No. 5, and 128, No. 11. SOUTHERN UTE: *Ibid.*,
p. 72, No. 43. ARAPAHO: Dorsey and Kroeber, FM, V, 122, No. 64, and 123,
No. 65. WICHITA: Dorsey, CI, XXI, 68, No. 8, and 87, No. 11. CROW: Lowie,
PaAM, XXV, 109; Simms, FM, II, 290, No. 12. ATSINA: Curtis, V, 127. —
WDL. CENT. OJIBWA: Jones-Michelson, PAES, VII (I), 33; Radin, GSCan,
II, 13, 27, 45, 64; Jones, JAFL, XI, 136, No. 7. — **WDL. N.E.** MICMAC:
Rand, p. 64, No. 8, and p. 245, No. 40. — **WDL. IROQ.** SENECA: Curtin-
Hewitt, RBAE, XXXII, 88, 136, 146, 217, 381, 537, 555; Curtin, *Seneca
Indian Myths*, pp. 130, 235, 344. — **S.W.** NAVAHO: Matthews, RBAE, V,
407; Matthews, MAFLS, V, 102. JICARILLA APACHE: Russell, JAFL, XI,
262; Goddard, PaAM, VIII, 203, No. 9. — Cf. **PLNS.** SHOSHONI: Lowie,
PaAM, II, 301. TETON: Dorsey, RBAE, XI, 497. — **S.E.** CHEROKEE:
Mooney, RBAE, XIX, 277, No. 30. —— SIBERIA: Jochelson, JE, VI, 368. —
European borrowings among American Indians: Thompson, CColl, II, 333,
409 ff. (incident D).

(*b*) *Vital bodily members* (E780). Severed members rejoin and bring their
owner to life again. Fragmentary references. — **MACK.** CARRIER: Morice,
TCI, V, 5. — **N. PAC.** TAHLTAN: Teit, JAFL, XXXIV, 353, No. 73; Emmons,

UPa, VIII, 168. TLINGIT: BBAE, XXXIX, 214. TSIMSHIAN: Boas, BBAE, XXVII, 231. TILLAMOOK: Boas, JAFL, XI, 136. — **CAL.** MEWAN: Merriam, p. 171. YOKUTS: Kroeber, UCal, IV, 209, No. 14. — **PLNS.** CROW: Lowie, PaAM, XXV, 126. PAWNEE: Dorsey, CI, LIX, 37, No. 5. CANADIAN DAKOTA: Wallis, JAFL, XXXVI, 84. — **WDL. IROQ.** SENECA: Curtin-Hewitt, RBAE, XXXII, 346, 388, 548; Curtin, *Seneca Indian Myths*, pp. 5, 6. — **S.E.** YUCHI: Gatschet, AA, old ser., VI, 282. — **S.W.** NAVAHO: Matthews, MAFLS, V, 103, 116. WHITE MOUNTAIN APACHE: Goddard, PaAM, XXIV, 113. PAPAGO: Mason, JAFL, XXXIV, 256.

247. *LXV. The Dog-Husband.* Girl has unknown lover, who is dog by day and man by night. She gives birth to puppies. She is deserted by tribe (S300). Crow hides fire for girl in clam shell (S352; cf. note 255). Girl changes dog-children to human by destroying their dog skins. Boys become prosperous. Crow visits them and takes home meat for her children. Starving tribe discover meat and are glad to be reconciled with daughter. — References: Boas, RBAE, XXXI, 785; Teit, JAFL, XXX, 463. — **ESK.** EAST GREENLAND, GREENLAND, PORT CLARENCE, POINT BARROW: Teit, *loc. cit.* SMITH SOUND, CUMBERLAND SOUND, UNGAVA, WEST HUDSON BAY: Boas, BAM, XV, 359. — **MACK.** KASKA, DOG RIB, HARE, TS'ETS'ÁUT, CARRIER: Teit, *loc. cit.* — **PLAT.** THOMPSON, LILLOOET: *Ibid.* CHILCOTIN: Farrand, JE, II, 7. NEZ PERCÉ: Spinden, MAFLS, XI, 198. — **N. PAC.** BELLA COOLA, KWAKIUTL, NOOTKA, COMOX, QUINAULT: Boas, RBAE, XXXI, 785. TAHLTAN, TLINGIT, COOS: Teit, *loc. cit.* TAHLTAN: Teit, JAFL, XXXIV, 248, No. 53. LOWER FRASER: Teit, MAFLS, XI, 130, No. 2. SKAGIT: Haeberlin, JAFL, XXXVII, 418. QUILEUTE: Farrand-Mayer, JAFL, XXXII, 272, No. 15. ALSEA: Frachtenberg, BBAE, LXVII, 125, No. 10, and 137, No. 11. COOS: Frachtenberg, CU, I, 167, No. 27 (= JAFL, XXII, 30). SHOALWATER BAY: Curtis, IX, 121. — **PLNS.** ARAPAHO: Dorsey and Kroeber, FM, V, 205–226, Nos. 90–92. CHEYENNE: Kroeber, JAFL, XIII, 181. BLACKFOOT: Wissler and Duvall, PaAM, II, 107. —— SIBERIA: Bogaras, AA, new ser., IV, 618. — General discussion: Boas, JAFL, IV, 14.

248. *Dog by day; man by night* (D621). A girl's paramour is a dog (or other animal) in the day and a man at night. Regular in the "Dog-Husband" story (note 247). — In addition to the references there given, see: **MACK.** KASKA: Teit, JAFL, XXX, 436, No. 1. — **N. PAC.** COOS: Frachtenberg, CU, I, 165, No. 26, and 171, No. 28. Cf. TAHLTAN: Teit, JAFL, XXXIV, 340, No. 62. HAIDA: Swanton, JE, X, 560, No. 47. — **CAL.** KATO: Goddard, UCal, V, 234, No. 30. MODOC: Curtin, *Myths of the Modocs*, pp. 3, 198, 221. — **PLNS.** PONCA: Dorsey, JAFL, I, 76. — **WDL. N.E.** MALECITE: Speck, JAFL, XXX, 482, No. 6. — **WDL. IROQ.** SENECA: Curtin-Hewitt, RBAE, XXXII, 87, No. 4, and 542, No. 113. — **S.E.** TUNICA: Swanton, JAFL, XX, 288. — **S.W.** ZUÑI: Cushing, p. 93. HOPI: Voth, FM, III, 349. —— SIBERIA: Jochelson, JE, VI, 151.

249. *Disenchantment by destroying animal skins* (D721). Occurs in most forms of "The Dog-Husband" (note 247) and of "The Swan-Maidens" (note 284). — In addition see: **ESK.** KODIAK: Golder, JAFL, XVI, 89. CUMBERLAND SOUND: Boas, BAM, XV, 224, No. 42. — **MACK.** KASKA: Teit, JAFL, XXX, 464, No. 18. — **PLAT.** CHILCOTIN, JE, II, 37, No. 22. — **N. PAC.** HAIDA: Swanton, BBAE, XXIX, 13. KWAKIUTL: Boas, *Sagen*, p. 147. NEWETTEE: *Ibid.*, pp. 170, 175, 203. NOOTKA: *Ibid.*, p. 121. COMOX: *Ibid.*,

p. 86. CHEHALIS: Hill-Tout, JAI, xxxiv, 349. KATHLAMET: Boas, BBAE, xxvi, 158. — **CAL.** MODOC: cf. Curtin, *Myths of the Modocs*, p. 127. — **PLNS.** ASSINIBOIN: Lowie, PaAM, IV, 157. Cf. TETON: Dorsey, JAFL, II, 137. — **S.W.** ZUÑI: Cushing, p. 162.—— SIBERIA: Jochelson, JE, VI, 370, 380. SOUTH AMERICAN INDIAN: Koch-Grünberg, Nos. 9, 15, 38, 64, 67.— Some analogous motifs are:

(a) *Disenchantment by beating* (D712). — **PLNS.** CANADIAN DAKOTA: Wallis, JAFL, xxxvi, 91, No. 22. — **WDL. IROQ.** SENECA: Curtin-Hewitt, RBAE, xxxii, 623, No. 119; 607, No. 118; 565, No. 116; cf. 487, No. 105.

(b) *Disenchanted person recognized by ornaments under skin* (H61.2).— References: Boas, RBAE, xxxi, 776. — **MACK.** Ts'ETS'ÁUT: Boas, *loc. cit.* — **N. PAC.** TSIMSHIAN, TLINGIT, HAIDA: *Ibid.* TAHLTAN: Teit, JAFL, xxxiv, 343, No. 64, and 344, No. 65.

250. *Bird carries food from deserted child to starving tribe* (S361). A part of both "The Dog-Husband" (No. LXV) and "The Deserted Children" (No. LXVII). — **N. PAC.** TSIMSHIAN, NASS, HAIDA, NEWETTEE, KWAKIUTL, NOOTKA, COWICHAN, CHEHALIS, SQUAMISH: Boas, BBAE, xxxi, 788.

251. *Deserted daughter's good fortune discovered by accident* (N771). — References: Boas, RBAE, xxxi, 785 (**PLAT.** CHILCOTIN. — **N. PAC.** TSIMSHIAN, NASS, HAIDA, TLINGIT, BELLA COOLA, KWAKIUTL, COMOX, NEWETTEE, COWICHAN, SQUAMISH, CHINOOK).

252. *LXVI. The Youth who joined the Deer.* A man goes to the underground kingdom of the deer. Temporarily becomes a deer and marries among the deer.— References: Boas, BBAE, xxxi, 738.— **ESK.** LABRADOR: Turner, RBAE, xi, 339. — **PLAT.** LILLOOET, THOMPSON, SHUSWAP: Boas, *loc. cit.* THOMPSON: Teit, MAFLS, xi, 40. — **N. PAC.** TSIMSHIAN, TLINGIT, KWA-KIUTL: Boas, *loc. cit.* — **PLNS.** SOUTHERN PAIUTE (SHIVWITS): Lowie, JAFL, xxxvii, 127; cf., pp. 124, 137; cf. (MAOPA): *Ibid.*, pp. 165, 192. — **WDL. N.E.** MICMAC: Michelson, JAFL, xxxviii, 34.—— SIBERIA: Jochelson, JE, VI, 378.

253. *Underground animal kingdom* (F127). — Besides references in note 252, see: **N. PAC.** TWANA: Curtis, IX, 166. ALSEA: Frachtenberg, BBAE, LXVII, 173, No. 15. — **PLNS.** SOUTHERN UTE: Lowie, JAFL, xxxvii, 63, No. 34. CROW: Lowie, PaAM, xxv, 216, 218, cf. 159. MANDAN: Maximilian, II, 185. ARIKARA: Dorsey, CI, xvii, 39, No. 12, and 114, No. 34. — **WDL. CENT.** Cf. MENOMINI: Skinner and Satterlee, PaAM, xiii, 456. — **WDL. IROQ.** SENECA: Curtin-Hewitt, RBAE, xxxii, 539, No. 113, and 654, No. 126. — **S.E.** CHEROKEE: Mooney, RBAE, xix, 324, No. 73. CHOCTAW: Bushnell, BBAE, xlviii, 32. CADDO: Dorsey, CI, xli, 11, No. 1. BILOXI: Dorsey and Swanton, BBAE, xlvii, 83. — **S.W.** HOPI: Voth, FM, III, 349. — An analogous motif is:

(a) *Animal village* (B220). — Besides the references in note 252 (goats or deer), see: **N. PAC.** TSIMSHIAN, BELLA COOLA, HAIDA: Boas, RBAE, xxxi, 740 (mosquitoes).

254. Some other tales of marriages with animals are:

(a) *The woman with a stallion as paramour* (B611.3). — References: Teit, MAFLS, xi, 53 (**PLAT.** THOMPSON. — **PLNS.** SHOSHONI, ARAPAHO, PAW-NEE, BLACKFOOT, GROS VENTRE, ASSINIBOIN).

(b) *Various animals tried as wives: only one accepted* (B600.1).—References: Jochelson, JE, VI, 366, 376; Skinner and Satterlee, PaAM, xiii, 377. — **ESK.** Jochelson, *op. cit.*, p. 366. — **N. PAC.** KATHLAMET: *Ibid.* TSIMSHIAN: *Ibid.*,

p. 376.— **WDL. CENT.** MENOMINI, EASTERN CREE, OJIBWA: Skinner and Satterlee, *loc. cit.* OJIBWA: Jones-Michelson, PAES, VII (II), 215, No. 20. ——SIBERIA: Jochelson, *loc. cit.*, and Bogaras, AA, new ser., IV, 629.

255. *LXVII. The Deserted Children* (S300). Children are deserted by a camp. They come to an old woman who kills them all except a boy and a girl. Flight. When they come to camp they are tied to a tree. Rescued and given fire by friendly animal. Boy kills game by glance; girl performs magic by glance. Starving camp returns to children for food The last incident is common to this story and the "Dog-Husband" tale (No. LXV, note 247). — **MACK.** Cf. KASKA: Teit, JAFL, XXX, 455, No. 12. — **PLAT.** THOMPSON: Teit, MAFLS, VI, 51 and XI, 34; Teit, JE, VIII, 230; Boas, *Sagen*, p. 17. LILLOOET: Teit, JAFL, XXV, 296; Hill-Tout, JAI, XXXI, 784 and XXXV, 201. NEZ PERCÉ: Spinden, MAFLS, XI, 196, No. 17. — **N. PAC.** TSIMSHIAN, HAIDA, BELLA BELLA: Boas, RBAE, XXXI, 785. TAHLTAN: Teit, JAFL, XXXIV, 230, No. 37, and 232, No. 38. SNOHOMISH: Haeberlin, JAFL, XXXVII, 415.—**CAL.** Cf. HUPA: Goddard, UCal, I, 193, No. 10.—**PLNS.** ARAPAHO, PONCA, SKIDI PAWNEE, CROW, BLACKFOOT, GROS VENTRE, ASSINIBOIN: Lowie, PaAM, XXV, 222. CHEYENNE: Kroeber, JAFL, XIII, 185. SHOSHONI: St. Clair, JAFL, XXII, 275. MANDAN: Will, JAFL, XXVI, 331. PAWNEE: Dorsey, CI, LIX, 95, No. 24. CANADIAN DAKOTA: Wallis, JAFL, XXXVI, 42. — **WDL. CENT.** KICKAPOO: Jones, PAES, IX, 55, No. 8. OJIBWA: Radin, GSCan, II, 67, cf. Laidlaw, OAR (1918 reprint), p. 54.—**WDL. N.E.** MICMAC: Parsons, JAFL, XXXVIII, 79, No. 12. — **WDL. IROQ.** SENECA: Curtin-Hewitt, RBAE, XXXII, 104, No. 9, and 152, No. 25.—**S.E.** BILOXI: Dorsey and Swanton, BBAE, XLVII, 77. — **S.W.** ZUÑI: Cushing, p. 132; Ten Kate, JAFL, XXX, 496. PAPAGO: H. R. Kroeber, JAFL, XXV, 95.

256. *LXVIII. The Princess who rejected her Cousin* (L431). A proud girl induces her lover to disfigure himself to prove his love. She then scorns him. He journeys to the supernatural people and is magically beautified. He then returns and humiliates her.—References: Boas, RBAE, XXXI, 767.— **N. PAC.** TSIMSHIAN, TLINGIT, HAIDA: Boas, *loc. cit.* CHEHALIS: Hill-Tout, JAI, XXXIV, 354. SONGISH: Hill-Tout, JAI, XXXVII, 346. SKAGIT: Haeberlin, JAFL, XXXVII, 433.— The following show somewhat remote analogies: **PLNS.** CROW: Lowie, PaAM, XXV, 192, 197. — **S.W.** HOPI: Voth, FM, VIII, 81, No. 18.

257. *Magic self-boiling kettle* (D1172). Cf. note 210, especially the Central Woodland references.

258. *Magic beautification by dismemberment and resuscitation* (D1865).— Cf. **WDL. IROQ.** SENECA: Curtin-Hewitt, RBAE, XXXII, 254, No. 48 (= Curtin, *Seneca Indian Myths*, p. 85), and 614, No. 119.

259. *Magic beautification* (D1860). Cf. notes 183, *Dirty-Boy* and 185, *Male Cinderella.*— **PLAT.** WISHRAM: Sapir, PAES, II, 65, No. 2. — **N. PAC.** TSIMSHIAN, TLINGIT, HAIDA, CHEHALIS, SONGISH: see references in note 256. TLINGIT: Swanton, BBAE, XXXIX, 234, No. 75. BELLA COOLA: Boas, JE, I, 109. SNOHOMISH: Haeberlin, JAFL, XXXVII, 415. CHINOOK: Boas, BBAE, XX, 33, No. 2. TAKELMA: Sapir, UPa, II, 66, No. 4.—**CAL.** HUPA: Goddard, UCal, I, 213, No. 16. MODOC: Curtin, *Myths of the Modocs*, pp. 127, 258.— **PLNS.** CROW: Lowie, PaAM, XXV, 154, 193. PAWNEE: Grinnell, *Pawnee Hero Stories*, p. 96; Dorsey, CI, LIX, 158, No. 42; Dorsey, MAFLS, VIII, 28, No. 5. WICHITA: Dorsey, CI, XXI, 39, No. 3, and 43, No. 4. ARAPAHO:

Dorsey and Kroeber, FM, v, 319, No. 133, and 348, No. 139. CHEYENNE: Kroeber, JAFL, XIII, 171, No. 14. OMAHA: Dorsey, CNAE, VI, 606. BLACK- FOOT: McClintock, p. 498. ARIKARA: Dorsey, CI, XVII, 132, No. 47. ASSINI- BOIN: Lowie, PaAM, IV, 135, 142. GROS VENTRE: Kroeber, PaAM, I, 81. TETON: Curtis, III, 117. — WDL. CENT. OJIBWA: Schoolcraft, *Hiawatha*, p. 72. MICMAC, PASSAMAQUODDY: Leland, p. 53. — S.E. BILOXI: Dorsey and Swanton, BBAE, XLVII, 78. — S.W. HOPI: Voth, FM, VIII, 150, No. 41.

260. *Resuscitation by boiling* (E15.1). Does not occur frequently in this form. — See N. PAC. TSIMSHIAN: Boas, RBAE, XXXI, 188. NOOTKA: *Ibid.*, p. 917. More often the resuscitation is by burning (*e.g.* PLNS. WICHITA: Dorsey, CI, XXI, 218, No. 31. — WDL. CENT. MENOMINI: Hoffman, RBAE, XIV, 231. — CAL. MODOC: Curtin, *Creation Myths*, p. xxix) or by sweating in a sweathouse (*e.g.* PLNS. CHEYENNE: Kroeber, JAFL, XIII, 180, No. 17. ARAPAHO: Dorsey and Kroeber, FM, v, 12, No. 5).

261. *Resuscitation by jumping (or stepping) over* (E13). — PLAT. LIL- LOOET: Hill-Tout, JAI, XXXV, 198. — N. PAC. TSIMSHIAN: Boas, RBAE, XXXI, 188. SKAGIT: Haeberlin, JAFL, XXXVII, 388, 389. — PLNS. SOUTH- ERN UTE: Lowie, JAFL, XXXVII, 68, No. 36.

262. *LXIX. The Fatal Swing.* An old woman wishing to marry her daughter's husband induces the young woman to swing over a pool of water. She causes the swing to break (K855), and the girl falls into the water, where she is taken by a water monster (R11.1, cf. note 235), but brought to the sur- face to nurse her human baby, she is rescued. — PLNS. ARAPAHO: Dorsey and Kroeber, FM, v, 11, No. 5. OSAGE: Dorsey, FM, VII, 26, No. 22. AS- SINIBOIN: Lowie, PaAM, IV, 157. — WDL. CENT. OJIBWA: Schoolcraft, *Indian in his Wigwam*, p. 116. CREE: Russell, p. 205. Fox: Jones, PAES, I, 101. — S.W. JICARILLA APACHE: Mooney, AA, old ser., XI, 210. Cf. PLNS. GROS VENTRE: Kroeber, PaAM, I, 87. BLACKFOOT: Wissler and Duvall, PaAM, II, 57.

263. *Drowned mother returns to suckle child* (E323.1). See references in note 262. — See also: PLAT. THOMPSON: Teit, MAFLS, XI, 44. LILLOOET: Teit, JAFL, XXV, 329. — CAL. MEWAN: Merriam, p. 131. — S.E. BILOXI: Dorsey and Swanton, BBAE, XLVII, 81. — S.W. HOPI: Voth, FM, VIII, 144, No. 39. — Cf. WDL. CENT. Fox: Jones, PAES, I, 155 (dead mother returns to rebuke her children's cruel stepmother). —— EUROPEAN: Bolte- Polívka, I, 96.

264. *Murder by stabbing in ear* (S115.1). Aside from this tale (Dorsey, FM, VII, 27) and PAWNEE: Dorsey, CI, LIX, 170, No. 45, and 506, No. 72, see references in Jochelson, JE, VI, 365 (ESKIMO and KORYAK).

265. *LXX. The Skin-shifting Old Woman.* Related to "The Fatal Swing" (No. LXIX). An old woman who covets her daughter's (or another younger woman's) husband kills the young woman and disguises herself in the vic- tim's skin. She is discovered and punished. — ESK. CUMBERLAND SOUND: Boas, BAM, XV, 185. WEST HUDSON BAY: Boas, RBAE, VI, 624. — MACK. Cf. KASKA: Teit, JAFL, XXX, 462. — N. PAC. TAHLTAN: Teit, JAFL, XXXIV, 252, No. 55. — CAL. YANA: Curtin, *Creation Myths*, p. 353. — PLNS. PAWNEE: Dorsey, CI, LIX, 167, No. 45, and 506, Nos. 71, 72. WICHITA: Dorsey, CI, XXI, 124, No. 17. — S.E. BILOXI: Dorsey and Swanton, BBAE, XLVII, 77.

266. Over a large part of the American continent the number four occupies

the same prominent place as the number three in European tales. In several European tales taken over by the Indians, the only substantial change is the shift of numbers. A new incident is added to the European tale in order to complete the conventional series of four.

267. *Disguised flayer (skin-shifter)* (K1941). An impostor dresses in the skin of his victim. See all references in note 265. — References: Boas, BBAE, LIX, 302. — **MACK.** CHIPEWYAN: Boas, *loc. cit.* — **PLAT.** SHUSWAP, THOMPSON, NEZ PERCÉ, WISHRAM: *Ibid.* CHILCOTIN: Farrand, JE, II, 41. THOMPSON: Teit, MAFLS, XI, 29. — **N. PAC.** HAIDA, CHEHALIS, ALSEA, TILLAMOOK, TAKELMA, COOS: Boas, *loc. cit.* TLINGIT, HAIDA: Boas, RBAE, XXXI, 870. COWLITZ: Hill-Tout, JAI, XXXIV, 371. SNOHOMISH: Haeberlin, JAFL, XXXVII, 409. — **CAL.** JOSHUA: Farrand-Frachtenberg, JAFL, XXVIII, 237. YANA: Sapir, UCal, IX, 158, 216; Curtin, *Creation Myths*, pp. 318, 359. — **PLNS.** SHOSHONI, OMAHA, PAWNEE, BLACKFOOT, ASSINIBOIN: Boas, BBAE, LIX, 302. SOUTHERN PAIUTE (SHIVWITS): Lowie, JAFL, XXXVII, 99, No. 1, and 141, No. 14; (MAOPA): *Ibid.*, p. 163, No. 3. TETON: Dorsey, JAFL, II, 137. PLAINS CREE: Skinner, JAFL, XXIX, 345. PLAINS OJIBWA: Skinner, JAFL, XXXII, 285. — **WDL. CENT.** OJIBWA, CREE, FOX, MENOMINI: Boas, *loc. cit.* — **S.E.** CHEROKEE: Mooney, RBAE, XIX, 268, No. 17. — **S.W.** ZUÑI: Boas, *loc. cit.* —— SIBERIA: Jochelson, JE, VI, 370. — An analogous motif is:

(a) *Skin tightened in order to look beautiful* (K1942). — References: Boas, RBAE, XXXI, 605, 860 (**PLAT.** LILLOOET, UTAMQT. — **N. PAC.** CHEHALIS).

268. LXXI. *The Child and the Cannibal* (G400–G599). Children are abducted by a giantess. A boy born from the mucus of mother's nose has miraculous growth and goes in search of brothers and sisters. Finds children seated on floor and a woman rooted to floor. Latter warns him of cannibal giantess. Flight. Tree refuge. Fugitives betrayed by reflection in water. Giantess asks hero how he happens to be so beautiful. He tells her his head was pressed between stones and thus persuades her to submit to the same treatment. He kills her but she revives, since she has external soul. Hero kills her again and escapes with brothers and sisters. — **N. PAC.** BELLA COOLA: Boas, *Sagen*, p. 249; Boas, JE, I, 83. KWAKIUTL: Boas and Hunt, JE, III, 87; Boas, CU, II, 117. BELLA BELLA: Boas, *Sagen*, p. 241. SQUAMISH: *Ibid.*, p. 57. Cf. the European tale of "Little Poucet" (No. LXXXI, note 292). Many of these parts appear separately:

(a) *Children kidnapped in basket deceive kidnapper and escape* (G441, K526). — References: Boas, BBAE, LIX, 296, note 5. — **PLAT.** CHILCOTIN, SHUSWAP, THOMPSON, LILLOOET, KUTENAI, NEZ PERCÉ: Boas, *loc. cit.* SAHAPTIN: Farrand-Mayer, MAFLS, XI, 176, No. 14. — **N. PAC.** BELLA COOLA, BELLA BELLA, COMOX, COWICHAN, FRASER DELTA, RIVERS INLET, SQUAMISH, CHEHALIS, CHINOOK: Boas, *loc. cit.* SNOHOMISH: Haeberlin, JAFL, XXXVII, 436. SKYKOMISH: *Ibid.*, p. 385. Cf. SKAGIT: *Ibid.*, p. 381. — **CAL.** KATO: Boas, *loc. cit.* — **PLNS.** SHOSHONI, OSAGE, ARAPAHO: *Ibid.* SOUTHERN UTE: Lowie, JAFL, XXXVII, 75, No. 46. CROW: Lowie, PaAM, XXV, 128. — **WDL. N.E.** MICMAC: Boas, *loc. cit.* — **S.W.** HOPI: *Ibid.* NAVAHO: Parsons, JAFL, XXXVI, 375. KERES: MAAA, VI, 224. WHITE MOUNTAIN APACHE: Goddard, PaAM, XXIV, 137.

(b) *Bodies of victims in front of cannibal's house* (G691). — References: Jochelson, JE, VI, 381 (KORYAK, KATHLAMET). — **CAL.** PAVIOTSO: Lowie, JAFL, XXXVII, 225, No. 10.

269. *Birth from mucus* (T542.1). — References: Boas, RBAE, xxxi, 734 (**PLAT.** Shuswap. — **N. PAC.** Tsimshian, Haida, Bella Coola, Kwakiutl, Nootka, Comox, Songish). — Cf. note 166*a*.

270. *Reflection betrays fugitive* (R351). — References: Boas, BBAE, lix, 306, note 1. Cf. note 230. — **MACK.** Kaska: Teit, JAFL, xxx, 433, No. 1. — **PLAT.** Chilcotin, Shuswap, Thompson, Kutenai: Boas, *loc. cit.* — **N. PAC.** Tsimshian, Haida, Kwakiutl, Bella Coola, Comox, Nootka, Quinault: *Ibid.* Tahltan: reference in Teit, JAFL, xxx, 433. — **PLNS.** Assiniboin, Osage: Boas, *loc. cit.* — **WDL. CENT.** Ojibwa: *Ibid.* Menomini: Skinner and Satterlee, PaAM, xiii, 441. — **S.E.** Caddo: Dorsey, CI, xli, 104. — **S.W.** Navaho: Matthews, MAFLS, v, 115. Zuñi: Parsons, JAFL, xxxi, 240, No. 15. Hopi: Voth, FM, viii, 70, No. 14. — Related incidents follow:

(*a*) *Diving for reflected enemy* (J1794.1). — References: Boas, RBAE, xxxi, 741. — **PLAT.** Shuswap: Boas, *loc. cit.* — **N. PAC.** Haida, Bella Coola, Kwakiutl, Nootka, Comox: *Ibid.* — **CAL.** Cahuilla: Hooper, UCal, xvi, 323. — **PLNS.** Canadian Dakota: Wallis, JAFL, xxxvi, 96, No. 24. — **WDL. CENT.** Ojibwa: Boas, *loc. cit.* Menomini: Skinner and Satterlee, PaAM, xiii, 420.

(*b*) *Diving for reflected woman* (J1793). — **N. PAC.** Tahltan: Teit, JAFL, xxxii, 220. Quinault: Farrand, JE, ii, 123. — **WDL. CENT.** Menomini: Skinner and Satterlee, PaAM, xiii, 315. —— Siberia: Jochelson, JE, vi, 379.

(*c*) *Shooting at enemy's reflection in water* (J1794). — References: Boas, BBAE, lix, 306 (**MACK.** Kaska. — **PLAT.** Chilcotin, Shuswap, Thompson, Kutenai. — **N. PAC.** Tahltan, Tsimshian, Haida, Kwakiutl, Bella Coola, Comox, Nootka, Quinault. — **PLNS.** Osage, Blackfoot, Assiniboin. — **WDL. CENT.** Ojibwa). —— European: Dähnhardt, *Natursagen*, iv, 230; Parsons, MAFLS, xiii, 106.

271. *False beauty-doctor* (K1013). Hero tells the ogre that he became handsome by having his head crushed between rocks. The ogre submits to the same treatment and is killed. — References: Boas, RBAE, xxxi, 762–766. — **ESK.** Alaska: Boas, *loc. cit.* Labrador: Turner, RBAE, xi, 334. — **MACK.** Loucheux: Boas, *loc. cit.* Kaska: Teit, JAFL, xxx, 432, 433. — **PLAT.** Lillooet, Sechelt, Thompson, Wishram, Wasco, Kutenai: Boas, *loc. cit.* Sanpoil: Gould, MAFLS, xi, 105. — **N. PAC.** Tsimshian, Haida, Bella Coola, Kwakiutl, Nootka, Kathlamet: Boas, *loc. cit.* — **CAL.** Maidu, Yana: *Ibid.* Cf. Miwok: Gifford, UCal, xii, 292, 334. — **PLNS.** Ponca, Osage: Boas, *loc. cit.* Plains Cree: Skinner, JAFL, xxix, 347, No. 2. Southern Ute: Lowie, JAFL, xxxvii, 49, No. 23. — **WDL. N.E.** Malecite: Boas, *loc. cit.* — **WDL. IROQ.** Huron-Wyandot: Barbeau, GSCan, xi, 166, 170, 171, Nos. 53-55. — **S.W.** Navaho: Parsons, JAFL, xxxi, 371. Keres: *Ibid.*, p. 227. Jicarilla Apache: Russell, JAFL, xi, 265; Goddard, PaAM, viii, 227, No. 30. Sia: Stevenson, RBAE, xi, 153. — **S.E.** Choctaw: Bushnell, AA, new ser., xi, 534. A world-wide motif. See Dähnhardt, *Natursagen*, iv, 239. — Some analogous motifs follow:

(*a*) *Sham doctor* (K1955). Hero masks as doctor and kills enemies. — References: Skinner and Satterlee, PaAM, xiii, 520; Lowie, PaAM, iv, 147. — **PLNS.** Pawnee, Omaha, Dakota, Assiniboin: Lowie, *loc. cit.* Shoshoni, Plains Ojibwa, Western Ojibwa, Plains Cree: Skinner and Satterlee, *loc. cit.* Cheyenne: Kroeber, JAFL, xiii, 190, No. 33. Blackfoot: Grinnell,

Blackfoot Lodge Tales, p. 152. — **WDL. CENT.** Ojibwa, Cree, Saulteaux, Fox, Menomini: Skinner and Satterlee, *loc. cit.* Cree, Menomini: Lowie, *loc. cit.* (additional references). Timiskaming Algonquin: Speck, GSCan, ix, 4. — Cf. note 109r.

(*b*) *Death through foolish imitation* (J2400.1). A widespread tale closely related to the *Bungling Host* (note 103). A trickster meets his death (or puts his family to death) by foolish imitation or by following foolish advice. See all references in note 271. — References: Boas, RBAE, xxxi, 680. — **ESK.** Greenland: Rink, p. 119. — **PLAT.** Shuswap, Kutenai: Boas, *loc. cit.* Thompson: Teit, MAFLS, vi, 68 and xi, 45. Wishram: Sapir, PAES, ii, 35. — **N. PAC.** Tsimshian, Nass, Tlingit, Haida, Newettee, Nootka: Boas, *loc. cit.* Tahltan: Teit, JAFL, xxxii, 208. Kawkiutl: Boas and Hunt, JE, iii, 345. Alsea: reference in BBAE, lix, 288, note 5. — **CAL.** Maidu: Dixon, PAES, iv, 83, No. 3. — **PLNS.** Southern Paiute (Shivwits): Lowie, JAFL, xxxvii, 144, No. 15. Southern Ute: Lowie, JAFL, xxxvii, 33, No. 19. Crow: Simms, FM, ii, 285, No. 4. Gros Ventre: Kroeber, PaAM, i, 70, No. 12. Plains Cree: Skinner, JAFL, xxix, 348. — **WDL. CENT.** Menomini: Skinner and Satterlee, PaAM, xiii, 270; Skinner, JAFL, xxvi, 80 (European). Ojibwa: Jones-Michelson, PAES, vii (ii), 45. Missisauga: Chamberlain, JAFL, v, 291. — **WDL. N.E.** Malecite: Mechling, GSCan, iv, 79, No. 18. Passamaquoddy: Leland, p. 183; Prince, PAES, x, 61, and 79, No. 12. — **S.E.** Muskhogean: Swanton, JAFL, xxvi, 198, No. 5, and 205, No. 14. Choctaw: Bushnell, BBAE, xlviii, 32. Biloxi: Dorsey and Swanton, BBAE, xlvii, 69. — **S.W.** Navaho: Matthews, MAFLS, v, 92. Zuñi: Parsons, JAFL, xxxi, 216, No. 1; Cushing, pp. 203 ff.; Handy, JAFL, xxxi, 455, No. 5; Lummis, *Pueblo Indian Folk-Stories*, No. 2. Jicarilla Apache: Russell, JAFL, xi, 262, 265, 267; Goddard, PaAM, viii, 227, No. 30. — Several well-defined groups appear in the list given above.

272. See note 246*b*.

273. *Resuscitation by rubbing* (*or beating*) (E11). — **PLAT.** Chilcotin: Farrand, JE, ii, 19, No. 7. Kutenai: Boas, BBAE, lix, 208. — **N. PAC.** Bella Coola: Boas, JE, i, 85. Takelma: Sapir, UPa, ii, No. 5. — **PLNS.** Southern Ute: Lowie, JAFL, xxxvii, 66, No. 36. Uintah Ute: Mason, JAFL, xxiii, 321. Crow: Lowie, PaAM, xxv, 124. Blackfoot: Wissler and Duvall, PaAM, ii, 122. Skidi Pawnee: Dorsey, MAFLS, viii, 73, No. 20. — **WDL. IROQ.** Seneca: Curtin-Hewitt, RBAE, xxxii, 607, No. 118.

274. *LXXII. The Cannibal who was burned* (G512). A cannibal is overcome and burned in a fire. The ashes turn into mosquitoes (or the like). — References: Waterman, JAFL, xxvii, 42 f. — **MACK.** Kaska: Teit, JAFL, xxx, 431, No. 1. — **N. PAC.** Tlingit, Haida, Comox, Kwakiutl, Skokomish: Waterman, *loc. cit.* Snuqualmi: Haeberlin, JAFL, xxxvii, 437. Quileute: Farrand-Mayer, JAFL, xxxii, 255, No. 2. — **CAL.** Paviotso: Lowie, JAFL, xxxvii, 231 f., No. 11. — **PLNS.** Dakota, Pawnee, Arapaho, Cheyenne, Blackfoot, Shoshoni, Assiniboin, Gros Ventre: Waterman, *loc. cit.* — **WDL. N.E.** Naskapi: Speck, JAFL, xxxviii, 27. — **S.W.** Zuñi: Waterman, *loc. cit.*

In a similar story, grizzly bear is killed by pouring hot pitch into her mouth. — References: Frachtenberg, BBAE, lxvii, 60 (**N. PAC.** Alsea, Molala, Coos, Lower Umpqua, Takelma. — **CAL.** Yana, Shasta, Athapascan). — Cf. note 167.

275. *Insects from burnt monster's body* (A2001).— References: Boas, RBAE, xxxi, 740. — **MACK.** KASKA: Teit, JAFL, xxx, 445, No. 7. — **N. PAC.** TSIMSHIAN, BELLA COOLA, HAIDA: Boas, *loc. cit.* TAHLTAN: Teit, JAFL, xxxiv, 351, Nos. 71 f. — **WDL. N.E.** MICMAC: Speck, JAFL, xxviii, 62; Parsons, JAFL, xxxviii, 57. — **WDL. IROQ.** Cf. SENECA: Curtin-Hewitt, RBAE, xxxii, 351, 354, 398, 488, 522, and IROQUOIS: Canfield, p. 125.

276. *LXXIII. The Conquering Gambler* (N1). A bankrupt gambler gets supernatural power and wins back his fortune. — **PLAT.** CHILCOTIN: Farrand, JE, II, 38, No. 23. — THOMPSON: Teit, MAFLS, VI, 53 and XI, 43, 56; Teit, JE, VIII, 375. LILLOOET: Teit, JAFL, xxv, 338, No. 32; Hill-Tout, JAI, xxxv, 199. WASCO: Curtin, PAES, II, 292. — **N. PAC.** HAIDA: Swanton, JE, V, 194, No. 18; 196, No. 24; 200, No. 37. TAHLTAN: Teit, JAFL, xxxiv, 233, No. 39. CHINOOK: Boas, BBAE, xx, 35, 220. — **CAL.** SHASTA: Dixon, JAFL, xxiii, 24, No. 14. — **PLNS.** WICHITA: Dorsey, CI, xxi, 194, No. 28. CROW: Lowie, PaAM, xxv, 200. — **S.W.** NAVAHO: Matthews, MAFLS, v, 82–86, 160 ff.; Matthews, JAFL, II, 89. JICARILLA APACHE: Goddard, PaAM, VIII, 214, No. 22; Russell, JAFL, XI, 268. For *Gambling contest* as part of the test theme (cf. notes 133–138), see **PLAT.** WISHRAM: Boas, RBAE, xxxi, 712, 812. — **N. PAC.** KWAKIUTL, NEWETTEE, NOOTKA, COMOX, CHINOOK, QUINAULT, TILLAMOOK: *Ibid.* — **CAL.** SOUTH SIERRA MIWOK: Barrett, UCal, xvi, 9, No. 6.

277. *Lives wagered* (N2, N2.1). See references in note 276. — Add **PLAT.** NEZ PERCÉ: Spinden, MAFLS, XI, 185, No. 5. — **N. PAC.** ALSEA: Frachtenberg, BBAE, lxvii, 25. — **CAL.** YANA: Dixon, UCal, IX, 227, No. 10. YOKUTS: Kroeber, UCal, IV, 238, No. 39, and 240, No. 40. WESTERN MONO: Gifford, JAFL, xxxvi, 352, No. 19. — **PLNS.** SOUTHERN PAIUTE (MAOPA): Lowie, JAFL, xxxvii, 160, 176. — **WDL. IROQ.** SENECA: Curtin-Hewitt, RBAE, xxxii, 179, 184, 205, 234, 247, 323, 351–353, 373, 439, 447, 449, 585; Curtin, *Seneca Indian Myths,* pp. 19, 29, 170, 334. — **S.E.** CHEROKEE: Mooney, RBAE, xix, 314, No. 63. — **S.W.** SAN CARLOS APACHE: Goddard, PaAM, xxiv, 22, 39. ZUÑI: Cushing, pp. 385 ff.

278. *LXXIV. The Deceived Blind Man* (*blind dupe*) (K333.1). A blind man's arrow is aimed for him by his mother (or wife), who deceives him into thinking he has missed his aim. She eats the slain game herself. He discovers the trickery. A friendly loon dives with him and thus restores his sight. He avenges his ill-treatment. — References: Boas, RBAE, xxxi, 825. — **ESK.** GREENLAND, SMITH SOUND, CENTRAL: Boas, *loc. cit.* — **MACK.** HARE, LOUCHEUX, CARRIER: *Ibid.* — **PLAT.** CHILCOTIN: *Ibid.* — **N. PAC.** TSIMSHIAN, TLINGIT, HAIDA, RIVERS INLET, KWAKIUTL: *Ibid.* TAHLTAN: Teit, JAFL, xxxiv, 226, No. 34. — **PLNS.** ARAPAHO, OSAGE, ASSINIBOIN: Boas, *loc. cit.* UTE (SOUTHERN): Lowie, JAFL, xxxvii, 78, No. 49; (UINTAH): Mason, JAFL, xxiii, 301.

279. *Healing water shown by animals* (B512). See the following versions of "The Deceived Blind Man" (note 278): — **ESK.** (Rink, Holm, Kroeber, Boas). — **MACK.** HARE, LOUCHEUX, CARRIER. — **PLAT.** CHILCOTIN.— **N. PAC.** TSIMSHIAN, KWAKUITL. Add HAIDA: Boas and Hunt, JE, V, 263, and X, 353). — **PLNS.** ASSINIBOIN. Add CROW: Lowie, PaAM, xxv, 190. — **WDL. CENT.** OJIBWA: Jones-Michelson, PAES, VII (II), 269, No. 26. —— EUROPEAN: Bolte-Polívka, I, 128.— Closely related motifs are:

(*a*) *Water of life* (E80). Water is used to restore life, or as a sovereign healing power.—References: Jochelson, JE, vi, 369.—**N. PAC.** Kwakiutl, Newettee, Bella Bella, Bella Coola: Jochelson, *loc. cit.* Rivers Inlet, Newettee, Kwakiutl: Boas, RBAE, xxxi, 667. Kwakiutl: Boas and Hunt, JE, x, 209. Chehalis: Hill-Tout, JAI, xxxiv, 309. Coos: Frachtenberg, CU, i, 121, No. 18.—**CAL.** Yana: Curtin, *Creation Myths*, p. 384. Maidu: Dixon, BAM, xvii, 97, No. 13; Dixon, PAES, iv, 189, No. 10, and 237, No. 17. Shasta: Dixon, JAFL, xxiii, 25, No. 16. Achomawi: Curtin, JAFL, xxii, 285, No. 2. Paviotso: Lowie, JAFL, xxxvii, 213, No. 3, and 231, No. 11.—**PLNS.** Southern Paiute (Shivwits): Lowie, JAFL, xxxvii, 123, No. 10. Ponca: Dorsey, JAFL, i, 205.—**WLD. CENT.** Ojibwa: Jones-Michelson, PAES, vii (ii), 395, No. 47.—**WDL. IROQ.** Seneca: Curtin-Hewitt, RBAE, xxxii, 187, 324, 381, 403.—**S.W.** Pima: Lloyd, *Aw-aw-tam*, p. 92; Neff, JAFL, xxv, 56.—— Siberia: Jochelson, JE, vi, 369.— European: Bolte-Polívka, i, 513 and ii, 400.

(*b*) *Water of life and death* (E82). A water which can be used both for killing and restoring life.—**N. PAC.** Kwakiutl: Boas, CU, ii, 465. Cf. also Kwakiutl: Boas and Hunt, JE, iii, 128. Tlingit: Swanton, BBAE, xxxix, 35, No. 8. Bella Coola: Boas, JE, i, 54.—— European: Bolte-Polívka, iii, 31.

280. *LXXV. The Girl who married her Brother.* A girl commits incest with her brother (cf. note 8). She then sets the world on fire (A1030; cf. note 57*d*). Tribe make sky-basket and ascend to sky. In spite of warning, one looks out (C300; cf. note 217), and whole tribe falls and is killed. In some versions the girl is Loon, and she makes a necklace of the hearts of the tribe. —**CAL.** Modoc: Curtin, *Myths of the Modocs*, p. 95. Shasta: Farrand-Frachtenberg, JAFL, xxviii, 212, No. 5; Dixon, JAFL, xxiii, 14 (defective). Achomawi: Dixon, JAFL, xxi, 165, 175. Yana: Sapir, UCal, ix, 34, No. 2, and 133, No. 10; Dixon, UCal, ix, 228, No. 12; Curtin, *Creation Myths*, p. 407. Maidu: Dixon, BAM, xvii, 71, No. 7. For another explanation of the loon's collar, see Teit, JAFL, xxxii, 209 (**MACK.** Carrier.—**PLAT.** Chilcotin, Shuswap, Lillooet, Thompson.—**N. PAC.** Tahltan).

281. *Lover identified by hair floating on water* (H75). Not otherwise found, at least to my knowledge, in American Indian myths. For European parallels, see Bolte-Polívka, iii, 33.

282. *Object as substitute for fugitive* (K525). Fugitives leave some object behind to deceive their captor into thinking they are still present. Cf. note 196, *Magic objects impersonate fugitive.* See references in note 268*a*, *Children kidnapped in basket deceive kidnapper and escape* and note 280, *The Girl who married her Brother.* In both, this motif is regular.—See also:**ESK.** Baffin Land: Boas, RBAE, vi, 634.—**PLNS.** Southern Paiute (Shivwits): Lowie, JAFL, xxxvii, 130, No. 12. Southern Ute: *Ibid.*, p. 11, No. 5.—**WDL. CENT.** Ojibwa: Jones-Michelson, PAES, vii (ii), 123, No. 7.—**WDL. IROQ.** Seneca: Curtin-Hewitt, RBAE, xxxii, 167, No. 29.—— Siberia: Jochelson, JE, vi, 364.

283. *Sky basket* (F51.2). See references in note 280.— See also: **ESK.** Kodiak: Golder, JAFL, xvi, 23.—**PLAT.** Thompson: Teit, MAFLS, vi, 24. Chilcotin: Farrand, JE, ii, 29, No. 12.—**N. PAC.** Haida: Swanton, JE, x, 733. Coos: Frachtenberg, CU, i, 29, No. 3.—**WDL. IROQ.** Huron-Wyandot: Barbeau, GSCan, xi, 57, No. 6.—**S.W.** Navaho: Matthews,

MAFLS, v, 121.——— SIBERIA: Bogaras, AA, new ser., IV, 591. Cf. note 28, *Sky window* and 48, *Sky rope*.

284. *LXXVI. The Swan-Maidens* (D361.1). A man sees on a lake some geese who have taken off their feathers and become women. He steals the feathers of one; the rest fly away as geese. She remains and marries him. One day she finds her feathers and she and her children fly away as geese. — References: Kroeber, JAFL, XII, 170.—**ESK.** GREENLAND, SMITH SOUND, BAFFIN LAND, POINT BARROW: Kroeber, *loc. cit.* CUMBERLAND SOUND: Boas, BAM, XV, 179. KODIAK: Golder, JAFL, XVI, 95.— **MACK.** ANVIK: Chapman, PAES, VI, 11, No. 1.—**PLAT.** THOMPSON: Teit, MAFLS, XI, 31; Teit, JE, VIII, 369.—**N.PAC.** TLINGIT: Swanton, BBAE, XXXIX, 56, No. 24, and 206, No. 54. HAIDA: Swanton, JE, V, 192, No. 13 (= BBAE, XXIX, 264). — **CAL.** Cf. WISHOSK: Kroeber, JAFL, XVIII, 103, No. 21. — **PLNS.** UTE: Kroeber, JAFL, XIV, 277, No. 10; (UINTAH): Mason, JAFL, XXIII, 322, No. 25. Cf. WICHITA: Dorsey, CI, XXI, 83, No. 11.— **WDL. CENT.** Cf. Fox: Owen, PFLS, LI, 90.—**WDL. N.E.** MICMAC: Hagar, AA, old ser., VIII, 38. PASSAMAQUODDY: Leland, p. 142; Prince, PAES, X, 59, No. 12.— **WDL. IROQ.** Cf. HURON-WYANDOT: Barbeau, GSCan, XI, 56, No. 6.— For the incident in obvious European borrowings, see Thompson, CColl, II, 366 ff. For European distribution, see Bolte-Polívka, III, 406, and Aarne-Thompson, *Types of the Folk-tale*, No. 400.

285. *LXXVII. The Death of Pitch.* The version of the tale here given is a continuation of the text of tale LVI, "The Visit to Chief Echo." Pitch is killed by being exposed to the sun.—References: Boas, RBAE, XXXI, 683. —**N. PAC.** TSIMSHIAN, NASS, TLINGIT, HAIDA, RIVERS INLET, NEWETTEE, KWAKIUTL, COMOX: Boas, *loc. cit.* TAHLTAN: Teit, JAFL, XXXII, 210.

286. *Trickster's false creations fail him* (J2175). Trickster creates men of excrement (or pitch) to help him. They melt.— References: Boas, RBAE, XXXI, 689; Skinner and Satterlee, PaAM, XIII, 528. — **ESK.** SMITH SOUND: Rasmussen, *People of the Polar North*, p. 104.—**PLAT.** UTAMQT: Boas, *loc. cit.* SHUSWAP: Teit, JE, II, 691. OKANAGON: Teit, MAFLS, XI, 75. CHILCOTIN: Farrand, JE, II, 16 f.— **N. PAC.** TSIMSHIAN, NASS, TLINGIT, HAIDA, KWAKIUTL: Boas, *loc. cit.* CHEHALIS: Hill-Tout, JAI, XXXIV, 356. SNOHOMISH: Haeberlin, JAFL, XXXVII, 400; cf. 403.— **PLNS.** BLACKFOOT, ASSINIBOIN: Skinner and Satterlee, *loc. cit.*— **WDL. CENT.** MENOMINI: Skinner and Satterlee, *op. cit.*, p. 382. TIMAGAMI OJIBWA: Speck, GSCan, IX, 70. OJIBWA: Schoolcraft, *Indian in his Wigwam*, p. 164; Jones-Michelson, PAES, VII (II), 415, No. 50. KICKAPOO: Jones, PAES, IX, 23, No. 4.——— SIBERIA: Jochelson, JE, VI, 373, 375.

287. Some additional motifs in native American Indian tales follow:

(*a*) *Dwarfs* (F495). — **PLNS.** SOUTHERN UTE: Lowie, JAFL, XXXVII, 76, No. 47. CROW: Lowie, PaAM, XXV, 165, 169, 171 f., 257. PLAINS CREE: Skinner, JAFL, XXIX, 362, No. 5.— **WDL. CENT.** OJIBWA: Jones, PAES, VII (II), 287, No. 29; cf. 193, No. 18 (water-fairies). — **WDL. N.E.** MONTAGNAIS: Speck, JAFL, XXXVIII, 23.

(*b*) *Invisible arrow* (D1656.1). A weapon is invisible except to one person. —**MACK.** KASKA: Teit, JAFL, XXX, 820.— **N. PAC.** TSIMSHIAN, NASS, TLINGIT, HAIDA, BELLA COOLA, BELLA BELLA, NEWETTEE, KWAKIUTL, NOOTKA, COMOX, CHEHALIS, COOS: Boas, RBAE, XXXI, 820. TAHLTAN: Teit, JAFL, XXXII, 235, No. 13. QUILEUTE: Farrand-Mayer, JAFL, XXXII,

252, No. 1.—**WDL. N.E.** Micmac: Rand, p. 87, No. 9.——Siberia and Asia (in general): Jochelson, JE, vi, 377; Boas, JAFL, iv, 19.

(c) *Person becomes a cannibal* (G30).—References: Jochelson, JE, vi, 371. —**ESK.** Greenland, Cumberland Sound: Jochelson, *loc. cit.*—**N. PAC.** Kwakiutl: *Ibid.*—**WDL. IROQ.** Seneca: Curtin-Hewitt, RBAE, xxxii, 118, No. 18 (= Curtin, *Seneca Indian Myths*, p. 369), and 232, 464.

(d) *One-sided man* (F525).—References: Jochelson, JE, vi, 367.—**MACK.** Dog Rib: Petitot, p. 363.—**N. PAC.** Bella Coola: Boas, *Sagen*, p. 256. —**PLNS.** Southern Paiute (Shivwits): Lowie, xxxvii, 122, No. 10; (Maopa): *Ibid.*, p. 189, No. 20.—**WDL. IROQ.** Seneca: Curtin-Hewitt, RBAE, xxxii, 473, No. 102.——Siberia: Jochelson, *loc. cit.*

(e) *Vampires* (E251).—**CAL.** Western Mono: Gifford, JAFL, xxxvi, 307–326, Nos. 5–8.—**PLNS.** Crow: Curtis, iv, 117; Lowie, PaAM, xxv, 127. Arapaho: Dorsey and Kroeber, FM, v, 231.—**WDL. N.E.** Abnaki: Harrington, JAFL, xiv, 160; Brown, JAFL, xv, 63.—**WDL. IROQ.** Curtin-Hewitt, RBAE, xxxi, 459, No. 97. Onondaga: Beauchamp, JAFL, i, 47; Smith, RBAE, ii, 87.—**S.E.** Cherokee: Terrell, JAFL, v, 125.

(f) *Many-headed monsters* (B15.1).—References: Jochelson, JE, vi, 368 f., —**N. PAC.** Bella Coola, Newettee, Comox, Squamish, Chehalis, Quinault, Kathlamet: Jochelson, *loc. cit.*—**WDL. IROQ.** Seneca: Curtin-Hewitt, RBAE, xxxii, 106, No. 11.——Siberia: Jochelson, *loc. cit.* (Cf. *Horned serpent.*—**WDL. N.E.** Micmac, Passamaquoddy, Penobscot: Parsons, JAFL, xxxviii, 60.—**S.W.** Hopi: *Ibid.*)

(g) *Unique deadly weapon* (Z312). One thing alone will kill a certain person.—**PLNS.** Southern Ute: Lowie, JAFL, xxxvii, 74 f., No. 46. Dakota: Wissler, JAFL, xx, 122. Cheyenne: Kroeber, JAFL, xiii, 184, No. 20. Ponca: Dorsey, CNAE, vi, 12.—**WDL. CENT.** Ojibwa: Schoolcraft, *Hiawatha*, p. 80; Jones-Michelson, PAES, vii (i), 31.—**WDL. N.E.** Micmac: Rand, p. 339, No. 60; Leland, p. 16. Malecite: Jack, JAFL, viii, 194. Passamaquoddy: Leland, p. 183.—**WDL. IROQ.** Seneca: Curtin-Hewitt, RBAE, xxxii, 330, No. 58. Huron: Hale, JAFL, i, 181.— **S.W.** Zuñi: Parsons, JAFL, xxxi, 240.—Of this number the following contain a pretended exchange of confidences as to what thing will kill: Cheyenne, Ojibwa, Micmac, Malecite, Passamaquoddy, Huron.

(h) *Fee-fi-fo-fum* (G532.1). Cannibal returning home smells the hidden hero and exclaims, "I smell human flesh," or the like (analogous to the European giant who exclaims "fee-fi-fo-fum!").—**ESK.** Greenland: Rink, p. 218.—**MACK.** Yukon: Schmitter, p. 22. Chipewyan: Lowie, PaAM, x, 192; Petitot, p. 352. Dog Rib: *Ibid.*, p. 321.—**N. PAC.** Chinook: Boas, BBAE, xx, No. 4.—**PLNS.** Southern Paiute (Maopa): Lowie, JAFL, xxxvii, 186, No. 19. Southern Ute: *Ibid.*, p. 77, No. 48. Blackfoot: Grinnell, *Blackfoot Lodge Tales*, p. 99; Uhlenbeck, VKAWA, xii, 53. Arapaho: Dorsey and Kroeber, FM, v, 242, No. 106.—**WDL. CENT.** Ojibwa: Jones-Michelson, PAES, vii (ii), 3 ff.; information from Laidlaw.—**WDL. IROQ.** Iroquois: Smith, RBAE, ii, 102. Cf. Seneca: Curtin-Hewitt, RBAE, xxxii, 78, No. 1.—**S.E.** Yuchi: Sapir, UPa, i, 146, No. 8.—**S.W.** Tusayan: Fewkes, JAFL, viii, 137; Voth, FM, iii, 350.

(i) *Image comes to life* (D435.1). The image may be either carved or drawn. —References: Jochelson, JE, vi, 370 f.—**ESK.** Baffin Land: Jochelson, *loc. cit.* Point Barrow: Nelson, RBAE, xviii, 479, 485.—**PLAT.** Chilcotin: Farrand, JE, ii, 42, No. 28. Shuswap: Teit, JE, ii, 691, No. 28, and 705, No. 33. Lillooet: Teit, JAFL, xxv, 358. Wasco: Curtin, PAES, ii, 290.—N. PAC. Tsimshian, Quinault: Jochelson, *loc. cit.* Puyallup: Curtis, ix, 17 ff. Tahltan: Teit, JAFL, xxxii, 215.—CAL. Mewan: Merriam, p. 159. Yuki: Kroeber, UCal, iv, 184.— PLNS. Arapaho: Dorsey and Kroeber, FM, v, 88, No. 44, and 397, No. 145. Pawnee: Dorsey, CI, lix, 124, No. 31; Dorsey, MAFLS, viii, 152, No. 39.—WDL. CENT. Ojibwa: Smith, JAFL, xix, 223. Timagami Ojibwa: Speck, GSCan, ix, 57. Menomini: Hoffman, RBAE, xiv, 228.—WDL. N.E. Micmac: Rand, p. 321, No. 56.—WDL. IROQ. Seneca: Curtin-Hewitt, RBAE, xxxii, 112, No. 14, cf. 219, 259, 710.— S.W. Zuñi: Cushing, p. 359. Hopi: Voth, FM, viii, 169, No. 51.—— Siberian: Jochelson, *loc. cit.*

(*j*) *Artificial whale made as strategem* (K922). Related to last motif cited, since an image of a whale is made and the image comes to life. The story has also resemblances to the *Trojan-horse* motif.—N. PAC. Tsimshian, Nass, Haida, Tlingit, Newettee, Comox, Nisqually, Songish, Quinault: Boas, RBAE, xxxi, 822; Bella Bella, Rivers Inlet, Newettee, Kwakiutl, Nootka, Comox: *Ibid.*, p. 714.

(*k*) *Large boot-supply for journey* (H1231).— References: Jochelson, JE, vi, 369 (ESK. — PLAT. Shuswap.— N. PAC. Chehalis, Kathlamet). —PLNS. Blackfoot: Grinnell, *Blackfoot Lodge Tales*, p. 96. Arapaho: Dorsey and Kroeber, FM, v, 134, No. 70.—— Siberia and Europe: Jochelson, *loc. cit.*

(*l*) *Hero hidden in protector's pocket* (G165).—MACK. Hare: Jochelson, JE, vi, 369.— WDL. N.E. Micmac: Michelson, JAFL, xxxviii, 36 ff. Montagnais: Speck, JAFL, xxxviii, 7.—— Siberia, Mongolia: Jochelson, *loc. cit.*

(*m*) *Chastity test* (H400). A magic test of a person's chastity.— References: Boas, RBAE, xxxi, 581, 780.— MACK. Kaska: Teit, JAFL, xxx, 440, No. 1. Ts'ets'áut: Boas, JAFL, ix, 267.— PLAT. Chilcotin, Lillooet, Sechelt: Boas, RBAE, xxxi, 780.— N. PAC. Kwakiutl: *Ibid.*, p. 581. Tsimshian, Tlingit, Haida, Bella Coola: *Ibid.*, p. 780. Tillamook: Boas, JAFL, xi, 137.— PLNS. Blackfoot: Wissler and Duvall, PaAM, ii, 34, 67, 147. Arapaho: Dorsey and Kroeber, FM, v, 73, No. 37, and 269, No. 120. — WDL. N.E. Passamaquoddy: Leland, p. 207.—— European: Bolte-Polívka, iii, 519, 531.

(*n*) *Boat towed by geese* (B558.1).—MACK. Beaver: Goddard, PaAM, x, 248. Chipewyan: *Ibid.*, p. 46; Lowie, PaAM, x, p. 189.— WDL. IROQ. Seneca: Curtin-Hewitt, RBAE, xxxii, 221, No. 41 (= Curtin, *Seneca Indian Myths*, p. 348), and 706, No. 135.

288. European tales borrowed by North American Indians have been studied by the editor in his *European Tales among the North American Indians* (CColl, ii), Colorado Springs, 1919. Some thirty well-defined European tales are there compared. The study has now been brought up to date with the help of Mrs. Llora B. Lydy, a graduate student in Indiana University. The results of this further investigation will probably appear as a second number of the original study.

289. *LXXVIII. The Seven-Headed Dragon.*— See Thompson, CColl, ii, 323 ff. (PLAT. Thompson, Kutenai, Shuswap.— PLNS. Osage, Black-

FOOT, PONCA, ASSINIBOIN, PLAINS CREE. — **WDL. CENT.** OJIBWA, PEORIA. — **S.E.** BILOXI).

290. *LXXIX. John the Bear.* — See *Ibid.*, pp. 334 ff. (**MACK.** LOUCHEUX. — **PLAT.** CHILCOTIN, THOMPSON. — **N. PAC.** KWAKIUTL. — **PLNS.** SHOSHONI, ASSINIBOIN. — **WDL. CENT.** OJIBWA. — **WDL. N.E.** MICMAC, MALECITE. —— MEXICO: TEHUANO, TEPECANO).

291. *LXXX. The Enchanted Horse.* — See *Ibid.*, pp. 347 ff. (**PLAT.** THOMPSON. — **PLNS.** CHEYENNE, DAKOTA, ASSINIBOIN. — **WDL. CENT.** OJIBWA, MENOMINI, KICKAPOO. — **WDL. N.E.** MALECITE, MICMAC).

292. *LXXXI. Little Poucet.* — See *Ibid.*, pp. 357 ff. (**PLAT.** THOMPSON, SHUSWAP. — **N. PAC.** BELLA COOLA. — **CAL.** MEWAN. — **PLNS.** UINTAH UTE, PONCA. — **WDL. CENT.** OJIBWA. — **WDL. N.E.** MALECITE). Cf. tales LXXI and LXXII above. It is sometimes difficult to draw the line between tales of this type which are borrowed and those which are native.

293. *LXXXII. The White Cat.* — See *Ibid.*, pp. 366 ff. (**PLAT.** CHILCOTIN, THOMPSON, SHUSWAP. — **PLNS.** ASSINIBOIN. — **WDL. CENT.** OJIBWA, MENOMINI. — **WDL. N.E.** MICMAC, PASSAMAQUODDY. — **S.E.** BILOXI, NATCHEZ. —— MEXICO: TEPECANO). — Cf. note 107, *The Sun Tests his Son-in-law;* 170, *The Son-in-Law Tests;* 284, *The Swan-Maidens.*

294. *LXXXIII. Cinderella.* — See *Ibid.*, pp. 382 ff. (**PLNS.** PIEGAN. — **WDL. N.E.** MICMAC. — **S.W.** ZUÑI).

295. *LXXXIV. The True Bride.* — See *Ibid.*, pp. 385 ff. (**PLAT.** THOMPSON. — **WDL. CENT.** OJIBWA. — **WDL. N.E.** PENOBSCOT. — **S.E.** ALABAMA. —— MEXICO: TEPECANO).

296. *LXXXV. The Magic Apples.* — See *Ibid.*, pp. 399 ff. (**WDL. N.E.** PENOBSCOT).

297. *LXXXVI. Making the Princess laugh.* — See *Ibid.*, pp. 411 ff. (**WDL. N.E.** MICMAC, MALECITE, PENOBSCOT. — **WDL. IROQ.** HURON-WYANDOT).

298. *LXXXVII. The Clever Numskull.* — See *Ibid.*, pp. 416 ff. (**PLAT.** THOMPSON, SHUSWAP. — **WDL. N.E.** MICMAC), and 419 ff. (**PLAT.** THOMPSON. — **PLNS.** WICHITA, DAKOTA. — **WDL. CENT.** OJIBWA. — **WDL. N.E.** MICMAC, MALECITE, PENOBSCOT. — **WDL. IROQ.** HURON-WYANDOT. — **S.E.** CREEK, YUCHI, ALABAMA, HITCHITI. — **S.W.** JICARILLA APACHE, ZUÑI, PIMA, HOPI, PUEBLO. —— MEXICO: POCHULTA, CHALINA, AZTEC, TUXTAPEC, TEPECANO).

299. *LXXXVIII. The Fox and the Wolf.* — See *Ibid.*, pp. 437 ff. (**MACK.** LOUCHEUX. — **PLAT.** THOMPSON, FLATHEAD. — **PLNS.** PONCA. — **WDL. CENT.** SAULTEAUX, MENOMINI, PEORIA, FOX. — **WDL. IROQ.** IROQUOIS, ONONDAGA. — **S.E.** CADDO).

300. *LXXXIX. The Tar-Baby.* — See *Ibid.*, pp. 440, 444 ff. (**N. PAC.** TAKELMA. — **CAL.** SHASTA, YANA. — **PLNS.** OSAGE. — **S.E.** YUCHI, NATCHEZ, CHEROKEE, CREEK, BILOXI. — **S.W.** JICARILLA APACHE).

301. *XC. The Turtle's Relay Race.* — See *Ibid.*, pp. 441, 448 ff. (**PLAT.** KUTENAI, KALISPEL. — **PLNS.** PIEGAN, ARIKARA. — **WDL. CENT.** OJIBWA. — **WDL. IROQ.** HURON-WYANDOT. — **S.E.** CHEROKEE, NATCHEZ, ALABAMA, CREEK, HITCHITI, CADDO. — **S.W.** JICARILLA APACHE, ZUÑI. —— MEXICO: POCHULTA).

302. *XCI. The Peace Fable.* — See *Ibid.*, p. 451 (**WDL. IROQ.** HURON-WYANDOT).

303. *XCII. The Ant and the Grasshopper.* — See *Ibid.*, p. 451 (**PLAT.** SHUSWAP. — **WDL. IROQ.** HURON-WYANDOT. — **S.E.** BILOXI).

304. For a discussion of Bible stories among the American Indians, see Thompson, "Sunday School Stories among Savages," *Texas Review*, III, 109, January, 1918. See also Thompson, CColl, II, 452, for a list of these stories.

305. *XCIII. Adam and Eve.* — See Thompson CColl, II, 452 (**PLAT.** THOMPSON. — **CAL.** DIEGUEÑO. — **WDL. IROQ.** MOHAWK, HURON-WYANDOT. — **S.E.** BILOXI).

306. *XCIV. Noah's Flood.* — See *Ibid.*, p. 452 (**PLAT.** THOMPSON, LILLOOET. —— MEXICO: TEPECANO).

307. *XCV. The Tower of Babel.* — See *Ibid.*, p. 552 (**S.E.** CHOCTAW. — **S.W.** PAPAGO). Cf. note 53, *Confusion of tongues*, for native parallels.

308. *XCVI. Crossing the Red Sea.* — See *Ibid.*, p. 452 (**PLNS.** CHEYENNE).

LIST OF MOTIFS DISCUSSED IN THE NOTES[1]

A. MYTHOLOGICAL MOTIFS
Gods and culture heroes

		NOTE
.1.	The woman who fell from the sky	27
.	Creator's grandmother	13
6.	Sun father-in-law	123
4.2.	Thunderbird	151c
5.	Mistress of the under world	2
1.	Culture hero pacifies monsters	12
0.	Divinity teaches arts and crafts	12
1.	Divinity's departure for west	11
5.	Dying culture hero	52a
5.	Departed deity grants requests to visitors	17
0.	Divinity's expected return	11a

Establishment of heavens and earth

5.	World parents	37
1.	Hierarchy of worlds	58
2.	World tree	56a
4.1.	The man who acted as the sun	66
8.1.	The sun snarer	65
5.	Pursuit of sun by moon	9
1.	The man in the moon	69
3.	The moon as wooer	6a
3.	Origin of the Pleiades	71
1.	Earth-mother	37a
0.	Primeval water	29
1.	Earth diver	30
5.	Earth from turtle's back	31
1.	Four world-columns	56
2.	Atlas	56b

Ordering of earth and human life

3.	Origin of tides	76a
10.	Deluge	57
12.	Flood from tears	57b
13.	Flood from belly	57c
30.	World fire	57d
11.	Empounded water	76
27.	The bird whose wings made the wind	74
50.	Determination of the seasons	60

		NOTE
A1151.	Theft of the seasons	60a
A1152.	Boneless man turned over to produce seasons	16
A1153.	Marriage of North and South	61
A1172.	Determination of night and day	62
A1200.	Creation of man	49
A1311.1.	The lizard-hand	59
A1313.3.	Misplaced genitalia	59a
A1320.	Determination of the span of life	60b
A1333.	Confusion of tongues	53
A1335.	Origin of death	51
A1411.	Theft of light	42
A1411.1.	Light kept in box or basket	45
A1411.2.	Theft of light by being swallowed and re-born	44
A1415.	Theft of fire	63
A1415.1.	Fire brought in flute	64
A1421.	Hoarded game	75
A1620.	Distribution of tribes	54

Vegetable and animal life

A2001.	Insects from burnt monster's body	275
A2101.	Fish made from wood	101
A2211.1.	Birds cling to sky in flood (cause of tail colors)	57a
A2330.1.	Wildcat gets a new face	99
A2601.	Origin of corn	77
A2731.1.	Trickster's burnt (or scratched) flesh becomes gum on trees	109l

B. ANIMALS
Mythical animals

B15.1.	Many-headed monster	287f
B31.1.	Roc	151
B220.	Animal villages	253a
B223.	Kingdom of fishes	236

Helpful animals

B300.	Helpful animals	146
B350.	Grateful animals	146a

[1]See note at end of p. 367.

NOTE

B431.   Rodent ally   147
B500.   Magic power from animals   146c
B512.   Healing water shown by ani-
          mals   279
B535.   Animal nurse   146b
B542.1.2. Bat rescue from height   151b
B550.   Animals help hero rescue
          woman   228a, 235

Animal marriages

B600.   Animal marriages   3
B600.1. Various animals tried as wives:
          only one accepted   254b
B611.1. Bear paramour   245
B611.3. Stallion paramour   254a
B613.1. Snake paramour   239
B651.   Fox-woman   233

Other animal motifs

B325.1. Sop to Cerberus   113c
B558.1   Boat towed by geese   287n
B575.1. Wild animals kept as dogs   113d
B576.1. Guardian animals avoided   113a

C. TABU

C10.   Tabu: profanely calling on
          spirit   217a
C15.   Wish for star husband real-
          ized   193
C26.   Wishing for animal husband   231
C31.   Offended supernatural wife   223a
C35.   Tabu: offending animal wife   223
C61.   The offended rolling stone   96
C111.   Tabu: incontinence   209a
C117.   Nuptial tabu   209
C211.   Tabu: eating in other world   217c
C250.   Tabu: drinking   217b
C300.   Looking tabu   217
C321.   Pandora's box   19
C322.   The bag of winds   72
C441.   Origin tabu   234
C523.   Digging tabu   197
C762.1. Tabu: using magic power too
          often   93

D. MAGIC

Transformation

D251.   Trickster becomes a dish   100
D263.   Person transformed to ring   228a
D275, D642. Transformation to feather
          to escape death   117a
D361.1. Swan-maidens   284

NOTE

D435.1. Image comes to life   287i
D482.   The stretching tree   199
D490.   Compressible objects   210a
D531.   Transformation by putting on
          skin   132
D550.   Transformation by eating or
          drinking   132a
D611.   Protean beggar   117d
D615.   Transformation combat   117e
D621.   Dog by day; man by night   247, 248
D641.   Transformation to reach dif-
          ficult place   117
D642.   Transformation to escape
          death   117b
D651.   Transformation to kill enemies   26
D655.   Transformation to receive
          food   117c
D657.1. The stolen harpoon   109x
D658.   Transformation to seduce
          women   109v
D671.   Transformation flight (trans-
          formed fugitives)   205b
D672.   Obstacle flight   205
D673.   Reversed obstacle flight   205a
D712.   Disenchantment by beating   249a
D721.   Disenchantment by destroying
          animal skins   249
D733.   Loathly bridegroom   188

Magic objects

D876.   Magic provider destroyed   109z
D902, D1361.4. Mist of invisibility   221b
D925, D1338.1. Fountain of youth   50a
D931.3. Symplegades   15
D990, D1312.2. Bodily members as ad-
          visers   150
D998, D1610.3, H451. Talking pri-
          vates   83a, 83b
D999, D1317.3. Buttocks watcher   83
D1001, D1611.1. Spittle impersonates
          fugitive   196a
D1001, D1456. Jewels from spittle   190
D1002, D1312.1. Talking excrements   83c
D1002, D1458. Jewels from excrements   190a
D1004, D1457. Jewels from tears   190b
D1031.   Inexhaustible food-supply   210
D1052, D1601.1. Magic self-returning
          robe   109i
D1053, D1067, D1361. Cloak (or cap)
          of invisibility   221a
D1065, D1521, D2121.3. Magic jour-
          ney   145

		NOTE
92, D1526.1.	Magic arrow flight	145a
18.	Magic airships	14d
21.2.	Magic self-moving boat	14a
21.3.	Magic hollow-log boat	14e
22.	Compressible canoe	14c
22.1.	Canoe created by magic	14b
22.2.	Island canoe	14
72.	Magic self-boiling kettle	257
56, D1526.2.	Magic ball flight	145b
12.	Advice from magic object	86b
13.	Magic objects point out road	86c
13.4.	Blinded trickster directed by trees	86a
20, D1612.	Magic objects betray fugitives	196b
51.	Magic parting of waters	15b
11.	Magic objects talk and delay pursuer	196
56.1.	Invisible arrow	287b

Magic powers

01.1.	Contest in magic	182
41.3.	Burning magically evaded	120
60.	Magic beautification	259
65.	Magic beautification by dismemberment and resuscitation	258
80.	Rejuvenation	50
90.	Magic aging	50b
04.	Love-compelling man sickens of bargain	19a
62.	Lousing	174
63.	Lulling to sleep by "sleepy" stories	162
91.1.	Rip Van Winkle	143
97.	Waking contest	137
06.	Forgetting by stumbling	109g
62.	Death by pointing	242a
64.	Death-giving glance	242
21.4.	Magic contraction of road	145c
31.	Magic underground journey	145e
35.	Magic journey through air	145d
50.	Magic storm	61b
55.1.	Porcupine as controller of cold	107
55.2.	Local winter	61c
59.	Weather contest	61a

RETURN FROM THE DEAD; THE SOUL

Resuscitation

.	Resuscitation by rubbing (or beating)	273
.	Resuscitation by jumping (or stepping) over	261

		NOTE
E15.1.	Resuscitation by boiling	260
E15.2.	Resuscitation by sweating	225
E25.	Resuscitation by frightening dead	153
E30.	Resuscitation by assembling members	114
E32.	Resuscitated eaten animal	114a
E33.	Resuscitation with missing member	114b
E34.	Resuscitation with misplaced head	114c
E55.	Resuscitation by music	153b
E66.	Resuscitation by breathing on corpse	153a
E80.	Water of life	279a
E82.	Water of life and death	279b
E161.	Killed game revives and flees away	109e
E175.	Death thought sleep	154

Ghosts

E251.	Vampires	287e
E323.1.	Drowned mother returns to suckle child	263
E381.	Ghost summoned by weeping	41
E481.	Shadow people	221

Reincarnation

E600.	Metempsychosis	216a

The soul

E700.	External soul	246a
E761.	Life-token	149
E780.	Vital bodily members	246b
E781.	Substituted eyes	94

F. MARVELS

Other-world journeys

F0.	Journeys to the other world	192
F10.	Ascent to sky	118
F15.	Visit to land of the stars	118c
F17.	Visit to land of the sun	118b
F51.	Sky rope	48
F51.1.	Spider-web sky rope	201
F51.2.	Sky basket	283
F52.	Ladder to upper world	204
F53.	Ascent to upper world on arrow chain	203
F54.	Tree to upper world	200
F59.	Sky window	28
F61.2.	Ascent to sky on feather	118a
F81.	Visit to the land of the dead	216

NOTE

F81.1.   Orpheus   215
F111.   Under-water world   236a
F127.   Underground animal kingdom   253
F152.   Rainbow-bridge to other
         world   204a

Marvelous beings

F420.1. Hero drowned by water-
         spirits   23
F495.   Dwarfs   287a
F525.   One-sided man   287d
F547.1. Vagina dentata   115

Marvelous places and things

F791.   Rising and falling sky   15a
F835.   Winking club   214

Remarkable occurrences

F913.   Victims rescued when swal-
         lower is killed   159a
F921.   Swallowed person becomes
         bald   159b
F1027.   Turtle's war party   108
F1035.   Disintegration: a man eats
         himself up or dismembers
         himself   109m

G. OGRES AND CANNIBALS

G30.   Person becomes a cannibal   287c
G61.   Relative's flesh unwittingly
         eaten   98, 226
G165.   Hero hidden in (giant) pro-
         tector's pocket   287l
G311.   Burr-woman   191e
G321.   Cliff ogre   163
G328.   Rectum snakes   161
G331.   Pot-tilter   157
G332.   Sucking monster   158
G333.   Path between monsters
         (Scylla and Charybdis)   113b
G341.   Sharp-elbowed women   181
G345.   Fire-moccasins   164
G400–G599. The child and the canni-
         bal   268
G441.   Ogre carries victims in sack   268a
G512.   The cannibal who was burned   274
G532.   Help from ogre's child (or
         wife)   171
G532.1. Fee-fi-fo-fum   287h
G691.   Bodies of victims in front of
         cannibal's house   268b

H. TESTS

Identity tests

NOTE

H58.   Tell-tale hand mark   7
H61.2.   Disenchanted person recog-
         nized by ornaments under
         skin   249b
H75.   Lover identified by hair float-
         ing on water   281
H161.   Picking out transformed wife
         and child from identical
         companions (prearranged
         signal)   224

Marriage tests

H310.   Son-in-law tests   170
H331.   Suitor contests: bride offered
         as prize   186
H400.   Chastity test   287m
H451.   Talking privates betray un-
         chastity   83d
H481.   Father test   212

Tests of prowess

H1001.   Quest for berries in winter   126c
H1212.1. Feigned dream to send hero on
          dangerous quests   191g
H1231.   Large boot-supply for jour-
          ney   287k
H1235.   Succession of helpers   211
H1360.   Quest for dangerous animals   126
H1371.   Impossible quests   126b
H1375.   Absurd quests   126b
H1511.   Heat test   120
H1511.1. Swallowing red-hot stones   120c
H1511.2. Burning food test   120b
H1511.3. Smoke test   120a
H1511.4. Smoking test: substitute for
          ordeal   191d
H1515.   Poisoned food test   140
H1521.   Clam test   130
H1522.   Killing trees threaten hero   160
H1531.   Spine test   168
H1532.   Wedge test   129
H1535.   Precipice test   122
H1536.   Toboggan test   173
H1538.   Drowning test   124

J. THE WISE AND THE FOOLISH

Fools

J1792.   Diving for reflected food   81
J1793.   Diving for reflected woman   270b

NOTE

.. Shooting at enemy's reflection in water 270c
..1. Diving for reflected enemy 270a
... Creaking limbs 85
.. Trickster joins bulrushes in dance 109dd
.. Trickster caught on fishhook 109y
.. Trickster puts on buffalo skull 86
.. Trickster eats medicines that physic him 109h
.. Trickster eats scratch-berries 109k
.. Coyote wears fox's rattle: caught in brush and injured 109bb
.. Trickster's false creations fail him 286
.. Sleeping trickster's feast stolen 84
..1. Death through foolish imitation 271b
.. The eye-juggler 92
.. The sharpened leg 95
.. Bungling host 103
.. Person frightened into falling down cliff 109f

K. DECEPTIONS

Contests won by deception

.. Trickster's race 90
Wrestling contest 137a
Climbing match 135
Diving match 136
Jumping contest 104
Shinny match 141
Shooting contest 142
Trapping contest 187
Harpooning contest 134
Tree-pulling contest 191f
Eating contest 137b
.1 Sham eating 191b
Scratching contest 109ee

Thefts and cheats

3.1. The deceived blind man (blind dupe) 278
.5. Trickster frightens people from food and eats it himself 109b

Deceptive escapes and captures

.4. Boy passes as girl to avoid decree of death on males 128
.2.1. Sham blood and brains 191a

NOTE

K525. Object substituted for fugitive 282
K526. Captor's bag filled with animals or objects while captives escape 268a
K528.1. Substitute smoker 191c
K550. False plea 109cc
K581. Drowning punishment for turtle 108
K711. Birds enticed into bag 82a
K736. Snapping door 113
K751. Game caught by feigning death 88

Fatal or disastrous deceptions

K825. Cormorant's tongue pulled out by putting louse on it 109aa
K826. Hoodwinked dancers 82
K894.1. Animals (or giants) enticed over precipice 91
K896. Beaver and porcupine 106
K922. Artificial whale made as stratagem 287j
K932. Trickster pollutes nest and brood of bird 109a
K951. Monster killed by throwing hot stones into throat 167
K952. Monster killed from within 159
K952.1. Animal killed from within by another which he is carrying across stream 104
K1013. False beauty-doctor 271
K1041. Trickster carried by birds and dropped (borrowed feathers) 80
K1081. The deceived blind men 89
K1084. Trickster tells lies to fishes 109j

Seduction and deceptive marriages

K1315. Seduction by sham doctor 109r
K1321.1. Trickster poses as woman and marries man 109n
K1387. Lecherous trickster seduces women from tree and loses them 195
K1391. Long-distance sexual intercourse 109u
K1392. Trickster and girls play obscene tricks on one another 109w
K1539. Death feigned to meet paramour 109t

Deceiver falls into own trap

K1615. Ogre's own moccasins burned 172
K1616. Marooned egg-gatherer 175

		NOTE
K1617.	Substituted arrows	121
K1618.	Swinging contest	169
K1681.	Originator of death first sufferer	52

Other deceptions

K1721.	Coyote proves himself a cannibal (vomit-exchange)	102
K1867.	Trickster shams death and eats grave offerings	109d
K1915.	The false bridegroom	189
K1932.	Impostor claims prize	183
K1941.	Disguised flayer	267
K1942.	Skin tightened in order to look beautiful	267a
K1955.	Sham doctor	271a
K1983.	Trickster poses as helper and eats women's stored provisions	109c
K2111.	Potiphar's wife	178
K2152.	Unresponsive corpse	105

L. VICTORY OF THE WEAK

Unpromising hero

L11.	Victorious youngest son	185
L100.	Unpromising child succeeds	185
L113.	Dirty-Boy	183

Modest choice best

L200.	Modest choice rewarded	18a

Pride before fall

L431.	The princess who rejected her cousin	256

N. FORTUNE

Gambling

N1.	The conquering gambler	276
N2.	Lives wagered	277
N2.1.	Gambler stakes own body	277

Accidents

N772.2.	Deserted daughter's good fortune discovered by accident	251

Influential helpers

N825.	Old woman adviser	180
N831.	Mysterious housekeeper	207

Q. REWARDS AND PUNISHMENTS

Q2.	Kind and unkind	18b
Q241.	Adultery revenged	240

		NOTE
Q339.	Immoderate request punished	18
Q385.	Captured animals avenge themselves	126a
Q478.	Eaten heart	241

R. CAPTIVES AND FUGITIVES

R11.1.	Girl abducted by monster	228, 228a, 231, 262
R31.	Light extinguished and woman stolen	237
R125.	Rescue of stolen woman by husband	235
R231.	Obstacle flight (Atalanta type)	232
R245.	Whale-boat	179
R246.	Crane bridge	227
R261.	Pursuit by rolling head	238a
R301.	Tree refuge	228, 230
R321.	Escape to the stars	71a
R351.	Reflection betrays fugitive	270

S. UNNATURAL CRUELTY

S11.	The jealous father	177
S71.	The jealous uncle	127
S115.1.	Murder by stabbing in ear	264
S141.	Abandonment in boat	131
S300.	Deserted children	255
S352.	Animal preserves fire for abandoned children	247, 255
S361.	Bird carries food from deserted child to starving tribe	250
S362.	Starving camp return to children for food	247, 255

T. SEX

Chastity

T381.	Imprisoned virgin (to avoid impregnation)	21b

Illicit sex relations

T411.1.	Lecherous father	109p
T415.	Brother and sister incest	8
T415.1.	Lecherous brother	109q
T417.	Lecherous son-in-law	109s
T471.	Trickster has tree for wife	109o

Conception and birth

T510.	Immaculate conception	166e
T511.	Conception from eating	166h
T521.	Impregnation from sunlight	21a
T522.	Conception from rain	166g
T524.	Impregnation by wind	21

		NOTE
.	Pregnancy from casual contact with man	166f
).	Miraculous birth	166
.	Birth from a wound	229
.1.	Blood-Clot-Boy	165
.	Birth from secretions of body	166b
.1.	Birth from mucus	269
.	Birth from tears	166a
.	Child born in jug	166c
.	Short pregnancy	116
.	Twins quarrel before birth	33
.	Pregnant man	166d
.	Child removed from dead mother	152, 166i
.	Many children at a birth	116a

Rearing of children

		NOTE
T615.	Supernatural growth	112

Z. MISCELLANEOUS GROUPS

Unique exceptions

Z311.	Achilles' heel	246
Z312.	Unique deadly weapon	287g

Heroes

Z411.	Dreadnaughts	156
Z420.	Twin adventurers	155

AUTHOR'S NOTE: These references to the *Motif-Index of Folk-Literature* were made in several years before the actual appearance of that work (6 vols., Helsinki, 1932-36; edition Copenhagen and Bloomington, 1955-58). The numbers are for the most part exact or so nearly so as to cause no confusion. The following changes, however, are to be noted: C61: C91.1.—D931.3: D1553.—D1991.1: D1960.1.—D1997: H1450.1.—G165: J2155.1.1.—H1001: H1023.3.—J2152: J2131.5.1.—J2153: J2134.2.—J2154: J2134.2.1.—J2155: J2186.—J2194: J2173.1.—N771: N732.2.—R125: R155.1.—T471: T461.3.—Z411: Z210.—Z420: Z210.

SOURCES

For titles of books see bibliography. The more extensive collections are starred.

I. **ESKIMO AREA.** GENERAL: Boas (*f, g*); Signe Rink (*a, b*); Wardle; Kroeber (*a*). EAST GREENLAND: *Holm. GREENLAND (GENERAL): *Rasmussen; Grønlandske Folkesagn; *Rink; Thalbitzer. SMITH SOUND: Kroeber (*h*). BAFFIN LAND: Rink and Boas; *Boas (*b, e*); H. I. Smith (*a*). LABRADOR: *Turner. WEST HUDSON BAY: *Boas (*e*); Hall; Simpson; Rae. CORONATION GULF: Jenness; Petitot (*b*). POINT BARROW: Murdoch. BERING STRAIT: *Nelson; Boas (*p*). KODIAK and ALEUTIAN: Golder (*a, b, c, d, e*).

II. **MACKENZIE RIVER AREA.** LOWER YUKON (ANVIK): Chapman (*a, b, *c*). UPPER YUKON: Schmitter. KASKA: *Teit (*g*). LOUCHEUX: *Barbeau (*b*); Russell (*a*); Petitot (*c*). HARE: J. M. Bell; Petitot (*c*). DOG RIB: J. M. Bell; Petitot (*c*). SLAVEY: Russell (*a*); R. Bell (*b*). TS'ETS'ÁUT: *Boas (*v*). CHIPEWYAN: Petitot (*c*); *Lowie (*b*); *Goddard (*c*); Schoolcraft (*b*); Hearne. BEAVER: *Goddard (*a*). CARRIER: Morice.

III. **PLATEAU AREA.** GENERAL: *Boas (*h*); *Farrand-Mayer (*b*); Hill-Tout (*a, e*). CHILCOTIN: *Farrand (*a*). SHUSWAP: Dawson; *Teit (*n*); Boas (*i*). THOMPSON: Teit (**d, *h, *k, *f*); Boas (*i*); Hill-Tout (*b, h*). LILLOOET: *Teit (*j*); Hill-Tout (*f*). SECHELT: Hill-Tout (*d*). OKANAGON: *Teit (*b*); Gould (*a*); Allison. SANPOIL: *Gould (*b*). KUTENAI: *Boas (*k*); Chamberlain (*a, d*); E. S. Curtis, VII. CŒUR D'ALÈNE: *Teit (*a*). PEND D'OREILLE (KALISPEL): Teit (*e*); E. S. Curtis, VII. FLATHEAD: McDermott. NEZ PERCÉ: Packard (*a*); Spinden (*a, *b*); E. S. Curtis, VIII. WASCO: *Curtin (*e*). WISHRAM: *Sapir (*d*); E. S. Curtis, VIII. WARMSPRING: Lewis (*a, b*).

IV. **NORTH PACIFIC COAST AREA.** TAHLTAN: Emmons; *Teit (*i, m*). TLINGIT: Deans (*c*); *Krause; Golder (*f*); *Swanton (*h*). HAIDA: Deans (*d, e, *f*); Harrison (*a*); Swanton (**b, *c, *d, f*). TSIMSHIAN: Boas (*i, s, *w, *x*); Deans (*a, b*). BELLA COOLA: Boas (*a, i, *n*). BELLA BELLA: Boas (*i, *x*). KWAKIUTL: Boas (*i, *l*); *Boas and Hunt; Hunt; N. Curtis (*b*). NEWETTEE: Boas (*i*). RIVERS INLET: Boas (*i*). NANAIMO: Boas (*i, q*). LOWER FRASER RIVER: Teit (*c*). COMOX: Boas (*i*); E. S. Curtis, IX. NOOTKA: Boas (*i, *x*); Jewett; Sapir (*a*). COWICHAN: Boas (*i*); E. S. Curtis, IX; Hill-Tout (*g*). COWLITZ: Hill-Tout (*g*). MAKA: Swan. SQUAMISH: Boas (*i*). SONGISH: Boas (*i*). TWANA: E. S. Curtis, IX. NISQUALLI: E. S. Curtis, IX. CHEHALIS: Boas (*i*). PUYALLUP: E. S. Curtis, IX. SKYKOMISH: Hill-Tout (*c*); Haeberlin. SNOHOMISH, SNUQUALMI, SKAGIT: *Haeberlin. CHINOOK: *Boas (*c*). KATHLAMET: *Boas (*j*). QUINAULT: *Farrand (*b*). QUILEUTE: *Farrand-Mayer (*a*). TILLAMOOK: *Boas (*u*). ALSEA:

*Frachtenberg (a). Coos: *Frachtenberg (b); St. Clair-Frachtenberg. TA-KELMA: *Sapir (b). LOWER UMPQUA: *Frachtenberg (c).

V. **CALIFORNIA AREA.** KLAMATH: Gatschet (b); Bancroft. MODOC: *Curtin (c); Gatschet (e). KAROK: Powers; Kroeber (e). CHIMARIKO: Dixon (a). SHASTA: Dixon (e, *f); Farrand-Frachtenberg; Kroeber (e). JOSHUA, TUTUTUNI: Farrand-Frachtenberg. ACHOMAWI: Dixon (i); Curtin (a); Powers; Kroeber (e). ATSUGEWI: Dixon (i). POMO: Barrett (a). YANA: *Sapir (e); *Curtin (b). SALINAN: Mason (a). YUROK: Powers; Kroeber (e). WISHOSK: Kroeber (j). HUPA: *Goddard (d). CHILULA: Goddard (b). KATO: *Goddard (f). LASSIK: Goddard (g). SINKYONE: Kroeber (g). YUKI: Kroeber (e). WAPPO: H. R. Kroeber (m); *Radin (d). WINTUN: Curtin (b). MAIDU: Dixon (*b, *c, g, h); Powers; Kroeber (e). MIWOK (MEWAN): *Merriam; *Gifford (a); *Barrett (b); Kroeber (e). COSTANOAN: Kroeber (e). YOKUTS: *Kroeber (e); Powers; Stewart. DIE-GUEÑO: DuBois (a, c, d, f, h); Waterman (c). LUISEÑO: DuBois (b, e, g); Waterman (a); James (a, b, c). CAHUILLA: *Hooper; Woosley. MONO: *Gifford (b). PAVIOTSO: *Lowie (e).

VI. **PLAINS AREA.** GENERAL: Maclean (c). PAIUTE: *Lowie (e); Sapir (c). SHOSHONI: *Lowie (d); St. Clair and Lowie. UTE: Kroeber (i); *Mason (b); *Lowie (e). COMANCHE: St. Clair and Lowie. KIOWA: Gatschet (a); Mooney (a); N. Curtis (b). WICHITA: Dorsey (*c, j). OSAGE: *Dorsey (h); Schoolcraft (b). ARAPAHO: *Dorsey and Kroeber; Dorsey (a); Voth (a); N. Curtis (b). CHEYENNE: Dorsey (b); Grinnell (c, h); *Kroeber (c); N. Curtis (b); Campbell. OTO: Kercheval. OMAHA: Kercheval; Dorsey (k, *s). PONCA: *Dorsey (s). PAWNEE: Dorsey (*d, e, *i); Grinnell (d, *e, f, g, i); N. Curtis (b). CROW: *Lowie (c); *Simms (b); E. S. Curtis, IV. DAKOTA (SIOUX, TETON): Dorsey (n, o, p, q, r); Eastman; N. Curtis (b); Riggs; McLaughlin; Meeker (a, b); Wissler (b); Zitkala-Ša; Wallis; E. S. Curtis, III; Schoolcraft (b, c). HIDATSA: Matthews (a); Will (c); E. S. Curtis, IV. MANDAN: Will (a, b, c); Will and Spinden; Maximilian; Hopkins; E. S. Curtis, V. ARIKARA: *Dorsey (f); E. S. Curtis, V. BLACKFOOT: *Wissler and Duvall; Grinnell (*a, b); *McClintock; *Uhlenbeck; Maclean (a, b); Petitot (c); Schultz. PIEGAN: Michelson (f, g, h). SARCEE: Goddard (j); Simms (c). GROS VENTRE (ATSINA): *Kroeber (d); E. S. Curtis, V. PLAINS CREE: Teit (l); Skinner (d). PLAINS OJIBWA: Skinner (b, *e). — ASSINIBOIN: *Lowie (a): Potts. BUNGEE (SWAMPY CREE): Simms (a); Cresswell.

VIIa. **WOODLAND AREA — CENTRAL.** GENERAL: Chamberlain (f); Hamilton (a, b); Young. SAULTEAUX: *Skinner (c). CREE: *Skinner (c); R. Bell (a); Hamilton (d); Swindlehurst; *Russell (b); Petitot (c). OJIBWA: *Schoolcraft (a, b); *Radin (c); P. Jones; W. Jones (c); **Jones and Michelson; Michelson (e); Carson; Jenks; Knight; Hoffman (c); *Laidlaw; H. I. Smith (b). TIMAGAMI OJIBWA: Speck (g). TIMISKAMING ALGONQUIN: Speck (g). OTTAWA: Schoolcraft (a, b); Rasles. MISSISAUGA: Chamberlain (b, g). MENOMINI: Hoffman (a, *b); *Skinner and Satterlee; Michelson (a); Skinner (a). WINNEBAGO: Radin (*b). (SAUK and) FOX: Jones (a, *b, d); Michelson (c); Lasley; Owen. POTAWATOMI: DeSmet. PEORIA: Michelson (d). KICKAPOO: *Jones (e).

VII*b*. **WOODLAND AREA — NORTHEAST.** Naskapi: Speck (*f*, *i*). Montagnais: *Speck (*f*); LeJeune (*a*). Abanaki: Brown; N. Curtis (*b*); Deming; Harrington (*a*); Frost. Micmac: *Rand; *Leland; Hagar (*a*, *c*, *d*); Michelson (*b*); *Parsons (*b*); Speck (*h*); LeClercq. Malecite: *Mechling (*a*, *b*); Speck (*e*); Leland; Jack. Passamaquoddy: Fewkes (*a*); Bateman; Prince (**a*, *b*). Penobscot: Speck (*d*, *j*, *k*). Wampanoag: M. F. Knight. Pequot: Speck (*l*). Mohegan; Prince (*c*); Schoolcraft (*b*). Lenâpé: Brinton.

VII*c*. **WOODLAND AREA — IROQUOIS.** Iroquois: Beauchamp (*a*, *b*, *c*, *d*); Canfield; Converse; Hewitt (**a*, *b*); Parker (*a*); *E. A. Smith. Seneca: *Curtin (*d*); *Curtin and Hewitt; Sanborn; Parker (*b*); Weitlaner. Onondaga: Beauchamp (*e*, *f*); *Hewitt (*a*). Mohawk: Chamberlain (*c*); *Hewitt (*a*). Caughnawaga: Harrington (*b*). Huron-Wyandot: Barbeau (**a*, *c*); Connelley (*a*, *b*); Hale; LeJeune (*a*, *b*); Schoolcraft (*b*).

VIII. **SOUTHEASTERN AREA.** Shawnee: Gregg; Schoolcraft (*c*); Spencer. Cherokee: Davis (*a*, *b*); Hagar (*b*); Mooney (*b*, **d*, *e*); Terrell; H. ten Kate. Catawba: Radin (*b*). Yuchi: Gatschet (*f*); *Speck (*c*). Creek: Gatschet (*c*); Speck (*b*). Choctaw: Bushnell (*a*, *b*). Muskhogean (Alabama, Hitchiti, Natchez): Swanton (*a*). Chitimacha: Swanton (*g*). Biloxi: Dorsey and Swanton; Dorsey (*t*). Louisiana Coast: Swanton (*e*). Texas: Hilder. Caddo: *Dorsey (*g*).

IX. **SOUTHWESTERN AREA.** Navaho: Matthews (*b*, **c*, *d*, *e*); Packard (*b*); Pepper; *Parsons (*d*); J. Stevenson; E. S. Curtis, i; Boas (*o*). Apache: Bourke (*b*); N. Curtis (*b*). Jicarilla Apache: Mooney (*c*); E. S. Curtis, i; *Russell (*c*); *Goddard (*e*). White Mountain Apache: Goddard (*i*). San Carlos Apache: Goddard (*h*). Pueblo (general): Lummis (*a*, *b*); Parsons (*f*). Zuñi: Parsons (*c*, *e*); Boas (*t*); Parsons and Boas; Cushing (**b*, *c*, **d*); *Handy. Laguna: Parsons (*c*). Acoma: Pradt. Isleta: Gatschet (*d*). Hopi (Moqui, Tusayan, Oráibi): Fewkes (*b*, *c*); Cushing (*a*); Voth (*b*, *c*, **d*); Stephen; Mindeleff (*a*, *b*); N. Curtis (*b*). Pima: Lloyd; *Russell (*d*); E. S. Curtis, ii; Neff. Papago: Neff; H. R. Kroeber (*k*, *l*); Mason (*c*). Sia: *Stevenson (*b*). Yuma: N. Curtis (*a*, *b*); E. S. Curtis, ii; J. P. Harrington. Mohave: Bourke (*a*); E. S. Curtis, ii; Kroeber (*f*). Mohave-Apache: Gould (*c*); N. Curtis (*b*). Tewa: *Parsons (*g*).

BIBLIOGRAPHY

BIBLIOGRAPHY

See the list of abbreviations on page 269.

In general, only original collections of tales are listed here. Much fugitive material later gathered into collections has been omitted.

Aarne, A., and Stith Thompson. *The Types of the Folk-tale*. FF Communications, No. 74. Helsingfors, 1928.

Allison, Mrs. S. S. "Account of the Similkameen Indians of British Columbia," JAI, xxi, 305.

Bancroft, Hubert Howe. *The Native Races of the Pacific States of America*. New York, 1874–76.

Barbeau, C.-Marius. (*a*) *Huron and Wyandot Mythology*. GSCan, xi. Ottawa, 1915.

    (*b*) "Loucheux Myths," JAFL, xxviii, 249.

    (*c*) "Wyandot Tales, including European Elements," JAFL, xxviii, 83.

Barnum, F. *Grammatical Fundamentals of the Innuit Language*. Boston, 1901.

Barrett, S. A. (*a*) "A Composite Myth of the Pomo Indians," JAFL, xix, 37.

    (*b*) *Myths of the Southern Sierra Miwok*. UCal, xvi. Berkeley, 1919.

Bateman, L. C. "The Passamaquoddy Indians of Maine," *Southern Workman*, xxxix, 17.

Beauchamp, W. M. (*a*) "The Great Mosquito," JAFL, ii, 284.

    (*b*) "Hi-a-wat-ha," JAFL, iv, 295.

    (*c*) "Indian Corn Stories and Customs," JAFL, xi, 195.

    (*d*) "Iroquois Notes," JAFL, v, 223.

    (*e*) "Onondaga Tale of the Pleiades," JAFL, xiii, 281.

    (*f*) "Onondaga Tales," JAFL, i, 44; ii, 261; vi, 173.

Bell, James M. "The Fireside Stories of the Chippewayans," JAFL, xvi, 73.

Bell, Robert. (*a*) "History of the Che-che-puy-ew-tis," JAFL, x, 1.

    (*b*) "Legends of the Slavey Indians of the Mackenzie River," JAFL, xiv, 25.

Blackbird, Andrew J. *History of the Ottawa and Chippewa Indians of Michigan*. Ypsilanti, 1887,

Boas, Franz. (*a*) "The Growth of Indian Mythologies," in Thomas, W. I., *Source Book for Social Origins*. Chicago, 1909.

    (*b*) *The Central Eskimo*. RBAE, vi. Washington, 1888.

    (*c*) *Chinook Texts*. RBAE, xx. Washington, 1894.

    (*d*) "Dissemination of Tales among the Natives of North America," JAFL, iv, 13.

    (*e*) *The Eskimo of Baffin Land and Hudson Bay*. BAM, xv. New York, 1901.

    (*f*) "Eskimo Tales and Songs," JAFL, ii, 123; vii, 45; x, 109.

    (*g*) "The Folk-lore of the Eskimo," JAFL, xvii, 1.

    (*h*) (Editor) *Folk-tales of Salishan and Sahaptin Tribes*. MAFLS, xi. New York, 1917.

    (*i*) *Indianische Sagen von der Nord-Pacifischen Küste Amerikas*. Berlin, 1895.

(*j*) *Kathlamet Texts.* RBAE, xxvi. Washington, 1901.
(*k*) *Kutenai Tales.* RBAE, lix. Washington, 1918.
(*l*) *Kwakiutl Tales.* CU, ii. New York, 1910.
(*m*)"Mythology and Folk-tales of the North American Indians," JAFL, xxvii, 374.
(*n*) *The Mythology of the Bella Coola Indians.* JE, i. New York, 1898.
(*o*) "Northern Elements in the Mythology of the Navaho," AA, old ser., x, 371.
(*p*)"Notes on the Eskimo of Port Clarence, Alaska," JAFL, vii, 205.
(*q*) "Notes on the Snanaimuq," AA, old ser., ii, 321.
(*r*) "Salishan Texts," *Proceedings of the American Philosophical Society,* xxxiv, 31.
(*s*) "Eine Sonnensage der Tsimschian," *Zeitschrift für Ethnologie*, xl, 776.
(*t*) "Tales of Spanish Provenience from Zuñi," JAFL, xxxv, 62.
(*u*) "Traditions of the Tillamook Indians," JAFL, xi, 23, 133.
(*v*) "Traditions of the Ts'ets'áut," JAFL, ix, 257 and x, 35.
(*w*) *Tsimshian Texts.* RBAE, xxvii. Washington, 1902.
(*x*) *Tsimshian Mythology.* RBAE, xxxi. Washington, 1916.
——. *See* Parsons, Elsie Clews.
—— and George Hunt. *Kwakiutl Texts.* JE, iii and x. New York, 1905–06.
—— and Henry Rink. "Eskimo Tales and Songs," JAFL, ii, 124.
Bogaras, Waldemar. (*a*) "The Folklore of Northeastern Asia, as compared with that of Northwestern America," AA, new ser., iv, 577.
(*b*) *Tales of the Yukaghir, Lamut, and Russianized Natives of Eastern Siberia.* PaAM, xx. New York, 1918.
Bolte, Johannes, and Georg Polívka. *Anmerkungen zu den Kinder- und Hausmärchen der Brüder Grimm.* 3 vols. Leipzig, 1913–18.
Bourke, John G. (*a*) "Cosmogony and Theogony of the Mojave Indians," JAFL, ii, 169.
(*b*) "Notes on Apache Mythology," JAFL, iii, 209.
Brinton, D. G. *The Lenâpé and their Legends.* Philadelphia, 1885.
Brown, Mrs. Wallace. "Wa-ba-ba-nal, or Northern Lights: a Wabanaki Legend," JAFL, iii, 213.
Bushnell, David I., Jr. (*a*) *The Choctaw of Bayou Lacomb, St. Tammany Parish, Louisiana.* BBAE, xlviii. Washington, 1909.
(*b*) "Myths of the Louisiana Choctaw," AA, new ser., xii, 526.
Campbell, Stanley. "Two Cheyenne Stories," JAFL, xxix, 406.
Canfield, Willam Walker. *The Legends of the Iroquois, told by "the Cornplanter."* New York, 1902.
Carson, William. "Ojibwa Tales," JAFL, xxx, 491.
Chamberlain, A. F. (*a*) "A Kootenay Legend: the Coyote and the Mountain Spirit," JAFL, vii, 195.
(*b*) "A Mississaga Legend of Naniboju," JAFL, v, 291.
(*c*) "A Mohawk Legend of Adam and Eve," JAFL, ii, 228.
(*d*) "Mythology and Folk-lore of the Kootenay Indians," *American Antiquarian*, xvii, 68.
(*e*) "Mythology of the Indian Stocks North of Mexico," JAFL, xviii, 111.
(*f*) "Nanibozhu amongst the Otchipwe, Mississagas and other Algonkian Tribes," JAFL, iv, 193.
(*g*) "Tales of the Mississaguas," JAFL, ii, 141 and iii, 149.

(*h*) "The Thunder-bird amongst the Algonkins," AA, old ser., III, 51.

Chapman, J. W. (*a*) "Athapascan Traditions of the Lower Yukon," JAFL, XVI, 180.

(*b*) "The Happy Hunting Ground of the Ten'a," JAFL, xxv, 66.

(*c*) *Ten'a Texts and Tales from Anvik, Alaska.* PAES, VI. Leyden, 1914.

Connelley, William E. (*a*) "Notes on the Folk-lore of the Wyandots," JAFL, XII, 116.

(*b*) *Wyandot Folk-lore.* Topeka, Kansas, 1899.

Converse, Mrs. Harriet Maxwell Clarke. *Myths and Legends of the New York State Iroquois.* Albany, 1908.

Cresswell, J. R. "Folk-tales of the Swampy Cree of Northern Manitoba," JAFL, XXXVI, 404.

Curtin, Jeremiah. (*a*) "Achomawi Myths," JAFL, XXII, 283.

(*b*) *Creation Myths of Primitive America.* Boston, 1898.

(*c*) *Myths of the Modocs.* Boston, 1912.

(*d*) *Seneca Indian Myths.* Boston, 1923.

(*e*) *See* Sapir, *Wishram Texts.*

—— and J. N. B. Hewitt. *Seneca Myths and Fictions.* RBAE, XXXII. Washington, 1918.

Curtis, Edward S. *The North American Indian.* 20 vols. Cambridge, Mass., 1908– .

Curtis, Natalie. (*a*) "Creation Myth of the Cochans (Yuma Indians)," *Craftsman*, XVI, 559.

(*b*) *The Indians' Book.* New York and London, 1907.

Cushing, Frank Hamilton. (*a*) "Origin Myth from Oraibi," JAFL, XXXVI, 163.

(*b*) *Outlines of Zuñi Creation Myths.* RBAE, XIII. Washington, 1896.

(*c*) "A Zuñi Folk-tale of the Underworld," JAFL, V, 49.

(*d*) *Zuñi Folk Tales.* New York and London, 1901.

Davis, J. B. (*a*) "The Liver Eater: a Cherokee Story," *Annals of Archæology and Anthropology of the University of Liverpool*, II, 134.

(*b*) "Some Cherokee Stories," *Ibid.*, III, 26.

Dawson, G. M. "Notes on the Shuswap People of British Columbia," *Trans. Royal Soc. Canada* (Sec. II, 1891), pp. 3–44.

Deans, James. (*a*) "The Daughter of the Sun: a Legend of the Tsimshians of British Columbia," JAFL, IV, 33.

(*b*) "A Creation Myth of the Tsimshians of Northwest British Columbia," JAFL, IV, 34.

(*c*) "The Doom of the Katt-a-quins, from the Aboriginal Folk-lore of Southern Alaska," JAFL, V, 232.

(*d*) "Legend of the Fin-back Whale Crest of the Haidas, Queen Charlotte Island, B.C.," JAFL, V, 43.

(*e*) "The story of the Bear and his Indian Wife," JAFL, II, 255.

(*f*) *Tales from the Totems of the Hidery.* Chicago, 1899.

de Jong, J. P. B. de Josselin. *Original Odjibwe-texts, with English translation, notes, and vocabulary.* Leipzig and Berlin, 1913.

Deming, Mrs. E. W. "Abenaki Witchcraft Story," JAFL, XV, 62.

DeSmet, Rev. Father. *Life, Letters and Travels of Father Pierre-Jean DeSmet, S.J., 1801–1873.* 4 vols. New York, 1905.

Dixon, Roland B. (*a*) *The Chimariko Indians and Language.* UCal, V, Berkeley, 1907–10.

(b) *Maidu Texts*. PAES, IV. Leyden, 1912.

(c) *Maidu Myths*. BAM, XVII. New York, 1905.

(d) "Mythology of the Central and Eastern Algonkins," JAFL, XXII, 1.

(e) "The Mythology of the Shasta-Achomawi," AA, new ser., VII, 607.

(f) "Shasta Myths," JAFL, XXIII, 8, 364.

(g) "Some Coyote Stories from the Maidu Indians of California," JAFL, XIII, 267.

(h) "System and Sequence in Maidu Mythology," JAFL, XVI, 32.

(i) "Achomawi and Atsugewi Tales," JAFL, XXI, 159.

Dorsey, George Amos. (a) *The Arapaho Sun Dance*. FM, IV. Chicago, 1903.

(b) *The Cheyenne*. FM, IX. Chicago, 1905.

(c) *The Mythology of the Wichita*. CI, XXI. Washington, 1904.

(d) *The Pawnee: Mythology*, part I. CI, LIX. Washington, 1906.

(e) "Pawnee War Tales," AA, new ser., VIII, 337.

(f) *Traditions of the Arikara*. CI, XVII. Washington, 1904.

(g) *Traditions of the Caddo*. CI, XLI. Washington, 1905.

(h) *Traditions of the Osage*. FM, VII. Chicago, 1904.

(i) *Traditions of the Skidi Pawnee*. MAFLS, VIII. Boston and New York, 1904.

(j) "Wichita Tales," JAFL, XV, 215 and XVI, 160.

—— and Alfred L. Kroeber. *Traditions of the Arapaho*, FM, V. Chicago, 1903.

Dorsey, James Owen. (a) "Abstracts of Ponka and Omaha Myths," JAFL, I, 74, 204.

(b) "Indians of the Siletz Reservation, Oregon," AA, old ser., I, 55.

(c) "Modern Additions to Indian Myths, and Indian Thunder Superstitions," JAFL, VI, 232.

(d) "Nanibozhu in Siouan Mythology," JAFL, V, 293.

(e) *A Study of Siouan Cults*. RBAE, XI. Washington, 1894.

(f) "A Teton Dakota Ghost Story," JAFL, I, 68.

(g) "Teton Folklore," AA, old ser., II, 143.

(h) "Teton Folklore Notes," JAFL, II, 133.

(i) *The Thegiha Language*. CNAE, VI. Washington, 1890.

(j) "Two Biloxi Tales," JAFL, VI, 48.

—— and John R. Swanton. *A Dictionary of the Biloxi and Ofo Languages*. BBAE, XLVII. Washington, 1912.

DuBois, Constance Goddard. (a) "Diegueño Myths and their Connection with the Mohave," *Congrès Internationale des Americanistes*, XV, 129. Quebec, 1907.

(b) "Mission Indian Religion: a Myth in the Making," *Southern Workman*, XXXIII, 353.

(c) "The Mythology of the Diegueños," JAFL, XIV, 181.

(d) "Mythology of the Diegueños," *International Congress of Americanists*, XIII, 101. New York, 1905.

(e) "Mythology of the Mission Indians," JAFL, XIX, 52.

(f) "Religious Ceremonies and Myths of the Mission Indians," AA, new ser., VII, 620.

(g) *Religion of the Luiseño Indians*. UCal, VIII. Berkeley, 1908.

(h) "The Story of the Chaup, a Myth of the Diegueños," JAFL, XVII, 217.

Duvall, D. C. *See* Wissler.

Eastman, Charles A. *Old Indian Days.* New York, 1907.
—— and Elaine Goodale. *Wigwam Evenings: Sioux Tales Retold.* Boston, 1909.
Eastman, Mrs. Mary Henderson. *Dahcotah, or Life and Legends of the Sioux around Fort Snelling.* New York, 1849.
Eels, Rev. Myron. "The Thunder Bird," AA, old ser., II, 329.
Ehrenreich, Paul. *Die Mythen und Legenden der südamerikanischen Urvölker.* Berlin, 1905.
Emerson, Mrs. E. R. *Indian Myths.* Boston, 1884.
Emmons, G. T. *The Tahltan Indians.* UPa, IV. Philadelphia, 1911.
Farrand, Livingston. (*a*) *Traditions of the Chilcotin Indians.* JE, II. New York, 1909.
(*b*) *Traditions of the Quinault Indians.* JE, II. New York, 1909.
—— and Leo J. Frachtenberg. "Shasta and Athapascan Myths from Oregon," JAFL, XXVIII, 207.
—— and Theresa Mayer. (*a*) "Quileute Tales," JAFL, XXXII, 251.
(*b*) *Sahaptin Tales.* MAFLS, XI, 135. New York, 1917.
Fewkes, Jesse Walter. (*a*) "Contributions to Passamaquoddy Folklore," JAFL, III, 257.
(*b*) "The Destruction of the Tusayan Monsters," JAFL, VIII, 132.
(*c*) *Tusayan Migration Traditions.* RBAE, XIX. Washington, 1902.
Frachtenberg, Leo J. (*a*) *Alsea Texts and Myths.* BBAE, LXVII. Washington, 1920.
(*b*) *Coos Texts.* CU, I. New York, 1913.
(*c*) *Lower Umpqua Texts.* CU, IV. New York, 1914.
——. *See* St. Clair.
Frost, Helen Keith. "Two Abenaki Legends," JAFL, XXV, 188.
Gatschet, Albert S. (*a*) "Creation Myth of the Kiowa," *Das Ausland* (November, 17, 1890), No. 46.
(*b*) *The Klamath Indians of Southwestern Oregon.* CNAE, II. Washington, 1890.
(*c*) *A Migration Legend of the Creek Indians.* Vol. I, Philadelphia, 1884 (Library of Aboriginal American Literature, No. 4); vol. II, St. Louis, 1888 (Transactions of the Academy of Science of St. Louis, V, 33–239).
(*d*) "A Mythic Tale of the Isleta Indians, New Mexico," *Proceedings of the American Philosophical Society,* XXIX, 208.
(*e*) "Oregonian Folklore," JAFL, IV, 141.
(*f*) "Some Mythic Tales of the Yuchi Indians," AA, old ser., VI, 279.
Gifford, Edward Winslow. (*a*) *Miwok Myths.* UCal, XII. Berkeley, 1917.
(*b*) "Western Mono Myths," JAFL, XXXVI, 301.
Goddard, Pliny Earle. (*a*) *The Beaver Indians.* PaAM, X. New York, 1916.
(*b*) *Chilula Texts.* UCal, X. Berkeley, 1914.
(*c*) *Chipewyan Texts.* PaAM, X. New York, 1912.
(*d*) *Hupa Texts.* UCal, I. Berkeley, 1904.
(*e*) *Jicarilla Apache Texts.* PaAM, VIII. New York, 1911.
(*f*) *Kato Texts.* UCal, V. Berkeley, 1909.
(*g*) "Lassik Tales," JAFL, XIX, 133.
(*h*) *Myths and Tales of the San Carlos Apache.* PaAM, XXIV. New York, 1920.

(i) *Myths and Tales from the White Mountain Apache.* PaAM, xxiv. New York, 1920.

(j) *Sarsi Texts.* UCal, xi. Berkeley, 1915.

Golder, F. A. (a) "Aleutian Stories," JAFL, xviii, 215.

(b) "Eskimo and Aleut Stories from Alaska," JAFL, xxii, 10.

(c) "A Kadiak Island Story: the White-faced Bear," JAFL, xx, 296.

(d) "The Songs and Stories of the Aleuts," JAFL, xx, 132.

(e) "Tales from Kodiak Island," JAFL, xvi, 16, 85.

(f) "Tlingit Myths," JAFL, xx, 290.

Gould, Marian K. (a) *Okanagon Tales.* MAFLS, xi, 98. New York, 1917.

(b) *Sanpoil Tales. Ibid.,* p. 101.

(c) "Two Legends of the Mojave-Apache," JAFL, xxxiv, 319.

Gregg, Josiah. *The Commerce of the Prairies.* New York and London, 1844.

Grinnell, George Bird. (a) *Blackfoot Lodge Tales.* New York, 1892.

(b) "A Blackfoot Sun and Moon Myth," JAFL, vi, 44.

(c) "A Cheyenne Obstacle Myth," JAFL, xvi, 108.

(d) "Development of a Pawnee Myth," JAFL, v, 127.

(e) *Pawnee Hero Stories and Folk-tales.* New York, 1889.

(f) "Pawnee Mythology," JAFL, vi, 113.

(g) "A Pawnee Star Myth," JAFL, vii, 197.

(h) "Some Early Cheyenne Tales," JAFL, xx, 169.

(i) "The Young Dog's Dance," JAFL, iv, 313.

Grønlandske Folkesagn, opskrevne og meddeelte af Indfødte, med dansk Over-sættelse. Godthaab, 1859. (Text in Eskimo; Danish translation.)

Haeberlin, Hermann. "Mythology of Puget Sound," JAFL, xxxvii, 371.

Hagar, Stansbury. (a) "The Celestial Bear," JAFL, xiii, 92.

(b) "Cherokee Star Lore," *Boas Anniversary Volume,* p. 354. New York, 1906.

(c) "Micmac Customs and Traditions," AA, old ser., viii, 31.

(d) "Weather and Seasons in Micmac Mythology," JAFL, x, 101.

Hale, Horatio. "Huron Folklore," JAFL, i, 180.

Hall, Capt. Charles Francis. *Narrative of the Second Arctic Expedition.* London, 1879.

Hamilton, James Cleland. (a) "The Algonquin Manabozho and Hiawatha," JAFL, xvi, 229.

(b) *Famous Algonquins; Algic Legends.* TCI, vi. Toronto, 1899.

(c) "Stellar Legends of the American Indians," *Transactions of the Royal Astronomical Society of Canada* (1905), pp. 47–50.

(d) "Two Algonquin Legends," JAFL, vii, 201.

Handy, Edward L. "Zuñi Tales," JAFL, xxxi, 451.

Harrington, John P. "A Yuma Account of Origins," JAFL, xxi, 324.

Harrington, M. Raymond. (a) "An Abenaki 'Witch Story,'" JAFL, xiv, 160.

(b) "Da-ra-sá-kwa: a Caughnawaga Legend," JAFL, xix, 127.

(c) "Shinnecock Notes," JAFL, xvi, 37.

Harrison, Rev. Charles. (a) *Ancient Warriors of the North Pacific: the Haidas, their Laws, Customs, and Legends.* London.

(b) "Religion and Family among the Haidas," JAI, xxi, 14.

Hearne, Samuel. *A Journey from Prince of Wales' Fort in Hudson's Bay to the Northern Ocean.* London, 1795.

Hewitt, J. N. B. (a) *Iroquoian Cosmology.* RBAE, xxi. Washington, 1903.

(*b*) "Raising and Falling of the Sky in Iroquois Legends," AA, old ser., v, 344.

—— *See* Curtin, Jeremiah.

Hilder, F. F. "A Texas Indian Myth," AA, new ser., I, 592.

Hill-Tout, Charles. (*a*) *British North America:* I. *The Far West, the Home of the Salish and the Déné.* London, 1907.

    (*b*) "Notes on the N'tlakápamaq of British Columbia, a branch of the great Salish stock of North America," BAAS, LXIX, 500.

    (*c*) "Notes on the Sk'qómic," BAAS, LXX, 472.

    (*d*) "Report on the Ethnology of the Síciatl of British Columbia," JAI, XXXIV, 20.

    (*e*) "Report on the Ethnology of the Southeastern Tribes of Vancouver Island, British Columbia," JAI, XXXVII, 306.

    (*f*) "Report on the Ethnology of the StlatlumH of British Columbia," JAI, XXXV, 126.

    (*g*) "Report on the StsEélis and Sk'aulits Tribes of the HalkomélEm Division of the Salish of British Columbia," JAI, XXXIV, 311.

    (*h*) "'Sqaktktquaclt' or the Benign Faced, the Oannes of the N'tlakápamaq, British Columbia," FL, X, 195.

Hoffman, Walter James. (*a*) "Mythology of the Menomini Indians," AA, old ser., III, 243.

    (*b*) *The Menomini Indians.* RBAE, XIV. Washington, 1896.

    (*c*) *The Midéwiwin or "Grand Medicine Society" of the Ojibwa.* RBAE, VII. Washington, 1891.

Holm, G. "Sagn og Fortællinger fra Angmagsalik," *Meddelelser om Grønland*, X, 237.

Hooper, Lucile. *The Cahuilla Indians.* UCal, XVI. Berkeley, 1920.

Hopkins, William John. *The Indian Book.* Boston, 1911.

Hunt, George. "The Rival, a Kwakiutl Story," *Boas Anniversary Volume*, p. 108. New York, 1906.

——. *See* Boas and Hunt.

Jack, E. "Maliseet Legends," JAFL, VIII, 193.

James, G. W. (*a*) *The Indians of the Painted Desert Region.* Boston, 1903.

    (*b*) "The legend of the Tauquitch and Algoot," JAFL, XVI, 153.

    (*c*) "A Sababo Origin Myth," JAFL, XV, 36.

Jenks, Albert Ernest. "The Bear Maiden," JAFL, XV, 33.

Jenness, Diamond. "Notes and Traditions from Northern Alaska, the Mackenzie Delta, and Coronation Gulf," *Report of the Canadian Arctic Expedition, Southern Party, 1913–16*, vol. XIII, part A, pp. 1–90a. Ottawa, 1924.

Jewett, J. R. *A Narrative of Adventures and Sufferings.* Middletown, 1815.

Jochelson, Waldemar. (*a*) *The Koryak.* JE, VI. New York, 1908.

    (*b*) "The Mythology of the Koryak," AA, new ser., VI, 413.

Jones, Peter. *History of the Ojebway Indians.* London, 1861.

Jones, William. (*a*) "Episodes on the Culture-Hero Myth of the Sauks and Foxes," JAFL, XIV, 225.

    (*b*) *Fox Texts.* PAES, I. Leyden, 1907.

    (*c*) "Ojibwa Tales from the North Shore of Lake Superior," JAFL, XXIX, 368.

(*d*) "Notes on the Fox Indians," JAFL, xxiv, 209.

(*e*) *Kickapoo Tales.* PAES, ix. Leyden, 1915.

Jones, William, and Truman Michelson. *Ojibwa Texts.* PAES, vii, (2 vols). New York, 1919.

Kercheval, George Truman. "An Otoe and an Omaha Tale," JAFL, vi, 199.

Knight, Julia. "Ojibwa Tales from Sault Ste. Marie, Michigan," JAFL, xxvi, 91.

Knight, Mabel Frances. "Wampanoak Indian Tales," JAFL, xxxviii, 134.

Koch-Grünberg, Theodor. *Indianermärchen aus Südamerika.* Jena, 1920.

Krause, Aurel. *Die Tlinkit-Indianer.* Jena, 1885.

Kroeber, Alfred L. (*a*) "American Culture and the Northwest Coast," AA, new ser., xxv, 1.

(*b*) "Animal Tales of the Eskimo," JAFL, xii, 17.

(*c*) "Cheyenne Tales," JAFL, xiii, 161.

(*d*) *Gros Ventre Myths and Tales.* PaAM, i. New York, 1908.

(*e*) *Indian Myths of South Central California.* UCal, iv. Berkeley, 1907.

(*f*) "Preliminary Sketch of the Mohave Indians," AA, new ser., iv, 276.

(*g*) "Sinkyone Tales," JAFL, xxxii, 346.

(*h*) "Tales of the Smith Sound Eskimo," JAFL, xii, 166.

(*i*) "Ute Tales," JAFL, xiv, 252.

(*j*) "Wishosk Myths," JAFL, xviii, 85.

———. *See* Dorsey and Kroeber.

Kroeber, Henriette Rothschild. (*a*) "Papago Coyote Tales," JAFL, xxii, 339.

(*b*) "Traditions of the Papago Indians," JAFL, xxv, 95.

(*c*) "Wappo Myths," JAFL, xxi, 321.

Laidlaw, George E. *Ojibwa Myths and Tales.* OAR, xxvii–xxx. Toronto, 1915–18, and special 1918 reprint.

Lanman, Charles. *Haw-ho-noo, or records of a tourist.* Philadelphia, 1850.

Lasley, Mary. "Sac and Fox Tales," JAFL, xv, 170.

LeClercq, Father Chrestien. *A New Relation of Gaspesia, with the Customs and Religion of the Gaspesian Indians.* Publication of the Champlain Society, v. Toronto, 1910.

LeJeune, Father Paul. (*a*) "Relation of what occurred in New France in the Year 1633," *Jesuit Relations*, v, 81. Paris, 1634.

(*b*) "Relation of what occurred in New France in the Year 1634," *Ibid.*, vi, 97. Paris, 1635.

Leland, Charles Godfrey. *The Algonquin Legends of New England.* Boston, 1885.

Lewis, L. M. (*a*) "Sunlight Legend of the Warmspring Indians," *Southern Workman*, xxxviii, 685.

(*b*) "The Warmspring Indian Legend of the Fox and the Spirits," *Ibid.*, xxxix, 94.

Lloyd, John William. *Aw-aw-tam Indian Nights, being myths and legends of the Pimas of Arizona.* Westfield, N. J., 1911.

Lowie, Robert H. (*a*) *The Assiniboine.* PaAM, iv. New York, 1910.

(*b*) *Chipewyan Tales.* PaAM, x. New York, 1912.

(*c*) *Myths and Traditions of the Crow Indians.* PaAM, xxv. New York, 1918.

(*d*) *The Northern Shoshone:* Part II, *Mythology.* PaAM, ii. New York, 1909.

(*e*) "Shoshonean Tales," JAFL, xxxvii, 1.

(*f*) "The Test-theme in North American Mythology," JAFL, xxi, 97.

——. *See* St. Clair.

Lummis, C. F. (*a*) *The Man who married the Moon, and other Pueblo Indian Folk-stories.* New York, 1894.

(*b*) *Pueblo Indian Folk Stories.* New York, 1910.

McClintock, Walter. *The Old North Trail, or life, legends and religion of the Blackfeet Indians.* London, 1910.

McDermott, Louisa. "Folklore of the Flathead Indians of Idaho," JAFL, xiv, 240.

Maclean, John. (*a*) "Blackfoot Indian Legends," JAFL, iii, 296.

(*b*) "Blackfoot Mythology," JAFL, vi, 165.

(*c*) *Canadian Savage Folk: the native tribes of Canada.* Toronto, 1896.

McLaughlin, Marie L. *Myths and Legends of the Sioux.* Bismarck, N. D., 1916.

Mason, John Alden. (*a*) *The Ethnology of the Salinan Indians.* UCal, x. Berkeley, 1912.

(*b*) "Myths of the Uintah Utes," JAFL, xxiii, 299.

(*c*) "The Papago Migration Legend," JAFL, xxxiv, 254.

Matthews, Washington. (*a*) *Ethnography and Philology of the Hidatsa Indians.* U. S. Geological and Geographical Survey, Miscellaneous Publications, No. 7. Washington, 1877.

(*b*) *The Mountain Chant, a Navaho Ceremony.* RBAE, v. Washington, 1887.

(*c*) *Navaho Legends.* MAFLS, v. Boston, 1897.

(*d*) *Navaho Myths, Prayers, and Songs.* UCal, v. Berkeley, 1907.

(*e*) "Naqoilpi, the Gambler: a Navaho Myth," JAFL, ii, 89.

Maximilian, Prince Alex. *Voyage en l'Amérique du Nord.* Paris, 1843.

Mechling, William H. (*a*) "Maliseet Tales," JAFL, xxvi, 219.

(*b*) *Malecite Tales.* GSCan, iv. Ottawa, 1914.

Meeker, Louis L. (*a*) "Siouan Mythological Tales," JAFL, xiv, 161.

(*b*) "The White Man, a Siouan Myth," JAFL, xv, 84.

Merriam, Clinton Hart. *The Dawn of the World: myths and weird tales told by the Mewan Indians of California.* Cleveland, 1910.

Mindeleff, Cosmos. *Localization of Tusayan Clans.* RBAE, xix. Washington, 1900.

Mindeleff, V. *A study of Pueblo Architecture, Tusayan and Cibola.* RBAE, viii. Washington, 1891.

Michelson, Truman. (*a*) "Menominee Tales," AA, new ser., xiii, 68.

(*b*) "Micmac Tales," JAFL, xxxviii, 33.

(*c*) "Notes on the Folk-lore and Mythology of the Fox Indians," AA, new ser., xiii, 694.

(*d*) "Notes on Peoria Folk-lore and Mythology," JAFL, xxx, 493.

(*e*) "Ojibwa Tales," JAFL, xxiv, 249.

(*f*) "A Piegan Tale," JAFL, xxix, 408.

(*g*) "Piegan Tales," JAFL, xxiv, 238.

(*h*) "Piegan Tales of European Origin," JAFL, xxix, 409.

——. *See* Jones and Michelson.

Mooney, James. (*a*) *The Calendar History of the Kiowa Indians.* RBAE, xvii. Washington, 1898.

(*b*) "Cherokee and Iroquois Parallels," JAFL, ii, 67.

(*c*) "The Jicarilla Genesis," AA, old ser., xi, 197.

(*d*) *Myths of the Cherokee*. RBAE, xix. Washington, 1900.

(*e*) "Myths of the Cherokee," JAFL, i, 98.

Morice, Father A. G. "Three Carrier Myths," TCI, v, 1.

Murdoch, J. "A Few Legendary Fragments from the Point Barrow Eskimos," *American Naturalist* (July, 1886), p. 594.

Neff, Mary L. "Pima and Papago Legends," JAFL, xxv, 51.

Nelson, Edward William. *The Eskimo about Bering Strait*. RBAE, xviii. Washington, 1899.

Nutt, Alfred. "Irish Tales among the Redskins," FL, ii, 130.

Owen, Mary Alicia. *Folklore of the Musquakie Indians of North America*. PFLS, li. London, 1904.

Packard, R. L. (*a*) "Notes on the Mythology and Religion of the Nez Percés," JAFL, iv, 327.

(*b*) "A Navaho Myth," *Transactions of the Anthropological Society of Washington*, i, 84. Washington, 1882.

Parker, Arthur C. (*a*) "Certain Iroquois Tree-myths and Symbols," AA, new ser., xiv, 608.

(*b*) *Seneca Myths and Folk-tales*. Buffalo Historical Society Publications, xxvii. Buffalo, 1924.

Parkman, Francis. *The Jesuits of North America in the Seventeenth Century*. Boston, 1867.

Parsons, Elsie Clews. (*a*) *Folk-tales of Andros Island, Bahamas*. MAFLS, xiii. New York, 1918.

(*b*) "Micmac Folk-lore," JAFL, xxxviii, 55.

(*c*) "The Nativity Myth at Laguna and Zuñi," JAFL, xxxi, 256.

(*d*) "Navaho Folk-tales," JAFL, xxxvi, 368.

(*e*) "The Origin Myth at Zuñi," JAFL, xxxvi, 135.

(*f*) "Pueblo-Indian Folk-tales probably of Spanish Provenience," JAFL, xxxi, 216.

(*g*) *Tewa Tales*. MAFLS, xix. New York, 1926. (Not included in notes to this volume.)

—— and Franz Boas. "Spanish Tales from Laguna and Zuñi, New Mexico," JAFL, xxxiii, 47.

Pepper, George H. "Ah-jih-lee-hah-neh, a Navajo Legend," JAFL, xxi, 179.

Petitot, Émile. (*a*) *La femme aux métaux*. Meaux, 1888.

(*b*) *Monographie des Esquimaux Tchligit du Mackenzie et de l'Anderson*. Paris, 1876.

(*c*) *Traditions indiennes du Canada nord-ouest*. Paris, 1886.

Pettazzoni, R. "The Chain of Arrows: the diffusion of a mythical motive," FL, xxxv, 151.

Potts, John William. "Creation Myth of the Assiniboines," JAFL, v 72.

Powell, John Wesley. *Sketch of the Mythology of the North American Indians*. RBAE, i. Washington, 1881.

Powers, Stephen. *Tribes of California*. CNAE, iii. Washington, 1877.

Pradt, George H. "Shakok and Miochin: origin of summer and winter," JAFL, xv, 88.

Prince, John Dyneley. (*a*) *Passamaquoddy Texts*. PAES, x. New York, 1921

(*b*) "Some Passamaquoddy Witchcraft Tales," *Proceedings of the American Philosophical Society*, xxxviii, 181.

(*c*) "A Tale in the Hudson River Language," AA, new ser., vii, 74.

Radin, Paul. (*a*) *Literary Aspects of North American Mythology*. GSCan, vi. Ottawa, 1915.
  (*b*) "Some Catawba Tales and Folk-lore," JAFL, xxvi, 319.
  (*c*) *Some myths of the Ojibwa of Southeast Ontario*. GSCan, ii. Ottawa, 1914.
  (*d*) *Wappo Texts* — first series. UCal, xix. Berkeley, 1924.
  (*e*) "Winnebago Tales," JAFL, xxii, 288.
Rae, John. *Narrative of an Expedition to the Shores of the Arctic Sea in 1846 and 1847*. London, 1850.
Rand, Silas Tertius. *Legends of the Micmacs*. Wellesley College Philological Publications. New York, 1894.
Rasles, Father Sébastien. "Letters to his Brother," *Jesuit Relations*, lxvii, 133.
Rasmussen, Knud. *Myter og sagn fra Grønland*. 3 vols. Kjøbenhavn, 1921–25. (Not included in notes.)
Reichard, Gladys A. "Literary Types and Dissemination of Myths," JAFL, xxxiv, 269.
Riggs, Stephen Return. *Dakota Grammar, Texts and Ethnography*. CNAE, ix. Washington, 1893.
Rink, Henry. *Tales and Traditions of the Eskimo*. Edinburgh, 1875.
——. *See* Boas and Rink.
Rink, Signe. (*a*) "A Comparative Study of two Indian and Eskimo Legends," *International Congress of Americanists*, xiii, 279.
  (*b*) "The Girl and the Dog — an Eskimo tale with comments," AA, old ser., xi, 181, 209.
Russell, Frank. (*a*) "Athapascan Myths," JAFL, xiii, 11.
  (*b*) *Explorations in the Far North*. University of Iowa Publication. Iowa City, 1898.
  (*c*) "Myths of the Jicarilla Apache," JAFL, xi, 253.
  (*d*) *The Pima Indians*. RBAE, xxvi. Washington, 1908.
St. Clair, Harry Hull, 2d, and Leo Frachtenberg. "Traditions of the Coos Indians of Oregon," JAFL, xxii, 25.
—— and Robert H. Lowie. "Shoshone and Comanche Tales," JAFL, xxii, 265.
Sanborn, John Wentworth. "Folk-lore of the Seneca Indians of North America," FLJ, iii, 196.
Sapir, Edward. (*a*) "A Flood Legend of the Nootka Indians of Vancouver Island," JAFL, xxxii, 351.
  (*b*) *Takelma Texts*. UPa, ii. Philadelphia, 1909.
  (*c*) "Two Paiute Myths," *University of Pennsylvania Museum Journal*, i, 15.
  (*d*) *Wishram Texts, together with Wasco Tales and Myths, collected by Jeremiah Curtin and edited by Edward Sapir*. PAES, ii. Leyden, 1909.
  (*e*) *Yana Texts, together with Yana Myths collected by Roland B. Dixon*. UCal, ix. Berkeley, 1910.
Sarat Chandra Nitra. "The Bear in Asiatic and American Ritual," *Journal of the Asiatic Society of Bombay*, vii, 467.
Schmitter, Ferdinand. *Upper Yukon Native Customs and Folk-lore*. Smithsonian Miscellaneous Collections, lvi, No. 4. Washington, 1910.

Schoolcraft, Henry Rowe. (a) *Algic Researches*. New York, 1839.
  (b) *The Indian in his Wigwam*. New York, 1845.
  (c) *The Myth of Hiawatha*. Philadelphia and London, 1856.
Schulz, James Willard. *Blackfoot Tales of Glacier Park*. Boston and New York, 1916.
Simms, Stephen Chapman. (a) "Myths of the Bungees or Swampy Indians of Lake Winnepeg," JAFL, xix, 334.
  (b) *Traditions of the Crows*. FM, ii. Chicago, 1903.
  (c) "Traditions of the Sarcee Indians," JAFL, xvii, 180.
Simpson, John. "Observations on the Western Esquimaux and the country they inhabit," *Further Papers Relative to the Recent Arctic Expeditions in Search of Dr. John Franklin*. London, 1855.
Skinner, Alanson. (a) "European Folk-tales Collected among the Menominee Indians," JAFL, xxvi, 64.
  (b) "European Tales from the Plains Ojibwa," JAFL, xxix, 330.
  (c) *Notes on the Eastern Cree and Northern Saulteaux*. PaAM, ix. New York, 1911.
  (d) "Plains Cree Tales," JAFL, xxix, 341.
  (e) "Plains Ojibwa Tales," JAFL, xxxii, 280.
—— and John V. Satterlee. *Folklore of the Menomini Indians*. PaAM, xiii. New York, 1915.
Smith, Harlan I. (a) "Notes on Eskimo Traditions," JAFL, vii, 209.
  (b) "Some Ojibwa Myths and Traditions," JAFL, xix, 215.
Speck, Frank G. (a) "An Algonkian Myth," *University of Pennsylvania Museum Journal*, i, 49.
  (b) *The Creek Indians of Taskigi Town*. MAAA, ii. Lancaster, Penn., 1907–15.
  (c) *Ethnology of the Yuchi Indians*. UPa, i. Philadelphia, 1909.
  (d) "European Folk-tales among the Penobscot," JAFL, xxvi, 81.
  (e) "Malecite Tales," JAFL, xxx, 479.
  (f) "Montagnais and Naskapi Tales from the Labrador Peninsula," JAFL, xxxviii, 1.
  (g) *Myths and Folk-lore of the Timiskaming Algonquin and Timagami Ojibwa*. GSCan, ix. Ottawa, 1915.
  (h) "Some Micmac Tales from Cape Breton Island," JAFL, xxviii, 59.
  (i) "Some Naskapi Tales from Little Whale River," *Ibid.*, p. 70.
  (j) "Penobscot Tales," *Ibid.*, p. 52.
  (k) "Penobscot Transformer Tales," *International Journal of American Linguistics*, i (1918), No. 3.
  (l) "A Pequot-Mohegan Witchcraft Tale," JAFL, xvi, 104.
Spencer, J. "Shawnee Folk-lore," JAFL, xxii, 319.
Spinden, Herbert, J. (a) "Myths of the Nez Percé," JAFL, xxi, 13.
  (b) *Nez Percé Tales*. MAFLS, xi, 180. New York, 1917.
——. *See* Will and Spinden.
Stamp, Harley. "A Malecite Tale: adventures of Bukschinskwesk," JAFL, xxviii, 243.
Stephen, A. M. "Legend of the Snake Order of the Moquis," JAFL, i, 109.
Stevenson, James. *Ceremonies of the Hasjelti Dailjis and Mythical Sand Painting of the Navajo Indians*. RBAE, viii. Washington, 1891.

Stevenson, Matilda Coxe. (*a*) *The Zuñi Indians, their Mythology, Esoteric Fraternities and Ceremonies.* RBAE, XXIII. Washington, 1905.
  (*b*) *The Sia.* RBAE, XI. Washington, 1894.
Stewart, George W. "A Yokuts Creation Myth," JAFL, XIX, 322.
Swan, J. G. *The Indians of Cape Flattery.* Smithsonian Contributions to Knowledge, No. 220. Washington, 1868.
Swanton, John R. (*a*) "Animal Stories from the Indians of the Muskhogean Stock," JAFL, XXVI, 193.
  (*b*) *Contributions to the Ethnology of the Haida.* JE, V. Leiden and New York, 1905–09.
  (*c*) *Haida Texts, Masset Dialect.* JE, X, Leiden and New York, 1908.
  (*d*) *Haida Texts and Myths.* BBAE, XXIX. Washington, 1905.
  (*e*) "Mythology of the Indians of Louisiana and the Texas Coast," JAFL, XX, 285.
  (*f*) "Notes on the Haida Language," AA, new ser., IV, 229.
  (*g*) "Some Chitimacha Myths and Beliefs," JAFL, XXX, 474.
  (*h*) *Tlingit Myths and Texts.* BBAE, XXXIX. Washington, 1909.
  (*i*) "Types of Haida and Tlingit Myths," AA, new ser., VII, 94.
——. *See* Dorsey and Swanton.
Swindlehurst, Fred. "Folklore of the Cree Indians," JAFL, XVIII, 139.
Teit, James A. (*a*) *Cœur d'Alène Tales.* MAFLS, XI, 119. New York, 1917.
  (*b*) *Okanagon Tales, Ibid.,* p. 65.
  (*c*) *Tales from the Lower Fraser River, Ibid.,* p. 129.
  (*d*) *Thompson Tales, Ibid.,* p. 1.
  (*e*) *Pend d'Oreille Tales, Ibid.,* p. 114.
  (*f*) "European Tales from the Upper Thompson Indians," JAFL, XXIX, 301.
  (*g*) "Kaska Tales," JAFL, XXX, 427.
  (*h*) *Mythology of the Thompson Indians.* JE, VIII. New York, 1912.
  (*i*) "Tahltan Tales," JAFL, XXXII, 198 and XXXIV, 223, 335.
  (*j*) "Traditions of the Lillooet Indians," JAFL, XXV, 292.
  (*k*) *Traditions of the Thompson River Indians.* MAFLS, VI. Boston, 1898.
  (*l*) "Two Plains Cree Tales," JAFL, XXXIV, 320.
  (*m*) "Two Tahltan Traditions," JAFL, XXII, 314.
  (*n*) *The Shuswap.* JE, II. New York, 1900–09.
ten Kate, Dr. H. "Legends of the Cherokees," JAFL, XXX, 496.
ten Kate, H. F. C. "A Zuñi Folk-tale," JAFL, XXX, 496.
Terrell, James W. "The Demon of Consumption, a Legend of the Cherokees of North Carolina," JAFL, V, 125.
Thalbitzer, William. *A Phonetic Study of the Eskimo Language.* Copenhagen, 1904.
Thompson, Stith. (*a*) *European Tales among the North American Indians.* CColl, II. Colorado Springs, 1919.
  (*b*) "Sunday School Stories among Savages," *Texas Review,* III, 109.
  (*c*) "The Transmission of Folk-tales," *Gayley Anniversary Volume.* Berkeley, 1922.
——. *See* Aarne and Thompson.
Turner, Lucien M. *Ethnology of the Ungava District, Hudson Bay Territory.* RBAE, XI. Washington, 1894.
Uhlenbeck, C. C. *Original Blackfoot Texts.* VKAWA, XII, XIV. Amsterdam, 1911, 1912.

386   TALES OF NORTH AMERICAN INDIANS

Voth, Henry R. (*a*) "Arapaho Tales," JAFL, xxv, 43.

   (*b*) *Four Hopi Tales.* FM, ix. Chicago, 1905.

   (*c*) *Orâibi Summer Snake Ceremony.* FM, iii. Chicago, 1902.

   (*d*) *The Traditions of the Hopi.* FM, viii. Chicago, 1905.

Wake, C. Stanisland. "A Widespread Boy-hero Story," JAFL, xx, 216.

Wallis, Wilson D. "Beliefs and Tales of the Canadian Dakotas," JAFL, xxxvi, 36.

Wardle, H. Newell. "The Sedna Cycle: a study in myth evolution," AA, new ser., ii, 568.

Waterman, T. T. (*a*) "Analysis of the Mission Indian Creation Story," AA, new ser., xi, 41.

   (*b*) "The Explanatory Element in the Folk-tales of the North-American Indians," JAFL, xxvii, 1.

   (*c*) *Religious Practices of the Diegueño Indians.* UCal, viii. Berkeley, 1908–10.

Weitlaner, R. J. "Seneca Tales and Beliefs," JAFL, xxviii, 309.

Will, George F. (*a*) "No-tongue, a Mandan Tale," JAFL, xxvi, 331.

   (*b*) "The Story of No-tongue," JAFL, xxix, 402.

   (*c*) "Some Hidatsa and Mandan Tales," JAFL, xxv, 93.

—— and H. J. Spinden. *The Mandans.* Papers of the Peabody Museum, iii. Cambridge, Mass., 1906.

Wilson, E. B. "On the Northwest Tribes of Canada," BAAS (1888), p. 244.

Wissler, Clark. (*a*) "Material Cultures of the North American Indians, AA, new ser., xvi, 447.

   (*b*) "Some Dakota Myths," JAFL, xx, 121, 195.

—— and D. C. Duvall. *Mythology of the Blackfoot Indians.* PaAM, ii. New York, 1909.

Woosley, David J. "Cahuilla Tales," JAFL, xxi, 239.

Young, Egerton Ryerson. *Algonquin Indian Tales.* New York, 1903.

Zitkala-Sa. *Old Indian Legends.* Boston and London, 1901.